The Routledge Companion to Strategic Risk Management

Managing risk in and across organizations has always been of vital importance, both for individual firms and for the globalized economy more generally. With the global financial crisis, a dramatic lesson was learnt about what happens when risk is underestimated, misinterpreted or even overlooked. Many possible solutions have been competing for international recognition, yet there is little empirical evidence to support the purported effectiveness of these regulations and structured control approaches, which leaves the field wide open for further interpretation and conceptual development.

This comprehensive book pulls together a team of experts from around the world in a range of key disciplines such as management, economics and accounting to provide a comprehensive resource detailing everything that needs to be known in this emerging area. With no single text currently available, the book fills a much-needed gap in our current understanding of strategic risk management, offering the potential to advance research efforts and enhance our approaches to effective risk management practices.

Edited by a globally recognized expert on strategic risk management, this book is an essential reference for students, researchers and professionals with an interest in risk management, strategic management and finance.

Torben Juul Andersen is Professor of Strategy and International Management, Director of the Center for Global Strategic Responsiveness at Copenhagen Business School, Denmark.

Routledge Companions in Business, Management and Accounting

Routledge Companions in Business, Management and Accounting are prestige reference works providing an overview of a whole subject area or sub-discipline. These books survey the state of the discipline including emerging and cutting-edge areas. Providing a comprehensive, up-to-date, definitive work of reference, *Routledge Companions* can be cited as an authoritative source on the subject.

A key aspect of these *Routledge Companions* is their international scope and relevance. Edited by an array of highly regarded scholars, these volumes also benefit from teams of contributors which reflect an international range of perspectives.

Individually, *Routledge Companions in Business, Management and Accounting* provide an impactful one-stop-shop resource for each theme covered. Collectively, they represent a comprehensive learning and research resource for researchers, postgraduate students and practitioners.

Published titles in this series include:

The Routledge Companion to Fair Value and Financial Reporting
Edited by Peter Walton

The Routledge Companion to Nonprofit Marketing
Edited by Adrian Sargeant and Walter Wymer Jr

The Routledge Companion to Accounting History
Edited by John Richard Edwards and Stephen P. Walker

The Routledge Companion to Creativity
Edited by Tudor Rickards, Mark A. Runco and Susan Moger

The Routledge Companion to Strategic Human Resource Management
Edited by John Storey, Patrick M. Wright and David Ulrich

The Routledge Companion to International Business Coaching
Edited by Michel Moral and Geoffrey Abbott

The Routledge Companion to Organizational Change
Edited by David M. Boje, Bernard Burnes and John Hassard

The Routledge Companion to Cost Management
Edited by Falconer Mitchell, Hanne Nørreklit and Morten Jakobsen

The Routledge Companion to Digital Consumption
Edited by Russell W. Belk and Rosa Llamas

The Routledge Companion to Strategic Risk Management

Edited by Torben Juul Andersen

Routledge
Taylor & Francis Group

LONDON AND NEW YORK

First published 2016 by Routledge

2 Park Square, Milton Park, Abingdon, Oxfordshire OX14 4RN
52 Vanderbilt Avenue, New York, NY 10017

Routledge is an imprint of the Taylor & Francis Group, an informa business

First issued in paperback 2019

British Library Cataloguing in Publication Data
A catalogue record for this book is available from the British Library

Library of Congress Cataloging-in-Publication Data
The Routledge companion to strategic risk management / edited by Torben Juul Andersen.
   pages cm. — (Routledge companions in business, management and accounting)
   Includes bibliographical references and index.
   ISBN 978-1-138-01651-4 (hardback) — ISBN 978-1-315-78093-1 (ebook)
 1. Risk management. 2. Strategic planning. I. Andersen, Torben Juul.
   HD61.R677 2016
   658.15'5—dc23
   2015023550

ISBN: 978-1-138-01651-4 (hbk)
ISBN: 978-0-367-86954-0 (pbk)

Typeset in Bembo
by Apex CoVantage

Contents

Contents

Contents

Figures

Tables

Appendices

Contributors

Torben Juul Andersen is Professor at the Center for Global Strategic Responsiveness at Copenhagen Business School, Denmark.

Laurel C. Austin is Associate Professor at Copenhagen Business School, Denmark.

Eyvind Aven is Vice President of risk management at Statoil ASA, Norway.

Terje Aven is Professor of risk analysis and risk management at the University of Stavanger, Norway.

Phil Bromiley is Dean's Professor in Strategic Management at the Paul Merage School of Business, University of California, USA.

Mark de Bruijne is Assistant Professor in the School of Technology, Policy and Management at Delft University of Technology, the Netherlands.

Kirsten Dunlop is Executive General Manager, Strategic Innovation, Suncorp Personal Insurance.

Kathleen Edmond is Partner at Robins Kaplan LLP and formerly chief ethics officer for Best Buy.

Denis Fischbacher-Smith is Professor and Research Chair in risk and resilience at the University of Glasgow, UK.

Baruch Fischhoff is Howard Heinz University Professor in the Department of Engineering and Public Policy at Carnegie Mellon University, USA.

Richard Friberg is Jacob Wallenberg Professor of Economics at the University of Stockholm, Sweden.

Maxine Loraine Garvey is Senior Operations Officer at the IBRD, World Bank.

Luca Gatti is Founding Partner and CEO of eLogus and Assistant Professor at the Collége de France.

Contributors

Carina Antonia Hallin is Assistant Professor in the Department of International Economics and Management at the Copenhagen Business School, Denmark.

Douglas J. Jondle is Research Director at the Center for Ethical Business Cultures at the University of St. Thomas, Minnesota, USA.

Andreas Klinke is a lecturer at the International Policy Institute, King's College London, UK.

Hans Læssøe is Head of strategic risk management at the LEGO Group.

T. Dean Maines is President at the Veritas Institute at the University of St. Thomas, Minnesota, USA.

Michael McShane is Associate Professor of finance in the College of Business and Public Administration at Old Dominion University, USA.

Kent D. Miller is Professor at the Eli Broad Graduate School of Management, Michigan State University, USA.

Mark Milliner is Chief Executive Officer, Suncorp Personal Insurance.

Leen Paape is Professor and Dean of degree programs and research at Nyenrode Business University, the Netherlands.

Don Pagach is Professor at the Jenkins Graduate School of Management, North Carolina State University, USA.

Devaki Rau is Associate Professor at Southern Illinois University, USA.

S. Abraham (Avri) Ravid is Sy Syms Professor of Finance and Economics at Yeshiva University, USA, and Visiting Research Professor at New York University Stern School of Business, USA.

Ortwin Renn is Professor of environmental sociology and technology assessment at the University of Stuttgart, Germany.

Emery Roe is a senior researcher and member of the RESIN (Resilient and Sustainable Infrastructure Networks) research team at the University of California at Berkeley, USA.

Oliviero Roggi is Professor of finance at the University of Florence, Italy, and visiting associate professor of finance at New York University, USA.

Michelle D. Rovang is Director at the Veritas Institute at the University of St. Thomas, Minnesota, USA.

Markus Schädeli is head of group risk management at Nestlé.

Eva Schiffer is net-mapper and leadership trainer at the World Bank, USA.

Peter Winther Schrøder is head of regulatory, governance and non-traded risk, Nordea, Denmark.

Paul Schulman is Professor of government at Mills College, University of California at Berkeley, USA.

Naciye Sekerci is a lecturer at the School of Economics and Management at Lund University, Sweden.

Gregory L. Shaw is Associate Professor of engineering management and systems engineering and a co-Director of the Institute for Crisis, Disaster and Risk Management at George Washington University, Washington, DC, USA.

Hersh Shefrin is Mario L. Belotti Professor of Finance at Santa Clara University, California, USA.

Roland F. Speklé is Professor at Nyenrode Business University, the Netherlands.

Kim B. Staking is Assistant Professor of finance at California State University, Sacramento, USA.

Simon Torp is Assistant Professor at Aarhus University, Denmark.

Michel van Eeten is a lecturer at Delft University of Technology, the Netherlands.

Richard Warr is Professor of finance at Jenkins Graduate School of Management, North Carolina State University, USA.

Peter C. Young is the 3M Endowed Chair in International Business at the Opus College of Business, University of St. Thomas, Minnesota, USA.

Introduction
Strategic risk management

Torben Juul Andersen

There has been an increasing focus on risk management in the wake of some spectacular collapses of major corporations, periodic stock market corrections, and economic recession spurred by a near breakdown of financial market trust garnered with recurring debt crises in major international markets. These events have had significant adverse effects on corporate value creation and societal wealth causing major disruptions to the quality of life of the people that inhabit the exposed economies. Hence, there should be little wonder that both political and business leaders have paid great tribute to these events with steadfast aims of imposing policies, rules, and regulations that would prevent something similar from happening again. However, as we know, it is human nature to do too much when it is too late, and too little when it is time to act. Hence, in hindsight executives and policy makers should act on early sightings of evolving changes that everybody nonetheless seems to ignore despite the warning signals for all to see. As argued by Harrison and Phillips (2014: p. 164): "it was apparent from the serious economic journalism of 2006, 2007 and early 2008 that there were many 'canaries in the cave' that anticipated the landscape of the financial crisis of 2008." In other words, there is a tendency to ignore even the most obvious signs of emergent risk events. With a bit of luck, this is what risk management practices might be able to circumvent by creating more risk conscious organizational settings.

Strategic risk management is a conceptual extension of risk management indicating that risk management somehow has become strategic. Using the term *strategic* may simply indicate that the derived concept is considered important with the aim of giving it a more imposing flair (Andersen, 2013). *Risk management* is typically conceived as the structured process of identifying and dealing with risks followed by monitoring and controls to minimize the negative downside effects of risk events and to maximize the positive upside potential of opportunities in line with corporate objectives.[1] Hence, according to the Institute of Risk Management (IRM), risk is the probability of an event and its consequences that can have both positive and negative outcomes. It is argued that anything that may obstruct, or create uncertainty about the ability to achieve organizational objectives at the strategic, tactical and operational levels constitutes a risk. COSO (2004)[2] describes enterprise risk management (ERM) as a process initiated by the board of directors involving management and personnel across the enterprise to identify potential risk events and manage them within a given risk appetite to ensure that organizational objectives can be achieved. These views establish a potential link between the risk management process and the ability to achieve intended outcomes that are considered to be of strategic importance. A recent practice-based view (PBV) of strategy scholarship (Bromiley and Rau, 2014) pinpoints the relevance of considering the potential effects of adopting specific techniques to ensure particular strategic aims or risk management outcomes even though these practices are exchanged between firms. This suggests that general management practices including enterprise risk management may in fact contribute with potential value despite the fact that it contravenes the basic assumptions of the resource-based view (RBV) suggesting that only practices that cannot be imitated by other firms can sustain corporate value creation.

The underlying risk management process is often formalized as advance identification, analysis, and assessments of risks, the effects of which can be handled through avoidance, mitigation, elimination, or transfer of unacceptable exposures that exceed an expressed risk appetite. The identified risk factors and implied risk exposures are subsequently monitored in internal management control systems to ensure that the agreed risk handling initiatives are in fact executed and that the organization retains preparedness for potential risk events. To ensure effective execution of these formal activities many organizations conduct periodic audits of the risk management process typically under the auspices of an independent audit function (Figure 0.1).

However, as the contemporary business environment in an increasingly globalized world becomes more complex, dynamic, and unpredictable (e.g., Bettis and Hitt, 1995), there is a greater need to cope with uncertain conditions that will challenge the relevance of prior objectives as things may evolve in new and unexpected ways. As a consequence, there is not a clear relationship between the risk management process and the achievement of predefined strategic, tactical, and operational objectives. Instead there is a fundamental need to adapt organizational activities in response to ongoing changes in the business environment and renew the strategy over time as a new environmental context emerges (Agerwal and Helfat, 2009). This resonates with recent discussions about the need for *dynamic capabilities* (Teece, 2007; Teece, Pisano and Shuen, 1997) and *strategic response capabilities* (Andersen, Denrell and Bettis, 2007) that allow the organization to adapt and maintain a proper fit with the environmental context. Hence, this is a recurring theme in the strategy literature where the view is that organizations must develop strategies, and structures to accommodate them, in ways that suit the environment; that

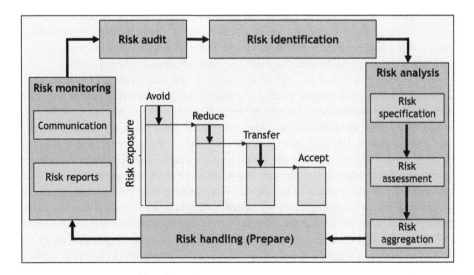

Figure 0.1   A generic risk management process

is, strategy and structure will have to be adapted as the external conditions change (Andersen, 2015). Accordingly, it has been argued that "the essence of management is coping with change" Chakravarthy (1982: p. 35). Therefore an essential aim of strategic risk management, or the management of strategic risk, is to ensure that the organization is able to adapt its business activities in view of emerging developments in the surrounding environment. This implies that the organization also must be able to exploit opportunities that arise out of the evolving uncertain context with a general awareness of new possibilities that can help the organization adapt its strategy, as things happen often in nonlinear and unpredictable ways.

Looking towards the field of strategic management a well-established contingent of strategy scholars sees strategy develop as a consequence of resource-committing decisions that are made by individual decision-makers throughout the organization partially inspired by strategic aspirations but also influenced by emerging events and social processes (e.g., Bower, 1970/1986; Bower and Gilbert, 2005). Strategic decisions are often considered to be those decisions that are concerned with the whole organization in view of the environment it operates in and the resources and people it engages to perform its organizational activities. As noted by Eisenhardt and Zbaracki (1992: p. 17), strategic decision-making is crucial "because it involves those fundamental decisions which shape the course of a firm." Lampel (2014) similarly suggests that strategic decision-making is the process of bringing choices into action that will affect the long-term welfare of the organization, often involving major organizational changes and investments that are difficult to reverse once they are implemented. That is, strategic decisions that commit resources in economic infrastructure and productive assets create irreversible exposures that should be managed. Hence, to the extent the risk management process can support and improve the quality of the underlying strategic decisions and subsequent monitoring of the outcomes of those decisions, this will constitute an important element of strategic risk management.

However, strategic decision-making is not as clearly structured as the formal risk management process may propose. Schwenk (1995: p. 473) states that "strategic decisions are often described as unstructured, un-programmed, and messy" and are influenced by internal conflicts, politics, cognitive biases and the behaviours of individual decision-makers. All the while, it is not clear that those strategic decisions are always made by the important people in the board of directors and the executive management team but are influenced by managerial decisions taken by multiple actors scattered throughout the organization. That is, many decisions and actions taken deep inside the organization may turn out to have subsequent strategic importance (e.g., Burgelman, 1996; Mintzberg, 1994). In short, the risk events that can affect the strategic development of the organization seem quite important and often constitute those exposures that affect corporate survival (Slywotzky and Drzik, 2005).

To help organizational decision-makers consider potential risk events, various management control systems and risk management frameworks propose more or less systematic ways to think through the type of events that could have significant effects of importance to the strategic development of the organization. The idea, of course, is that to the extent potential events have been considered in advance, the higher the level of preparedness within the organization will lead to better outcomes, everything else being equal. However, there is no single authorized approach to support this identification and analysis, although it usually considers a majority of external factors that are beyond the control of corporate management while being cognizant of internal issues that can cause trouble, if they are seriously mismanaged (Figure 0.2). A typical framework may distinguish between different externally driven categories of risk, such as *hazard risks* caused by industrial accidents and the like, *operational risks* linked to regulatory compliance, *financial risks* caused by underlying market volatilities, and *strategic risks* derived from the industry context and competitive conditions of the organization in general. In other words, the typical

Figure 0.2 A typical risk identification framework

risk identification approaches suggest that there is a particular risk category we can refer to as being strategic in nature in the sense that they comprise external factors that may affect the strategic position of the organization.

The strategic risk management concept

However, the concept of strategic risk management has not been well defined by any means. In view of the preceding overview, one might suggest that the concept can be framed by an ex ante strategic risk identification perspective and an ex post strategic risk management perfor- mance perspective. That is, one valid interpretation of the concept of managing strategic risks arguably relates to the advance, or ex ante, task of identifying different types of risk events of a strategic nature that might affect the organization's ability to carry out its underlying purpose and prepare it to deal better with those risks. Another valid interpretation of the strategic risk management concept relates to post hoc assessments of the organization's realized ability to deal with all major risk events of strategic importance that actually did occur when looking back over a certain period of time.

The ex ante interpretation of managing strategic risk relates to the initial elements in the generic risk management process of identifying and assessing various risks that might affect organizational performance. While this seems a plausible approach, it certainly has its limita- tions because we know that the turbulence of contemporary business environments always will present strategic managers with unforeseen events that failed to hit the radar screen with suffi- cient lead time for a formal treatment within the systematic risk management process. On the other hand, we also know that the borderline between *risk* and *uncertainty* is fine and is partially influenced by the prevalence of conscious risk management practices (Andersen, Garvey and

Roggi, 2014). That is, to an ignorant person all forthcoming events will emerge and appear as unexpected situations and will, therefore, represent circumstances characterized by very high levels of uncertainty. In contrast, an alert and attentive person will be more cognizant about possible things that may happen, and this can be used actively to measure potential effects and establish some advanced preparedness that leads to a more effective handling of those events if and when they happen. In this case, these future events represent measurable risks that can be described and assessed actuarially. So, the principles of the generic risk management approach can help advance better responses to emerging (strategic) events simply because uncertainty to some extent is converted to quantifiable risk constructs that can be assessed and managed in a more tangible manner.

Hence, first we note that effective strategic risk management requires that people in the organization are alert to environmental changes and conscious about possible responses one can make to those emerging events, and second we note that there will always be a limit to how far one can foresee future events. Consequently, an effective and well-managed organization is in a better position to deal effectively with unexpected events in the future (e.g., Weick and Sutcliffe, 2001). This also means that without an organization of engaged and alert employees, the risk management process might turn out to have limited effect, just as singular adherence to refinements and perfection of elaborate managerial practices may deliver little economic value because it can drown in a bureaucratic quagmire with little sense of the major things that happen around the organization. We know that even extensive control procedures tend to erode over time as people find ways to circumvent them, so they eventually fail to serve the purpose they were intended to accomplish. Tight control frameworks possibly spurred by public policy initiatives will also have the potential adverse effect of stifling innovation and thereby reducing the ability to take immediate responses when unexpected things happen. Hence, stringent adherence to extensive control systems can actually be detrimental to the organization's ability to deal effectively with emerging strategic events in a turbulent environment. There are also proactive reasons for enabling decentralized entrepreneurial risk taking within the organization (Andersen et al., 2014), as it facilitates exploration for new opportunities and possible responses to changing environmental conditions where new ideas and business initiatives are tried out that may prove to be the proper solutions for future corporate responses. So, managing risks is not just about avoiding downside losses, it is also a process of developing and probing innovative and responsive ideas that can help the organization gain new experiential insights about the opportunities that arise as the environmental conditions change.

According to Gary Klein (2013: p. 139), the engineering of management control systems can become "dumb by design" to the extent that they systematically hone in and focus on predefined types of information that tend to narrow the vision and the ability to discern new unexpected environmental patterns. Hence, there is a need for broader reconnaissance of various things that happen in and around the organization to be able to sense new emerging developments and trends that may veer off in different directions than were observed in the past. In other words, it takes many eyes and minds in different parts of the organization to observe all the subtle things that go on around the periphery of the enterprise and that eventually might constitute the early warning signals about impending environmental changes that need strategic responses. This also means that an effective risk managing organization must indulge and allow informal practices to take place allowing individual agents to act and experiment to learn about emerging changes in the surrounding environment (e.g., Andersen, 2010).

The ex ante approach to risk identification adheres to the suggested practices of identifying potential future risk events of some significance with the aim of preparing for these events in advance. This is where a simple risk classification framework might be useful as the means to inspire the advance risk identification process and ensure that all important risk categories are taken into consideration. While there is no claim to a singular best approach, the practices proposed in the various frameworks may be summarized in a simple and quite useful format (Figure 0.3). According to this scheme strategic risks belong to a certain category of events that with some weight can be argued to have a specific "strategic" nature. These include competitor moves, new regulations, political events, social changes, changes in taste, new technology shifts, and so forth. What is so characteristic of these types of risk is that they can be hard to quantify because they take place in new and unique ways every time they occur, which will defy statistical measurement and calculations. What is more, they can also be very difficult to uncover in advance because dynamic and complex environments evolve in a nonlinear manner where concrete outcomes are impossible to predict or determine in advance. So, strategic risks are typically much more uncertain and unpredictable than any of the other risk categories. However, that is not to say that, for example, financial or actuarial markets always develop in predictable ways. We have seen major corrections in price relations caused by various crisis events, such as default on Russian government debt, collapsing markets for subprime loans, loss of confidence in interbank markets, and so forth.

The ex post interpretation of strategic risk management takes a historical look upon the past ability of the organization to deal effectively with major events, or risk factors, in the internal and external environments whatever their origins. In other words this view in principle spans across all major effects caused by any of the listed risk categories (Figure 0.3). The ability to manage strategic risks, and by implication the ability to deal with all important events, would typically be measured as the firm's propensity to maintain stable earnings and cash flows patterns over time compared to their peers in comparable industries that are embedded in the same environmental context (e.g., Andersen, 2008, 2009). This measure of strategic risk management effectiveness implies that major risk effects with important implications for performance outcomes can have many different sources including areas that do not necessarily per se fall within the predefined category of strategic risk factors. For example, the financial crisis during 2008

Figure 0.3 Strategic risks and strategic risk management – an illustrative framework

taught us that prices in financial markets can take dramatic jumps way outside the ranges proposed by the Gaussian normal distribution and emphasizes the potential strategic importance of taking all risk areas into consideration even though they represent vastly different types of risk.

Taleb (2013: p. 227) implies that "we use models of uncertainty to produce certainties" where the underlying "scientific" methods systematically misestimate the role of the rare events that by experience will occur from time to time. Hence, it is a fact that the competitive landscape is changing and the business environment is becoming increasingly uncertain and harder to predict (Figure 0.4). When conditions are certain and information is available, we are really dealing with problems that have numerical optimization solutions that can be found through mathematics and computational modeling. Hence, no risk management practices are needed here and would only complicate things. The formal risk management process is geared to handle foreseeable risk events where potential effects and outcomes within reason can be determined actuarially. However, this process is not geared to handle uncertain events that are hard to quantify and maybe even difficult to forecast. When we try to impose the formal risk management process on these types of events one is likely to misjudge the potential for extreme outcomes, thus leaving the organization to operate under a false sense of security way beyond prudent risk limits.

Empirical studies have found that organizations with effective strategic risk management capabilities are good at handling all the different risk categories they are exposed to and show a general willingness to experiment with new approaches to become more responsive including the use of enterprise risk management techniques (e.g., Andersen, 2008). Conversely, the organizations that display poor strategic risk management capabilities seemingly fail to manage any of the risk categories including those areas with relatively well-developed hedging mechanisms, such as interest rate and currency risks. This suggests that all risk categories need attention but in many cases may also need people and functions with special expertise and capabilities to be

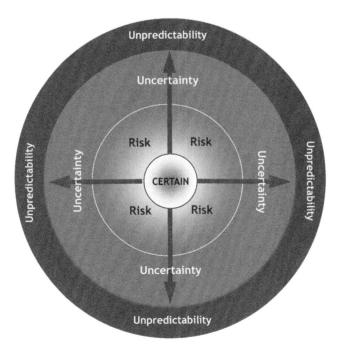

Figure 0.4 A changing strategic risk landscape – unpredictability and unknowability

handled effectively, including the structuring of proper reinsurance arrangements, financial hedging techniques, operational and supply chain processes, and even managing strategic risks. So, while a portfolio approach might suggest that there should always be full integration across all the risk categories to determine an aggregate corporate exposure, this is probably a truth with modifications, because you still need specialized expertise to deal effectively in specific risk markets.

However, it is true that the organization should be attentive to all risk categories that can affect the organization's long-term earnings capacity, including those events that constitute unusual tail events outside the boundaries of the normal distribution. This is also one of the reasons why risk management is such a multifaceted cross-disciplinary area of study that spans the actuarial sciences, economics, finance, accounting, management control, psychology, human cognition, decision-making, information processing, strategy, management, and so forth. This accentuates a need for better cross-disciplinary insight and understanding and also points to the need for specialized organizational entities to deal professionally with specific risk categories. All the while, there is a need for integrative analysis to manage ongoing information processing, without adopting excessively bureaucratic practices but rather imposing a set of "living" risk management practices that are continuously modified and improved along the way.

So, which one of the two strategic risk management perspectives is the more appropriate? The answer probably depends on what we want to use them for. The ex ante perspective is appropriate and useful when you engage in the risk management practice of identifying and assessing risk factors in advance as part of the generic risk management process. The ex post perspective is relevant and useful when you want to analyze the effects of effective strategic risk management capabilities and determine what may cause the extreme risk outcomes. This suggests that both perspectives serve a useful purpose but it is a matter of the analytical purpose that determines the approach one want to adopt. We see a similar dichotomy in the field of strategic management in the discussion between the appropriateness of an ex ante analytics-driven process to determine future strategy content and direction (Schendel and Hofer, 1979) versus analyzing strategy ex post as a pattern of decisions and actions taken over time (Mintzberg, 1979). Both of these approaches serve practical purposes as approaches to either gain insights to discuss relevant strategic issues in advance or to conduct post hoc analyses to better understand how the stochastic development of strategic events are handled by different organizational approaches with different degrees of effectiveness. These analytical approaches can complement each other. The ex ante analyses can be useful as a way to deal with and prepare for predictable and foreseeable events, whereas the ex post analyses can be useful as a way to better understand how the different elements of the complex risk management process evolve with the possibility to discern important contingencies that influence the risk management outcomes.

The risk management process of identifying and assessing emergent risks while broadly discussing the contours of the future risk landscape can clearly lead to better strategic decisions that avoid the adverse effects of risk and uncertainty while reaping potential benefits from the opportunities that arise out of the changing business conditions. It is also this ability to be proactive and respond effectively to ongoing environmental changes that defines good management, or as Andersen et al. (2014: p. 168) expressed with other words: "Good risk management is simply good management!"

Overview of *Companion*

Seeing strategic risk management, or the ability to manage strategic risk, as an outcome of many resource committing decisions made by managers and individuals throughout the organization within a network of stakeholders, it seems obvious that the underlying processes will be influenced by many different things. These include the basic principles of corporate governance, or risk governance, the application of economic and managerial rationales, the development of firm-specific corporate practices, biases imposed by human cognition and individual psychological factors, and alternative ways to update and process risk information. The *Routledge Companion to Strategic Risk Management* presents different aspects of these themes comprised by a mixture of deep insights from prominent established scholars, unique experiences from a select group of distinguished executives, and new risk management perspectives from promising researchers. Together this diverse collection of chapters provides a unique single source to comprehend and think about the multifaceted nature of strategic risk management, and to better understand how this may or may not lead to better strategic decisions that enhance economic efficiencies and value creation.

In principle, strategic risk management constitutes a set of practices and perspectives adopted to achieve better resource committing decisions without imposing excessive premature risk exposures. There is generally found to be a positive relationship between ex post measures of strategic risk management effectiveness and performance. However, the analyses of risk management effects depend on specific measures of enterprise risk management adopted in the studies while there are essential leadership contingencies at play that influence the viability of strategic risk management. The high-performing strategic risk management organizations show openness to new ways of challenging their exiting abilities to deal with future risk events and are always on the lookout to gain improvements. Hence, it is a pleasure to also include in the volume a number of contributions where we can learn from process effectiveness in high reliability organizations and new methods to improve the cognitive understanding of evolving risk influences and promising techniques to obtain updated strategic risk reconnaissance from the organizational frontlines as a way to better inform ongoing strategic decisions.

The underlying themes include the importance of corporate values in risk management, the implications of discrepancies between officially stated and practiced principles, the challenge of clearly defining the strategic risk management concept, and the fascinating implications of cognitive biases on risk management outcomes in social systems comprised by organizations and societies. The distinct and highly personal views from a number of prominent practitioners tells us that behind the successful application of strategic risk management practices there are some highly dedicated and unique individuals whose intuitive managerial creativity develops specific systems that work in their own organizations. So while strategic risk management might adhere to some common guidelines, the execution of concrete practices are often uniquely adapted to the individual organizations, and do not just represent standardized processing of risk information but rather unique ways of thinking and acting.

The various themes are structured around several main sections including "Risk governance perspectives," "The management of strategic risk," "Corporate risk management insights," "The managerial impact on risk outcomes," "Effects on enterprise risk management," and "Other aspects of strategic risk management." While this reflects an attempt by the editor to devise a simple organization of the material, it is also clear that the complexity of the topic defies a simple categorization of relevant themes, where every article makes a unique and distinct contribution in its own right. Hence, I am proud and thankful that it has been possible to assemble these unique contributions, and I sincerely hope it will provide valuable insights to readers in academia and practice with an interest in strategic risk management issues.

Notes

1   ISO 31000 talks about managing the effect of uncertainty on objectives.
2   The Committee of Sponsoring Organizations of the Treadway Commission (COSO).

References

Agerwal, R. and Helfat, C. E. (2009). Strategic renewal of organizations, *Organization Science* 20(2): 281–293.

Andersen, T. J. (2015). 'Strategic adaptation', in Wright, J. D. (ed.), *International Encyclopedia of the Social & Behavioral Sciences* (2nd ed.) 23: 501–507. Elsevier: Oxford.

Andersen, T. J. (ed.). (2014). *Contemporary Challenges in Risk Management: Dealing with Risk, Uncertainty and the Unknown*, Palgrave Macmillan: Basingstoke.

Andersen, T. J. (2013). *Short Introduction to Strategic Management*, Cambridge University Press: Cambridge.

Andersen, T. J. (2010). Combining central planning and decentralization to enhance effective risk management outcomes, *Risk Management* 12(2): 101–115.

Andersen, T. J. (2009). Effective risk management outcomes: Exploring effects of innovation and capital structure, *Journal of Strategy and Management* 2(4): 352–379.

Andersen, T. J. (2008). The performance relationship of effective risk management: Exploring the firm-specific investment rationale, *Long Range Planning* 41(2): 155–176.

Andersen, T. J. (2006). *Global Derivatives: A Strategic Risk Management Perspective*, Financial Times – Prentice Hall: Harlow.

Andersen, T. J., Denrell, J. and Bettis, R. A. (2007). Strategic responsiveness and Bowman's risk-return paradox, *Strategic Management Journal* 28: 407–429.

Andersen, T. J., Garvey, M. and Roggi, O. (2014). *Managing Risk and Opportunity: The Governance of Strategic Risk-Taking*, Oxford University Press: Oxford.

Andersen, T. J. and Schrøder, P. W. (2010). *Strategic Risk Management Practice: How to Deal Effectively with Major Corporate Exposures*, Cambridge University Press: Cambridge.

Bettis, R. A. and Hitt, M. A. (1995). The new competitive landscape, *Strategic Management Journal* 16(Special issue): 7–19.

Bower, J. L. (1986). *Managing the Resource Allocation Process*, Harvard Business School Press: Boston. (first published in 1970)

Bower, J. L. and Gilbert, C. G. (eds.). (2005). *From Resource Allocation to Strategy*, Oxford University Press: New York.

Bromiley, P. and Rau, D. (2014). Towards a practice-based view of strategy, *Strategic Management Journal* 35(8): 1249–1256.

Burgelman, R. A. (1996). A process model of strategic business exit: Implications for an evolutionary perspective on strategy, *Strategic Management Journal* 17(S1): 193–214.

Chakravarthy, B. S. (1982). Adaptation: A promising metaphor for strategic management, *Academy of Management Review* 7(1): 33–44.

COSO. (2004). Enterprise Risk Management-Integrated Framework.

Eisenhardt, K. M. and Zbaracki, M. J. (1992). Strategic decision making, *Strategic Management Journal* 13: 17–37.

Harrison, G. W. and Phillips, R. D. (2014). 'Subjective beliefs and statistical forecasts of financial risks: The chief risk officer project', in Andersen, T. J. (ed.), *Contemporary Challenges in Risk Management: Dealing with Risk, Uncertainty and the Unknown*, Palgrave Macmillan: Basingstoke.

Klein, G. (2013). *Seeing What Others Don't: The Remarkable Ways We Gain Insights*, Nicholas Brealey: London.

Lampel, J. B. (2014). 'Strategic decision-making', in Augier, M. and Teece, D. (eds.), *The Palgrave Encyclopedia of Strategic Management*, Palgrave Macmillan: Basingstoke.

Mintzberg, H. (1994). The fall and rise of strategic planning, *Harvard Business Review* 72(1): 107–114.

Mintzberg, H. (1979). Patterns in strategy formation, *International Studies of Management & Organization* 9(3): 67–86.

Schendel D. E. and Hofer C. W. (1979). *Strategic Management: A New View of Business Policy and Planning*. Boston: Little, Brown and Company, 1979.

Schwenk, C. R. (1995). Strategic decision making, *Journal of Management* 21(3): 471–493.

Slywotzky, A. J. and Drzik, J. (2005). Countering the biggest risk of all, *Harvard Business Review* 83(4): 78–88.

Taleb, N. H. (2013). 'The fourth quadrant: A map of the limits of statistics', in Brockman, J. (ed.), *Thinking: The New Science of Decision-Making, Problem-Solving, and Prediction*, HarperCollins: New York.

Teece, D. J. (2007). Explicating dynamic capabilities: The nature and microfoundations of (sustainable) enterprise performance, *Strategic Management Journal* 28: 1319–1350.

Teece, D. J., Pisano, G. and Shuen, A. (1997). Dynamic capabilities and strategic management, *Strategic Management Journal* 18: 509–533.

Weick, K. E. and Sutcliffe, K. M. (2001). *Managing the Unexpected*, Jossey-Bass: San Francisco.

Part I
Risk governance perspectives

1

Complexity, uncertainty and ambiguity in inclusive risk governance

Ortwin Renn and Andreas Klinke

Deciding the location of hazardous facilities, setting standards for chemicals, making decisions about clean-ups of contaminated land, regulating food and drugs, as well as designing and enforcing safety limits all have one element in common: these activities are collective endeavours to understand, assess and handle risks to human health and the environment. These attempts are based on two requirements. On the one hand, risk managers need sufficient knowledge about the potential impacts of the risk sources under investigation and the likely consequences of the different decision options to control these risks. On the other hand, they need criteria to judge the desirability or undesirability of these consequences for the people affected and the public at large (Horlick-Jones, Rowe and Walls 2007; Renn and Schweizer 2009; Rowe and Frewer 2000). Criteria on desirability are reflections of social values such as good health, equity or efficient use of scarce resources. Both components – knowledge and values – are necessary for any decision-making process independent of the issue and the problem context.

Anticipating the consequences of human actions or events (knowledge) and evaluating the desirability and moral quality of these consequences (values) pose particular problems if the consequences that need to be considered are complex and uncertain and the values contested and controversial. Dealing with complex, uncertain and (value) ambiguous outcomes often leads to the emergence of social conflict. Questions of how to deal with complex, uncertain and controversial risks demand procedures for dealing with risks that go beyond the conventional risk management routines. Numerous strategies to cope with this challenge have evolved over time. They include technocratic decision-making through the explicit involvement of expert committees, muddling through in a pluralist society, negotiated rule-making via stakeholder involvement, deliberative democracy or ignoring probabilistic information altogether (see reviews in Brooks 1984; Nelkin and Pollak 1979, 1980; Renn 2008: 290ff.) The main thesis of this chapter is that risk management institutions need more adequate governance structures and procedures that enable them to integrate professional assessments (systematic knowledge), adequate institutional process (political legitimacy), responsible handling of public resources (efficiency) and public knowledge and perceptions (reflection on public values and preferences). These various inputs require the involvement of several actors in the risk assessment and risk management process. The structures that evolve from the cooperation of various actors in all phases of the risk handling process are subsumed under the term risk governance (IRGC 2005; Renn 2008: 8).

Hutter (2006: 215) characterizes the move from governmental regulation to governance in the following manner:

> This decentring of the state involves a move from the public ownership and centralized control to privatized institutions and the encouragement of market competition. It also involves a move to a state reliance on new forms of fragmented regulation, involving the existing specialist regulatory agencies of state but increasingly self-regulating organizations, regimes of enforced self-regulation . . . and American-style independent regulatory agencies.
>
> *(2006: 215)*

Governing choices in modern societies are seen as an interplay between governmental institutions, economic forces and civil society actors, such as nongovernmental organizations (NGOs). *Risk governance* involves the 'translation' of the substance and core principles of governance to the context of risk and risk-related decision-making (Hutter 2006). It includes, but also extends beyond, the three conventionally recognized elements of *risk analysis* (risk assessment, risk management and risk communication). It requires consideration of the legal, institutional, social and economic contexts in which a risk is evaluated, and involvement of the actors and stakeholders who represent them. Risk governance looks at the complex web of actors, rules, conventions, processes and mechanisms concerned with how relevant risk information is collected, analysed and communicated, and how management decisions are taken.

Based on our previous work on risk governance and risk evaluation (Klinke, Dreyer, Renn, Stirling and van Zwanenberg 2006; Klinke and Renn 2001, 2002, 2010, 2012; Renn 2008; Renn and Klinke 2013; Renn, Klinke and van Asselt 2011), we will expand in this chapter on a normative-analytical model of a risk governance process that interlinks diverse actors and their claims, elaborates the institutional means to process diverse input and discusses the prospects and implications for adaptive capacity. The focus will be on collectively binding risk management decisions rather than on private risk management decisions. Such collective decisions are not only a product of governmental policy making but are joint products by a wide variety of actors including scientists, the private sector, civil society and governmental agencies.

In this chapter we will first analyze the major characteristics of risk knowledge and then address major functions of the risk governance process: pre-estimation, interdisciplinary risk estimation (including scientific risk assessment and concern assessment), risk characterization and risk evaluation as well as risk management including decision-making and implementation. Furthermore, we will explicate the design of an effective and fair institutional arrangement including four different forms of public and stakeholder involvement in order to cope with the challenges raised by the three risk characteristics. Finally, the chapter will conclude with some general lessons for risk governance.

Three characteristics of risk knowledge

Integrative risk governance is expected to address challenges raised by three risk characteristics that result from a lack of knowledge and/or competing knowledge claims about the risk problem. Transboundary and collectively relevant risk problems such as global environmental threats (climate change, loss of biological diversity, chemical pollution etc.), new and/or large-scale technologies (nanotechnology, biotechnology, offshore oil production etc.), food security or pandemics are all characterized by limited and sometimes controversial knowledge with respect to their risk properties and their implications (Horlick-Jones and Sime 2004). They need to be handled by transnational entities such as the European Union or the United Nations. The three characteristics are complexity, scientific uncertainty and socio-political ambiguity (Klinke et al. 2006; Klinke and Renn 2002, 2010; Renn 2008).

Complexity

Complexity refers to the difficulty of identifying and quantifying causal links between a multitude of potential candidates and specific adverse effects (cf. Lewin 1992; Underdal 2009). A crucial aspect in this respect concerns the applicability of probabilistic risk assessment techniques. If the chain of events between a cause and an effect follows a linear relationship (as for example in car accidents or in an overdose of pharmaceutical products), simple statistical models are sufficient to calculate the probabilities of harm. Such simple relationships may still be associated with high uncertainty, for example, if only few data are available or the effect is stochastic by its own nature. Sophisticated models of probabilistic inferences are required if the relationship between cause and effects becomes more complex (Renn and Walker 2008). The nature of this difficulty may be traced back to interactive effects among these candidates (synergisms and antagonisms, positive and negative feedback loops), long delay periods between cause and effect, inter-individual variation, intervening variables and others. It is precisely these complexities that make sophisticated scientific investigations necessary, since the cause–effect relationship is neither obvious nor directly observable. Nonlinear response functions may also result from feedback loops that constitute a complex web of intervening variables. Complexity requires therefore sensitivity to nonlinear transitions as well as to scale (on different levels). It also needs to take into account a multitude of exposure pathways and the composite effects of other agents that are present in the exposure situation. Examples of highly complex risk include sophisticated chemical facilities, synergistic effects of potentially eco-toxic substances on the environment, failure risk of large interconnected infrastructures and risks of critical loads to sensitive ecosystems.

Scientific uncertainty

Scientific uncertainty relates to the limitedness or even absence of scientific knowledge (data, information) that makes it difficult to exactly assess the probability and possible outcomes of undesired effects (cf. Aven and Renn 2009; Filar and Haurie 2010; Rosa 1997). It most often results from an incomplete or inadequate reduction of complexity in modeling cause–effect chains (cf. Marti, Ermoliev and Makowski 2010). Whether the world is inherently uncertain is a philosophical question that is not pursued here. It is essential to acknowledge in the context of risk assessment that human knowledge is always incomplete and selective and, thus, contingent upon uncertain assumptions, assertions and predictions (Functowicz and Ravetz 1992; Laudan 1996; Renn 2008: 75). It is obvious that the modeled probability distributions within a numerical relational system can only represent an approximation of the empirical relational system that helps elucidate and predict uncertain events. It therefore seems prudent to include additional aspects of uncertainty (van Asselt 2000: 93–138). Although there is no consensus in the literature on the best means of disaggregating uncertainties, the following categories appear to be an appropriate means of distinguishing between the key components of uncertainty:

* *Variability* refers to different vulnerability of targets such as the divergence of individual responses to identical stimuli among individual targets within a relevant population such as humans, animals, plants, landscapes etc.
* *Inferential effects* relate to systematic and random errors in modeling including problems of extrapolating or deducing inferences from small statistical samples, from animal data or

experimental data onto humans or from large doses to small doses etc. All of these are usually expressed through statistical confidence intervals.

- *Indeterminacy* results from genuine stochastic relationship between cause and effects, apparently noncausal or noncyclical random events, or badly understood nonlinear, chaotic relationships.
- *System boundaries* allude to uncertainties stemming from restricted models and the need for focusing on a limited amount of variables and parameters.
- *Ignorance* means the lack of knowledge about the probability of occurrence of a damaging event and about its possible consequences.

The first two components of uncertainty qualify as statistically quantifiable uncertainty and, therefore, can be reduced by improving existing knowledge, applying standard statistical instruments such as Monte Carlo simulation and estimating random errors within an empirically proven distribution. The last three components represent genuine uncertainty components and can be characterized to some extent by using scientific approaches, but cannot be completely resolved. The validity of the end results is questionable and, for risk management purposes, additional information is needed, such as a subjective confidence level in risk estimates, potential alternative pathways of cause–effect relationships, ranges of reasonable estimates, maximum loss scenarios and others. Examples of high uncertainty include many natural disasters, such as earthquakes, possible health effects of mass pollutants below the threshold of statistical significance, regional impacts due to global climate change and long-term effects of introducing genetically modified species into the natural environment.

Socio-political ambiguity

While more and better data and information may reduce scientific uncertainty, more knowledge does not necessarily reduce ambiguity. Ambiguity thus indicates a situation of ambivalence in which different and sometimes divergent streams of thinking and interpretation about the same risk phenomena and their circumstances are apparent (cf. Feldman 1989; Zahariadis 2003). We distinguish between interpretative and normative ambiguity, which both relate to divergent or contested perspectives on the justification, severity or wider 'meanings' associated with a given threat (Renn 2008: 77; Stirling 2003).

Interpretative ambiguity denotes the variability of (legitimate) interpretations based on identical observations or data assessments results, e.g. an adverse or nonadverse effect. Variability of interpretation, however, is not restricted to expert dissent. Laypeople's perception of risk often differs from expert judgments because it is related to qualitative risk characteristics such as familiarity, personal or institutional control, assignment of blame and others. Moreover, in contemporary pluralist societies diversity of risk perspectives within and between social groups is generally fostered by divergent value preferences, variations in interests and very few, if any, universally applicable moral principles; all the more if risk problems are complex and uncertain. Examples for high interpretative ambiguity include low dose nonionizing radiation, low concentrations of genotoxic substances, or the impacts of alien species to natural environments (How far do I go back in time for determining what species is alien and what domestic?).

That leads us to the aspect of *normative ambiguity*. It alludes to different concepts of what can be regarded as tolerable, referring e.g. to ethics, quality of life parameters, distribution of risks and benefits etc. A condition of ambiguity emerges where the problem lies in agreeing on the appropriate values, priorities, assumptions, or boundaries to be applied to the definition of possible outcomes. Normative ambiguities can be associated, for example, with exposure to noise, aquaculture in sensitive areas, prenatal genetic screening and genetically modified food. In these cases, science is very familiar with the risks and there is little uncertainty and interpretative ambiguity about cause–effect relationships. Yet there is considerable debate whether the application is tolerable or not. Another example may be the use of phthalates in toys. All analysts are aware that these substances are potentially carcinogenic, but given the known exposure and the dose-response functions there is hardly any possibility for young children to be negatively affected (Wilkinson and Lamb 1999). Yet the mere idea of having a carcinogenic substance in children's toys has incited a fierce debate about the tolerability of such an ingredient in rubber toys.

Most risks are characterized by a mixture of complexity, uncertainty and ambiguity. Passive smoking may be a good example of low complexity and uncertainty but high ambiguity. Nuclear energy may be a good candidate for high complexity and high ambiguity but relatively little uncertainty. The massive emission of aerosols into the atmosphere to combat the effects of greenhouse gases might be cited as an example for high complexity, uncertainty and ambiguity.

Towards an inclusive risk governance model

The ability of risk governance institutions to cope with complex, uncertain and ambiguous consequences and implications has become a central concern to scientists and practitioners alike. In 2005, the International Risk Governance Council suggested a process model of risk governance (IRGC 2005; Renn 2008). This framework structures the risk governance process in four phases: preassessment, appraisal, characterization and evaluation and risk management. Communication is conceptualized as a constant companion to all four phases of the risk governance cycle. The framework's risk process, or risk handling chain, is illustrated in Figure 1.1.

Since its publication in 2005, the IRGC Risk Governance Framework has been applied to diverse risk governance issues in various case studies. Publications of these case studies are available

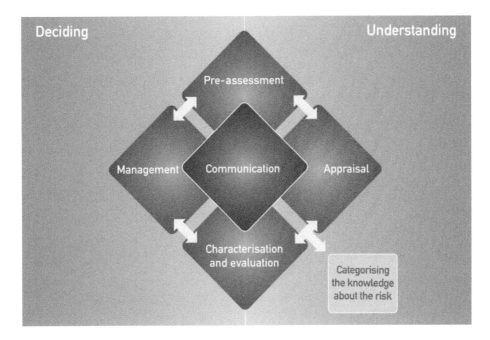

Figure 1.1 The risk governance framework

on the IRGC's home page (http://www.irgc.org/Publications.html). The case studies deal with emerging risks such as air quality, bioenergy, carbon capture and storage, critical infrastructure, nanotechnology, pollination services and synthetic biology. Furthermore, the IRGC has commissioned several case studies as tests of the applicability, efficacy and practicability of the risk governance framework (Renn and Walker 2008). The applications have shown that the framework can be used as broad conceptual guidance on the critical elements of the risk governance process. To date, the framework has been discussed and partially applied to a number of institutions and organizations, including most prominently the European Food Safety Authority (Vos and Wendler 2009) and the Health Council of the Netherlands (Health Council 2006). Reports using the framework have been given by the German Occupational Health and Safety Committee (Bender 2008), the International Occupational Safety Association (Radandt, Rantanen and Renn 2008), the UK Treasury (UK Treasury Department 2005), the US Environmental Protection Agency (EPA; 2009), and several private organizations. In addition, the framework was applied for strategic risk management of the US Joint Chiefs of Staff (Rouse 2011). The model has been used for major military operations and has, according to the source, improved the risk management process considerably.

The framework was primarily developed to deal with technological risks. It has been criticized as overstating the demarcation line between assessment and management, as being too rigid in its phasing of the governance process and in being not specific enough on stakeholder involvement and participation (see Renn and Walker 2008; van Asselt 2005). For the purpose of developing a more adaptive and inclusive version of the framework, Klinke and Renn (in press) and Renn et al. (2011) suggest a slightly modified version illustrated in Figure 1.2.

Governance institution

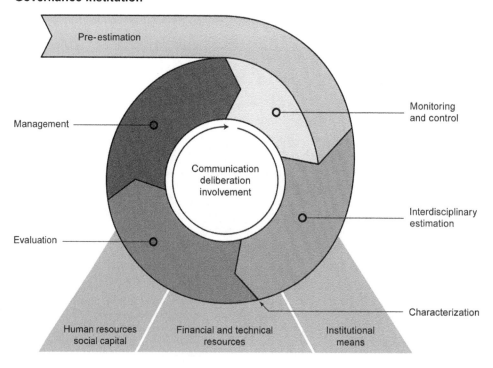

Figure 1.2 Adaptive and integrative risk governance model

The modified framework consists of these steps: pre-estimation, interdisciplinary risk estimation, risk characterization, risk evaluation and risk management. This is all related to the ability and capacity of risk governance institutions to use resources effectively (see Figure 1.2). Appropriate resources include institutional and financial means as well as social capital (e.g. strong institutional mechanisms and configurations, transparent decision-making, allocation of decision-making authority, formal and informal networks that promote collective risk handling, education), technical resources (e.g. databases, computer software and hardware), and human resources (e.g. skills, knowledge, expertise, epistemic communities). Hence, the adequate involvement of experts, stakeholders and the public in the risk governance process is a crucial dimension to produce and convey adaptive and integrative capacity in risk governance institutions (cf. Pelling, High, Dearing and Smith 2008). Since the social acceptance of any response of risk governance to risk problems associated with complexity, uncertainty and/or ambiguity is critical, risk handling and response strategies need to be flexible and the risk management approaches need to be iterative and inclusionary.

Pre-estimation

Risks are not straightforwardly objective phenomena. They are also mental constructions that reflect how people perceive uncertain phenomena and the ways in which their interpretations and responses are determined by social, political, economic and cultural contexts and judgments (cf. Luhman 1993; IRGC 2005; OECD 2003). The introduction of risk as a mental construct is contingent on the presumption that human action can prevent harm in advance. The conceptualization of risk as a mental construct has major implications for how risk is considered. Risks are created and selected by human actors. What counts as a risk to someone may be a destiny explained by religion or even an opportunity for a third party. Although societies have over time gained experience and collective knowledge of the potential impacts of events and activities, one cannot anticipate all potential scenarios and be worried about all the many potential consequences of a proposed activity or an expected event. By the same token, it is impossible to include all possible options for intervention. Therefore, societies have been *selective* in what they have chosen to consider worth addressing and what to ignore.

The insight that risks are not objective entities that need only to be discovered but mental constructs of how people select signals from their environment in order to be better prepared if a hazard strikes leads to the necessity to establish (culture-sensitive) institutions for early warning. Many such institutions exist – particularly on the national level. However, an adequate international mechanism for the *detection and early warning* of some globally relevant potential future harm (e.g. regarding global environmental threats, global food security) is lacking in spite of the fact that some specialized organizations (e.g. International Atomic Energy Agency, Pacific Tsunami Warning Center, National Hurricane Center in Miami, Centers for Disease Control and Prevention in Denver, Colorado) have been established to monitor specific hazards and to detect hints of future problems on an international scale.

A systematic review of the stages in pre-estimation would start with *screening* as an exploration of a large array of actions and problems looking for those with a specific risk-related feature. It is important to explore what major political and societal actors such as governments, companies, epistemic communities, NGOs and the public identify as risks and what types of problems they label as problems associated with risk and uncertainty. This is called *framing*, and it specifies how society and politics rely on schemes of selection and interpretation to understand and respond to those phenomena that are socially constructed as relevant risk topics (Kahneman and Tversky 2000; Reese, Gandy and Grant 2003). Interpretations of risk experience depend on frames of reference (Daft and Weick 1984). The process of framing corresponds with a multi-actor and multi-objective governance structure since governmental authorities (national, supranational and international agencies), risk and opportunity producers (e.g. industry), those affected by risks and opportunities (e.g. consumer organizations, environmental groups) and interested bystanders (e.g. the media or an intellectual elite) are all involved and often in conflict with each other over the appropriate frame to conceptualize the problem. What counts as risk may vary among these actor groups. Whether an overlapping consensus evolves about what requires consideration as a relevant risk depends on the legitimacy of the selection rule. For example, the risks and benefits of biomass conversion for energy purposes can be seen under the frame of energy security, national independence, climate protection or economic development opportunities for rural areas. Depending on the frame, different types of risks and benefits may emerge; furthermore, some benefits under one frame (e.g. national independence) may be a risk for another frame (economic opportunities for developing countries).

Interdisciplinary risk estimation

For politics and society to come to reasonable decisions about risks in the public interest, it is not enough to consider only the results of (scientific) risk assessment. In order to understand the concerns of people affected and various stakeholders, information about both risk perceptions and the further implications of the direct consequences of a risk is needed and should be taken into account by risk management.

Interdisciplinary risk estimation thus includes scientific assessment of risks to human health and the environment and assessment of related concerns as well as social and economic implications (cf. IRGC 2005; Renn and Walker 2007). The interdisciplinary estimation process should be clearly dominated by scientific analyses but, in contrast to traditional risk regulation models, the scientific process includes both the natural/technical as well as the social sciences, including economics. The interdisciplinary risk estimation consists of two stages:

(1) *Risk assessment*: Experts from the natural and technical sciences produce the best estimate of the physical harm that a risk source may induce.
(2) *Concern assessment*: Experts from the social sciences, including economics, identify and analyze the issues that individuals or society as a whole link to a certain risk. For this purpose, the repertoire of the social sciences such as survey methods, focus groups, econometric analysis, macro-economic modeling, or structured hearings with stakeholders may be used.

There are different approaches and proposals regarding how best to address the issue of interdisciplinary risk estimation. The German Advisory Council on Global Change (WBGU) has developed a set of eight criteria to characterize risks beyond the established assessment criteria (Klinke and Renn 2002; WBGU 2000). Some of the criteria have been used by different risk agencies or risk estimation processes (for example HSE 2001). These criteria include:

- *Extent of damage*: Adverse effects in natural units, e.g. death, injury, or production loss.
- *Probability of occurrence*: Estimate of relative frequency, which can be discrete or continuous.
- *Incertitude*: How do we take account of uncertainty in knowledge, in modeling of complex systems or in predictability in assessing a risk?
- *Ubiquity*: Geographical dispersion of damage.
- *Persistence*: How long will the damage last?
- *Reversibility*: Can the damage be reversed?

- *Delay effects:* Latency between initial event and actual damage.
- *Potential for mobilization:* The broad social impact. Will the risk generate social conflict or outrage etc.?
    - *Inequity and injustice* associated with the distribution of risks and benefits over time, space and social status.
    - *Psychological stress and discomfort* associated with the risk or the risk source (as measured by psychometric scales).
    - *Potential for social conflict and mobilization,* or the degree of political or public pressure on risk regulatory agencies.
    - *Spill-over effects* that are likely to be expected when highly symbolic losses have repercussions on other fields such as financial markets or loss of credibility in management institutions.

These four subcriteria of the last category reflect many factors that have been proven to influence risk perception. The 'appraisal guidance' published by the UK Treasury Department in 2005 recommends a risk estimation procedure that is similar to our proposal and includes as well both the results of risk assessment and the direct input from data on public perception and the assessment of social concerns (UK Treasury Department 2005).

Risk evaluation

A heavily disputed task in the risk governance process relates to the procedure of how to judge a given risk and justify an evaluation about its societal acceptability or tolerability (see Figure 1.2). In many approaches, risks are ranked and prioritized based on a combination of probability (how likely is it that the risk will occur) and impact (what are the consequences if the risk does occur). In the so-called traffic light model (see Figure 1.3), risks are located in the diagram of probability versus expected consequences and three areas are identified: *acceptable* (a green light),

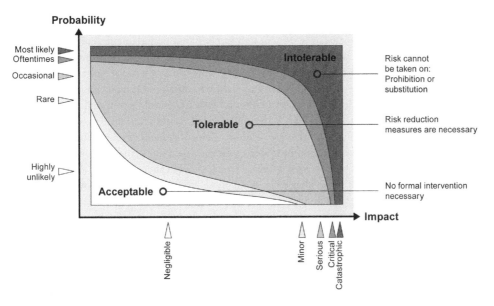

Figure 1.3   Risk areas

tolerable (a yellow light) and *intolerable* (a red light) (Klinke and Renn 2002; Renn 2008: 149ff.). A risk falls into the acceptable area if the occurrence is highly unlikely and the impact is negligible. No further formal intervention is necessary. A risk is seen as tolerable when serious impacts might occur occasionally. The benefits are worth the risk, but risk reduction measures are necessary. Finally, a risk is viewed as intolerable when the occurrence of catastrophic impacts is most likely. Possible negative consequences of the risk are so catastrophic that in spite of potential benefits it cannot be tolerated.

Drawing the lines between acceptable, tolerable and intolerable risk is one of the most controversial tasks in the risk governance process. The UK Health and Safety Executive developed a procedure for chemical risks based on risk–risk comparisons (Löfstedt 1997). Some Swiss cantons such as Basel experimented with round tables as a means to reach consensus on drawing the two demarcation lines, whereby participants in the round table represented industry, administrators, county officials, environmentalists and neighborhood groups. Irrespective of the selected means to support this task, the judgment on acceptability or tolerability is contingent on making use of a variety of different knowledge sources. One needs to include the data and insights resulting from the risk assessment activity, and additional data from the concern assessment.

Attempting to draw fixed and precise lines in the traffic light model has been criticized as simplistic. To meet this objection, we have introduced gradual transition zones to allow more differentiation in the evaluation of risks. If a given risk based on the risk assessment results cannot definitely be classified as acceptable, but it is plausible that the occurrence is rather rare and the impact is rather minor, the risk would be assigned to the transition zone between acceptable and tolerable. Furthermore, we would locate a given risk in the transition zone between tolerable and intolerable, if the risk cannot clearly be characterized as intolerable and, at the same time, the benefits to society are seen at least partially worthwhile.

Risk evaluations in general rely on causal and principal beliefs as well as worldviews (cf. Goldstein and Keohane 1993). Causal beliefs refer to the scientific evidence from risk assessment, whether, how and to what extent the hazard potential causes harm to the environment or to human health. This dimension emphasizes cause–effect relations and provides factual guidance on which strategy is appropriate to achieve the goal of risk avoidance or reduction.

However, the question of what is safe enough implies a moral judgment about the acceptability of risk and the tolerable burden that risk producers can impose on others. The results of the concern assessment can provide insights into what kind of associations are present and which moral judgments people would prefer in a choice situation. Of major importance is the perception of just or unjust distribution of risks and benefits. How these moral judgments are made and justified depends to a large degree on cultural values and worldviews. They affect personal thinking and evaluation strategies and are shaped by collectively shared ontological and ethical convictions. The selection of strategies for risk handling is, therefore, understandable only within the context of broader worldviews. Hence, society can never derive acceptability or tolerability from looking at the evidence alone. Likewise, evidence is essential if we are to know whether a value has been violated or not (or to what degree).

In those cases where there is unanimous agreement about the underlying values and even the threshold of what is regarded as acceptable or tolerable (i.e. interpretive ambiguity), evidence in the form of risk estimates may be sufficient to locate the risk within the risk area diagram. A judgment can then best be made by those who have most expertise in risk and concern assessments, in which case it makes sense to place this task within the domain of risk estimation by experts. However, with respect to values and evidence we can distinguish three dimensions of socio-political ambiguity that make it difficult to simply delegate risk estimation to experts.

Interpretive and normative ambiguity have already been discussed. These refer to ambiguity in relation to the interpretation of evidence and in relation to the underlying values that should be considered by risk managers, respectively. For example, the definition of adverse effects relating to an exposure to a chemical may raise concerns about the nature of adverse effects (focusing only on physical health impacts or also including psychological anxieties) and of the attached significance to specific symptoms (e.g. the impact of electromagnetic fields on brain activity). If there is disagreement about the interpretation of results, for example, whether a change in the environment due to human intervention is an adverse effect or not (such as adding nutrients to a lake), expertise alone does not resolve the issue. In this case, an epistemic or interpretative discourse among those who are knowledgeable about the subject is necessary in order to collect evidence on impacts and arguments about their evaluation. The US National Academy has labeled such a discourse as analytic-deliberative (Stern and Fineberg 1996). Even more deliberation is needed for resolving normative ambiguity. If the underlying values of what could be interpreted as acceptable or tolerable are disputed, while the evidence of what is at stake is clearly given and noncontroversial, the judgment needs to be based on a discourse about values and their implications. Such a discourse should be part of risk management by the legitimate decision-makers.

A third dimension evolves when both interpretive and normative ambiguity are 'present', that is, where both the evidence and the values are controversial. This would imply that assessment should engage in an activity to find some common ground for characterizing and qualifying the evidence and risk management needs to establish agreement about the appropriate values and their application. A good example for this third case may be the interpretative and normative implications of global climate change. The Intergovernmental Panel on Climate Change (IPCC) has gone through considerable efforts to articulate a common characterization of climatic risks and their uncertainties. Given the remaining uncertainties and the complexities of the causal relationships between greenhouse gases and climate change, it is both a question of contested evidence and of conflicting values whether governments place their priorities on prevention, mitigation or adaptation (Keeney and McDaniels 2001).

Since the last case includes both issues of the other two, the process of judging the tolerability and acceptability of a risk can be structured into two distinct components: risk characterization and risk evaluation (IRGC 2005). The first step, *risk characterization*, determines the evidence-based component for making the necessary judgment on the tolerability and/or acceptability of a risk. The second step, *risk evaluation*, determines the value-based component for making this judgment. The separation of evidence and values underlying the distinction between characterization and evaluation is, of course, functional and not necessarily organizational (Renn 2008: 153f). Since risk characterization and evaluation are closely linked and each depends on the other, it may even be wise to perform these two steps simultaneously in a joint effort by both risk assessment experts and risk management decision-makers (Frewer and Salter 2007). The US regulatory system tends to favor an organizational combination of characterization and evaluation, while European risk management tends to maintain the organizational separation, e.g. in the food area (Löfstedt and Vogel 2001).

Risk management

Risk management starts by reviewing all relevant data and information generated in the previous steps of interdisciplinary risk estimation, characterization and risk evaluation. The systematic analysis of risk management options focuses on still tolerable risks and those where tolerability is disputed (the transition zones between acceptable and tolerable, and between tolerable and intolerable). The other cases (acceptable and intolerable) are fairly easy to deal with. Intolerable risks demand prevention and prohibition strategies as a means of replacing the hazardous activity with another activity leading to identical or similar benefits. The management of acceptable risks is left to private actors (civil society and economy). They may initiate additional and voluntary risk reduction measures or to seek insurance for covering possible but rather minor or negligible losses. If risks are classified as tolerable, or if there is a dispute as to whether they are in the transition zones of tolerability, public risk management needs to design and implement actions that make these risks either acceptable or at least tolerable by introducing reduction strategies. This task can be described in terms of classic decision theory (cf. Aven and Vinnem 2007; Klinke and Renn 2010):

- Identification and generation of generic risk management options
- Assessment of risk management options with respect to predefined criteria
- Evaluation of risk management options
- Selection of appropriate risk management options
- Implementation of risk management options
- Monitoring and control of option performance.

By meeting the different challenges raised by complexity, scientific uncertainty and socio-political ambiguity, it is possible to design general strategies for risk management that can be applied to four distinct categories of risk problems, thus simplifying the process step of risk management mentioned earlier (Klinke and Renn 2002).

The first category refers to linear risk problems: they are characterized as having low scores on the dimensions of complexity, uncertainty and ambiguity. They can be addressed by *linear risk management* because they are normally easy to assess and quantify. Routine risk handling within risk assessment agencies and regulatory institutions is appropriate for this category, since the risk problems are well known, sufficient knowledge of key parameters is available and there are no major controversies about causes and effects or conflicting values. The management includes risk–benefit analysis, risk–risk comparisons or other instruments of balancing pros and cons.

If risks are ranked high on complexity but rather low on uncertainty and ambiguity, they require a systematic involvement and deliberation of experts representing the relevant epistemic communities for producing the most accurate estimate of the complex relationships. It does not make much sense to integrate public concerns, perceptions or any other social aspects for resolving complexity unless specific knowledge from the concern assessment helps to untangle complexity. Complex risk problems therefore demand *risk-informed management* that can be offered by scientists and experts applying methods of expanded risk assessment, determining quantitative safety goals, consistently using cost-effectiveness methods, and monitoring and evaluating outcomes.

Risk problems that are characterized by high uncertainty but low ambiguity require *precaution-based management*. Since sufficient scientific certainty is currently either not available or attainable, expanded knowledge acquisition may help to reduce uncertainty and, thus, move the risk problem back to first stage of handling complexity. If, however, uncertainty cannot be reduced by additional knowledge, risk management should foster and enhance precautionary and resilience-building strategies and decrease vulnerabilities in order to avoid irreversible effects. Appropriate instruments include containment, diversification, monitoring and substitution.

Finally, if risk problems are ranked high on ambiguity (regardless of whether they are low or high on uncertainty), *discourse-based management* is required demanding participative processing. This includes the need to involve major stakeholders as well as the affected public. The goal of discourse-based risk management is to produce a collective understanding among all stakeholders and the concerned public on interpretative ambiguity or to find legitimate procedures of justifying collectively binding decisions on acceptability and tolerability. It is important that a consensus or a compromise is achieved between those who believe that the risk is worth taking (perhaps because of self-interest) and those who believe that the pending consequences do not justify the potential benefits of the risky activity or technology.

Communication, deliberation and involvement of nongovernmental actors

The effectiveness and legitimacy of the risk governance process depends on the capability of management agencies to resolve complexity, characterize uncertainty and handle ambiguity by means of communication and deliberation.

Instrumental processing involving governmental actors

Dealing with linear risk issues, which are associated with low scores of complexity, scientific uncertainty and socio-political ambiguity, requires hardly any changes to conventional public policymaking. The data and information of such linear (routine) risk problems are provided by statistical analysis, law or statutory requirements determine the general and specific objectives, and the role of public policy is to ensure that all necessary measures of safety and control are implemented and enforced. Traditional cost–benefit analyses including effectiveness and efficiency criteria are the instruments of political choice for finding the right balance between under- and overregulation of risk-related activities and goods. In addition, monitoring the issue area is important as a reinsurance that no unexpected consequences may occur. For this reason, linear risk issues can well be handled by an instrumental involvement of departmental and agency staff and enforcement personnel of state-run governance institutions. The aim is to find the most cost-effective method for a desired regulation level. If necessary, stakeholders may be included in the deliberations as they have information and know-how that may provide useful hints for being more efficient.

Epistemic processing involving experts

Resolving complex risk problems requires dialogue and deliberation among experts. Involving members of various epistemic communities that demonstrate expertise and competence is the most promising step for producing more reliable and valid judgments about the complex nature of a given risk. Epistemic discourse is the instrument for discussing the conclusiveness and validity of cause–effect chains relying on available probative facts, uncertain knowledge and experience that can be tested for empirical traceability and consistency. The objective of such a deliberation is to find the most cogent description and explanation of the phenomenological complexity in question as well as a clarification of dissenting views (e.g. by addressing the question of which environmental and socioeconomic impacts are to be expected by specific actions or events). The deliberation among experts might generate a profile of the complexity of the given risk issue on selected inter-subjectively chosen criteria. The deliberation may also reveal that there is more uncertainty and ambiguity hidden in the case than the initial appraisers had anticipated. It is advisable to include natural as well as social scientists in the epistemic discourse so that potential problems with risk perception can be anticipated. Controversies would occur less as a surprise than now.

Reflective processing involving stakeholders

Characterizing and evaluating risks as well as developing and selecting appropriate management options for risk reduction and control in situations of high uncertainty pose particular
challenges. How can risk managers characterize and evaluate the severity of a risk problem
when the potential damage and its probability are unknown or highly uncertain? Scientific
input is, therefore, only the first step in a series of steps during a more sophisticated evaluation
process. It is crucial to compile the relevant data and information about the different types of
uncertainties to inform the process of risk characterization. The outcome of the risk characterization provides the foundation for a broader deliberative arena, in which not only policy
makers and scientists, but also directly affected stakeholders and public interest groups ought
to be involved in order to discuss and ponder the 'right' balances and trade-offs between over-
and under-protection. This reflective involvement of stakeholders and interest groups pursues
the purpose of finding a consensus on the extra margin of safety that potential victims would
be willing to tolerate and potential beneficiaries of the risk would be willing to invest in in
order to avoid potentially critical and catastrophic consequences. If too much precaution is
applied, innovations may be impeded or even eliminated; if too little precaution is applied,
society may experience the occurrence of undesired consequences. The crucial question here
is how much uncertainty and ignorance the main stakeholders and public interest groups are
willing to accept or tolerate in exchange for some potential benefit. The nature and scope
of uncertainty may have implications on the range of groups to be involved and procedures
appropriate to address uncertainties and to debate how decisions should be made in the light
of unresolved uncertainty. The reflective involvement of policy makers, scientists, stakeholders
and public interest groups can be accomplished through a spectrum of different procedures
such as negotiated rule-making, mediation, roundtable or open forums, advisory committees,
and so on (cf. Beierle and Cayford 2002; Klinke 2006; Rowe and Frewer 2000; Stoll-Kleemann
and Welp 2006).

Participative processing involving the wider public

If risk problems are associated with high ambiguity, it is not enough to demonstrate that risk
regulation addresses the issues of public concerns. In these cases, the process of evaluation needs
to be open to public input and new forms of deliberation. This starts with revisiting the question of proper framing. Is the issue really a risk problem or is it an issue of lifestyle or future
vision? Often the benefits are contested as well as the risks. The debate about designer babies
may illustrate the point that observers may be concerned not only about social risks of intervening into the genetic code of humans but also about the acceptability of the desired goal to
improve the performance of individuals (Hudson 2006). Thus the controversy is often much
broader than dealing with the direct risks only. The aim here is to find an overlapping consensus
on the dimensions of ambiguity that need to be addressed in comparing risks and benefits and
balancing pros and cons. High ambiguity would require the most inclusive strategy for involvement because not only directly affected groups but also those indirectly affected should have
an opportunity to contribute to this debate. Resolving ambiguities in risk debates necessitates a
participatory involvement of the public to openly discuss competing arguments, beliefs and values. Participatory involvement offers opportunities to resolve conflicting expectations through a
process of identifying overarching common values, and in defining options that allow a desirable
lifestyle without compromising the vision of others. Critical to success here is the establishment
of equitable and just distribution rules when it comes to common resources and to activating

institutional means for achieving common welfare so that all can benefit. The set of possible procedures to involve the public includes citizen panels or juries, citizen forums, consensus conferences, public advisory committees and similar approaches (cf. Abels 2007; Beierle and Cayford 2002; Hagendijk and Irwin 2006; Klinke 2006; Renn 2008: 284ff.; Rowe and Frewer 2000).

An overview of the different participation and stakeholder involvement requirements with respect to linear, complex, uncertain and ambiguous risks is displayed in Figure 1.4. As is the case with all classifications, this scheme shows a simplified picture of the involvement process and it has been criticized for being too rigid in its linking of risk characteristics (complexity, uncertainty and ambiguity) and specific forms of discourse and dialogue (van Asselt 2005). In addition to the generic distinctions shown in Figure 1.4 it may, for instance, be wise to distinguish between different types of risks and different types of regulatory cultures or styles (Löfstedt and Vogel 2001; Renn 2008: 358ff). To conclude these caveats, the purpose of this scheme is to provide a general orientation and to explain a generic distinction between ideal cases rather than to offer a strict recipe for participation.

The classification in Figure 1.4 offers a taxonomy of requirements for stakeholder and public inclusion based on the characteristics of risk knowledge. These general guidelines can be further specified by looking into each phase of the risk governance cycle (Renn 2008; Renn and Walker 2008: 356f).

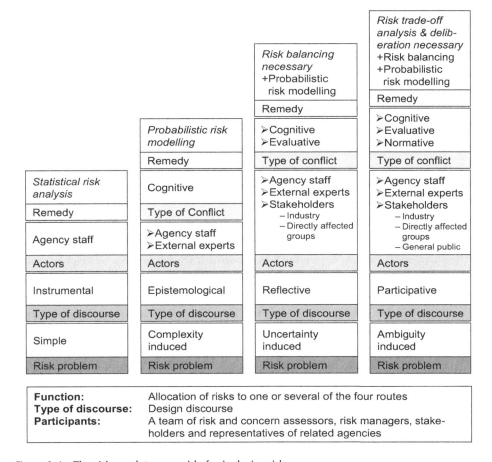

Function:	Allocation of risks to one or several of the four routes
Type of discourse:	Design discourse
Participants:	A team of risk and concern assessors, risk managers, stakeholders and representatives of related agencies

Figure 1.4 The risk escalator: a guide for inclusive risk governance

Conclusions

The goal of this chapter has been to illustrate how the different components of pre-estimation, interdisciplinary risk estimation, risk characterization, risk evaluation, risk management as well as communication and involvement interact with each other and to demonstrate how the various combinations of complexity, uncertainty and ambiguity can be addressed by different risk management strategies.

The proposed modifications to the IRGC framework were partly based on critical remarks in the literature and partly informed by the experiences and lessons drawn from empirical case studies. The modified framework offers substantial advantages over conventional models of risk governance. First, it joins the two crucial elements of risk governance: analysis (i.e. knowledge generation) and management (i.e. decision-making). These two elements are kept separate from an analytical perspective but work hand in hand operationally. Second, the analytic distinction of risk characteristics – complexity, uncertainty and ambiguity – helps to tackle governance issues where complex technologies are concerned. This distinction not only highlights deficits in our knowledge about a risk issue but also shows the way forward by pointing out management options. Furthermore it underscores the importance for transnational risk management, for example by the European Union or the UN. Third, the risk governance framework attributes public and stakeholder participation as well as risk communication – an important function in the risk governance process. The framework suggests efficient and adequate public/stakeholder participation. Concerns of stakeholders and/or the public are integrated in the risk appraisal phase via concern assessment. Furthermore, stakeholder and public participation are an established part of risk management. The optimum participation method thereby depends on the characteristics of the risk issue. Finally, the framework helps to identify governance gaps and deficiencies. At the same time, it proposes alternative actions.

The risk governance framework broadens the stakeholder's views towards an interactive, dialogical and systematic tool for reflecting the best available knowledge on physical risks as well as societal concerns and designing decision-making processes that considers both the likely consequences of the management measures as well as their impact on the various groups in society.

References

Abels, G. (2007). Citizen Involvement in Public Policymaking: Does It Improve Democratic Legitimacy and Accountability? The Case of pTA, *Interdisciplinary Information Science*, 13(1), pp. 103–116.

Aven, T. and Renn, O. (2009). The Role of Quantitative Risk Assessments for Characterizing Risk and Uncertainty and Delineating Appropriate Risk Management Options, with Special Emphasis on Terrorism, *Risk Analysis*, 29(4), pp. 587–600.

Aven, T. and Vinnem, J.E. (2007). *Risk Management: With Applications from the Offshore Petroleum Industry* (Heidelberg: Springer).

Beierle, T.C. and Cayford, J. (2002). *Democracy in Practice. Public Participation in Environmental Decisions* (Washington, DC: Resources for the Future).

Bender, H.F. (2008). Ergebnisse der Projektgruppe Risikoakzeptanz des AGS. *Gefahrstoffe- Reinhaltung der Luft*, 68(7/8), pp. 287–288.

Brooks, H. (1984). The Resolution of Technically Intensive Public Policy Disputes, *Science, Technology, and Human Values*, 9, pp. 39–50.

Daft, R.L. and Weick, K.E. (1984). Toward a Model of Organizations as Interpretation Systems, *Academy of Management Review*, 9(2), pp. 284–295.

Feldman, M.S. (1989). *Order without Design: Information Production and Policy Making* (Stanford, CA: Stanford University Press).

Filar, J.A. and Haurie, A. (Eds.). (2010). *Uncertainty and Environmental Decision Making* (New York: Springer).

Frewer, L.J. and Salter, B. (2007). Societal Trust in Risk Analysis: Implications for the Interface of Risk Assessment and Risk Management. In M. Siegrist, T.C. Earle and H. Gutscher (Eds.), *Trust in Cooperative Risk Management: Uncertainty in Scepticism in the Public Mind*, pp. 143–158 (London: Earthscan).

Functowicz, S.O. and Ravetz, J.R. (1992). Three Types of Risk Assessment and the Emergence of Post-Normal Science. In S. Krimsky and D. Golding (Eds.), *Social Theories of Risk*, pp. 251–273 (Westport, CT: Praeger).

Goldstein, J. and Keohane, R.O. (1993). Ideas and Foreign Policy. An Analytical Framework. In J. Goldstein and R.O. Keohane (Eds.), *Ideas and Foreign Policy. Beliefs, Institutions, and Political Change*, pp. 3–30 (Ithaca, NY: Cornell University Press).

Hagendijk, R. and Irwin, A. (2006). Public Deliberation and Governance: Engaging with Science and Technology in Contemporary Europe, *Minerva*, 44, pp. 167–184.

Health Council of the Netherlands. (2006). Health Significance of Nanotechnologies. Publication No. 2006/06E (The Hague: Health Council of the Netherlands).

Horlick-Jones, T. (2007). On the Signature of New Technologies: Materiality, Sociality, and Practical Reasoning. In R. Flynn and P. Bellaby (Eds.), *Risk and the Public Acceptance of New Technologies*, pp. 41–65 (Basingstoke: Palgrave).

Horlick-Jones, T., Rowe, G. and Walls, J. (2007). Citizen Engagement Processes as Information Systems: The Role of Knowledge and the Concept of Translation Quality, *Public Understanding of Science*, 16, pp. 259–278.

Horlick-Jones, T. and Sime, J. (2004). Living on the Border: Knowledge, Risk and Transdisciplinarity, *Futures*, 36, pp. 441–456.

HSE, Health and Safety Executive. (2001). *Reducing Risk – Protecting People* (London: Health and Safety Executive).

Hudson, K.L. (2006). Preimplantation Diagnosis: Public Policy and Public Attitudes, *Fertility & Sterility*, 58(6), pp. 1638–1645.

Hutter, B.M. (2006). Risk, Regulation, and Management. In P. Taylor-Gooby and J. Zinn (Eds.), *Risk in Social Science*, pp. 202–227 (Oxford: Oxford University Press).

IRGC, International Risk Governance Council. (2005). *Risk Governance: Towards an Integrative Approach*, White Paper No. 1, O. Renn with an Annex by P. Graham (Geneva: IRGC).

Kahneman, D. and Tversky, A. (Eds.). (2000). *Choices, Values, and Frames* (Cambridge: Cambridge University Press).

Keeney, R. and McDaniels, T. (2001). A Framework to Guide Thinking and Analysis Regarding Climate Change Policies, *Risk Analysis*, 21(6), pp. 989–1000.

Klinke, A. (2006). *Demokratisches Regieren jenseits des Staates. Deliberative Politik im nordamerikanischen Große Seen-Regime* (Opladen: Barbara Budrich).

Klinke, A., Dreyer, M., Renn, O., Stirling, A. and van Zwanenberg, P. (2006). Precautionary Risk Regulation in European Governance, *Journal of Risk Research*, 9(4), pp. 373–392.

Klinke, A. and Renn, O. (2001). Precautionary Principle and Discursive Strategies: Classifying and Managing Risks, *Journal of Risk Research*, 4(2), pp. 159–173.

Klinke, A. and Renn, O. (2002). A New Approach to Risk Evaluation and Management: Risk-Based, Precaution-Based, and Discourse-Based Strategies, *Risk Analysis*, 22(6), pp. 1071–1094.

Klinke, A. and Renn, O. (2010). Risk Governance: Contemporary and Future Challenges. In J. Eriksson, M. Gilek and C. Ruden (Eds.), *Regulating Chemical Risks: European and Global Perspectives* (Berlin: Springer).

Klinke, A. and Renn, O. (2012). Adaptive and Integrative Governance on Risk and Uncertainty. *Journal of Risk Research*, 15(3), pp. 273–292.

Laudan, L. (1996). The Pseudo-Science of Science? The Demise of the Demarcation Problem. In L. Laudan (Ed.), *Beyond Positivism and Relativism. Theory, Method and Evidence*, pp. 166–192 (Boulder, CO: Westview Press).

Lewin, R. (1992). *Complexity: Life at the Edge of Chaos* (New York: Macmillan).

Löfstedt, R.E. (1997). *Risk Evaluation in the United Kingdom: Legal Requirements, Conceptual Foundations, and Practical Experiences with Special Emphasis on Energy Systems*, Working Paper No. 92 (Stuttgart: Center of Technology Assessment).

Löfstedt, R. and Vogel, D. (2001). The Changing Character of Regulation: A Comparison of Europe and the United States, *Risk Analysis*, 21(3), pp. 393–402.

Luhmann, N. (1993). *Risk: A Sociological Theory* (Berlin: de Gruyter).

Marti, K., Ermoliev, Y. and Makowski, M. (Eds.). (2010). *Coping with Uncertainty. Robust Solutions* (Berlin: Springer).

Nelkin, D. and Pollak, M. (1979). Public Participation in the Technological Decisions: Reality or Grand Illusion?, *Technology Review*, 6, pp. 55–64.

Nelkin, D. and Pollak, M. (1980). Problems and Procedures in the Regulation of Technological Risk. In C.H. Weiss and A.F. Burton (Eds.), *Making Bureaucracies Work*, pp. 233–253 (Beverly Hills, CA: Sage).

OECD (Organisation for Economic Co-operation and Development). (2003). *Emerging Systemic Risks: Final Report to the OECD Futures Project* (Paris: OECD Press).

Pelling, M., High, C., Dearing, J. and Smith, D. (2008). Shadow Spaces for Social Learning: A Relational Understanding of Adaptive Capacity to Climate Change within Organisations, *Environment and Planning A*, 40, pp. 867–884.

Radandt, S., Rantanen, J. and Renn, O. (2008). Governance of Occupational Safety and Health and Environmental Risks. In H.-J. Bischoff (Ed.), *Risks in Modern Society*, pp. 127–258 (Heidelberg: Springer).

Reese, S.D., Gandy, O.H., Jr. and A.E. Grant (Eds.). (2003). *Framing Public Life: Perspectives on Media and Our Understanding of the Social World* (Mahwah, NJ: Lawrence Erlbaum Associates).

Renn, O. (2008). *Risk Governance. Coping with Uncertainty in a Complex World* (London: Earthscan).

Renn, O. and Klinke, A. (2013). Space Matters! Impacts for Risk Governance. In D. Müller-Mahn (Ed.), *The Spatial Dimension of Risk. How Geography Shapes the Emergence of Riskscapes*, pp. 1–21 (Milton Park: Routledge).

Renn, O., Klinke, A. and van Asselt, M. (2011). Coping with Complexity, Uncertainty and Ambiguity in Risk Governance: A Synthesis. *AMBIO*, 40(2), pp. 231–246.

Renn, O. and Schweizer, P. (2009). Inclusive Risk Governance: Concepts and Application to Environmental Policy Making, *Environmental Policy and Governance*, 19, pp. 174–185.

Renn, O. and Walker, K. (2008). Lessons Learned: A Re-Assessment of the IRGC Framework on Risk Governance. In O. Renn and K. Walker (Eds.), *The IRGC Risk Governance Framework: Concepts and Practice*, pp. 331–367 (Heidelberg: Springer).

Rosa, E. (1997). Metatheoretical Foundations for Post-Normal Risk, *Journal of Risk Research*, 1(1), pp. 15–44.

Rouse, J. (2011). *The Chairman of the Joint Chiefs of Staff Risk Assessment System. Incorporation of the International Risk Governance Council Framework*. Paper at the Annual Meeting of the Society for Risk Analysis in Salt Lake City, December 6 (Washington, DC: Arete Associates).

Rowe, G. and Frewer, L.J. (2000). Public Participation Methods: A Framework for Evaluation, *Science, Technology and Human Values*, 25(1), pp. 3–29.

Stern, P.C. and Fineberg, V. (1996). *Understanding Risk: Informing Decisions in a Democratic Society*, National Research Council, Committee on Risk Characterization (Washington, DC: National Academy Press).

Stirling, A. (2003). Risk, Uncertainty and Precaution: Some Instrumental Implications from the Social Sciences. In F. Berkhout, M. Leach and I. Scoones (Eds.), *Negotiating Change*, pp. 33–76 (London: Edward Elgar).

Stoll-Kleemann, S. and Welp, M. (Eds.). (2006). *Stakeholder Dialogues in Natural Resources Management: Theory and Practice* (Heidelberg: Springer).

UK Treasury Department. (2005). Managing Risks to the Public: Appraisal Guidance (London: HM Treasury). Accessed May 2011 at http://www.hm-treasury.gov.uk/media/0/B/Managing_risks_to_the_public.pdf

Underdal, A. (2009). Complexity and Challenges of Long-Term Environmental Governance, *Global Environmental Change*, 20, pp. 386–393.

US Environmental Protection Agency. (2009). *Potential Nano-enabled Environmental Applications for Radionuclides*, EPA-402-R-06–002 (Washington, DC: EPA).

van Asselt, M.B.A. (2000). *Perspectives on Uncertainty and Risk* (Dordrecht: Kluwer).

van Asselt, M.B.A. (2005). The Complex Significance of Uncertainty in a Risk Area, *International Journal of Risk Assessment and Management*, 5(2–4), pp. 125–158.

Vos, E. and Wendler, F. (2009). Legal and Institutional Aspects of the General Framework. In M. Dreyer and O. Renn (Eds.), *Food Safety Governance. Integrating Science, Precaution and Public Involvement*, pp. 83–109 (Berlin: Springer).

WBGU, German Advisory Council on Global Change. (2000). *World in Transition: Strategies for Managing Global Environmental Risks* (Heidelberg: Springer).

Wilkinson, C.F. and Lamb, J.C. (1999). The Potential Health Effects of Phthalate Esters in Children's Toys. A Review and Risk Assessment, *Regulatory Toxicology and Pharmacology*, 30(2), pp. 140–155.

Zahariadis, N. (2003). *Ambiguity and Choice in Public Policy. Political Decision Making in Modern Democracies* (Washington, DC: Georgetown University Press).

2

The governance of strategic risk-taking

Maxine Lorraine Garvey[1]

Defining governance

Where you stand on defining governance depends on where you sit. Ideas on public governance, corporate governance, network governance, e-governance, collective governance, global governance and environmental governance make for a lively 'governance conversation' among practitioners and academics. This conversation covers a rainbow of competing and complementary conceptual approaches to understanding, analyzing and prescribing action.

Whenever people organize for a common purpose, governance becomes a concern. Essentially governance is concerned with the exercise of power of the organized group for the agreed purpose.[2] In a state, institution or firm with dysfunctional governance, the power and resources of the group are diverted to purposes not envisaged when the entity was established or when power was granted by the group. Often the diversion serves a particular subgroup, which has appropriated power.

Although governance of the corporation has been a concern since the establishment this type of legal form, the term did not come into common in usage until the 1960. In business literature, the specific term corporate governance is credited to Richard Eells (1960), who used it to denote "the structure and functioning of the corporate polity."[3] Many early discussions of corporate governance addressed 'representative government' within corporates. Concerned with corporate democracy, the discussion of corporate suffrage dominated much of the literature about corporations. However, it was from economics and the corporate finance field that the strong impetus for rigorous study of corporate governance evolved to become the dominant paradigm.

This chapter discusses the role of the board in governance of the corporation and the board responsibility for the oversight of strategic risk-taking. It starts with a discussion of the corporate governance concept then introduces some elements of risk and risk-taking. It closes by bringing the two themes together and looking at emerging consensus around main issues in the governance of strategic risk-taking.

Corporate governance: perspectives from the dominant paradigm

Corporate governance refers to the mechanisms used by suppliers of finance (debt holders and shareholders) to assure that they will receive a fair return on their investment.[4] Ultimately it is about the exercise of power in the corporation (Insert 2.1). The use of this definition signals that this chapter cleaves to the finance-economics perspective of corporate governance. We find this appropriate given that that this perspective focuses on value creation and the uses of risk-adjusted cash flows in assessing value. This approach is congruent with the main objective of strategy risk-taking: the creation of value for the firm and in particular, for its shareholders.

Insert 2.1 Definitions of corporate governance

There are many workable definitions of corporate governance, which either add nuance to the financial economics perspective or add other useful dimensions to the governance concept, such as explicitly taking a stakeholder approach. As with risk, there is still no single consensus definition.

- *Corporate governance is concerned with the resolution of collective action problems among dispersed investors and the reconciliation of conflicts of interest between various corporate claimholders.*[5]
- *A corporate governance system is the complex system of constraints that frame the ex post bargaining over the quasi rents that are generated by an enterprise.*[6]
- *Corporate governance is the system by which companies are directed and controlled.*[7]
- *Corporate governance involves a set of relationships between a company's management, its board, its shareholders and other stakeholders. Corporate governance also provides the structure through which the objectives of the company are set and the means of attaining those objectives and monitoring performance are determined. Good corporate governance provides incentives for managers and directors to pursue objectives which are in the interest of the company and its shareholders.*[8]

Governance versus management in a corporate context

Regardless of the definition of governance favored by particular practitioners or academics, there is general agreement that governing a corporation and managing a corporation are distinct activities. Bob Tricker (2012) sliced to the heart of the difference when he argued that if corporate management was about running a business, then corporate governance was about seeing that the business was well run.[9] Both managing and governing are vital activities in creating value, and every corporation needs managing as well as governing.

Governing and managing a corporation are bound in a hierarchical relationship. In a well-governed enterprise, the shareholders (or the representatives of their choosing) are the governing actors, enjoying the upper hand and providing oversight. Managers are responsible for operational decision-making and action subject to this active oversight (Figure 2.1).

A vivid line from a film helps us visualize this relationship. The film's protagonist declares: "You see, in this world there's [*sic*] two kinds of people, my friend. Those with loaded guns and those who dig. You dig."[10] Coarsely extended, if the movie was about a well-structured corporate governance world, the shareholders would be holding the loaded guns and the managers (and employees) would be digging.

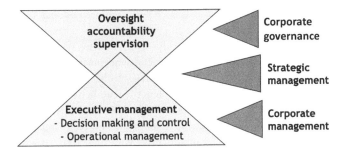

Figure 2.1 A simple view: management vs. governance

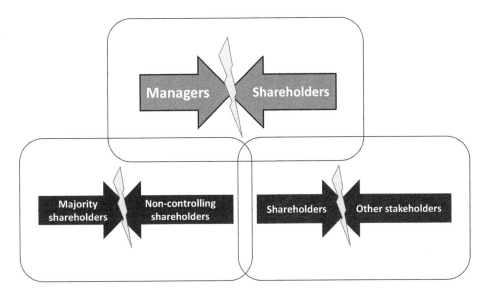

Figure 2.2 Three key governance conflicts

Corporate governance: avoiding greed, sloth and fear

A series of scandals including Enron, Tyco, Parmalat, Satyam, Lehman Brothers and so forth made corporate governance a familiar term in the nightly news and daily newspapers.[11] However, governance of the corporation has been a challenge from the founding of the first limited company. It was Berle and Means that brought incisive thinking to this issue and turned on academics to untangle the moral hazards arising from the separation of ownership and control characteristic of the corporate form. One essential issue is that corporate insiders need not (and often do not) act in the best interests of the owners and debt holders.[12] In running an enterprise, the corporate insiders are the agents of the providers of financing, many of whom are not insiders. Corporate governance is then concerned with conflicts between various claimants to the quasi-rents arising from the firm (Figure 2.2).

What exactly do suppliers of finance have to fear from insiders, particularly from managers? Recent scandals provide us with a litany of potential sources of loss arising from managers stealing, self-dealing, awarding themselves excessive perks, empire building, using entrenchment strategies, taking undeserved compensation and hiding poor performance using accounting manipulations. These maladies are typical of poorly governed firms with widely dispersed, small shareholders. These misbehaviors dominate the public perception of governance failures due to the media focus on listed enterprises. The public has also been treated to lurid headlines on corporate governance disputes in family firms, such as the feud between the Ambani brothers of Reliance Enterprises in India. This dispute arose, as seen often in family firms, upon the founder's death as the heirs wrestled over ownership. Even if no one dies, family members who are managers and controlling shareholders frequently clash with their relatives who are owners but not managers. State-owned enterprises also have their peculiar corporate governance failures, usually arising from multiagency conflicts arising from citizen-shareholders and lack of clear commercial objectives.

Practitioners and academics take two broad approaches to coping with moral hazards arising from the agency problems in corporations: alignment of incentives and monitoring.[13] Performance-based compensation, implicit incentives (e.g., threat of dismissal or reputation impairment) and product market competition help make managers work to ensure the well-being of the firm and its shareholders. Good incentive devices ensure that managers, the firm and shareholders gain or lose jointly.

In practice, designing appropriate incentives proves the cliché that the devil is in the details. Managers are paid in three ways, through salary, shares, and stock options plans. The latter two are structured as performance incentives. The press focuses on the level of pay but it is the structure of the compensation package that concerns governance specialists. Bonuses are usually paid using accounting-based measures of firm performance. The most popular bonus measures used by firms include earnings per share, total shareholder return, return on equity, return on capital employed and return on assets. However, accounting measures are subject to manipulation by managers and tend to encourage a focus on short-term outcomes. Stock and stock options gained popularity for a longer-term orientation and lower susceptibility to managerial manipulation. However, they too have proved to have their shortcomings. For example, when their stock options are underwater, managers may be tempted to take aggressive risks to try to bump up stock prices. It has been almost impossible to design an optimal incentive system that aligns the interests of managers and shareholders.

The providers of financing increasingly rely on monitoring by boards, rating agencies, external analysts, bankers, bondholders, auditors, activist investors, corporate raiders, large shareholders, regulators and other parties to reign in corporate abuses and resolve conflicts. Various associations of monitors have developed numerous codes, professional practice norms and rules to make monitoring foolproof. However, the continued flow of corporate governance failures indicates how difficult it is for external monitors to detect and act on poor conduct. Furthermore, many of the monitors find themselves with conflicts of interest when performing their supposed independent roles. For example, prior to the enforcement of the Sarbanes-Oxley rules in the US, many accountants earned such large fees from consulting to the firms they were monitoring that their auditing lost fervor and objectivity. Effective monitoring occurs only if the monitors remain committed and effective. In practice, the uncomfortable question of how to monitor the monitors remains unanswered.

Recent research has focused on using monitoring and performance incentives as complements rather than substitutes in effectively handling agency problems. Different combinations of governance mechanisms (i.e., governance bundles) may serve providers of financing in different ways depending on the firm's size, structure and stage in organizational life cycle (i.e., start-up vs. mature). In one study using high profitability as the outcome measure, researchers found that the effectiveness of board independence and CEO nonduality (i.e., where the CEO was not the chairperson) depended on how the mechanisms were combined in a bundle as complements.[14]

Although corporate governance mechanisms are concerned with both the rights of debt holders and shareholders, it is the latter group that attracts the bulk of efforts to create incentives and to monitor. This is as shareholders are generally more vulnerable to moral hazard than debt holders. Of course, shareholders also have more to gain as they have residual claims to upside gains from the firm. The debt holders can only regain their principal and the earned interest. Holders of debt often have collateral and are protected by well-developed bankruptcy laws. Often their legal contracts allow creditors to act individually to retrieve their money from firms and their deviant managers.

Despite the higher potential upside, shareholders have no collateral for their investment. Once they have taken the plunge and paid over their cash, they obtain rights to vote for a board and on other matters at the annual general meetings as set out in their respective articles of association and charters. If they are unhappy with how the firm in which they have invested is doing, they have a right to sell at the going rate to another potential investor. If they wish to keep their stake but to unseat the managers, then they will have to persuade other shareholders to join their action in voting or in filing in the courts. Both paths are painful. Both require resources, time and money to organize the required collective action (Figure 2.3). Varied corporate governance codes, laws and regulations provide corporate governance mechanisms to help shareholders to surmount this collective action problem.

Addressing the collective action problem

- Electing a board of directors who represent shareholders' interests and to which the CEO is accountable
- Facilitating takeovers or corporate raiders that temporarily concentrate voting power to remove an inefficient manager
- Ensuring active, continuous monitoring by the holder of a large block of shares
- Aligning of managerial interests with shareholders through design of the managers' compensation contracts
- Defining fiduciary duties clearly for CEO and directors in the law and then facilitating a lawsuit (usually a class action).

Countries have different devices for monitoring managers, varied incentives for alignment of interests and a range of collective action mechanisms. These combine with country culture, local legal and judiciary traditions, varied enforcement capabilities, corporate traditions and other local features to produce idiosyncratic country-specific governance environments. These corporate governance environments fall within four general groupings: (1) Anglo-Saxon common law legal traditions (e.g., Britain, the US), (2) Latin European civil law legal traditions (e.g., France, Italy, Spain), (3) Northern European civil law traditions (e.g., Germany, Scandinavia) and (4) Asian corporate governance traditions (e.g., Japan, Korea). Notwithstanding these regional groupings, within each there is wide variability between individual countries. However, strains of these four traditions are identifiable worldwide, as many former colonies adopted the legal traditions and corporate governance environments of their former colonizers. Due to their histories, the former Soviet republics have a different patchwork of governance environments.

China, with its powerful hybrid economy, has its own novel corporate governance arrangements. These national institutional environments, exogenous to each firm, determine the outcome of corporate governance conflicts as it sets shareholder and debt holders' rights.

The corporate governance environment – countries differ

Possible dimensions of national governance differences:

- Disclosure requirements and accounting standards
- Securities regulations and stock exchange rules
- Shareholders rights, proxy rules
- Mergers and acquisitions practices
- Shareholding patterns
- Fiduciary duties of directors, officers and controlling shareholders
- Bankruptcy and creditors' rights
- Financial media and analysts
- Credit rating agencies
- Role of state-controlled enterprises
- Role of sovereign funds
- Role of family companies, ethnic and network ties
- Labor relations and laws
- Financial sector practices
- Tax and pension policies
- Judicial and regulatory enforcement
- Understanding of corporate citizenship
- Competition on product and capital markets
- Market for managers, labor and corporate control
- Universities and civil society.

Studies show that the different legal systems provide very different levels of investor protection and the different levels of investor protection drive patterns of ownership of debt and equity in that country.[15] For example, where there is strong investor protection, as is usually found in common law countries, firms have widely held shareholdings. Even more far-reaching, poor investor protection reduces corporate risk-taking.[16] Managers (and insiders) in countries with weak investor protection are able to appropriate a good chunk of corporate assets for their own personal welfare. Often they invest more conservatively to protect these private benefits. They avoid even value-enhancing risk opportunities if there is any possibility that their private benefits will be threatened. Conversely, strong investor protection encourages managers (and insiders) to engage in more value enhancing risk-taking.

Of the collective action mechanisms, boards have carried increasing responsibilities over the last decade. Twenty years ago a newly appointed corporate director could expect a cushy role with good perks, enjoying comradeship with managers. In this kind of boardroom, it was easy to forget that shareholders nominated directors to monitor the managers. However, the vivid outrage at boards (some of it unfair and misplaced) arising after the corporate governance scandals worldwide have led directors to sharpen their focus on their fiduciary duties to the shareholders.

To support this change to increased accountability, many countries and international organizations have delivered new corporate governance codes outlining the specific responsibilities on directors. While the details vary, there is wide consensus that the director's role is one of oversight, not to undertake operational duties. Directors approve corporate strategy and major decisions such as asset disposals, acquisitions and mergers. They also oversee compensation of managers, risk-taking and the integrity of internal controls and financial reporting. The entire board has responsibility for oversight, although it often assigns specific tasks to board committees for governance, risk, audit and compensation.[17]

The role of directors according to the Organisation for Economic and Co-operative Development (OECD)[18]

A. Board members should act on a fully informed basis, in good faith, with due diligence and care, and in the best interest of the company and the shareholders.

B. Where board decisions may affect different shareholder groups differently, the board should treat all shareholders fairly.

C. The board should apply high ethical standards. It should take into account the interests of stakeholders.

D. The board should fulfill certain key functions, including reviewing corporate strategy, risk policy, monitoring governance practices, selecting key executives and aligning their remuneration, ensuring transparent board nominations, managing potential conflicts of interest, ensuring the integrity of accounting and reporting with appropriate systems of control, systems for risk management, and compliance with law and standards.

E. The board should be able to exercise objective independent judgment on corporate affairs implying (e.g., assigning a sufficient number of nonexecutive board members and well-defined committees of the board).

F. In order to fulfill their responsibilities, board members should have access to accurate, relevant and timely information.

A director has a tricky job. She has to monitor the manager. This same manager enjoys the benefit of greater information flow about the firm than she does. The director has to act as advisor to manager. She has fiduciary duties to the shareholders. She has to help the manager make social and business connections but she cannot materially benefit from her connections to the board on which she serves. She cannot herself undertake managerial actions but can find herself excoriated for the firm's failures. Directors could argue, with more than a modicum of reason, that the job is impossible to get right.

Broadening the governance concept

In the discussion so far, the predominant thought and tools in corporate governance draw upon agency theory – from finance and economics. It is far too early to argue that these theoretical perspectives will eventually lose preeminence. It is correct, however, to say that other approaches are gathering growing respect. Increasingly academia argues for opening the governance concept beyond the confines of agency and the rights of investors. New views include looking at corporate governance questions from the perspectives of stewardship, stakeholder, resource dependency and social capital. An emergent strain of this rethinking comes from management research, where voices from within the academy are positing a new view of governance to include different levels of analysis, varieties of contexts, new processes and temporal shifts. The editors of a leading management journal offered a definition of corporate governance as leadership systems of management controls over delegated decisions and similar practices of authority and mandates for action.[19]

For this discussion, however, this essay uses the finance perspective as the guiding theoretical framework. From this perspective, one can say that good corporate governance arrangements restrain an agent's greed without encouraging sloth and fear. Greed is seen when managers or large shareholders make decisions for their own benefit, which impairs the benefits of the shareholder community. Sloth arises when managers are so tightly controlled they lose their flair for the risk-taking needed to build value. Instead of displaying value-seeking verve and enterprise, they apply themselves to administration and bureaucracy. Fear makes managers nervous and fearful of their investors, unable to attend creatively to execution of their jobs and reluctant to communicate frankly with the suppliers of finance. Achieving good governance arrangements requires having balance between the various governance mechanisms and a sensible approach by all stakeholders.

The next section will discuss risk and risk-taking. Then the final section of the chapter combines the discussion of risk and governance and extends the discussion to risk governance practice and the role of a board in strategic risk-taking.

Risk and risk-taking

There is no consensus on a single definition of risk.[20] This discussion will rely on the financial perspective from which risk is understood as the standard deviation of a variable from its expected value.[21] Seeing risk as a variability of return draws upon the statistical sciences and it is one of the keystones of the treatment of risk within the field of finance. The definition contains implications for managerial actions as risks are future uncertain events that may interfere with an entity realizing its strategic and financial objectives.

Upside and downside of risk-taking

Any worthwhile definition of risk must capture an essential duality of risk as both danger and opportunity. Views of risk in terms of randomness and variability recognize that variability is not unidirectional thus outcomes can be above or below expectations. This view of risk-taking with both upside and downside effects is important, as defining risk in terms of only negative outcomes reduces risk management to just risk mitigation or hedging.[22] To include discussions of the returns above expectation highlights a key element of risk-taking, particularly strategic risk-taking: that it offers opportunities for excess returns and enhancing the value of the enterprise.

Understanding risk as a mix of danger and opportunity emphasizes that in business you cannot have one (opportunity) without the other (danger or threats), and that offers that look too good to be true (offering opportunity with little or no risk) are deceptive. By emphasizing the upside potential as well as the downside dangers, this definition also serves to remind us of an important truth about risk: where there is a downside, there is an upside (and vice versa). Booms and busts will come and go, and robust enterprises must prepare for both. Managers that excel at risk-taking cope with risk situations with sangfroid and look to manage risk actively in both good times and bad. They scout for opportunities during bad times and in good times they plan for future crises, which will certainly come.

How people perceive and behave when coping with risks

The litany of corporate failures attributed to poor risk-taking tells a story of bemusing behavior by people entrusted with shareholder investments. Some of the reported conduct borders on fraudulence, but many billions were lost by individuals that inadvertently acted in a manner that defied rational thinking, especially when looked at with hindsight. Other studies explore the specific incidents, but in this section we focus on how humans behave when faced with risk. Behavioral finance, social construction perspectives and an exploration of corporate culture offer instruction to shareholders and board members on how managers (and their staff) behave when they encounter risks.

Behavioral finance tells us that humans are not economic men, the rational information-processing machines commonly described in classical economics textbooks. Instead, humans often behave badly in surprising and inconsistent ways.[23] Several of these idiosyncratic behaviors were seen repeatedly in recent crises. For example, we become risk-seeking demons when the chips are down. Generally, under normal conditions humans tend to be risk averse, with women and older persons being more risk averse than young men. However, this risk aversion is not constant by person. Individuals behave in a more risk-averse manner when the stakes are large than when they are minor. Under some circumstances, humans can become desperately risk-seeking. Individuals that have lost money tend to take enormous risk to recoup the losses. This, the break-even effect, often causes losses to pile up as the hapless risk-taker seeks to break even on previous losses. In another breakaway from risk aversion, humans are drawn to take risks if the potential gain is large in spite of the probability of winning being small (the long-shot bias). Consistent with these two types of risk-seeking behaviors, a quick review of press on banks that suffered losses in the recent crisis would find many stories of traders trying to recover initial losses by taking big, long-shot bets that resulted in even more damage to shareholder wealth.

Common features of the rogue trader

- Relatively young male trader seen as a 'star'
- Internal pressure to bring high profits
- Risk-taking cultural environment
- Profitable departments
- Initial warning signs are ignored
- Initial smaller loss trader tried to cover up leads to big gambles.

In another departure from rationality, losses are felt more keenly than equal (but opposite) gains are enjoyed. This is called loss aversion. Further, whether a choice is seen as risky or not (and the level of risk perceived) is very dependent on how the matter is framed.[24] Also, it is true that risk perceptions change over time depending on the external economic conditions (Insert 2.2). This importance of context has significant implication for managerial and board-level discussions, as skillful presentations can obscure the true perils that lie underneath. In another human quirk with risk-taking implications, everyone finds it easier to gamble with money they came by easily (the 'house money effect'). This is not only an individual-level phenomenon; in organizational contexts the appearance of excessive 'slack' and excess resources can lead to reckless risk-taking.

Insert 2.2 Changes in risk perception over time[25]

The higher the perceived risk, the higher the compensation the investor wants in terms of future returns. The extra compensation required to invest in risky assets is expressed by the difference between the risky bond rate and the risk-free rate referred to as the default spread. Investors see more risk in equity and, therefore, will demand higher expected returns as compensation. The difference between the expected return on equities and the risk-free rate is called the equity risk premium (ERP). Looking at the default spread of a Moody's-rated Baa corporate bond with intermediate default risk and the equity risk premium in the US over the period from 1960 to 2009, we notice dramatic changes in the risk compensation over time (Figure 2.3).

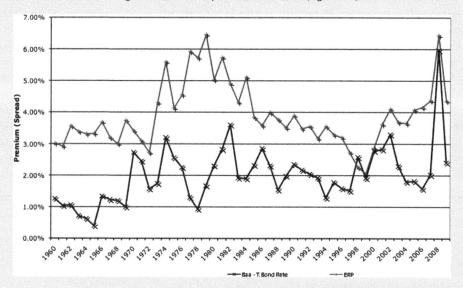

Figure 2.3   Default spreads of equity and corporate bonds 1960–2009

It is quite clear that while investors have stayed risk averse through history (the premiums would be zero if that were not the case), both assessments of risk and the price of risk have changed over time. Investors were charging far higher prices for risk in 1978 than they were in 1999, and again in 2008, after the banking crisis, than in 2007. In other words, the investment and general business climate changes over time and affects the way investors and corporate decision-makers perceive risk and value financial assets and commercial ventures.

Social constructivists argue that organizations and societies are engaged in forming the conceptualization of risks into their perceived existence. Products, practices and activities are seen as dangerous, or risky, through a process of developing shared meanings among people within an organization or across a community. This constructivist approach differs from the realist approach often observed in professional fields like medicine, economics, finance and engineering, where risks often are conceived as objective, measurable, assessable and independent of the related social processes. Constructivists explore risk as social phenomena resulting from value judgments, belief systems, social biases, moral positions, shared past history and political processes. Societies decide, consciously and unconsciously, what, whom and when something is risky and or not.[26] For example, societal selection processes are what give rise to public concern about war, pollution, immigrants, ethnic groups and seeing certain chemicals as dangerous and risky. Organizations are also systems of shared meaning and their internal social interactions and culture shape the context in which risk-taking occurs.[27]

The cultural context within which risk-taking takes place should be one of the main concerns of a board. The firm's leadership creates and manages the organizational culture and should set the tone from the top.[28] Organizational culture is the basic assumptions and beliefs shared by members of an organization. It is a learned product of group experience where the group has repeatedly shared success in solving the problems of integration and survival. Cultural elements are both visible and invisible. The most visible elements are the physical artifacts seen in firms, the deeper elements of values (what ought to be), whereas the shared underlying assumptions (the deepest and real level of culture) are less so.

Within organizations, there are subcultures where different departments may develop slightly different cultures. The business press increasingly speaks of risk cultures with organizations referring to the values that guide their risk-taking behaviors. The values provide a normative moral guide on how to deal with risk situations, particularly around uncertain, uncontrollable, and rapidly evolving events. Risk cultures would also include the behaviors related to risk-taking enforced by the kinds of conduct that are rewarded and praised. When risk-taking situations arise in the absence of written rules or clarity, the risk culture acts as the dominant control and guidance mechanism.

The main point is that risk is a complex concept, and risk-taking has both an upside and a downside. Furthermore, good strategic risk-taking requires that both quantitative and qualitative factors are brought into the analysis before any actions are taken.

Having deepened the understanding of both corporate governance and risk, the next section address the oversight of risk-taking. The board's guiding of risk-taking is a particularly difficult due to the asymmetry of information between managers and directors, which is often exacerbated when risk-taking occurs in real time in rapidly changing contexts.

Risk governance

As the economic recession of 2008 swept through the industrialized economies, it became clear that something had gone seriously awry with how banks and other firms handled their risk-taking activities.[29] The trouble at firms that were previously lionized as corporate exemplars, such as Citibank, Deutsche Bank, Royal Bank of Scotland, and UBS, revealed widespread weaknesses in how boards undertook the oversight of risk in their enterprises.

Risk management and governance are complex and dynamic activities. In many corporate failures, directors often lacked the knowledge and risk vocabulary to engage effectively in overseeing the senior executives, which impaired their ability to execute their fiduciary duties. This failure threatened the very survival of the firms they governed.

Risk governance is a relatively new term with little consensus definition in the field of corporate governance. However, for the purposes of discussion, we will treat risk governance in firms as concerned with how directors authorize, optimize and monitor the risk-taking within an enterprise. It includes the skills, infrastructure (i.e., organization structure, controls and information systems) and culture deployed as directors exercise their risk oversight. Good risk governance provides clearly defined accountability, authority, communication and reporting mechanisms.

The risk oversight role is the responsibility of the entire board of directors. However, some boards use risk committees to assist them in fulfilling their responsibilities. The risk committee may be set up independently or its work may be combined with that of the audit task and assigned to a combined audit and risk committee (Appendix 2.1).

Risk governance versus risk management

Earlier we looked at the difference between corporate governance practices and corporate management and pointed out an essential difference as oversight activities versus operational activities.[30] Risk governance and risk management bear a similar relationship to each other (Figure 2.4). Risk governance responsibilities fall to the directors as a part of their fiduciary oversight duties.

Risk management is not the same activity as risk hedging. Over time some interpretations of risk management started to mean risk hedging with the main objective of eliminating and dampening risk exposures. Perhaps three sources of influence – human nature, the bankers and agency conflicts – are to be blamed for this creeping redefinition of risk management.[31] Humans remember losses (the downside of risk-taking) far more clearly than they recall profit (the upside of risk-taking). After market downturns and natural disasters, we latch on to risk-hedging products and pay hefty fees to the purveyors of such pain-sparing products. Even in good economic times, bankers and others that create insurance, derivatives and swap products hawk them vigorously as risk management products.[32] As these are revenue generators for the financial community, they have a vested interest in highlighting the virtues of risk hedging. From a corporate governance perspective, the tendency to insure against risks could arise from the conflict of interests between managers and stockholders. As pointed out by Berle and Means (1932), this potential conflict is inherent in the separation of management from ownership in most publicly traded firms. Managers tend to try to protect their jobs by insuring against risk rather than seek value-enhancing risk-taking. They do this even if the suppliers of financing gain nothing from the hedging activities.

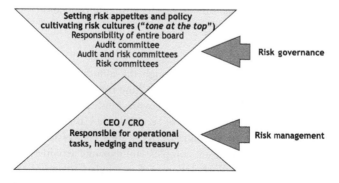

Figure 2.4   Diagram: risk governance vs. risk management

Strategic risk managment versus hazard, financial, project risk and enterprise risk management

Over time several subdisciplines have arisen in the risk management practice largely driven by the placing of these activities into different organizational departments and units. The risk management (RM) practices thus cover several different activities including traditional hazard, financial and project risk management. However the umbrella enterprise risk management (ERM) and strategic risk management (SRM) approaches engage the entire organization, its senior executives and board members, as these risk activities require the highest levels of organizational attention.

Traditional risk management (TRM) is often undertaken by the insurance department, emphasizing pure risk coverage tools and techniques including risk prevention, protection and coverage through transfer to third parties (insurance policies and other risk transfer instruments).[33] This approach contributes to the creation of value, the guiding principle of corporate finance, by minimizing downside risk and includes processes known as crisis management, risk forecasting and business continuity. These techniques have the general objective of handling pure risks that may arise during the life of an enterprise.

Financial risk management (FRM) is typically undertaken by the treasury unit mainly addressing the challenges of managing financial risks originating from fluctuating market conditions, e.g., interest rates, foreign exchange rates, and commodity prices. FRM is most widespread and developed in banks and financial institutions, but it is also growing among nonfinancial enterprises due to the wide use of derivative instruments on foreign exchange and interest rates. The large variety of tools introduced to the derivatives market provides a number of new ways to cover profit risks with opportunities to reorganize the capital structure.

Project risk management (PRM) is typically used by technical specialists responsible for implementing large public and private projects, where identified risks are analyzed and handled. PRM is particularly applicable to construction, large public works and advanced mechanical industries including aeronautics, aerospace and naval engineering, but can also be applied across commercial investment projects in any firm. The objective of the project is typically to build and manage a given structure, so the key objective of PRM is often to limit downside risks generated during the project execution. When dealing with major structures that can be very complex, there can be risks of service interruption caused by meteorological events and geologic incidents. In addition, the project may be exposed to effects of postponed cash flows from unexpected project delays and so forth.

ERM is intended to provide a more comprehensive and holistic approach to managing risk, thus avoiding the pitfalls of a silo approach where different risks are handled separately without considering interacting effects between risks. Prior to more widespread use of ERM, organizations tended to isolate the management of different risks without assessing how they could affect each other. For example, the treasurer managed currency exposures, the sales or credit manager managed credit risk, and commodity traders and purchasing officers managed commodity price risks. Insurance risk managers handled hazard risks. Personnel managed human resources risks. Quality and production managers were responsible for containing production risk. Marketing and strategy departments attended to competitive risks and so on. However, there was little effort devoted to an overview of aggregated exposures and coordinated risk management activities across the enterprise, where risks might augment each other (and multiply) or cancel out across diversified exposures.

Hence, the aim of ERM is to create an overview of corporate risks and coordinate risk management activities throughout the enterprise as needed. For example, a conglomerate where one division is long in currency A and another division is short in the same currency, each responsible divisional manager may purchase separate currency hedges if the firm adheres to a silo approach. However, this is not value-enhancing when viewed from an enterprise-wide approach because the conglomerate already has a natural diversification hedge. With good ERM this risk diversification advantage will be enhanced and executed effectively. However, diversification from natural hedges is not the only effect observed across complex organizations. In the recent economic recession, we saw that many risks were positively correlated with reinforcing effects under the extreme stress of financial crisis. The coordination function of ERM is often vested in a chief risk officer (CRO) position as head of a corporate risk office, which reflects increased risk governance activity with direct board oversight.

Enterprise approaches to risk management also use valuation techniques at various points in the process to ensure that the risk decisions taken will have positive value effects. These valuation efforts typically deploy the discounted cash flow methodology used in the capital asset pricing models. In adopting these valuation methods, the risk analysts need to estimate the effect of each risk on firm value and determine the cost of managing each of these risks. Hence, if a risk reduction initiative is costly, the decision-makers must decide whether the benefit to firm value can justify the costs of risk handling.

It is natural to think of SRM as an extension of the broader ERM concept as a way to emphasize the importance of managing operational and strategic risk factors to achieve longer-term corporate objectives. Hence, the SRM approach is involved in identifying, measuring and handling both pure and financial risks but also takes a special interest in speculative strategic risks with particular concerns for proactive risk-taking initiatives. RM and FRM are focused on a limited number of pure and market-related risks and, therefore, constitute subsets of the techniques presented under the name of ERM with broader concerns for enterprise-wide risk effects. PRM has a more limited and focused range of actions related to specific project activities that may, however, be linked to the firm's strategy execution. Hence, SRM can be seen as the highest level of corporate risk-taking considerations that make up RM and FRM as well as PRM and ERM approaches while supporting directors in their concerns for risk governance. We will discuss these issues further in subsequent chapters.

Role of the board in risk-taking

An important task for boards related to their corporate strategy work is the approval of risk-taking business initiatives and formulating the related risk-taking policies. A firm's risk-taking policy must be aligned with its strategic aims, capital budgeting plans, financial and compensation structures.

Ultimately the objective of governing and managing risk is to make the firm more valuable. For directors and managers, this is the primary objective, regardless of whether they view this as value to shareholders or value to a wider group of stakeholders. Fortunately, classical finance provides robust techniques for valuing enterprises. The most frequently used method, drawn from finance and economics, is the discounting of future cash flow to the firm at a risk-adjusted cost of capital.

A risk-taking policy involves specifying the types and degree of risk a company is willing to accept in pursuit of its overarching goals. It is thus a crucial guide for executives that must manage risks to meet the company's desired risk profile and performance targets (Insert 1.3).[34] The board is also instrumental in driving the development of an appropriate risk culture, which regulates the spirit of risk-taking behavior, particularly in new, rapidly evolving situations where written policy is not yet promulgated.

The attitude towards risk-taking among decision-makers in an enterprise (or more formally their risk aversion) will be reflected, in aggregate, in the corporate risk-taking policy whether this policy is explicitly stated or is implied through behavioral actions. In strategic risk-taking, there are various managerial decision points where the decision-makers' attitude to risk will drive the actions taken.

Insert 2.3 Tea and coffee plantation in Kenya

A commercial Kenyan farm producing tea and coffee for the European, Asian and US markets faces a range of risks. These risks include the vagaries of weather, particularly drought, changes in government policy, ethnic strife affecting the workforce, commodity price fluctuations and exchange rate fluctuations. The farm is owned and operated by the second generation of the founding family. The board consists of the three siblings running the business, their accountant and the export sales manager. The directors have taken a decision that they will not retain any foreign exchange risks as the siblings are of the view that they do not have the expertise to cope with foreign exchange fluctuations. They are confident that their knowledge of Kenya enables them to assess, evaluate and treat the weather and political risks. As result of their aversion to foreign currency risk, their risk-taking policy is to avoid or hedge this risk almost completely. They sell their produce to a middleman trading company that sets the contracts in Kenyan shillings. In addition, forward contacts are used to limit exposure on any inputs that need to be purchased in foreign currency.

For directors to meet their obligations in guiding risk-taking, they must have sufficient grasp of risk issues to engage the managers and executives in the firm. The board members in the risk committee must have a high level of competence in skills related to risk-taking. Each of the directors should understand the breadth of risks that confront the enterprise and how these risks reinforce or cancel out where risk assessments consider the perspective of multiple stakeholders.

Risk aversion, policy, tolerance, capacity, appetite, culture, limit and so forth

One of the most perplexing features of the risk governance and management world since the financial crisis of 2008 is the rapidly expanding nomenclature around risk oversight by boards. Risk appetite, risk appetite framework, risk tolerance, risk culture, risk tolerance, risk universe, risk limits and risk capacity are newer terms in the risk-taking lexicon that have come into vogue with a change in usage, particularly among the corporate governance and accounting community. The precise meaning and metrics of these terms are evolving, and thus there is still considerable inconsistency in their use. In time, academics in finance, economics and management will come to the aid of practice by developing more robust constructs backed by theoretically and empirically rigorous work.

The term *risk aversion* has the benefit of long use in the corporate finance community and thus there is consensus about the concept, its measurement and its implications for behavior. Fortunately, the current governance usage of *risk appetite* and *risk tolerance* appears to be rooted in the more robust concepts of risk aversion and risk policy. Individuals show various attitudes to risk: they may dislike risk (risk averse), be neutral to risk (risk neutral) or they love taking risks (risk loving).[35]

However, risk appetite is one of the terms now used within the governance community in a different way than it has been used for years by economists. The economists developed theoretical (based on models) and atheoretical (based on statistical analysis of market data) economic risk appetite indices to test market sentiment for risk-taking.[36] This view of risk appetite is a macroeconomic perspective rather than the micro-perspective in which the governance community is starting to use the term. These market indices measure the willingness to take risks, with the risk appetite depending on (1) the risk aversion or the degree investors are repelled by uncertainty about consumption in the future and (2) the perception of the factors that drive the uncertainty about future consumption. Risk aversion is a personal characteristic and thus is fairly stable as it reflects deep preferences. However, risk appetite fluctuates as investors respond to macroeconomic uncertainty about fundamental factors that drive asset prices. When the market has low risk appetite then cost of capital rises, restricting business investment. When the risk appetite is high, booms in credit and asset prices are evident. Economists measure risk appetite using changes in risk premium and making inferences from changes in investor's portfolios. The International Monetary Fund, the Bank of International Settlements, Bank of England, Goldman Sachs, JP Morgan and others track market sentiment using risk appetite indices. Of course, the macroeconomic view of risk appetite as a market aggregate is related to the risk appetites of individuals and firms that make up that market.

Risk appetite statements by the board

Since 2008, the extended corporate governance community has taken up use of risk appetite in managerial policy making and board oversight, encouraging and mandating boards to formally approve their firm's *risk appetite statement*. We expect this trend to intensify, making approval of risk appetite statements a routine part of a board's annual work cycle. It should be noted that this is not necessarily a simple and straightforward task due to the somewhat ambiguous nature of the risk appetite concept.[37] However, discussions about risk appetite in the board will undoubtedly elevate the risk awareness, which is useful in its own right.

While there is no consensus, there is a distinct trend to view a firm's risk appetite as comparable to the risk objective required by investment advisors for individuals wishing to build an investment portfolio. The potential investor is asked (or their preferences are evaluated by questionnaire) to know if she or he is risk-seeking and thus suited to investing aggressively in equity and derivatives, or conservative and wishing to buy safer financial instruments such as treasury bonds. Similarly, risk appetite can be understood to be the amount of risk the firm is willing to undertake to achieve its strategic objectives and to secure value for its stakeholders.

Standard and Poor's (S&P), the rating agency, and an influential monitor as seen from the agency theory perspective discussed earlier, perhaps triggered the widespread use of this term when they started to assess ERM frameworks in 2006 as a part of their rating methodology applied to financial firms. S&P announced that a strong ERM would include a well-defined risk appetite framework. Further impetus for financial institutions to use this risk appetite approach also came from the Committee of European Insurance and Occupational Pension Supervisors, who in a consultation paper asserted that a clearly defined risk strategy included a risk appetite statement and related risk limits. The Financial Stability Board (FSB) added to this direction when in February 2013, after a peer review on risk governance, it recommended that national supervisory authorities provide specific guidance to their financial services firms on the key elements of a risk appetite framework. The FSB argued that risk governance frameworks should consist of three lines of defense: (1) the board and front office, (2) the entity-wide risk management framework and (3) an audit function that provides an independent of risk governance.[38]

Nonfinancial firms, many of whom also fell into trouble during the Great Recession have also joined the move to using risk appetite statements.

The risk appetite construct should be tied to the firm's strategy as a part of good risk governance. However the linkage mechanisms are still unclear and are likely to differ by industry and by firm. In 2010, S&P announced that it now assessed the integration of the risk appetite process with the firm's strategy and culture. This new emphasis recognizes a shift within firms from using the risk appetite framework for protecting value (coping with risk downside) to also creating value (exploiting the risk upside).

For boards that are starting to craft risk appetite statements there is a dearth of fine examples to follow. Many of the published materials on risk appetite are often contradictory as the governance and risk practice communities feel their way toward more refined approaches. Notwithstanding the relative disarray, a review of several recent practice-oriented contributions can provide some useful information on how this active conversation on risk appetite and its linkage to strategic planning is developing. To this end, we provide summaries of discussions of risk appetite offered by the Institute of Risk Management (IRM; 2011), the Society of Actuaries in Ireland (SAI; 2011), the Committee of Sponsoring Organizations of the Treadway Commission (COSO; 2012), the Casualty Actuarial Society (CAS; 2012) and the Financial Stability Board (FSB; 2014).

The Institute of Risk Management (IRM; 2011)

The Institute of Risk Management (IRM) produced definitions of the terms risk appetite and risk tolerance as follows.[39]

- Risk appetite: The amount of risk an organization is willing to seek or accept in pursuit of its long-term objectives.
- Risk tolerance: The boundaries of risk-taking outside of which the organization is not prepared to venture in the pursuit of long-term objectives. Risk tolerance can be stated in absolutes, for example: "We will not deal with a certain type of customer" or "We will not expose more that X% of our capital to losses in a certain line of business."
- Risk universe: The full range of risks that could impact either positively or negatively on the ability of the organization to achieve its long-term objectives.

The Society of Actuaries in Ireland (SAI; 2011)

The Central Bank of Ireland issued a corporate governance code requiring credit institutions and insurance firms to establish a board-approved risk appetite. In response, the SAI offered a guidance note on setting a risk appetite and its relationship to the risk management framework and strategic planning.[40] The SAI defines risk appetite as the qualitative and quantitative statement that defines the organization's general attitude to a desired risk level. Risk tolerance is the maximum variation from this level that the firm was willing to accept.

The first step in setting the risk appetite is the analysis of the firm's business strategy. A risk appetite framework takes a risk-based view of the strategy and should answer questions such as:

- What risks fit with the firm's overall strategic plan?
- What risk-taking limits can the firm accept and is it capable of monitoring?
- What risks do not fit and therefore should be avoided by the firm?
- What risks are not sought but will become a part of doing business to which the firm will need to be reactive?

The board setting the risk appetite needs to understand the risks (and risk categories) faced by the firm as it pursues its strategic plan. It should understand how the risks interact by using correlation frameworks, scenarios, statistical copulas or expert judgment. Using an appropriate measure, a risk objective is stated either at the individual risk level or the risk category level for a time horizon. This stated objective is risk appetite. For example, if capital is the measure, the target may be (1) maintain a particular economic capital cover, (2) maintain a certain credit rating and (3) maintain sufficient solvency so as to withstand a specific stress scenario. If the earnings are the target, then the objective may be (1) maximum allowed earnings volatility and (2) minimum acceptable profitability (measured as return on capital, margins) for a new or existing business. Once the objective is set and a tolerance for variation selected, the board needs to review it, approve it and monitor compliance.

The Committee of Sponsoring Organizations of the Treadway Commission (COSO; 2012)

COSO defines risk appetite as the amount of risk on a broad level that an entity accepts in pursuit of value. Risk appetite influences the organization culture and operating style, it guides resource allocation and it helps align the infrastructure to respond and monitor risks.[41] Risk tolerances are tactical and apply the risk appetite to specific objectives. Operating within risk tolerances keeps the firm within its broader risk appetite. Risk tolerance communicates flexibility while the risk appetite sets a rigid limit beyond which risk-taking is forbidden (see Inserts 2.4 and 2.5 for examples).

Insert 2.4 Aerospace supplier's (AS) objective, risk appetite and risk tolerance[42]

As a part of its strategic plan, AS sets an objective to grow revenue and operating revenue by 8% a year by working with customers to improve products and market share. Its risk appetite related to this objective is that while the company seeks growth, the acquisitions should not put the capital structure at risk. There is low risk appetite for allowing the capital to be so leveraged that it hinders the company's future flexibility. The tactical risk tolerances are at the operations, reporting and compliance levels.

- *Operations tolerance:* Low risk tolerance for failing to meeting customer orders on time.
- *Reporting tolerances:* Very low risk tolerances concerning the possibility of significant or material deficiencies in internal controls.
- *Compliance tolerances:* Near-zero risk tolerance for violations of regulatory requirements.

COSO proposes that the board's oversight of the entity's risk appetite encompasses (1) discussing the entity's objectives and risk appetite, (2) ensuring that the compensation plan is consistent with the risk appetite, (3) monitoring risk identification by managers when the entity is pursuing strategies, (4) looking actively for any unintended consequences when pursuing objectives and (5) reviewing the appropriateness of the risk appetite and tolerances.

Casualty Actuarial Society (CAS; 2012)

The CAS published a detailed set of case studies demonstrating how risk appetite can be tightly linked to strategy in insurance companies.[43] Their fundamental step in developing a risk appetite framework was seeking the input of the board in defining the enterprise's ability and eagerness to take risks. Risk appetite is the high-level view of risks to be taken in the pursuit of value. The optimal level of risk-taking is selected with the objective of increasing shareholder value. The risk appetite is set after an analysis of the firm's core competencies and the market situation as well as with a sense of the constraints arising from other interests including regulators, rating agencies, bond holders and employees. In the CAS view, the risk appetite framework has three levels: (1) the enterprise tolerance, (2) a risk appetite for each category of risks and (3) a risk limit. The risk limits are the most detailed and the tolerances the least so.

Enterprise tolerance is the aggregate level of authorized risk-taking (by the board) and is best expressed in terms of capital adequacy, earning volatility and credit rating targets. This is a long-term view to be unchanged unless the strategy and market shifts. A risk appetite is developed for each risk category by allocating the risk tolerance across the lines of business and their related risks. For an insurance company, this may mean deciding how much life insurance business versus property insurance business to seek, or how much market and liquidity risks to accept. The risk appetite measures are quantitative (e.g., Value-at-Risk [VAR] measures like capital/equity at risk and earnings at risk) and qualitative (e.g., credit ratings, risk priorities and franchise value). With this risk analysis, the company's resources including capital are allocated to areas in which the enterprise perceives it has competitive advantages. Appropriate analysis should help the enterprise select business activities that have a high risk-adjusted return where the most granular level is the risk limits converting the risk appetite into risk-monitoring measures.

Insert 2.5 Examples of risk tolerance statements

Financial strength rating: Maintain an AA (S&P) on a global basis and keep a buffer of more than 50% of one year's net income above minimum capital requirement for AA rating.

Earnings at risk: The probability of a negative earnings (measured by International Financial Reporting Standards [IFRS]) for one year is less than 5%.

Examples of risk appetite statements:

- The company will not participate in any strategy that bets on the direction and magnitude of the foreign exchange movements.
- The firm will not invest in any bonds that have a credit rating below BBB.
- The company maintains liquidity for a 1-in-200 year event over a time horizon of three months.
- The company cannot lose more than 20% of IFRS equity in a terrorism event.

According to the CAS formulation the risk appetite established and approved by the board and the strategic planning process sets a number of constraints presenting the 'field of play'. It is within this ring of limits that all profit-seeking activities can take place. An astute strategist will also notice that the firm could build strategies that can shift these constraints in the longer term. For example, the enterprises can shift a constraint by working with industry groups to persuade the regulators to revise capital adequacy rules and so forth.

The Financial Stability Board (FSB; 2014)

The FSB published a well-received set of principles for an effective risk appetite framework in November 2013 and a framework for assessing risk culture in 2014, both of which provide additional guidance, particularly to the financial sector.

The FSB defines risk appetite as "the aggregate level and types of risk a financial institution is willing to assume within its risk capacity to achieve its strategic objectives and business plan."[44] The risk appetite is arrived at by way of an organization-wide iterative conversation. The board includes assessment of the risk appetite in all strategic risk-taking including plans for growth, new business lines, mergers and acquisitions. The board approves the risk appetite as a part of approving a wider risk appetite framework that also includes the risk limits (i.e., quantitative measures allocating the risk appetite to business lines) and assigns specific roles to the board (i.e., approval and monitoring) as well as key managers (i.e., development, implementation, being held accountable). The risk framework sets the parameters within which managers are expected to execute the business strategy.

The discussion of risk culture asserts that a sound risk culture bolsters sound risk-taking. Arguing that weak risk cultures are the root cause of many organizational failures, the FSB encourages bank regulators to understand the relationship between level of soundness and safety and each institution's risk culture.

Indicators of a risk culture are: (1) the 'tone at the top', which includes the board leading by example; assessing the appropriateness and implementation of espoused values; ensuring a common understanding of risk, including of non-financial risk; and learning from experiences; (2) clear accountability including the clearly assigned ownership of risks; specific escalation and whistleblowing processes; clear consequences for breaches of policy; (3) effective communication including openness to alternative views, challenging of models/assumptions and ensuring that the control functions (i.e., risk management, internal audit and compliance) enjoy appropriate organizational status; and (4) well-calibrated incentives that encourage sound risk-taking including performance evaluation, promotions, talent development and pay.

Conclusion

This discussion reviewed risk, risk management and risk governance and argues that value creating strategic risk-taking is an essential activity in a well-governed and well-managed enterprise. Risk governance is perhaps more an art than a science, and consequently directors must take a commonsense approach. Establishing risk cultures that are resilient and provide guidance when new situations arise is an important part of a board's work. However, it is essential to create a dynamic process that exploits upside potential and fends off excessive downside losses as new risks emerge. In the final analysis, in their oversight of strategic risk-taking, boards as a whole and directors individually must keep their eyes to the prize: value to creation for stakeholders.

Notes

1 The World Bank Group, CGIAR Fund Office, Washington, DC. This article draws on Garvey, M.L., 'Risk, risk management, and risk governance', in Andersen, T.J., Garvey, M.L., and Roggi, O. (2014). *Managing Risk and Opportunity* (Oxford: Oxford University Press, 2014): pp. 5–34.
2 Clarke, T. (ed.). (2004). *Theories of Corporate Governance: The Philosophical Foundations of Corporate Governance*. Oxford: Routledge.
3 Eells, R.S.F. (1960). *The Meaning of Modern Business: An Introduction to the Philosophy of Large Corporate Enterprise*. New York: Columbia University Press.

4 Shleifer, A., and Vishny, R. (1997). A Survey of Corporate Governance, *Journal of Finance*, 52(2), 737–783.

5 Claessens, S., and Yurtoglu, B. (2012). *Corporate Governance and Development – An Update*. Washington, DC: Global Corporate Governance Forum, International Finance Corporation.

6 Zingales, L. (1998). 'Corporate governance', in *The New Palgrave Dictionary of Economics and Law*. London: Macmillan.

7 Cadbury Report. (1992). *The Financial Aspects of Corporate Governance*. London: Burgess Science Press.

8 Organisation for Economic Co-Operation and Development. (2004). *The OECD Principles of Corporate Governance*. Paris: OECD.

9 Tricker, B. (2012). *Corporate Governance: Principles, Policies and Practices*. Oxford: Oxford University Press.

10 Said by Blondie in the movie *The Good, the Bad and the Ugly*, Sergio Leone (director). United States: United Artists, 1968.

11 Already the Asian crisis of 1987 had awakened interest in corporate governance among regulators, international organizations and academics after decades of inactivity in this sphere.

12 Berle, A., Jr., and Means, G. (1932). *The Modern Corporation and Private Property*. New York: Commerce Clearing House.

13 Tirole, J. (2005). *The Theory of Corporate Governance*. Princeton, NJ: Princeton University Press.

14 Misangyi, V.F., and Acharya, A.G. (2014). Substitutes or Complements? A Configurational Examination of Corporate Governance Mechanism, *Academy of Management Journal*, 57, 1681–1705.

15 La Porta, R., Lopez-de-Silanes, F., and Shleifer, A. (1999). Corporate Ownership Around the World, *Journal of Finance*, 54(2), 471–517.

16 Kose J., Litov L., and Yeung, B. (2008). Corporate Governance and Risk Taking, *Journal of Finance*, 63(4), 1679–1728.

17 Tirole, *The Theory of Corporate Governance*.

18 Extracted and summarized from the OECD principles (Principle VI, in particular, provides useful guidance on the responsibilities of directors).

19 Tihanyi, L., Graffin S., and George, G. (2014). Rethinking Governance in Management Research, *Academy of Management Journal*, 57(6), 1535–1543.

20 Roggi, O., and Altman, E. (2012). *Managing and Measuring Risk: Emerging Global Standards and Regulations after the Financial Crisis*. World Scientific Series in Finance, 5. Singapore: World Scientific Press.

21 Roggi, O. (2008). *Rischio d'Impresa, Valore e Insolvenza: Aspetti Teorici e Processi di Gestione del Rischio*. Milan: Franco Angeli.

22 Damodaran, A. (2008). *Strategic Risk Taking: A Framework for Risk Management*. Upper Saddle River, NJ: Pearson Education, Wharton School Press.

23 See, for example, Shefrin, H. (2008). *Ending the Management Illusion: How to Drive Business Results Using the Principles of Behavioral Finance*. New York: McGraw-Hill.

24 Tversky, A., and Kahneman, D. (1981). The Framing of Decisions and the Psychology of Choice, *Science*, 211(January), 453–458.

25 This example draws on Aswath Damodaran's website with permission (Damodaran Online: http://pages.stern.nyu.edu/~adamodar/).

26 Douglas, M., and Wildavsky, A. (1982). *Risk and Culture*. Berkeley: University of California Press.

27 Smircich, L. (1983). 'Organizations as shared meanings', in Pondy, L.R., Frost, P.J. Morgan, G., and Dandridge, T.C. (eds.), *Organizational Symbolism* (pp. 55–65). Greenwich, CT: JAI Press.

28 Schein, E.H. (1985). *Organizational Culture and Leadership*. San Francisco: Jossey-Bass.

29 Several would argue that the financial crisis was apparent since 2007, whereas others note 2009 as the nadir.

30 This is a rough approximation, as corporate governance mechanism extends beyond oversight activities.

31 Damodaran, *Strategic Risk Taking*.

32 See, for example, Andersen, T.J. (2006). *Global Derivatives: A Strategic Risk Management Perspective*. New York: FT Prentice Hall, Pearson Education.

33 This risk classification draws on Roggi, *Rischio d'Impresa, Valore e Insolvenza*.

34 A firm's risk profile is a snapshot at a specific time of perceived risk exposures from the perspective of its managers.

35 In classical economics the Arrow-Pratt coefficient of risk aversion is often used to summarize these attitudes.

36 Illing, M., and Aaron, M. (2005, June). A Brief Survey of Risk-Appetite Indexes, *Financial Systems Review* (June), 37–43.

37 Power, M. (2009). The Risk Management of Nothing, *Accounting, Organizations and Society*, 34(6–7), 849–855.

38 See Financial Stability Board. (2013, February). *Thematic Review of Risk Governance: Peer Review Report*.

39 See Anderson, R. (2011). *Risk Appetite and Tolerance*. London: Institute of Risk Management (IRM).

40 See Society of Actuaries in Ireland. (2011, March). *Constructing a Risk Appetite Framework: An Introduction*. Dublin: Society of Actuaries in Ireland.

41 See Rittenberg, L., and Martens, F. (2012). *Enterprise Risk Management: Understanding and Communicating Risk Appetite*. Durham, NC: Committee of Sponsoring Organizations of the Treadway Commission (COSO).

42 This example draws on Rittenberg and Martens, *Enterprise Risk Management*.

43 See Kailan, K., and Chen, Z. (2012). *Risk Appetite: Linkage with Strategic Planning*. Schaumburg, IL: Society of Actuaries.

44 See Financial Stability Board. (2013). *Principles for an Effective Risk Appetite Framework*. Basel, Switzerland: Financial Stability Board (FSB).

Appendix 2.1

Risk committee practices

A good committee will have the practices under the 'good' column and the best risk committees will achieve practices under the column labeled 'best'.

Creation	Good	Better	Best
Any written document, including board resolution	•		
Incorporated in bylaws or corporate governance guidelines		•	
Incorporated in corporate charter of articles of association			•
The board has considered if separate risk and audit committees are required and has established the risk committee separately if needed (e.g., in the case of financial institutions)			•
Broad role			
Ensures that senior management takes the steps necessary to identify, measure, monitor and control risks	•		
Oversees the enterprise's risk policies, its risk management processes and the linkage of risk-taking to the entity's strategy. See 'Specific responsibilities – RM, ERM and SRM'.		•	•
Establishes that the entity's risk-taking policies aims for creation of value (upside) as well as mitigating losses (downside)			•
Reviews the adequacy of the entity's capital and allocation to various business units considering the type and size of risks of those business units			•
Reviews the entity's compensation policy and risk culture to ensure they encourage ethical risk-taking with the objective of enhancing short- and long-term shareholder value		•	•
Composition			
Composed of at least three board members	•	•	
Composed of at least three but no more than five board members			•
Includes a material presence of nonexecutive board members	•		
The majority are independent board members			•

Creation	Good	Better	Best
The majority are nonexecutive board members		•	
Has an annual rotation of members			•
Limit on number of memberships on other board committees			•
No more than one committee member serves on both the risk policy and audit and compliance committees. That shared member may be the committee chair.			•
Individual committee membership qualifications			
Overall committee possesses requisite skills and knowledge adequate for overseeing the entity's risk management program	•		
Each member of the committee has the requisite skills and knowledge adequate for overseeing the entity's risk management program		•	•
Members possess the time and desire to fulfill obligations	•	•	•
Each new member receives an introductory briefing	•	•	•
Each new member receives periodic professional education/training		•	•
Attending fewer than 70% of meetings in a single year is criteria for automatic non-reappointment			•
Chairperson characteristics			
Appointed by nonexecutive board chair or board as a whole	•	•	•
Is an independent board member			•
Does not chair any other board committees nor the board of the entity		•	•
Possess requisite skills and knowledge adequate for overseeing the entity's risk management program	•	•	•
Appointment to the committee			
Appointed by board chair, board as whole or corporate governance/nominations committee	•	•	•
Where nomination is by board chair or corporate governance/nominations committee, appointments are ratified by the full board	•	•	•
Fixed terms, preferably annual, but in no case to exceed board terms	•		
One-year renewable terms		•	•
Compensation			
Solely related to fulfilling the obligation as a committee member. No forms of payment that compromise independence (e.g., salary or consulting/finder's fees).	•	•	•
Payment as committee fees and/or meeting fees is preferred form	•		
Level of payment is adequate for creating the expectation of responsibility		•	•
Annual committee fees		•	•
Additional per meeting fees		•	•
Additional fee for chair		•	•
Schedule and conduct of meetings			
May be called by the committee chair	•	•	
May be called by the committee chair or by any two committee members			•
Has an approved annual calendar of meetings in place		•	•
Held at least semiannually	•		
Held at least quarterly.		•	•
May be requested by the board chair, CEO, CFO and chief risk office	•	•	•

(Continued)

Creation	Good	Better	Best
May be in person, by telephone, web or other electronic communication means agreeable to the committee		•	•
Attendance and notice			
Quorum required	•		
Quorum required with simple majority as a minimum		•	•
Advance noticed required; may be waived with unanimous written consent	•	•	
Minimum of 48 hours' notice required; may be waived with unanimous written consent		•	
Minimum of one week's notice required; may be waived with unanimous written consent			•
Approved annual calendar of regular meetings	•	•	•
Minutes prepared and distributed to committee members. The board has access to review them.	•	•	•
Agenda and related materials provided in advance unless chair (or other convener) believes confidentiality requires otherwise, in which case a general description of the subject of the meeting will be circulated, with a statement from the chair as to reasons of confidentiality	•	•	•
Chief risk officers attend committee meetings by standing invitation	•	•	•
Chief of internal audit, external auditor, chief compliance officer and other executives receive notice of all meetings and are invited as needed		•	•
Independent and nonexecutive committee members meet without executive officers present for an interval during each meeting			•
Reporting to the board and shareholders			
Provides verbal and written reports to the board as needed	•		
Provides written report or minutes to the board following each committee meeting		•	•
Provides annual written report to the board	•	•	•
A general report on the activities of the risk policy committee is included in the entity's annual report		•	•
That general report includes qualitative and quantitative data, enabling shareholders and general public to understand the entity's risk profile and policies			•
Evaluation			
An annual evaluation of the work the committee performed during the preceding year is conducted		•	•
An annual evaluation of the committee's effectiveness, including processes and procedures, is conducted		•	•
A periodic evaluation of the committee's charter (or terms of reference) is conducted, with a written report to the board suggesting improvements, if any		•	•
A periodic independent evaluation of the committee's effectiveness is conducted			•
Access to resources			
Committee has access to all internal resources and personnel	•	•	•

Creation	Good	Better	Best
Access to internal resources is available without necessarily going through the entity's hierarchy (however the hierarchy will be respected absent compelling reasons to avoid it)		•	•
Can recommend hiring outside resources such as risk management consultants or counsel as needed	•		•
Has the right to hire outside resources without executive approval		•	•
Receives an annual budget sufficient to meet its needs and is able to access additional funds for unforeseen circumstances			•

Specific responsibilities – RM, ERM and SRM

Creation	Good	Better	Best
Establishes a risk management (RM) approach for the entity	•		
Establishes and monitors implementation an enterprise-wide risk management (ERM) framework for all companies in the group and at all levels		•	•
Establishes and monitors implementation a strategic risk management (SRM) framework for all companies in the group and at all levels			•
Reviews entity's risk management infrastructure and control systems to ensure that it is adequate for enforcing the entity's risk policies.	•	•	•
Ensures that management (e.g., CEO and chief risk officer) develops a comprehensive risk management program including limits and monitoring. Approves high-level limits and reviews monitoring policies. Receives selected exception reports.		•	•
Ensures both quantitative and qualitative factors and cognitive biases are taken into account in risk-taking throughout the entity	•	•	•
Oversees the chief risk officer and the annual plan for his/her activities	•	•	•
Reviews management's determination of what constitutes key balance sheet and off-balance sheet risks	•	•	•
Meets periodically with audit committee and other parties as needed	•	•	•
Requires periodic independent assessment of the risk governance framework and function (e.g., by internal audit, external audit firms or consultants)		•	•
Ensures that risk measurement/management function has adequate expertise, resources and objectivity/independence to fulfill its responsibilities		•	•
Is consulted by the CEO regarding appointment and performance evaluation of the chief risk officer	•	•	•
Reviews and recommends to the board (for approval) the risk measurements and rating methodologies. These might include value at risk, economic capital, risk adjusted return on capital, credit rating, internal measures and so forth.		•	•
Reviews assumptions used in risk measurements models, insuring that model risk issues have been properly considered			•
Reviews entity's preparedness to respond to crisis and other special risks (e.g., those with low probability but high impact or highly correlated risks). Approves contingency planning.		•	•
Approves the risk appetite and profile if the enterprises uses this approach in its risk policy			•

(Continued)

Creation	Good	Better	Best
Regularly receives high-level summary risk data from the responsible managers (CEO, chief risk officer) and compares the data to the approved risk policies	•	•	•
Periodically receives disaggregated data on major risk categories from the responsible managers (CEO, chief risk officer)	•	•	•
Receives and acts on compliance and internal audit reports that are relevant to the risk function	•	•	•
Reviews exposures to major clients, counterparties, countries and economic sectors			•
Additional responsibilities in the financial services industry firms			
Reviews and recommends to board, in conjunction with executive officers, proposed aggregate loss limit targets for various risk categories (e.g., loan losses and operational risk), paying special attention to capital adequacy and liquidity requirements	•	•	•
Approves management's recommendations for overall credit and market risk limits, as well as country risk limits for nondomestic exposures		•	•
Approves maximum credit exposures for top clients and counterparties so as to ensure diversification	•	•	•
Reviews and recommends to the board (for approval) the risk measurements, management and rating methodologies to be reported to regulators	•	•	•
Receives regular reports from the asset liability committee and credit risk committees	•	•	•
Reviews reports on financial compliance issues such as compliance risk and money-laundering risks (unless specifically reserved for the audit and compliance committee)		•	•
Reviews stress and scenario tests on credit, liquidity, market and operational risk, and approves contingency planning	•	•	•

3

Risk management and ethical cultures

Peter C. Young, Douglas J. Jondle, T. Dean Maines,
and Michelle D. Rovang

While all organizations manage risk to some degree, this International Standard establishes a number of principles that need to be satisfied to make risk management effective. This International Standard recommends that organizations develop, implement and continuously improve a framework whose purpose is to integrate the process for managing risk into the organization's overall governance, strategy and planning, management, reporting processes, policies, values and culture.

(ISO, 2009)

Over the past 15 years a number of guidelines, frameworks, and standards have emerged, all pressing for a more comprehensive approach to risk management. Arguably one of the more frequently referenced, but seldom examined, aspects of these documents is the assertion that risk management should align with an organization's culture and its values. Although this assertion – perhaps 'assumption' is a better word – is nowhere fully explained, the implication seems to be that a comprehensive approach to risk management represents a fundamental change in an organization and that organizations will resist such change if it is inconsistent with culture and values.

In a conversational context, the idea that risk management is an expression of an organization's values seems sensible enough, but how is alignment between values and risk management discerned and assured? And if alignment is achieved, does not that suggest that risk management might be subject to quite different interpretations from organization to organization and from culture to culture? (This leads to an interesting sidebar question: Beyond bare-bones framing, does it even make sense to aspire to a global uniform standard of practice?)

The purpose of this chapter is to search for a means of linking risk management with organizational values, first by reviewing present thinking regarding organizational values; then considering how risk management presently looks at values; and finally evaluating the means through which a firmer connection between risk management practices and values may be found, measured and examined. Alongside this discussion, the concept of ethical risks (or 'risks arising from values') also will receive attention.

The ethical organizational culture

Schein (2004) writes that organizational culture, at its root, is composed of individuals whose learned responses at the fundamental level are derived from an organization's taken-for-granted homologous 'assumptions and beliefs'. Organizational cultures are manifestations of formal and informal systems, processes, and interactions, according to Cohen (1993). *Formal characteristics* integrate into organizational culture through the quality and persistence of the organization's leadership. They are further integrated into organizational culture through the organization's ability to manage processes and people, and its overarching business and governance structures, policies, and socialization mechanisms to regulate employee behavior, employee reward systems, and decision-making processes. *Informal elements* of organizational culture, in turn, rely on values, implicit behavioral norms, role models, organizational myths and rituals, organizational beliefs, historical anecdotes, and language (Dion, 1996; Trevino and Nelson, 2004).

Ardichvili and Jondle (2009) note that ethical business culture is based on an alignment between formal structures and processes and informal recognition of heroes, stories, and rituals that inspire organizational members to behave ethically. This includes personal moral development and exhibition of authenticity by leaders. When developing and sustaining ethical culture, organizations must be willing to address not only formal compliance requirements (baseline and minimal expectations), but focus on the identification of corporate values and the alignment of those values with all other elements of the culture. Ardichvili, Mitchell and Jondle (2009) at the Center for Ethical Business Cultures (CEBC) identified a model of ethical business cultures (the CEBC Model) consisting of five characteristics: Values-Driven, Leadership Effectiveness, Stakeholder Balance, Process Integrity, and Long-term Perspective (Figure 3.1).

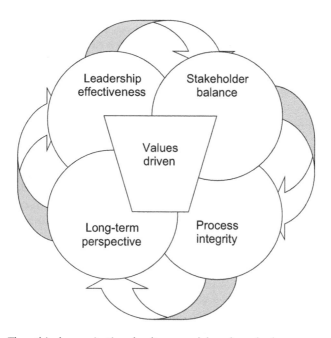

Figure 3.1   The ethical organizational culture model: a closer look

In validating the ethical business cultures model and ensuing survey instrument Jondle, Ard-ichvili and Mitchell (2014) reported on a construct consistent with the five characteristics just mentioned. They hypothesized that the ethical cultures of organizations are the resultant expression of specific combinations of organizational values – each organization models a unique ethical culture.

It is no accident the CEBC Model presents a platform on which corporate conscience is imprinted. By focusing on the five characteristics of an ethical business culture, organizations have specific directions to take in building and sustaining their organizational culture based on ethical principles and metrics to measure progress.

At the core of the CEBC Model is the *Values-Driven* characteristic. Values define an organi-zation's character (Freeman, Gilbert and Hartman, 1988; George, 2003), 'not to be compromised for financial gain or short-term expediency' (Collins and Porras, 1994). For an organization the 'core values' (Carroll and Buchholtz, 2009) not only build the superstructure on which accepted employee behavior is based, but more importantly they functionally and strategically capture and instill a sense of purpose that is transparent and actually 'mean[s] something' towards build-ing organizational consensus (Lencioni, 2002). To put it in the context of the CEBC Model, values define organizational culture; organizational culture defines how its leaders lead and employees behave, how stakeholders are treated, how internal processes function, and the degree to which the organization's perspective is long term.

According to Goodpaster (2007), an ethical culture is delineated by two distinct languages. One originates from *espoused values*; the other is a language of *values-in-action*. In corporations with a conscience – that is, those based on ethical cultures – alignment exists between core (stated, formal, or espoused) values and the values-in-action. The former are indicative of an organization's codes of conduct and ethics, and mission and value statements, while the latter are 'driven by the incentives, rewards, hiring and promotion systems of the organization' (Good-paster, 2007, p. 152).

The concept of dual values, formal and informal, is not new (Schein, 2004). Formal or stated values are those embraced and promoted by the organization to influence behavior and direct organizational goals. Informal or practiced values are unwritten, behavioral in nature, and actively practiced within the organization. They evolve through employee experiences and interactions with the organization and possess the power to both adversely or beneficially moderate behavior and affect goal achievement. Tension between stated and practiced values can impact operational effectiveness. As the misalignment between stated and practiced values increases, dysfunction increases within the organization. Goodpaster (2007) states, 'when the two come into conflict, the second language inevitably prevails' (p. 153). In other words, success within the organization rests upon the dynamic interaction between the stated values that characterize desired behavior and the practiced values that moderate and reinforce the actual behavior within the organiza-tion's core business functions and processes.

According to Jondle et al. (2014),

> stated values form the basis of ethical business culture, and include trust, integrity and hon-esty. They are the values posted on the walls of organization's lobbies. They are the essential elements of any organization that wishes to operate in an environment cognizant of its stakeholders. Within the framework of an ethical culture are constructs directing behavior that instill organizational purpose and provides direction and aspiration to its employees. An organization's mission, vision, and values are those constructs defining stated values and principles that establish expectations of behavior within the organization.
>
> *(p. 13)*

An ethical organization begins to define itself through its purpose, as articulated through its mission statement. In the ability to motivate its employees towards an aspirational outcome the organization relies on its vision statement. For an ethical organization to both survive and thrive, it must assiduously select the values that delineate acceptable and expectable individual and organizational behavior. Values must align with mission, vision and to each other to foster a high performance culture, and they must integrate freely and systemically throughout the organization to become the source of operational norms that drive desired behavior (i.e., codes of conduct and ethics). An ethical corporate culture is optimized when alignment exists between organizational and individual values, and between the processes that reinforce desired behavior and the organization's core business functions – for example, through the ways in which it manages risk.

Although the Values-Driven component of the model is of central interest to this chapter, it is worthwhile to briefly map out the other components as they do have relevance to the challenge of linking risk management to cultures and values.

Effective organizations have effective leaders (Bass and Steidlmeier, 1999; Brown and Trevino, 2006). *Leadership Effectiveness* stresses that an ethical culture starts at the top and is conveyed by example. Leadership, most notably senior management, must embody the organization's values in its own behavior and must articulate those values in a way that is compelling for employees and all other stakeholders.

Stakeholder Balance references the central premise of stakeholder theory: an organization and its managers have fiduciary responsibilities and other duties to various stakeholder groups with vested interests in the success of their organizations (Freeman, 1994). The organization is responsible to numerous stakeholders (Goodpaster, 2010). Stakeholder Balance suggests that tensions can and do exist between multiple stakeholders. Nor does the model suggest that the tensions between stakeholders will disappear for the ethical organization. It does, however, create an environment conducive for discussion and consideration of various stakeholder groups. The goal is to maintain a balance among all stakeholders (e.g., customers, employees, owners, community, and competitors) in all its decision-making and to work with all stakeholders on a consistently ethical and values-oriented basis (Goodpaster, 2007; Handy, 2002).

Process Integrity describes the institutionalization of the company's values throughout its business functions and includes key functional units of the business, for example, recruiting, hiring, firing, evaluating, compensating, promoting, communicating, and managing risk (Gabler, 2006; Small, 2006; Trevino, Weaver, Gibson and Toffler, 1999). Numerous challenges exist, including establishing desired behavioral standards, aligning the systems to consistently reinforce desired behavior, and monitoring behavior on an ongoing basis.

Long-term Perspective is characterized by the question, 'What is the organization's purpose?' (Ardichvili et al., 2009; Handy, 2002). Is it to maximize shareholder value or balance the needs of various stakeholders? Implicit in the Long-term Perspective is balancing between the short and long term. It necessitates doing what is right, not easy, and not doing things in the short term that create harm in the long term (Collins and Porras, 1994; Handy, 2002). It recognizes that, because employees are the ones who deliver service to customers, all employees need to be treated respectfully and compensated fairly. Concern for the environment and the desired role and responsibility of organizations to its environmental stewardship is another key feature of the Long-term Perspective. Leadership and its ability to lead is influenced by its ability to establish a strategy focused on consistent long-term growth that is *not* influenced by short-term gains (Ardichvili et al., 2009; George, 2003).

Returning to the core characteristic of the CEBC Model (Values-Driven), what exactly are the values of an ethical organizational culture? It is proposed here that ethical cultures are quite different in terms of the array of values espoused by any particular organization, and that it would perhaps be more useful to understand how organizational values can be identified and assessed, especially with reference to their connections to risk management. In other words, the best use of time may not be in searching for a universally acceptable set of values but in determining the best way in which values (whatever they are in a particular organization) can be found. Nevertheless, some attention will have to be paid to the matter of the influence of specific values on risk management.

One issue warranting separate study (it will be examined briefly later) is the question: Does ISO 31000 itself imply the acceptance of certain values? This latter question turns out to be important, for if implementation of ISO 31000 means the acceptance of its underlying values, does not that directly contradict the idea that risk management derives from a specific organization's own values and culture?

Sidebar: ethical risks

It is useful here to pause and briefly reflect on the concept of 'ethical risks'. Young (2004, 2010) sought to determine whether values actually produce risks, which led to the consideration of the idea of 'ethical risks'. His conclusion was that while categories of risk are relatively arbitrary, there would seem to be some value in alerting managers to the fact that organizational values play a role in the shape of an organization's risk environment. Such an orientation may be illuminating especially because, as Young notes, the process for identifying and assessing risks should acknowledge that an organization's culture and values are not just exposures to risk, but plausibly sources of risk as well.

Perhaps most importantly for this paper, the CEBC Model highlights the distinction between *espoused* values and *values-in-action*, which may give rise to a 'space' within which many so-called ethical risks can be said to originate. As Young (2004) noted, commenting on earlier insights from Goodpaster (1997), the concept of teleopathy (goal sickness) may be a useful starting point for exploring the concept of ethical risks within an organization. Teleopathy posits the view that an organization's Values, Goals, and Means stand in balance with one another and that upsets to that balance tend to produce ethical issues (or risks). However, as the CEBC Model asserts, there is a linkage that precedes the Values, Goals, and Means connection and that is the link between Espoused Values and Values-in-Action. Breaks or distortions in that link, arguably, provide a basis for further linkage of difficulties between Values–Goals, Goals–Means, and Means–Values. Additionally, there exists an overarching link between an organization's espoused and practiced values and broader societal values. As Young noted, there may be internal consistency linking goals and means to socially reprehensible values and thus separation between social and organizational values also serve as a space for the emergence of ethical risks.

Values: a risk management perspective

An environment of expectations has emerged over the past 15–20 years with respect to the practice of risk management. Evidence can be found in wide ranging sources: regulator and rating agency interests in corporate resiliency; internal and external audit requirements; citizen expectations for local government responsiveness to community safety issues; or broader global expectations for meaningful responses to climate change, just to name a few examples.

There are numerous reasons why this has happened. At the widest societal level, writers like Ulrich Beck (1992) have observed that these rising expectations are actually linked to many aspects of modern life: to information systems and the influence of the media, to fears arising from new and highly mysterious (at least mysterious to the public) risks, to greater degrees of global interconnectivity, and paradoxically, to the intensifying focus on residual risk as science and technology improve quality of life in wide-ranging ways (e.g., controlling infectious diseases, improved public safety). On a slightly smaller scale, many of these expectations also have emerged in response to specific events: sensational cases of corporate fraud and malfeasance, oil spills, volcanoes, terrorism, and financial crises as catalogued by the World Economic Forum's annual *Global Risks Report* (2014).

As noted in the introduction to this chapter, the sharpened edge of modern expectations is seen in a proliferation of guideline/standards documents focused on risk management (ISO 31000 is a particularly notable current example), and various nation-specific frameworks and standards. Further, as Figure 3.2 suggests, there are many other direct and indirect ways in which risk management has become an expectation (or even a requirement) in the service of addressing a specific risk issue: financial regulation, trade rules, labor practices.

Taken as a whole, but even when taken individually, these instruments of modern expectations provide a general picture of the type of risk management 'expected'. It is holistic, integrated, comprehensive, policy-driven, and systematic. The term enterprise risk management (ERM) is often used in reference to this form of risk management, though in fact ERM is just one version of this idea. For simplicity purposes, the authors will rely on the term risk management in this chapter as the vehicle for conveying the main characteristics of modern risk management thinking and practice.

Risk management is reasonably well framed and – at least among specialists in the field – fairly well understood (though there are many remaining or new issues; for example, see Smith and Fischbacher, 2009). Broadly, organizations are expected to devote attention to developing an approach to risk management that is attuned to the environmental conditions and the context of

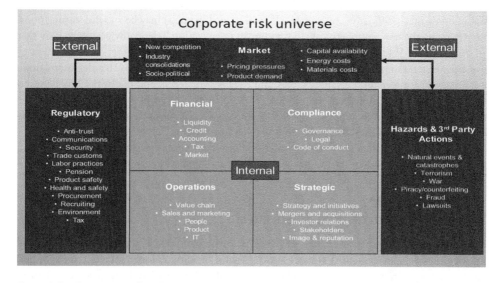

Figure 3.2 Corporate risk universe

an organization's current situation. This is variously expected to include (1) an understanding of the history (of the organization or situation), (2) an evaluation of the external and internal environments, including (3) some form of stakeholder assessment and (4) an evaluation of the organization's goals, purposes, and intentions. Once the context has been established, risk management involves risk assessment, response to/treatment of risks, evaluation and monitoring, and effective communication to stakeholders. Figure 3.3 shows, for example, how ISO 31000 frames the risk management process.

Underlying this framework are several ideas that also are present in most of the current guidelines, standards, and frameworks.

- Risk management exists to directly support the fulfillment of organizational (or situational) objectives, and thus is seen as an element of the policy-setting, strategy-setting governance dimension of management, and leadership (Andersen and Schrøder, 2010, chapter 1).
- While top management is the target for some clear expectations, there is a general view that the actual implementation and practice of risk management is something that is dispersed throughout the entire organization and embedded in processes and systems. 'All managers are risk managers within the scope of their specific responsibilities' is a phrase often cited in support of this general notion (Schrøder, 2006).
- Risk is seen as producing both positive outcomes (via opportunities) as well as negative outcomes (via hazards). Owing to this ecumenical view of risk, the purposes of risk management broadly are not focused only on eliminating or reducing risk, but on finding a proper balance of risk taking/risk mitigation (Williams, Smith and Young, 1998, chapter 2).

Additionally, risk management is expected in some way to connect itself to organizational culture and organization values. ISO 31000, the most recent (and perhaps the most ambitious) guidance, references the embedding of risk management in an organization's culture, arguing that risk considerations should be a part of managing the organization so business processes are embedded in prevailing behaviors and practices (ISO, ISO 31000, 2009).

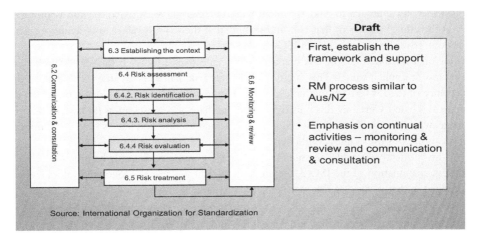

Figure 3.3 ISO 31000 risk management process

Establishing a 'values' context for risk management

The current academic and practitioner work in risk management seems to anticipate an eventual link-up with organizational ethics but does not present easy and obvious ways for this to happen. Equivalently, the ethical organizational culture concept anticipates an inclusion of risk-related perspectives but does not engage the issue of assessing and addressing ethical risks. How can this gap be bridged; and specifically, how is risk management explicitly connected with organizational values?

To begin thinking about this, consider what might be called a values dimension of the concept of risk. ISO 31000 defines risk as the 'effect of uncertainty on objectives', underscoring the document's distinct managerial orientation. Objectives derive from an organization's strategy, mission and vision, and thus the meaning of risk is tied to its impact on the intentions of the organization, which are informed by its values. Not all objectives are exclusively values-driven, but ISO does imply that risk is defined in relation to organizational values.

Adopting a more historic perspective, risk also may be defined as 'variation around expectation', which establishes its own way of tying risk to organizational values (Williams et al., 1998, chapter 1).

(1) Expectation is determined by objective observation, but also is influenced by cultural filters and the implicit values therein. For example, cultures establish beliefs and values related to 'the other' (that is, those not within the group), and these values establish expectations as to future behavior of those not within the group. Additionally, even when expectation derives from highly scientific methodologies, the selection of a subject for evaluation or the selection of methodologies (e.g., Do we conduct product experimentation with animals?) involves values-based choices.
(2) Variation may be mathematically measured, but the meaning of various outcomes is not mathematically determined. What does it mean to a manager to be told that there is a 95 percent probability a product defect is not likely to injure customers?

Thus can it be argued that values not only influence the dimensions of risk (expectation and variation), but they – at least indirectly – define the exposure to risk (objectives). This would suggest that any approach to risk assessment would be well served, first, to include a consideration of the ethical aspects of that risk, and second, that the express values underlying organizational objectives be identified in an ISO-guided risk assessment process.

One final word here on the risk management perspective of values. Is ISO 31000 itself based on express or implicit values? This question challenges risk managers because it could mean that acceptance of the ISO 31000 methodology also requires acceptance of the values on which the statement is based. Certainly this is intriguing, and perhaps also troubling, as ISO asserts that risk management must be driven by specific organizational culture and values – so what does an organization do if ISO values conflict with organizational culture and values?

As this is, effectively, a sidebar issue for this chapter, comments can only be provisional. Nevertheless, examination of the ISO 31000 document indicates that the following values seem to be implied in that version of risk management:

• Respect for logic, rationality, and reason; the intellectual tradition
• Long-term time orientation, including a respect for the past (the importance of remembering)
• Vigilance
• Fairness and respect

- Personal and corporate responsibility for actions and consequences
- Openness, transparency, and honesty.

Other values may be discerned; the list here is only indicative. One could see conflict arising from several of these implied values and the values (espoused or values-in-action) of a particular organization – or, perhaps more likely – while ISO values may align with espoused values, they may not align with values-in-action. This would be an interesting finding from a diagnostic standpoint, but the larger point here is that ISO 31000 is not a value-free document, and difficulties in implementation may come down to the fact that external values are entering the frame as well as recommended practices. Indeed, since ISO 31000 is a human creation, how could it be value-free?

A possible methodology

The Veritas Institute has developed a set of assessment and improvement tools that help for-profit and not-for-profit organizations evaluate whether their management systems and cultures support and sustain their espoused values. These tools enable firms to assess the distance or 'gap' between the values they profess and their values-in-action, and to take corrective action to close that gap. Use of the tools also fosters improved clarity about the nature and practical implications of a firm's espoused values. The tools may help leaders form an ethical business culture by aiding values deployment and values alignment.

The Institute's tools are based upon a method known as the Self-Assessment and Improvement Process (SAIP). The SAIP method seeks to integrate insights from corporate ethics, spirituality, and total quality management. More specifically, its underpinnings include the principle of moral projection, the practice of conscience examination, and the organizational self-assessment process used within the Baldrige Performance Excellence Program.

Following the Baldrige model, the SAIP translates a set of ethical principles into a systematic inventory of questions concerning an organization's management system, that is, the operating policies, processes, and practices that shape how it performs its work. By answering the questions within the inventory on the basis of evidence – for example, documentation describing how the organization currently operates, and data indicating the outcomes it has achieved – and then scoring these responses using a set of evaluation guidelines, a firm can determine the degree to which it has integrated vital moral aspirations within its operating policies and procedures. By highlighting strengths and deficiencies, the assessment helps leaders formulate and launch improvement initiatives designed to more comprehensively embed moral principles within their firm's management system.

Assessment tools based on the SAIP method potentially place risk management at the service of a firm's moral commitments. By enabling leaders and managers to discern how their organization's processes and practices may be in tension with its values, they create the possibility of systematically identifying value-specific risks, and of initiating corrective action to mitigate risks through improved alignment between moral aspirations and action. Furthermore, since these tools are intended to be applied periodically and not simply as a one-time event, they help establish the management of ethical risk as an ongoing discipline within a firm.

An illustration

One of the Veritas Institute's SAIP-based assessment tools, the Catholic Identity Matrix (CIM), enables Catholic health systems and hospitals to examine themselves from the inside out. That is, the CIM helps a Catholic healthcare institution identify the extent to which values and princi-ples rooted in the Catholic moral tradition have been integrated within its management system, to advance its mission and benefit stakeholders. The forerunner of the CIM was developed in 2006 by Ascension Health, the largest Catholic and not-for-profit health system in the US. As-cension Health partnered with the Veritas Institute in 2007 to integrate the SAIP method within this prototype, thereby making it more rigorous and evidence-based.

The CIM is grounded in six principles of Catholic moral teaching specific to the ministry of healthcare: solidarity with the poor, holistic care, respect for life, participatory community of work, stewardship, and acting in communion with the Church. The CIM evaluates a Catholic healthcare institution in light of each principle and a framework for organizational maturity and development. This framework describes the steps necessary to implement a principle within an organization's management system, namely, through effective planning, aligning leaders through reporting metrics and incentives, operationalization in work processes, training, and the assess-ment of outputs and impact.

A CIM application yields both a qualitative portrait of the current state of an organiza-tion's management system and a quantitative appraisal of the extent to which the six principles have been embedded within this system. This information allows leaders to identify opportu-nities for improvement and to formulate initiatives designed to help their organization embody more fully the mission and aspirations of Catholic healthcare. Periodic use of the CIM enables Catholic healthcare organizations to establish a discipline of sustained, ongoing improvement in response to the challenge of mission integration (Brinkmann and Johnson, 2011).

This illustration predates the insertion of *explicit* risk management elements within the assess-ment. The Veritas Institute is now planning to include questions that directly address such ele-ments. Under current consideration, for example are:

- Questions concerning uncertainties and risks tied to each element of the matrix ('We ex-pect X to happen (or not happen), but what if we are wrong . . . what are the consequences of unexpected or unintended outcomes?' Alternatively: 'What is the risk of incorrectly framing our analysis of organizational values?').
- Questions addressing possible factors outside the normal managerial range of vision that might influence the organization's ability to live up to its moral values and aspirations.
- Questions concerning risks arising from a commitment to specific principles within the assessment framework, which otherwise would not exist for the organization? In other words, is adherence to particular values in and of itself a source of risk?
- Questions regarding issues of risk tolerance ('How much risk are we *willing* to tolerate? How much risk are we *able* to carry? At what point does stress on our values and beliefs actually fracture the connection between espoused values and values-in-action?').

The CIM has been recognized as a best practice in Catholic health care. To date, it has been applied within six health systems in the US. Plans for extending the CIM to Catholic hospitals in other countries are now emerging.

In addition, the Veritas Institute is collaborating with its partners to address the needs of organizations outside of healthcare. The latest SAIP tool is the Business Ethics and Assessment Method (BEAM). This assessment allows a company to audit its management system and cul-ture through pointed queries based on standards taken from ISO 26000 and – notably – general components of ISO 31000. By using this tool to systematically examine the values reinforced by its management system (including risk management), as well as those present within its culture, a corporation can begin a journey whose destination is not simply effective compliance but formal processes and a culture that consistently supports and reinforces ethical conduct (United States Sentencing Commission, 2004).

Concluding comment

The approach described earlier addresses one issue discussed in this chapter: it provides a way for a risk-analytic approach to be inserted into an ethical assessment exercise and to extend the scope of analysis by focusing on what might provisionally be called ethical risks. Consideration of measures that might be taken to treat those risks also becomes part of the analysis.

Less obviously, the Veritas Institute's methodology provides a basis for articulating the values that should inform an organization's risk management efforts. As stated earlier, those values, the arraying of those values, and the relative importance of those values will differ from organization to organization. Nevertheless, the articulation of values in light of the ethical organizational culture concept should provide direction to an ISO 31000-inspired effort to structure risk management in alignment with the organization's espoused values.

There are numerous other areas of inquiry when considering both the challenge of managing ethics-based risks and reflecting organizational values in risk management policy and practice – and indeed, the authors encourage additional investigation, as there is not a lot of research currently available on this general subject area. Of particular interest would be the following:

- There is a potentially lively discussion between directors of risk or chief risk officers and corporate ethics officers (and for that matter, compliance officers, sustainability leaders, and corporate social responsibility [CSR] managers). Their responsibilities have many common features: multidisciplinary, organization-spanning, subject matter that is embedded in virtually all organizational activities, and so on. Can ethics (and the other focus areas) and risk management efforts coordinate or leverage off one another?
- How exactly does an assessment of vulnerability to ethical risks connect to more tangible risk exposures? For example, how can an assessment of the ethical dimension of financial risks be fitted into the quantitative assessment of the financial risk itself? The recent/current financial crisis clearly shows that financial institutions did not fall victim to bad mathematics alone but to a combination of technical problems and human behavior. It would be interesting to assess how well financial and operational risk management efforts have been integrated in financial institutions post-2008.
- There does need to be a clearer examination of ISO's implied values as conceivably there are potential conflicts between those values and an adopting organization's values. Indeed, there are at least two dimensions to this: first, differences between espoused organizational values and ISO implied values, and second, differences between espoused and practiced organizational values and the relationship between that gap and ISO implied values. For example, it has been recently observed that transparency, which has seeming importance as a goal of ISO 31000, may run afoul of top manager concerns about 'too much transparency'.

References

Andersen, T.J. and Schrøder, P.W. (2010). *Strategic Risk Management Practice: How to Deal Effectively with Major Corporate Exposures*. Cambridge: Cambridge University Press.

Ardichvili, A. and Jondle, D. (2009). Ethical business cultures: A literature review and implications for HRD. *Human Resource Development Review* 8(2): 223–244.

Ardichvili, A., Mitchell, J. and Jondle, D. (2009). Characteristics of ethical business cultures. *Journal of Business Ethics* 85: 445–451.

Bass, B.M. and Steidlmeier, P. (1999). Ethics, character, and authentic transformational leadership behavior. *Leadership Quarterly* 10: 181–218.

Beck, U. (1992). *Risk Society: Towards a New Modernity*. London: Sage.

Boatright, J.R. (2011). *The Ethics of Risk Management: A Post-crisis Perspective*. White paper. Chicago: Loyola University.

Brinkmann, B. and Johnson, E. (2011). *The Catholic Identity Matrix – Seeing Mission in All We Do*. Ascension Health (internal publication).

Brinkmann, B., Maines, T.D., Naughton, M. J, Stebbins, J.M. and Weimerskirch, A. (2006). Bridging the gap. *Health Progress* 87: 43–50.

Brown, M. and Trevino, L. (2006). Ethical leadership: A review and future directions. *Leadership Quarterly* 17: 595–616.

Carroll, A. and Buchholtz, A. (2009). *Business & Society: Ethics and Stakeholder Management*. Mason, OH: South-Western Cengage Learning.

Cohen, D. (1993). Creating and maintaining ethical work climates: Anomie in the workplace and implications for managing change. *Business Ethics Quarterly* 3: 343–358.

Collins, J. and Porras, J. (1994). *Built to Last: Successful Habits of Visionary Companies*. New York: Harper Business.

Dion, M. (1996). Organizational culture as matrix of corporate ethics. *International Journal of Organizational Analysis* 4: 329–351.

Feldman, S. (2007). Moral business cultures: The keys to creating and maintaining them. *Organizational Dynamics* 36: 156–170.

Freeman, R.E. (1994). The politics of stakeholder theory: Some future directions. *Business Ethics Quarterly* 4(4): 409–421.

Freeman, R.E., Gilbert, D.R. and Hartman, E. (1988). Values and the foundation of strategic management. *Journal of Business Ethics* 7: 821–834.

Gabler, D. (2006). Is your culture a risk factor? *Business and Society Review* 111: 337–362.

George, B. (2003). *Authentic Leadership: Rediscovering the Secrets to Creating Lasting Value*. San Francisco: Jossey-Bass.

Goodpaster, K.E. (1997). Moral projection, principle of. In P.H. Werhane and R.E. Freeman (eds.), *Blackwell Encyclopedic Dictionary of Business Ethics*, p. 432. Malden, MA: Blackwell.

Goodpaster, K.E. (2007). *Conscience and Corporate Culture*. Malden, MA: Blackwell.

Goodpaster, K.E. (2010). Business ethics: Two moral provisos. *Business Ethics Quarterly* 20(4): 740–742.

Handy, C. (2002). What's a business for? *Harvard Business Review* 80(12): 49–55.

ISO (International Organization for Standardization). (2009). *ISO: 31000, Risk Management – Principles and Guidelines, Final Draft*. Geneva: International Organization for Standardization.

Jondle, D., Ardichvili, A. and Mitchell, J. (2014). Modeling ethical business culture: Development of the ethical business culture survey and its use to validate the CEBC model of ethical business culture. *Journal of Business Ethics* 119(1): 29–43.

Lencioni, P. (2002). Making your values mean something. *Harvard Business Review* 80(7): 113–117.

Maines, T.D. (2011). Self-assessment and improvement process for organizations. In L. Bouckaert and L. Zsolnai (eds.), *The Palgrave Handbook of Spirituality and Business*, pp. 359–368. New York: Palgrave Macmillan.

Paine, L. and Deshpandé, R. (2005). Up to code: does your company's conduct meet world-class standards? *Harvard Business Review* 83(12): 122–133.

Power, M. (2009). The risk management of nothing. *Accounting, Organizations & Society* 34(6/7): 849–855.

Schein, E.H. (2004). *Organizational Culture and Leadership*. San Francisco: Jossey-Bass.

Schminke, M, Arnaud, A. and Kuenzi, M. (2007). The power of ethical work climates. *Organizational Dynamics* 36: 171–183.

Schrøder, P.W. (2006). Impediments to effective risk management. In T.J. Andersen (ed.), *Perspectives on Strategic Risk Management*, pp. 65–87. Copenhagen: Copenhagen Business School Press.

Small, M. (2006). Management development: Developing ethical corporate culture in three organizations. *Journal of Management Development* 25: 588–600.

Smith, D. and Fischbacher, M. (2009). The changing nature of risk and risk management: The challenge of borders, uncertainty and resilience. *Risk Management* 11(1): 1–12.

Trevino, L. and Nelson, K. (2004). *Managing Business Ethics: Straight Talk about How to Do It Right*. New York: Wiley.

Trevino, L., Weaver, G.R., Gibson, D. and Toffler, B. (1999). Managing ethics and legal compliance: What works and what hurts. *California Management Review* 41: 131–150.

United States Sentencing Commission. (2004). 2004 Federal Sentencing Guidelines. Washington, DC: Office of Public Affairs.

Williams, C.A., Smith, M.S. and Young P.C. (1998). *Risk Management and Insurance*. New York: McGraw-Hill.

World Economic Forum. (2014). *Global Risks 2014 Report* (9th ed.). Geneva: World Economic Forum.

Young, P.C. (2004). Ethics and risk management: Building a framework. *Risk Management* 6(3): 23–34.

Young, P.C. (2010). Risk management. In J. Boatright (ed.), *Finance Ethics: Critical Issues in Financial Theory and Practice*, pp. 495–509. New York: Wiley-Blackwell.

4

The key to sustainable risk governance

Strong core values, delegation and accountability

Gregory L. Shaw and Torben Juul Andersen[1]

Abstract

This chapter brings attention to the importance of corporate values and concrete leadership enactment of those values as a necessary condition for effective risk management outcomes. The content is based on practice-based research experiences supported by relevant literature on risk governance and values-based management complemented with insights from case analyses and empirical studies. The chapter explains why formal risk management approaches have limitations and outlines how the presence of official policies and codes of conduct is insufficient to deal with dynamic and complex high-impact situations where strong core values heeded by the corporate leadership, in contrast, leads the way to better risk behaviors throughout the organization. Major disasters in British Petroleum over the past decade illustrate how a formal code of conduct failed to do the job when the leadership in reality gave first priority to profits at the expense of the stated environmental values. The prioritized code of the US Coast Guard is used to illustrate the circumstances where core values support effective crisis, disaster and risk management outcomes. The findings go against conventional wisdom of imposing tighter rules and regulations with formal controls as a panacea to cope with major disasters and shows why simpler means of guiding core values combined with delegation of responsibility to act under unexpected conditions is important in both private and public enterprise.

Major crises have regularly affected highly reputed business enterprises and public institutions over the past decades with significant negative impacts on value creation and social welfare. Many of these events seemingly happened without ill-intended human interventions and despite seemingly good governance practices, executive intents and managerial efforts. However, these cases often display a striking discrepancy between what executives thought, and said, was being done and what actually took place within the organization as business activities were carried out in practice. To remind ourselves we can just think of Lehman Brothers during the financial crisis and British Petroleum (BP) in the Mexican Gulf.[2] Lehman Brothers had excellent risk management capabilities but the board still accepted higher exposures to the market for subprime loans. BP had a clear code of conduct emphasizing safety and environment as prime concerns but still pushed the organization into risky drilling ventures. These crises were caused by a diversity of factors ranging from lack of oversight and excessive risk-taking to the impacts of operational hazards and external economic phenomena. Yet, as a typical trait across incidents there was a shortage of behavioral guidance and core values, or if they were in place, they were somehow not respected or adhered to when push came to shove. In short, the organizations were exposed to poor risk governance and leadership practices that beg the questions why such events happen time and again, and what top managers and directors can do to safeguard against these kinds of devastating outcomes.

More often than not the response to major crises and reported scandals has been to impose more regulation, tighter rules, increased scrutiny and more detailed reporting to enforce compliance such as the imposition of the Sarbanes–Oxley Act in 2002. However, there is little evidence to show that these approaches actually advanced the cause they were intended to support. At best we see no effect from intensified monitoring and tighter controls and at worst it increases the burden of bureaucracy and kills creative efforts devoted to search for better responses to unexpected conditions. Instead we suggest that good risk management behaviors derive from relatively mundane but essential and fairly costless leadership traits. We find it is important that essential *core values* are instituted and followed by the top executives both in spirit and in terms of specific actions because the example of good leadership decisions inspires people in the organization to follow the lead. It might be necessary to express the core values in words displayed in a formal code of conduct in general view for everybody, but it is insufficient to formalize the principles in glossy policy documents. The values and the principles behind the codes and core values must be enacted from the highest level of the organization through executive deeds and concrete actions.

If the leaders in charge pay lip service to the core values of the organization and make decisions without any regard for them, or apply incentives that contravene these values, then people working in the organization cannot be expected to adhere to the underlying principles either. Good risk behaviors derive from good leadership conduct as practiced by the top executives, and by extension, by the managers that operate at all levels of the organization leading the daily execution of business activities. Investing in extensive risk management systems without supportive leadership in spirit and action can be a waste of money and effort and may become an excuse for inactive leadership. Sometimes poor leadership traits derive from engrained behaviors embedded in the way organizational members think and act as implanted by generally accepted conduct over prolonged periods of time, which is often referred to as the *corporate culture*. In particular, executives that gained most of their managerial experience in a single organization with the same contextual background should be cognizant of this phenomenon, but we all are prone to it.

Since corporate cultures to a large extent are established, influenced and subsequently changed by the executive echelons, it may take a strong and diverse board to identify such traits and actively engage to have them instituted across the organization in a proactive and effective manner. Humans, and thereby also executives, are exposed to particular perceptions and views of the world that derive from their own personal experiences, and hence it is sound practice to involve people with diverse backgrounds and experiences in major decisions about complex strategic issues and potential disaster scenarios. That is, good risk management practices entail attentiveness and engagement at all levels of the organization with open and honest communication about what may turn out to be early warning signals revealing emergent risks and potential opportunities.

Every streak of risk events seems to stir an urge towards legislative, regulatory and corporate governance initiatives with the intent of restraining similar events from ever happening again by imposing more elaborate and comprehensive restrictions. While well intended, this can unfortunately lead us into a false belief about our ability to control human behaviors in highly dynamic and complex environments. It also displays the human shortcoming of not being able to see low-probability high-impact events in advance while seeing too many shadows pointing in that same direction after a major event has occurred. This bias often results in the futile exercise of "closing the barn door after the horse has left," and closing it with a slam. But doing things too late does not help, no matter how hard they are done. A better response might be to try to understand how the adverse situations arose in the first place and then learn from the mistakes.

In the early 2000s we saw a number of corporate scandals caused by executive misbehavior in some cases bordering on fraudulent actions including corporations like Enron, Global Crossing, WorldCom and Tyco where executives purposely misreported for personal gains. The Sarbanes–Oxley (SOX) legislation was a direct outgrowth of these events and imposed new reporting demands on US-listed firms while holding executives personally responsible. These requirements would encourage top managers to engage in stringent compliance exercises hiring external consulting outfits to implement state-of-the-art control systems and demonstrate that best efforts had been made. However, this inadvertently promotes a protective and defensive behavior, where the exercise has more concern for covering one's behind rather than ensuring the organization is more alert, engaged, responsive and on its toes to deal with the unexpected that always will arise along the way. To little surprise then, we saw that a SOX-compliant super-bank, Société Générale, was able to lose close to €5 billion in January 2008 due to an individual so-called rogue trader, Jérôme Kerviel.[3] During the evolving financial market crisis in 2008, we saw other compliant financial institutions budge due to reckless risk-taking pursued by dominant executives condoned by their boards in established companies like Bear Stearns[4] and Lehman Brothers.[5] In these cases, the shareholders lost most if not all of their invested money, while the executives continued to rake in their sizeable bonuses.

Other events are more subtle in nature and not necessarily ill-intended, although the disastrous consequences often will be the same. Two examples from the United States National Aeronautics and Space Administration (NASA) organization include the *Columbia* and *Challenger* disasters, both caused by systemic internal priorities arising from an institutional environment of budget controls and an accounting culture that gradually induced decision-makers to ignore the potential for major disasters (Vaughan, 2005). In the corporate sector some comparable examples may include the major explosions at the Texas City refinery and the Deepwater Horizon platform operated by BP in the Mexican Gulf. While the corporate governance practices at BP for all intents and purposes appeared to be perfect and run by the book, it was still possible for the company to incur two major industrial disasters within a relatively short period of time despite corrective changes in the executive management team. This pinpoints a number of challenges, such as: how to establish an effective culture of risk awareness throughout the organization; how to ensure that risk is handled by all organizational members in accordance with the corporate aims; how to motivate employees to act as effective risk managers; and how executives and directors can engage to ensure better risk leadership.

We believe an important part of the answer to these essential questions lies in the leadership approach taken by the executive team and the directors that oversees it. It is not a question of control and compliance, which represents a false sense of security in dynamic, complex and unpredictable environmental settings. The issue rather becomes how to ensure that early warning signals identified throughout the organization are communicated, probed, and interpreted in a timely and proactive manner, so the corporate executives are in a better position to deal with the unexpected event that can lead to crisis and disaster. This requires clear moral standards and prioritized core values imposed on the organization and enforced through executive example.

It further demands delegation of authority where local managers and employees in general can act knowing that their superiors support them and trust their ability to respond properly while they are accountable for actions taken or not taken.

Avoiding gaps between intentions and actions

So, why do we observe the apparent discrepancies between well-intended policies and general guidelines issued by the executive leadership and experienced external directors in the board? We think the answer to this question is linked to discrepancies between what the executives and the board members preach and what they practice in reality as they make major decisions on corporate resource utilization and promote people based on achieved outcomes. That is, if the official core values heeded by senior management cannot be recognized in the actual decisions made around the daily operations, people in the organization will act in accordance with the true values that motivate those decisions. Hence, we argue that managing the core values of an organization is one of the major responsibilities of top executives and directors and heeding those values is essential to good crisis, disaster and risk management practices.

According to *values-based management*, one of the principal leadership tasks is to establish the core values to be adopted across the organization as guiding principles to prioritize the many resource committing decisions taken over time (Anderson, 1997). Whereas different people and groups in the firm have diverging personal interests, the core values serve to balance diverse aims by promoting a concise set of ethical principles and corporate priorities. That is, the core values constitute the means to balance the concerns and interests of the organization's important stakeholders and ensure collaboration for a common cause. The core values reflect the shared beliefs embedded in the corporate culture that influence how corporate actions are executed by people through the influence of informal leadership (Wieland, 2005). *Stakeholder theory* argues that business conduct is about how various stakeholders, such as customers, suppliers, employees, financiers, communities and managers, act together and create value (Freeman, Harrison, Wicks, Parmar and De Colle, 2010). This view suggests that there is a need to impose core values to prioritize essential stakeholder interests and ensure long-term performance through stakeholder collaboration where the absence of such is likely to create fundamental conflicts as the basis for future risk incidents and crises.

Hence, the ability to mitigate and manage foreseeable risks while preparing for the emergence of unpredictable events is the essence of good risk management practice. The comprehensive risk management frameworks, often referred to as enterprise risk management (ERM), including the Committee of Sponsoring Organizations of the Treadway Commission (COSO) and ISO 31000 standards, are superbly geared to deal with foreseeable risks based on well-described processes of identifying, assessing, handling and managing the embedded exposures. However, unpredictable events are by definition very hard, if not impossible, to foresee in advance and yet the organization must be able to deal with these emergent crisis situations. This is where core values embedded in the corporate culture play an important role. In contrast, the use of formal policies and codes of conduct works well where the operating conditions are well known and little new is happening in the business environment (Figure 4.1).

The conventional use of ethical guidelines and codes of conduct suffice when the organization deals with decisions of relatively low significance under situational conditions that are known. If the stakes increase and the decisions take on higher significance, the standards should be complemented by good practices and managerial judgment supplemented by more advanced risk analysis to assess the consequences as proposed by the formal risk management frameworks (Figure 4.1).

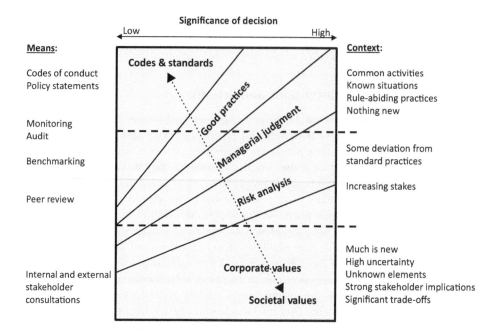

Adapted from *Risk Based Decision Making Framework*, United Kingdom Offshore Operators Association (1999).

Figure 4.1 Means of risk management against decision significance and context

However, the real challenge arises when the organization is faced with contexts where things are constantly changing and in flux where much is new and evolving, thus creating a high level of uncertainty with many unknown elements. Under these circumstances the standard approaches to risk management will not suffice because they provide general guidance with little flexibility to accommodate new and unexpected circumstances. Here the core values embedded in the corporate culture become essential as a guide to individual responsive actions throughout the organization and help prioritize decision alternatives in new, not previously encountered situations (Figure 4.1). In the case of truly high-stakes decisions, it also becomes important to consider the societal values that might be affected and influenced by the potential outcomes.

This illustrates why the presence of core values is indispensable beyond formal codes and standards, particularly in organizations operating in highly uncertain and unpredictable environments. It also pinpoints that formal codes and standards compared to core values and corporate culture are distinctly different risk management means. That is, we cannot just assume that the imposition of formal codes of conduct and policy standards automatically will lead to the existence of strong and durable core values.

The prevalence of core values with a good sense of direction and behavioral clues will help individuals dispersed throughout the organization act more effectively and consistently when confronted with unexpected events and unforeseeable circumstances. The establishment of core values embedded in a corporate culture can, for example, derive from a clear mission statement outlining the general aspirations with stated prioritization of essential stakeholder concerns and general behavioral guidelines (Andersen and Schrøder, 2010).

Schein (2004) argues that a corporate culture is imposed by the beliefs, values and assumptions of the founder(s), experiences among people as the company evolves, and beliefs, values and assumptions brought in by new people hired into the organization. Hence, the core values reflect the morality of the top executives and the members of the board and they earn confidence and loyalty among employees through their role modeling actions (De Hoogh and Den Hartog, 2008). That is, the moral stance of the senior executives influence the predominant core values and inspire the behavior of organizational members when the values are adhered to in practice by the corporate leaders. In other words, core values with impact will evolve from established ethical principles reinforced through the personal commitment and conduct displayed by corporate leadership.

Assessing and managing the exposures of major identifiable risks is a relatively straightforward task in the case of financial, insurable and economic exposures where outcomes typically can be documented based on readily available public data. However, the same cannot be applied to unpredictable events although simulation techniques, scenario analyses and stress-testing exercises may be useful to assess potential outcome effects. Instead the ability to prepare for unpredictable and unforeseeable events requires a risk-aware corporate culture where a core value induces individuals at all levels in the organization to stay alert to emergent risks and be ready to deal with the unexpected. This also provides the ability for a central risk function to collect early warning signals from dispersed organizational members where decentralized responsive actions are encouraged to fend off the preliminary effects of emergent risk situations.

Effective risk management under uncertain conditions entails conjoint efforts of analytical and coordinating activities by a central risk function and decentralized observance and responsiveness among dispersed employees operating in the grapevines of the organization where the new events typically will be visible first (Andersen, 2011). Hence, part of effective risk management entails engaging the right people to operate within a decision structure with open information and communication systems and flexible interactive controls. It implies that decision power is delegated, so organizational members can act fast within their areas of responsibility, and that the leadership trusts their ability to respond properly while they remain accountable for eventual outcomes.

The corporate leadership can enhance and support the ability to deal with uncertainty and unexpected events by developing an organizational culture with proper core values where the risk behavior primarily is driven by the character of the corporate executives and the line managers (see Figure 4.2). In addition, corporate leadership can support the enactment of effective risk practices by imposing organizational structures and decision-making processes with business policies, procedures and practices that are conducive to good risk management behaviors (Figure 4.2).

In the case of BP,[6] very elaborate and highly visible policy guidelines on corporate behaviors expressed in a formal code of conduct were imposed when Tony Hayward was put in place in 2007 as new group CEO after the Texas City Refinery explosion (see Insert on British Petroleum). But despite these concerted efforts to guide the right behavior, the company experienced another path-breaking event, when an oil rig under their command exploded in the Gulf of Mexico in 2010. We now know that the discrepancy between deed and action was due to the fact that codes and standards are unable to deal effectively with new unknown situations and because the executives in reality prioritized short-term profits more than the values expressed in the official guidelines. The fact that the board gave first priority to profits was expressed implicitly by the chairman Carl-Henric Svanberg at the time: "The BP board is deeply saddened to lose a CEO whose success over some three years in driving the performance of the company was so widely and deservedly admired."[7] In other words, when the board of directors

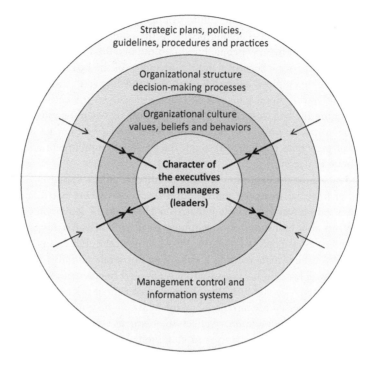

Adapted from Pauchant, T.C. and Mitroff, I.I. (1992). *Transforming the Crisis-Prone Organization: Preventing Individual, Organizational, and Environmental Tragedies*. Jossey-Bass Publishers: San Francisco, CA.

Figure 4.2 Leadership influences on organizational risk behaviors here

represented by their chairman signals that profits is the primary focus, it is no wonder that the executives under their supervision, and the managers reporting to them throughout the organization, give foremost attention to this concern. Writing a nice and possibly well-meaning story about concerns for safety and environment in an official code of conduct can do little to change this, even though it portrays the board as showing great care for societal issues.

British Petroleum (BP)

Major risk incidents and environmental Disasters

BP experienced a number of risk incidents over a relatively short period of time that had some devastating impacts on their key stakeholders while hurting their own bottom line and the market value of the company.

The Group Executive Officer John Brown was famously known for BP's 'Beyond Petroleum' campaign aimed at changing the corporate focus towards more sustainable energy sources. He turned BP into the largest global oil conglomerate among other things through the megamerger with Amoco. However, in March 2005 a major explosion at BP's Texas City refinery that killed 15 workers and injured more than 170 people changed the course. The incident was caused by a number of confluent factors including ineffective equipment, poor maintenance and insufficient safety precautions that had a catastrophic outcome. As a consequence John Brown retired prematurely in May 2007 and Tony Hayward became new group executive just before a panel (led by former US Secretary of State James Baker III) released a devastating report on the incident. BP was fined close to $50 million for environmental violations with claims of more than $1.6 billion in compensation. The explosion hurt the confidence in corporate management and the stock price on BP shares suffered in the aftermath compared to its peers in the industry (Figure 4.3).

Figure 4.3 BP

The investigative report stated that BP had failed to provide effective process safety leadership and had not established adequate process safety across its U.S. refineries, and found instances lacking operating discipline while tolerating serious deviations from safe operating practices.[8] These were serious allegations and caused BP to instate clear codes of conduct emphasizing safety and environmental consciousness (see following). Still the Centre for Public Integrity reported that the refiner, together with another BP facility in Toledo, Ohio, accounted for 97 percent of all serious violations in the US refining industry identified by inspectors over the previous three years.[9] So, things did not really improve.

With the changes in executive leadership one should think that the board and top management would make sure things were changed. However, we know that another environmental disaster happened, as the Deepwater Horizon rig operated by BP in the Mexican Gulf exploded in April 2010. That is, Tony Hayward spent three years in charge to restore the corporate reputation for safety after the Texas City blast, but despite these efforts the company still faced another disastrous event. It happened despite imposing a clear code of conduct prioritizing safety and environmental concern and the board abiding by all best practice governance requirements.

The code covers key areas of business operations of which the first is:
– health, safety, security and the environment –
fundamental rules and guidance to help us protect the natural environment, the safety of the communities in which we operate, and the health, safety and security of our people

Some argued that the company had taken safety risks to save money long before the explosions, possibly stemming from a market-driven obsession with profits that had become an unavoidable trait of the corporate culture. Other human factors might also be in play to enhance events, namely the inability to estimate the probability of unlikely events with extreme cost effects. Since the directors, executives and operating managers had never experienced a rig explosion, they could not conceive it as happening in reality. Yet, the adverse impact on the BP stock price was very real and it continues to suffer compared to major competitors (Figure 4.4).

Figure 4.4   BP

BP faced hundreds of lawsuits in federal court in New Orleans including claims by families of workers killed in the explosion of the drilling rig. Under the circumstances, the board decided to replace Tony Hayward as group executive and sell $30 billion of corporate assets (around 10% of the entire balance sheet) to offset costs connected to the oil spill, with expected future claims estimated as high as $49 billion.

We can draw on comparable examples from public sector, not-for-profit organizations to illustrate the importance of institutional core values combined with trust, delegation and accountability in driving effective crisis, disaster and risk management practices (see Insert on the United States Coast Guard).[10] Hence, if you are faced with central commanders that try to impose controls under strained conditions due to lack of trust in their subordinates, things are likely to go wrong. Field officers need the authority, trust and support from the central office to focus on the demands of unfolding local actions when unexpected events happen to accomplish the overarching mission and safeguard the crew. This projects a model of decentralized responsiveness among operating officers in the field as they deal with uncertain evolving circumstances supported by strong core values to guide the responsive actions they take.

The United States Coast Guard

Governance Based on Mutual Respect, Trust and Open Communication

The United States Coast Guard is a military armed force with all uniformed personnel (supported by civilian employees and volunteer personnel) subjected to very specific conduct requirements laid out in the Unified Code of Military Justice (see following). For the purpose of this case study, the analogy is made of the general governance, command structure and code of conduct of the military structure to the governance, leadership and policies of a generic organization.

The general governance philosophy of the United States Coast Guard is conveyed in its core values of Honor, Respect and Devotion to Duty reflected in personal integrity, teamwork and accountability to the public trust. Of course, these high-level statements, operationalized through organizational strategies, goals and objectives do not ensure 100% compliance at all levels of the military structure. As a microcosm of society in general, violations requiring correction and/or disciplinary action do occur. At the unit level, these organizational goals and objectives are supplemented and reinforced by more specific unit goals and objectives, policies and procedures, and most importantly, the expressed and demonstrated leadership philosophy and style of the unit commanders.

The operation of a Coast Guard cutter requires myriad knowledge elements, skills and abilities in areas which are the province of crew members with the requisite training, experience and qualifications. No commanding officer possesses technical and operational expertise across all these areas, and she or he must place trust in the cutter's officers and crew and provide the necessary support for them to accomplish their responsibilities to the best of their ability. The commanding officer is totally responsible and accountable for the safe operation and mission of his or her unit and must establish oversight and communication channels to meet this absolute responsibility.

The commander's trust of individual crew members is earned through their observed and reported performance and is lost when performance does not meet accepted standards without sufficient reason. Trust works both ways, however. A commanding officer must continually model the core values of honor, respect and devotion to duty to earn and maintain the trust of the officers and crew who place their safety in her or his hands on a daily basis. Performing the missions of the United States Coast Guard onboard cutters is dangerous business often conducted in the worst of weather conditions under significant stress and uncertainty. To perform safely and professionally, the crew must place their complete trust in their commander to do the right thing. There can be no perception that the commander is more concerned with his or her personal agenda and advancement than with the safety and well-being of the crew and the requirements of the mission. Once lost, trust is seldom if ever earned back, and can have a negative impact on morale and performance.

Core values merely expressed in words and not followed from the top down and from the bottom up in both spirit and action are a recipe for poor organizational governance and will most likely have adverse consequences. An organization whose leaders do not believe in, follow, and visibly support their own core values cannot expect the same from those people they lead. Within the United States Coast Guard, the very best units in terms of safety, morale, and mission performance are those who believe in the Coast Guard's core values supported and modeled by their leaders.

Officers are evaluated on a periodic basis using standard forms and required documentation that are based upon personal and professional qualities consistent with the core values of the Coast Guard. These evaluations largely determine promotions and future duty assignments. Personal and professional qualities requiring detailed evaluation include: Initiative – originating and acting on new ideas; Judgment – making sound decisions and providing valid recommendations based upon risk assessment and analytic thought; Responsibility – Acting ethically, courageously, and dependably and inspiring the same in others; and Professional Presence – Bringing credit to the Coast Guard through one's actions, competence, demeanor and appearance. The evaluation process reflects the overall Coast Guard culture and belief in its core values. Officers who do not attain and maintain the highest standards in general have very limited career advancement and enhancement opportunities and those that do comprise the current and future leaders of the Coast Guard.

Honor

Integrity is our standard. We demonstrate uncompromising ethical conduct and moral behavior in all of our personal and organizational actions. We are loyal and accountable to the public trust.

Respect

We value our diverse workforce. We treat each other and those we serve with fairness, dignity, respect and compassion. We encourage individual opportunity and growth. We encourage creativity through empowerment. We work as a team.

Devotion to Duty

We are professionals, military and civilian, who seek responsibility, accept accountability and are committed to the successful achievement of our organizational goals. We exist to serve. We serve with pride.

Hence, we see that the same approach seems to work across different types of organization whether it constitutes a private company generating returns to their owners by showing concern for other stakeholders or a public institution providing a common good for society. This approach builds on strong core values supported straight from the top combined with trustful delegation of authority that leaves room for local responses to evolving events where individual actors are accountable for action as well as inaction.

Discussion and conclusion

The core values and the cultural context within which crisis, disaster and risk management takes place should be a main concern of the board of directors and the executive management team. The corporate leadership creates and manages the organizational culture and the tone is set by the executive echelons. The corporate culture is comprised of the basic assumptions and beliefs shared by all members of the organization, which will affect how things are done. It is learned from practical experience where group members engage in repeated tasks and share in successful problem-solving exercises that over time become the behavioral standard for people operating in the organization. The cultural traits are both visible and invisible where the most visible elements are the physical artifacts displayed in the firm, while the deeper elements of values constitute the invisible shared assumptions, beliefs and accepted behaviors throughout the organization.

The importance of core values is further supported by recent evidence collected among professional market participants after the financial market crisis in 2008–09 in the RiskMinds 2009 Risk Managers' Survey. This study indicated that the specification and development of risk management competencies was critical for the events. However, despite good risk management systems they were not expected to make a difference without changes in the corporate culture. This is because the effectiveness of risk management, governance and internal controls depends on the leadership and organizational climate that drives the behaviors in the organization. As a consequence, risk culture and ethical principles should be brought to the top of the agenda among corporate executives and members of the board as well as regulators and law makers.

This verdict suggests that those responsible for overseeing the actions of the executives were not competent enough, not rigorous enough, and maybe not sufficiently powerful to influence things in the right direction. However, as the press release from the BP chairman Carl-Henric Svanberg seems to indicate, the entire company board supported the prevailing practices and was as instrumental in maintaining the existing cultural traits as were the executives they had engaged. Hence, specifying the relevant risk management competence is crucial, but it will not have lasting effects without a strong corporate culture backed by core values, because the effectiveness of risk management depends on the climate in which practice is enacted. In other words, risk culture and business ethics need to be at the top of the agenda both in the board rooms and the regulators' suites.

Risk management and governance are complex dynamic activities. In many corporate failures, the directors often lacked the knowledge to effectively oversee the executives, which impaired their ability to execute their fiduciary obligations. However, this can threaten the very survival of the firm. That is, good risk governance includes the skills, infrastructure (i.e., decision structure, incentive systems, management information and control processes) and corporate culture imposed by the directors as they exercise their risk oversight duties. In short, effective management of crisis, disaster and risk requires adherence to strong core values, trust in people, delegation of authority and individual accountability.

Notes

1 Gregory L. Shaw, George Washington University, Institute for Crisis, Disaster, and Risk Management, Washington, DC 20052, USA; Torben Juul Andersen, Copenhagen Business School, Center for Global Strategic Responsiveness, Department of International Economics and Management, DK-2000 Frederiksberg, Denmark.

2 See, for example, the cases 'Lehman Brothers (B)', Case Centre Ref. no. 310–266–1 (Andersen 2010) and 'British Petroleum: From Texas City to the Gulf of Mexico and Beyond', Case Centre Ref. no. 714–017–1 (Andersen 2014).

3 Jérôme Kerviel was convicted in the 2008 trading loss for breach of trust and forgery as the bank claimed he worked on his own and without authorization. He later published a book in 2010 where he argues that his superiors knew about his doings as part of common practice.

4 Bear Stearns was a sizeable issuer of asset-backed securities with increasing exposures to sub-prime mortgage-backed assets where the Federal Reserve Bank of New York intervened to save the company but eventually instigated a sale to JP Morgan Chase for $10 a share, which was approved by the Bear Stearns shareholders on May 29, 2008.

5 Lehman increased its investment in subprime mortgage-related assets extending the leverage ratio of assets over equity to around 31:1. As the market turned, Lehman Brothers filed for bankruptcy on Sept. 15, 2008. The CEO, Richard Fuld, received a US$22 million bonus in March 2008.
6 This draws on the case 'British Petroleum: From Texas City to the Gulf of Mexico and Beyond' (Andersen 2014).
7 BP Corporate Website, Press Release on July 27, 2010.
8 Extracts from the Baker Report, 2007.
9 AFP, August 10, 2010.
10 This draws upon Gregory Shaw's experience and insights from 27 years of active duty as a US Coast Guard officer and as commanding officer of four Coast Guard cutters.

References

Andersen TJ. 2010. Lehman Brothers (B). The Case Centre. [http://www.thecasecentre.org]

Andersen TJ. 2011. Combining central planning and decentralization to enhance effective risk management outcomes. *Risk Management* 12(2): 101–115.

Andersen TJ, Andersen CB. 2014. *British Petroleum: From Texas City to the Gulf of Mexico and Beyond*. Frederiksberg, Denmark: Copenhagen Business School (CBS).

De Hoogh AHB, Den Hartog DN. 2008. Ethical and despotic leadership, relationships with leader's social responsibility, top management team effectiveness and subordinates' optimism: A multi-method study. *Leadership Quarterly* 19: 297–311.

Freeman RE, Harrison JS, Wicks AC, Parmar BL, De Colle S. 2010. *Stakeholder Theory – The State of the Art*. Cambridge University Press: Cambridge.

Schein EH. 2004. *Organizational Culture and Leadership*. Jossey-Bass: San Francisco.

Vaughan D. 2005. System effects: On slippery slopes, repeating negative patterns, and learning from mistake? In Starbuck WH, Farjoun M., *Organization at the Limit: Lessons from the Columbia Disaster*. Blackwell: Malden, MA.

Wieland J. 2005. Corporate governance, values management, and standards: A European perspective. *Business & Society* 44: 74–93.

5

The risk management paradox

Enhanced focus on risk management seemingly doesn't pay off!

Peter Winther Schrøder

Abstract

It is argued that corporate scandals, in the newspaper headlines, most likely will continue to unfold as further attention is paid to internal controls and formal risk reporting as prevalent elements of current risk management practice, which is at the detriment of good risk governance. Risk governance is pivotal in accomplishing effective risk management outcomes. It starts at the top of the organization, and accounts for how the board of directors and the executive management board discuss, determine and communicate the company's risk appetite. It is argued that proper decision-making processes that can compensate for the distortions ingrained in the human mind as well as establishing decision-making forums with a broader range of personal characteristics can avoid a uniform mind-set. However, the effectiveness of risk management and governance depends heavily on the organizational climate in which they take place. It is reasoned that effective risk governance must encourage risk awareness throughout the organization. This includes appropriate training to impart knowledge and confidence around the applied risk methodology fostering a common understanding of the company's risk management norms. Incentives and sanction structures should be designed to encourage sound risk assessment in a risk-aware organization. It is argued that proper risk governance can lead to more effective risk management practices. Accordingly, regulators and other stakeholders are encouraged to consider qualitative rather than quantitative checklist-oriented controls in the risk management practice and evaluate the quality of the company's risk management system to reduce the propensity for corporate scandals in the future.

Risk management has long been a standard management activity, although the risk focus generally has been limited to those exposures that can be observed, measured, and mitigated through various controls, insurance contracts, and other financial hedging products aimed at protecting the company against the adverse economic effects of potential risk events.

However, there has been a growing public pressure for more systematic and comprehensive approaches to risk management as the news about corporate scandals have hit the newspaper headlines over the past decades. These events have also paid much attention to the integrity and personal accountability of corporate executives. The examples of corporate scandals (see

Appendix 5.1) include excessive trading practices in Barings Bank (1995), Société Générale (2008), and UBS (2011), where traders took unauthorized positions in various financial contracts, falsified documents, kept trades hidden by booking the transactions on unused error accounts, and/or made unauthorized use of the bank's computer systems. The collapse of the American energy company Enron (2001), the American telecommunication company Worldcom (2002), the Italian dairy product company Parmalat (2003), and Bernard Madoff's wealth management arm (2008) revealed that reported profits were sustained by a planned and systematic use of forgeries and accounting fraud.

As a result, new enhanced risk management approaches were introduced commonly known under the general heading of enterprise risk management (ERM) frameworks. For example, the German Control and Transparency in Business Act (KonTraG) was imposed in 1998, setting new standards of corporate governance for German publicly listed companies; while the Turnbull Report was published in the UK in 1999 (and revised 2005), and focused on directors obligations with respect to good internal controls. The Enron scandal was a key factor behind the creation of the Sarbanes–Oxley Act in the US in 2002, probably the most notable legislative initiative, holding boards, CEOs, and other senior executives accountable for potential corporate risk outcomes. Finally, the Committee of Sponsoring Organizations of the Treadway Commission (COSO) in the US, which originally was formed in 1985 to inspect, analyze, and recommend on fraudulent corporate financial reporting, developed the COSO ERM framework in 2004 with a new set of principles to manage corporate risks.

The financial crisis in 2008 had a severe societal impact and was to a large extent caused by failures in organizational cultures and ethical principles including remuneration practices that encouraged excessive risk exposures and showed severe shortcomings in the engagement of the board in overseeing risk management. All the while, organizational cultures often inhibited effective challenges to the excessive risk-taking where easy access to capital and inadequate accounting and regulatory standards led to pervasive asset overvaluation.[1]

As a result of the financial crisis, new and comprehensive regulatory measures were considered and are currently introduced via Basel III[2] aimed at increasing the banking industry's resilience to absorb various shocks from different sources, improving management and governance practices, and strengthening transparency and disclosure. In addition to formally meeting the Basel III requirements, global systemically important financial institutions are imposed a higher loss absorbency capacity to reflect the significant influence they pose to the financial system. The enhanced requirements to formal risk management and governance entail among other things official requirements for managerial duties with a vastly increased workload on elaborate sign-off and documentation schemes. For example, it is not uncommon to see board material in financial institutions well in excess of several hundred pages per meeting, of which much is material that board members must approve in accordance with the regulatory requirements. The magnitude of this documentation means that there might not be sufficient time for evaluation and discussion on relevant risk issues for the organization.

Ideally, an ERM framework should support managers in efforts to limit the potential for downside losses from major exposures while helping them to think more systematically about opportunities that represent future upside potential (e.g., Henriksen and Uhlenfeldt, 2006). However, the new formalized risk management practices imposed on the business community serve to ensure that the company maintains a stringent internal control framework to circumvent potential risks as well as to enhance corporate accountability for the consequences of their occurrences. As a result, the risk management process in many organizations has become a stale checklist drill, which serves as a convenient tool to satisfy regulators and other stakeholders as well as convincing executives and board members that they have done their duty if things should go wrong. The risk management perception evolves with a predominant focus on routine system errors, operational malfunctions, uncontrolled employees, and the personal accountability of corporate executives that can be managed by a central corporate risk management function (Power, 2007). Such an approach often promotes a defensive mentality that works against the development of a proper risk-awareness culture, and worse, potential changes in the risk landscape might not be identified in a timely manner because it is forgotten in formal reporting practices. For example, the use of certifications and standards within information security and general IT controls are endemically focused on having formal controls in place that cater to the external and internal environments, while focusing less on establishing awareness about information security risk associated with social engineering and so forth.

Although it is undisputable that the financial crisis in 2008 and the many reported corporate failures have had severe repercussions for society as they exposed organizations and their stakeholders, the imposition of comprehensive, resource demanding, and control-oriented risk management frameworks on corporate business activities will hardly prevent the advents of severe corporate scandals in the future. Hence, the Bernard Madoff (2008),[3] Société Générale (2008), and UBS (2011)[4] issues happened after the introduction of more extensive ERM practices.[5] While the various ERM frameworks relate to risk governance, the attention given to internal controls and formal risk reporting has been pronounced, to the detriment of proper risk governance that deserves more attention.

Risk governance was pivotal in the discussions and recommendations in the UK in light of the financial crisis (The Walker Report, 2009). It is pinpointed that "the most critical need is for an environment in which effective challenge of the executive is expected and achieved in the boardroom before decisions are taken on major risk and strategic issues" and "board-level engagement in risk oversight should be materially increased, with particular attention to the monitoring of risk and discussion leading to decisions on the entity's risk appetite and tolerance" (The Walker Report, 2009: 12).

Whichever business model a company pursues it entails risk, and accordingly strategic decisions cannot be taken without considering the exposures such decisions may give rise to. Consequently, risk management is not a box-ticking exercise that can be delegated to be managed by a central corporate risk management function, but is a core activity that should be considered an integrated part of the strategic decision-making process to ensure that an appropriate risk-reward trade-off is established when major resources are committed. For example, most companies outsource part of their noncore activities and/or move production to cheaper geographical locations, and have formal checklist risk management procedures in place to consider the risks associated with the handover. However, while such an approach is correct from a narrow strategic point of view, the interests of and potential reactions from key stakeholders including employees, unions, nongovernmental organizations (NGOs), and local and federal governments should also be evaluated, which requires nonroutine evaluations and assessments engaging various expert views (The Walker Report, 2009: 12). Thus, higher dedication and engagement from members in the boardroom as well as the executive management board is needed as a prerequisite for a more prudent risk culture in the organization that will be paramount in establishing a risk-resilient and responsive organization.

Embedding risk management at the top: overcoming the obstacles

Insufficient engagement in the company's risk management practice might be ascribed to the fact that risk management often is considered a rather abstract and intangible discipline. However, a higher level of risk consciousness can be accomplished in a pragmatic manner based on an open mind-set rather than a comprehensive set of risk management qualifications. Scenario planning,[6] i.e., creating plausible scenario story lines, is a useful and pragmatic tool to guide open discussions and determine the company's risk environment and appetite for risk due to its relative ease of outlining complex chains of events with potential losses offering the advantage of transparency with limited use of complex statistical models. For example, an information technology (IT) outage could materialize for most companies, while criticality off-course depends on the specific business model adopted by the firm. A story framed as shown in Insert 5.1 does not require specific risk management expertise but rather a readiness to discuss potential implications, what to do about the implied risk with involvement from functional experts and business owners to determine acceptable risk levels. The story is fictive, but nevertheless a model example that can be used to evaluate, discuss, and train an IT-dependent organization on how to deal with particular risk events.

Insert 5.1 Irregular Behavior

This morning a database administrator was informed about irregular behavior and an unexpected increase of translations in a critical database. The database specialist has pointed out that no changes were made related to this database during last weeks. At the same time, the organization experienced a high market activity, which to some extent could explain the specialist's concern and observation.

A few hours later, the database administrator reports that the backup database restarted without obvious reason. The customer-facing teams have reported an outstanding number of password-reset requests during the last hour. Further, it is reported that clients are having difficulties logging in to most web applications. It seems that clients are unable to execute trades. In addition, the organization discovers that account overview is shown incorrectly both for the company and clients.

As the specialists are investigating these rather alarming issues, an external person contacts the organization who claims responsibility for recent technical issues. He states he has control over some of the key systems within the organization and he is ready to misuse this control if his demands are not met. To prove his intentions, he has changed some of the trading limits forcing systems to close several client accounts. As a result, it is unclear to the organization whether trading limits have been breached and action is required.

The organization has just received another message from the perpetrator, in which it is stated that if his demands are not met in four hours he will change limits for additional active clients, and login names together with their passwords will be published in the social media, which can be misused. Finally, he will erase information so the organization cannot reconstruct clients' portfolio.

The IT specialists confirm that there are some unusual activities on some of the systems.

Determining the company's risk appetite, i.e., the amounts and types of risk the company is prepared to accept in pursuit of its business objectives, can be supported by elaborating scenarios that are unlikely, but not unthinkable, and that potentially could have a severe impacts on the business under abnormal or extreme market conditions. The outcome of such scenarios might imply that the line of business will be faced with impossible requirements, which is one reason why scenarios should consider severe circumstances as the basis for more balanced discussions for decision-making purposes. While scenario discussions based on normal market conditions allows the company to consider minor adjustments to its current business model, the result of a more extreme scenario is to force the decision-makers to assess whether current business strategies are in fact viable or at least acceptable, and if so, think about the mitigating initiatives and preparedness a potential future crisis might require. For example, it might be acceptable that the company is exposed to a severe IT outage, if the direct loss can be transferred by taking an insurance coverage while reducing reputational risk by devising appropriate business continuity plans. In contrast, using a major subcontractor in Bangladesh might not be acceptable due to a potential exposure to improper working conditions that could draw negative media coverage, even though the direct risks of, e.g., missing deliverables due to production shutdown, could be mitigated by engaging multiple backup suppliers in different regions.[7]

When determining the risk appetite executive management and board members must exercise judgment on the relevant scenarios where abnormal market conditions that should be considered as a balanced representation of event with potential operational severity and strategic challenges. However, there are a number of well-documented psychological traps ingrained in the human mind, cognitive biases, that affect the way decision-makers can achieve balanced judgment in important business decisions (Bazerman and Watkins, 2004; Hammond, Keeney and Raiffa, 1998). For example, we tend to give disproportionate weight to initial impressions, past events or trends and thus anchor subsequent thoughts and evaluations around a fairly narrow-minded foundation. Further, we are reluctant to make changes and rather prefer to maintain status quo and therefore display strong biases against possible alternatives. This may be ascribed to the fact that it is more pronounced to blame people for making bad decisions than for doing nothing, which may refrain people from taking action because if can lead to personal criticism. We subconsciously decide what we want to do before we figure out why we want do it. Thus, we are inclined to cherry-pick and interpret information in a way that supports our established views while ignoring or giving less emphasis to information that contradicts predominant beliefs. We tend to have unrealistic expectations about the future, being overconfident about the accuracy of our forecasts and capabilities thus exposing the company to far greater risk than is generally realized. We are blinded by past decisions, rarely admitting mistakes or acknowledging poor decisions, which paves the way for (personal) criticism, and are therefore prone to make choices in a manner that justifies former decisions even though the decisions no longer seem valid. Finally, we don't want to invest in preventing a problem that we have not personally experienced or witnessed before and supported by unquestionable documentation.

It is hard to eliminate these distortions ingrained in the human mind, but it is possible to establish a decision-making process that can compensate for those errors in our thinking, and avoid that mental flaws become errors in judgment and faulty business decisions. Some of the key measures that can be considered in the decision-making process are as follows (Bazerman and Watkins, 2004; Hammond et al., 1998):

- Identify alternative options and evaluate plusses and minuses with equal rigor.
- Ensure that a problem is viewed from different perspectives – be open and actively seek conflicting information and opinions from a variety of people and sources.
- Listen carefully to the view of people who are not burdened by former decisions.
- Think on your own before consulting others.
- Be careful not to influence the people you consult – your own preconception might come back.
- Acknowledge that some good ideas sometimes lead to bad outcome. Create an internal environment that permits and encourages the organization to learn from past mistakes.

In addition to the psychological traps in the human mind, the fact that sense-making occurs in a social environment where people are not just sensitive to what is being said but also who is saying it means that there is a tendency to select people that perceive, appreciate and decide on matters in the same manner as oneself, whereas individuals that differ from this are considered less attractive and reliable. Consequently, most organizations are prone to adopt a uniform mind-set and subconsciously subscribe to group thinking (Day and Schoemaker, 2006).

For example, it is not uncommon that people in the driver's seat (e.g., executive decision makers) are charismatic, eloquent, persuasive, impatient, and action oriented, while qualifications, position, prestige, and personality features may curb the audience's inclination to raise critical voices even when they are explicitly encouraged to express their points of view.

Ideally, opposites complement each other as different approaches to a problem ensure greater variance in developing alternative solutions and a higher likelihood to uncover things that otherwise would be overlooked. Therefore, in order to eliminate biases from individual behaviors and attitudes, executive management and the board of directors should ensure that relevant decision fora are composed in a way that ensures a broad range of personal characteristics, knowledge, and insights to create variance in discussions and decision-making alternatives. This is no doubt a challenging task. For example, two polar opposites in a management group are often represented by introvert fact-based staff function managers (e.g., risk management officials) and extravert and action-oriented sales managers. The introvert functional specialists who generally seek depth of knowledge look for minor details and prefer to organize information through order, structure, and schedules and are regarded as tiresome people looking for issues rather than opportunities. The extravert marketing people that generally emphasize action and new possibilities and seek breadth of knowledge while spending less time on reflection and analysis are regarded as frivolous opportunists. If these fundamental differences in human behavior are not understood and accepted, people in the organization are not likely to work together well. However, by being self-aware as the basis for developing emotional intelligence that enhance the understanding and acceptance of human differences, it is possible to find the right balance between excessive conformity and conflict where differences are not so pronounced that things end up in a bun.[8]

The risk management tune in the middle

Establishing a formalized risk management structure across all organizational entities is not sufficient, as the risk landscape the company is faced with typically is complex. Some risks are relatively predictable and thus easier to control, whereas other risk factors are known but still highly uncertain to predict, maybe even hard to foresee at all. In addition, the prediction of aggregate corporate exposures are complicated by the complexity of internal specialization and external business interactions that make risk events fall outside the scope of conventional control approaches to risk management. Furthermore, whereas predictable risks can be controlled centrally, unpredictable risks characterized by unknowable conditions and high complexity are impossible to control centrally and, therefore, should be managed through decentralized actions. Therefore, the organization of risk management activities within the company calls for an appropriate balance between central management controls and decentralized responsiveness, which means that risk management must form part of everyone's duties in tandem with other tasks, and not just an activity delegated to a central specialist function such as the risk management office (RMO). Nonetheless, general risk management responsibility is rarely, if ever, incorporated explicitly in individual job descriptions or descriptions of operational functions outside the proper risk management departments. Similarly, employment contracts while often incorporating the company's security policy, compliance policy, and so forth that must be observed where noncompliance can lead to disciplinary actions – they rarely impose a risk awareness requirement.

However, it is an advantage to engaging each and everybody in the organization to use knowledge about risk more effectively, because operational managers and staff positioned at lower hierarchical levels in the organization very often possess essential knowledge, that rarely reach those who formulate the strategies and manage aggregate risks at the corporate center.

The risk management office is a specialist unit that serves in an advisory capacity liaising with members of the board and executive management on risk appetite and monitoring of exposures. An important role of the risk office is to spearhead the translation of board-determined risk appetite statements into specific risk measures and exposure limits appropriately tailored to each of the business lines. At the same time, the risk management function should provide appropriate coaching and training company-wide to foster an understanding of the boundaries for acceptable risks and the implications of these boundaries.

The risk management office should also facilitate identification of risks by organizing and assisting business process owners in the risk identification and exposure monitoring as well as assisting business process owners in addressing control deficiencies that surface as a result of a loss event and exposures identified during an investigation.

The initial identification of risks across the company can be carried out by means of workshops for the various business areas headed by the RMO and participants from among key process and risk owners. Beyond identifying and assessing risk, such workshops constitute formal training sessions to impart risk knowledge and create confidence in the applied risk methodology. As the organization's risk maturity increases, the training workshops should be replaced by risk self-assessments, where process owners themselves identify and assess relevant risks as part of their daily duties – often complemented by a view on how the risk is mitigated. Subsequently, the RMO challenges and provides feedback on the risk assessments as well, as it collects data for executive reporting purposes and so forth.[9] Constructive feedback to and dialogue with the risk owners, not least in relation to the mitigation of risks, are crucial in establishing a prudent risk awareness as it becomes transparent how the information is applied and why it is valuable.

In addition, recording of incidents and near misses within the organization and open sharing of this information should be implemented, as this can facilitate learning how to avoid major incidents and keeping the margins for error low. The company should create an internal environment that will permit employees to learn from past mistakes and use them as learning experiences. This takes time and requires strong support from upper management, as recording of incidents and near misses entails some challenges (e.g., few want to confess their own misdoings as it exposes them). Hesitance to "blame" colleagues and team members that may give rise to "annoying" questions and increased workload and so forth may work against imposing effective risk alertness (Hain, 2009). Nevertheless, establishing such an environment will enhance general risk awareness. For example, in hindsight of major internal risk events it is revealed time after time that someone lower in the hierarchy felt that something was amiss, but this suspicion was never passed on. The reason for inaction is in many cases caused by insufficient managerial encouragement and a realization that it requires extra effort to sort things out and get assurance that there is something to be done.

Further to reinforce the decentralized risk awareness, elaborating and practicing contingency plans around worst-case scenarios is valuable, because it enables employees to engage in discussions about how their actions may affect the organization as well as it enhances the understanding of competencies needed to manage the various risk events, competencies that subsequently can be developed if required. Formal contingency planning to deal with potential crisis situations will typically include a number of sequential steps (Turpin, 2006).

- Conduct a crisis audit to determine the company's vulnerability to, for example, product defects, hazards, key managers, employees, customers, partners, and so forth.
- Set up a crisis organization and determine who within the chain of command is in charge in a crisis situation and distribute roles and responsibilities.
- Prepare monitoring processes and recovery plans to enhance preparedness.
- Develop alert systems in order to determine when it is appropriate to react.
- Anticipate potential emergency responses in order to prepare how to react.
- Identify the key stakeholders including journalists and media, and elaborate how they should be informed.
- Rehearse for effective action.

Managing contingency planning requires detailed knowledge of the company's operating model and calls for participation from experts with "engine room" insight. Therefore, in setting up the chain of command much can be learned from the practice pursued in HROs, or high reliability organizations (Weick and Sutcliffe, 2001). Shifting of leadership roles is pronounced in HROs. They may have an underlying hierarchical structure but have a built-in operational dynamic that enables them to shift to command mode when extraordinary conditions require it. This is achieved by combining a hierarchical decision structure with a specialist decision structure that allows expertise at the bottom of the organization to migrate upward when needed. This means that decision authority moves towards the expertise and knowledge so those organizational members that are closest to the problem are empowered to make important decisions. Last but not least, it creates enhanced engagement and motivation and thus reinforces general risk awareness.

Companies' incentive structures very often reward staff in a biased manner, encouraging them to increase sales or profit without regard to the risk undertaken, e.g., practiced unethical behaviors in order to increase short-term sales (OECD, 2009; The Walker Report, 2009). Furthermore, the incentive structures are rarely linked to the company's risk management practice, as for example stated in the company's risk policy, an issue that is crucial to incentivize each individual in the organization to contribute to a prudent risk culture, for example, by providing first quality risk information, reacting to potential risk events in a prudent manner, and so forth. Consequently, the company should implement an incentive and sanction structure that is designed in a way that encourages sound risk management practices as well, as it punishes divergence from the company's established risk policy. While various reports on remuneration practice (cf. OECD, 2009; The Walker Report, 2009) primarily focus on senior executives and high-end employees' remuneration, the mentioned incentive and sanction structure should cover all organizational levels.

Therefore, internal recognition such as promotion, salary increases, bonuses, and so forth should explicitly adhere to the company's stated risk management norms to account for and encourage individuals to comply with the risk policies. In contrast, deviance from stated risk management norms should result in sanctions like warnings, firings, or similar penalties as it articulates the importance of a proper risk management practice. Accordingly, the company should develop measurable indicators of adherence to stated risk management norms, including not only compliance with hard exposure limits but also with clearly stated behavioral expectations that link these indicators to the company's performance measures (Hain, 2009).

Conclusion

Major corporate scandals will most likely continue to unfold even as the public demands more robust risk management systems with enhanced personal accountability of corporate executives for corporate failures. The imposition of comprehensive control-based frameworks can often lead to the implementation of defensive, auditable, and formal enterprise risk management and reporting practices. So, even though enterprise risk management frameworks might be useful, they are not a sufficient condition for effective risk governance. The reason is that there is too much focus on having the technical risk analyses and formal reporting right, whereas less attention is paid to how risk management is actually practiced throughout the organization. Effective risk management starts at the top, where the board of directors and executive management should discuss, determine, and communicate the company's risk appetite as part of their strategic discussions. This requires that executive managers and directors on the board must exercise judgment and, therefore, entertain decision-making processes that can compensate for the distortions that inevitably engrain the human mind as well as establish decision-making forums composed by a broader range of people with diverse interpersonal characteristics to avoid uniformity of mind-set and ensure open discussions with sufficient diversity to create viable decision alternatives.

However, nothing will really happen without a cultural foundation within the organization, because the effectiveness of risk management outcomes depends on the organizational climate in which all decisions are made at different levels and parts of the firm. Therefore, effective risk governance must encourage general risk awareness throughout all members of the organization to ensure that risk considerations is a natural part of everybody's duties on an equal footing with other operating tasks. The risk management office is an "accelerator" in this process, as it should serve in an advisory capacity liaising with the board of directors, executive management, and operational managers throughout the organization. Hence, the risk managers should provide appropriate coaching and training to impart knowledge of and confidence with the general risk methodology as well as foster an understanding of the company's stated risk management norms and the implications of the risk management process. To emphasize the importance of a risk-aware organization, the company should implement an incentive and sanction structure designed in a way that encourage sound risk management practice as well as disfavor divergence from the risk policy, so each and every individual in the organization is incentivized to contribute with prudent behavior in a risk-aware culture.

An enhanced focus on risk governance to guide how risk management is carried out in the company will without a doubt lead to a more risk-resilient and responsive organization and, therefore, a more effective risk management practice. As a result, corporate scandals should be less pronounced, although corporate risk events and even corporate failures will continue to unfold as a natural consequence of calculated risk-reward decisions. Regulators and other stakeholders should focus on these qualitative concerns (see Appendix 5.2) within prevailing risk management practices as the basis for evaluating the durability of the risk management systems.

Notes

1 See Moore, Carter & Associates and Cranfield School of Management (2010) and OECD (2009).
2 The regulatory framework Basel II that was introduced in 2002 incorporated self-monitoring and internal control systems as focal elements to regulate institutions in the international financial markets.
3 The largest accounting fraud scandal in American history at the time.
4 The biggest fraud in UK history at the time.
5 At the time of writing, the publicly traded Spanish global Wi-Fi provider Gowex is filing for bankruptcy after the founder and CEO of the company, Jenaro Garcia, has admitted that he has inflated the revenues. The financial fraud came to light, when the investment firm Gotham City Research published a report asserting "that more than 90 percent of reported Gowex revenues "do not exist," and putting a $0 price target on its stock." *Chicago Tribune*, 11 July 2014.
6 The scenario planning technique is described in Andersen and Schrøder (2010).

7 In September 2008, the Norwegian telecommunication company Telenor announced that it had been made aware of unacceptable working conditions at a subcontractor to a supplier in Bangladesh. The example is not applied pertaining to criticize Telenor, but used as an example to illustrate that even though the direct impact can be mitigated, the risk might not be acceptable due to the potential contagious impact on the company's reputation. In all fairness, Telenor actually practiced a systematically audit of their subcontractors in order to provide assurance that their products are sourced sustainably, but the audit in question suffered from flaws further down the value chain – underpinning again that audit/risk frameworks are not bulletproof.

8 It is beyond the scope of this article to describe those aspects that must be taken into account when establishing such a team. However, Myers–Briggs type indicator assessment is for example a useful tool in putting together effective teams.

9 The approach to identify and assess risks is described in Andersen and Schrøder (2010).

10 Société Générale characterized it as rogue trading. However, although Kerviel was convicted in 2008, the categorization as rogue trading was met by skepticism by former colleagues and so forth. Kerviel alleged that his superiors knew of his trading activities and that the practice was very common.

11 At a point in time, the potential liabilities amounted to more than £7 billion.

References

Andersen, T.J. and Schrøder, P.W. (2010). *Strategic Risk Management Practice – How to Deal Effectively with Major Corporate Exposures*. Cambridge: Cambridge University Press.

Bazerman, M.H. and Watkins, M.D. (2004). 'Cognitive Roots: The Role of Human Biases', Chapter 4 in *Predictable Surprises: The Disaster You Should Have Seen Coming, and How to Prevent Them* (pp. 71–94). Cambridge, MA: Harvard Business School Press.

Day, G.S. and Schoemaker, P.J.H. (2006). 'Interpreting: What the Data Mean', Chapter 4 in *Peripheral Vision: Detecting the Weak Signals That Will Make or Break Your Company*. Cambridge, MA: Harvard Business School Press.

Hain, S. (2009). Managing operational risk: Incentives for reporting and disclosing. *Journal of Risk Management in Financial Institutions* 2(3), pp. 284–300.

Hammond, J.S., Keeney, R.L. and Raiffa, H. (1998). The hidden traps in decision making. *Harvard Business Review* 76(5), pp. 47–48.

Henriksen, P. and Uhlenfeldt, T. (2006). 'Contemporary Enterprise-Wide Risk Management Frameworks: A Comparative Analysis in a Strategic Perspective', Chapter 6 in T.J. Andersen (Ed.), *Perspectives on Strategic Risk Management*, pp. 107–130. Copenhagen: CBS Press.

Moore, Carter & Associates and Cranfield School of Management. (2010). *The RiskMinds, 2009. Risk Managers' Survey – The Causes and Implications of the 2008 Banking Crisis*.

OECD. 2009. *Financial Market Trends, 2009: The Corporate Governance Lessons from the Financial Crisis*. Paris: OECD.

Power, M. (2007). *Organized Uncertainty: Designing a World of Risk Management*. London: Oxford University Press.

Turpin, D. (2006). When disaster strikes: Communicating in a crisis. *European Business Forum* 25.

The Walker Report. (2009, July). *A Review of Corporate Governance in UK Banks and Other Financial Industry Entities*. http://webarchive.nationalarchives.gov.uk/+/http://www.hm-treasury.gov.uk/d/walker_review_261109.pdf

Weick, K.E. and Sutcliffe, K.M. (2001). 'What Business Can Learn from High Reliability Organizations' (Chapter 1, pp. 1–23) and 'A Closer Look at Process and Why Planning Can Make Things Worse' (Chapter 3, pp. 51–83) in *Managing the Unexpected*. San Francisco: Jossey-Bass.

Appendix 5.1

Baring Brothers

In 1995, the highly esteemed institution Baring Brothers went bankrupt due to a loss of £827 million incurred as a result of rogue trading in their Singapore branch, where a derivatives trader, Nick Leeson, took unauthorized positions in various futures contracts and kept them hidden by booking the transactions on an unused error account.

Rogue trading[10] threw the French bank Société Générale into turmoil in 2008 due to unauthorized use of the bank's computer systems by the trader Jérôme Kerviel resulting in trading losses of approximately EUR 5 billion.

In September 2011, the biggest fraud in UK history was revealed when the Swiss bank UBS announced that it had lost over £1.5 billion due to unauthorized trading carried out by the trader Kweku Adoboli in their London office.[11] Late 2008, he began his illicit and off-the-book trades, which initially generated substantial profits. These were kept in a secret account and drip by drip moved back on to the regular books. However, the trades began to make a loss when the European markets hit turmoil in the summer of 2011, which he attempted to recoup with ever-bigger bets.

At the end of 2001, the American energy company Enron filed for bankruptcy after it was revealed that reported profits to a large extent was sustained by a planned and systematic use of accounting fraud, where a number of complex tax schemes were set up enabling the company to shift debt into a series of almost nonexistent companies while the company engaged in transactions with no true business purpose other than to appear profitable. These activities seemed consciously performed and acknowledged by Chairman Kenneth Lay, CEO Jeffrey Skilling, and CFO Andrew Fastow, who gained personal benefits from these arrangements.

In 2002, the American telecommunication company WorldCom failed. It was revealed that the company, directed by CEO Bernard Ebbers for several years, had used fraudulent accounting methods – such as inflating revenues with bogus accounting entries and book selected cost items as capital expenditures – to disguise decreasing earnings inflating the company's assets by about $11 billion. This was the largest accounting fraud scandal in American history at the time – later surpassed by Bernard Madoff's $64 billion Ponzi scheme in 2008, where it was disclosed that Bernard Madoff was practicing a Ponzi scheme paying returns to current investors with the proceeds from new investors.

At the end of 2003, the Italian dairy product company Parmalat declared bankruptcy with a EUR 14 billion hole in its accounts as a result of forgeries and fraud. The company founder Calisto Tanzi was formally charged for constructing a series of shell companies and using forged documents to conceal losses and divert cash to a daughter enterprise and elsewhere.

Appendix 5.2

Qualitative aspects of risk management

The following list provides selective examples of questions that can assess the qualitative aspects of an organization's risk management practices:

- How is the "tone from the top" communicated throughout the organization?
- To what extent do all managers and employees understand the organization's approach to risk and what it means for their operations?
- What are criteria that underlie the selection of relevant scenarios?
- To what extent are there tangible examples on discussions of and rationales for chosen and discarded scenarios?
- To what extent are there tangible examples on discussions among executive management boards, boards of directors, and other executives and managers with regard to risk?
- To what extent do such discussions lead to significant differences in the decision-making with regard to strategic initiatives, revenue target, and so forth?

- To what extent are there tangible examples that the strategic planning process in the various business areas includes discussions relating to risk-appetite?
- To what extent can the various business areas provide tangible examples on discussions related to risk implications of potential new business initiatives?
- How is the adherence to and deviation from the company's risk management policy incorporated in the company's remuneration practice?

Part II
The management of strategic risk

6

Risk and uncertainty – a taxonomy of strategies

Richard Friberg[1]

The outcome of almost any business decision partly depends on risk and uncertainty. Consider for example a European clothing retail chain that during summer places orders for the winter collection from suppliers in Asia. Will the designs appeal to consumer tastes? What designs will the closest competitors choose? How will exchange rate changes affect the cost of goods? Will political uncertainty or strikes affect the functioning of the supply chain? The question that we address in this chapter is how such risks and uncertainties should affect decisions by firms. Should the firm in question use financial instruments such as forward contracts or options to hedge exposures? Should it take higher fixed costs to build flexibility into its operations? Should it use several suppliers of the same good to create alternatives if one supplier fails?

Unfortunately the topic of how firms should respond to risk has been compartmentalized. The old adage that to the person with a hammer, every problem looks like a nail is highly relevant in the field of risk management. Listen to the teachings from financial economics and you will most likely be led to financial hedging strategies. Proponents of real options analysis tend to see real options everywhere. Each view comes with their own set of tools that are likely to appear complex and opaque to a practitioner. Some theories from the management literature are perhaps easier to digest, but what does it mean to build dynamic capabilities and how can we determine when it is worth it to do so? Furthermore, Nassim Nicholas Taleb has had a substantial impact with his writing, arguing that risk management as commonly practiced does more harm than good, and emphasizing new concepts such as black swans and wild randomness (Taleb, 2007, 2012). It becomes clear that the task for executives who want to pursue research-based decisions in the face of risk and uncertainty is not an easy one.

In this chapter I outline a suggested way for considering how risk and uncertainty can map into firm strategy. We take as given the basic strategy of a firm – we take it as given that a firm by and large has a particular place in the competitive landscape such as for instance "we are a supplier of premium outdoor clothes." The question we pose is: How should risk and uncertainty affect the firm's decisions, if at all? To address this question we proceed in several steps. First we clarify what we mean by risk and uncertainty. Our use of the terms goes back to Frank Knight, who in his 1921 book *Risk, Uncertainty and Profit* defined risk as randomness that can be described by probability distributions, and uncertainty as randomness that is not apt to be described by probability distributions. We then proceed to consider the relative roles of risk and uncertainty in different stylized situations using what we term a risk-uncertainty matrix (RUM). With that groundwork laid we ask: Why should a firm let risk and uncertainty considerations affect its decisions? If you've been exposed to ideas in finance you might ask if isn't better to leave profits risky and let owners choose a diversified portfolio that reflects their preferences vis-à-vis risk. We will be clear on the reasons for letting risk and uncertainty affect strategy – in essence, cases where the expected value of the firm increases as a result of tending to risk and uncertainty. We will also highlight that risks are often hedgeable using financial instruments whereas uncertainty by and large needs to be dealt with by other means. As a mental device for structuring discussion and analysis we finally propose four strategies for dealing with risk and uncertainty and connect their suggested use to the risk-uncertainty matrix. The presentation of the material is perhaps somewhat dense – heavy on figures and light on examples. The going is fairly easy, however, and hopefully the reader will come away with a set of tools that can be used to study choice under risk and uncertainty. In particular we hope to deepen the understanding the relative merits of risk management by financial means on the one hand, and risk management using strategic decisions such as what and where to produce on the other hand. A book-length treatment of these issues is found Friberg (2015): *Managing Risk and Uncertainty: A Strategic Approach*. As will become clear, the framework that we propose is based on the standard toolbox of economics. The novelty mainly lies in drawing out the implications of Knight's distinction between risk and uncertainty for firm decision making.[2]

Risk versus uncertainty

Let us consider three investment situations, which we can use to illustrate the concepts of risk and uncertainty:

(1) A bet on the roll of a die.
(2) A bet on the price of gold in U.S. dollars six months from now.
(3) Starting a new company that aims to compete in the market for digitally provided music.

All three investments require decision before we know the realizations of random variables that affect the outcome. To be able to discuss how the three situations differ it is useful to know some terminology, and let us turn to this now using the framework that was laid down by Leonard Savage in his *The Foundations of Statistics* (1954/1972). First of all, we need a word for what can possibly happen, such as a die coming up with the number 3, or the price of gold as $39.20 per gram. We use *state of the world*, or *state* for short, to describe this. The three cases differ in the ease with which we can describe the states of the world. For the throwing of a die, there are typically just six states, and they are easily described by the number 1 through 6 that comes up on the die. For the price of gold the state will be given by a price. The description of the states are linked to your role as a decision maker, however – you may want to distinguish between the states "the price of gold is 1.40 and there is a major war in my region" and "the price of gold is 1.40 and there is peace in my region." Nevertheless, the part of the state that is linked to the price of gold is easy to describe – it's simply a particular amount in some currency. In contrast, in the last case considered, digital music, the states of the world are much harder to describe. As for many corporate investments, even just describing the relevant states of the world can be a challenge. For one, the number of possible states can easily expand beyond the astronomical. Thus describing the states of the world necessarily involves simplification. Furthermore, some possible states are hard to foresee. A new technology that you had not anticipated can crowd you out of the market. A frequently cited statement on the difficulty of describing the states of the world is by former U.S. Secretary of Defense Donald Rumsfeld: "There are known knowns; there are things we know that we know. There are known unknowns; that is to say, there are things that we now know we don't know. But there are also unknown unknowns; there are things we do not know we don't know." The latter, "unknown unknowns," highlights our difficulties in describing all relevant states of the world beforehand when there is uncertainty.

Our fundamental concern is decision making, and we use the word *action* to describe a choice that is made out of a set of possible actions. For instance, one action is to bet 10 euro on the number 4 coming up on the die or to buy 1 kg of gold or to launch the streaming service on the Japanese market. Finally, we are interested in *outcomes*. Outcomes will depend on both actions and states of the world. An action associates a particular outcome to every state of the world. An outcome, for instance, can be that you lose $100 as a result of your action (bet $100 on number 2) and the state of the world (number 4 came up).

The central concern in decision making is the mapping from actions to outcomes. We want to select actions that yield high outcomes in states that we think are likely to materialize. How can we think about the likelihood of different states of the world? In the first case we know the probability distribution for a die toss. The probability of each of the outcomes is equal to 1/6 if the die is fair and the die follows a uniform distribution. We do not know the state of the world beforehand, but we can use an objective probability distribution to guide our decisions. It is easy to add additional observations from experiments under identical conditions to learn about the probability distribution. This is clearly a case of risk in Knight's terminology. In the case of the price of gold we are less fortunate. We are not sure what distribution that future changes will follow, but we can nevertheless use historical observations and our understanding of how markets work to make statistically founded predictions of the likelihood of different values. In Figure 6.1 we graph the distribution of month-to-month changes in the price of gold between 2002 and 2012. We have overlaid a normal probability distribution – if changes in the price of

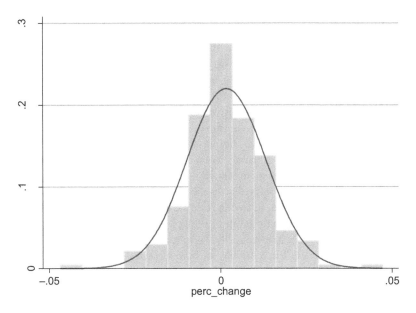

Figure 6.1 Month-to-month changes in the price of gold in U.S. dollars (percent), November 1992–November 2012

gold followed a normal distribution, the bars and the curve would match up more or less perfectly. As seen the fit is not abysmal, but there are important differences; in particular, the tails are fatter than predicted by the normal distribution. In practice this means that if we were to use the normal distribution to predict changes we would underestimate the likelihood of large changes in either direction.

How one should view distributions in cases such as these is partly a philosophical question – we cannot add observations under identical conditions at will. On the other hand I believe that it is nevertheless useful to see also cases such as this risk. We are outside the world of gambling, but the tools of statistics are nevertheless likely to serve us well, in particular if we couple them with some humility. The normal distribution is but one of many distributions that we have in our toolbox and we may believe that the empirical distribution is stable, in particular if we have access to a long time series (or data from many similar markets). Also variables that follow very different patterns – such as the size of cities or of firms (both dominated by a scattering of very large observations) – can in some cases be remarkably well described by stable distributions (in these cases, so-called power law distributions; see Gabaix, 1999, Axtell, 2001, or Clauset et al., 2009).

For the firm pondering whether to enter the market for digitally provided music, however, the situation is different. It might glean insights from other cases in business history but essentially it is faced with a unique set of circumstances. Many of the relevant outcomes are going to be affected by strategic interaction – how a small set of competitors and negotiating partners act, both on their own and in response to your actions. We might make guesses on the likelihood of various states, but we are clearly in the case of uncertainty if we use Knight's terminology.

For business decisions we may be interested in considering different situations and markets and letting our course of action be affected by whether there is high risk or high uncertainty. Higher risk is defined as a probability distribution that is more spread out and that has more weight in the tails. More weight in the tails can come about for instance via more extreme values and/or via higher probability of extreme observations. One way of defining higher risk follows Rothschild and Stiglitz (1970) and uses a *mean preserving spread* as the operational way of defining risk. A mean preserving spread of a distribution puts more weight in the tails but keeps the expected value unchanged. Higher uncertainty is trickier to define, but one alternative is to operationalize it as situations where knowledgeable observers find it harder to agree on the likelihood of different states – and where it is harder to think of what the relevant evidence would be that could be brought to bear on the prediction exercise (see Crès et al., 2011, for an investigation along such lines). Situations where we expect much risk would then be those where prices of important inputs or the finished product have the potential for large swings – such as in commodity markets, shipping or other highly competitive markets with the potential for large shifts in supply or demand. Prime examples of situations characterized by high uncertainty are those where there is strategic interaction with a few other customers, competitors or partners. In a strategic setting the optimal action for me depends on what I believe about your payoffs and how you see the game, and what is optimal for you depends on what you believe about me. These situations frequently result in multiple equilibria even in the stylized models used in game theory (see, e.g., Harrington, 2009) – in reality the range of possible outcomes may be even larger and there is also the possibility of pure surprises, strategic moves that we hadn't foreseen. Few comparable cases to ponder, a long time horizon and the possibility for drastic innovations – new products that effectively outcompete existing products – are all associated with more uncertainty. We summarize the preceding discussion in Table 6.1, and note that the list should not be seen as exhaustive.

Table 6.1 Examples of situations pointing in the direction of higher risk and more uncertainty

Situations associated with higher risk	Situations associated with more uncertainty
Volatile prices of inputs or outputs	Importance of strategic interaction with few competitors, few customers or few strategic partners
Important part of operations affected by volatile exchange rates	Rules of the game subject to complex political process
Highly competitive markets	Markets characterized by drastic innovations – competition for the market rather than in the market
Long time horizon	Long time horizon
	Few comparable cases

Table 6.2 A risk-uncertainty matrix (RUM)

		Uncertainty	
		Low	High
Risk	Low	Local ski area with stable snow pack	Pharmaceutical products
	High	Raw material extractionFarming of cash crops	Airlines

RUM – a risk-uncertainty matrix

Using the categorization implicit in our discussion thus far we may use a matrix to depict different combinations of risk and uncertainty. An example of a situation with low risk and low uncertainty would be a service firm with a large number of small customers, stable input prices and little potential for competition or regulatory changes. A ski resort in an area with stable snow cover would be another example. A copper mine or grower of coffee would be typical examples of situations characterized by low uncertainty and high risk. A firm specializing in developing new medicines would be an example of high uncertainty and low risk – the success of the research process and potential competition is highly uncertain. Negotiations with and approval from authorities may add to the uncertainty. On the other hand, costs (largely wages) are likely to be stable and controllable by the firm. Competition in airline markets finally would be an example of a situation with both high uncertainty (entry/exit of competitors matters much, sensitive to regulatory changes) and high risk (affected by exchange rates and prices of jet fuel). We use the RUM in Table 6.2 to highlight the distinctions.

Clearly the location in the matrix of a market can change with conditions. It would probably have made great sense to place the major airline carriers in the 1960s in the low risk/low uncertainty quadrant. Entry and pricing were regulated in most markets and prices of jet fuel were low and comparatively stable – a situation very different from the one they are faced with today. In the following we will relate the consequences of different strategies for a firm to the extent of risk and uncertainty that the firm faces. Before doing so, however, it is useful to briefly lay out the foundation for why a firm should – or should not – manage risk (the case of why you should manage uncertainty is less worked out in the literature, and for simplicity we stick to risk management in this short exposition, which will get us far in terms of intuition). The use of diagrams makes the material appear perhaps a tad removed from strategic management issues. I nevertheless believe that it affords a very efficient way to convey

Richard Friberg

the main insights from the financial literature of risk management and as such an excellent stepping stone for a strategic discussion.

Why manage risks?

A benchmark – linear exposure and risk neutral owner

As a first benchmark, consider a risk-neutral owner of a firm whose profit depends in a linear way on risk. Thus, consider an exporter whose revenue from export sales can be described schematically as in Figure 6.2.

The exchange rate is denoted by s and a depreciation of the exchange rate (higher s) is associated with higher profits in the exporter's currency. If the exchange rate is 0.7, profit is 70; if the exchange rate is 1.3, profit is 130; and if the exchange rate is 1, profit is 100. Consider first case where the probability is 0.8 that the exchange rate is 1, and 0.1 on each of the more extreme outcomes. Expected profits are then $0.1 \times 70 + 0.8 \times 100 + 0.1 \times 130 = 100$. Consider instead a situation of higher risk where the probabilities of $s = 0.7$ and $s = 1.3$ are both 0.5 and thus the probability of the middling exchange rate equal to 0. The expected value $E(s)$ is equal to 1 also with this more dispersed distribution since $0.5 \times 0.7 + 0.5 \times 1.3 = 1$. The change to the distribution is thus an example of a mean preserving spread: higher weight in the tails of the distribution but the same expected value. What are expected profits now? Quick calculation establishes that they are still 100: $0.5 \times 70 + 0.5 \times 130 = 100$. Expected profits are unaffected by the riskiness. This holds generally for linear functions. In this case, then, there is no reason to manage risk – some times are good and some times are bad, but the good times are as good as the bad times are bad and there is no reason to limit variability.

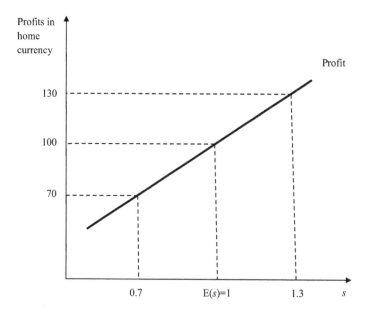

Figure 6.2 Linear profits

Risk-averse owner – a reason to lower risk?

Next consider the case where the firm in question is owned by a risk-averse owner whose sole source of income is the profit she receives as owner of this firm. She has a utility of profits that can be described as $u = \ln(\text{profit})$. This means that higher values of profits are attached a lower weight in her utility. If all her wealth came from this one firm, her expected utility in the first case would thus be $0.1 \times \ln(70) + 0.8 \times \ln(100) + 0.1 \times \ln(130) \approx 4.60$ and in the case of higher risk the expected utility is $0.5 \times \ln(70) + 0.5 \times \ln(130) \approx 4.56$. Her expected utility is thus lower in the case of higher risk. We say that a person who is risk averse has a (strictly) concave utility function (in a nutshell, a function is strictly concave if an imaginary string tied between two points on the curve traced out by the utility function is always below the curve). While strict concavity may sound like a mathematical concept far removed from the world of business, note that it is just another way of saying that the more wealth you have, the less further additions in wealth are worth to you.

Note, however, that she need not have all her wealth tied to this single firm. If capital markets function well, she would be well advised to make whatever investments that maximize the value of the firm and then trade in capital markets in a way that captures her preferences toward risk. This is the intuition for what is sometimes known as the Fisher separation theorem (following Irving Fisher, 1930): the firm should undertake whatever investments that maximize its net present value, irrespective of the preferences of the owners. The notion that firm policy should be independent of the risk profiles of owners is also associated with Modigliani and Miller (1958). These are important points and remain highly valid. It is also the case, however, that the reason not to manage risk, in the case just presented, hinges on that it is *owners' preferences* that create the concavity.

Why variability might *lower* the value of the firm

Consider next a firm as the one just mentioned, but now assume that profits fall sharply as they drop below a certain threshold. It is a simple way to capture the intuition that if a firm's profitability is low enough, this in itself may trigger additional difficulties. For instance, valuable employees are more likely to leave and customers may require rebates to compensate for fears regarding a lack of after-sales service or falling value of the product in secondhand markets. As explored in an influential paper by Froot et al. (1993), the ability to finance investments can create a value of staying above a lower threshold for profits. In the simplest possible setups a firm is always able to find additional finances if the ideas are strong enough. However, if there are informational asymmetries a firm, or its current owners, need to be able to commit sufficient amounts of own funds to be able to attract outside investors. Now revisit the firm that we studied in Figure 6.2 and assume that such a threshold exists at a profit of 90. With the steeper slope of profits below the threshold we now have profit of only 30 when $s = 0.7$. Expected profits for the first exchange rate distribution that we considered are now $0.1 \times 30 + 0.8 \times 100 + 0.1 \times 130 = 96$. In the case studied in Figure 6.2 the expected profits were higher, at 100. If the exchange rate is equal to 1 the profit is 100 in both cases, but the possibility of low realization of profits is lowering the expected value of profits in the case studied here. If we now consider the same mean preserving spread as in the discussion of Figure 6.2 we find that expected profits are now falling further to $0.5 \times 30 + 0.5 \times 130 = 80$. Thus increasing risk lowers expected profits and lowers the value of this firm in this case. Note the difference relative to the case of preferences. Here again it is concavity of the function that we use to evaluate profits that yields the result that the

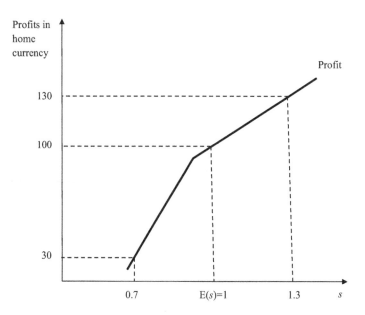

Figure 6.3 Steeper fall in profits as a lower threshold is crossed – an example of strictly concave profits

expected value of profits decreases as we increase risk. Here, though, concavity stems from the profit function rather than from preferences of owners. Diversification by owners will not make the negative relation between risk and expected profits disappear. When it is crucial to keep profits above a lower threshold there is thus a clear motivation for risk management. Taxes are another reason that might create a concave profit function (Smith & Stulz, 1985, is the seminal reference for that insight). More generally, a host of other aspects related to how costs depends on quantity, demand and behavior of competitors can generate concavity of the profit function (Figure 6.3).

And why variability might *raise* the value of the firm

Should you then always strive to lower risk? No, not necessarily. Return to the linear case of Figure 6.2 and consider a firm that is more flexible than the benchmark. Consider for instance a French exporter of wine that has determined to sell 10,000 bottles of wine to the U.S. market at $10 a bottle. If the euro depreciates, profits when measured in euros will increase. If the euro moves from 1 euro per dollar to 1.10 euros per dollar, for instance, the profit will increase by (10,000 × 10) × 1.10 − (10,000 × 10) × 1 = 10,000 euros (we can disregard costs since they are the same in both cases, given that quantity is fixed). A further depreciation to 1.20 would raise profits by an additional 10,000 euros. It is thus clear that profits vary one-for-one with the exchange rate and are linear, just as in Figure 6.2. What if the firm were more flexible though? A firm that was not committed to a fixed quantity and a fixed price would expand volumes as conditions are favorable, and cut back to limit the harm when the exchange rate is less favorable. It would presumably do better than a firm that followed a "passive" strategy. We illustrate such a flexible situation in Figure 6.4.

Assume that profits for a flexible firm are 150 at the depreciated level of the exchange rate and 80 under the stronger exchange rate. Expected profits are now 0.1 × 80 + 0.8 × 100 + 0.1 × 150 = 103 euros under the baseline case and 0.5 × 80 + 0.5 × 150 = 115 in the high-risk case. Thus, in this case higher risk increases expected profits of the firm.

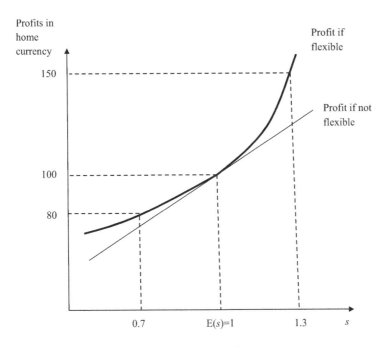

Figure 6.4   Profits under flexibility – strictly convex profits

This is an example of strictly convex profits, and a general feature of strictly convex profit functions is that expected profits are increasing in risk (in a classic result Oi, 1961, establishes that expected profits of a price-taking firm are increasing in price variability for this reason). We say that a function is strictly convex if an imaginary string tied between two points on the curve traced out by the function is everywhere above the curve. In the case of a profit function strict convexity implies that profits are increasing at an increasing rate as conditions become more favorable. Many business decisions related to real options feature such strict convexity (see Chevalier-Roignant & Trigeorgis, 2011, for an overview). For instance, opening and closing a mine or oil well depending on fluctuating market prices will yield a profit curve that is shaped like a hockey stick (strictly convex). As prices are low the resource is kept idle, but after a threshold is reached operations start, and profits are then an increasing function of the market price (see Moel & Tufano, 2002, for a study of the real options implicit in the opening and closing of gold mines).

We have now established reasons why a firm would like to limit risk or seek out risk. Conversely, for a given amount of risk the preceding discussion highlights why a firm would try to make profits more convex by investing in flexibility. Starting with the first part, how a firm can limit risk, we turn to the role of financial instruments.

Financial versus operational hedging and the role of incomplete markets

One view sometimes heard is "Why should a firm care about risk – why not just let owners choose a portfolio that reflects their risk appetite?" This is the issue that we just covered.

A complementary view sometimes heard is: "If you want to limit risk – just use derivative instruments. They are cheaper and easier to reverse than changes to operations." Both views contain important truths – but can also be misleading if unthinkingly applied as we explored earlier for the first question and will explore next for the second question. Return to the case depicted in Figure 6.3, where expected profits are independent of risk. If there exist forward contracts for the currency in question the firm could in this case rid itself of risk by using such forward contracts. By creating an offsetting exposure, the firm shields profits from the effect of the exchange rate – losses stemming from operations as the exchange rate strengthens will be counterweighed by gains made on the forward contract.

If there exist financial instruments like this to shield against all risk we say that we have a situation of complete markets. In contrast, we have *incomplete markets* if there are many states of the world for which no state contingent contracts exist. Why might such contracts fail to exist? For one, the benefits have to be sufficiently large for some agents to take the fixed costs associated with creating such markets. The experience of collateralized debt obligations (CDOs) from the 2000s illustrate the potential for financial innovation – but also the difficulties of correctly pricing and evaluating the riskiness of new state contingent claims. A fundamental reason for the lack of many state contingent claims and a lack of derivative instruments is that many of the uncertainties that affect firm profits are subject to asymmetric information. A firm itself knows much more about these uncertainties, and how it will respond to them, than what outside parties do.

To highlight such asymmetric information let us illustrate with the help of a specific case, the U.S. firm Textron, which makes products such as Cessna airplanes and Bell helicopters. The U.S. Securities and Exchange Commission (SEC) requires that firms above a certain size publish annual reports according to a format known as a 10-K. Under heading 1A in those forms corporations discuss the risk factors that they are facing (in the SEC terminology they do not distinguish between risk and uncertainty). Of the risk factors that Textron mentions, 17 relate to factors that we might most aptly describe as uncertainty and only one to what we would describe as risk, the latter being (Textron, 2013, p. 14): "Currency, raw material price and interest rate fluctuations may adversely affect our results." Clearly for shorter horizons there are derivative instruments that can be used to hedge such exposures, and indeed Textron does so. Naturally, a mere headcount does not imply that uncertainty is more important than risk. But it does point to the fact that many important uncertainties are not easily covered by financial instruments. Of the factors that we might label as uncertainty we can for instance highlight the following: "U.S. Government contracts may be terminated at any time and may contain other unfavorable provisions." The U.S. government is an important customer for Textron and the statement exemplifies how reliance on one or a few partners generates uncertainty. What if Textron would want to insure against this risk in financial markets? One difficulty is that the firms that would be most likely to want such insurance are precisely the ones that are most likely to have their contracts terminated. This is something that is harder to observe for potential insurers. In consequence, the development of such instruments is hampered by *adverse selection* (Akerlof, 1970). A firm that is covered from business risks that it can influence itself is also liable to be more reckless since it is partly sheltered from the consequences of losing a customer. Such *moral hazard* will also hinder the development of state contingent claims. There is a clear link between whether a risk factor is seen as risk or uncertainty – and whether financial instruments are available for hedging that exposure – either via standard contracts or via tailor-made instruments. In a slight caricature we may say that risk is hedgeable on financial markets or with insurers whereas uncertainty is much less likely to be hedgeable with financial instruments.

Four strategies – a taxonomy

Return now to our key question of whether the strategy of a firm should be affected by where it places itself in the risk-uncertainty matrix. Next we present four strategies to deal with risk and uncertainty. The four strategies that we present pull together insights from many different fields of research and cast them into a common setting – which is highly stylized as will become evident. We hope that the very stylized nature may make it helpful as a mental framework for organizing thought and discussion. We think of strategy as a set of actions taken "today" that govern how risk and uncertainty will affect profit in the future ("tomorrow"). Profits are affected by two types of shocks. One type of shock is described as risk denoted by s (as in spot rate) and assumed to follow a known probability distribution. The expected value for this variable is denoted $E(s)$. The other shock can be described as being due to uncertainty and the decision maker has no probability distribution for this. We do, however, assume that there is a worst-case scenario associated with this shock that the decision maker is willing to contemplate. This worst case is denoted Li, where i refers to one of four strategies. Let us now describe the strategies in turn.

We call the first strategy "benchmark." It is the strategy that is optimal if s were close to $E(s)$ and if uncertainty is disregarded. Note that such a firm need not be naïve about risks and uncertainties; it may simply have determined that they are minor enough for it not to change its main course or that, even if the profit consequence of shocks are large, it has a strong enough position to be able to take the shock on the chin without flinching. Figure 6.5 illustrates this strategy. Profits are a positive function of the random variable s and in the case depicted are linear – providing there is no reason to engage in hedging if unless owners of the firm are more averse to risk. Realized profits "tomorrow" will however not only depend on the level of s that prevails at that time, but also on the realization of the uncertainty shock. In Figure 6.5 we also depict the worst case for the uncertainty shocks that the firm is willing to contemplate. As seen,

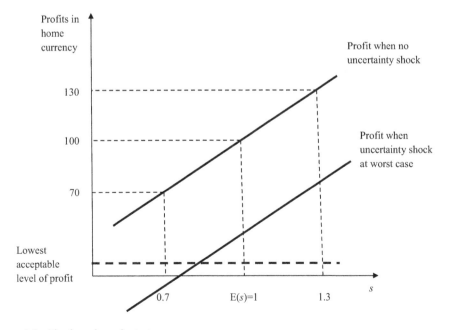

Figure 6.5 The benchmark strategy

the overall profits depend on both variables – if the firm is hit with an uncertainty shock at the same time as s is low, the profits are particularly low. We allow for the possibility that there is a lowest acceptable level of profits for the firm, marked by the horizontal dashed line. This can be seen as shorthand for the notion that if the profits or value of the firm fall too low it will go bankrupt and value might be destroyed. The more value destruction and the less access the firm has to external finance to help it through rough times, the higher is such a threshold likely to be.

Turn now instead to the strategy that we denote as "flexible." This strategy picks up on the intuition from above that, by making profits a strictly convex function of s, expected profits will increase. In Friberg (2015) we describe at length what such flexibility might consist of. It can for instance refer to making marginal costs a flatter function of quantity – an idea that goes back to Stigler (1939). By having expansions in sales associated with a lesser increase in costs the firm is in a better position to benefit from variability. As economists we don't believe that good things come to us as costless free lunches and thus we assume that such flexibility is associated with higher fixed costs. Flexibility can also refer to an ability to set different prices on different markets in response to shocks, or even more generally as freeing the firm from constraints (Silberberg, 1971). Flexibility can also refer to the way that firms are managed and how information is created and transmitted within the firm – in particular on whether decisions should be centralized or decentralized. Overall the literature suggests that the more risk there is, the more you want to decentralize (such a broad generalization of course hides many nuances – see for instance Alonso, Dessein & Matouschek, 2008, for an inroad to this field of study). In Figure 6.6 we illustrate profits under a flexible strategy and compare to profits under the benchmark strategy. The more risk there is in s, the more attractive is the flexible strategy – for the same reason as we explored in connection with Figure 6.4. Higher risk raises expected profits under this strategy. As illustrated in Figure 6.6 we further assume that the flexible strategy makes the firm less sensitive to uncertainty shocks. Intuitively, being more flexible implies a greater potential to

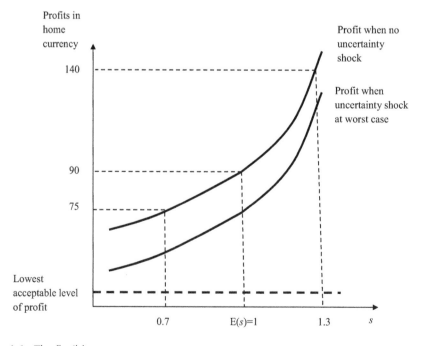

Figure 6.6 The flexible strategy

respond to all kinds of shocks and we therefore expect the flexible strategy to be able to keep profits above a lower threshold to a greater extent.

The third strategy we term "financial hedging." The key point of financial hedging is that it strives to make the value of the firm insensitive to changes in s. To highlight this we therefore assume that this strategy completely insulates profits from shocks to s, as illustrated in Figure 6.7. We assume that the potential for shocks due to uncertainty are identical to those in the benchmark. The strategy can be seen as a caricature of a financial hedging strategy – do whatever is optimal in a real sense and if various factors lead you to want to limit variability (such as one of the factors behind concavity that we pointed out earlier) then use financial instruments. We assume a relatively minor cost of the financial hedging strategy, but clearly if s equals E(s), the profits are lower under the financial strategy.

Note that even if financial instruments in this strategy only hedge against risk they also work in the direction of helping the firm keep profits up in the face of uncertainty shocks. By neutralizing the effect of low s on profits the financial strategy avoids the double whammy that firms were exposed to in the benchmark strategy – that a negative uncertainty shock hits at the same time as profits are low due to a low s. Much work indeed shows that many firms use financial derivatives to hedge risks (see for instance Servaes et al., 2009; Bodnar et al., 2011). However, there are several puzzles if we believe that financial derivatives are the main way that firms deal with risk and uncertainty. Much of the usage of derivatives is for relatively short horizons, and usage is more common among large firms – which is surprising since large firms are more likely to have diversified ownership. In addition evidence by Guay and Kothari (2003) shows that at the time of their study the derivatives portfolios held by large U.S. firms were too small to act as an important hedge with regard to the overall exposure of these firms. The survey in Bodnar et al. (2011) also points to the fact that respondents view operational hedging as a more important way of managing risks for most sources of risk and uncertainty (the exception is foreign exchange rate risk). This observation thus brings us to the last of the proposed strategies.

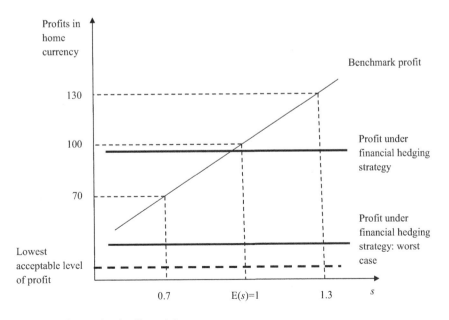

Figure 6.7 Profits under the financial strategy

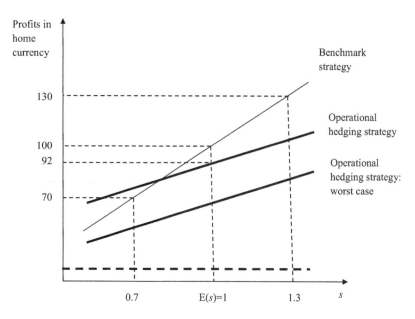

Figure 6.8   The operational hedging strategy

The last strategy that we highlight is "operational hedging." The aim here is to make profits less sensitive to both changes in *s* and to uncertainty shocks. It may for instance be motivated by the stabilizing cash flows to avoid the concerns identified by Froot et al. (1993) but noting that financial hedges can only deal with parts of the exposure. The motivation for doing so stems from a want to avoid low profits, but the price for this is in part made up of lower profits for higher values of *s*. An illustration is provided in Figure 6.8.

Treanor et al. (2014) exemplify operational hedging with the case of an airline that invests in more fuel-efficient planes. This limits the harm of high prices of jet fuel, but also makes the impact on profits of falling prices of jet fuel lower. Again, for it not to be a free lunch we would need the more fuel-efficient planes to be less profitable when jet fuel is around its average prices. Another way of operationally hedging is to organize as a conglomerate. Matvos and Seru (2015) for instance establish that being in a conglomerate is associated with lower profitability and inefficient allocation of capital within the conglomerate, but also with higher survival chances in times of crisis. We can also classify the holding of large cash reserves for precautionary purposes as an operational hedging strategy (Bates et al., 2009, document a sharp increase in cash holdings among U.S. firms and find that higher risk is associated with more cash holdings). We assume that operational hedging not only makes a firm less sensitive to shocks in *s*; we also assume that it provides better protection against uncertainty shocks.

A comparison of strategies

The final goal of the foregoing analysis is to create a frame of mind within which to analyze and recommend strategy for firms facing different conditions. Let us illustrate all strategies in Figure 6.9.

Evaluating different strategies in expected terms is hampered by the fact that we are not able to form expectations for variables that are uncertain. We propose to evaluate the strategies by the following criterion: choose the strategy that maximizes expected profit subject to the criterion

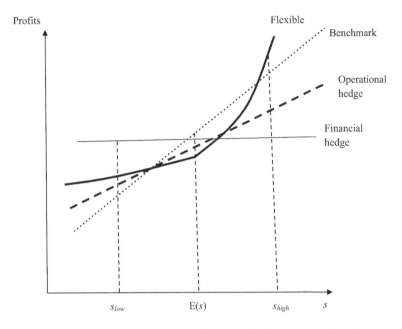

Figure 6.9 Four stylized strategies – the case when no shocks to uncertainty have occurred

that ex post profits are high enough under the worst-case scenarios that the firm is willing to ponder.[3]

In the case of low risk and low uncertainty the benchmark strategy is preferred. Some possibility for randomness exists in all lines of business, but consider for instance a monopoly supplier of a service in a sheltered section of a market facing stable supply – taking any major action to respond to risk or uncertainty is unlikely to be worth it. Now consider the case of raising the risk – this makes the flexible strategy more attractive since the expected profits are then increasing the risk. If profits under low realizations of *s* are a concern, and the costs of the flexible strategy are high enough, then the financial hedging strategy is favored. Turning to the case of high uncertainty we note that the operational hedging strategy will be favored as a way of keeping profits sufficiently high also under negative shocks. Note that the financial strategy is largely ineffective in doing this if shocks are mainly described as the result of uncertainty rather than by risk. For the case where both risk and uncertainty are high the flexible strategy becomes attractive; whether it dominates the operational hedging strategy depends on the relative costs of implementing the two. Schematically we can therefore suggest different strategies for the different combinations of risk and uncertainty as shown in Table 6.3. In terms of costs we assume that at the expected level of the random variable *s* the benchmark strategy yields the highest profits, followed by the financial hedging strategy and the operational hedging strategy; finally, the flexible strategy is the costliest to implement.

It is important to stress that the taxonomy and mapping between situations and strategies are meant to organize the mind and clarify discussions only. The limit between operational hedging and flexibility is rather blurry, for instance. Having several suppliers for the same good is a part of the operational hedging strategy. If we are willing in addition to shift the relative importance between suppliers as costs change, it becomes a flexible strategy. Many firms will mix between the different strategies – hedging some short-term exposures financially to simplify

Richard Friberg

Table 6.3 Strategy in the face of risk and uncertainty

| | | Uncertainty | |
		Low	High
Risk	Low	Benchmark	Operational hedging
	High	Flexible	Flexible
		Financial hedging	Operational hedging

cash management while overall going for a flexible strategy. I nevertheless believe and hope that the kind of distinctions that we make here can help improve discussions in firms and clarify what one wants to achieve. For instance, flexibility is frequently hailed as important and one can easily be led to believe that flexibility is key for the success of all firms. But if we are talking flexibility in earnest it comes at a cost, and only if you are faced with high risk is it worth investing in flexibility.

Concluding remarks

While the distinction between risk and uncertainty has a long tradition – dating back to Frank Knight (1921) – it has not been the main way of looking at risk for economists or academics working in finance. Rather economics and finance have by and large followed the path suggested, but not necessarily endorsed, by Keynes (1937), whose definition of uncertainty is close to that of Knight:

> By "uncertain" knowledge, let me explain, I do not mean merely to distinguish what is known for certain from what is only probable. The game of roulette is not subject, in this sense, to uncertainty; nor is the prospect of a Victory bond being drawn. . . . The sense in which I am using the term is that in which the prospect of a European war is uncertain . . ., or the obsolescence of a new invention, ... About these matters there is no scientific basis on which to form any calculable probability whatever. We simply do not know. Nevertheless, the necessity for action and for decision compels us as practical men to do our best to overlook this awkward fact and to behave exactly as we should if we had behind us a good Benthamite [after British economist Jeremy Bentham – in this case meaning expected utility] calculation of a series of prospective advantages and disadvantages, each multiplied by its appropriate probability, waiting to be summed.

> *(pp. 212–213)*

Thus, in the spirit suggested by Keynes's passage we might say that we have largely handled uncertainty by treating it as risk – Savage (1954/1972) gives the foundations for such an approach and in many ways it has served us well (for those wanting to explore the deeper roots of such distinction see Gilboa, 2009). The events leading up to the financial crisis of 2008 have highlighted some dangers with an approach that relies heavily on treating relatively short time series as appropriate measures of uncertainty. What I argue here is that an alternative approach that separates risk and uncertainty can be a useful way of evaluating strategy. I also believe that the expanding possibilities which we have to use computer simulations allow us to combine simulations of profits under risk for different scenarios subject to uncertainty in a way that can be highly useful. A fuller treatment of how investments can be evaluated in this way is given in Friberg (2015).

Notes

1   Richard Friberg, Jacob Wallenberg Professor of Economics, Stockholm School of Economics.
2   For a full clarification as to where the novelty of the approach lies I refer the reader to Friberg (2015). Within financial economics a related notion to Knight's uncertainty, ambiguity aversion, has generated substantial interest in the last few years. The focus of that work is quite different from what we do here, however. See Epstein and Schneider (2010) for a survey.
3   While not standard, the criterion is close to what is proposed under various versions of what is sometimes termed robust optimization (see for instance Ben-Tal et al., 2009). Note that while intuitively appealing to many it may not be clear that striving for survival of the firm is the optimal policy to pursue – it may be sacrificing too much expected profit in the name of prudence. See Oprea (2014) for an example of the interplay using theory and students in an experimental setting. Foster et al. (2008) examine links between firm survival and growth and profitability among U.S. firms. The academic study of survival versus profitability is still relatively undeveloped, however, and we note that if survival is not a concern the decision maker may simply set the lower threshold low enough that it never binds.

References

Akerlof, G.A. (1970). The market for "lemons": Quality uncertainty and the market mechanism. *Quarterly Journal of Economics* 84(3), 488–500.

Alonso, R., Dessein, W. & Matouschek, N. (2008). When does coordination require centralization? *American Economic Review* 98(1), 145–179.

Axtell, R.L. (2001). Zipf distribution of US firm sizes. *Science* 293, 1818–1820.

Bates, T.W., Kahle, K.M. & Stulz, R.M. (2009). Why do US firms hold so much more cash than they used to? *Journal of Finance* 64(5), 1985–2021.

Ben-Tal, A., El Ghaoui, L. & Nemirovski, A. (2009). *Robust Optimization*. Princeton, NJ: Princeton University Press.

Bodnar, G.M., Giambona, E., Graham, J.R., Harvey, C.R. & Marston, R.C. (2011). *Managing risk management*. Manuscript. Available at http://ssrn.com/abstract=1787144

Chevalier-Roignant, B. & Trigeorgis, L. (2011). *Competitive Strategy: Options and Games*. Cambridge, MA: MIT Press.

Clauset, A., Shalizi, C.R. & Newman, M.E.J. (2009). Power-law distributions in empirical data. *SIAM Review* 51(4), 661–703.

Crès, H., Gilboa, I. & Vieille, N. (2011). Aggregation of multiple prior opinions. *Journal of Economic Theory* 146(6), 2563–2582.

Epstein, L. & Schneider, M. (2010). Ambiguity and asset markets. *Annual Review of Financial Economics* 2, 315–346.

Fisher, I. (1930). *The Theory of Interest*. New York, NY: Macmillan.

Foster, L., J. Haltiwanger, and C. Syverson. (2008). Reallocation, firm turnover, and efficiency: Selection on productivity or profitability? *American Economic Review* 98, 394–425.

Friberg, R. (2015). *Managing Risk and Uncertainty: A Strategic Approach*. Cambridge, MA: MIT Press.

Froot, K.A., Scharfstein, D.S. & Stein, J.C. (1993). Risk management: Coordinating corporate investment and financing policies. *Journal of Finance* 48(5), 1629–1658.

Gabaix, X. (1999). Zipf's law for cities: An explanation. *Quarterly Journal of Economics* 114(3), 739–767.

Gilboa, I. (2009). *Theory of Decision under Uncertainty*. Cambridge: Cambridge University Press.

Guay, W. & Kothari, S.P. (2003). How much do firms hedge with derivatives? *Journal of Financial Economics* 70(3), 423–461.

Harrington, J.E., Jr. (2009). *Games, Strategies and Decision Making*. New York, NY: Macmillan.

Keynes, J. M. (1937). The general theory of employment, *Quarterly Journal of Economics* 51(2), 209–223.

Knight, F.H. (1921). *Risk, Uncertainty and Profit*. New York, NY: Hart, Schaffner and Marx.

Matvos, G. & Seru, A. (2015). Resource allocation within firms and financial market dislocation: Evidence from diversified conglomerates. *Review of Financial Studies*, forthcoming.

Modigliani, F. & Miller, M.H. (1958). The cost of capital, corporation finance and the theory of investment. *American Economic Review* 48(3), 261–297.

Moel, A. & Tufano, P. (2002). When are real options exercised? An empirical study of mine closings. *Review of Financial Studies* 15(1), 35–64.

Oi, W.Y. (1961). The desirability of price instability under perfect competition. *Econometrica* 29(1), 58–64.

Oprea, R. (2014). Survival versus profit maximization in a dynamic stochastic experiment. *Econometrica* 82(6), 2225–2255.

Rothschild, M. & Stiglitz, J.E. (1970). Increasing risk: I. A definition. *Journal of Economic Theory* 2(3), 225–243.

Savage, L.J. (1972). *The Foundations of Statistics*. New York, NY: Dover. (Original work published 1954)

Servaes, H., Tamayo, A. & Tufano, P. (2009). The theory and practice of corporate risk management. *Journal of Applied Corporate Finance* 21(4), 60–78.

Silberberg, E. (1971). The Le Chatelier principle as a corollary to a generalized envelope theorem. *Journal of Economic Theory* 3(2), 146–155.

Smith, C.W. & Stulz, R.M. (1985). The determinants of firms' hedging policies. *Journal of Financial and Quantitative Analysis* 20(4), 391–405.

Stigler, G. (1939). Production and distribution in the short run. *Journal of Political Economy* 47(3), 305–327.

Taleb, N.N. (2007). *The Black Swan: The Impact of the Highly Improbable Fragility*. New York, NY: Random House.

Taleb, N.N. (2012). *Antifragile: Things that Gain from Disorder*. New York, NY: Random House.

Textron. (2013). Annual Report. Available at http://investor.textron.com/

Treanor, S.D., Simkins, B.J., Rogers, D.A. & Carter, D.A. (2014). Does operational and financial hedging reduce exposure? Evidence from the US airline industry. *Financial Review* 49(1), 149–172.

7

Reflections on integrated risk management

Kent D. Miller[1]

Risk researchers in the various fields of business have tended to examine particular sources of risk in isolation (Miller, 1992). International management researchers highlight risks owing to political and economic instability, government policy changes, or social unrest. Finance researchers focus on managing the categories of risk for which hedging and insurance instruments apply, such as movements in commodity prices, interest rates, and exchange rates. Operations and management researchers consider hazards arising within particular functional activities, across supply chains, and in dynamic markets.

A strategic management perspective encompasses all of these concerns, and brings a particular emphasis to the role of competitive strategies in creating and ameliorating organizational risk. Moves by rivals, new entrants, and technological breakthroughs present risks and rewards as they transform industries. Strategists have available a diverse repertoire of possible responses to manage risk, including avoidance or control of risky situations, collaboration with other organizations to reduce uncertainty, imitation or follow-the-leader coordination, and developing operational and strategic flexibility.

Strategic managers are uniquely positioned to consider the organization in relation to its environment, and to do so in a way that encompasses intra-organizational, industry, and general environmental risks. Strategic managers are charged with assessing and managing diverse risks, and they need ways to think about, discuss, and carry out these complex responsibilities. My 1998 article, "Economic Exposure and Integrated Risk Management," contributed to the conceptual framing and methodology of assessing and managing diverse risk exposures in an integrated manner. Viewing the organization in relation to its environment with a view toward enhancing firm value, as that article does, reflects defining concerns in the strategy field.

Integrated risk management considers the organization's diverse risk exposures simultaneously. Some risks may be independent and, when this is the case, they can be assessed and managed in isolation; however, many of the risks of concern to strategic managers are interdependent. The integrated risk management perspective recognizes that organizational exposures to diverse contingencies are often correlated and, as such, can be neither assessed nor managed in isolation. Risk management often involves tradeoffs between exposures to various uncertain contingencies. Reduction of the risk associated with a particular exposure may increase or otherwise alter exposures to other contingencies. Assessment of particular risk exposures in isolation will differ from their assessment taking into consideration correlated contingencies. Hedging practices focused on particular contingencies will be inefficient relative to integrated risk management. Actions to manage distinct exposures can be offsetting and even can heighten risk unintentionally.

These understandings carry important implications for managers. Because uncertain contingencies affecting firm value often are correlated, risk management requires central oversight. Risk cannot be managed simply through delegation to divisional or functional units. Financial, operational, and strategic risk management must be coordinated. Risk assessment and management should be aspects of firms' ongoing strategy processes. Firms should take on and hedge exposures to the extent that doing so is consistent with enhancing firm value.

"Economic Exposure and Integrated Risk Management" presented an implementable method for measuring business organization exposures to a set of relevant environmental contingencies. An estimable multivariate model of economic exposures takes the form:

$$R_v(t) = \sum_{i=1}^{n} \beta_i R_i(t) + \eta(t)$$

where $R_v(t)$ is the rate of return to shareholders in period t, $R_i(t)$ is the rate of change in environmental contingency i in t, β_i is the estimable coefficient reflecting exposure to contingency i, and $\eta(t)$ is the error term.[2] Implementing this model requires identifying a set of contingencies with measurable rates of change over time that correlate – either positively or negatively – with shareholder returns. A broad set of regressors can be narrowed to a parsimonious set of n contingencies by eliminating those that are redundant to others included in the model (as indicated by an assessment of multicollinearity).

Key challenges to implementing this method arise from unstable and asymmetric coefficients. Coefficient instability should be expected when changes occur in the firm's strategy or industry. For an exposure model to be estimable, the periods for measured shareholder returns and regressors must be short enough to provide sufficient time series data for model identification between shifts in exposures. In dynamic contexts, this requirement may not hold. When lack of data precludes estimation (because the multivariate model is unidentified), managers' qualitative assessments of firm-specific exposures still can inform their management of strategic risk.

Asymmetric exposures occur when a firm's operating and strategic responses differ depending on which direction environmental contingencies move (see Miller & Reuer, 1998). For example, a company may change its sourcing depending on whether currency movements favor a particular country. By reducing downside risk while allowing companies to take advantage of upside potential, operational and strategic flexibility make exposure coefficients asymmetric; the exposure coefficients differ depending on whether rates of change in environmental contingencies are positive or negative. In such situations, separate coefficients for positive and negative changes in regressors can be estimated using a spline function. Acknowledging flexibility in organizations' responses to environmental contingencies connects discussions of strategic risk management and real options.

What I labeled "integrated risk management" anticipated later developments in "enterprise risk management." Enterprise risk management (ERM) emerged in the late 1980s and gained influence among risk management practitioners during the 1990s, with consulting firms being major proponents. The ERM perspective holds that company-wide risk should be managed through a coordinated, comprehensive program. ERM oversight responsibility often is given to a chief risk officer (CRO), a title that spread along with ERM practice (Lam, 2014: ch. 4). Experiences with ERM lead us to appreciate the challenges associated with trying to manage the diverse array of exposures that companies face. Implemented ERM programs tend toward either (1) taking a strategic view of risk and managing it qualitatively or (2) taking an operational view and managing risks quantitatively (Mehta, 2010: ch. 4). In complex organizations with multiple divisions and separated functions, managing strategic, operational, and financial risk in an integrated fashion is extremely challenging, despite being compelling in principle. Reasonable goals for ERM in such contexts may be to identify and prioritize key risks relevant to strategic decision making for top management attention, while allowing responsibility for operational risks to remain decentralized. Bridging the disparity between the ideal of integrated risk management and its practice remains an ongoing area for organizational learning to which researchers can contribute. "Economic Exposure and Integrated Risk Management" described the challenge managers face, but did not address the roles, processes, and practices associated with organizing around the mandate to assess and manage risk integratively.

The approach to risk assessment in my 1998 article was correlational rather than processual (see Chiles, 2003). Its framing was in terms of correlates of company value, without trying to delve into the causal mechanisms producing the correlations. Focusing on correlates without trying to develop a causal model greatly simplifies the task of risk assessment. It also simplifies hedging because management needs only to make investments in assets with payoffs that offset the company's measured exposures. In contrast, analyzing the processes that generate a company's risks requires modeling the organization and its environment as a complex interdependent system. Perrow's (1999) research on accidents in organizations and Beck's (1992) writings on societal risk illustrate processual analysis of the origins of risk in complex sociotechnical systems. Difficulties arise in ERM implementation because organizations identify risks with specific processes, and associate expertise to manage particular risks with features of the organizational-environmental system. Although a correlational approach supports a practical method for risk assessment, it offers limited insights into potential actions to manage risk through interventions in organizations and their environments. Correlational framing motivates clearly the need for an integrated approach to risk management, but assessment of company-specific risks and insights about creative responses to mitigate these risks require in-depth knowledge of organizational-environmental systems.

Notes

1   Kent D. Miller, The Eli Broad Graduate School of Management, Michigan State University, 632 Bogue Street, N475 Business College Complex, East Lansing, MI 48824-1122, Tel: (517) 353-6428, Fax: (517) 432-1111, E-mail: millerk@broad.msu.edu.
2   See equation (9) and its derivation in the article.

References

Beck, U. (1992). *Risk Society: Towards a New Modernity*. London: Sage.
Chiles, T.H. (2003). Process theorizing: Too important to ignore in a kaleidic world. *Academy of Management Learning and Education*, 2(3), 288–291.
Lam, J. (2014). *Enterprise Risk Management: From Incentives to Controls*, 2nd ed. Hoboken, NJ: Wiley.
Mehta, S. (2010). *Enterprise Risk Management: Insights and Operationalization*. Morristown, NJ: Financial Executives Research Foundation.

Miller, K.D. (1992). A framework for integrated risk management in international business. *Journal of International Business Studies*, 23(2), 311–331.

Miller, K.D. (1998). Economic exposure and integrated risk management. *Strategic Management Journal*, 19(5), 497–514.

Miller, K.D., & Reuer, J.J. (1998). Asymmetric corporate exposures to foreign exchange rate changes. *Strategic Management Journal*, 19(12), 1183–1191.

Perrow, C. (1999). *Normal Accidents: Living with High-Risk Technologies*. Princeton, NJ: Princeton University Press.

Economic exposure and integrated risk management

Kent D. Miller*

KRANNERT GRADUATE SCHOOL OF MANAGEMENT, PURDUE UNIVERSITY, WEST LAFAYETTE, INDIANA, U.S.A.

Most corporate risk management research focuses on particular risk exposures to the exclusion of other interrelated exposures. By contrast, this study models corporate risk exposures using a multivariate approach integrating the distinct exposures of interest to finance, international business, and strategy researchers. The paper addresses the implications of multivariate modeling for corporate risk management, some key methodological issues arising in empirical estimation of corporate economic exposures, and directions for research on integrated risk management. © 1998 John Wiley & Sons, Ltd.

Strat. Mgmt. J. *Vol. 19, 497–514 (1998)* Reprinted with permission.

Exposure refers to the extent to which external environmental contingencies affect a company's performance. If we conceptualize strategy as the alignment of the firm with its external environment (see, for example, Andrews, 1971; Porter, 1980), then the measurement and management of exposures are central concerns for strategists.

While scholars have acknowledged economic exposure as the relevant basis for corporate risk assessment, risk management practices for the most part continue to reflect accounting-based notions of exposure assessment (Batten, Mellor, and Wan, 1993; George and Schroth, 1991; Rawls and Smithson, 1990; Rodriguez, 1981). Although there appears to be growing interest in economic exposure among managers, only a few large multinationals have implemented economic exposure assessment and management (Kohn, 1990; Lewent and Kearney, 1990).

The lack of clear guidelines for measuring economic exposure is a major obstacle to implementing economic exposure assessment and hedging. While Dufey (1972) drew attention to the need to rethink foreign exchange exposure in economic rather than accounting terms, finance research has not adequately addressed the practical issue of how to measure corporate economic exposures when firms are simultaneously exposed to multiple uncertain environmental contingencies. Ahkam (1995) recently drew attention to the need for explicit attention to the measurement of corporate economic exposures.

This paper addresses the measurement and management of corporate economic exposures. The measurement perspective adopted is that of top managers concerned with a variety of uncertain environmental contingencies affecting corporate performance. The general management perspective requires integrating the risk exposures considered in the strategy field (e.g., competitive, input supply, market demand, and technological risks) with those of interest to finance and international business scholars. In developing a conceptual and operational basis for measuring economic exposure, the study also lays the groundwork for strategy research directed at understanding the role of corporate strategy (e.g., diversification or real options) in economic exposure management. The insights from this study have important practical implications for corporate risk assessment and management.

The paper begins with background on the concept of economic exposure. The subsequent section presents multivariate modeling of corporate economic exposures. The starting point for this model is corporate foreign exchange exposure but the model is also extended to an integrated framework incorporating other uncertain environmental contingencies. This is followed by a discussion of the theoretical and managerial implications of multivariate assessment of economic exposure. Next, the paper seeks to resolve some key methodological issues that must be addressed in order to actually measure corporate economic exposures. The final section discusses directions for extending research on integrated risk management.

Assessing and managing exposures

Accounting and economic exposure

In the past, scholarly interest in corporate risk exposure has come almost exclusively from the accounting and finance fields. Exposure assessment has received greatest attention from managers and scholars interested in smoothing the impacts of foreign exchange rate movements on accounting profits. Recognition of foreign exchange exposure arose from the practical need to consolidate the financial statements of foreign operations to local currencies (translation exposure) and the possibility of incurring accounting gains or losses on receivables and payables denominated in foreign currencies (transaction exposure).[1] While much attention has been given to foreign exchange exposure, finance researchers have also considered exposures to movements in other financial market variables, such as interest rates and commodity prices. Such exposures can be managed through the use of financial hedging instruments such as futures and forward contracts, options, and swaps.

Whereas the accounting concepts of transaction and translation exposure have been codified in accounting standards (e.g., FASB 52), no such standard definition exists for economic exposure. One point of confusion in the existing discussions of economic exposure regards the choice of the dependent variable. Economic exposure has been discussed in terms of the sensitivity of cash flows, accounting profits, and the real value of the firm to exchange rate movements (Lessard, 1986; Bishop and Dixon, 1992; Oxelheim and Wihlborg, 1987a). These varying perspectives on economic exposure point out the need to clarify the choice of the dependent variable in defining and measuring economic exposure.

In his early work, Shapiro (1975, 1977) focused on cash flow sensitivity to nominal movements in foreign exchange rates. The emphasis on cash flows is also found in corporate managers' attempts to assess and hedge economic exposure to foreign exchange rate movements (Kohn, 1990; Lewent and Kearney, 1990). Later, Shapiro (1984) acknowledged that the emphasis on nominal cash flows was inappropriate and, following Cornell (1980) and Wihlborg (1980), asserted real cash flows as theoretically appropriate for measuring economic exposure. The need to use real cash flows, as opposed to nominal values, is, however, not explicit elsewhere in Shapiro's writings on measuring economic exposure (Garner and Shapiro, 1984; Shapiro, 1992).

While focusing on real cash flows is superior to looking simply at nominal cash flows, the emphasis on cash flows needs to be questioned. Looking at the magnitude of net cash flows is clearly incorrect when a firm's level of capitalization changes over time. Consider a firm that raises new capital through debt or equity financing or simply through retention of earnings. Investment of this capital in projects generating returns equal to the cost of capital does not increase shareholder value (Rappaport, 1986). Such investments do, however, increase net cash flows.

Even for firms with constant levels of capitalization, emphasizing real cash flow sensitivity overlooks the distortions in current cash flows. Short-term cash flows provide little information about the value created by a firm's strategy. For example, new strategic initiatives often require several years of negative cash flows before entering into a period of positive cash flows. These negative cash flows may result from intensive investment in R&D, plants and equipment, and marketing, and limited initial sales. The deficiencies of cash flow or net income as dependent variables in estimating economic exposures bring into question the approach used in recent empirical studies (e.g., Ahkam, 1995; Moens, 1995) and advocated in papers directed towards managers (e.g., Lewent and Kearney, 1990).

From a value creation perspective, we are actually interested in the sensitivity of a firm's present value to exchange rate movements. Present value takes into consideration the discounted cash flows over the life of an investment. Since short-term cash flows are not a direct measure of value creation, cash flows and firm value can present quite divergent criteria for estimating a firm's economic exposure. Unlike current cash flows, present value is a direct measure of firm value.

Calculation of a firm's present value is, however, problematic, given the high uncertainty surrounding forecasted cash flows and the need to make appropriate assumptions regarding the discount rate and time horizon for a firm's operations. On the other hand, if capital markets are not fooled by accounting numbers (i.e., capital markets are able to ascertain the underlying value of the firm's competitive position), market valuation of shareholder equity can be used to measure firm value. This suggests that the market value of a firm's equity can be used as the dependent variable in determining a firm's economic exposure.

Hence, this study follows Adler and Dumas (1984), Garner and Shapiro (1984), and Shapiro (1992) in defining economic exposure as the sensitivity of the real value of a company to fluctuations in environmental contingencies. This focus on economic valuation, while consistent with the emphasis on shareholder value creation in strategic management (e.g., Rappaport, 1986), conflicts with accounting exposure defined in terms of the book values of assets and liabilities denominated in foreign currencies. Economic exposure is a forward-looking concept considering future cash flows rather than historical accounting values.

Why should managers be concerned about economic exposure?

The aforementioned assumption of efficient capital markets raises the question of why firms should be willing to invest resources in exposure assessment and management.[2] Assessment of exposures and establishment of hedging policies are independent decisions. Some justification is needed for investing corporate resources in each of these activities.

Assessment of corporate economic exposure identifies the set of environmental contingencies relevant to shareholder value creation. Hence, measuring economic exposures is very much in keeping with the tradition in strategy research of equipping managers with tools for assessing the company's strategic position with respect to its environment. Such information is fundamental to strategic decisions since it allows management to assess the performance implications of alternative environmental scenarios. The assessment of exposures may have value for understanding the position of one's own firm or those of competitors. This analytical value exists regardless of whether hedging is undertaken.

Based on exposure assessments, management may seek to increase or decrease corporate exposures to certain environmental contingencies. Strategic managers presumably possess inside information useful for predicting the direction of environmental changes affecting their industries. Such inside information allows them to place selective bets which increase corporate exposures but are likely to result in positive pay-offs to shareholders.

More controversial are the decisions to selectively reduce exposures below the levels inherent in their line of business. What justification could be offered for hedging economic exposures? We consider two rationales for hedging economic exposures. Neither conflicts with the assumption of semi-strong capital market efficiency.

The first rationale is that many organizational stakeholders do not hold the broadly diversified portfolio assumed in asset pricing models. Many stakeholders simply cannot diversify their firm-specific investments. Buyers, suppliers, alliance partners, managers, and employees have sunk investments in firm-specific knowledge which tie a disproportionate share of their future earnings to the fate of the firm. While all these stakeholders seek claims to the resources of the firm, their interests are aligned with those of shareholders to the extent that increasing the overall value of the firm is consistent with meeting the firm's ongoing obligations. Firm growth and the generation of slack resources may be wholly consistent with the long-term interests of diverse stakeholders, despite conflicts over claims to current cash flows. Compensation systems designed to alleviate agency problems (e.g., employee stock ownership plans or bonuses tied to shareholder returns) align the interests of management and employees with those of shareholders by tying large components of their earnings to company-specific stock returns. Such compensation systems purposely skew portfolio holdings of key stakeholders by mandating large, undiversifiable stakes in a single company.

Even shareholders with broadly diversified domestic portfolios often do not hold internationally diversified portfolios. Hence, they care a great deal whether exchange rate movements help or hurt domestic firms relative to international competitors. The most extreme example of a stakeholder with a domestic-focused portfolio may be government. Since the revenue base of government is tied to the economic activity within its jurisdiction, government is far from indifferent between the success of domestic and foreign competitors.

Thus, for less than fully diversified stakeholders, downsizing, bankruptcy, and reorganization within a company have large effects on their wealth. Such stakeholders care a great deal about changes in the competitive position of the firm, which are also reflected in the firm's share prices. This creates an incentive to reduce downside movements in the value of the firm even when such practices may be costly. While this motivation for managing economic exposure may conflict with the interests of broadly diversified shareholders, this is not necessarily the case. The alternative to paying for corporate risk reduction is to pay the diverse stakeholders for their risk bearing. Such payments take the form of discounts to buyers, improved compensation packages for management and employees, and premium prices to suppliers. Thus, from the diversified shareholders' perspective, hedging economic exposures is value-enhancing if it is more economical than paying the various stakeholders for risk-bearing. Following this argument, even using efficiently priced financial instruments (futures and forward contracts, options, and swaps) to hedge economic exposures may enhance shareholder value.

An alternative rationale for hedging economic exposures, consistent with shareholder interests, is that markets for strategic hedges may not be efficient. This is the argument implicit in strategy research presenting the acquisition of real options as enhancing shareholder value (e.g., Sanchez, 1993). Just as theorists developing the resource-based view of the firm argue markets for strategic resources are imperfect (e.g., Amit and Schoemaker, 1993; Barney, 1991), markets for options on such resources are also imperfect. Unlike financial options which are highly liquid and trade on organized exchanges, real options are idiosyncratic. The high uncertainty and complexity associated with real options may preclude efficient market transactions. Such inefficiency results in the potential for value enhancement through internal development or acquisition of real options.

Although the approach to assessing economic exposure developed in this paper assumes equity market efficiency, arguing that equity markets are efficient does not preclude inefficiencies in pricing strategic resources or options on such resources. While the overall value of a firm may be efficiently assessed, the price of any particular strategic resource or real option may be very difficult to determine for both those inside and outside a firm. Barney (1988) developed similar theoretical arguments to specify the conditions under which acquisitions can enhance shareholder value. Barney's argument rests on the assumption that while the acquired assets themselves may be difficult to price and trade, once the acquisition is completed equity markets efficiently include the contribution to expected cash flows from the acquisition in the acquiring firm's share price. Presumably private information about the value of the acquisition to the acquirer which was not revealed during the bidding process is revealed shortly after announcing the terms of the acquisition.

The implementation of financial and strategic hedges is considered in greater depth after discussing the multivariate nature of economic exposures.

Multivariate exposure

Most corporate risk management research to date reflects a 'particularist' view (Miller, 1992; Werner, Brouthers, and Brouthers, 1996). That is, researchers focus on particular risk exposures to the exclusion of other interrelated exposures. Finance researchers have focused on the exposures for which there are well-developed markets and hedging instruments such as foreign exchange, interest rate, and commodity prices. International business scholars have given extensive attention to political risk. In the strategy field, researchers have focused on competitive, input supply, market demand, and technological risk exposures. Given the focus on particular risk exposures, there has been little conceptual and modeling work integrating the various categories of corporate risk exposures. Most research on economic exposure considers simple bivariate relations between firm value (or cash flows) and a single environmental variable, most frequently a foreign exchange rate. Finance researchers have increasingly recognized the shortcomings of the 'particularist' approach and the need for well-developed multivariate models of economic exposures which explicitly take into account the interrelations among various exposures (Cornell, 1980; Froot, Scharfstein, and Stein, 1994; Kaufold and Smirlock, 1986; Oxelheim and Wihlborg, 1987b; Schnabel, 1989; Shapiro and Titman, 1986).

Since most of the work on economic exposure has taken the form of simple bivariate models of foreign exchange exposure, we take such a model as our starting point in this section. We then elaborate the implications of expanding a model of foreign exchange exposure to include additional uncertain environmental contingencies.

Economic exposure to multiple foreign exchange rates

Adler and Dumas (1984) and Garner and Shapiro (1984) proposed simple bivariate linear models of exchange exposure. Following their work, we would express the exposure of a dollar-priced asset to movements in the dollar–pound exchange rate as:

$$V(t) = \beta_0 + \beta_1 S_{\pounds}(t) + \epsilon(t) \qquad (1)$$

where $S_\pounds(t)$ denotes the real spot dollar price of one pound at time t, $V(t)$ is the real dollar value of the firm, and $\epsilon(t)$ is the random error term. As specified, the U.S. dollar is assumed to be the relevant numeraire for valuing the firm.[3] We further assume the error term is normally distributed with mean zero and a constant variance, i.e., $\epsilon(t) \sim N(0, \sigma^2)$. In this simple bivariate model, the coefficient reflecting the exchange rate exposure, β_1, equals $\text{cov}[V(t), S_\pounds(t)] / \text{var}[S_\pounds(t)]$.[4]

While Garner and Shapiro (1984) noted that the bivariate model (1) can be extended to multivariate models allowing for asset exposures to multiple currencies, they did not consider the important implications of switching from bivariate to multivariate exposure measures.[5] Although simplification to the bivariate case is useful for illustrative purposes, focusing on bivariate relations can greatly distort estimated exposures. Bivariate estimates of exposure coefficients overlook the interrelations among exposures. Consider the following model expressing economic exposure in terms of two currencies:

$$V(t) = \beta_0 + \beta_1 S_\pounds(t) + \beta_2 S_\yen(t) + \epsilon(t), \epsilon(t) \sim N(0, \sigma^2) \tag{2}$$

$S_\yen = (t)$ denotes the real spot dollar price of one yen at time t and the other variables are defined as before. In this multivariate case the coefficient reflecting exposure to movements in the dollar price of the pound sterling, β_1, partials out the effect of the real spot price of the yen, $S_\yen = (t)$. Similarly, the yen exposure coefficient, β_2, partials out the effect of the real pound spot price, $S_\pounds(t)$.[6]

These observations have very important practical implications for corporate risk assessment. If the true model is Equation 2, estimating two bivariate models similar to Equation 1 can greatly distort the estimated exposure coefficients. While the estimated pound exposure coefficient from the bivariate Equation 1 may be significant, the estimated pound coefficient in the multivariate Equation 2 may not be significant. Alternatively, an insignificant relation in Equation 1 may be significant in the multivariate Equation 2. Furthermore, the signs of significant parameters may reverse themselves when moving from bivariate to multivariate modeling of exposure coefficients. In short, all the problems associated with specification error due to omitted variables (see Kenny, 1979: 62–65) apply to the misspecification of economic exposure models as simple bivariate relations.

If you have prior knowledge that your firm is exposed to only the pound and not to the yen, then this knowledge should be incorporated in the specification of the exposure model by eliminating the yen exchange rate, as in Model 1. Similarly, if you have predetermined that your firm will hedge the pound but not the yen, then the appropriate model would exclude the yen exchange rate. However, if you lack prior knowledge that certain exposure coefficients are equal to zero and have made no *a priori* choice of a single focal currency for your hedging strategy, then specifying the multivariate Model 2 yields the appropriate exposure coefficient estimates for exposure assessment.

Exchange rate exposure in an integrated risk management framework

The previous section contrasted bivariate and multivariate models of foreign exchange risk exposure. Taking the multivariate conceptualization of exposures one step further, it is important to recognize that in addition to exposures to multiple foreign currencies, companies have exposures to a variety of other uncertain environmental contingencies. Oxelheim and Wihlborg point out: 'managing exchange rate exposure per se is not clearly meaningful without considering the interdependence between the exchange rate and other variables related to the exchange rate in a general equilibrium system such as inflation rates and interest rates' (1987a: 88). Consistent with this reasoning, Grammatikos, Saunders, and Swary (1986) considered the joint implications of exchange rate and interest rate risks for U.S. banks. Kawai and Zilcha (1986) modeled export firm behavior under foreign currency and commodity price uncertainties.

While finance researchers have broadened the concept of corporate exchange risk management to include interrelated macroeconomic variables, they neglect the interrelated risk exposures of most interest to corporate strategists.[7] Competitive, input supply, and product demand risks are often interrelated with movements in real exchange rates. Since industry variables affecting the competitive position of a firm may be interrelated with movements in exchange rates, the effect of exchange rates may be negligible after partialing out such variables. By focusing on exchange rate and other macroeconomic exposures, previous finance research may have overlooked the most relevant economic exposures such as exposures to strategic moves by competing firms.

For example, if Japanese exporters to the United States reduce real dollar prices in response to yen devaluations, this increases the economic exposure of competing U.S. firms to movements in the real value of the yen. If Japanese exporters' response is symmetric (i.e., they raise real dollar prices in response to yen appreciation), the magnitude of the economic exposure of U.S. firms is further increased. On the other hand, if Japanese exporters maintain constant dollar prices in the face of yen appreciation or depreciation, the yen exposure of U.S. competitors is reduced. Hence, the strategic variable of product pricing by Japanese competitors affects the foreign exchange exposure of U.S. firms, even U.S. firms producing and selling exclusively in their home market.

Expanding on the model developed earlier, we could incorporate the real dollar price of competing Japanese products, $P(t)$, into the economic exposure model.

$$V(t) = \beta_0 + \beta_1 S_\mathcal{L}(t) + \beta_2 S_\yen = (t) + \beta_3 P(t) + \epsilon(t), \epsilon(t) \sim N(0, \sigma^2) \tag{3}$$

If as the yen decreases in real value, Japanese exporters seek to increase their U.S. market shares through reductions in their real dollar price, $P(t)$ would be positively correlated with $S_\yen = (t)$.[8] Hence, the OLS estimate of the yen exposure coefficient, β_2, in Equation 3, may be quite different from that estimated using Equation 2.[9]

As noted earlier, foreign exchange rates and the prices of foreign competitors' exports are just two types of variables that may affect firm value. We could also incorporate other variables such as the prices for inputs, substitutes, and domestic competitors' goods. A general model for economic exposures would take the form:

$$V(t) = X'(t)\beta + \epsilon(t), \epsilon(t) \sim N(0, \sigma^2) \tag{4}$$

where the vector of independent variables, $X(t)$, consists not only of exchange rates and foreign competitors' prices, but also other macroeconomic and industry contingencies.[10] β is a vector of exposure coefficients. Some independent variables may be continuous (e.g., macroeconomic variables or input, competitor, and substitute prices) while others may be expressed as discrete indicator variables (e.g., technological state or political and government policy variables).

Changes in the estimated foreign exchange coefficients are not the only implications of the expanded multivariate model. A significant foreign exporter price coefficient may suggest very different hedging practices than would a model incorporating only the variables of primary interest in finance research — exchange rates, interest rate, or commodity prices. Exposure to competitor prices may require strategic risk management responses rather than hedging through the use of financial market instruments. The next section elaborates some implications of the integrated approach to risk assessment and management.

Implications of multivariate assessment of economic exposures

The multivariate approach to economic exposure has important implications for corporate risk assessment and hedging. These implications have been broadly overlooked in previous research on economic exposure and corporate risk management.

A fundamental conclusion from the earlier discussion is that specifying simple bivariate models of foreign exchange exposure can result in very different assessments of corporate exposures than estimating a multicurrency exposure model. Using a series of bivariate models is inappropriate given the failure of such an approach to take into consideration the correlations among real exchange rates.

These observations have very important ramifications for corporate hedging practices. Hedging based on simple bivariate exposure estimates will generally result in suboptimal risk management. Firms may engage in inadequate or excessive hedging to cover their currency exposures if they fail to take into consideration the correlations among various currencies. If the real spot prices of two currencies have a nonzero correlation, the bivariate and multivariate model coefficients will indicate different quantities of each currency to be bought or sold in order to fully hedge. Significant exposure coefficients estimated in a series of bivariate models may be insignificant in a combined multivariate model. Conversely, insignificant coefficients from bivariate models may be significant in a multivariate model. The signs of significant relations may even be reversed in moving from a bivariate to a multivariate model. The implication of this latter observation is that firms engaging in hedging practices based on bivariate exposure estimates may actually increase their aggregate exposure relative to the 'unhedged' position.

Furthermore, movements in foreign exchange rates may be correlated with other environmental contingencies. Examples of such variables include interest rates, input prices, and the prices of competing, substitute, or complementary goods. Even political and social risks affecting MNCs could have significant inverse relations with the value of a country's currency. Hence, competitive, macroeconomic, and political risk – facets of corporate risk management generally treated in isolation from foreign exchange risk – may be best modeled in a single multivariate model to determine corporate exposures.[11]

While the implications of including noncurrency variables in a model of foreign exchange exposure are similar to the implications of moving from a single currency to a multiple currency model, the inclusion of these additional variables suggests very different corporate hedging practices. While financial market instruments exist for hedging currency, interest rate, and commodity price exposures, financial hedging instruments may not be available to hedge movements in many critical environmental contingencies such as the prices of noncommodity inputs or competitors' goods. Corporate responses to these risks may require strategic rather than financial hedging practices. For example, firms facing uncertainty regarding the price of a noncommodity input may seek to vertically integrate to control a key supplier. Exposure to competitors' prices may be reduced through a strategy of product differentiation increasing customer brand loyalty and switching costs, thereby reducing the price elasticity of demand.

The integrated risk management perspective reflected in the multivariate estimation of exposure coefficients suggests a complementary role for financial and strategic hedging practices. Where appropriate financial instruments exist, they may be relatively inexpensive (i.e., low transaction cost) means to hedge short-term economic exposures. However, financial hedging instruments cover only a limited subset of the environmental contingencies affecting firm value and the time frame for corporate economic exposures frequently exceeds the terms for financial hedging instruments.

Where appropriate financial hedging instruments do not exist, firms have available a variety of strategies to deal with economic exposures. These include gaining control over external contingencies, cooperating with suppliers, buyers, or competitors, and developing flexibility. Diversification into new product or geographic markets, and operational flexibility have option characteristics that can be used to hedge corporate downside risk in a manner analogous to financial options. As noted earlier, the markets for such idiosyncratic investments may be inefficient due to information asymmetry. Hence, such hedging has the potential to increase firm value.

Whereas financial hedging instruments can be tailored to specific financial market contingencies (e.g., particular foreign exchange rates, interest rates, or commodity prices), changes in strategy are likely to have broad implications across a corporation's set of exposure coefficients.[12] This observation indicates that rather than a simple one-to-one mapping between exposures and relevant hedging instruments, prescribing hedging practices involving changes in strategy must take into consideration the entire risk exposure profile of a firm. As such, it may often be inadequate to make simplistic assertions about the appropriateness of strategic changes as responses to particular risk exposures.

Consider, for example, the case of a firm with a significant negative exposure to input prices. Such a firm may be encouraged to engage in backward vertical integration through developing an in-house capacity to produce the inputs. Such a strategy would reduce the variability of input prices in local currency terms. At the same time, however, vertical integration could increase the firm's exposure to foreign exchange rate movements. This becomes evident if we consider a situation in which the local exchange rate appreciates making foreign inputs cheaper than the firm's own in-house inputs. Since the company continues to source inputs through its in-house production, the availability of lower cost imported inputs to competing firms would put the company at a competitive disadvantage, thereby reducing the competitiveness and value of the firm. Hence, the prescription available to reducing input price volatility involves increased exposure to foreign exchange rate movements. Such exposure tradeoffs must be explicitly considered in determining the role of strategic responses in corporate hedging.

If the proposed change in strategy involves acquiring an existing firm, estimates of the firm's own exposures and the acquisition candidate's exposures using a multivariate model could be compared to indicate the potential exposure coefficients associated with running the two firms as a single entity. The validity of such an assessment depends on whether management intends to significantly change the strategy of the acquired (or acquiring) unit after acquisition. For full hedging, the ideal candidate for a firm with exposure coefficients given by the vector β would be a firm of equivalent size with an exposure vector $-\beta$. It is unlikely that such an ideal candidate would be found. Most acquisition candidates would have some exposure coefficients which are opposite in sign from those of the acquiring firm and other exposures with the same sign. Hence, acquisitions which reduce the firm's exposure along certain dimensions will increase the exposure to other environmental contingencies. While the 'ideal' acquisition candidate is unlikely to exist, a linear combination of various acquisition candidates may approximate full hedging. Such linear combinations may involve partial or full acquisition, or even taking short positions.[13] More realistically, firms will select acquisition candidates based foremost on their strategic implications. Risk management is generally viewed as subordinate to consideration of the competitive ramifications of corporate strategic decisions (Kenyon, 1990: Ch. 9). Even when strategic rather than hedging considerations drive the selection of acquisition candidates, assessment of the risk implications may be an important input into the acquisition decision.

Unlike acquisitions or divestitures, the use of options has the potential to eliminate downside losses without eliminating the potential for upside gains. Currency options provide a good illustration of this property. If a firm is exposed to downside risk in the event of depreciation in the pound relative to the dollar, this downside risk can be averted through selling a pound put option or buying a dollar call option. Elimination of downside risk results from the option holder's flexibility to exercise the option or allow it to expire unexercised. To fully eliminate the downside economic risk, the exercise price must be equivalent to the current spot price. For such an 'at the money' spot option, the writer of the option bears the full downside risk and receives the option premium for this risk-bearing service.

While the pay-offs associated with options traded on financial markets are generally described in terms of just one contingency variable (e.g., a single foreign exchange rate), it is possible to reconceptualize option pay-offs in terms of multiple contingencies. In fact, such a multivariate conceptualization may be much more appropriate than the typical univariate perspective when we seek to describe the risk management implications of corporate strategies with option characteristics. An ideal multivariate call option for a firm with exposure coefficients given by the vector β would have a pay-off expressed as max $\{0, -X'(t)\beta - P_e\}$, where $X(t)$ is the vector of values for the uncertain environmental contingencies and P_e is the exercise price reflecting the initial capital investment needed to implement the strategy. Such complex options can be implemented through changes in strategies resulting in increased flexibility (Ware and Winter, 1988). Options traded on financial markets could be used in combination with changes in strategic flexibility to achieve management's desired option hedge. Hence, financial market instruments and strategic choices have complementary roles in hedging economic exposure. As argued earlier, however, the inefficiency of real options markets may make such investments more value enhancing than investments in options traded in financial markets.

Estimation of economic exposures

Up to this point, we have considered theoretical arguments supporting multivariate modeling of economic exposures and the implications of this approach for corporate exposure assessment and hedging. We turn now to the practical issues involved in specifying and estimating multivariate models of corporate economic exposures.

Specifying an estimable model

While the above specifications of economic exposure equations using firm value as the dependent variable are useful for theoretical discussion, such specifications present problems for estimation. Using the total market value of the firm is problematic because shifts in the size of the firm over time may not reflect shareholder wealth creation. For example, dividend payments reduce firm value. Public offerings of new shares of stock increase the total market value of the firm but will only change the value of previously outstanding shares if the newly raised capital is invested in projects earning a rate of return which differs from the cost of capital. These observations indicate that using the total market value of equity as the dependent variable does not result in estimable exposure coefficients using time series data from a single firm if new shares are issued or dividends paid. For similar reasons, the use of total firm value precludes cross-sectional comparison of exposure coefficients.

For estimation purposes, it is useful to specify firm value as a nonlinear function. The relations previously expressed in Equation 3 can be respecified as

$$V(t) = \beta_0 S_£(t)^{\beta_1} S_¥(t)^{\beta_2} P(t)^{\beta_3}(t). \tag{5}$$

This specification does not solve the problems with the earlier specifications but it can be used to derive an estimable equation. After logarithmic transformation and taking the derivative of Equation 5 with respect to time, we have

$$[dV(t) / dt] / V(t) = \beta_1[dS_\pounds(t) / dt / S_\pounds(t)]$$
$$+ \beta_2[dS_\yen(t) / dt] / S_\yen(t) \tag{6}$$
$$+ \beta_3[dP(t) / dt] / P(t) + \eta(t)$$

where the error term, $\eta(t) = [d\epsilon(t) / dt] / \epsilon(t)$. The coefficients in this equation can be interpreted as the elasticities of firm value with respect to each of the independent variables (Glaister, 1978: 117–118). For example, β_1 measures the elasticity of firm value with respect to movements in the dollar spot price of the pound (controlling for all other variables in the model). As such, these coefficients can be interpreted as hedge ratios (Bilson, 1994). For example, complete hedging of exposure to the pound involves taking a position of $-\beta_1$ times the total dollar market value of the firm. For $\beta_1 > 0$, this implies taking a short position. This contrasts with estimation of the coefficients in Equation 3 which can be interpreted as the dollar magnitudes of firm exposures.

Using discrete data, we can express the Equation 6 relations in terms of the rates of change of each of the variables:

$$R_V(t) = \beta_1 R_\pounds(t) + \beta_2 R_\yen(t) + \beta_3 R_P(t) + \eta(t) \tag{7}$$

Treating $R_V(t)$ as the rate of return in period t to shareholders for a specific firm, this equation provides a basis for estimating exposure coefficients using time series data.[14] Unlike models of economic exposure using cash flows or market value of equity as the dependent variable, expressing the dependent variable as the rate of return to shareholders results in a model which is invariant to changes in the size of the firm over time. Estimated parameters from Equation 7 are also comparable across organizations.

The general form of Equation 5 for a model of economic exposure using n independent variables would be

$$V(t) = \prod_{i=1}^{n} \beta_0 X_i(t)^{\beta_i} \in (t) \tag{8}$$

As before, using a logarithmic transformation and taking the derivative with respect to time gives rise to the estimable rate of return model:

$$R_V = \sum_{i=1}^{n} \beta_i R_i(t) + \eta(t) \tag{9}$$

where R_V is rate of return to shareholders and R_i is the rate of change of X_i.

Equation 9 has several desirable properties. It offers a multivariate model of exposures, the coefficients are interpretable as elasticities and comparable across organizations, and the model is estimable using corporate time series data. One limitation arises from the requirement that all variables must be transformed into discrete rates of change. Hence, it is preferable that each explanatory variable, X_i, be continuous. Ordinal scale variables could be used, but nominal scale (i.e., indicator) variables could not be included. During periods of dramatic change in the explanatory variables, stock prices may not adjust instantaneously, hence evaluation of outlier observations may be an important supplemental analysis to obtain robust parameter estimates.

Deviations from expectations or total variability?

Equation 9 presented an estimable multivariate model of corporate economic exposures. As specified, changes in shareholder returns are a function of changes in a set of independent variables. Hence, this specification measures economic exposures with respect to total movements in the independent variables rather than focusing solely on movements that are deviations from expectations. Since other researchers have argued for specifying economic exposure only in terms of deviations from expectations, it is worthwhile to consider whether deviations from expectations or total variability are most appropriate.

Hodder (1982) and Adler and Dumas (1984) argued economic exposure to foreign exchange rates should be defined in terms of random deviations from expected real rates. Oxelheim and Wihlborg state:

> There are reasons to distinguish between exposure to anticipated and unanticipated changes in, for example, the exchange rate. The firm can incorporate the former in its budget and planning process, while exposure to unanticipated changes constitutes the firm's risk exposure.
>
> *(1987a: 88)*

Emphasizing unanticipated currency movements accommodates hedging using available financial instruments. The primary financial hedging tools (futures and forward contracts, options, and swaps) allow firms to hedge unexpected deviations from the market's expected price but do not hedge total price variability. Financial hedging instruments do not, therefore, eliminate exposure to widely expected price changes.

Despite the arguments for specification of exposure models in terms of deviations from expectations, most models purporting to measure economic exposure as a regression coefficient do not incorporate expectations (e.g., Garner and Shapiro, 1984; Jorion, 1990; Oxelheim and Wihlborg, 1987b; Rawls and Smithson, 1990; Shapiro, 1992: 242–243). Presumably, forward market prices could be incorporated into such models but, in order to simplify their models, these researchers have chosen not to incorporate available market expectations proxies. If, however, variables were included in the economic exposure model for which there are no existing forward markets to generate proxies for expected future prices (e.g., the price of noncommodity competitors' goods), the lack of data would present a significant obstacle to exposure model estimation.

Beyond the pragmatic concern of data availability, there are theoretical arguments for using the total variability of the independent variables rather than just deviations from expectations. From a top management perspective, exposure to both predictable and unpredictable changes are important. This is an important point separating strategy and finance perspectives on risk management.[15] Downside potential rather than unpredictability is the essence of risk for strategic decision makers (Aaker and Jacobson, 1990; Baird and Thomas, 1990; March and Shapira, 1987; Miller and Leiblein, 1996; Miller and Reuer, 1996). Consider, for example, the perspective of an incumbent firm in an industry where new technology is replacing existing technology. While information about the emerging technology may be widely known, firms unable to appropriate the technology stand to lose sales, or at the extreme, be completely displaced by competitors and new entrants with the resources necessary to exploit the technology. Hence, while the technological change is predictable, it constitutes a threat, and hence a risk, for the incumbent firm. Similarly, movements in prices may be predictable but not all firms will be equally capable of reacting to expected changes. That firms may be incapable of strategic responses, despite their managements' foresight, is a fundamental premise of the resource-based view of competitive advantage.

Since managers are interested in how the variability of environmental contingencies affects corporate performance regardless of whether the variability is foreseen or not, it makes sense to specify models of economic exposure in terms of total variability of the independent variables. While defining economic exposure just in terms of unanticipated movements in the independent variables accommodates the properties of financial market hedging instruments, such a definition is inconsistent with managers' concerns about the performance impacts of both foreseeable and unforeseeable contingencies.

Selection of regressors

The model of economic exposure expressed in Equations 8 and 9 leaves open the question of which regressors should be included. In order to estimate multivariate exposure models, we need a theoretical basis for the selection of regressors. Furthermore, we need to deal with the potential problem of multicollinearity among the chosen regressors. The objective is to specify a parsimonious model with neither omitted variables nor redundant variables.[16]

The environmental contingencies relevant to explaining corporate returns to shareholders may vary across industries and firms within industries. This point was made by Robock (1971), Kobrin (1982), and Simon (1982) whose discussions of political risk contrasted firm-specific 'microrisks' with general 'macrorisks' applicable across firms. This contention also underlies strategy perspectives grounded in both industrial organization economics (e.g., Porter, 1980) and resource-based theory (e.g., Barney, 1991; Wernerfelt, 1984). Differences in strategies and hedging practices across firms create different exposure profiles. Hence, any attempt to empirically derive a set of regressors that explain returns across all firms is unlikely to be a fruitful exercise. Empirical estimates of foreign exchange exposures at the industry level or some other aggregation of firms (e.g., Bodnar and Gentry, 1993; Amihud, 1994) overlook intercompany differences in exposure coefficients.

Our objective ought to be to glean from existing theory a typology of potentially relevant environmental contingencies. Some such contingencies may prove significant across a wide range of firms, while others may affect few firms. Assessment of the significance of particular environmental variables across different industries and firm strategies within industries is an interesting empirical issue for future research.

Previous theoretical treatments of corporate risk have done little to develop a comprehensive typology of relevant environmental contingencies. Given the emphasis on particular environmental contingencies in most of the previous risk management research, it is necessary to draw from a broad range of literature (finance, international business, and strategy) to formulate a more comprehensive view of corporations' risk profiles.

The typology of uncertain environmental contingencies offered by Miller (1992) sought to respond to the need for an integrated framework for corporate risk assessment.[17] As such, the typology provides one possible starting point from which to develop empirical proxies for the contingencies relevant to corporate risk assessment. The typology categorized environmental uncertainties into two broad categories: (1) general environmental and (2) industry. General environmental uncertainties include political, government policy, macroeconomic, social, and natural contingencies. This suggests economic exposure models include measures of political and social risk, fiscal, trade, and regulatory policies, and macroeconomic performance, as well as the contingencies often given attention in finance studies – foreign exchange and interest rates, and the performance of the overall stock market. Industry dynamics involve input market, product market, competitive, and technological uncertainties. Relevant proxies include input and product market prices, measures of competitor behaviors, and the rate of new patent applications.

Environmental analysis, using the Miller (1992) typology or some other framework found in the strategy field (e.g., Austin, 1990; Porter, 1980), is the starting point for identifying relevant contingencies to include in an economic exposure model. Such firm-specific analysis lays the groundwork for maximizing the explanatory power of an exposure model and reduces the likelihood of omitting key variables. Such analyses may offer key qualitative insights into the economic exposures of the firm, even if model estimation is not undertaken. This link between industry analysis and the assessment of economic exposures involves an integration of finance and strategic management research which has not been adequately developed.

Using theory-grounded analysis to select a broad set of regressors to include in a model of corporate risk exposure, we are likely to encounter multicollinearity. Correlations among the regressors may be spurious or involve causal relations. For example, currency values may be pegged to one another. Comovements in interest rates and currency values may reflect causal relations or be due to other macroeconomic variables. The earlier example of pricing exports in the home currency rather than the export market currency (and thereby gaining market share when the home currency devalues) illustrated that even competitive variables may be correlated with currency values. Hence, in order to empirically estimate a multivariate model of economic exposure, we must assess and deal with multicollinearity. Econometric research provides guidelines for dealing with multicollinearity in model specification (e.g., Belsley, Kuh, and Welsch, 1980).

Temporal stability of exposure coefficients

Finance researchers have cautioned that corporate economic exposures may be unstable over time (Adler and Dumas, 1984; Garner and Shapiro, 1984; Shapiro, 1992). Oxelheim and Wihlborg (1987b: 115) stress exposure coefficient stability using time-series estimation depends on the government policy regime, including both domestic and foreign fiscal and monetary policies.

While instability of exposure coefficients over time is viewed as problematic in finance research, temporal instability is of fundamental interest in the field of strategy. Largely overlooked in finance discussions of economic exposure is the observation that changes in corporate strategy give rise to changes in economic exposure. Corporate changes in strategy and hedging policies may be much more influential in shifting economic exposure coefficients than changes in the government policy regime. If so, the period for time series estimation of corporate economic exposure coefficients should be limited to the duration of the corporate strategy. As noted earlier, shifts in strategy such as acquisitions, divestitures, or changes in strategic flexibility (i.e., strategies with option characteristics) influence corporate exposure coefficients. Whether exposure coefficients can be estimated for any given firm is a function of the frequency of strategy changes and the periodicity of the model variables.

Research directions

In the past, strategy and finance research has sought to measure risk as a single corporate or business-level construct reflecting financial performance variability. The emphasis on risk measures such as the variance of accounting returns, stock returns beta and unsystematic risk, and the variance of analysts' earnings forecasts reflect this orientation toward general measures of firm risk (Miller and Bromiley, 1990). The primary applications of such measures in strategy research have been studies on corporate risk–return relations, and the risk implications of specific strategies (corporate diversification being the research domain most widely incorporating risk measures) and business environments. In focusing on general measures of risk, previous research has not addressed the managerial concern for determining exposures to specific environmental contingencies and developing appropriate hedges for identified exposures. This previous research also fails to take into consideration the possibility that changes in strategy may have little impact on the overall risk of the firm despite changing significantly the exposures to particular environmental contingencies. By dealing at the level of general measures of risk, strategy research offers little guidance as to how specific risks affect strategies and vice versa.

The integrated risk management perspective elaborated in this paper offers an alternative approach to that of earlier strategy and finance research. Multivariate modeling of economic exposures offers the possibility of assessing corporate exposures along many different dimensions. Distinguishing among exposures is likely to be quite important for explaining firm strategic responses. Casual observation suggests companies respond quite differently to exposures to political and government policy, macroeconomic, input and product market, and competitive factors that affect firm value. Breaking the risk construct into distinct exposures to multiple environmental contingencies allows for more precise specification of the relations between risks and strategies. The development and testing of multivariate models linking corporate exposures to strategies could provide valuable guidelines for strategic risk management.

While this study provided general guidance regarding the choice of regressors when specifying economic exposure models, further conceptual and empirical development is needed. Case studies identifying relevant firm-specific environmental contingencies may prove insightful for managers and researchers alike.

As is frequently done in econometrics, this study made the simplifying assumption that all model constructs are observable and measured without error. While the assumption of direct observability often holds for economic variables (e.g., foreign exchange rates, prices of competitors' products, input prices), we may have only indirect indicators of other relevant environmental contingencies. For example, government policy, social, and technological variables may be complex constructs with multiple indicators. In such instances, the structural economic exposure model could be augmented by an explicit measurement model with multiple indicators of latent variables. In such a case, assessments of reliability and validity should be undertaken (see, for example, Bagozzi, Yi, and Phillips, 1991). As before, the coefficients of a structural equations model containing latent variables are the elasticities of firm value with respect to each of the variables. Hedging exposures to latent constructs requires looking beyond available financial hedging instruments to insurance (e.g., political risk insurance) and investments in strategic flexibility (e.g., purchasing real options on emerging technologies).

Assessment of economic exposure is an important complement to an emerging stream of strategy research applying option theory (Bowman and Hurry, 1993; Chi and McGuire, 1996; Folta and Leiblein, 1994; Hurry, Miller, and Bowman, 1992; Kogut, 1991; Kogut and Kulatilaka, 1994; Sanchez, 1993). Viewing strategic moves resulting in increased flexibility as options provides a useful theoretical perspective for thinking about strategic flexibility as a means to hedge corporate exposures. However, modeling the option characteristics of strategies is much more complex than modeling financial options. Strategy research cannot assume the simple one-to-one mapping between exposures and hedging instruments generally followed in finance research. Just as economic exposure is multidimensional, so changes in strategies alter exposures to many different environmental contingencies. Changes in strategies resulting in increased flexibility can be viewed as the purchase of options with pay-offs contingent on multiple environmental contingencies (Ware and Winter, 1988). This suggests moving beyond option theory models of strategic flexibility as responses to a single environmental contingency such as a foreign exchange rate (Kogut and Kulatilaka, 1994) or technological turbulence (Folta and Leiblein, 1994; Hurry et al., 1992). Incorporating multiple environmental contingencies should provide a more complete picture of the role of strategic flexibility responses in corporate risk management.

The instability of corporate exposure coefficients over time offers an interesting research opportunity. Future research could consider both the implications of corporate exposure profiles for subsequent changes in strategies and, conversely, the implications of strategy changes for corporate exposures. We know of no previous research looking at the shifts in exposure coefficients following changes in corporate strategies. Such research could provide practical risk management guidance to corporate strategists.

Whereas finance research has struggled to explain hedging by firms given the efficiency of capital markets, this study offered two explanations as to why management of economic exposures may be consistent with shareholder interests even under the assumption of capital market efficiency. The two alternative arguments are based on (1) undiversified stakeholders needing to be compensated for risk bearing and (2) inefficiencies in the market for strategic resources and real options. These perspectives, derived from stakeholder and resource-based views of the firm, are firmly grounded in strategic management theory and deserve further attention in finance research.

Conclusion

This study sought to clarify a number of issues left unaddressed in previous research on economic exposure. The guidelines offered for specifying estimable models of economic exposure included clarification of the choice of the dependent variable and regressors, and the functional form of the relations. While cash flows have been widely recommended as the focus for exposure assessment, this study pointed out shortcomings of that approach and emphasized shareholder returns as an appropriate dependent variable. The recommendation to incorporate total variability of regressors, rather than deviations from expectations, reflects a divergence in the strategic management perspective from previous treatments of economic exposure in finance.

Many of the issues highlighted in this study arise from the recognition that the various exposures corporations face must be assessed and managed from an integrated perspective. The integrated risk management perspective encompasses the risk exposures considered in the strategy field (e.g., competitive, input supply, market demand, and technological risks) and those of interest to finance and international business scholars (e.g., interest rate, foreign exchange, and political risks). Drawing from econometrics research, the study indicated the problems associated with exposure assessments that isolate particular uncertain environmental contingencies from others. Hedging strategies based on separate bivariate exposure estimates are suboptimal.

The multivariate approach to exposure assessment has implications for theory development. In particular, this study points out the need to distinguish among exposures in explaining firms' strategic risk management actions. Research seeking to explain strategic risk management responses such as acquisitions and the purchase of real options requires theory development incorporating multiple environmental contingencies.

Acknowledgements

The author wishes to thank Tim Folta, Jeffrey Reuer, and the anonymous referees for comments on earlier drafts. Funding from Krannert's Center for International Business Education and Research is gratefully acknowledged.

Notes

* Correspondence to: Kent D. Miller, Krannert Graduate School of Management, Purdue University, 1310 Krannert Building, West Lafayette, IN 47907-1310, U.S.A.
  Key words: risk measurement; risk management; economic exposure; real options.
1 International finance and accounting texts (e.g., Choi and Mueller, 1992; Shapiro, 1992) provide extensive discussions of translation and transaction exposure.
2 Adler and Dumas (1983), Dufey and Srinivasulu (1984), and Logue and Oldfield (1977) provide summaries and critiques of the arguments underlying the efficient capital markets perspective on corporate hedging. These arguments, as well as those put forth more recently by Smith and Stulz (1985) and Froot, Scharfstein, and Stein (1993), focus on the management of current cash flows rather than economic exposure.
3 Since Equation 1 expresses the value of the firm in real terms, the choice between a single-currency numeraire and a basket of currencies is irrelevant. The model and its implications would be equally valid if the real value of a basket of currencies were chosen as the numeraire. This contrasts with Eaker's (1981) conclusion which considered accounting exposure where nominal exchange rates deviate from purchasing power parity.
4 The fully hedged position involves taking a position $\beta\star$ in pounds, which offsets the existing exposure, β_1. This can be represented by the extended form of Equation 1:

$$V(t) = \beta_0 + \beta_1 S_\mathcal{L}(t) + \beta\star S_\mathcal{L}(t) + \epsilon(t)$$

Solving for the fully hedged value of $\beta\star$, we have:

$$\partial V(t) \, / \, \partial S_\mathcal{L}(t) = \beta_1 + \beta\star = 0$$

or

$$\beta\star = -\beta_1$$

Thus, for an estimated exposure coefficient $b_1 > 0$, full hedging involves selling b_1 pounds for dollars. If $b_1 < 0$, a hedging strategy of purchasing b_1 pounds with dollars would eliminate the exposure. If b_1 is not significantly different from zero, there is no exposure to movements in the dollar–pound exchange rate. The best estimate of the residual variance associated with the fully hedged position is s^2, the estimator of σ^2, equal to the mean of the squared residuals.
5 An initial step towards considering the implications of multi-variate foreign exchange exposure modeling was Schnabel's (1989) brief article.
6 These conditional relations can be shown as follows. Let c_{ij} be the estimated coefficient from a simple bivariate regression model (which includes an intercept term) where the first subscript denotes the dependent variable and the second subscript denotes the independent variable. The OLS estimates for the Model 2 regression coefficients β_1 and β_2, call them b_1 and b_2, can be expressed in terms of the bivariate regression coefficients, c_{ij}. These relations take the following form (see Land, 1969: 12–14).

$$b_1 = (c_{V\mathcal{L}} - c_{V\yen} c_{\yen\mathcal{L}}) \, / \, (1 - c_{\mathcal{L}\yen} c_{\yen\mathcal{L}}) \qquad \text{(f1)}$$

$$b_2 = (c_{V\yen} - c_{V\mathcal{L}} c_{\mathcal{L}\yen}) \, / \, (1 - c_{\yen\mathcal{L}} c_{\mathcal{L}\yen}) \qquad \text{(f2)}$$

These expressions indicate each regression coefficient in Model 2 is a function of the bivariate coefficients expressing the relations between the predictor variables, $c_{\yen L}$ and $c_{L\yen}$, as well as the bivariate coefficients involving the endogenous variable, $c_{V\yen}$ and c_{VL}. Hence, for any nonzero covariance between the spot prices of the yen and the pound, the Model 2 multivariate exposure coefficients will differ from the coefficients derived by running separate bivariate OLS regressions for each currency.

For exposure regression models with more than two explanatory variables, the parameter estimates can also be expressed in terms of the bivariate coefficients between the predictor variables, and predictor-endogenous variable coefficients. The expressions are, however, more complex than Equations f1 and f2.

7 Lessard's work on operating exposure (e.g., Flood and Lessard, 1986; Lessard, 1986) is a notable exception.

8 We assume that due to lags in price adjustments or possible asymmetries in pricing responses to exchange rate movements, Japanese export prices are not perfectly correlated with movements in the real value of the yen. If movements in Japanese export prices and the real yen exchange rate were perfectly correlated, Model 3 could not be estimated. Furthermore, if the two variables were perfectly correlated, the firm could simply estimate Model 2 and use the yen exposure coefficient as the basis for exposure assessment and hedging.

9 The pricing-to-market literature (e.g., Krugman, 1987) con- tends pricing decisions in an international market may differ depending on whether the host country currency appreciates or depreciates. Alternatively, prices may only respond to large exchange rate movements and not to minor changes. The way to handle such inconsistencies in the exposure coefficients is to separate the time series data into distinct subperiods for exposure model estimation. Such an approach also allows explicit testing of whether exposure coefficients differ among subperiods. This is an interesting empirical issue − one that has not been addressed in finance treatments of economic exposure.

10 This is a reduced form equation which does not model the relations among explanatory variables. In the context of measuring economic exposures, we have no need to estimate the parameters associated with structural relations among explanatory variables. Our interests are limited to the relations of the explanatory variables to firm value controlling for other variables in the model.

11 It also follows from the discussion above that if a particular environmental contingency is orthogonal to other corporate contingencies, it need not be included in an integrated assessment of risk exposures. This is a very restrictive condition and it is difficult to conceive of such risks. Recognizing the restrictiveness of the orthogonality condition highlights the general inappropriateness of assessing and managing individual risks to the exclusion of other risks.

12 It should be noted, however, that even hedging by purchasing an option tied to a particular financial market price will affect other corporate exposure coefficients to the extent that movements of the hedged currency are correlated with movements of other environmental contingencies.

13 This discussion of hedging through acquisition is intended to be illustrative, not normative. Many such acquisitions may fail the value creation criterion. See Barney (1988) for a discussion of the conditions necessary for an acquisition to enhance shareholder value.

14 There are several studies using such models with a single currency proxy. Booth and Rotenberg (1990) considered movements in the Canadian dollar relative to the U.S. dollar to the exclusion of all other foreign currencies that could affect the stock returns of Canadian companies. Other studies used trade-weighted sums of nominal or real foreign exchange rates as their foreign exchange proxies (Amihud, 1994; Bodnar and Gentry, 1993; Jorion, 1990).

15 For further discussion on the discrepant assumptions underlying strategy and finance risk management discussions, see Bettis (1983).

16 These are the ideals advocated in econometrics. Practical issues regarding data availability and underdevelopment of theory generally preclude realizing these ideals. Nevertheless, the ideals of completeness and parsimony are relevant criteria for evaluating alternative model specifications.

17 For an application of the Miller (1992) typology to strategy research see Brouthers (1995).

References

Aaker, D.A. and R. Jacobson (1990). 'The risk of marketing: The roles of systematic, uncontrollable and controllable unsystematic, and downside risk'. In R.A. Bettis and H. Thomas (eds.), *Risk, Strategy, and Management*. JAI Press, Greenwich, CT, pp. 137–160.

Adler, M. and B. Dumas (1983). 'International portfolio choice and corporation finance: A synthesis', *Journal of Finance*, **38**, pp. 925–984.

Adler, M. and B. Dumas (1984). Exposure to currency risk: Definition and measurement', *Financial Management*, **13**(2), pp. 41–50.

Ahkam, S.N. (1995). 'A model for the evaluation of a response to economic risk by multinational companies', *Managerial Finance*, **21**(4), pp. 7–22.

Amihud, Y. (1994). 'Exchange rates and the valuation of equity shares'. In Y. Amihud and R. Levich (eds.), *Exchange Rates and Corporate Performance*. Irwin, Burr Ridge, IL, pp. 49–59.

Amit, R. and P.J.H. Schoemaker (1993). 'Strategic assets and organizational rent', *Strategic Management Journal*, **14**(1), pp. 33–46.

Andrews, K.R. (1971). *The Concept of Corporate Strategy*. Dow Jones-Irwin, New York.

Austin, J.E. (1990). *Managing in Developing Countries: Strategic Analysis and Operating Techniques*. Free Press, New York.

Bagozzi, R.P., Y. Yi and L.W. Phillips (1991). 'Assessing validity in organizational research', *Administrative Science Quarterly*, **36**, pp. 421–458.

Baird, I.S. and H. Thomas (1990). 'What is risk anyway?: Using and measuring risk in strategic management'. In R.A. Bettis and H. Thomas (eds.), *Risk, Strategy, and Management*. JAI Press, Greenwich, CT, pp. 21–52.

Barney, J.B. (1988). 'Returns to bidding firms in mergers and acquisitions: Reconsidering the relatedness hypothesis', *Strategic Management Journal*, Summer Special Issue, **9**, pp. 71–78.

Barney, J.B. (1991). 'Firm resources and sustainable competitive advantage', *Journal of Management*, **17**, pp. 99–120.

Batten, J., R. Mellor and V. Wan (1993). 'Foreign exchange risk management practices and products used by Australian firms', *Journal of International Business Studies*, **23**, pp. 557–573.

Belsley, D.A., E. Kuh and R.E. Welsch (1980). *Regression Diagnostics: Identifying Influential Data and Sources of Collinearity*. Wiley, New York.

Bettis, R.A. (1983). 'Modern financial theory, corporate strategy and public policy: Three conundrums', *Academy of Management Review*, **8**, pp. 406–415.

Bilson, J.F.O. (1994). 'Managing economic exposure to foreign exchange risk: A case study of American airlines'. In Y. Amihud and R.M. Levich (eds.), *Exchange Rates and Corporate Performance*. Irwin, New York, pp. 221–246.

Bishop, P. and D. Dixon (1992). *Foreign Exchange Handbook*. McGraw-Hill, New York.

Bodnar, G.M. and W.M. Gentry (1993). 'Exchange rate exposure and industry characteristics: Evidence from Canada, Japan, and the USA', *Journal of International Money and Finance*, **12**, pp. 29–45.

Booth, L. and W. Rotenberg (1990). 'Assessing foreign exchange exposure: Theory and application using Canadian firms', *Journal of International Financial Management and Accounting*, **2**, pp. 1–22.

Bowman, E.H. and D. Hurry (1993). 'Strategy through the option lens: An integrated view of resource investments and the incremental-choice process', *Academy of Management Review*, **18**, pp. 760–782.

Brouthers, K.D. (1995). 'The influence of international risk on entry mode strategy in the computer software industry', *Management International Review*, **35**(1), pp. 7–28.

Chi, T. and D.J. McGuire (1996). 'Collaborative ventures and value of learning: Integrating the transaction cost and strategic option perspectives on the choice of market entry modes', *Journal of International Business Studies*, **27**, pp. 285–307.

Choi, F.D.S. and G.G. Mueller (1992). *International Accounting* (2nd ed.). Prentice-Hall, Englewood Cliffs, NJ.

Cornell, B. (1980). 'Inflation, relative price changes, and exchange risk', *Financial Management*, **9**(3), pp. 30–34.

Dufey, G. (1972). 'Corporate finance and exchange rate variations', *Financial Management*, **1**(2), pp. 51–57.

Dufey, G. and S.L. Srinivasulu (1984). 'The case for corporate management of foreign exchange risk', *Financial Management*, **12**(4), pp. 54–62.

Eaker, M.R. (1981). 'The numeraire problem and foreign exchange risk', *Journal of Finance*, **36**, pp. 419–426.

Flood, E. and D. Lessard (1986). 'On the measurement of operating exposure to exchange rates: A conceptual approach', *Financial Management*, **15**, pp. 25–36.

Folta, T.B. and M.J. Leiblein (1994). 'Technology acquisition and the choice of governance by established firms: Insights from option theory in a multinomial logit model'. In D.P. Moore (ed.), *Best Papers Proceedings: Academy of Management*, pp. 27–31.

Froot, K.A., D.S. Scharfstein and J.C. Stein (1993). 'Risk management: Coordinating corporate investment and financing policies', *Journal of Finance*, **48**, pp. 1629–1658.

Froot, K.A., D.S. Scharfstein and J.C. Stein (1994). 'A framework for risk management', *Harvard Business Review*, **72**(6), pp. 91–102.

Garner, C.K. and A.C. Shapiro (1984). A practical method of assessing foreign exchange risk', *Midland Corporate Finance Journal*, **2**(3), pp. 6–17.

George, A.M. and C.W. Schroth (1991). 'Managing foreign exchange for competitive advantage', *Sloan Management Review*, Winter, pp. 105–116.

Glaister, S. (1978). *Mathematical Methods for Economists* (revised ed.). Basil Blackwell, Oxford, UK.

Grammatikos, T., A. Saunders and I. Swary (1986). 'Returns and risks of U.S. bank foreign currency activities', *Journal of Finance*, **41**, pp. 671–683.

Hodder, J.E. (1982). 'Exposure to exchange-rate movements', *Journal of International Economics*, **13**, pp. 375–386.

Hurry, D., A.T. Miller and E.H. Bowman (1992). 'Calls on high-technology: Japanese exploration of venture capital investments in the United States', *Strategic Management Journal*, **13**(2), pp. 85–101.

Jorion, P. (1990). 'The exchange rate exposure of U.S. multinationals', *Journal of Business*, **63**, pp. 331–345.

Kaufold, H. and M. Smirlock (1986). 'Managing corporate exchange and interest rate exposure', *Financial Management*, **15**(3), pp. 64–72.

Kawai, M. and I. Zilcha (1986). 'International trade with forward-futures markets under exchange rate and price uncertainty', *Journal of International Economics*, **20**, pp. 83–98.

Kenny, D.A. (1979). *Correlation and Causality*. Wiley, New York.

Kenyon, A. (1990). *Currency Risk and Business Management*. Basil Blackwell, Cambridge, MA.

Kobrin, S.J. (1982). *Managing Political Risk Assessment*. University of California Press, Berkeley, CA.

Kogut, B. (1991). 'Joint ventures and the option to expand and acquire', *Management Science*, **37**, pp. 19–33.

Kogut, B. and N. Kulatilaka (1994). 'Operating flexibility, global manufacturing, and the option value of a multinational network', *Management Science*, **40**, pp. 123–139.

Kohn, K. (1990). 'Are you ready for economic-risk management?', *Institutional Investor*, **24**(11), pp. 203–207.

Krugman, P. (1987). 'Pricing to market when exchange rate changes'. In J.D. Richardson (ed.), *Real-Financial Linkages among Open Economies*. MIT Press, Cambridge, MA, pp. 49–70.

Land, K.C. (1969). 'Principles of path analysis'. In E.F. Borgatta (ed.), *Sociological Methodology 1969*. Jossey-Bass, San Francisco, CA, pp. 3–37.

Lessard, D.R. (1986). 'Finance and global competition: Exploiting financial scope and coping with volatile exchange rates'. In M.E. Porter (ed.), *Competition in Global Industries*. Harvard Business School Press, Boston, MA, pp. 147–184.

Lewent, J.C. and J.A. Kearney (1990). 'Identifying, measuring, and hedging currency risk at Merck', *Continental Bank Journal of Applied Corporate Finance*, **2**(4), pp. 19–28.

Logue, D.E. and G.S. Oldfield (1977). 'Managing foreign assets when foreign exchange markets are efficient', *Financial Management*, **6**(2), pp. 16–22.

March, J.G. and Z. Shapira (1987). 'Managerial perspectives on risk and risk taking', *Management Science*, **33**, pp. 1404–1418.

Miller, K.D. (1992). 'A framework for integrated risk management in international business', *Journal of International Business Studies*, **23**, pp. 311–331.

Miller, K.D. and P. Bromiley (1990). 'Strategic risk and corporate performance: An analysis of alternative risk measures', *Academy of Management Journal*, **33**, pp. 756–779.

Miller, K.D. and M.J. Leiblein (1996). 'Corporate risk–return relations: Returns variability versus downside risk', *Academy of Management Journal*, **39**, pp. 91–122.

Miller, K.D. and J.J. Reuer (1996). 'Measuring organizational downside risk', *Strategic Management Journal*, **17**(9), pp. 671–691.

Moens, L.C. (1995). 'The effect of dollar appreciation on U.S. manufacturing corporate profits: An empirical investigation'. In H.P. Gray and S.C. Richard (eds.), *International Finance in the New World Order*. Elsevier Science, Oxford, UK, pp. 157–173.

Oxelheim, L. and C. Wihlborg (1987a). 'Exchange rate-related exposures in a macroeconomic perspective'. In S.J. Khoury and A. Ghosh (eds.), *Recent Developments in International Banking and Finance*, Vol. 1. Lexington Books, Lexington, MA, pp. 87–102.

Oxelheim, L. and C. Wihlborg (1987b). *Macroeconomic Uncertainty: International Risks and Opportunities for the Corporation*. Wiley, New York.

Porter, M.E. (1980). *Competitive Strategy*. Free Press, New York.

Rappaport, A. (1986). *Creating Shareholder Value*. Free Press, New York.

Rawls, S.W. and C.W. Smithson (1990). 'Strategic risk management', *Journal of Applied Corporate Finance*, **2**(4), pp. 6–18.

Robock, S.H. (1971). Political risk: Identification and assessment', *Columbia Journal of World Business*, July–August, pp. 6–20.

Rodriguez, R.M. (1981). 'Corporate exchange risk management: Theme and aberrations', *Journal of Finance*, **36**, pp. 427–439.

Sanchez, R. (1993). 'Strategic flexibility, firm organization, and managerial work in dynamic markets: A strategic-options perspective'. In P. Shrivastava, A. Huff and J. Dutton (eds.), *Advances in Strategic Management*, Vol. 9. JAI Press, Greenwich, CT, pp. 251–291.

Schnabel, J.A. (1989). 'Exposure to foreign exchange risk: A multi-currency extension', *Managerial and Decision Economics*, **10**, pp. 331–333.

Shapiro, A.C. (1975). 'Exchange rate changes, inflation, and the value of the multinational corporation', *Journal of Finance*, **30**, pp. 485–502.

Shapiro, A.C. (1977). 'Defining exchange risk', *Journal of Business*, **50**, pp. 37–39.

Shapiro, A.C. (1984). 'Currency risk and relative price risk', *Journal of Financial and Quantitative Analysis*, **19**, pp. 365–373.

Shapiro, A.C. (1992). *Multinational Financial Management* (4th ed.). Allyn & Bacon, Boston, MA.

Shapiro, A.C. and S. Titman (1986). 'An integrated approach to corporate risk management'. In J.M. Stern and D.H. Chew, Jr. (eds.), *The Revolution in Corporate Finance*. Blackwell, Boston, MA, pp. 215–229.

Simon, J.D. (1982). 'Political risk assessment: Past trends and future prospects', *Columbia Journal of World Business*, Fall, pp. 62–71.

Smith, C.W. and R.M. Stulz (1985). 'The determinants of firms' hedging policies', *Journal of Financial and Quantitative Analysis*, **20**, pp. 391–405.

Ware, R. and R. Winter (1988). 'Forward markets, currency options and the hedging of foreign exchange risk', *Journal of International Economics*, **25**, pp. 291–302.

Werner, S., L.E. Brouthers and K.D. Brouthers (1996). 'International risk and perceived environmental uncertainty: The dimensionality and internal consistency of Miller's measure', *Journal of International Business Studies*, **27**, pp. 571–587.

Wernerfelt, B. (1984). 'A resource-based view of the firm', *Strategic Management Journal*, **5**(2), pp. 171–180.

Wihlborg, C. (1980). 'Economics of exposure management of foreign subsidiaries of multinational corporations', *Journal of International Business Studies*, **11**(3), pp. 9–18.

8

Can strategic risk management contribute to enterprise risk management?

A strategic management perspective

Phil Bromiley, Devaki Rau, and Michael McShane

Within the discipline of enterprise risk management (ERM), strategic risk management (SRM) has become a subject of increasing interest to practitioners and academics. To our knowledge, the term strategic risk management first appeared in the management literature in 1985 and 1986 (Figenbaum and Thomas, 1986; Jammine, 1985) and in the academic finance literature in 1990 (Rawls and Smithson, 1990), although early usage of the term did not clearly relate to later conceptions. The phrase has been in use even longer than ERM (Bromiley, McShane, Nair, and Rustambekov, 2014). Even with this longevity, the meaning of the term remains unclear, with confusion increasing with the advent of ERM. For example, does SRM mean the management of a specific category of risks known as "strategic risks" (AICPCU, 2013), or does SRM mean strategic actions/responses taken to mitigate major uncertainties facing the enterprise? Can any type of risk potentially become a strategic risk, or are only certain types of risk strategic? Is SRM a separate type of risk management or a subset of ERM?

This chapter deals with these issues. Specifically, we adopt a strategic management perspective to examine: what "strategic" means in SRM; the relation between SRM and ERM; the issues associated with identifying a separate category of risks termed "strategic"; and the outlook for value creation by SRM. In a preview of our discussion, we conclude that SRM is a subset of ERM and that strategic risk is more usefully defined as applying to risks that have strategic importance rather than a specific kind of risk. We begin by defining strategic risks and SRM, and by examining the relations between SRM and ERM.

In several places, we will use banking examples to illustrate issues. We do this not because our discussion applies most directly to banks, but because we assume most readers will be relatively familiar with banking and bank lending. Furthermore, nonbanking businesses vary so much that risk terminology and kinds of risks faced may not be interpretable for individuals from other industries. The issues illustrated apply equally well to nonbanking organizations.

Defining strategic risk

Any discussion of SRM must address the usage of the term strategic risk. What SRM means depends on what dimension or dimensions we use to differentiate between strategic and other risks. Let us begin by considering some of the definitions of strategic risk and strategic risk management provided by professional bodies, scholars, and practitioners. Table 8.1 lists these definitions/descriptions.

Table 8.1 Definitions/descriptions/discussions of strategic risk and strategic risk management

Baird and Thomas (1985)	**Strategic risk-taking:** Corporate strategic moves that cause returns to vary, that involve venturing into the unknown, and that may result in corporate ruin – moves for which the outcomes and probabilities may be only partially known and where hard-to-define goals may not be met.
Figenbaum and Thomas (1986)	Argued that while the market-based measure is important from a "financial markets" perspective, the accounting-based measure (or "total risk") is valuable from a **strategic risk management** perspective.
Miller and Bromiley (1990)	Defined risks in three categories: income stream, stock returns, and **strategic risks**. They measured **strategic risks** as debt-to-equity ratio, capital intensity, and research and development (R&D) intensity.
Rawls and Smithson (1990)	Discussed **management of strategic exposures** facing firms: exposure to changes in foreign exchange rates, interest rates, or commodity prices that affect firm market value – that is the present value of the expected future cash flows.
Miller (1992)	Discussed **strategic moves that can potentially mitigate the risks** associated with uncertainties. Uncertainty means the unpredictability of environmental or organizational variables that impact corporate performance or the inadequacy of information about these variables.
Collins and Ruefli (1992)	Developed a unique ordinal measure of **strategic risk**, as opposed to most other measures that are cardinal.
Clarke and Varma (1999)	Discussed an integrated **strategic risk management** approach that allows companies to consistently deliver superior performance while proactively managing risks. Risk management is a strategic business process, but is often treated tactically and piecemeal.
Chatterjee, Lubatkin, Lyon, and Schulze (1999)	Discussed three types of risk: tactical, normative, and strategic risk. **Tactical risk** is rooted primarily in information asymmetries, **strategic risk** in imperfections in the resource and output markets, and **normative risk** in the forces that underlie institutional norms.
Roberts, Wallace, and McClure (2003)	**Strategic risk management** identifies, monitors, and manages the risk profile of the organization. **Strategic risk** relates to risk at the corporate level, and it affects the development and implementation of an organization's strategy.
Lam (2003), p. 229	**Business risk** is the risk of adopting the wrong business strategy, or failing to execute the right strategy.

(Continued)

Table 8.1 Continued

Committee of European Banking Supervisors (2004)	**Strategic risk** is the current or prospective risk to earnings and capital arising from changes in the business environment and from adverse business decisions, improper implementation of decisions, or lack of responsiveness to changes in the business environment.
Slywotzsky and Drzik (2005)	**Strategic risk** is the array of external events and trends that can devastate a company's growth trajectory and shareholder value.
Chapman (2006), pp. 224–225.	**Strategy risk** is risk associated with the initial strategy selection, execution, or modification over time, resulting in a lack of achievement of overall objectives.
Sehn (2006)	**Strategic risk management** is a process designed to keep both the risks associated with doing business and the costs to a minimum. Strategic risk management is a planning and management tool to minimize the cost of risk and the cost of doing business.
Crouhy, Galai, and Mark (2006), pp. 32–33	**Strategic risk** refers to the risk of significant investments for which there is high uncertainty about success and profitability.
Standard and Poor's (2007)	**Strategic risk management** is the process that an insurer uses to incorporate the ideas of risk, risk management, and return for risk into the corporate strategic decision-making processes. Risk capital is usually a key concept in these processes. Standard & Poor's analysis of SRM starts with understanding the risk profile of the insurer and getting management to explain the reasons for recent changes in the risk profile and the changes it expects to make in future.
Hampton (2009), pp. 127–129	**Strategic risk** is the positive or negative impact of risk on an organization. **Strategic risk management** encompasses all activities intended to identify risks, solve problems, adapt to change, and successfully execute plans. It includes goals and strategies, resources, organizational structure, capabilities of people, systems, and risk identification.
Andersen and Schroder (2010), p. 77	**Strategic risk** factors may include major competitor moves, product innovations, process improvements, new business designs, and technology leaps, all which constitute exposures that can be difficult to identify in advance and hard to quantify. The main focus of ERM has been on downside exposures (hazard, financial, and operational). The inclusion of strategic risk management has added a focus on opportunities.
Fraser and Simkins (2010), p. 510	**Strategic risks** group includes external and internal risk factors. The external factors essentially refer to the likelihood that industry, economy, legal, and regulatory changes and competitors will cause the breakdown of operations or variability in the firm's earnings. The internal factors risk related to the likelihood that the firm's reputation, strategic focus, patent, and trademark types of company-specific risk factors will cause variability in the revenues or net earnings of the firm. **Operational risks** are the cause–effect related pressures on the revenues and net earnings of the firm resulting from the supply-chain discontinuities, customer satisfaction, cycle time, manufacturing processes (process risks); others may be caused by environment, regulations, policy and procedures, and litigations (compliance risks); and yet others may be cause by factors such as human resources, employee turnover, performance incentives, and training factors (people risks).

Economist Intelligence Unit (2010)	**Strategic risks** are those that pose a threat to a company's ability to set and execute its overall strategy.
	Strategic risk management encompasses the interdisciplinary intersection of strategic planning, risk management, and strategy execution in managing risks and seizing opportunities, not only for protection against losses, but for reducing uncertainties and seizing opportunities, thus enabling better performance in achieving the organization's objectives and greater resilience in an uncertain environment.
RIMS (2011)	**Strategic risk management** is a business discipline that drives deliberation and action regarding uncertainties and untapped opportunities that affect an organization's strategy and strategy execution.
Segal (2011), pp. 117–118	**Strategic risks** are a category of risks related to unexpected changes in key elements of strategy formulation or execution. This is highly variable by company and must be customized.
Frigo and Anderson (2011)	**Strategic risk management** is a process for identifying, assessing, and managing risks and uncertainties, affected by internal and external events or scenarios, that could inhibit an organization's ability to achieve its strategy and strategic objectives with the ultimate goal of creating and protecting shareholder and stakeholder value. It is a primary component and necessary foundation of enterprise risk management.
Kaplan and Mikes (2012)	There are three categories of risk:
	Strategy risks are risks taken for superior strategic return.
	Preventable risks arise from within the organization, are controllable, and ought to be eliminated or avoided.
	External risks arise from events outside the company and are beyond its influence or control.
Tonello (2012)	**Strategic risks** are those risks that are most consequential to the organization's ability to execute its strategies and achieve its business objectives. These are the risk exposures that can ultimately affect shareholder value or the viability of the organization.
	Strategic risk management is the process of identifying, assessing and managing the risk in the organization's business strategy – including taking swift action when risk is actually realized. Strategic risk management is an area that merits the time and attention of executive management and the board of directors.
Mohammed and Sykes (2013)	**Strategic risks** can be defined as the uncertainties and untapped opportunities embedded in your strategic intent and how well they are executed. As such, they are key matters for the board and impinge on the whole business, rather than just an isolated unit.
	Strategic risk management is your organization's response to these uncertainties and opportunities. It involves a clear understanding of corporate strategy, the risks in adopting it and the risks in executing it.
AICPCU (2013)	There are four risk categories:
	Strategic risks arise from trends in the economy and society, including changes in the economic, political, and competitive environments, as well as from demographic shifts.
	Operational risk arises from people, processes, and controls.
	Financial risk arises from the effect of market forces on financial assets or liabilities.

(Continued)

Table 8.1 Continued

	Hazard risk arises from property, liability, or personnel loss exposures. **Strategic risk management** is not intended to be an alternative to ERM, but to provide a higher-level perspective for the organization's leaders.
Deloitte (2013a)	There are four types of risk: **Strategic risks** are risks that affect or are created by an organization's business strategy and strategic objectives. **Operational risks** are major risks that affect an organization's ability to execute its strategic plan. **Financial risks** include areas such as financial reporting, valuation, market, liquidity, and credit risks. **Compliance risks** relate to legal and regulatory compliance.
Deloitte (2013b)	**Strategic risks** are risks that have a major effect on a company's business strategy decisions, or are created by those decisions. So they tend to have a larger and more widespread impact than the other types of risk that businesses have traditionally focused on, in areas such as operations, finance, and compliance.
Standard and Poor's (2013)	**Strategic risk management** is the process through which insurers facilitate the optimization of risk-adjusted returns, starting with a view of the required risk capital and a well-defined process for allocating capital among different products, lines of business, and risk factors. **The strategic risk management** subfactor assesses the insurer's program to optimize risk-adjusted returns and to evaluate and prioritize strategic options on a level playing field.
Andersen, Garvey, and Roggi (2014), pp. 24, 51	**Strategic risk management** is an extension of the ERM concept and a way to emphasize the importance of managing operational and strategic risk factors to achieve longer-term corporate objectives. The SRM approach is involved in identifying, measuring, and handling both pure and financial risks, but also takes a special interest in speculative strategic risks with particular concerns for proactive risk-taking initiatives. **Strategic risks** are characterized by high uncertainty and predictability for which there is little concrete data and include economic risks, competitor risks, political risks, social trends, new technologies, and innovations.
Louisot and Ketcham (2014), p. 105	**Strategic risks** are risks that impact the organization's ability to achieve its broader goals and objectives, such as risks to market position or reputation, or the risk that a business plan to which major resources and effort are committed will ultimately not be successful due to lack of acceptance in the market place. **Strategic risk** is sometimes referred to as the risk associated with "doing the right thing." **Strategic risk management** is a critical component ultimately driving enterprise risk management. **Strategic risk** is associated with adopting or not adopting the correct strategy for the organization in the first place, or once adopting, not adapting the chosen strategy in response to competition or other forces. **Strategic risk management** contemplates the integration of strategic planning, the setting of organizational objectives and the identification of "risk" with the organization's enterprise risk management program.

The AICPCU argues that strategic risk derives from trends in the economy and society including changes in economic, political, and competitive conditions and demographic shifts (AICPCU, 2013). Similarly, Slywotzky and Drzik (2005) define strategic risks as the array of external events and trends that can devastate a company's growth trajectory and shareholder value. Slywotzky and Drzik (2005) identify seven major classes of strategic risk including industry, technology, brand, competitor, customer, project, and stagnation, and suggest counter-measures for each class of risk. In a similar fashion, Andersen and Schroder (2010) list several risk factors related to strategic risks: competitor moves, new regulations, political events, social changes, changing tastes, and new technologies.

These three definitions emphasize strategic risk as stemming from external factors. This creates two specific problems. First, internal factors can offer strategic risks just as well as external factors. Consider, for example, a drug company. Developing a new drug is clearly an internal issue, but a failure to foresee adverse side effects is a strategic risk in that it could bankrupt the company. Likewise, manufacturing a drug is an internal issue, but a serious quality failure is a strategic risk. In the banking industry, subprime lenders' internal policy decisions to issue 100% loan-to-value mortgages to high-risk individuals resulted in the bankruptcy of many such lenders.

Second, identifying trends in external factors as a source of strategic risks, as the AICPCU and Slywotzky and Drzik (2005) definitions do, is also problematic. While trends that management has not identified could pose risks, for well-informed managers, predictable known trends should pose little risk. It is the deviations from known trends that pose risks. That the baby boom generation is nearing retirement in the US, for example, is not a risk but rather a completely predictable pattern that may have positive or negative impacts on firms.

Another set of definitions emphasizes strategic in terms of achieving corporate objectives. Frigo and Anderson's (2011) definition of SRM as a process for identifying, assessing, and managing risks and uncertainties, affected by internal and external events or scenarios, that could inhibit an organization's ability to achieve its strategy and strategic objectives with the ultimate goal of creating and protecting shareholder and stakeholder value, overcomes the problems that stem from defining strategic risks solely in terms of external factors. By adding goals to create and protect shareholder and stakeholder value to the definition, however, Frigo and Anderson (2011) create a new problem: that of assuming that the corporate goal is one of creating both shareholder and stakeholder value, when in reality, a massive debate exists over possible conflicts between shareholder and stakeholder value.

Paralleling Frigo and Anderson's (2011) theme of creating value, the Risk and Insurance Management Society (RIMS), a professional association and standard-setting body, defines SRM as a business discipline that drives deliberation and action regarding uncertainties and untapped opportunities that affect an organization's strategy and strategy execution (RIMS, 2011). The RIMS definition thus explicitly includes identification of opportunities whereas the others emphasize the traditional view of risk as something that hurts performance.

Kaplan and Mikes (2012) identify three types of risks: preventable, external, and strategy. Preventable risks and external risks are downside risks. Preventable risks are internal risks that the firm should eliminate cost effectively, typically using rules-based, internal audit methods. External risks (for example political risks and natural disasters) are not preventable; hence, the company should mitigate their impact, for example with lobbying and business continuity plans or by transferring the risks using insurance. Strategy risks, in contrast to preventable and external risks, are risks that the company consciously takes on with the goal of increasing firm value.

Defining strategic risks as those the firm chooses to take on to increase firm value creates two problems. First, it makes a strategic risk depend on the firm's thinking around undertaking that risk. The firm that blithely does something without considering a potential problem does not face a strategic risk from that problem, while the firm that carefully considers a potential problem does. A firm that takes a given action to increase value has a strategic risk, whereas another firm that does the same thing in the same circumstances with a different motive does not. Making what is a strategic risk dependent on firm motivation seems undesirable. Furthermore, many would assume that all risks the firm takes on are taken on consciously with the hope the risk will help the firm achieve its goals; this would make all risks strategic.

Second, the "take on to increase firm value" approach makes the definition of strategic risks dependent on the company's reference point and intent. A firm intending to grow could define an external factor as risky while a firm trying to maintain the status quo might not. Paralleling the "it's not a defect, it's a feature" logic, this might be fine, but it dramatically complicates the situation. What happens when a growth firm looks at the risk and, upon assuming it cannot grow, decides to revise its objectives? Has it eliminated the risk? This creates the potential for circularity, or what researchers refer to as the endogeneity problem. Clarke and Varma's (1999) definition of SRM illustrates this problem. Clarke and Varma (1999) define SRM as an integrated risk management approach that allows companies to deliver consistently superior performance while proactively managing risks. This definition includes the desired output of SRM (consistently superior performance) as part of its definition. This is problematic because if a firm takes a given set of actions and succeeds it is SRM, but if it takes the same actions and it fails it is not.

Furthermore, the common usage of "strategic" depends to a substantial extent on the importance of the decision to the entity. For example, managers in an extremely large bank like Bank of America or Wells Fargo would not consider buying a small bank strategic. These large banks routinely purchase small banks to acquire their facilities and customer bases. However, these large banks would see acquiring another very large bank as strategic. Likewise, management might not view the launch of a single product line extension as strategic, but would consider the launch of some major new products strategic. If management does not see a given decision as strategic, it seems hard to classify the risk associated with that decision as strategic and vice versa.

A strategic management approach to defining strategic risks

An alternative approach, more consistent with usage in strategic management, would see strategic as connoting important or key decisions of all types (Nutt and Wilson, 2010). Strategic decisions have the following characteristics: they are

> elusive problems that are difficult to define precisely; require an understanding of the problem to find a viable solution; rarely have one best solution, but often a series of possible solutions; questions about trade-offs and priorities appear in the solutions; solution benefits are difficult to assess as to their effectiveness, in part because they lack a clear final end point against which effectiveness can be judged; other problems in the organization are connected to solutions for a focal problem; high levels of ambiguity and uncertainty are associated with solutions; realizing hoped for benefits has considerable risk; strategic decisions have competing interests that prompt key players to use political pressure to ensure that a choice aligns with their preferences.
>
> *(Nutt and Wilson, 2010, p. 4)*

Strategic decisions differ from other decisions in that "once implemented, a strategic decision stipulates premises that guide the operational decisions that follow" (Nutt and Wilson, 2010, p. 4). Often, the highest level of management makes strategic decisions. In this approach, strategic aligns with the responsibilities normally ascribed to top management and boards of directors. Strategic risk then means the risk associated with factors that the company considers strategic.

Strategic risks defined in this fashion would include both the risks inherent in the company's strategic decisions and the macro structural decisions that determine internal risk-taking. Whether one acquires another company or enters a new market falls in the first portion of the definition, namely, "the risks inherent in the company's strategic decisions." The parameters and structure under which one manages the rest of the firm's risk fall into the second. These parameters and structure set the stage for subsequent decisions; they determine and constrain the kinds of operational decisions (and their attendant risks) that organizational members would make while implementing the strategic decision.

While not part of the definition, a fundamental question underpins the earlier definition of strategic risk and indeed, any discussion of risk management in general. Does the firm manage the risk because the risk per se is an issue or because the risk defined in terms of negative potential outcomes can influence expected value? For strategic risks, the answer is that we care about risks because a bad outcome in this domain could have major implications for the continuing existence or prosperity of the company. Strategic risks can result from a single major decision or a set of policies that lead the firm to take a number of inappropriate small risks. This contrasts with operational risk management decisions where we are not concerned with the risk per se, but rather with the impact of the risk on the expected return level. A banking example may illustrate the difference.

Consider a retail bank. Whether the bank makes a significant acquisition, begins trading derivatives, or starts making consumer loans are clearly strategic choices. The other portion of the bank's risk comes from the interaction of policies, procedures, and criteria that determine how the bank engages in derivatives trading or what specific loans the bank makes. The composition of a bank's entire lending portfolio, for example, is an SRM problem; an excessively risky or undiversified portfolio can lead the bank into bankruptcy. At the same time, a bank with a policy of not verifying borrowers' credit histories or addresses before issuing a loan *and* with a policy of making the loan process as easy for customers as possible would face a strategic risk because the interaction of these two policies strongly influences the loans the bank makes and its consequent loan portfolio.

The bank's operational risk management problem, in contrast, comes in what loans to reject and what prices to offer potential borrowers of given risk levels. Here, the bank is not directly concerned with the negative consequences of a given loan. The problem is to appropriately price and select loans to achieve an appropriate expected return. Unlike strategic risks, the bank should not be concerned with risk per se, but rather should focus on the expected value. Thus, for an appropriately high interest rate, loans to individuals who have a relatively high probability of default can be profitable. At the same time, individuals may have very low default probability but may command such a low interest rate that lending to them is not profitable. Thus, at the operational level, the bank should be concerned largely with expected value of each loan, but at the firm or strategic level, the bank should be concerned with the possibility that either a single big loan or the portfolio of loans, and the set of policies or criteria the bank will use to make loans, will damage the organization significantly.

This approach of defining strategic risk as the risks inherent in a company's strategic decisions and in the macro structural decisions that determine internal risk-taking makes the definition of strategic risk dependent on the usage within a given company. From a research standpoint, this creates problems. Specifically, how can we differentiate between strategic and nonstrategic risks? Potentially, could any type of risk be a strategic risk? One answer would be no: if every risk is strategic, then nothing is. Power (2004) argues that the proliferation of risk management techniques to encompass a multitude of decisions (termed the "risk management of everything") has a detrimental effect. The "risk management of everything" may extend the risk management logic from areas in which it works effectively to areas in which we have no idea whether it works effectively. Researchers in strategic management have dealt with this problem of differentiating strategic decisions from others by studying decisions that appear to be strategic for most corporations – mergers, divestitures, corporate outlays on R&D or capital expenditures, and so forth. This set of decisions will probably be smaller than the set of decisions any specific company sees as strategic.

While definitions can have better and less functional features, they remain essentially arbitrary. By taking a strategic management perspective to examine SRM, we lean toward a strategic management approach that views strategic risk as risk associated with factors that the company would consider strategic. Organizations already have made some allocation of decision responsibility to the top for what is often termed strategy or strategic decisions. To define strategic risk such that strategic risks do not generally apply to strategic decisions opens immense opportunities for confusion.

This also aligns with a legal allocation responsibility to top management and boards. Top management and the board have responsibility for the major strategic choices of the company. When it comes to risk, they have a responsibility to assess or make sure someone assesses appropriately the risks of their decisions and that they consider such assessments. They also have responsibility for the aggregate supervision of risk management processes and controls in their companies. US corporate law assigns these responsibilities to top management and corporate boards.

Both corporate practice and law define certain activities as strategic and demanding of attention from top management and the board of directors. To define strategic risk as risk associated with such activities (including major systems choices), simply aligns usage with prior usage of strategic rather than developing a new definition of strategic in strategic risk that differs from usage of strategic elsewhere in management. Any definition of strategic risk that does not align with the risk of strategic choices seems destined to create confusion.

How does SRM relate to ERM?

We next turn to the relation between SRM and ERM. Understanding this relation requires an understanding of the history of ERM. ERM evolved from traditional risk management (TRM) (Bromiley et al., 2014; Nair, Rustambekov, McShane, and Fainshmidt 2014). TRM was originally insurance management for hazard risks and operational actions related to safety issues. Vestiges of the "insurance and risk management" approach continue to appear in the names for educational programs, organizational units, and journals. Following the development of the options pricing model in the early 1970s, TRM expanded to involve financial risk management, which, however, developed in a separate silo from managing hazards.

In the late 1990s, the concept of ERM arose from TRM. Two main features distinguished ERM from TRM. First, in ERM, the firm should manage all risks – not just hazard and financial risks, but also operational and strategic risks. Second, the firm should see these risks as portfolios spanning functional or organizational divisions, not silos where different groups independently handle different risks. Under ERM, the management of "all" risks inherently includes strategic risks, consolidated across functions and organizational units, and leaning towards risk management at the strategic level of the organization. ERM rhetoric has implicitly, and often explicitly, included managing strategic risks as part of ERM.

Several authors have taken this view. Louisot and Ketcham (2014), for example, criticizes efforts to establish SRM as a new discipline as unnecessary and deriving from ERM implementations not living up to the ERM philosophy of managing all risks in a portfolio. Skipper and

Kwon (2008) describes risk management as an evolution that starts with hazard risk management, then adds some operations risk management (such as safety training), then financial risk, and finally reaches full integration with the addition of strategic risk. Bromiley et al. (2014) list more than 20 definitions/descriptions of ERM found in both the academic and practitioner literatures between 1995 and 2011. Most of the definitions/descriptions indicate that ERM should manage all risks, and some of the more recent ones imply a close relation between ERM and the achievement of strategic objectives. We could thus view SRM as part of the next generation of ERM (ERM 2.0) that has reached its conceptual potential to include strategic risks. Indeed, one could argue that ERM cannot be "enterprise" risk management if it ignores the risks that could influence the entire organization (or enterprise).

This then raises the question of why some have promoted SRM as a discipline separate from ERM. Part of the answer may lie in turf battles among different risk management silos in both the corporate and academic worlds. The rise of ERM has increased the power of whatever function controls ERM. In many companies, internal audit oversees the ERM process, although a chief risk officer (CRO), typically reporting to the CFO or CEO, often has overall responsibility. Many companies have not assigned responsibility for SRM to any specific group. Consequently, SRM could change the power relations within organizations. It also could generate a substantial amount of consulting as organizations that implemented ERM now need to pay consultants to help them implement SRM. In the academic world, silos have remained intact even as research on ERM demands cross-disciplinary collaboration.

The appearance of SRM as separate from ERM also reflects that ERM research and practice have been slow to include strategic risks. Indeed, the main purpose of Bromiley et al. (2014) was to stimulate ERM research by management scholars on these types of risk for which other disciplines are not suited. Given the difficulties in defining and identifying strategic risks that we discussed earlier, however, the question comes up as to why we should bother or care to delineate SRM as a part of ERM. There are both several explanations for this and reasons why it may be desirable. We examine these in the next section.

Why bother with SRM?

The categorization of risks into categories such as strategic, financial, operational, and so forth has both potential benefits and drawbacks. On the upside, risk categories are useful for grouping risks to determine processes and responsibilities. At an individual level, sorting risks into broad categories or groups overcomes some of the time and attention-related constraints facing managers (Cyert and March, 1963) by directing managers' attention towards certain types of risk and helping them decide what to do about these risks (Damodaran, 2008). Grouping coincides with specialization that allows greater expertise; the skills necessary to manage factory safety and related insurance issues differ greatly from the skills necessary to manage currency exchange and other financial transactions. At the senior levels of the firm, sorting risks into categories can free a board to focus on broader strategy issues facing the firm instead of focusing on the risks facing each individual division (Protiviti, 2014).

At the organizational level, grouping risks helps assign responsibility and allocate resources for managing these risks. The expertise benefits noted earlier mean that risk categories could lead to more accurate budgeting and reporting. Further, the risks differ fundamentally across many different categories of risks; financial risks, for example, are distinctly different from operational risks for many firms. Bundling disparate risks together (rather than treating them as belonging to distinct categories) can create analytical confusion over what tools or frameworks to apply and what benchmarks to use to evaluate the extent to which it has mitigated each type of risk.

On the downside, risk categories may constrain managerial thinking about risk and encourage the treatment of risk in silos. This, in turn, may prevent the organization from identifying a common cause underlying different types of risk, or the interactions among different types of risk (Bharathy and McShane, 2014). Organizations that use risk categories as a means of risk identification may also neglect important sources of risk. Furthermore, the portfolio benefits from ERM require the aggregation of risks across categories.

Practically, whether risk categorizations help or hinder the ERM prescription that organizations treat risks as a portfolio remains problematic. While the benefits of aggregating risks are unquestionable, it is hard to treat risks as a portfolio in the financial sense when different systems define and attempt to manage different kinds of risks. Portfolio treatment assumes a common metric for risk and understanding of correlations among risks. Let us examine why it may be difficult to achieve these. Think about how firms evaluate risks, and more specifically, the extent to which conventional risk management tools apply in particular domains. To apply conventional risk management tools, we need good estimates of the probabilities of potential outcomes. Often, this means we have to deal with domains in which we have substantial experience. To the extent that certain groups have been lent to historically, the retail bank we discussed earlier can draw on long histories of lending experience (both its own and that of other organizations) in assessing the risk of lending to particular groups. In contrast, for some strategic and operational categories we cannot apply conventional risk management tools because we cannot estimate variances or covariances. This was part of the problem in the subprime debacle. Because no one had ever loaned to this particular category of borrower under these terms, history did not provide appropriate data on which to assess the long-term risk of such loans.

While data problems are generally more challenging for strategic than operational risks, often objective data does not exist for operational risk management either. In many organizations, managers assess operational risks on scales of 1 to 5 because management cannot see how to assess real probabilities at reasonable cost. The available data clearly depend on a variety of factors, both externally and internally determined. The lower the probability of an event, the more data we need to estimate the probability accurately, but risk management usually tries to lower the frequency of negative events.

Now consider how most organizations evaluate strategic risks. As we noted earlier, conventional risk management tools often do not apply to these kinds of risks because of difficulties related to data collection. As a substitute, organizations usually rely on qualitative methods (e.g., scoring methods where managers rate the likelihood and impact of various risks) to estimate these risks. We know of no validated techniques for the analysis of a portfolio that combines quantitative and qualitative risk estimations. Lacking such validated tools, portfolio-based decisions could be worse than traditional practices. Hubbard (2009), in fact, goes further and terms qualitative risk assessments "worse than useless" because individuals interpret qualitative descriptions differently resulting in inconsistent use of scales. Even if we mitigate this concern by carefully standardizing the meaning of the descriptions and ensuring that the users understand the scales, we still face the fundamental problem that we lack validated tools to estimate the risk of a portfolio based on a combination of qualitative and quantitative risk assessments.

Even in the rare instances where historical data on strategic risks exists, strategic decisions often differ within categories such that historical averages may not be very helpful. This appears, for instance, in the literature on acquisitions where the average return from acquiring another company may be slightly negative, but almost half the companies have positive returns from acquisitions.

A further complication comes from the ERM idea that a firm should think of risks it can handle efficiently as a potential source of value. We noted the difficulties of analyzing portfolios where we only have qualitative risk assessments on some of the risks. The potential for gains from risk management further complicates the analysis. As a practical matter, it is unclear how many companies are ready to manage coherently enterprise risk that incorporates both concern for downside risks and exploitation of risk-based opportunities.

Often, assessing and evaluating strategic risks rests on managerial judgment. However, there are good reasons to question managerial judgment in risk assessment. People have enormous difficulty learning to assess and deal effectively with risky events. An entire division of psychology termed behavioral decision theory is devoted to how people deviate from the prescriptive models in handling uncertainty and risk. This does not mean people cannot be trained to some extent to assess risk better, but that training will be domain specific. For example, meteorologists may be reasonably well calibrated so that when they say a 50% chance of rain, it on average rains half the time (Sjörberg, 1979). This does not mean, however, that meteorologists are any better at assessing other forms of risk than anyone else. Likewise, someone could be good at handicapping horses at the track, but not necessarily good at handling other kinds of risk.

People have difficulty learning to assess risks accurately. To learn to do something effectively, it helps to do it, see the outcome, and repeat, but in learning to assess risk this often does not suffice. Meteorologists do not learn strictly by trial and error, but rather learn scoring rules and other research-based shortcuts to improve prediction. Managers face many situations even if they wanted to do the analysis; the situations themselves do not structure the data and the world in a way that would enhance or facilitate learning.

For example, take something as simple as a bank making loans to companies. The individual loan officer makes a loan. In assessing the borrower's risk, the bank cares whether some modest or not so modest proportion of the loans goes bad over the next 5 years. For example, with a low risk assessment, a 2% failure might be a good outcome and a 10% failure a very bad outcome. Often, however, loan officers' risk assessments suffer from systematic biases (McNamara and Bromiley, 1997, 1999). Ideally, the loan officer would learn the association of borrower characteristics with differences in actual probabilities, but many organizations do not even systematically feed back outcomes to those who make probabilistic assessments. For example, lenders who make loans do not necessarily know what happened to those loans 2, 3, 4, and 5 years later. Even if they do have the data, unless the loan officer undertakes systematic statistical analyses, the loan officer is unlikely to be able to learn the relations between specific levels of borrower characteristics and specific loan default probabilities. The immense majority of lenders do not even know the statistical techniques necessary to estimate such relations. Even more generally, we suspect many ERM implementations do not systematically analyze the accuracy of risk assessments.

When the choice is not random (and we hope our bank is not lending completely randomly), assessing the impact of a choice on an outcome presents significant statistical problems. Indeed, a rapidly developing area of econometrics and statistics is devoted to developing tools to analyze the impact of treatments when the treatments are not randomly applied (see, for instance, Stata, 2013). Where we want to understand the impact of an action on an outcome and the action is not random, naïve analyses of data can be terribly misleading.

Consider now the issues associated with estimating strategic risks, whether assessing the probabilities associated with outcomes of specific major choices (e.g., an acquisition or new product launch) or assessing the probabilities associated with outcomes of internal control choices (e.g., level of flexibility given to division managers allocating resources). Here the problem is much worse than for our lender. A given individual only observes a very small set of comparable choices, and in many cases only one. Very few managers see a statistically viable sample of acquisitions. Likewise, they see a very limited set of internal control choices and almost never observe what would have happened if they made different choices. In such situations, there is no reason to believe that the individual will become skilled at assessing the probabilities of different outcomes given specific choices.

Some might argue that firms select managers on their ability to assess and manage risk so we can assume they can do so effectively. However, few if any firms actually have managers stipulate risk assessments, and use a comparison of outcomes to such assessments in judging managers. In many companies for many important decisions, managers do not even write down risk assessments. Many firms punish managers who take risks that turn out badly, but this is very different from judging whether the managers can assess a range of risk probabilities accurately.

To summarize, we have argued that the primary distinction between strategic and other risks is that that strategic risks deal with strategic issues. We also note that strategic risks generally imply risks large enough that the firm should care about the risk per se whereas for operational risks the focus should be on expected values. Furthermore, the firm seldom has good data on which to assess strategic risks. Whether managing strategic risk in an ERM framework will benefit firms remains an open empirical question. In the next section, we expand on why SRM may be valuable to firms, and how long it may provide value.

Will the value of SRM and ERM diminish over time?

A strategic view of SRM raises the question whether it can provide competitive advantage. Strategy scholars concern themselves with whether a given set of activities will help the firm perform better than its competitors and whether that better performance is fleeting or sustainable.

The resource-based view (RBV) of the firm presents a popular approach in strategic management to explain how firms create value and generate sustained competitive advantage (Barney, 1986; Peteraf, 1993). In essence, the RBV proposes that only rare, valuable, and hard-to-imitate and substitute resources or capabilities can give firms persistent competitive advantage.

SRM and ERM are capabilities that may protect and create value by allowing firms to improve performance by reducing the negative impact of unanticipated events, as well as anticipating how changes in environmental or internal conditions could create opportunities for value creation that other firms may miss. However, as more firms begin to use SRM, it will no longer be particularly rare. The standardization of SRM in the form of steps or processes outlined by consultants or organizations (such as RIMS) may mean that SRM should not even be particularly hard to imitate. In this case, will SRM still create value?

To answer this question, we turn to some recent research on firm practices. Based on a vast quantity of empirical evidence from a variety of management fields, Bromiley and Rau (2014) argue that even publicly available practices can create value for firms. RBV assumes that the majority of firms in an industry show "normal" returns, with a few firms showing above-normal returns; the presence of rare or valuable resources within these firms explains their above normal performance. Even a cursory examination of the distribution of returns in most industries, however, reveals a wide distribution of returns. Many firms perform below average, some close to average, and a few show truly superior performance. Bromiley and Rau (2014) suggest that firms that perform below or slightly above average can improve their performance if they adopt practices that have created value in other firms – in this case, SRM.

Before we turn to assessing the actual value creation potential and outlook for SRM, perhaps the first question we need to ask is whether the broader practice of ERM as practiced actually delivers. Schrand and Unal (1998) and McShane, Zhang, and Cox (2012), for example, find evidence of risk allocation by banks and insurance companies where these institutions appear to transfer risks in which they have no comparative information advantage so that they can take on more risk in areas where they do have an advantage or core competence. However, the academic literature on ERM is not chockablock with studies showing that ERM per se reduces risk, let alone improves financial performance.[1]

It may seem obvious that using ERM to manage risk will result in better risk management and better corporate performance, but it is not that simple. First, a firm that really cares about controlling risk might reduce the firm's risk level regardless of the techniques it uses. Put differently, the desire to reduce risk might result in firms adopting ERM and reducing risk even if ERM had no impact on risk whatsoever. Second, ERM is not free. ERM usually requires significant amounts of management time (often taken from other duties) and the real costs may be much greater than the dollar cost of management time. Whether ERM benefits the company overall depends on the relative impact of the improvement in risk management versus the potential damage of having less management time paid to other concerns like operations.

The literature on safety raises an even more troubling possibility. Some academics on safety claim that making cars safer simply results in drivers driving more dangerously. These academics argue that drivers want a particular level of risk, and if improvements in the car or the road remove that risk, they will drive in a more risky manner to compensate. In a corporate setting, would a top management that believed it had excellent internal risk management processes take more strategic risk than one less confident in its internal risk management? Would those risks on average have positive expected value? We do not have evidence for these inherently empirical questions. In the end, we simply do not have a substantial literature demonstrating that ERM (let alone SRM) as practiced in most companies has the desired impact. Clearly, this is an important area for future research.

Even if we assume that ERM and SRM could positively affect a company, the extent to which a firm realizes these benefits may vary for a few reasons. While many organizations have offered guidance on implementing ERM, there remains enormous variation in how firms actually implement ERM. However, the problem is not just standardizing ERM (and by extension SRM), but whether we can standardize them on extremely desirable models – and whether firms can implement these models correctly and consistently.

The example of total quality management (TQM) is instructive. TQM is risk reduction. Measuring quality as the inverse of error rates meant high quality equals low risk. Probability of errors is just another risk measure. Thus, in one sense, operational risk management is like TQM in that it tries to reduce operational probabilities of errors/failures.

TQM was extremely popular in the late 20th century. While many firms that used TQM did find an increase in the level of product quality across many product categories (Hendricks and Singhal, 1997), many other firms that did TQM didn't see a significant improvement in performance and often quit using it (Staw and Epstein, 2000). Whether this is because they did not do it long enough or they did not do it for long because it was not working is unclear (Hendricks and Singhal, 1999).

Even whether a firm can estimate the risk impact of ERM or SRM is questionable. To assess the risk impact of ERM or SRM, we need to estimate the difference in riskiness of outcomes with and without ERM/SRM. In addition to the statistical problems noted earlier, at the corporate level we often are concerned with relatively low probability events like financial distress during a recession. Historically, the frequency of recessions is less than every 10 years. Assessing a probabilistic outcome generally requires more than one or two relevant observations. Few managers will see any assessment that takes 10 years or more as timely or relevant.

We should also worry that, like TQM, SRM and ERM may be fads. With a fad, large numbers of firms adopt the practice, but many drop it when it fails to produce obvious, immediate results. Those that do persist are likely to have seriously implemented the practice and developed skills in its use. In the persisting population, ERM and SRM may become more technical (and therefore less susceptible to the opinions of generalists), improving their contributions to firm performance (David and Strang, 2006).

Even firms that adopt an extremely desirable model of SRM (and implement it both correctly and consistently) may find that SRM does not create value. Consider, for example, the effects of organizational characteristics – in particular, organizational structure – on the outcomes of a practice. A central idea in Andersen and Schroder (2010) is that the management of strategic risks needs a different organizational structure than that required for managing hazard, financial and operational risks. Specifically, SRM needs central risk monitoring at the senior manager level to understand interdependencies between risks. At the same time, SRM also needs a dispersed awareness of risks at all levels of the organization. Dispersed awareness allows employees at the middle and lower levels of the organization to monitor risks and feed that information back up to the higher levels of the organization, thereby enabling senior managers to become aware of trends and emerging risks and opportunities. Dispersed awareness of risks can best be achieved with a loosely coupled, decentralized structure. Overall, therefore, SRM requires an ambidextrous structure, combining central risk monitoring with decentralization. Effective management of nonstrategic risks, on the other hand, requires a more centralized and uniform structure (in the form of internal control, accounting systems, etc.). An organization with an existing ERM system that would like to implement SRM cannot do so just by introducing new SRM related routines; it also has to change its structure simultaneously, from a centralized one to an ambidextrous one. Given the notorious difficulty of this latter task, an organization that attempts to add SRM to its existing ERM system without a corresponding change in structure may find that, ironically, the very presence of ERM limits the value the firm will obtain from the adoption of SRM.

Conclusion

In this article, we proposed a definition of SRM and examined its relation to ERM. We see the practice of SRM as having the potential to contribute to the field of ERM and to create value for firms. At the same time, however, we see the need for substantial advances both in research and practice before SRM can achieve its potential.

Note

1   For a review of the mixed findings on the relation between ERM and firm performance, see McShane, Nair, and Rustambekov (2011) and Eckles, Hoyt, and Miller (2014).

References

AICPCU. 2013. *Enterprise Risk Management*. Edited by Michael W. Elliott. Malvern, PA: The Institutes.

Andersen, T.J., Garvey, M., & Roggi, O. 2014. *Managing Risk and Opportunity: The Governance of Strategic Risk-Taking*. Oxford: Oxford University Press.

Andersen, T.J., & Schroder, P.W. 2010. *Strategic Risk Management Practice: How to Deal with Major Corporate Exposures*. Cambridge: Cambridge University Press.

Baird, I.S., & Thomas, H. 1985. Toward a contingency model of strategic risk taking. *Academy of Management Review*, 10(2): 230–243.

Barney, J. B. (1986). Strategic factor markets: Expectations, luck, and business strategy. *Management science*, 32(10): 1231–1241.

Bharathy, G., & McShane, M. 2014. Applying a systems model to enterprise risk management. *Engineering Management Journal*, 26(4), 38–46.

Bromiley, P., McShane, M., Nair, A., & Rustambekov, E. 2014. Enterprise risk management: Review, critique and research directions. *Long Range Planning*, forthcoming.

Bromiley, P., & Rau, D. 2014. Towards a practice based view of strategy. *Strategic Management Journal*, 35(8): 1249–1256.

Chapman, R.J. 2006. *Simple Tools and Techniques for Enterprise Risk Management*. West Sussex: Wiley.

Chatterjee, S., Lubatkin, M.H., Lyon, E.M., & Schulze, W.S. 1999. Toward a strategic theory of risk premium: Moving beyond CAPM. *Academy of Management Review*, 24(3): 556–567.

Clarke, C.J., & Varma, S. 1999. Strategic risk management: The new competitive edge. *Long Range Planning*, 32(4): 414–424.

Collins, J., & Ruefli, T. 1992. Strategic risk: An ordinal approach. *Management Science*, 38(12): 1707–1730.

Committee of European Banking Supervisors. 2004. *The Application of the Supervisory Review Process under Pillar 2 (CP03)*. Accessed September 11, 2014, at https://www.eba.europa.eu/cebs-archive/publications/consultations/2004/cp03

Crouhy, M., Galai, D., & Mark, R. 2006. *The Essentials of Risk Management*. New York: McGraw-Hill.

Cyert, R.M., & March, J.G. 1963. *A Behavioral Theory of the Firm*. Englewood Cliffs, NJ: Prentice Hall.

Damodaran, A. 2008. *Strategic Risk Management: A Framework for Risk Management*. Upper Saddle River, NJ: Wharton School Publishing.

David, R.J., & Strang, D. 2006. When fashion is fleeting: Transitory collective beliefs and the dynamics of TQM consulting. *Academy of Management Journal*, 49(2): 215–233.

Deloitte. 2013a. *Exploring Strategic Risk: 300 Executives around the World Say Their View of Strategic Risk Is Changing*. Accessed September 12, 2014, at http://deloitte.wsj.com/riskandcompliance/files/2013/10/exploring_strategic_risk.pdf

Deloitte. 2013b. *Risk Angles: Five Questions on Strategic Risk*. Accessed September 12, 2014, at http://www.deloitte.com/view/en_US/us/Services/additional-services/governance-risk-compliance/risk-angles/085e42767e642410VgnVCM2000003356f70aRCRD.htm

Eckles, D.L., Hoyt, R.E., & Miller, S.M. 2014. The impact of enterprise risk management on the marginal cost of reducing risk: Evidence from the insurance industry. *Journal of Banking and Finance*, 43: 247–261.

Economist Intelligent Unit. 2010. *Fall Guys: Risk Management in the Front Line*. Accessed September 12, 2014, at https://www.rims.org/resources/ERM/Documents/EIU%20Research%20on%20Strategic%20Risk%20Management%20November%202010.pdfFigenbaum, A., & Thomas, H. 1986. Dynamic and risk measurement perspectives on Bowman's risk-return paradox for strategic management: An empirical study. *Strategic Management Journal*, 7(5): 395–407.

Fraser, J., & Simkins, B.J. 2010. *Enterprise Risk Management: Today's Leading Research and Best Practices for Tomorrow's Executives*. Hoboken, NJ: Wiley.

Frigo, M.L., & Anderson, R.J. 2011. What is strategic risk management? *Strategic Finance*, April. Available at http://www.markfrigo.com/What_is_Strategic_Risk_Management_-_Strategic_Finance_-_April_2011.pdf

Hampton, J.J. 2009. *Fundamentals of Enterprise Risk Management*. New York: AMACON.

Hendricks, K.B., & Singhal, V.R. 1997. Does implementing an effective TQM program actually improve operating performance? Empirical evidence from firms that have won quality awards. *Management Science*, 43(9): 1258–1274.

Hendricks, K.B., & Singhal, V.R. 1999. Don't count TQM out. *Quality Progress*. April, 35–42.

Hubbard, D.W. 2009. *The Failure of Risk Management: Why It's Broken and How to Fix it*. Hoboken, NJ: Wiley.

Jammine, A.P. 1985. *Product Diversification, International Expansion, and Performance: A Study of Strategic Risk Management in U.K. Manufacturing*. Ph.D. dissertation, London Business School: London.

Kaplan, R.S., & Mikes, A. 2012. Managing risks: A new framework. *Harvard Business Review*, 90(6): 48–60.

Lam, J. 2003. *Enterprise Risk Management: From Incentives to Controls*. Hoboken, NJ: Wiley.

Louisot, J.P., & Ketcham, C. 2014. *Enterprise Risk Management: Issues and Cases*. West Sussex: Wiley.

McNamara, G., & Bromiley, P. 1997. Decision-making in an organizational setting: Cognitive and organizational influences on risk assessment in commercial bank lending. *Academy of Management Journal*, 40(5): 1063–1088.

McNamara, G., & Bromiley, P. 1999. Risk and return in organizational decision-making. *Academy of Management Journal*, 42(3): 330–339.

McShane, M., Nair, A., & Rustambekov, E. 2011. Does enterprise risk management increase firm value? *Journal of Accounting, Auditing, and Finance*, 26: 641–658.

McShane, M., Zhang, T., & Cox, L. 2012. Risk allocation across the enterprise: Evidence from the insurance industry. *Journal of Insurance Issues*, 35: 73–99.

Miller, K.D. 1992. A framework for integrated risk management in international business. *Journal of International Business Studies*, 23: 311–331.

Miller, K., & Bromiley, P. 1990. Strategic risk and corporate performance: An analysis of alternative risk measures. *Academy of Management Journal*, 13(4): 756–779.

Mohammed, A., & Sykes, R. 2013. *Sharpening Strategic Risk Management*. PricewaterhouseCoopers. Accessed September 12, 2014, at http://www.pwc.com/gx/en/governance-risk-compliance-consulting-ser vices/resilience/publications/sharpening-strategic-risk-management.jhtml

Nair, A., Rustambekov, E., McShane, M., & Fainshmidt, S. 2014. Enterprise risk management as a dynamic capability. *Managerial and Decision Economics*, 35(8), 555–556.

Nutt, P.C., & Wilson, D.C. 2010. Crucial trends and issues in strategic decision making. In *Handbook of Decision Making* (pp. 3–29). Hoboken, NJ: John Wiley & Sons.

Peteraf, M.A. 1993. The cornerstones of competitive advantage: A resource-based view. *Strategic Management Journal*, 14(3): 179–191.

Power, M. 2004. The risk management of everything. *Journal of Risk Finance*, 5(3): 58–65.

Protiviti. 2014. 10 Lessons in Integrating Risk Management with Strategy. *Bulletin*, 5(7). Accessed August 14, 2014, at http://www.protiviti.com/en-US/Documents/Newsletters/Bulletin/The-Bulleti n-Vol-5-Issue-7-Lessons-Risk-Mgmt-Strategy-Protiviti.pdf

Rawls, S.W., & Smithson, C.W. 1990. Strategic risk management. *Journal of Applied Corporate Finance*, 2(4): 6–18.

RIMS, 2011. *Why Strategic Risk Management?* RIMS white paper. Accessed August 12, 2014, at http:// www.rims.org/resources/ERM/Documents/FAQ%20on%20SRM%20and%20ERM%20FINAL%20 April%2020%202011.pdf

Roberts, A., Wallace, W., & McClure, N. 2003. *Strategic Risk Management*. Edinburgh Business School, Edinburgh. Accessed September 11, 2014, at http://www.ebsglobal.net/documents/course-tasters/english/ pdf/h17rk-bk-taster.pdf

Schrand, C., & Unal, H. 1998. Hedging and coordinated risk management: Evidence from thrift conversions. *Journal of Finance*, 53(3): 979.

Segal, S. 2011. *Corporate Value of Enterprise Risk Management: The Next Step in Business Management*. Hoboken, NJ: Wiley.

Sehn, F.P. 2006. *Strategic Risk Management*. Accessed September 11, 2014, at http://www.asse.org/prac ticespecialties/riskmanagement/docs/Francis%20Sehn%20Article.pdf

Sjörberg, L. 1979. Strength of belief and risk. *Policy Sciences*, 11: 39–57.

Skipper, H.D., & Kwon, J.W. 2007. *Risk Management and Insurance: Perspectives in a Global Economy*. Victoria, Australia: Blackwell.

Slywotzky, A.J., & Drzik, J. 2005. Countering the biggest risk of all. *Harvard Business Review*, 83(4): 78–88.

Standard and Poor's. 2007. *Summary of Standard & Poor's Enterprise Risk Management Evaluation Process for Insurers*. Accessed September 12, 2014, at http://www.standardandpoors.com/ratings/articles/en/ us/?assetID=1245193859443

Standard and Poor's. 2013. *Enterprise Risk Management*. Accessed September 12, 2014, at http://www.stand ardandpoors.com/spf/upload/Ratings_US/Enterprise_Risk_Management_5_7_13.pdf

Stata. 2013. *Stata Treatment Effects Reference Model: Potential Outcomes/Counterfactual Outcomes. Stata Release 13*. College Station, TX: Stata Press.

Staw, B.M., & Epstein, L.D. 2000. What bandwagons bring: Effects of popular management techniques on corporate performance, reputation, and CEO pay. *Administrative Science Quarterly*, 45(3): 523–556.

Tonello, M. 2012. *Strategic Risk Management: A Primer for Directors*. Accessed September 12, 2014, at http:// blogs.law.harvard.edu/corpgov/2012/08/23/strategic-risk-management-a-primer-for-directors/

9

The symbiosis of failure

The strategic dynamics of risk and resilience

Denis Fischbacher-Smith[1]

If an event or a kind of behavior meets a predetermined criterion, whatever the criterion is, then we say it is a success. If the criterion is violated, then a failure occurs.

(Cai, 1996, p. 115)

Adding the word failure implies that an abnormality has to be rectified through some intervention process.

(Hughes, 2007, p. 97)

The notion of failure permeates many aspects of society. News reports provide accounts of failures in service provision as well as the failures of professionals to protect those in their care. There are also accounts of failures in the products and core processes of organisations, sometimes with catastrophic consequences. Even governments are not immune from failures of policy. In all cases, the questions that are asked after the event are essentially along the lines of 'How could this happen, why were the risks of failure not identified and acted upon'? Any discussion of failure – whether it is framed in terms of healthcare interventions, engineering, policy making, or management practices, amongst others – is plagued by a core problem of the definition of failure when framed within a particular context (Morris, LaForge, & Allen, 1994; Watson & Everett, 1999). Even in the areas of risk and resilience the definition of 'failure' (along with that of crisis) and its relationship to other terms has been the source of some ambiguity (Smith, 2006; Smith & Fischbacher, 2009). Failure is, therefore, in many respects in the eyes of the beholder, but as a systems state it does not exist in isolation. Failure is also dependent on a range of elements at work within the system and against which that 'failure' is judged. This symbiotic nature of failure sits at the core of the literature on risk and resilience. Irrespective on the definition of failure used, there is a sense that the objectives of the system have not been met in full and that the host organisation has not been operating at the level of effectiveness required to ensure that failure did not occur.

In commenting on the nature of failure in healthcare, Hughes (2007), in the second epigraph, highlights the notion that failure implies that there is some abnormality that needs to be addressed, thereby suggesting that any corrective action taken by the organisation has the potential to rectify this abnormal phenomenon. One might argue that risk, resilience, and crisis management each have a focus on the processes of intervention by seeking to identify, prevent, and respond to organisational abnormalities that have the potential to cause harm. There is a case to be made, therefore, for linking these processes to the wider mechanisms by which strategy is developed, operationalised (Mitroff, Pearson, & Pauchant, 1992; Power, 2005; Smith, 1992), and seeks to achieve organisational effectiveness and resilience (Fischbacher-Smith, 2014b). Within the literature, there is considerable agreement that organisations need to consider the nature of risk as an integral part of the strategic management process, but there appears to be a dislocation between these aspirations to integrate the processes conceptually and the realities of practice (Mikes, 2009, 2011). One area where there has been a more extensive consideration of the relationships between risk and strategy has been in the area of supply chain management, although this has been a relatively recent phenomenon (Uta, 2005; Zachary, Jason, & Stephen, 2008). More recent work on resilience has recognised that its processes have an inherently strategic nature and that embedding these demands in the structures and processes of organisations and communities should be a core aspect of that approach (Carmeli & Markman, 2011; Hamel & Valikangas, 2003; Norris, Stevens, Pfefferbaum, Wyche, & Pfefferbaum, 2008; Somers, 2009). The obvious question to pose then is, why do the relationships between them appear to be so fractured when there is considerable agreement of the significance of the relationships between risk, resilience, and strategy?

There is little doubt that failures within the core technologies and processes of an organisation can generate problems for its strategy, especially where that organisation is already experiencing problems. For example, the loss of two Malaysia Airlines aircraft in 2014, both in controversial circumstances, led to a severe decline in the company's share price and resulted in job cuts and the development of a revised strategy to turn the company around (Topham, 2015). Conversely, an organisation's strategy can also shape the generation of the conditions that lead to catastrophic failure (Turner, 1976). An example of this relationship can be found in the accident on board the Deepwater Horizon oil rig that resulted in loss of life, caused a severe environmental impact, and has been seen as a failure in the governance processes within the strategy of deep-water drilling (Osofsky, 2013). This accident ultimately generated a multi-level crisis for both BP and the US government (Audra & Jennie, 2013; Smithson & Venette, 2013). Its genesis, however, could be seen to lie in the heavy dependence that Western countries have on oil imports and the geopolitics of the oil-producing regions. These factors have resulted in the search for additional sources of hydrocarbon resources, often in increasingly hostile environments with the attendant risks of working in such a setting. In the aftermath of the accident, the role of politicians in shaping a risky strategy of deep-water drilling was overshadowed by the blame that fell on BP as the main contractor. Whilst BP clearly bears responsibility for the accident, they are not the only villains in the case (Houck, 2010). On the basis of these examples alone, it could be argued that that risk and resilience are intrinsically linked to the strategic management process in what amounts to a symbiotic relationship – each has the potential to feed off the other. Why, then, are these processes not considered more systematically and holistically by organisations, academic research, and business education?

Our aim in this chapter is to consider this question and it does so by considering how four interrelated elements of the failure process can interact together to generate problems for organisations in integrating resilience (as capability) and strategy (as intent). In addition to dealing with some of the ambiguities and nuances around the nature of risk, the chapter sets out three other elements that are relevant to shaping strategic failures. The first of these concerns the indeterminate nature of many of the hazards facing organisations, especially within a highly connected and complex environment. Second, it highlights the importance of transformation processes within the emergence of new forms of hazard and the organisation's responses to those challenges. Finally, it considers the ways in which the range of hazards facing the organisation are framed and judged to be acceptable, or otherwise, by key decision-makers. These four elements – set out using the acronym RITA (risk, indeterminate nature, transformations, and acceptability) – are used to highlight the scale of the underlying issues that inhibit organisations from taking a more holistic perspective on the relationships between failure and strategy. The chapter seeks to contextualise these issues by setting the challenges that they present within the processes of risk and resilience research and to frame them within the wider contexts of strategic management that operate within organisations. The core argument developed here concerns the nature and utilisation of knowledge by managers within the context of uncertain and highly damaging events. In essence, the chapter seeks to consider how organisations deal with an ever more complicated portfolio of hazards and do so within a complex environment where the potential for emergent conditions is high. The discussions reflect the literatures on what Mikes (2009) has termed 'calculative cultures', in which the power of technical expertise has been a dominant element in the determination of risk.

The demand for greater certainty around the management of risk is a long-standing challenge for management and one that has transcended a number of organisational contexts in which risk is considered (see, for example, Irwin, Smith, & Griffiths, 1982; Mikes, 2009; Power, 2004, 2008). This search for greater certainty has become an ever more elusive construct as organisational systems become increasingly complex, operate over longer distances, and have to contend with increasing demands for certainty and control. As a first step in exploring the challenges for the strategic management of these issues, we first need to reflect on the nature of organisational failure.

Organisational failure – fragments of a failure in strategy

The future is totally unpredictable. Organizations are unpredictable. Efforts to control organizations are futile, even harmful to organizations. Planning stifles strategic thinking. What is to be done? . . . Surprisingly, there is much that can be done.

(Sherden, 1998, p. 241)

Any attempt to explain organizational failure will not be complete unless the interplay between contextual forces and organizational dynamics is taken into account.

(Mellahi & Wilkinson, 2004, p. 34)

The quotes that open this section highlight the pervasive nature of organisational failure, the holistic nature of the causal factors that generate it, the role of uncertainty as a critical element within the management of risk, and the constraints around attempts at organisational control. At its core, failure can be seen an essentially perceptual construct. Within our daily organisational lives we can see failure defined and redefined depending on the vantage point and vested interest of the individual who is making the judgement. There are, of course, clearly defined failures within organisations that are not easily reconfigured no matter how effective the organisation's public relations capabilities might be. Catastrophic accidents, especially those involving loss of life and resource, cannot be redefined in a positive light. They point to the ineffectiveness of the organisation in controlling its activities and the failure of managers to anticipate and prevent these adverse events from occurring (Fischbacher-Smith, 2014a). It is with such catastrophic forms of failure that have clear strategic impacts that this essay is concerned.

The globalised nature of modern organisations ensures that the interactions between elements of the RITA acronym occur across space and time, and this adds a layer of complexity for managers to contend with. Highly interconnected organisations may experience a crisis if the vulnerabilities inherent in the organisation are exposed at points within this global landscape of activities. Mellahi and Wilkinson remind us of the importance of the various interactions that occur both within the organisation and as a result of its interaction with its environmental contexts. The plurality of environmental settings in which organisations operate, across a global network of interactions, serves to create fractures in organisational controls that generate varying degrees of vulnerability at different points in space-time. The distributed and interconnected nature of supply chains and the instantaneous coverage of catastrophic events by global news networks will ensure that the reputational aspects of any crisis become problematic for organisations. The range of task demands generated by shifts in the relationships between an organisation's environment and its capabilities has the effect of moving an organisation away from its designed-for state. They do so in a way that can create conditions that can exceed the contingency capabilities that are in place to deal with the anticipated perturbations that may affect the wider system (Hodge & Coronado, 2007; Smith, 2005; Tsoukas, 1999). As organisations extend the scale and locations of their activities, they increase the interactions that occur between the elements of that this wider system. The result is the creation of a complex mosaic of interactions that generate emergent conditions, which then serve to challenge the dynamic capabilities (Eisenhardt & Martin, 2000; Teece & Pisano, 1994) that the organisation has in place. These perturbations can also create the conditions where the various control systems that are in place are unable to prevent harm from occurring (Fischbacher-Smith, 2014b; Smith, 2005).

Failure is often defined in multiple ways depending on the circumstances in which it is judged (Dörner, 1996) but it is seen as both pervasive and inevitable, especially in sociotechnical systems (Petroski, 1985). At an organisational level, failure can be seen to occur when the organisation does not have sufficient fit between its internal capabilities and the external task demands imposed upon it (Miles & Snow, 1994). The notion of 'misfit' is identified by Miles and Snow as a critical element in the failure process, but it is also one that is seen to defy prediction on occasions:

> Occasional situations of misfit and failure are beyond managerial anticipation and/or influence ... managers cannot foresee or prevent some forms of organizational failure.
>
> *(Miles & Snow, 1994, p. 66)*

Thus, the abilities of management, as both a functional area and as a set of processes, are central to the generation of failure conditions, either as a result of acts of commission or omission, and over space and time. The incubation of failure has been an issue that has attracted considerable attention (Collingridge, 1992; Turner, 1978, 1994), and the incremental nature of the process is seen to be of importance:

> One of the most troublesome aspects of misfit and failure is that the process by which they occur is incremental, interactive, and cumulative. If harmful changes occur over a long enough period, both the changes and the adaptations made to them may well become so deeply ingrained in the organization that the next generation of manager takes them as given.
>
> *(Miles & Snow, 1994, p. 68)*

As a consequence, the processes around failure can be seen to be intrinsically linked to the actions of human operators – through the decision-making process, the manner in which technical expertise is used to justify decisions (especially where the extent of uncertainty is high), and the acceptability of key decisions involving risk and uncertainty. Failure is, therefore, a term that is related to a number of other elements that coalesce around it.

The situation becomes more complicated when human actors are involved in the failure process. Human actions that serve to precipitate failure can be accidental (slips and lapses) or intentional acts (mistakes and violations) (Reason, 1990), and both groups of actions can create significant challenges around the development and maintenance of control. In addition, these actions can be latent (delayed in effect) or active (immediate in effect), with the result that human interventions have the potential to shape the conditions of failure at multiple levels and across different timelines. In addition to generating the conditions that precipitate strategic failure, human actions can also serve to erode the processes around mitigation and control.

The strategic nature of organisational failure (in its various guises) is a concept that has a long history within the academic literature (Pauchant & Mitroff, 1992; Reason, 1993a, 1997; Smith, 1992, 1995; Tenner, 1996; Turner, 1978, 1994). Despite this history, business schools have been seen as somewhat reluctant both to incorporate crisis concepts within mainstream programmes (Comer, 2013) and to do so in a manner that recognises the role that managerial decision-making plays in the process (Fischbacher-Smith & Fischbacher-Smith, 2013). These decisions can generate acute problems around failures by creating the conditions for active errors, whilst also generating more chronic (or latent) errors (Collingridge, 1992; Reason, 1990, 1993b). As a result, the relationships between the strategy process and failure can be seen to operate at two levels. The first occurs as a result of the creation of a set of conditions in which human operators working within the sociotechnical system are forced into error traps (Reason, 1987, 1990). The second relates to decisions taken in which their consequences are not immediately realised but instead error cost is embedded, or incubated, within the system (Collingridge, 1992; Turner, 1978, 1994). Inherent in both forms of error generation are a range of processes around the generation of uncertainty within the decision-making process and the manner in which expertise and the organisation's knowledge base is brought to bear on the decision problem.

The actions of managers in designing, shaping, and adapting these controls or by generating activities that can exceed their boundaries can create additional vulnerabilities within the organisation (Reason, 1997; Turner, 1994). For some, this terrain of activities represents failures of both foresight and hindsight in dealing with the range of hazards facing the organisation and the set of problematic practices that have emerged and which have the potential to cause harm (Reason, 1997; Toft & Reynolds, 1994; Turner, 1978). If we add to this the intentional actions of hostile actors – those malevolent individuals who actively seek to cause harm by exposing vulnerabilities in controls – then any control processes have to be able to constantly adapt to meet the demands of an ever-changing threat matrix. Organisations need to adapt without creating further emergent conditions that lead to new forms of unrecognised vulnerability. This is often especially problematic when the failures occur in those underpinning critical infrastructures on which organisations rely but which lie outside of their control and are effectively ignored (Boin & Smith, 2006). The effect is the generation of what is effectively an arms race between a set of emergent conditions that are constantly evolving and a set of controls that management has put in place to prevent certain harmful events from occurring.

Organisations are, therefore, faced with a set of operational and strategic challenges around the management of hazards and the associated failure potential. These challenges include: the collection, analysis, synthesis, and distribution of information relating to systems performance; the maintenance of capabilities that allow for the control of processes, technologies, and material flows and transformations; the effective control of human resources on an increasingly global scale and in a way that negates any threats arising from hostile insiders; and the management of a range of transformative processes that operate at different levels of scale, speed, and reach in ways that reflect the balance between effectiveness, efficiencies, and the risk of failure. These issues generate both considerable and challenging task demands for the strategic management of organisations.

The intellectual and practical challenge for managers is to be able to identify and act on a range of such failure modes and effects – a task for which, it could be argued, the management function is invariably ill-prepared. In part, this is a function of the difficulties associated with the control of a diverse, but essentially synergistic, range of potential hazards and the requirement to do so over increased spatial and temporal contexts. Given the highly interactive and coupled nature of modern organisations, it is not surprising that the speed and range of these failures can often generate the potential for catastrophic failure (Perrow, 1981, 1984, 2011). A particular problem in prediction concerns that category of failures described as extreme events (low-probability, high-consequence hazards) as these are often deemed to be of such a low probability of occurrence that effective control mechanisms are not put in place to deal with them – the assumption is that existing controls will prevent the escalation of any perturbation to the point of catastrophic failure. This 'Titanic Syndrome' (Smith, 1995) can lead to the suppression of concerns about potential failure modes or mitigations strategies because there is no a priori evidence to support such a failure scenario. However, like the sinking of the Titanic, the scale of the failure can lead to a paradigm shift around causality and result in a range of postcrisis legitimation issues for an organisation (Sipika & Smith, 1993; Smith, 1990; Smith & Sipika, 1993), and especially around the role of risk management within the strategy process.

There has been discussion within both practice and the academy about the abilities of organisations to integrate the principles of risk management within the strategy process (Mikes, 2009, 2011). One of the challenges here concerns this predictive capability of risk analysis. Risk analytical techniques are at their strongest when dealing with phenomena where the failure modes and effects are known and understood and where the probabilities associated with such failures are also known and with a reasonable degree of accuracy. Invariably, this predictive capability is eroded when the issues considered are strategic rather than operational. Space and time also contribute to this increased uncertainty as they increase the potential for emergent conditions to generate intervening variables that confound the predictive process.

Figure 9.1 takes the four elements that were identified earlier – risk (and its relationship to disaster and crisis), the indeterminate nature of prediction for extreme events, the transformations that take place as part of the routines and rituals of the organisation, and the overall acceptability of the various parts of an organisation's risk portfolio – and highlights a range of additional issues that are felt to have an impact on the strategic dynamics of failure. We can now turn our attention briefly to each of the major elements of this framework, starting with the nature of risk itself.

The ambiguities of risk

Risk, and the manner in which ambiguities are incorporated within decision-making, have been widely discussed within the academic literature (Curley, Yates, & Abrams, 1986; Ellsberg, 1961; Haisley & Weber, 2010; Knight, 1921; Rigotti & Shannon, 2012). The ambiguities inherent within a risk-based problem have been shown to impact upon the perceptions that individuals have of that risk (Camerer & Weber, 1992; Ghosh & Ray, 1997; Riddel, 2009), and these ambiguities can be related to the understanding of the phenomena, its probabilities of occurrence and the associated consequences of a hazard, and the manner in which information about that hazard is communicated and evaluated (Fox & Tversky, 1995; Frisch & Baron, 1988). Against such a background it is not surprising that organisations seem to struggle to incorporate risk-related

Figure 9.1 The nature of failure and resilient organisations

concepts into their strategies in a way that is both transparent and meaningful. A core element that is associated with the generation of ambiguities around risk concerns the definition of the main elements of the term.

At a basic level, risk can be seen to consist of a source of hazard or harm, the probability of that hazard being realised, and the consequences associated with it. For many forms of hazard, there is considerable uncertainty associated with both the probabilities of the hazard generating different consequences as well as the cause-and-effect relationships that exist within a particular set of hazard pathways. The interactions between these elements can also serve to generate a set of challenges around the ways in which we attempt to manage that risk. Thus, we can argue that whilst the concept of risk may have its origins in actuarial approaches to failure (Sherden, 1998), it does not provide the certainty around cause and effect that such actuarial approaches might imply. Neither does it provide a sense of the predictive validity around the probabilities attributed to different forms of hazard. It is because of the complexities within the management of risk that some have argued that it is essentially a social construction (Beck, 1992; Nelkin, 1989; Short, 1984). Such views are clearly at odds with those held in many parts of the risk industry, but the reality is likely to be somewhere between the two extremes. For certain types of risk it is possible to calculate group-based probabilities for harm – the life insurance industry is based on such calculations. However, such group-based approaches cannot accurately predict such risks at the level of the individual based on such aggregate information due to the intervening variables that can impact on those risks. Similar problems exist in the criminal justice system where calculations of offending risks are also based on group data. Thus, one might argue that risk analysis is essentially indicative rather than predictive and that the interpretation of the information available in risk assessments becomes a social construction as a consequence. If we extend the processes around risk generation over space and time, then the strategic nature of risk management becomes an even more complex task and it begins to encompass more of the uncertainty facing decision-makers.

The management of 'risk' should be a central component of management practices, especially within a strategic context. However, despite its significance, it can be seen as being largely a marginal element of management theory (especially in terms of strategy) and certainly does not seem to occupy the central role within the practice agenda that one might expect (Bolton & Galloway, 2014; Currie, Knights, & Starkey, 2010; Fischbacher-Smith & Fischbacher-Smith, 2013; Mikes, 2009). Whilst there is little doubt that the attention given to risk has increased over the last 30 years, the pervasive nature of its role within organisations remains something an elusive challenge for organisational scholars. There are several reasons why the management of risk has proved problematic. These include: the need for risk management to be holistic in its approach (Bolton & Galloway, 2014); the development of 'calculative cultures' (Mikes, 2009) that often assume that risks can be effectively predicted and controlled; the meanings and ambiguities of the various terms that are associated with risk; and the requirements for risk management to reflect a range of knowledge domains and managerial spans of control.

Conventional risk analytical tools are at their strongest when dealing with events that have an actuarial basis for analysis, where the frequency of occurrence is such that it allows for the assessment of the probabilities of failure and does so with a high degree of reliability. For low-probability, high-consequence events, or those events involving human agency, actuarial approaches to determining risk are invariably more problematic. Within this context, uncertainty drives the decision-making process and the knowledge available to decision-makers becomes a key factor in determining organisational effectiveness. When those decisions are extended in space and time and the cause-and-effect relationships between elements are correspondingly difficult to identify, then the processes around the use of risk analysis becomes even more problematic. Even within routine decision problems, uncertainty plays an important role in shaping the actions of organisations and especially the human operators within them. Uncertainty is, therefore, a critical element with the processes of managing harmful events. If there is no uncertainty then there will be no need for individuals and groups to make a decision as the outcomes will be known and understood by all parties concerned – risk will, therefore, be predictable. Clearly, the absence of uncertainty has no bearing on reality and our lives are invariably interwoven with the uncertainty of both occurrence and outcome in terms of our decision-making. Managers exist to deal with this uncertainty but they may also play a significant role in shaping it as a function of their behaviours, decisions, knowledge, and understanding. A central component of the arguments developed here concerns the role of human actors within the strategic risk management process. In particular, the ways in which expert judgment and leadership style can contribute to the potential for failure is an important element in the embedding of error cost within the strategy process.

Much of the debate within the academic literature has looked at risk in the aftermath of major adverse events (Dörner, 1996; Gigerenzer, 2002; Knight, 1921; Reason, 1997; Shubik, 1954; Turner, 1978), and this discussion has taken on a new perspective within the postmodern approaches to dealing with the nature of hazard, especially within the context of a globalised environment (Fox, 1999; Giddens, 1990, 1999). It is in this interconnected environment that 'risk' has become a central element of debates around a range of issues, and a central dynamic of the discussion relates to the ways in which the nature of risk is constructed, perceived, and acted upon. Within this globalised setting, risk is also framed within a strategic process in which the relationships between cause and effect can be extended across space and time, with both the spatial and intergenerational effects of the hazards proving to be significant factors in their management (Fischbacher-Smith & Hudson, 2010; Hudson, 2009). This has generated problems around the role of technical expertise within risk-based decision-making, the burden of proof, and the ways in which powerful interests can serve to shape debates around risk generation (Oreskes, 2004; Pigliucci & Boudry, 2014; Walton, 1988).

Discussions around the so-called risk society (Beck, 1986, 1992) have seen a focus on the argument that many forms of risk assessment are essentially social constructions (Douglas & Wildavsky, 1982; Gergen, 2001), and that actuarial approaches to risk are limited in their scope and invariably fail to predict the realisation of a hazard in a manner that is helpful to organisational decision-makers (Bulkeley, 2001; Sherden, 1998). A central element of many of these discussions relates to the role of human actors in the failure process through a range of factors including: the role of decision-making in the design of systems and the incubation of failure potential and the development of error cost within them; the role of human intervention around the escalation of an incident into a major accident; and the direct actions of individuals in causing harm (as accidental or intentional acts) (Collingridge, 1992; Colwill, 2009; Reason, 1997; Turner, 1994). The very nature of sociotechnical systems highlights the symbiotic role that human actors play in the management of technologies, and it is the interaction between technological process and human activities that generates important questions about the strategic nature of risk management and the potential that these have for the generation of crises.

The management of risk and its relationship to social expectations creates a series of challenges for the decision-making processes within organisations (Douglas & Wildavsky, 1982; Power, 2008, 2009). Social expectations are such that there are demands around the prediction of risk that cannot be delivered (Power, 2004, 2009), and this generates organisational responses around the production of structured analyses in an attempt to determine what is essentially the indeterminate probability and consequences of hazards. The result is the creation of an ever more complex set of analyses and the generation of a calculative culture (Mikes, 2009) in which the technocratic processes effectively serve to overrule accountability by making the processes of risk analysis more opaque to strategic decision-makers. Within this context any ambiguities within the process of analysing risk have the potential to generate additional indeterminacy due to the lack of an effective burden of proof and the interventions from different 'expert' groups.

Indeterminacy and uncertainty in the generation of strategic failure

Uncertainty creates problems for action. Actors' organizations resolve these problems by following rules of thumb, using rituals, relying on habitual patterns, or, more self-consciously, by setting goals and making plans to reach them. These devices provide the determinateness and certainty needed to embark upon organizational action in the present.

(Turner, 1976, p. 378)

A key aspect of the challenge around risk assessment relates to the indeterminate nature of some of the information available to decision-makers, and this challenges the nature of the knowledge and understanding in areas where the accuracy of that information is critical. This has echoes of Rumsfeld's (2002, 2011) notion of what is known and the range of things that remain unknown. In the case of the latter, it is possible for organisations to be aware of the limitations of their knowledge (the known unknowns), but there is also the potential for some of this knowledge to be indeterminate (the unknown unknowns). These unknown unknowns can arise from a number of factors. These include: the paradigm blindness that constrains the acquisition of new knowledge; the role of new forms of hazard that arise out of emergent conditions within sociotechnical systems; and the limitations of domain-specific expertise when dealing with new forms of hazard (Erikson, 1994; Fischbacher-Smith, 2012; Perrow, 1984).

A number of factors contribute to the problems surrounding the nature of indeterminacy within risk assessment. First, the nature of complexity within the sociotechnical systems in which the failure is situated serves to undermine deterministic and calculative approaches to prediction (Sherden, 1998). The nature of emergent conditions within systems – essentially those unforeseen elements that arise out of the interactions between systems components – serves to generate problems around predicting likely event scenarios (Smith, 2005). Second, the situational context in which such risk assessments are undertaken is also seen to be problematic (Sherden, 1998). Here, psychological processes that impact upon the decision-making process have a major effect in shaping the ways in which we see the world sometimes resulting in paradigm blindness (Kahneman, 2011; Sabatier, 1987, 1988; Weick, 1993, 1995). The core beliefs, values, and assumptions of decision-makers are important elements in serving to shape the ways in which they see the world (Fischbacher-Smith, 2012; Pauchant & Mitroff, 1992). Third, and in a related manner, the nature of expert judgement is also a key element of the process of determining risk, but it can be coerced by powerful interests (Collingridge & Reeve, 1986). Finally, the prediction of failure becomes more problematic as we extend that assessment out over space and time, thereby encompassing more uncertainty into the decision-making process.

Despite the limitations of our abilities to deal with the indeterminate nature of many forms of hazard and the constraints that exist around our knowledge and understanding, organisations are willing to make a set of assumptions about the nature of the hazards that they face. Turner (1976) highlights the ways in which organisations make assumptions around how those routine processes can lead to the incubation of failure. Sociotechnical systems also generate emergent conditions that can result in sudden, unforeseen task demands that further compound the problems around decision-making (Gavetti, 2005; Jackson & Dutton, 1988; Kiesler & Sproull, 1982). In this setting, the knowledge base of the organisation and the nature of technical expertise within it are important elements in shaping the discourse around risk and uncertainty. It is here that the notion of what the organisation knows and understands relative to what it does not fully know, that shapes the nature of debates around risk. There are clear echoes here of Rumsfeld's categorisation of knowledge where we need to distinguish between what it is that we know and fully understand and those areas where the knowledge base is incomplete and uncertainty is high (Rumsfeld, 2002, 2011). In the latter context, organisations can be both aware or unaware of the exact nature of their knowledge boundaries. Risk management should, in an ideal context, reflect the known elements around the various hazards and it should allow for the determination of the probabilities of failure with a high degree of reliability. In addition, the failure modes and effects associated with the hazard should be clear and understood. As we move into those areas where the balance between the established knowledge base and the unknown characteristics of the system shifts in the direction of the latter, then the uncertainty that this generates has the potential to incubate the potential for crisis and erode the organisation's abilities to manage hazards in an effective manner (Fischbacher-Smith, 2014a).

Within the context of this uneven terrain of knowledge, there have been calls to widen the base of recognised sources of expertise (Michael, 1992). The result has been the emergence of 'citizen science' (Irwin, 1995, 2001) in which it is recognised that public groups often hold relevant and valid knowledge about the potential hazards generated by organisations (Irwin, Dale, & Smith, 1996; Wynne, 1992, 1996). This construct changes the parameters of legitimised expertise, especially where the phenomena in question is poorly understood, and it challenges the traditional power of expertise and the legitimacy of the various parties involved in risk debates. In those conflicts where the potential for harm is significant, it may lead to calls for a more precautionary approach to dealing with the hazards (Calman & Smith, 2001; Fischbacher-Smith & Calman, 2010). Strategically, this generates challenges for organisations in terms of their abilities to anticipate public concerns about their activities and the abilities to communicate the nature of the risk. These are inherently strategic processes that are central to the ways in which the organisation utilises its knowledge and expertise within the decision-making process. These strategic processes are also framed within spatial and temporal settings and harms are often realised in a sense of place, and it is to an examination of these interactions that the chapter now turns.

Transforming hazards

A key element within the realisation of risk and the generation of harm relates to the processes by which transformations take place within the system. Systems are designed against a set of parameters, and unless these parameters are reassessed on a regular basis there will be the potential for the system to move from its designed-for state into a state that is far from its equilibrium position. This can arise over space and time as adaptation occurs differentially in response to perturbations. These perturbations, or disruptions, that impact upon the system have the effect of stimulating a response from the organisation either as local adaptations or more systematic changes in operational protocols (Smith, 1995, 2005). Over time, organisations can adapt to these new ways of working but without changing their core protocols for dealing with the new set of conditions. This can lead to a movement away from the designed-for state of the system and may result in problems around contingency responses to events. Similarly, as the environment changes – moving from ordered through complex to chaotic – it will generate different task demands that may exceed the organisation's abilities to respond in a time frame that allows them to remain effective (Fischbacher-Smith, 2014b; Kauffman, 1993).

In the first instance, organisations are faced with a set of environmental challenges that are either benign or threatening. The uncertainty inherent in this process can generate problems for the organisation at multiple levels. If these challenges are perceived to generate a threat to the organisation's current stability, then decision-makers within the organisation will seek to make sense of it and, in doing so, will deal with it through processes of enactment – the rules for systems use – in which previously held assumptions around the nature of threat–response relationships have generated a set of processes and procedures (controls) that shape response (Hall, 1984; Hodge & Coronado, 2007; Smith, 2005; Tsoukas, 1999). For many types of events, the actions are seen as arising from a set of routine processes – possibly generating a condition of mindlessness – and occur as a function of scripts that guide behaviours based on past experience (Ashforth & Fried, 1988; Cohen, Levinthal, & Warglien, 2014). However, there are also issues arising out of the relationships between the individual and the group – the notion of collective (group) mind (Weick & Roberts, 1993). The result of this collective process can result in the generation of such processes as groupthink (Esser, 1998; Janis, 1971, 1972) or paradigm blindness (Fischbacher-Smith, 2012, 2013); in both cases it results in organisational decision-makers being unable to recognise the fundamental flaws in their decisions. This is especially significant in those settings where the task demands of the event move beyond the experience base of those making the decisions. In these cases, the selection of adaptive strategies becomes more problematic as previous experiences will not serve to guide behaviours, and the impacts of groupthink and paradigm blindness will impact upon the selection of alternative perspectives (that might run counter to the dominant paradigm) and shape group decision behaviours. The organisational recipes that arise from this process are often used as a means of shaping attempts at effectiveness (Bernard, 1998).

Moving a system away from its designed-for state is a function of a number of factors that reflect the complexity inherent within the system and especially the speed and extent of those interactions. This reflects the processes identified by Perrow (1981, 1984, 2011) around tight coupling and interactive complexity and the potential that this has to generate the revenge effects identified by Tenner (1996). Figure 9.1 identified some of the elements that typify transformations towards failure. Again, this is only indicative of the processes that take place around transformations.

Space, place, and time are important in shaping the dynamics of the harms that arise from various forms of hazards. Hazards exist within space and are located in places. Time is an important element in shaping both exposure to the hazard and the framing of the population at risk. Taken in its totality, a hazard generates harms across multiple distances, over different time frames, and across multiple spaces (either as levels within activities or across activities – which may be interconnected). Thus, risk (which is the probability of a particular hazard occurring and the consequences associated with it) exists in space and time and is contextualised within a sense of place. This has the effect of generating different levels of risk across space and time, which will generate different levels of acceptability amongst those populations who are deemed to be at risk. From a strategic perspective, this introduces a further layer of complexity into the process.

Acceptability of risk

'Riskiness' means more to people than 'expected number of fatalities'. Attempts to characterize, compare, and regulate risks must be sensitive to the broader conception of risk that underlies people's concerns.

(Slovic, Fischhoff, & Lichtenstein, 1982, p. 92)

The final group of issues raised in Figure 9.1 concerns the processes that surround the acceptability of risk. Acceptability is shaped by the RITA components and can be seen as a function of the ways in which we make sense of the information that is available to us. This is shaped, in turn, by the paradigmatic and heuristic lenses that we use within the sense-making process and is shaped by the transformations that take place at particular points in space and time. In addition, there are issues surrounding the comparability of certain forms of risk in allowing individuals to make judgements about their acceptability (Johnson, 2004). If, as some suggest, risk assessment is a social construction (Beck, 1992; Douglas & Wildavsky, 1982), then any ambiguities and uncertainty within the calculation of risk and its expression will have a potential impact on different levels of acceptability. The ways in which the potential victims of a hazard have a level of trust in those who are communicating the risk is also an important variable in shaping the processes around risk acceptability (Earle, 2010; Poortinga & Pidgeon, 2005; Smith & Irwin, 1984), as are the networks through which people communicate and make sense of the issues (Short, 1984).

In an increasingly globalised context, the management of risk becomes problematic as hazardous activities are exported in response to different regulatory environments and levels of public concern (Hudson, 2009; Nanda & Bailey, 1988). This has been seen as a reflection of domestic practices in which low-income areas are often chosen to be the location for hazardous activities (Marbury, 1995; Pastor, Sadd, & Hipp, 2001). The diverse nature of such communities can also play a role in shaping the nature of harms as a result of lifestyle and social behaviours (Dunn & Alexeeff, 2010), and they are also less likely to be able to deal with the power of polluting companies and regulatory authorities. Invariably, the diversity within such populations will also impact upon different approaches to dealing with the ambiguities in data and uncertainty within the determination of harm.

In addition to the spatial dynamics of acceptability, there are also issues around the context in which the particular hazards are set. There are certain types of hazards that are deemed to be more unacceptable than others. As with the export of hazards, the notion of a vulnerable population is an important factor in shaping the acceptability of risk. Young children, or other vulnerable populations, will often generate a lower level of tolerance around risk generation because these groups are seen as being unable to resist against any attempts at control from outside the community. The debates around the use of the measles, mumps, and rubella (MMR) vaccine in the UK, for example, illustrates how problems can emerge around the standards of behaviour within professional groups (Clements & Ratzan, 2003). Here, it is the professional nature of healthcare professionals, along with the nature of the population at risk, that can generate a lower tolerance around risk acceptability. The manner in which the evidence is reported in the media and the manner in which technical evidence is mediated through a journalist's lens, can serve to increase the uncertainty surrounding the issue (Clarke, 2008; Dixon & Clarke, 2013) as well as lead to unintended consequences (Flaherty, 2011; Serpell & Green, 2006).

As a result, the issues around risk acceptability become typified by their multilevel nature and the variations that can occur over space and time. Risk acceptability is intrinsically linked into the other elements of the RITA framework and it is the combination of the factors outlined in Figure 9.1 that makes the incorporation of these issues into the strategy process problematic and difficult to deal with. The acceptability of risk is, therefore, a problematic aspect of the success of organisational strategies in communication as perception is seen as a critical aspect of acceptability (Delfosse, 2005). This raises issues around the ethical behaviours of organisations in terms of the ways in which they communicate risk and utilise expertise in the framing of that communication (Collingridge & Reeve, 1986). There is potential here for the organisation's strategies around risk communication to generate the potential for further conflict and may ultimately result in the onset of a crisis for the organisation. Thus, the processes set out around the RITA framework should be seen as circulatory as well as operating at multiple levels. The interactions between the elements are such that they generate a range of challenges for organisations, which are configured as a consequence of the spatial and temporal settings in which they are set. The result is a constantly evolving set of task demands around hazards that are interpreted differently at various points within the system.

Conclusions

The learning that should follow failure often does not occur, and when it does occur, it often teaches the wrong lessons.

(Baumard & Starbuck, 2005, p. 295)

The strategic nature of failures within organisations remains a potentially significant issue for management theory and practice. This chapter has sought to set out a range of issues that could be seen to account for the criticisms of organisational practices around the lack of synergies between risk, resilience, and strategy (Mikes, 2009, 2011). The interconnections that exist between the activities of organisations serve to generate emergent conditions that have the potential to exceed the contingency plans that organisations have put in place. These perturbations have a significant impact on the performance of individual decision-makers within the organisation and raise issues around the incorporation of knowledge, uncertainty, and ambiguity within attempts to develop effective organisational strategies.

At the core of this process is the role and behaviours of human actors – both as decision-makers and enactors of organisational strategies. Within debates involving complex sociotechnical systems, where there is a potentially high level of harm, there is often an overlay of technical expertise within the assessment of risk, where the potential for the incubation of errors within the decision-making process remains high. One antidote to these processes is often framed within the construct of organisational learning. This has been a constant theme within the risk literature, but it does raise some important questions about the potential barriers that might exist to that learning (Smith & Elliott, 2007). If organisations are going to become more effective at integrating risk management processes within their strategies, then they will need to develop more effect mechanisms for learning from the experiences of others, both within and outside of their own organisational boundaries.

The complexities associated with the RITA elements developed in this chapter provide a set of parameters around which organisations should seek to develop their own learning and ensure that staff at various levels within the organisation are familiar with the ambiguities that such elements generate. A failure to frame the RITA elements in a holistic way will ensure that the management of risk and the development of resilience will remain hampered by the fractured landscape that is developed as a result of a reductionist approach to dealing with the issues. Strategic management practice necessitates a greater degree of integration of the main concepts associated with risk and resilience with those that are core to the processes of strategic management. Business education has a central role to play here, but it has largely failed to see this as a key set of debates within the undergraduate and postgraduate curriculum. Unless and until there is a wholesale increase in the awareness of the nuances around risk and the limitations that exist within the decision-making process around such issues, then the fractures between risk and strategy will persist.

Acknowledgements

The author would like to acknowledge the comments made on an earlier version of this paper by Moira Fischbacher-Smith. As always, all errors of commission and omission remain those of the author.

Note

1   Denis Fischbacher-Smith, University of Glasgow.

References

Ashforth, B.E., & Fried, Y. 1988. The mindlessness of organizational behaviors. *Human Relations*, 41(4): 305–329.

Audra, R.D., & Jennie, D. 2013. Synchronizing crisis responses after a transgression. *Journal of Communication Management*, 17(3): 252–269.

Baumard, P., & Starbuck, W.H. 2005. Learning from failures: Why it may not happen. *Long Range Planning*, 38(3): 281–298.

Beck, U. 1986. *Risikogesellschaft: Auf dem Weg in eine andere Moderne*. Frankfurt: Suhrkamp Verlag.

Beck, U. 1992. *Risk Society. Towards a New Modernity* (M. Ritter, Trans.). London: SAGE.

Bernard, B. 1998. Recipes for organisational effectiveness. Mad, bad, or just dangerous to know? *Career Development International*, 3(3): 100–106.

Boin, A., & Smith, D. 2006. Terrorism and critical infrastructures: Implications for public-private crisis management. *Public Money and Management*, 26(5): 295–304.

Bolton, D., & Galloway, C. 2014. The holistic dilemma: Helping management students deal with risk. *International Journal of Management Education*, 12(2): 55–67.

Bulkeley, H. 2001. Governing climate change: the politics of risk society? *Transactions of the Institute of British Geographers*, 26(4): 430–447.

Cai, K.-Y. 1996. System failure engineering and fuzzy methodology An introductory overview. *Fuzzy Sets and Systems*, 83(2): 113–133.

Calman, K., & Smith, D. 2001. Works in theory but not in practice? Some notes on the precautionary principle. *Public Administration*, 79(1): 185–204.

Camerer, C., & Weber, M. 1992. Recent developments in modeling preferences: Uncertainty and ambiguity. *Journal of Risk and Uncertainty*, 5(4): 325–370.

Carmeli, A., & Markman, G.D. 2011. Capture, governance, and resilience: Strategy implications from the history of Rome. *Strategic Management Journal*, 32(3): 322–341.

Clarke, C.E. 2008. A question of balance: The autism-vaccine controversy in the British and American elite press. *Science Communication*, 30(1): 77–107.

Clements, C.J., & Ratzan, S. 2003. Misled and confused? Telling the public about MMR vaccine safety. *Journal of Medical Ethics*, 29(1): 22–26.

Cohen, M.D., Levinthal, D.A., & Warglien, M. 2014. Collective performance: Modeling the interaction of habit-based actions. *Industrial and Corporate Change*, 23(2): 329–360.

Collingridge, D. 1992. *The Management of Scale: Big Organizations, Big Decisions, Big Mistakes*. London: Routledge.

Collingridge, D., & Reeve, C. 1986. *Science Speaks to Power: The Role of Experts in Policy Making*. London: Pinter.

Colwill, C. 2009. Human factors in information security: The insider threat – Who can you trust these days? *Information Security Technical Report*, 14(4): 186–196.

Comer, D.R. 2013. Educating students to prepare for and respond to crises that affect organizations: An introduction to the special issue. *Journal of Management Education*, 37(1): 3–5.

Curley, S.P., Yates, J.F., & Abrams, R.A. 1986. Psychological sources of ambiguity avoidance. *Organizational Behavior and Human Decision Processes*, 38(2): 230–256.

Currie, G., Knights, D., & Starkey, K. 2010. Introduction: A post-crisis critical reflection on business schools. *British Journal of Management*, 21: s1–s5.

Delfosse, E.S. 2005. Risk and ethics in biological control. *Biological Control*, 35(3): 319–329.

Dixon, G.N., & Clarke, C.E. 2013. Heightening uncertainty around certain science: Media coverage, false balance, and the autism-vaccine controversy. *Science Communication*, 35(3): 358–382.

Dörner, D. 1996. *The Logic of Failure. Recognising and Avoiding Error in Complex Situations*. Reading, MA: Perseus Books.

Douglas, M., & Wildavsky, A. 1982. *Risk and Culture: An Essay on the Selection of Technological and Environmental Dangers*. Berkeley: University of California Press.

Dunn, A.J., & Alexeeff, G.V. 2010. Beyond risk assessment: Principles for assessing community impacts. *International Journal of Toxicology*, 29(1): 78–87.

Earle, T.C. 2010. Trust in risk management: A model-based review of empirical research. *Risk Analysis*, 30(4): 541–574.

Eisenhardt, K.M., & Martin, J.A. 2000. Dynamic capabilities: What are they? *Strategic Management Journal*, 21(10–11): 1105–1121.

Ellsberg, D. 1961. Risk, ambiguity, and the savage axioms. *Quarterly Journal of Economics*, 75(4): 643–669.

Erikson, K. 1994. *A New Species of Trouble. Explorations in Disaster, Trauma, and Community*. New York: W.W. Norton.

Esser, J.K. 1998. Alive and well after 25 years: A review of groupthink research. *Organizational Behavior and Human Decision Processes*, 73(2–3): 116–141.

Fischbacher-Smith, D. 2012. Getting pandas to breed: Paradigm blindness and the policy space for risk prevention, mitigation and management. *Risk Management*, 14(3): 177–201.

Fischbacher-Smith, D. 2013. Paradigm blindness. In K. Penuel, M. Statler, & R. Hagen (Eds.), *Encyclopedia of Crisis Management* (pp. 716–720). Thousand Oaks, CA: SAGE.

Fischbacher-Smith, D. 2014a. The dark side of effectiveness – risk and crisis as the "destroyer of worlds". *Journal of Organizational Effectiveness: People and Performance*, 1(4): 338–348.

Fischbacher-Smith, D. 2014b. Organisational ineffectiveness: Environmental shifts and the transition to crisis. *Journal of Organizational Effectiveness: People and Performance*, 1(4): 423–446.

Fischbacher-Smith, D., & Calman, K. 2010. A precautionary tale – the role of the precautionary principle in policy making for public health. In P. Bennett, K. Calman, S. Curtis, & D. Fischbacher-Smith (Eds.), *Risk Communication and Public Health* (pp. 197–211). Oxford: Oxford University Press.

Fischbacher-Smith, D., & Fischbacher-Smith, M. 2013. Tales of the unexpected: Issues around the development of a crisis management module for the MBA program. *Journal of Management Education*, 37(1): 51–78.

Fischbacher-Smith, D., & Hudson, R. 2010. Exporting Pandora's box – exploitation, risk communication and public health problems associated with the export of hazard. In P. Bennett, K. Calman, S. Curtis, & D. Fischbacher-Smith (Eds.), *Risk Communication and Public Health* (pp. 245–260). Oxford: Oxford University Press.

Flaherty, D.K. 2011. The vaccine-autism connection: A public health crisis caused by unethical medical practices and fraudulent science. *Annals of Pharmacotherapy*, 45(10): 1302–1304.

Fox, C.R., & Tversky, A. 1995. Ambiguity aversion and comparative ignorance. *Quarterly Journal of Economics*, 110(3): 585–603.

Fox, N.J. 1999. Postmodern reflections on "risk", "hazards" and life choices. In D. Lupton (Ed.), *Risk and Sociocultural Theory. New Directions and Perspectives* (pp. 12–33). Cambridge: Cambridge University Press.

Frisch, D., & Baron, J. 1988. Ambiguity and rationality. *Journal of Behavioral Decision Making*, 1(3): 149–157.

Gavetti, G. 2005. Cognition and hierarchy: Rethinking the microfoundations of capabilities' development. *Organization Science*, 16(6): 599–617.

Gergen, K.J. 2001. *Social Construction in Context*. London: SAGE.

Ghosh, D., & Ray, M.R. 1997. Risk, ambiguity, and decision choice: Some additional evidence★. *Decision Sciences*, 28(1): 81–104.

Giddens, A. 1990. *The Consequences of Modernity*. Cambridge: Polity Press.

Giddens, A. 1999. *Runaway World. How Globalisation Is Reshaping Our Lives*. London: Profile Books.

Gigerenzer, G. 2002. *Reckoning with Risk. Learning to Live with Uncertainty*. London: Allen Lane/Penguin Press.

Haisley, E.C., & Weber, R.A. 2010. Self-serving interpretations of ambiguity in other-regarding behavior. *Games and Economic Behavior*, 68(2): 614–625.

Hall, R.I. 1984. The natural logic of management policy making: Its implications for the survival of an organization. *Management Science*, 30(8): 905–927.

Hamel, G., & Valikangas, L. 2003. The quest for resilience. *Harvard Business Review*, 81(9): 52–65.

Hodge, B., & Coronado, G. 2007. Understanding change in organizations in a far-from-equilibrium world. *Emergence: Complexity and Organizations*, 9(3): 3–15.

Houck, O.A. 2010. Worst case and the Deepwater Horizon blowout: There ought to be a law. *Tulane Environmental Law Journal*, 24(1): 1–18.

Hudson, R. 2009. The costs of globalization: Producing new forms of risk to health and well-being. *Risk Management*, 11(1): 13–29.

Hughes, I. 2007. Confusing terminology attempts to define the undefinable. *Archives of Disease in Childhood*, 92(2): 97–98.

Irwin, A. 1995. *Citizen Science. A Study of People, Expertise and Sustainable Development*. London: Routledge.

Irwin, A. 2001. Constructing the scientific citizen: Science and democracy in the biosciences. *Public Understanding of Science*, 10(1): 1–18.

Irwin, A., Dale, A., & Smith, D. 1996. Science and Hell's Kitchen – The local understanding of hazard issues. In A. Irwin & B. Wynne (Eds.), *Misunderstanding Science? The Public Reconstruction of Science and Technology* (pp. 47–64). Cambridge: Cambridge University Press.

Irwin, G.A., Smith, D., & Griffiths, R.F. 1982. Risk analysis and public policy for major hazards. *Physics in Technology*, 13(6): 258–265.

Jackson, S.E., & Dutton, J.E. 1988. Discerning threats and opportunities. *Administrative Science Quarterly*, 33(3): 370–387.

Janis, I.L. 1971. Groupthink. *Psychology Today*, 5(6): 43–46.

Janis, I.L. 1972. *Victims of Groupthink: A Psychological Study of Foreign-Policy Decisions and Fiascoes*. Boston: Houghton Mifflin.

Johnson, B.B. 2004. Risk comparisons, conflict, and risk acceptability claims. *Risk Analysis*, 24(1): 131–145.

Kahneman, D. 2011. *Thinking, Fast and Slow*. London: Allen Lane.

Kauffman, S.A. 1993. *The Origins of Order. Self Organization and Selection in Evolution*. New York: Oxford University Press.

Kiesler, S., & Sproull, L. 1982. Managerial response to changing environments: Perspectives on problem sensing from social cognition. *Administrative Science Quarterly*, 27(4): 548–570.

Knight, F.H. 1921. *Risk, Uncertainty and Profit*. Boston: Houghton Mifflin.

Marbury, H.J. 1995. Hazardous waste exportation: The global manifestation of environmental racism. *Vanderbilt Journal of Transnational Law*, 28(1): 251–249.

Mellahi, K., & Wilkinson, A. 2004. Organizational failure: A critique of recent research and a proposed integrative framework. *International Journal of Management Reviews*, 5–6(1): 21–41.

Michael, M. 1992. Lay discourses of science: Science-in-general, science-in-particular, and self. *Science, Technology & Human Values*, 17(3): 313–333.

Mikes, A. 2009. Risk management and calculative cultures. *Management Accounting Research*, 20(1): 18–40.

Mikes, A. 2011. From counting risk to making risk count: Boundary-work in risk management. *Accounting, Organizations and Society*, 36(4–5): 226–245.

Miles, R.E., & Snow, C.C. 1994. *Fit, Failure and the Hall of Fame. How Companies Succeed or Fail.* New York: Free Press.

Mitroff, I.I., Pearson, C., & Pauchant, T.C. 1992. Crisis management and strategic management: similarities, differences and challenges. *Advances in Strategic Management,* 8(2): 235–260.

Morris, M.H., LaForge, R.W., & Allen, J.A. 1994. Salesperson failure: Definition, determinants, and outcomes. *Journal of Personal Selling & Sales Management,* 14(1): 1–15.

Nanda, V.P., & Bailey, B.C. 1988. Export of hazardous waste and hazardous technology: Challenge for international environmental law. *Denver Journal of International Law & Policy,* 17(1): 155–206.

Nelkin, D. 1989. Communicating technological risk: The social construction of risk perception. *Annual Review of Public Health,* 10(1): 95–113.

Norris, F., Stevens, S., Pfefferbaum, B., Wyche, K., & Pfefferbaum, R. 2008. Community resilience as a metaphor, theory, set of capacities, and strategy for disaster readiness. *American Journal of Community Psychology,* 41(1–2): 127–150.

Oreskes, N. 2004. Science and public policy: What's proof got to do with it? *Environmental Science & Policy,* 7(5): 369–383.

Osofsky, H.M. 2013. Multidimensional governance and the BP Deepwater Horizon oil spill. *Florida Law Review,* 65(5): 1077–1137.

Pastor, M., Sadd, J., & Hipp, J. 2001. Which came first? Toxic facilities, minority move-in, and environmental justice. *Journal of Urban Affairs,* 23(1): 1–21.

Pauchant, T.C., & Mitroff, I.I. 1992. *Transforming the crisis-prone organization. Preventing individual organizational and environmental tragedies.* San Francisco: Jossey-Bass.

Perrow, C. 1981. Normal accident at Three Mile Island. *Society,* 18(5): 17–26.

Perrow, C. 1984. *Normal Accidents.* New York: Basic Books.

Perrow, C. 2011. Fukushima and the inevitability of accidents. *Bulletin of the Atomic Scientists,* 67(6): 44–52.

Petroski, H. 1985. *To Engineer Is Human. The Role of Failure in Successful Design.* New York: Barnes and Noble Books.

Pigliucci, M., & Boudry, M. 2014. Prove it! The burden of proof game in science vs. pseudoscience disputes. *Philosophia,* 42(2): 487–502.

Poortinga, W., & Pidgeon, N.F. 2005. Trust in risk regulation: Cause or consequence of the acceptability of GM food? *Risk Analysis,* 25(1): 199–209.

Power, M. 2004. *The Risk Management of Everything: Rethinking the Politics of Uncertainty.* London: Demos.

Power, M. 2005. Organizational responses to risk: The rise of the chief risk officer. In B. Hutter & M. Power (Eds.), *Organizational Encounters with Risk* (pp. 132–148). Cambridge: Cambridge University Press.

Power, M. 2008. *Organized Uncertainty: Designing a World of Risk Management.* Oxford: Oxford University Press.

Power, M. 2009. The risk management of nothing. *Accounting, Organizations and Society,* 34(6–7): 849–855.

Reason, J.T. 1987. An interactionist's view of system pathology. In J.A. Wise & A. Debons (Eds.), *Information Systems: Failure Analysis* (pp. 211–220). Berlin: Springer-Verlag.

Reason, J.T. 1990. *Human Error.* Oxford: Oxford University Press.

Reason, J.T. 1993a. The identification of latent organizational failures in complex systems. In J.A. Wise, V.D. Hopkin, & P. Stager (Eds.), *Verification and Validation of Complex Systems: Human Factors Issues* (Vol. 110, pp. 223–237). Berlin: Springer.

Reason, J.T. 1993b. Managing the management risk: New approaches to organisational safety. In B. Wilpert & T. Qvale (Eds.), *Reliability and Safety in Hazardous Work Systems. Approaches to Analysis and Design* (pp. 7–22). Hove: Lawrence Erlbaum.

Reason, J.T. 1997. *Managing the Risks of Organizational Accidents.* Aldershot: Ashgate.

Riddel, M. 2009. Risk perception, ambiguity, and nuclear-waste transport. *Southern Economic Journal,* 75(3): 781–797.

Rigotti, L., & Shannon, C. 2012. Sharing risk and ambiguity. *Journal of Economic Theory,* 147(5): 2028–2039.

Rumsfeld, D. 2002. DoD News Briefing – Secretary Rumsfeld and Gen. Myers. News Transcript. US Department of Defense, Office of the Assistant Secretary of Defense (Public Affairs). Accessed August 17, 2011 at http://www.defense.gov/Transcripts/Transcript.aspx?TranscriptID=2636

Rumsfeld, D. 2011. *Known and Unknown. A Memoir.* New York: Sentinel.

Sabatier, P.A. 1987. Knowledge, policy-oriented learning, and policy change. *Science Communication,* 8(4): 649–692.

Sabatier, P.A. 1988. An advocacy coalition framework of policy change and the role of policy-oriented learning therein. *Policy Sciences,* 21(2): 129–168.

Serpell, L., & Green, J. 2006. Parental decision-making in childhood vaccination. *Vaccine,* 24(19): 4041–4046.

Sherden, W.A. 1998. *The Fortune Sellers. The Big Business of Buying and Selling predictions.* New York: Wiley.

Short, J.F., Jr. 1984. The social fabric at risk: Toward the social transformation of risk analysis. *American Sociological Review*, 49(6): 711–725.

Shubik, M. 1954. Information, risk, ignorance, and indeterminacy. *Quarterly Journal of Economics*, 68(4): 629–640.

Sipika, C., & Smith, D. 1993. From disaster to crisis: the failed turnaround of Pan American Airlines. *Journal of Contingencies and Crisis Management*, 1(3): 138–151.

Slovic, P., Fischhoff, B., & Lichtenstein, S. 1982. Why study risk perception? *Risk Analysis*, 2(2): 83–93.

Smith, D. 1990. Beyond contingency planning – Towards a model of crisis management. *Industrial Crisis Quarterly*, 4(4): 263–275.

Smith, D. 1992. The strategic implications of crisis management: A commentary on Mitroff et al. In P. Shrivastava, A. Huff, & J. Dutton (Eds.), *Advances in Strategic Management* (pp. 261–269). Stamford, CT: JAI Press.

Smith, D. 1995. The dark side of excellence: Managing strategic failures. In J. Thompson (Ed.), *Handbook of Strategic Management* (pp. 161–191). London: Butterworth-Heinemann.

Smith, D. 2005. Dancing with the mysterious forces of chaos: Issues around complexity, knowledge and the management of uncertainty. *Clinician in Management*, 13(3/4): 115–123.

Smith, D. 2006. Crisis management – practice in search of a paradigm. In D. Smith & D. Elliott (Eds.), *Key Readings in Crisis Management. Systems and Structures for Prevention and Recovery* (pp. 1–12). London: Routledge.

Smith, D., & Elliott, D. 2007. Exploring the barriers to learning from crisis: Organizational learning and crisis. *Management Learning*, 38(5): 519–538.

Smith, D., & Fischbacher, M. 2009. The changing nature of risk and risk management: The challenge of borders, uncertainty and resilience. *Risk Management: An International Journal*, 11(1): 1–12.

Smith, D., & Irwin, G.A. 1984. Public attitudes to technological risk: The contribution of survey data to public policy-making. *Transactions of the Institute of British Geographers*, 9(4): 419–426.

Smith, D., & Sipika, C. 1993. Back from the brink – post crisis management. *Long Range Planning*, 26(1): 28–38.

Smithson, J., & Venette, S. 2013. Stonewalling as an image-defense strategy: A critical examination of BP's response to the Deepwater Horizon explosion. *Communication Studies*, 64(4): 395–410.

Somers, S. 2009. Measuring resilience potential: An adaptive strategy for organizational crisis planning. *Journal of Contingencies and Crisis Management*, 17(1): 12–23.

Teece, D., & Pisano, G. 1994. The dynamic capabilities of firms: An introduction. *Industrial and Corporate Change*, 3(3): 537–556.

Tenner, E. 1996. *Why Things Bite Back. Technology and the Revenge Effect.* London: Fourth Estate.

Toft, B., & Reynolds, S. 1994. *Learning from Disasters.* London: Butterworth.

Topham, G. 2015. Malaysia Airlines chief promises turnaround for "bankrupt" carrier. *Guardian*, June 2, p. 16.

Tsoukas, H. 1999. David and Goliath in the risk society: Making sense of the conflict between Shell and Greenpeace in the North Sea. *Organization*, 6(3): 499–528.

Turner, B.A. 1976. The organizational and interorganizational development of disasters. *Administrative Science Quarterly*, 21: 378–397.

Turner, B.A. 1978. *Man-Made Disasters.* London: Wykeham.

Turner, B.A. 1994. The causes of disaster: Sloppy management. *British Journal of Management*, 5: 215–219.

Uta, J. 2005. Supply chain risk management. *International Journal of Logistics Management*, 16(1): 120–141.

Walton, D.N. 1988. Burden of proof. *Argumentation*, 2(2): 233–254.

Watson, J., & Everett, J. 1999. Small business failure rates: Choice of definition and industry effects. *International Small Business Journal*, 17(2): 31–47.

Weick, K.E. 1993. The collapse of sensemaking in organizations: The Mann Gulch disaster. *Administrative Science Quarterly*, 38: 628–652.

Weick, K.E. 1995. *Sensemaking in Organizations.* Thousand Oaks, CA: SAGE.

Weick, K.E., & Roberts, K.H. 1993. Collective mind in organizations: Heedful interrelating on flight decks. *Administrative Science Quarterly*, 38(3): 357–381.

Wynne, B. 1992. Misunderstood misunderstanding: Social identities and public uptake of science. *Public Understanding of Science*, 1(3): 281–304.

Wynne, B. 1996. May the sheep safely graze? A reflexive view of the expert–lay knowledge divide. In S. Lash, B. Szerszynski, & B. Wynne (Eds.), *Risk, Environment and Modernity. Towards a New Ecology* (pp. 44–83). London: Sage.

Zachary, W., Jason, E.L., & Stephen, A.L. 2008. Supply chain security: An overview and research agenda. *International Journal of Logistics Management*, 19(2): 254–281.

10

Innovation
Managing strategic risk

Luca Gatti

Abstract

This chapter establishes that Strategic Risk – the "biggest risk of all" – is a problem of governance that derives from definitional ambiguity and the recourse to obsolete paradigms. The chapter explores the extent of the problem, particularly in the light of recent market experiences, and articulates a solution. The solution offered is derived from recognition of the idiosyncratic qualities of Strategic Risk and application of a paradigm of strategy that is better suited to decision-making in conditions of uncertainty. Its value is that the solution offers a robust argument for substantive investment in innovation and a disciplined and prudent approach to innovation activities.

Decision-making in Strategic Risk demands a representation of the problem that evolves, frames uncertainty and invests it with relevance, so that activities can be put in place that over time will furnish data, information, intelligence and the capabilities to mitigate, adapt, innovate and, where opportune, commit to new business models. Decision-making, when it comes to Strategic Risk, is therefore exercised over an extended time frame. The notional starting point in the cycle is the identification of relevant strategic risks; this then demands a mandate to articulate a portfolio of strategic options; the options will eventually lead to new strategic commitments that will rest on a reconceptualisation of the business identity. At this point, a new cycle begins.

Having thus established a robust conceptual framework for the management of Strategic Risk and the leveraging of strategic innovation, the chapter reviews general principles for developing capabilities, embedding processes and designing tools.

The problem

Innovation and the governance of uncertainty

Born of the breaking down of geographical barriers and of extraordinary intellectual breakthroughs, the modern world was aptly named the risk society.[1] That world structured its growth and dynamic progress around the capability to radically reduce uncertainty by modelling it. Abundant and consistent data sets and the new probability theory with which to interpret them were leveraged to make sense of the future and thus venture into discovery, invention and enterprise.

Luca Gatti

Yet, its very progress, the opening up this induced to multiple new aspirations, and the exponential technological development it fostered to realise them have by the same measure increased complexity. Most importantly, for decision-making that progress has also multiplied the instances of contexts relevant to us and has increased the speed in the transition we experience from one state of the context to the other. The emerging postmodern society is fast, multidimensional, nonlinear and random in its evolution (Figure 10.1).[2] This uncertainty challenges the generation of relevant intelligence about changes, the possibility of informed choices, the timeliness of action and the effectiveness of new commitments.

Risk is a "measurable uncertainty",[3] but in a postmodern society there are only few instances in which what is measurable is also most relevant to the governance process. When anticipating the nature and evolutions of our context, a reliance on probability is of fast diminishing value.[4] In fact, it is now a cognitive bias in governance that limits access to possibilities that lie outside the cone of probability, and thereby constrains the strategic conversation and commits to courses of action that can prejudice viability in the future. The dominant quality of our context already is, and increasingly will be, 'unmeasurable' uncertainty, a condition that can only be resolved by emergent, discursive, contingent processes of perpetual learning and self-renewal. The implication for institutions and organisations is a need to recognise the ineffectiveness of governance systems anchored to a Newtonian worldview of evident structures, linear evolutions, general laws and predictable dynamics. Effective strategic decision-making under these new circumstances demands a conceptual leap forward, an updating of its paradigms that severs the ties with a modernist perception of context as determined by linearity in its progress and of identity as an effect of consistency of being.

Decision-making systems must establish relevance of the multiple emerging changes, anticipate their implications and mitigate their effects. They must adapt and then learn to leverage those changes with a sustained investment in imagination, experience and possibilities. Success here depends on the flexibility of a strategic identity, on the speed at which it transforms, and on whether that identity can supply itself with a diverse range of options to conceive of new models for strategic renewal. Going forward this will prove to be the most effective approach to

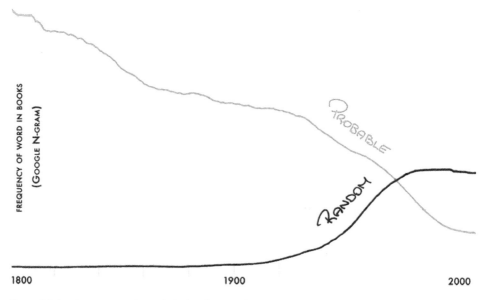

Figure 10.1   Frequency of words in books over last 200 years

managing the unpredictable and idiosyncratic qualities of contexts of experience and activity. And here lies a formidable argument for innovation and a rationale for sustained investments in building capabilities to support and enhance renewal efforts.

Change is changing, but the degree to which change is relevant, and thus an appropriate object of interpretation and a rationale for action, is not in its happening, but in its happening to 'us'. It is not the 'fact' of change that matters, but its relevance, the significance it assumes on account of an agent's identity. It is seldom appreciated in the innovation effort, in the design of its policies and of organisational systems that are intended to make it happen, that innovation has a transitive property: there is 'something' here that wants to renew itself, that makes itself the object of a process of renewal. It is this 'thing', this identity at play that establishes a principle of coherence and thus provides discipline to choices, investments and activities in the innovation effort. It is our sense of self, the robustness of the critical reflection that generates it, the extent of the engagement it emerges from, the richness of its representation that ultimately gives human systems the all-important values of relevance and, therefore, of engagement and effectiveness.

A fulsome appreciation of the idiosyncratic significance of one's relation to change is fundamental to resilience and eventually to generating competitive advantages predicated on distinctiveness and appropriate timing. It is here that risk becomes meaningful, that choices can be argued and purposeful actions can be taken to resolve uncertainty. It is here that strategic leadership matters.

The leadership qualities called for in the renewal of an identity are 'critical', as in capability to engender an organisational reflective 'crisis', an interrogation of fundamental assumptions that acknowledges the need for difference in the way of being. There is an imperative to innovate echoing across social systems, markets, organisations, lecture theatres, design labs and beyond, but there is also a blindness to this effort, a hit-and-run inefficiency that seldom is questioned. With this is a tension between the urgency of innovation (proportional to the increased frequency in change) and the averseness to it of prudent governance (proportional to an increased focus on efficiency and control). To reduce the uncertainty of outcome, risk-averse organisations with renewal intent seek and apply funnelling and evidence-based processes of innovation. What they reduce, instead, is the very stuff of which innovation is made: diversity, dynamic and open exchanges, creativity, obliquity,[5] serendipity, experimentation and learning. The effect is an overwhelming reliance on opportunistic and incremental developments of current value propositions: a tactical, and often very wasteful, innovation activity lacking the relevance and rigour of a robust strategic rationale.

The paradoxical consequences of this approach are strategic single-mindedness, operational short-termism, the funnelling down and the modesty of organisational innovation efforts. This is a consequence of governance systems where decision-makers adjudicate innovation rather than being responsible for fostering it, arguing its case and leveraging its value. All of this ultimately entails a diffuse lack of prudence. If innovation is a response to change, and change is constant and erratic, modest and reductive approaches to innovation can only increase the risk to viability of an entity, thus challenging the prudential concerns of responsible decision-makers.

Strategic Risk can unlock a purposeful and coherent commitment of leadership and governance to ensuring resilience and competitiveness through continuous innovation. The challenge, in leveraging such a strong rationale for innovation, lies in the fact that Strategic Risk is currently stagnating in a quagmire of conceptual haziness, of regulatory contradiction and of governance short-sightedness. All of this merits addressing and solving, for Strategic Risk, when it is fully recognised and managed, when it is the object of a sustained effort of intellectual enquiry and pragmatic solutions, resolves the taxing paradox that decision-makers experience, that is the conflict between stewardship and entrepreneurship.

Strategic Risk: a problem of definition

Absence from governance concerns, the challenging leadership qualities required by what is ultimately an effort of intelligence and interpretation, and lack of strong commitment to its robust management have all resulted in varied and ambiguous definitions of what Strategic Risk actually is.

Often no working definition is to be found as reference in management systems; when available or implicit, definitions range from that which is so 'big' in its effects as to substantially compromise the organization's viability (hence its frequent conflation with systemic risk), to that which, in representing a deviation from the intent and objectives of a strategic plan, affects execution and performance as measured with respect to that plan (hence its frequent conflation with operational risk).[6]

As for the causes of Strategic Risk, external changes are most often referred to; sometimes the quality of internal decision-making; occasionally a combination of both. Though all of these elements may be at play in Strategic Risk, none of these definitions is robust enough to support effective management and none places the problem in the context of decision-making that is specific to strategy and its concerns with resilience and renewal. An additional ambiguity emerges from the unresolved semantic difference between the management of Strategic Risk (which is the specific concern of this chapter) and Strategic Risk management (which often is seen as elevating system-wide risk management protocols to strategic decision-making).

There is a sector in the market where these definitional ambiguities have affected governance and performance very negatively, and to such a degree as to cause a systemic crisis: financial services. The macroscopic importance of the Strategic Risk problem, and the extent to which it is still awaiting an effective management solution, emerge clearly from recent evolutions in its regulation. Given the intermediary and infrastructural nature of the financial services sector its experience has universal relevance, providing arguments for reflecting on the general governance implications of Strategic Risk and for developing an original and robust solution to the problem it represents.

Strategic Risk in financial services

The Global Financial Crisis (GFC) was a turning point in the approach to Strategic Risk, at least in terms of recognising its significance: the "biggest Risk of all".[7] The crisis highlighted the potential impact of complexity and uncertainty when qualitative decision-making, and robust processes to support it, were missing. Weakness in the governance of financial institutions has been recognised as the principal cause of the crisis:[8] at the heart of the problem, and possibly the very source of it, was mismanagement of Strategic Risk.[9]

Ominously, just as the GFC was about to unfold, the regulators were beginning to recognise Strategic Risk as an important concern. The clearest representation of their concern, and of the definitional and management problems associated to it, is the approach taken in 2004 by the Basel Committee. Listing the various risk classes that institutions needed to consider to assess resilience in terms of "overall capital adequacy", the Committee ended with "other risks":

> Although the Committee recognizes that "other" risks, such as Reputational and Strategic Risk, are not easily measurable, it expects industry to further develop techniques for managing all aspects of these risks.[10]

Anything placed at the end and labelled "other" is unlikely to be given priority. There is a concern here with how to measure compliance, rather than with the full articulation of governance principles. Since both of those risks aren't "easily measurable" – reputation being a function of opinion in the market and Strategic Risk a function of uncertainty about the future – the industry was left to find its way, which we now know it didn't and still hasn't. Slighting of Strategic Risk was not the Committee's intent, but its approach had this effect.

In Basel II the preoccupation with sustainability is expressed mostly in terms of capital management. A call for stress testing[11] would appear to single out adverse effects of changes in the context, but the uncertainty of the nature and dynamics of changes, and the long-term concerns this should raise with respect to the resilience of any 'stable' system, were left unrecognised. Only after the GFC did 'long-term' become an explicit reference and the demand for stress testing – a very quantitative paradigm – enriched with a call for more qualitative solutions, such as scenarios and reverse testing, better suited to dealing with uncertainty.[12]

The preoccupation of regulators with Strategic Risk has, since the crisis, increased significantly but has followed a wayward and inconclusive path. The European Banking Supervisors sought to amend the original vagueness of Basel II and attempted to define Strategic Risk, calling out "changes in the business environment" and the quality of "responsiveness" to those changes.[13] But then the GFC happened, so escalation and contagion became primary concerns. Basel III, a response to the crisis, aimed to increase prudential constraints and effectiveness of supervision, hoping to shift from reaction to prevention. For a while, systemic risk and Strategic Risk conflated in the minds of decision-makers and supervisors so that, remarkably, there is no mention in Basel III of Strategic Risk: as the systemic effects of contagion were unravelling, its causes were obscured.

The omission of Strategic Risk in Basel III is really very surprising: clearly, the urgency of introducing system-wide standards and controls side-lined what was not "easily measurable". The problem would not go away, though, and to focus attention on long-term sustainability and quality of governance the regulators eventually had to turn to Strategic Risk.

In a paper delivered at a conference on resilience in the financial system, the Australian regulator's chairman defined Strategic Risk as

> External risks to the viability of a banking institution arising from unexpected adverse changes in the business environment with respect to the economy, the political landscape, regulation, technology, social mores and the actions of competitors.[14]

The challenge of managing Strategic Risk is evident in the view of the Australian Prudential Regulation Authority (APRA) that, despite it being "very difficult to quantify", it is "nonetheless real, and potentially very large".[15] There is a tension in this statement, an unresolved struggle with the nonordinary qualities of Strategic Risk that makes standard paradigms, approaches and controls ineffective. It emerges again when defining how the regulator will exercise its supervisory function:

> [APRA] will need to satisfy itself that the ADI has tested its key planning assumptions under some pessimistic but nonetheless plausible business scenarios.[16]

What we can see at play here, and in all the earlier and subsequent regulatory references to Strategic Risk, is a paradox born of the application of standard frameworks: that which is "very difficult to quantify" is also most important in affecting long-term resilience and quality of decision-making. APRA's choice of words reveals several conceptual constraints that effective management of Strategic Risk will eventually need to challenge and remove. Business scenarios that are "pessimistic but nonetheless plausible" assumes that structural changes that are relevant to the concern of decision-makers should be "plausible": this limits access to that which is "unexpected",[17] therefore not necessarily "plausible", and is accessible with multiple scenarios rich in diversity and possibility ('relevant' is, therefore, a better paradigm). Furthermore, "pessimistic" locks out the entrepreneurial leveraging of insights about changes with which to generate distinctive strategies and competitive advantages. In both instances the deficit in imagination often singled out as the challenge of strategic governance is likely to be confirmed by these constraints.

The ambiguity between the higher conceptual order of the assumptions that a governance system makes (about change, business-model effectiveness, need for strategic flexibility and ultimately strategic innovation) and the operational devices of strategy (a plan with its objectives) is evident throughout all the efforts to deal with Strategic Risk.[18] In fact, what we have seen emerging at various stages in the regulation of Strategic Risk is a tension with the first half of the Strategic Risk definitional problem: strategy. The reference to "key planning assumptions" is trying to move away from a plan and its objectives and locate the issue in organisational entrepreneurial "assumptions" which reside in the individual and collective views of the decision-makers responsible for strategy and the organisational commitments that follow from it.

Ineffectiveness in understanding and managing Strategic Risk is the compound effect of two paradigms, strategy and risk, neither of which in its standard form is useful for developing a robust solution. Given the extent to which risk is the dominant concern in the literature, in the regulation and in the practice of managing Strategic Risk, we turn to it first.

APRA's supervisory instrument, the Probability and Impact Rating System, reveals just how thorny is the conceptual ground the regulator is traversing. APRA acknowledges, very forcefully, the importance of Strategic Risk: "the most fundamental of business risks".[19] The challenge, though, is that APRA is required to 'measure' the risk of the entities it supervises, and Strategic Risk, by its own admission, is "very difficult to quantify".[20] APRA expects the institutions it monitors to address as very significant "any uncertainty in relation to the business operations", whether they be "statistically quantifiable or not", whilst relying for its own supervisory activity on an instrument that is exclusively quantitative in its approach to risk. Clearly, there is a paradox at play here.

A considerable part of the problem is the inability of 'letting go' of the necessity of information to model, support, direct and reassure decision-makers; and yet, this is the 'new' objective quality of the context: it is 'unmeasurable'. The role of strategic leadership here is to resolve uncertainty by determining relevance and thus to provide guidance for those activities that over time furnish intelligence, capabilities and solutions. The role might not be 'new', but the frequency and the intensity with which it needs to be exercised certainly are: systems, organisations and institutions will need to be designed to reflect a new role of governance, new paradigms and principles, and new ways with which to ensure resilience and renewal.

Where APRA lands on firmer conceptual ground is in calling out effects of structural changes in context on the viability of a business-model. APRA seems to recognise that resilience is a function of strategic slack: a "demonstrated capacity to respond to a changing environment" by adapting an entity's business model "to more permanent changes in the competitive environment" as a function of diversification of business activities.[21]

Governance implications

Much of the conceptual weakness we have observed so far stems from the fact that the problem of Strategic Risk has been addressed almost exclusively from the perspective of 'risk', thus with a strong bias for leveraging quantitative modelling to forecast events, measure impacts and mitigate effects.[22] Yet, the traditional paradigm of risk as 'measurable' is unsuited to something which on account of emergent properties, scale of complexity and random dynamics is, in fact, 'unmeasurable': the paradigm needs to be challenged and, at least, stretched. Notably, risk management, an important aggregator of research in the field, has recently called for a sustained effort in this direction, recognising that "the dynamic nature of emergent hazards requires new techniques and analytical frameworks for dealing with low probability high consequence events."[23]

There is a growing unease with disciplinary and organisational boundaries and approaches that privilege "efficiency, control, constancy and predictability – all attributes at the core of desires for fail-safe design and optimal performance. Those desires are appropriate for systems where uncertainty is low."[24]

The decisions that risk demands, and Strategic Risk most obviously so, are with respect to contextual dynamics that very often "lack the a priori evidence that would render them predictable to any degree".[25] This raises important questions about the role of current risk management control systems:

> These controls may inhibit the required levels of adaptation to environmental changes and may, therefore, result in a shift in the very equilibrium that the controls were designed to protect in the first place. This raises a question on how organizations can develop the dynamic capabilities that are required to cope with such challenges.[26]

Those organisations can better "control" and "develop the dynamic capabilities" by establishing that Strategic Risk is an object of qualitative judgement expressed by governance systems that recognise the idiosyncratic nature of the problem they attend to. There is a need to resolve uncertainties, learn about the nature and dynamics of structural changes that determine the degree of relevance they have for the organisation. This can help mandate management to establish an adequate portfolio of strategic options with which to address the problem and its implications, and leverage the organization competitively over time.

The GFC has revealed the extent to which the system is, in effect, global: its control functions to be efficient need to be at scale. Hence, the rapid rise in influence of the Financial Stability Board (FSB). Once it has managed 'systemic risk' by identifying systemically important financial institutions and dealing with them on special terms, the FSB will turn to "analysis of the fundamental, strategic risks that underlie the sustainability of financial institutions' business models".[27]

This statement opens up conceptually to the idiosyncratic and unsystemic nature of Strategic Risk, an important conceptual shift that has two implications: it removes the problem from the standard risk management approaches, and it recognises the organisation-specific business model as the object of concern.

As the FSB seeks to meet its objective – to ensure stability – the particular paradigm of resilience it adopts will frame its actions. As Strategic Risk comes into its focus, the FSB and other market agents will find the currently dominant paradigm of 'stability' ill-suited and likely to induce a reactive and conservative approach to change. Strategic Risk demands, instead, an open and adaptive approach, a 'responsiveness' characterised by spread and quality of options, dynamic management of a portfolio and robustness of strategic arguments for commitment to innovation.

Dealing with the complexity of Strategic Risk requires recognition of the emergent and fast properties of the system; a shift from organizational 'stability' to organic 'resilience'; a systemic strength of evolution rather than recovery of state; and insightful and adaptive pragmatism rather than blunt aspirational objectives and goals.

Regulators may well play a creative role in feeding these principles into governance systems whilst ensuring "that boards are focused on the higher-level strategic and risk issues".[28] In fact, one thing is clear in the muddled waters of Strategic Risk: most stakeholders recognise its importance to long-term resilience and thus for key decision-makers and management.[29] A 2005 *Harvard Business Review* paper[30] gave Strategic Risk a high profile: it documented the degree to which historically Strategic Risk has been the biggest source of loss of shareholder value, and helped enormously in alerting directors and executives to its significance. Ten years on, the experience in financial services has confirmed this case. Unfortunately, the extent to which Strategic Risk is not 'easily measurable' has caused that industry, very biased toward the 'easily measurable', to fail in developing appropriate governance principles and management 'techniques': the Basel Committee's expectation that the industry would develop appropriate solutions has, so far, been disappointed. That is a real problem: Strategic Risk is 'the biggest risk of all'.

Uncertainties that are not 'measurable' should be the object of qualitative judgement, the core of strategic leadership. The USA Financial Crisis Inquiry Commission set up to reflect on the causes of the GFC recognised how 'judgment' rather than modelling was a key to effective decision-making: in "too many instances" decision-makers have "embraced mathematical models as reliable predictors of risks, replacing judgment".[31] The judgement one would expect to see exercised is strategic, and the regulatory pattern is clear: Strategic Risk, and the critical long-term decision-making it demands, is principally the responsibility of boards, with the Group of Thirty advocating that an appropriate time frame of concern be set from 5 to 20 years. "Looking at the next two years is not strategic; it is tactical. Boards must oversee the present and ensure the future."[32]

Ensure is very much a keyword: governance of the future calls for a management rationale of hedging through rich and effective options. Strategic Risk is ultimately a problem of decision-making under conditions of complexity and uncertainty that test resilience, whilst sustaining an entrepreneurial intent by developing adaptive capabilities and future strategic commitments. Establishing Strategic Risk as a focus of board attention has an important effect: this level of governance is instrumental in leading a gradual transition from managing the uncertainty on which Strategic Risk is predicated to renewing the business assumptions on which decisions are based, thus allowing for and leveraging business model innovation. A good, simple, useful paradigm that frames the problem and allows for robust decision-making is called for. Rather than being brushed aside as 'complicated' on account of a lack of 'measurability' and of the 'softness' of the leadership skills that are called for, Strategic Risk requires, instead, to be addressed head-on: adopting effective conceptual frameworks that resolve its complexity and that will structure behaviours, decisions and solutions.

The determination of relevance is a function of qualitative judgement, as is the articulation of robust arguments for commitments to renewal: the solution to the problem of Strategic Risk has in the qualitative nature of strategic decision-making its key design principle. Judgment, if it is to be expressed collegiately and with respect to as difficult a matter as Strategic Risk, demands terms of reference: it is important, therefore, that organisations cultivate in people and embed across functions a sense of strategy that is simple and systemic, and support it with processes so robust as to make it become a pervasive organisational sense of self. Particularly important also is that their governance systems attribute a more anticipatory, reflective and active role to directors: in the governance of Strategic Risk, what matters most is the quality of conversation among decision-makers (its openness and its constancy) and the depth of engagement with its issues (the richness with which this engagement feeds insights and opportunities).

The solution

Strategy as coherence: a paradigm for the governance of Strategic Risk

By far the greatest challenge in managing Strategic Risk is that 'risk' has received most of the attention; and yet, 'strategy' is at the heart of the problem and constitutes the truly significant term in the Strategic Risk compound. The two terms, in fact, sit uncomfortably together: they reach solutions following distinct heuristics – one qualitative, the other quantitative. Given the nature of the problem as outlined earlier, it could be argued that Strategic Risk is a misnomer,[33] were it not for the fact that the solution, as we shall see, is one that transits from significant uncertainty that escapes modelling, to informed uncertainty that allows for the structuring of choice and future commitments.

As decision-makers turn to strategy, though, they struggle with the ineffectiveness of the dominant paradigm as embedded in organisations and their governance systems. Despite advances in the theoretical understanding of strategy towards more dynamic and resource-based models,[34] the paradigm of strategy dominating organisational cultures and systems, which structures mind-sets, behaviours and activities, derives from industrial processes, typified by the American manufacturing corporation:[35] determination of aspirational objectives, mostly financial and short term, and articulation of a plan on which to invest resources and align efforts. The strategic 'plan' is an operational device with which conceptually lazy organisations seek to transform a challenging, discursive and dynamic process of reflection, insight and choice into an object.

The effect is a dangerous concentration of commitment on the assumptions that underpin the plan and in the activities that support achieving an organisational goal. This strategy paradigm assumes stability over time in the business environment and in the firm's identity and purpose, and seeks to maximise efficiency by leveraging scale, hierarchy and rigid control systems. It fosters a governance bias for stability, consistency and compliance. It is a paradigm fundamentally at odds with structural, rapid and random changes in the nature and dynamics of social experience and of the context of business in particular, and, consequently, with changes in the nature of the business firm and in the needs and expectations of customers and other agents. The practice of strategy it fosters is ineffective in supporting governance systems that are called to determine relevance, resolve uncertainty and effect renewal, and thus weakens the determination to address Strategic Risk and the possibility of managing it effectively over time.

A conceptual architecture is called for that can establish and help apply a diffused risk-taking rationale that does not threaten the resilience of the organisation, but in fact enhances it by managing structural shifts in the context to generate consistent competitive advantage. This framework must enable the decision-makers to be creative and entrepreneurial, and therefore allow them to take on more risk than they typically might do, whilst being rigorous in applying the discipline of good, prudent business management.[36] A simple rationale must be embedded that will harness renewal efforts with a discipline of decision-making informed by relevance, intelligence and ongoing learning that eventually will lead to the design of new forms.

Strategy is an intellectual pursuit demanding critical thinking, interpretive effort and creative capability. Furthermore, negotiating the rationale for action in human systems is a complex political activity, and to that extent it is essentially a process of social learning. Strategy emerges from an iterative negotiation of differences. It is pragmatic in recognising contingency, fluid in responding to its constraints and reflective in generating meaningful and effective responses; it demands critical questioning of the self and its status in time. That interrogation engenders recognition of the degree to which any adjustment made to the self, in order for that entity to be resilient and successful, calls for access to relevant externalities: What 'out there' matters? How and when will it change? What do I need to change of myself to survive and thrive? Where do I find the resources to do so? And what models should I design and graft my new self into?

In the process of strategy there is an underlying richness of elements and a dynamic complexity that needs reducing to furnish decision-makers with a stronghold on the overarching concern. Strategy can be 'made' simple by resolving its complexity in terms of a system's view, which allows us to think of it as the activity by which human systems establish and manage a coherent relationship between who they are and why they are there, and their environment or context.

Luca Gatti

Figure 10.2   As context changes, so must identity to stay coherent

Any agent that has a will to be is at play in a context, with respect to which it seeks to maximise its purpose – to last in time and to do so meaningfully. On account of this intent it interprets the nature and dynamics of the context and understands the value of its own position with respect to it.

As the context changes, so must the agent, to adapt and better leverage the new configuration (Figure 10.2).

The abstract system's view of what is fundamentally a relational dynamic empowers a cognitive appreciation of what is essential to the problem of strategy and Strategic Risk, and thus structures our approach to it, ultimately allows us to effectively solve it. A human system needs to be coherent with context and its evolutions over time. Therefore, coherence between identity and context is the true object of strategic thinking and strategic decision-making.

The main conceptual value this simplification provides is the degree to which 'quality' is a function of two terms that stand in relation to each other whereby decision-makers can better comprehend and resolve an extremely high level of complexity. This paradigm establishes a relational system that evolves dynamically as each of the terms changes. The control and design of this dynamic relationship is necessarily emergent and evolutionary: it is an activity, not a 'thing'. The adaptive properties of this conceptual solution are better suited to the speed and random directions of change, to the scale of complexity of the environment in which institutions and organisations need to operate effectively and competitively.

Coherence has no metrics and is an eminently 'qualitative' paradigm. Strategic decision-making can, on account of the articulation and application of this framework, shift from a passive and reactive focus on quantitative modelling (based on retrospection and past performance data) to an active focus on qualitative interpretation of the future (based on insight and learning). One is the object of measurement; the other an effect of judgement. It is now possible, therefore, to address and satisfy the most important concerns to have emerged with respect to Strategic Risk: the decision-making at the board and executive levels as to the resilience and competitiveness of a current business model.

The focus on coherence has an important effect: it shifts the object of strategy away from either identity or from context. The object of design in strategy is coherence. Incoherence, therefore, is the risk.

A systemic and structurally simple understanding of strategy enables an effective definition of Strategic Risk: if strategy works to produce coherence between an identity and its future context, then Strategic Risk is the possibility of an incoherence occurring between those same two terms.

A robust definition of Strategic Risk is an important outcome, for it has so far eluded governance systems. Strategic-risk emerges from changes, mostly external, that an organisation will experience and that would have an impact on its survival and performance. This risk is a function of incoherence between the current identity and future relevant evolutions of the context.

The safest – statistically most robust – assumption to make about the future is constancy of change and randomness of the reconfigurations that emerge. Incoherence is, therefore, an unavoidable condition in the dynamic relationship between an identity and its future context, hence the need to embed processes and functions to constantly and effectively manage it.

Defining Strategic Risk as the possibility of a mis-relationship between an identity and a future context offers an organic understanding of 'risk': the role of strategy being the constant negotiation of incoherencies produced by dynamics of change. This definition furnishes decision-makers with clear terms of reference with which to prudently manage Strategic Risk. It requires participants to address the 'qualitative' nature of the problem.

Identity and Context

If resilience and competitiveness depend on strategic coherence, then adequate self-awareness (Identity) and good distributed intelligence about drivers of change and future environments (Context) are necessary for robust strategic decision-making: both terms need articulating and representing for the relationship to be managed.

Identity is a state of self-recognition, an awareness that comes out of interaction and negotiation with a Context and its difference, alterity, plurality and dynamics over time. Strategic self-awareness starts with critical self-reflection. When engaging with Strategic Risk, therefore, the first step is to articulate a systemic representation of Identity. This is a conceptual snapshot, an organisational rationale that captures three dimensions: what need explains its existence, what resources are used and transformed to engage with the need, and what contextual elements are necessary for this exchange.

The output of this activity is the most important for the purpose of identifying Strategic Risks, for it is by reference to it that relevance of changes in the context will be derived. It is an 'image' that emerges from a social conversation; it organises knowledge, establishes a shared sense of Identity and aligns a system around it. The image must resolve differences and ambiguities, and must extend beyond a mere description of activities and products toward an understanding of the rationale at play, one where causality matters a lot more than finality. The output needs to identify the structural elements, synoptically visualise the relations between them and represent the gravitational forces that make the system dynamic. It must have a mnemonic effect standing as a constant term of reference to foster recognition, insights and foresight. When executed, it will stay as an organisational asset, a self-portrait that is the object of ceaseless critical reflection and representation, a pivot of strategic insight and intent.[37]

Whether this 'strategic' conversation happens and the degree to which it is deep, challenging and rich in the complexity it discovers and addresses are a function of the quality of leadership in the organisation. It would be hard to underestimate the importance of this reflective conversation: most institutions and organisations become irrelevant when the need they serve has shifted and they fail to notice.

Coherence is a function of change: it is change to the Self that ensures resilience over time. The situations and problems we encounter are the outcome of choices already taken. The object of strategic decision-making, therefore, is how an Identity will be, or may not be, coherent with states of its Context in time: the tense of Strategy, in other words, is the Future.

In the past, experience has served us well and allowed us to identify patterns that we could project forward to probabilistically model the next stages of evolution in the Context. Today, relying on information from the past does little to enhance resilience and nothing to generate competitiveness. What is possible and relevant is strategically more important than what is probable: a focus on the probable has the effect of substantially reducing the range of possible future evolutions of the Context that are made available for observation, experience and interpretation. Imagination and good judgement at the highest level of decision-making are needed to conceive of that which is possible and to interpret its relevance. The problem of dealing with the Future is that it beams no data back to us; it is truly «uncertain». This problem has no obvious solution. All we can do is pragmatically recognise that and deal with it creatively.

Lack of knowledge of the Future is best resolved through imagination: by means of a representation that which does not exist in 'fact' can be made to exist in 'meaning'. The purpose of imagination is not to approximate reality, but to establish possibility and relevance: the value of meaningful representations of the Future is pragmatic and contingent, not absolute. In imagining possible Futures what matters is whether they work to stimulate insights and actions: a robust representation of a possible Future allows capturing its significance. Generating iconic forms that synoptically resolve complexity in meaningful representation of the Future is the better effort. Snappy, symbolic and challenging representations, built around one particular element in the Future, distribute intelligence and focus the interpretive effort. What will make the stories 'robust' is their collective effect: by whichever means,[38] the stories need to represent changes in the Context that would substantially reconfigure the world and will need to communicate their significance in such a way as to induce engagement and determine relevance.

Narrative representation of the Future is a human activity with a long history: meaning resolves complexity and in so doing empowers choice and action. But if narratives about the Future are very effective in framing the infinite complexity of Future time, they do not, however, have any superior order of certainty about how the Future will emerge. We all know, intuitively, that a story about the Future is not 'true', thus any decision based on it retains a significant amount of uncertainty: best be constantly aware and resolutely manage the complexity that derives from this. The experience of uncertainty is, of course, uncomfortable: deferred decision-making does not rank high in performance metrics, and there is an executive bias toward 'closure', the selection of a single assumption about the Future on which to base a seemingly reliable course of actions.

The only effective way of dealing with the fundamental uncertainties of the Future is, therefore, to adopt a portfolio approach to its possibilities:[39] because we know our story of the Future to be not true or sufficient, prudence demands that we have a good spread of such stories. The quality of a portfolio of possible Futures depends on its breadth: the latitude of the spread is here more important than the depth of the individual stories, for that range determines whether attention has been given to possibilities that are unexpected, surprising and therefore more disruptive.

Managing Strategic Risks

Quantitative modelling of Strategic-Risk is not merely ineffective: it is positively dangerous. It induces decision-makers to focus exclusively on the landscape of data available at a point in time: they look at what is considered to be probable, which is merely a fraction of what might be possible given the evolving and random dynamics of complexity over time. Availability and amount of data are in no way indicators of significance.

When a rich, varied and engaging spectrum of Futures is brought to bear on the representation of Identity, a sense of possible and relevant incoherencies arises. This process is a virtual 'wind tunnelling' that highlights aspects of Identity that would no longer be sustainable in those Futures. When we reflect on the significance of a wide range of possible future changes and we can observe consistency in the specific incoherencies that emerge across the spectrum, we are developing cognitive robustness and deriving a strong rationale for mitigating actions.

The outcome of this interpretive effort, to be fully appreciated and to adequately inform governance processes, needs to be communicated and represented effectively, where persuasion is a function of relevance and clarity in the representation. Shifts in the nature and dynamics of complex systems, and the relevance this may have, can only be resolved through powerful abstractions: the representation of Strategic Risk is an abstract form that synthetically organises and controls the relevance of its underlying materials. Its structure is simple, and emerges as a visual statement from the following query: what about us now is incoherent with what has changed in our Context in the Future? This representation consolidates insights and concerns, making them available for qualitative judgement, providing a reference for reflections and a structure to the strategic conversations. Its form purposefully denies the possibility and the recourse to a quantitative view of the problem. It is at this critical point that a process of constant and collective qualitative judgement gradually and meaningfully resolves the uncertainty. Judgement with respect to this order of Risk can only be expressed in terms of degrees of relevance and strategic concern (or incoherence). On the 'quality' of this judgement rests the determination to act to better understand, to resolve, and eventually renew.

The Strategic Risks that are identified and articulated must remain an object of interpretation and enquiry: they are assumed into governance systems as emergent possibilities, uncertainties framed by relevance. There is a very idiosyncratic quality to Strategic Risk, which is a function of the relevance of a change dynamic to an individual, distinct entity. That relevance in relation to dynamics of change is the object of prudent positioning and of strategic learning. By negotiating change in its Context an organisation learns, develops needed capabilities and thereby increases its agility: it can do so most effectively by developing Strategic Options.

Strategic options

Good management of Strategic Risk is, ultimately, an effect of timely renewal: Strategic Innovation.

To develop relevant knowledge about the world, and thus re-conceptualise their position with respect to that world, human systems learn. Systems learn by negotiating and responding to a difference in their state:[40] Strategic Innovation, therefore, is a function of learning. Organisations rarely structure themselves to optimise their learning capabilities and to leverage them effectively to engender a new sense of Self.

Learning in human systems occurs as a cycle of phases[41] that progresses (Figure 10.3) from a concept (the representation of reality or of a problem), to action (a decision to move into reality, a determination to do), to experience (an observation of reality, first-hand engagement), to reflection (the interpretation of effects and significance) and back to concept (rearticulation of the original concept, innovation).

The paradigm of learning brings to the management of Strategic Risk the knowledge that the constant possibility of incoherence between an Identity and its Context can be managed through a cycle of conceptualisation, action, experience, reflection and, if need be, renewal. It is the design and deployment of Strategic Options that most effectively induces a learning cycle in organisations and thus enables Strategic Innovation. Having Options in strategy is prudent and the most effective and competitive way of managing Strategic-Risk: after all, it is the capacity to produce a difference in the Self so as to adapt to new environmental conditions that matters in evolution.

Strategic Options are learning devices. They take a position with respect to change that provides experience and intelligence necessary to evolve the business identity.[42] A Strategic Option can be anything that delivers the value of being designed for future strategic action: a service, a product, a project, research, acquiring or developing a capability, investing and so forth. On the other hand, no matter what the Option might be, it must be 'strategic' in the sense that it sustains or develops coherence with a future Context. Each Strategic Option is designed to carry a possibility of Innovation, to generate an intelligence derived from experience that can, at an opportune moment in future time, renew, transform or enrich a structural element in the current Identity.

The ability to design Strategic Options is a core competence: these 'devices' have a positional value, offer experiential insights, develop strategic resources, identify new models and ultimately carry to full maturity an argument for Strategic Innovation. That effort demands rare qualities: an understanding of Strategic Risk and its implications; appreciation of an Identity in

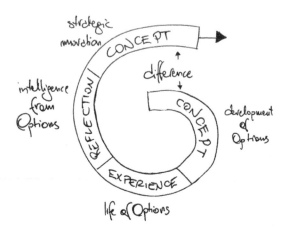

Figure 10.3   The strategic learning cycle

terms of its systemic and emergent properties; insightful and visionary understanding of the of future structural changes to the Context; a multi-trans-inter-disciplinary design competence with extraordinary intelligence functions; deep functional engagement within the organisation; robust skills of strategic communication with internal and external stakeholders.

Strategic Options have significance in that they hedge uncertainty about changes in Context: hence, a single Option is, clearly, insufficient in managing the spectrum of uncertain possibility. Rather than selecting one or two Options through funnelling processes of prioritisation and selection, good basic risk-management prudence suggests a contrary approach: articulate a broad portfolio of Options with which to hedge against the unexpected. Just as the individual Options are an object of strategic design – for which robust and sophisticated processes are required – so is a portfolio.

A robust portfolio of Strategic Options minimises risk and maximises opportunity by articulating a range of possible actions that hedge against loss of value. It is here that designers and key-decision-makers dynamically manage their Strategic Risks; here is where significant sense-making occurs, where relationships are activated and leveraged, where triggers are monitored, resources developed and acquired. And it is in here and from here that persuasive arguments for renewal are drafted. The relevance, the richness, the dynamism, the intelligence and the designerly approach make this the centre of resilience and renewal. Embedding such a capability in any organisation today is a strategic imperative: not doing so is imprudent and denies access to the possibility of Strategic Innovation.

Coherent, purposeful, informed change, from which resilience and competitiveness are derived, is a function of the time during which Strategic Options have been at play and the manner in which their value has been recognised and leveraged. Only at this point have key decision-makers fully addressed the implications of Strategic-Risk. Where time, intelligence and capital are used to develop and leverage an effective portfolio of Options by which to enhance adaptive strategic flexibility, the effect is not merely in terms of resilience:[43] in the case of business organisations, evidence suggests that over 15 years, they will "be worth an average of 40% more" than those companies – the majority – that do not have the same approach.[44]

Management of Strategic Risk rests, ultimately, on making a change to the nature of the Self: at the right time, with robust intelligence about the context, leveraging new competencies and applying new forms and models. Success in Strategic Innovation is, ultimately, an effect of leadership. At the very core of it is – there should be – an entrepreneurial intent, a willingness to take risk and a capability to structure choices that will support and satisfy that intent over time. This is the stuff of entrepreneurship, but entrepreneurship is often at odds with executive mindsets and management practices, especially when a turbulent and uncertain business environment appears to argue strongly for a modest assumption of risk.

Quality, in Strategic Leadership, is a function of a distinctive and organically coherent sense of Self, of participative processes and social engagement, of pragmatic intelligence and distinct capabilities, exercised over time.[45] It is over time that stewardship and entrepreneurship blend their intents: over time, the availability of Options will increase resilience and generate sustained value. At the heart of the conceptual framework presented here is the possibility to express qualitative judgement over time and across change: capabilities, processes and tools must be developed, embedded and designed to make the expression of judgement robust and effective.

A strategic innovation capability

Innovation is an emergent quality of environments that are rich in diversity, open to change, quick at transforming, smart at evolving. Innovation does not lend itself to being directed to meet a pre-established objective: it is a process in which opportunities arise obliquely[46] and unexpectedly. However robust the process of Strategic Risk management is, its innovation potential can only be sustained if the culture of the organisation allows emergence and has the capability to make innovation happen. Generating Strategic Options will prove ineffective if the system producing them is unwilling to engage in critical thinking or is incapable of changing. Innovation is a function of culture and of leadership: creating organisational contexts that allow for sufficient 'slack' and leadership qualities conducive of innovation may well be the most critical responsibility of any innovation effort.

The adoption of a Strategic Risk framework enables an organisation to engage in a sustained activity of Strategic Innovation. Implementing of this activity, however, requires appropriate governance systems and focused execution: if resilience is the effect of renewal with respect to change in Context, then this demands a functional capability that can induce and support renewal, by providing a rationale (Strategic-Risk) and the means (Strategic Options). Such a functional capability is responsible for the set of activities that fully sediments the conceptual framework of Strategic Risk into the organisation; its core mandate is to initiate and support the process by which Strategic Risks are identified and managed and Options are developed, held and eventually exercised. In this sense, it directs resources, practices and outputs to create resilience over time and constantly develop capabilities to stay competitive.

To enable intelligence flows, any Strategic Innovation function must have a lean, flexible, dynamic and open structure that manages and leverages an extensive network within and outside of the organisation, ultimately creating and leveraging an ecosystem it relates to osmotically and structures within it which it 'feeds' on symbiotically. This functional Strategic Innovation System is essentially a hub with soft organisational boundaries; it is a centre of strategic intelligence that seeds and sustains innovation by leveraging partnerships and a co-creative interdisciplinary approach to developing Strategic Options; it also makes design capabilities available across its ecosystem to leverage intelligence and identify immediate opportunities in those areas of the organisation that can best develop competitive services and products in the current Context. The latter is an important outcome of any innovation effort, if appropriately recognised and channelled, for it builds momentum and retains support for an activity that resolves itself on longer time frames.

The design of strategic options

Change in Context as seen through the exercise of projecting an Identity in a spectrum of possible Futures acquires a specific relevance that is both idiosyncratic (it is relevant to us) and consolidated (it emerges as an interpretive effort across multiple distinct possibilities).

The articulation of a set of Strategic Risks that is specific to a particular agent means that a strong filter of relevance has been applied. A much reduced, and very significant, landscape of structural shifts in the future is now available, to become the object of interest and positioning. Structural Changes are, to this extent, the necessary reference point for the design of Strategic Options: it is with respect to their relevance and uncertainty that Options will need to be deployed.

Options are learning hypotheses, positions through which to experience and reflect on the dynamics of change in the environment and develop insights and capabilities with which to modify the business identity and thus enhance resilience and competitiveness. For an effective process of design a robust general working definition is needed:

> An option is a position we are in with respect to action that we may and can execute at an opportune moment in time.

The value of this working definition is that it provides a backbone structure with respect to which we can articulate design principles and identify features for the generation of Options (Figure 10.4).

The Option can be said to be 'strategic' if it satisfies the purpose of enabling coherence. There is considerable variety as to what may give the positional value of an Option: it can be a project, a product, an investment, a research program, etc. What is essential is that the Option is a position that is taken 'now', that is, that the experiential value that it might give is immediately activated. The action that the Option prepares for is a decision of strategic nature, it is the commitment in the market that will be the function of the determination of a new identity. The core value of an Option is the extent to which it sustains a choice and establishes the possibility of an argument for change. The experiential dimension is designed to develop capabilities, find and attract resources, design new business-models and deliver solutions. An option is executed when its argument is realised, when the possibility of action is turned into actual engagement. The time at which an option is executed must be a function of opportunity, of the recognition that there are optimal conditions in the market at which to succeed: that opportunity will emerge in the future.

The process for designing Strategic Options has a general architecture (see Appendix 10.1) that has three structural elements: Argument, Choice and Design.

The Argument establishes a rationale for the organisation to commit to a Strategic Option and articulates the terms of reference for concrete investment in the present. The Argument addresses a Structural Change to manage the Strategic Risks that emerge from it, and derives its logical structure from an identified area of Change. As the nature of Structural Changes is uncertain, the Argument resolves the uncertainty by inducing an imaginative representation of elements in a future context that would be of strategic interest.

Choice is the point in the development of a Strategic Option when, on account of the Argument, a determination can be made that shifts the focus of attention from the future to the present. The concern now turns away from the uncertainty of the Structural Change towards the firmness of the surrounding ground: from 'there' to 'here', and to where 'here' we can establish a Position from which to observe the nature and dynamics of change in the context and learn how to be coherent with it. Once this determination is articulated, information about the chosen ground is assembled and material elements gathered with which an effective Option can be designed.

Design is where the substantiation occurs of a Strategic Argument into a prototyping and executive blueprint. Here a material output is generated that, if activated, would create a point of experience, would return strategic intelligence, would gather, develop and attract resources, and ultimately would enable strategic innovation. The intent in this phase is to design a strategic learning device, and to do so by reference to a set of specifically articulated design principles. To achieve

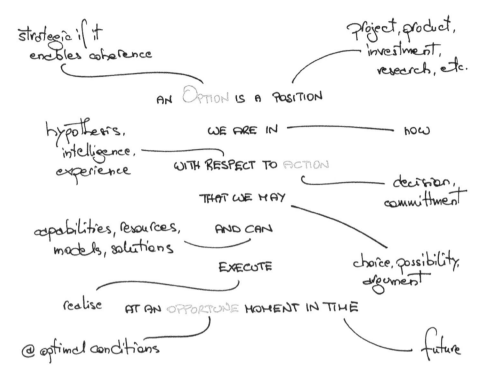

Figure 10.4 Working definition of strategic option

this, the possible solutions are explored and prototyped, and from these iterations a blueprint eventually emerges that supports effective communication, attribution of value and selection.

Dynamic Strategic Risk reporting and decision-making

The intent of governance systems is to affect organisational behaviour and actions by taking decisions based on the significance given to data considered sufficiently reliable.[47] The challenge with Strategic Risk, and with the nature and dynamics of the changes that are significant to it, is that data is either not available, or is available in forms that do not allow for robust determination.[48] Organisations seeking effective governance of Strategic Risk, therefore, need to develop and implement a dynamic reporting system to enable qualitative strategic decision-making.

Conditions of fundamental uncertainty induce decision-making biases that lead governance systems to either not consider the problem relevant, or to rely on what data happens to be available, regardless of its actual importance. It should be apparent, by now, that Strategic Risk does not lend itself to the standard protocol of risk reporting. It is essential that the design of a reporting system acknowledges the extraordinary complexity that Strategic Risk subsumes. To this end, it is dynamic and interactive visualisation that must be leveraged.

Visualisation is an emergent concern in the practice of risk management. As the 'bigness' of data explodes and its excess supply challenges its interpretation, the synoptic, intuitive, interactive and dynamic qualities of visualisation of data will become increasingly valuable. In the case of Strategic-Risk, though, uncertainty is a function of dearth of data, of ambiguity, of speed of change, of systemic complexity, random emergence, turbulence, and any of the properties of complex systems dynamics. So, the principle value of visualisation in reporting Strategic-Risk

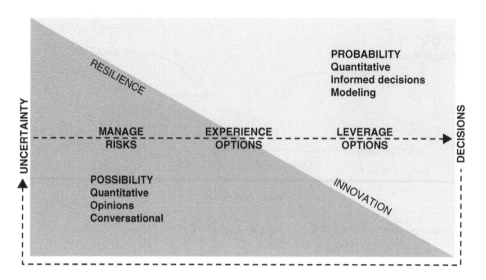

Figure 10.5   Option design process

is that of making synoptically available all the structural elements that are constitutive of the decision-making activity, and provide a constant reference and support to the exploration of the problem landscape (Appendix 10.1).

Conclusion

The complexity of Strategic Risk, and the conceptual ambiguity and operational ineffectiveness this has induced, can be resolved: to do so in the terms I have done in this chapter resolves a taxing paradox between the intents of stewardship and entrepreneurship, and articulates a strong argument for sustained investment in innovation. That effort, to be effective, calls for the articulation and adoption of a simple and robust paradigm of Strategy. From here can be derived a definition of Strategic Risk and can be designed processes by which to manage it well and competitively (Figure 10.5).

The outcome is a set of dynamic capabilities with which to resiliently and competitively negotiate change in the context. Organisational instances in which such an approach has been embedded[49] make a compelling case for leveraging Strategic Risk in developing advanced innovation capabilities, that leverage intelligence, design, experience and learning. There is a strong need to refresh the role of strategic governance in these terms, so that they may induce processes of renewal and lead them effectively.

Notes

1 Beck, 1992.
2 Nowotny, 2008.
3 Knight, 1921.
4 Taleb, 2008.
5 Kay, 2011.
6 Acharyya, 2010.
7 Slywotzky & Drzik, 2005.
8 Financial Crisis Inquiry Committee, 2001, p. xix.

9 The event that stands out as symbolically most representative of the crisis, the collapse of Lehman Brothers, has in fact been explained as a failure to manage strategic risk (McConnell, 2012). Strategic risk has been associated also with several other failures in financial services, such as Northern Rock, IKB Bank, Bears Sterns, LTCM and BCCI (Acharyya, 2010, pp. 86–87). Two other important cases would be the collapse of Equitable Life in the UK, on account of an unsustainable strategic commitment to customer focus (O'Brien, 2006) and HIH in Australia (HIH Royal Commission, 2003).

10 Bank for International Settlements, 2004, p. 742.

11 Bank for International Settlements, 2004, p. 726.

12 Bank for International Settlements, 2010, p. 8.

13 As quoted in Allen, 2007.

14 Laker, 2007.

15 Australian Prudential Regulation Authority [APRA], 2007, p. 10.

16 Ibid.

17 Laker, 2007.

18 See, for instance, the USA's Comptroller of the Currency: "the risk to current or anticipated earnings, capital, or franchise or enterprise value arising from adverse business decisions, poor implementation of business decisions, or lack of responsiveness to changes in the banking industry and operating environment. This risk is a function of a bank's strategic goals, business strategies, resources, and quality of implementation" (Comptroller of the Currency. Administrator of National Banks, 2010, p. 60).

19 APRA, 2007, p. 13, 7.4.

20 APRA, 2007, p. 10.

21 Ibid. For an exploration of the effects of innovation and capital structure in relation to strategic slack, see Andersen, 2009.

22 Strategic Risk has not figured prominently in Enterprise Risk Management. Surprisingly, given that a 2004 study of the 100 companies with the largest stock price losses during the ten year period 1995–2004 concluded that 66 suffered from Strategic Risk. The same study concluded that there appears to be a management bias toward focusing on risks that are either more common or more easily predictable (Gates, 2006, p. 82).

23 Smith & Fischbacher, 2009, p. 1.

24 Ibid., p. 8.

25 Ibid., p. 2.

26 Ibid., p. 10.

27 Financial Stability Board, 2012, p. 1.

28 Ibid., p. 6.

29 According to a survey by Schmidt and Chao (2010, p. 10), 53% of the interviewed board members believed that strategic risk was the biggest threat to the company, whilst only 15.7% identified financial risk as a key concern. One would expect this to be different in financial services: the challenge here, though, is that the concentration of financial risk appears to have reduced attention to strategic risk. According to Schmidt and Chao, only 28 out of 50 banks reviewed recognise strategic risk, and of these 28, only 15 provide a definition of it.

30 Slywotsky & Drzik, 2005. Shortly after Slywotsky, Mango focused on the insurance business and published a paper that had as a principle merit that of recognising the importance of a qualitative approach to managing a risk that does not lend itself to standard treatment (Mango, 2007). In more recent times the subject of strategic risk in systemically important financial institutions has been taken up by Patrick McConnell, who has highlighted the importance of an adequate management of the risk, considerable differences in the way the problem is dealt with in several entities and the extent to which strategic risk should be principally a Board concern (McConnell, 2012).

31 Financial Crisis Inquiry Committee, 2001, p. xix.

32 Group of Thirty, 2012, pp. 20 and 40. See also OECD, 2009, p. 9.

33 Allen, 2007.

34 Teece, Pisano, & Shuen, 1997.

35 Chandler, 1962.

36 Andersen, Garvey, & Roggi, 2014.

37 Where the concern is that of a business, there are many descriptive formulae to represent it and its activities. All of them tend to create a company-centred view of the world: a view structured around "need" shifts the focus and allows for an outside-in perspective to be generated that singles out the structural elements that matter and captures systemically the relationships at play.

38 The methodology by which the stories are created can be one of many available (of which Scenarios in the Shell tradition would stand out as the most tried).

39 As to how to arrange the portfolio's spread, I would suggest, like Markowitz, that ultimately the quality of the portfolio depends on good judgment (Markowitz, 1952, p. 91). The guiding principle of that judgment should be the quest to capture meaningful, possible and distinctive features of the future. Following the GFC there has been a very significant attention on the part of the regulators towards "stress testing". It is important to observe that once again the regulators run against the limitations of standard quantitative modelling. Hence an increasing call for more qualitative representations of change to support reflection, and ultimately action, on the part of key decision-makers. Regulators have, in fact, started referring to scenarios and, very interestingly, to reverse testing: it is the latter, in particular, that reveals the extent to which regulators are concerned about "failures of imagination" and the effect this has on the resilience of financial institutions (Basel Committee on Banking Supervision, 2009, p. 13).

40 Luhmann, 1995, pp. 59–102.

41 Kolb & Fry, 1975.

42 Bowman & Hurry, 1993.

43 Andersen, 2009.

44 Hall, Lovallo, & Musters, 2012.

45 The recognition of trigger points and the opportunity of commitments will, instead, be a function of the quality of decision-making at a specific point in time and as supported by the robustness of argumentation inherent in the options. Attention to strategic risk exposes short-termism and exclusive concentration on current opportunities as imprudent: given the current concerns with the quality of governance and the use of longer time frames in key decision-making, this must in itself be of value.

46 Kay, 2010.

47 Peters, 2008, p. 296.

48 If information is sufficiently and reliably available, one should deal with it in the terms of standard operational decision-making and risk management protocols.

49 See chapter 13, this volume.

References

Acharyya, M. (2010). The role of operational risk and strategic risk in the enterprise risk management framework of financial services firms. *International Journal of Services Sciences, 3*(1), 79–102.

Allen, B. (2007, September 1). The best-laid plans . . . *Risk Magazine*. Retrieved from http://www.risk.net/risk-magazine/analysis/1506621/the-laid-plans

Andersen, T.J. (2009). Effective risk management outcomes: Exploring effects of innovation and capital structure. *Journal of Strategy and Management, 2*(4), 352–379.

Andersen, T. J., Garvey, M., & Roggi, O. (2014). *Managing Risk and Opportunity. The Governance of Strategic Risk-Taking*. Oxford: Oxford University Press.

Australian Prudential Regulation Authority. (2007). *Implementation of the Basel II Capital Framework. 10 Supervisory Review Process*. Sydney: APRA Public Affairs Unit.

Australian Prudential Regulation Authority. (2012). *Probability and Impact Rating System*. Sydney: Author.

Bank for International Settlements. (2004, June). *Basel II: International Convergence of Capital Measurement and Capital Standards: A Revised Framework*. Retrieved from http://www.bis.org/publ/bcbs107.pdf

Bank for International Settlements. (2010, October). *Principles for Enhancing Corporate Governance*. Basel Committee on Banking Supervision. Retrieved from http://www.bis.org/publ/bcbs176.pdf

Basel Committee on Banking Supervision. (2009). *Principles for sound stress-testing and supervision*. Basel, Switzerland: Bank for International Settlements.

Beck, U. (1992). *Risk Society: Towards a New Modernity*. London: Sage.

Bowman, E. H., & Hurry, D. (1993, Oct). Strategy throug the option lens: an integrated view of resource investments and the incremental-choice process. *The Academy of Management Review, 18*(4), 760–782.

Chandler, A. (1962). *Strategy and Structure*. Cambridge, MA: MIT Press.

Comptroller of the Currency. Administrator of National Banks. (2010). *Comptroller's Handbook. Large Bank Supervision*. Washington, DC: Author.

Financial Crisis Inquiry Committee. (2001). *Final Report of the National Commission on the Causes of the Financial and Economic Crisis in the United States*. Retrieved from http://fcic-static.law.stanford.edu/cdn_media/fcic-reports/fcic_final_report_full.pdf

Financial Stability Board. (2012). *Increasing the Intensity and Effectiveness of SIFI Supervision*. Basel, Switzerland: Author.

Gates, S. (2006). Incorporating Strategic Risk into Enterprise Risk Management: A Survey of Current Corporate Practice. *Journal of Applied Corporate Finance, 18*(4), 81–90.

Group of Thirty. (2012). *Toward effective governance of Financial Institutions*. Washington, DC: Author.

Hall, S., Lovallo, D., & Musters, R. (2012, March). How to put money where your strategy is. *McKinsey Quarterly.*

HIH Royal Commission. (2003). *The Failure of HIH: A Corporate Collapse and Its Lessons*. Retrieved from http://www.hihroyalcom.gov.au/finalreport/index.htm

Kay, J. (2010). *Obliquity*. New York: The Penguin Group.

Kay, J. (2011). *Obliquity: Why Our Goals Are Best Achieved Indirectly*. London: Profile Books.

Knight, F. H. (1921). *Risk, Uncertainty and Profit*. Boston: Houghton Mifflin.

Kolb, D. A., & Fry, R. (1975). Toward an applied theory of experiential learning. In C. Cooper (Ed.), *Theories of group processes*. London: John Wiley.

Laker, J. F. (2007). The evolution of risk and risk management—a prudential regulator's perspective. *Structure and Resilience of Financial Markets*. Kirribilli: Reserve Bank of Australia. Retrieved from http://www.rba.gov.au/publications/confs/2007/pdf/laker.pdf

Luhmann, N. (1995). *Social Systems*. Stanford: Stanford University Press.

Mango, D. (2007). An introduction to insurer Strategic Risk. *Enterprise Risk Analysis*, 144–172.

Markowitz, H. (1952, March). Portfolio Selection. *The Journal of Finance, 7*(1), 77–91.

McConnell, P. (2012a). Lehman – A case of strategic risk. *Cass-Capco Institute Paper Series on Risk, 34*(3), 51–62.

McConnell, P. (2012b). *Strategic risk management: Disclosure by systemically important banks*. Sydney: Macquarie Applied Finance Research Centre Research Paper.

Nowotny, H. (2008). *Insatiable Curiosity: Innovation in a Fragile Future*. Cambridge: Massachusetts Institute of Technology.

O'Brien, C. (2006). The downfall of Equitable Life in the United Kingdom: The mismatch of strategy and risk management. *Risk Management and Insurance Review, 9*(2), 189–204.

OECD. (2009). *Corporate Governance and the Financial Crisis*. Paris: OECD.

Peters, E. (2008). Preferred data visualisation techniques may not lead to comprehension and use of hazard information. In A. Bostrom, S. P. French, & S. J. Gottlieb (Eds.), *Risk assessment, modelling and decision support* (pp. 296–305). Atlanta: Springer-Verlag.

Schmidt, M., & Chao, L.-S. (2010). Managing Growth Risk: lessons from the current crisis. *Centre Emile Bernheim. Working Papers, 10*(27).

Slywotzky, A., & Drzik, J. (2005, April). Countering the biggest risk of all. *Harvard Business Review*, 78–88.

Smith, D., & Fischbacher, M. (2009). The changing nature of risk and risk management: The challenge of borders, uncertainty and resilience. *Risk Management, 11*(1), 1–12.

Supervision, B.C. (n.d.).

Taleb, N. N. (2008). *The Black Swan: The Impact of the Highly Improbable*. London: Penguin UK.

Teece, D. J., Pisano, G., & Shuen, A. (1997, August). Dynamic capabilities and Strategic Management. *Strategic Management Journal, 18*(7), 509–533.

Appendix 10.1

Process for designing strategic options

The process for designing Strategic Options (Figure 10.6) goes through different stages of activities, each with its distinctive rationale, output and effect. The Hypothesis represents, engages with and zooms into an element of particular interest, something about that Change that we would have a strong interest in observing and learning about. The Hypothesis is an imaginary representation, a thought experiment about quality of life and dynamics of social interaction: it is derived inductively from elements that have been established in the articulation of the Structural Change. Within the Structural Change the Hypothesis addresses a broad area of interest, and with respect to it imagines individual and social experiences, bringing into play significant asymmetries. The narrative makes interactions emerge and traces their patterns, thus bringing into relief archetypal social, cultural and business structures. The discovery of needs,

Figure 10.6 The strategic risk and innovation decision-making cycle

the identification of emerging value attributed to resources and the means by which these are accessed generate a robust representation of the context and of the systems of exchange. The Hypothesis furnishes a richer understanding of the future landscape of human experience under different circumstances. The intent is to support inductively a determination as to what the Option recognises as significant and therefore is aimed at understanding, managing and leveraging.

In Position we determine where from we can most effectively look at an element of a Structural Change and its dynamics, so we can observe it, understand its evolutions and leverage its effects. What that element is, and the nature of our interest in it, is what was selected in Hypothesis. The Position is a clearly articulated statement of intent about where to ground an Option in the current context so that it can generate and deliver its strategic value. The Position is, therefore, an important point of revolution in the process of developing an Option, in which attention turns from the uncertainty and ambiguity of the Structural Change to the relative certainty and concreteness of the present. This rotation resolves uncertainty and supports material activity: the articulation of a Position statement establishes coordinates for the activity of reconnaissance and for the generation of design insights.

Reconnaissance is the activity by which information is gathered about the Position that was determined in the previous phase. This activity seeks to identify people, companies, resources, models etc., in fact anything that is available there and constitutes references and materials with which to design an Option (the models, colours, mediums and brushes of a painter). The information is derived from a surface scan of the ground and the results of this search activity are collated and laid out for collective review. Insights are derived from the assembled material and gradually consolidated and synthesised through conversation, clustering, interpretation. The output thus generated supports and feeds into the articulation of design principles.

The articulation of Design Principles is the second pivotal moment in the Options development process; Design Principles allow a shift of focus and effort to occur, from argumentation and sense-making to production of the Blueprint. Design Principles emerge from consolidation of the constitutive elements of the argument; they precipitate the interpretive output that occurs during the insight phase of Reconnaissance; and they establish universal and specific criteria of strategic optionality. They are also a factor of creativity as they establish generative terms of reference to initiate and help structure the activity of material production of the Option. Design Principles induce a formal discipline, determine necessary constraints, support the material rendition of the argument, and act as factors of coherence in the expression of the strategic value of an Option. Design Principles derive significance from all preceding phases of the development process and give form to the essential features of a Blueprint. Principles establish meaning and give form, effecting a seamless transition from concept through matter to action.

Blueprint is the objectification and substantiation of the argument, the phase in which effort, resources and activities are directed, structured and set up for realisation. This is where the material representation of what the Option can be goes through several prototypical iterations. This allows for definition, calibration, research and eventually arrangement in a form that enables immediate commitment. In Blueprint, design and planning combine to materialise the strategic argument and provide an opportunity for experience and learning. Blueprint is the tangible effect of the intellectual effort and strategic argument embedded in a Strategic Option, and is a structural constituent of the Brief that instructs decision-making.

Appendix 10.2

Design principles for strategic governance

To support the design of a Strategic Risk governance tool I have articulated design principles that are derived from the argument presented in this chapter. Though general and propaedeutic, these principles emerge from the experience of applying the framework in two major financial institutions. They are intended to support the development of a Strategic Risk governance tool that institutions and organisations can use to both identify Strategic Risks and effectively manage their implications. The Design Principles for a Strategic Risk reporting mechanism that follow have been articulated in terms of four features: the rationale it serves, the qualities it needs, the activities it supports and the effects it has.

Structure

synoptic in the rendering of all structural elements in a single 'image', a visual organising architecture that makes immediately available the systemic relationships between them, is conceptually coherent and induces reflection and learning

relevant as a function of the application of a strategic conceptual framework that establishes which elements are necessary, sufficient and at play

meaningful in representing qualitative judgment about the object of decision-making

deep in its access to material information aggregated and displayed in terms of structures and relations

Qualities

SIMPLE:

attracts, subsumes and arranges all 'noise': is coherent, intuitive, fast and seamless

DYNAMIC:

supports continuity of oversight in time leading to new or renewed strategic commitments

represents in a timely way shifts and evolutions in judgment as information is fed into the system and intelligence derived from it

reflects changes and effects over time, monitors the problem diachronically

INTERACTIVE:

enables individual 'dashboard' interaction with the representation of the Strategic Risk landscape such that the tension inherent in the risk is adequately evaluated, the task of deepening the investigation easily performed, the user's individual judgment easily collected.

REAL-TIME:

provides access to emerging inputs/outputs so as to enable an effective representation of all current and emerging elements relevant to decision-making

OPEN:

extends access, inquiries and conversations beyond the system's material boundaries

links to sources and intelligence that are coherent with the intent.
is unconstrained in its capability to morph scale, linkages and reach into other systems

ENGAGING:

establishes the users' ownership with the underlying problem and develops a sense of responsibility over the outcome of interaction

STIMULATING:

generates questions that structure conversations and induce cognitive and behavioural activity

Activity

INSIGHTFUL EXPLORATION:

supports individual mapping of the problem landscape
induces an inquisitive approach to the search for explanations
establishes associations, encouraging interdisciplinarity and allowing serendipity
enables the generation, the capture and the consolidation of individual and collective views as to
the causes and the effects of elements internal and external to the system.

COHERENT PARTICIPATION:

creates a common understanding
makes uniformly available relevant content in order to stimulate a participated recognition of
the problem, a negotiation of the different evaluations, a conversation that results in a collective judgment of the degrees of uncertainty and relevance inherent in the Strategic Risk
and in a mandate for management activities.

SHARED SENSE-MAKING:

engages decision-makers in an exchange of their interpretive effort and has them generate
meaning and purpose from the experience.
socialises insights and significance to produce collective and negotiated significance
switches naturally between interpretation of system dynamics and representation of its effects

Effect

QUALITATIVE GOVERNANCE:

decisions emerge from the review of the available material as propositions and not as conclusions
de-biases through exposure, conversations, negotiation, referencing

ORGANIC REPORTING:

represents a complex problem leveraging and linking into all available risk management activities and outputs, and any other information system that both needs the Strategic-Risk
significance and contributes to it

TIMELY MONITORING:

triggers timely decision-making that effectively sees opportunities and leverages new business-
models.

Part III

Corporate risk management insights

11

The LEGO Group implementation of strategic risk management

Hans Læssøe[1]

Abstract

The LEGO Group established its strategic risk management function in 2007. Initially, the function was very humbly project based, but has developed into a sophisticated and active management tool involved in strategy development as well as strategy implementation and execution. The core focus has been simplicity and business impact rather than technical proficiency and accuracy. The approach is based on a combination of three systematic and coherent processes deployed with high level of executive support and attention. It enables management in balancing risk-taking with pursuit of ambitious targets. As is, the LEGO Group has for the past decade been successful well beyond the level of the industry. This chapter is an open and personal description of how the strategic risk management at the LEGO Group approach has emerged over the years as seen from the point of view of the head of strategic risk management, Hans Læssøe. The article also describes how the LEGO Group works with strategic risk management in 2015.

The offset

The LEGO Group was struggling with declining sales and massive losses in the beginning of the millennium. From 2005, a new executive team took charge and changed a vast number of processes and initiatives to rectify the dire situation.

In 2006, Hans Læssøe, an M. Sc. in electrical power engineering, was a corporate strategic controller and as such a part of the corporate finance organization, where he prepared benchmark analyses and so forth to pinpoint where there were options to improve performance. In those days Læssøe already had almost 25 years of LEGO Group seniority spanning from IT to manufacturing, product development, strategic planning and business controlling – a background which already then provided him with significant overview and insight into the dynamics of the LEGO Group.

In February 2006 the head of finance came to Læssøe and said, "We need some strategic risk management, don't you think?" Læssøe had never heard about this before and had no idea what it was, but he assessed that from the mere wording it sounded "fair enough." The head of finance then asked Hans to "figure out how to do this in a simple and effective way ... you may spend a day a week on that for now. If you need more time, come see me." Hans asked for any background material on this, and he was simply directed to "try the Internet, there is so much stuff out there."

In February of 2006, Læssøe started searching on Google for "strategic risk management." This gave a lot of links and stuff to read – which drove the thinking in a wide range of possible directions, and Læssøe was utterly confused about this. Therefore, Læssøe contacted the LEGO Group head of insurance and discussed the issue with him – as well as a finance business consultant who happened to know something about strategic risk management, and who was already "in the house."

Based on that Læssøe discovered that risk management is essentially a matter of responding to three questions:

- What can hit you?
- How important is it?
- What are you going to do about it?

It has to be admitted that the clarity of these statements came somewhat later.

The next step was to look at risk management at the LEGO Group. Læssøe found that a lot of it was already implemented systematically:

- Operational risks like lack of vendor deliveries, machine breakdowns, periods of sickness, changes of demands and so forth were well cared for in a systematic sales and operations planning process Læssøe knew from his solid experience.
- Insurable risks like floods, fires, director/officer, travel, assets and such risks were covered by a global insurance function led by a highly experienced person.
- Financial risks like currencies and credit risk were well cared for by the treasury function.
- IT security risk was already a full-time position within IT with defined processes and guidelines.
- Employee health and safety was being deployed in compliance with the ISO 18000 standard.
- Legal risks, which covered both legal breaches on behalf of the LEGO Group but also – and more prominently – protection of the LEGO Brand from inappropriate competitor infringement, were and are a part of the legal function responsibilities.

Some of these risks may be operational in nature, but the impact could still be quite severe if not addressed prudently.

"What are strategic risks?"

Having identified risk management at LEGO System, Læssøe was still to define what are strategic risks. An eye-opener occurred when Læssøe found an analysis made in the US on companies losing significant market value over a short period – and what was the cause of this. The analysis indicated that 68% of the reasons were strategic risks, of which the three most prominent were:[2]

- Loss of core product demand
- Poor merger/acquisition integration
- Competitor infringement on core market.

Læssøe then defined strategic risks as "risks which impact our strategy or the implementation of this," and sketched an overview of risk types, as shown in Figure 11.1.

Læssøe found that this further entails that there is a significant paradigm difference between strategic risks and most other risks. Whereas the head of treasury "owns" the currency risk and hedges currencies based on policies and guidelines he has often written himself, and the head of insurance owns the insurance program she needs – the head of strategic risk management cannot own the strategic risks – without eventually owning the strategy.

Invariably, the role of a strategic risk management function must resemble that of a budgeting function, for example:

- They own the process and the tools
- They own the reporting
- They have the obligation to speak up if/when things goes astray
- They have the obligation to challenge performance

But

- They do not own the content.

It is not the budgeting function that earns or spends the money – nor can it be the strategic risk management function that takes or mitigates the risks.

This realization has been pivotal in the subsequent development of the strategic risk management function at the LEGO Group.

Figure 11.1 Risk types

Getting started

As indicated by the three questions listed earlier, the first step of managing is "seeing" the risks, that is identifying the risks that may hamper your pursuit of targets. A "risk identification work-shop" was initiated. Rather than asking top executives for the risks they saw, Læssøe was recom-mended to use his vast network of specialists throughout the LEGO Group. He made a session with approximately 30 senior specialists from all over the organization (product development, procurement, planning, finance, legal, etc.).

Sticky notepads were used to avoid group-thinking and lemming effects (based on a hint from a process consultant). The specialists were asked to look at everything they could think of, and "shoot – write down whatever you, from your perspective, can see may hamper our development and growth of our brand, company or people – anything you find potentially important."

The participants were given 30 minutes to "shoot." Hereafter, the risks seen were shared – one by one. In total, about 250 more or less tangible risks surfaced from that session. In essence – the session to a full working day – was seen as enlightening to many of the specialists and a good opportunity to raise concerns they had never had a forum for before.

Læssøe had been looking for the possibility of a supporting IT system, but rapidly faced that he had very little know-how of what such a system was supposed to do – and decided it would be next to impossible to find the right system. Instead, he decided to develop a database himself using his significant experience with spreadsheets.

His third attempt at a database appeared to work (and is today still the base of the risk reg-ister), and hence Læssøe listed all the risks, grouped them and found that they included a num-ber of overlaps, which were then pruned out. Risks were grouped based on a business system approach. It turned out that one area apparently was "risk-free," which led to a second, more focused session with a few of the specialists participating in the workshop.

By the fall of 2006 Læssøe had a first register of the strategic risks of the LEGO Group. It might not have been complete, but it constituted a response to the first of the risk management question, "What can hit you?"

The next natural step was assessing the risks, and Læssøe discussed this step with a number of people. Assessing risks can be done in many ways – but based on reading, input and discussions it was decided to base the assessment on a combination of impact and likelihood.

Speed was considered as a parameter (and still is from time to time), but has so far been dis-regarded, as it is evaluated that all else being equal, "fast" risks will tend to have a greater impact than "slow" ones. Hence the information is already implicitly embedded in an impact assess-ment. Vulnerability was also considered, but has been discarded as it was seen that vulnerability was essentially a combination of impact and mitigation capability, which is covered separately. This is not to state that looking at speed and/or vulnerability is wrong or a waste of time, but merely to provide a rationale as to the decision to stick with impact and likelihood.

From collected input, Læssøe was warned up-front about asking business leaders, who had never systematically addressed a risk before, about the impact and likelihood of the identified risks. Before doing that, Læssøe recognized that we needed a guided framework in terms of impact and likelihood scales and assessment.

First, it was found that whereas a 3 × 3 scale may very well be too coarse to really focus the subsequent prioritization, a 7 × 7 scale would probably be too complex for business leaders to handle. Hence, it was decided to use a 5 × 5 scale (i.e. Very Low, Low, Medium, High and Very High) on both impact and likelihood.

Based on recommendations, the first focus was on impact, because in several instances you end up "deciding" the impact. What is the impact of a failed product launch? In an industry as that of the LEGO Group, where 20 new themes are launched every year, the impact may be rather small if it is one of the lesser prioritized launches that does not deliver, or if it is a major launch that does not fully meet expectations, potentially only in a single market. However, we may also face a massive failure of a high-priority launch, which will have a massive impact. The former are (hopefully, and generally) more likely than the latter.

It was decided to define an impact scale, which is purely financial and based on the planned profitability of the LEGO Group. "Very High" was hence the loss of a defined share of the planned profits.

Subsequent levels were half of the above, that is when "Very High" is 100 (or more than 100), then "High" is 50, "Medium" is 25, "Low" is 10 (well, technically 12.5 – but that is suggesting an accuracy we cannot justify), and "Very Low" is 5 (or anything less than 5).

Læssøe also defined a likelihood scale, where:

- Very High is 90%
- High is 30%
- Medium is 10%
- Low is 3%
- Very Low is 1% or less

This scale has been found reasonably effective, as it does not indicate an accuracy that cannot be justified, yet it does drive prioritizations. Later experiences shows that if a business leader sees a risk with a 30% likelihood – it really does not matter whether the actual likelihood is 20%, 30%, 40% or even close to 50% – what the leader is inclined to do is exactly the same.

The framework lead to a 5 × 5 "heat map," as shown in Figure 11.2.

The next step was guiding the business leaders into some consistent assessment. Læssøe was warned that if not guided, some leaders would be "cool customers" and decide this was a low-impact, very-low-likelihood risk – whereas other leaders would get "scared" and easily see the impact to be high and the likelihood at least medium. Hence, without guidance, we would get assessments "all over the place."

Instead, Læssøe decided to team up with two senior colleagues and discussed with them what the impact and likelihood could be for each risk. Hence, for each of the 100+ risks, this team defined:

- What is the potential (bad case) impact of this risk – based on the defined scale?
- What, as a verbal description, is the rationale behind this assessment? This could be "loss of 25% of planned sales in region A," essentially describing a plausible micro-scenario for that risk.

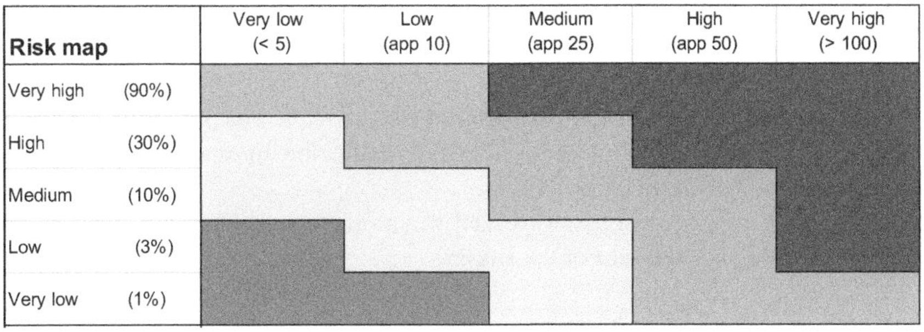

Risk map		Very low (< 5)	Low (app 10)	Medium (app 25)	High (app 50)	Very high (> 100)
Very high	(90%)					
High	(30%)					
Medium	(10%)					
Low	(3%)					
Very low	(1%)					

Figure 11.2 Heat map

- What is the likelihood of this happening within the next 3 years (the defined time frame of the strategic risk management), that is the probability that this risk will hit us as hard as defined by the impact.
- Describe verbally: How did that conclusion emerge?

It was quickly seen that this became a rather systematic process. Læssøe recognized that the assessments might very well be wrong, but there was a trust that they were at least internally consistent, which is actually more important that metric accuracy.

We included the verbal descriptions to support the business leaders in their feedback, but Læssøe also found that they were immensely powerful additions to the assessment, as someone not taking part in the assessment will find it hard to address "High" impact. This learning was subsequently deployed throughout the LEGO risk management.

The risk description and the assessments including rationales were sent to two or three relevant business leaders each to get their professional feedback and validation of the draft assessments made. Several of the risk assessments were altered: some were made more severe, others less so. The outcome was an assessment that was aligned with the belief of and buy-in from relevant business leaders.

This stage was completed in early 2007, and based on this a 5 × 5 heat map was defined. Each cell designated a level of priority ranging from first (most severe) to fifth (least severe), as shown in the heat map of Figure 11.2.

The business leaders were contacted again and asked, "What do we do about this?" and "When we do this, what is the impact and likelihood?" This process naturally started with the first-priority risks and worked through the lower-priority risks. Quite some time passed before all risks had defined mitigating actions, that is, some are deliberately specified *not* to be mitigated, as the cost of reasonably effective mitigation cannot be justified by the impact and likelihood. Naturally, one should not spend US$10 million to mitigate a risk that has a 3% risk of costing US$20 million – it is simply not cost effective.

Having defined mitigating actions, in mid-2007 Læssøe was ready to prepare the first enterprise risk management (ERM) report to management and the board of directors. It was further found that including the strategic risk management meant that the LEGO Group now had a comprehensive ERM approach.

However, whereas textbooks and standards refer to ERM as being the umbrella of all risk management, the LEGO Group chose a slightly different approach, as shown in Figure 11.3.

Læssøe became responsible for ERM, but the head of treasury did not report organizationally to Læssøe, nor did the head of insurance or environmental health and safety (EHS) or any other department. In the LEGO Group implementation it was hence decided that ERM is only the reporting on risks. The management happens in the rim of the Figure 11.3 "umbrella," where the ERM was only the reporting made on behalf of treasury, insurance and so forth, as well as the strategic risks.

At this point in time, management recognized that strategic risk management and ERM reporting was no longer a part-time project, but needed to be an established functional area. Læssøe was asked to take on this responsibility.

During the next 18 months Læssøe worked to complete and refine the draft spreadsheet tools and enhance the management of the risks:

- Each risk was assigned to a designated business owner who would be the one responsible for prudent and effective mitigation of the risk.
- Risks were linked to cover for the fact that if risk A materializes, then some element of risks

Figure 11.3   Enterprise risk umbrella

X,Y and Z will (no doubt) come right after. This is done using a one level "bill-of-material" approach, where risk A is 100%, but then assign some 25% of X, 10% to Y and 50% to Z. The full impact will then be larger than just the assessed impact of A – in some cases even significantly larger.

Consolidation and risk tolerance

When a risk register, as is the case for the LEGO Group, holds 100+ risks, a number of these may materialize any given year. Læssøe was pushed by the executive team to derive some way of showing whether the risk exposure of the total register was bigger than the LEGO Group would or could handle.

It is easy when all risk impact is monetized, as shown in Table 11.1, to multiply the impact and the likelihood of each risk and then add up the totals. However, this might be an extremely dangerous approach, as the resulting number essentially describes the average exposure over a very long time.

However, risk management is not about averages. If it were, no one would ever buy insurance, as it does not pay in average. Take home insurance as an example. Risk management is about the extremes, where it almost does not matter that the likelihood of your home burning to the ground is very small. You buy an insurance policy anyway, because you cannot live with the scenario where the house has burned down and you still hold the mortgage.

The Monte Carlo simulation was introduced to enable deriving some metric of consolidated worst-case exposure to any combination of risks, which may materialize the same year.

Table 11.1 Average exposure calculation

Risk	Impact	Likelihood	Impact likelihood
A	500	3%	15
B	200	10%	20
C	100	10%	10
D	300	1%	3
E	50	30%	15

The mechanics of Monte Carlo simulation are that you have a computer generate a huge number of "random" scenarios, and if risk A has a 10% likelihood, then risk A materializes in 10% of the generated scenarios. For each scenario, the computer calculates and logs the combined exposure of whatever risk materializes in that scenario. This is done on gross (prior to mitigation) as well as net (after mitigation). The results are then shown as a graphic such as Figure 11.4.

A Monte Carlo tool is then able to tell what the 3% worst-case scenario loss is, for example, with the known combination of risks – each described with an impact and a likelihood.

The exposure number (not shown, but based on the vertical delimiters) shows a worst-case combined loss, that is the exposure. Management has to decide what is acceptable. Læssøe supported a discussion in the executive team on which level of risk and with which likelihood is acceptable for the *net* exposure, that is including the effect of the defined mitigating actions – based on the planned earnings – and a defined share came up as the defined risk tolerance. This definition of the risk tolerance was subsequently approved by the LEGO Group board of directors.

This means that Læssøe was now able to show that whereas the overall risk tolerance is X, then the overall exposure is Y. If and when Y is larger than X, then management must do more to mitigate the risks taken. If, as it is the case for the LEGO Group, Y is smaller than X, then management can allow itself to take more risks if needed to meet the aspirations, or even raise the bar and aim for higher goals (Figure 11.5).

The executive team further defined that whereas the total risk tolerance is 100%, they wished to have controlled risk-taking, and were not prepared to take risks above 50% as long as the business climate in which the LEGO Group operates is not very hostile. They also limited risk-taking above 75% to known severe situations recognizing an immediate need for aggressive risk-taking.

In fact, Læssøe has been in the situation where he turned risk management upside-down as the LEGO Group at a point in time appeared to be missing out on a target, whilst also being exposed to risk well below the risk tolerance. Læssøe used this to write top management and emphasize that the purpose of risk management is to "provide a reasonable assurance that targets will be met with the actions taken," and hence suggest (or even recommend) that management take additional risks (and indicate one possible avenue of actions) in order to enhance the likelihood of meeting the defined target.

It clearly came as somewhat of a surprise to the managers that Læssøe recommended taking on more risks, and although the suggestions were not followed, it made the managers aware that risk management is *not* about risk avoidance. By year-end, the targets were met without added actions taken.

The overall risk exposure versus risk tolerance is today a systematic part of the ERM reporting and discussion amongst management and with the board of directors – clearly underlining that risk management is not about risk aversion but about making conscious choices.

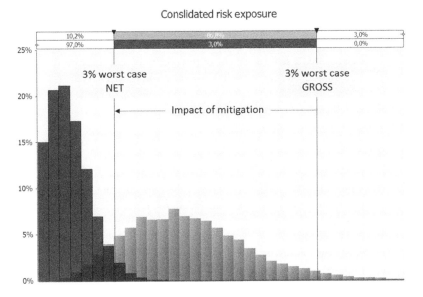

Figure 11.4 Monte Carlo simulation outcome

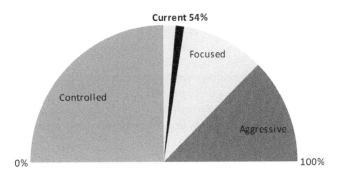

Figure 11.5 Risk tolerance speedometer

As an analogy, adding risk management is like adding brakes to a car. Brakes are not installed in order to drive slower, but to allow yourself to more safely drive faster. This is why the best brakes on any car are on a Formula 1 racecar. These brakes allow the driver to go full throttle just a little closer to the curve than the competitor, brake fast, turn and then speed up again. On the other end of the scale, you can just imagine having to drive home tonight safely, but without using the brakes – it is going to be a very long, slow ride.

Today, the LEGO Group reports on the enterprise risk exposure every 6 months. The seasonal nature of a toy industry makes quarterly reporting less relevant, as first- and third-quarter reports rarely will have new insights.

The ERM database is being systematically updated using a defined cadence. Some risks are very volatile (e.g. currencies) and are systematically reviewed and updated for every report. Other risks such as competitor risks are looked at annually to address the all-important Christmas season. A few are more standard (e.g. building fire) and are updated every second year to ensure these are not "forgotten," yet balance the workload of updating. Updates are based on requested feedback from risk owners as well as that of relevant "challengers" – people with alternate insights from other parts of the organization.

Today, we have also added a self-assessment of the quality of risk mitigations, where we ask early warning and mitigation owners to explicitly address and qualify:

- How precisely do you know what you are monitoring/doing?
- How precisely do we know who is doing it?
- How precisely do we know when to act (for early warnings) or that it works (for mitigations)?

All based on a defined 5-point scale. The average is then the calculated "maturity" of the early warning or risk mitigation. This has then been included in the strategic risk management policy, whereby there are minimum criteria for the maturity of handling first- and second-priority risks to balance efforts and impact.

Finally, every third year the report includes a "back-testing" where the actual events of the past 3 years are compared to the risk register and commented on:

- Did anything significant happen, which we had not included in the risk register? What and why?
- Amongst the incidents that were foreseen, did they happen somewhat as expected according to the risk assessments? If not, why?
- Were there risks that "should have happened" but did not? Why?
- What can we learn from this?

When doing this, we are very much aware that the fact that the risk register was "spot on" over the past period is by no means a proof of this being complete, or that it indicates that we have addressed the important issues. Alternatively, if something unforeseen and significant *did* happen, then we can use this as a clear indicator of identification inadequacy.

Adding strategy implementation – project-risk management – active risk and opportunity planning (AROP)

Active as it may be, ERM is to a large extent "damage control." Targets have been set and strategies are defined and deployed . . . now make it happen, even when something "goes wrong." Læssøe wished to move one step up in the decision process and also impact strategy implementation.

At the LEGO Group, whenever a strategy or other initiative is implemented, it is deployed through a project using a project model/approach, which is universally applied throughout the organization whether it is market entry, an IT project, or any other initiative. This project approach is "owned" and driven by a team of subject matter experts (SMEs), whom Læssøe contacted.

The approach did include some risk management, but this was entirely focused on "what can hamper us from delivering on-time and on-budget." The risks of lack of top management attention, lack of time and lack of resources could be entered as the default key risks.

In close collaboration with the SMEs the process was adjusted on a number of issues and points.

In risk identification,

- The process was enhanced to include opportunities (of exceeding the defined project target) as well as risks. It is known from other organizations as well as subsequent) LEGO Group experience that this creates a lot of "energy" in a competitive project team.
- The process was made explicitly holistic to encompass risks and opportunities emerging *from* the project as much as risk, including externally invoked, emerging *to* the project.

This has the consequence that all stakeholder groups now need to be heard in risk identification, as the project owner and manager no longer have the needed insight to spot a tax risk, for example, when entering a new market.

Strategic risk management at LEGO Group do this part in a plenary session amongst the stakeholders to allow them to be inspired by each other. Each member write down the risks and opportunities they see on sticky notes. This individual step is deployed to ensure everyone is heard, and we get unbiased input from even the most introverted members and avoid group-thinking in the brainstorm identification process.

In risk assessment,

- The former 3 × 3 High/Medium/Low scale was seen as too coarse and expanded to a 5 × 5 including Very High/Very Low on both impact and likelihood.
- The impact likelihood scales were explicitly defined (by project), as we had past experiences that a risk was agreed to be "high" impact amongst a team, where every member has his or her own notion of what "high" meant.
- The impact scale was explicitly defined based on the same approach as ERM, but naturally now aligned with project targets and/or impact. Further, we allowed for supporting scales where, for example, delayed delivery was calculated once to align with the financial impact, and allowing all risks related to late delivery to be assessed based on this scale rather than recalculating manually.
- The likelihood scale was "fixed" to match the scale applied in ERM.

This element is the most intellectually complicated part of the risk management process, but it has also served to significantly change the focus of project managers who realized through the assessment, "hey, it doesn't really matter that I deliver 2 months later than planned, as long as productivity is secured." A fictitious example of the scale setting is shown in Table 11.2.

The assessment process is done in small groups, generally with two or three risk owners and ideally the financial controller. The small team discusses each risk/opportunity any one of them owns and describes first (in case of a risk) a bad case impact of the risk. Focus not on the worst case imaginable – as these tend to be somewhat academic – but a plausible "bad" case. This is assessed versus the defined impact scale and the rationale is described in the tool to enable others to address the assessment as described previously.

Now the team has a "micro scenario" for the risk in terms of how hard this risk may hit us. This enables a discussion of the likelihood. Impact and likelihood are interdependent, but alas there is no mathematical relation to deploy. Hence we often end up "deciding" in the plausible impact of a risk and then define the likelihood of that (or similar) materializing.

Table 11.2 Example of impact and likelihood scale

Grade	Rationale	Very high	High	Medium	Low	Very low
Probability/ likelihood	The Very High probability is defined to be below 100%, as 100% is a "sure thing" and not a risk. The below scale is found by dividing by 3 to get to a 1% level.	**90%**	**30%**	**10%**	**3%**	**1%**
. . . meaning **Note:** This scale is presumed "fixed" for all projects		This will most likely happen.	This may very well happen, something like once in 3 years or in every third project.	This may happen, something like once in 10 years or in every tenth project.	This is unlikely to happen, something like once in 30 years.	This is very unlikely to happen, something like once in 100 years/ times, **but it cannot be ignored.**
Financial impact	Generally baseline for alignment of other scales	10	mDKK			
Grade	**Very high "definition"**	**Very high**	**High**	**Medium**	**Low**	**Very low**
Financial impact (mDKK)	Based on expected ball park savings	App. or above 10	App. 5	App. 2.5	App. 1	App. or below 0.5
Productivity	Cover 50% of processing with a cost base of 100 mDKK based hereon	20%	10%	5%	2%	1%
Implementation delays	Aligned with one year's planned benefit	12 months	6 months	3 months	1 month	2 weeks

This approach, and including opportunities as well as risks, yields a dual "heat map" as the one applied at the LEGO Group and shown as Figure 11.6.

Once impact and likelihood is defined, the tool provides a four-priority level, where we generally use the rules that:

- First-priority risks are "illegal" and must be mitigated to lower levels – first-priority opportunities must be actively pursued. Hence, first-priority risks must be mitigated to a lower level of priority.
- Second-priority risks should, if not prohibitively expensive, be mitigated or pursued.
- Third-priority risks may be mitigated or pursued if and when prudent cost/benefit advocates it.
- Fourth-priority risks are only addressed if an easy and next to "free" handling is immediately available.

In risk handling,

- Early warning metrics and monitoring are applied for those risks/opportunities where this is possible and relevant. Based on Bayesian mathematics, these may serve to show the likelihood of a risk increasing – or decreasing quite significantly – and hence redirect mitigating efforts.
- Ownership to *one* person is assigned to avoid a situation in which two people share a risk, the risk materializes, and suddenly each owner has only 1% of the responsibility (or in other words, "a success has many fathers, but a failure is an orphan").

Risk owners need not be the ones that do the mitigation, but are qualified and responsible individuals ensuring that the mitigation is done.

Risk owners are assigned right after the identification.

- For actions taken, the cadence/timing is defined to enable easy validation of whether this is actually done in time.
- Increasingly, we explicitly assess the "quality" of the defined handling (i.e. mitigations of risks and actions to pursue opportunities) and may apply a level of risk policy where, for example, first-priority risks must be mitigated at a quality level above 4 (on a 5-point scale) as we do with the enterprise risks (albeit somewhat more simple).
- Based on the assumed effect of the risk handling, the residual or net impact and likelihood is assessed explicitly, and hence evaluated as to whether or not this is acceptable.

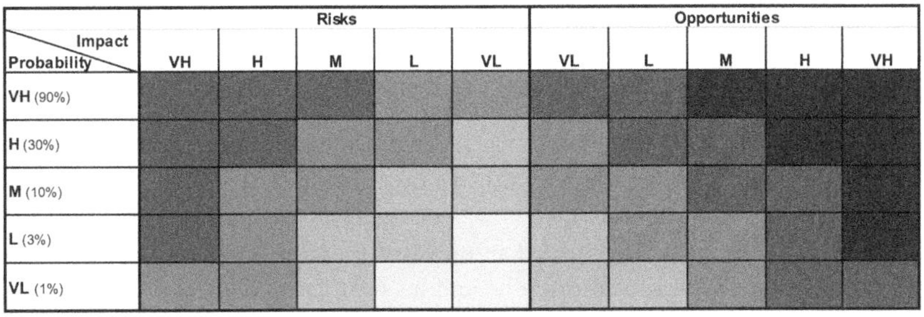

Probability \ Impact	Risks					Opportunities				
	VH	H	M	L	VL	VL	L	M	H	VH
VH (90%)										
H (30%)										
M (10%)										
L (3%)										
VL (1%)										

Figure 11.6 The double-sided active risk and opportunity planning (AROP) "heat map"

We have seen risk management tools where risks are identified and assessed and mitigated, implicitly assuming that the mitigations are adequate and bring the risk to an acceptable level. We do not assume we assess explicitly.

This step is often done in the same teamwork and session as the previous assessment step. Beyond that, a number of enhancements were made:

- In collaboration with the SME team, we created a spreadsheet-based tool developed to support project managers in their risk and opportunity management.
- We benefitted from having all the data of the risks and opportunities systematically listed and defined standard reporting on risk and risk exposure.

This proved to be a benefit to the project manager, who could not report on risks and opportunities by simple cut and paste from the tool. It also proved to be beneficial to the steering group member, who now saw a consistent layout of the reporting across projects – allowing him or her to focus on the content.

- We enabled use of Monte Carlo simulation–based consolidation of risk and opportunities and hence created an ability to show the outcome range of each project.
- The process and tools were (and are continuously) trained and deployed and defined mandatory (by top management) for projects above a defined threshold.
- The tool and process includes a follow-up step, which allows the project team to update the AROP database for milestone sessions and to define the "status" of risks/opportunities.

This status can be "active," meaning it can happen tomorrow, or "waiting," meaning it can happen later. It cannot be "resolved," meaning we are now past the time where this could happen and we know whether it did (and what was the impact) or not (and thus there was no impact).

Subsequently, and yet to be fully deployed, we developed a cross-project consolidation approach, which enabled exposure mapping and key risk/opportunity identification on a portfolio of projects.

Today, the LEGO Group use the active risk and opportunity planning (AROP) process for all business projects above a defined threshold – as well as for the implementation of business plan for each management area. Hence, the AROP is becoming a standard operating process throughout the LEGO Group. With this, we believe that projects and hence strategy implementation are being managed to support the purpose of making reasonably certain that targets will be met with the actions taken. The approach is also a strong driver of making conscious choices in the projects and initiatives that drives the company forward.

Adding strategy definition (i.e. scenario thinking) to risk management – prepare for uncertainty

Having explicit risk and opportunity management for implementation of strategies may be good. Nevertheless, what if the strategy is risky to begin with and/or based and depending on assumptions, which may not hold?

Invoked by colleagues from a network, Læssøe saw this, and based on insights and inspiration from other companies and organizations – he and his team created a scenario-based workshop process to validate the resilience of strategies. The process has become (internally) known as "Prepare for Uncertainty."

A first attempt to deploy scenario thinking in 2008 failed, as this was based on expert-created and very in-depth documented scenarios, which gave way to strong and good discussions. However, the discussions did not lead to actions or influence decisions, as none of the executives discussing the scenarios could link these to their area of responsibility or strategy . . . and hence essentially ignored these once they were "back in office." The key learning was that "ownership" is quintessential to successful use − also when it comes to scenarios.

The Prepare for Uncertainty process is now a 5-hour workshop with a leadership team, focusing on their strategy or the initiative at hand. There are five steps:

1. Define two key uncertainties
2. Define/describe the derived scenarios
3. Identify strategic issues to address
4. Prioritize the issues
5. Explicitly address the defined "act" issues.

The scenario definition is based on a 2 × 2 matrix defined by two key uncertainties. This ensures that both "pet futures" and their opposites are discussed.

The purpose of the process is to help leaders "think the unthinkable" and identify risks and opportunities before (the former) become black swans − and hence to support the definition of a resilient strategy and direction.

Step 1: Define key uncertainties

Strategic risk management facilitates the process and brings along a set of predefined uncertainties related to the strategy for discussion. These are made in "cards" where one statement/development is at one end and the opposite is at the other.

- Will we get a "free-trade world," where goods and money can flow freely and efficiently, or will we (based, for example, on the financial crisis) see a world of 1,000 restrictions where each country has implemented a number of barriers for foreign companies to operate (to protect their own workforce and job creation)?
- Will technology be a value driver in products, as this is what the consumer wishes to focus on, or will technology be "OK, but not important" for consumers?
- Will the political environment be totally dominated by large or supernatural authorities like the US Congress and the EU Commission, whereby legislation is broad but slow and predictable, or will it be locally overwhelmed and based on anarchy driven by nongovernmental organizations (NGOs), as local politicians "must" follow the trend of the day?

For all cards it is important that the uncertainty is external (versus the strategy and business area) and that both "ends" are seen as plausible futures. Not equally likely − but if one end, such as the NGO−driven legislation, is not seen as a plausible future, then the uncertainty is no longer that relevant (Figure 11.7).

The team is allowed to define its own driving uncertainties. It is our experience that whereas many teams start doing that most end up using two of the predefined cards. However, the possibility of defining new uncertainties is vital to ensure ownership of this along with the next steps of the process.

Whichever uncertainties are chosen, these must be external as mentioned, but the two must also be mutually independent, at least to a reasonable degree whereby one may change without the impacting the other − at least intuitively.

Global consumer			Individualistic consumer
Children watch the same movies, hear the same music, see the same TV programs ... and like the same concepts/products.	**Consumers**		Children are brought up to be special and want customized and personalized products and services.

Free trade world			1000 restrictions
Trade is pivotal, and WTO is increasingly successful. Everyone can freely move goods from anywhere to anywhere.	**Political**		Based on "protectionism", all imaginable types of barriers and legislative restrictions emerge – hampering international trade.

Figure 11.7 Example uncertainty drivers

It may appear that choosing two cards from among 20 is simple, but experience shows us that this leads to hefty and engaged discussion and easily takes an hour to do. As facilitators, we coach the team not to exceed 1 hour.

STEP 2: DEFINE SCENARIOS

With two axes of key uncertainties, the two most important uncertainties for the strategy discussed – crossing these yields a 2 × 2 map of four distinctly different but inherently plausible scenarios as shown in Figure 11.8. The likelihood of these will not be the same, but we do not know more than that any one of the scenarios may materialize.

In real life, none of the scenarios will materialize strictly as described, but the future will be some amalgamation of elements of all four scenarios. I will revert to this later.

(a) A "random" scenario is chosen to start. This is to be the extreme combination of the two outcomes of the cards in that "corner." It is not a wishy-washy, middle position but an extreme situation.

The team members are requested to describe "what the world looks like" in this scenario, seen from their perspective and related to the strategy. We use sticky notes for this to avoid lemming effects, and give the team some 10–15 minutes to describe the scenario by characteristics and/or key success factors.

The team shares and discuss the different descriptions and get to an aligned (not 100%) "image" of this scenario. The team is subsequently asked to name the scenario for later reference. This may take some 30–40 minutes to do in total.

(b) The team is requested to repeat the process on the directly opposite scenario, a process that often leads to heated discussions and easily takes another 30–40 minutes.
(c) The team is asked to look at the two in-between scenarios and define what differentiates either of these from their neighbours. It is intuitively easy to define the scenario by "cloning" – but that is not truly adding value – so instead, what are the differentiators. This is done for each of the two remaining and is done using some 20 minutes each, including the naming.

The team has now, based on their own choice of key uncertainties, defined four plausible and quite different images of the future.

As the next step is quite different, we normally give the team (which has now been working for 3 hours straight) a 15–30 minute break to clear their minds.

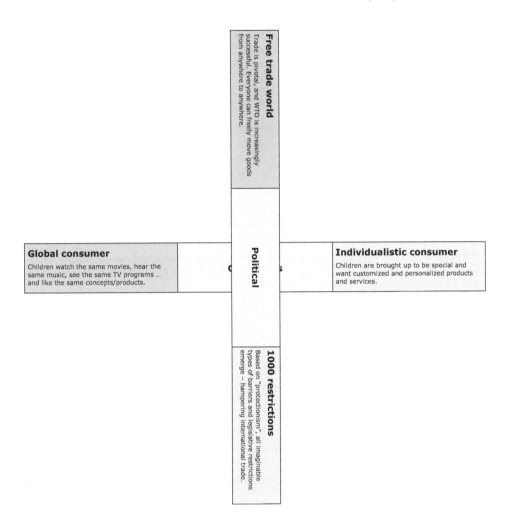

Figure 11.8 Example scenario "cross"

STEP 3: IDENTIFY ISSUES

The purpose of the defined scenarios is (solely) to inspire leaders to contemplate a future, which is not a mere plan based extrapolation of past years. Team members are now encouraged to identify strategic issues that we "need" to address.

Strategic issue may be an opportunity if we pursue this well and in time. If we ignore the issue, it may become a risk – and if that is not seen and addressed in time, it may materialize and constitute a problem.

The team is asked to be openly inspired by the scenarios they have just created. One scenario may inspire some issues, a combination of two scenarios (i.e. the one key uncertainty) may inspire other issues and the two scenarios combined with something one read in the news the other day makes one think of this issue. How the individual came to think about the issue does not matter – the issues does.

Again, to avoid group-thinking, we use sticky notes for the individual brainstorm and give the team approximately 15 minutes to do this. It is our experience that after 15 minutes, the issues tend to become increasingly academic or artificial as the urge to deliver exceeds the imagination.

As with the scenario description (as well as the risk and opportunity identification used in the AROP process) we share the issues. This is done in combination with the next step of prioritization.

STEP 4: PRIORITIZING ISSUES

It is assumed that identified issues are potentially important or impactful. At least, we do not expect any team member to spot an issue 4–5 years ahead of time and already be able to state "this is not really important."

Instead, for prioritization, we focus on a 2 × 2 (again) using likelihood and speed as the parameters. On likelihood, we ask: "Do we believe this issue will materialize (but then again, it may not) or don't we believe it will materialize (but it may)?" On speed, we ask: "If this materializes can we adapt to it once we know, or will it impact us so fast that if we are not prepared we're in trouble?" (i.e. slow- or fast-moving issues – compared to our adaptability in the relevant area).

We have named the Park/Adapt/Prepare/Act prioritization the PAPA model (Figure 11.9).

Low likelihood, slow changing issues are **P**arked issues – not forgotten, but maybe reconsidered 2 years from now to see if anything has happened. At the LEGO Group, we have seen parked issues that when readdressed 2 years later were close to full fruition.

High-likelihood, slow-changing issues need to be **A**dapted to. This is not where we change a lot here and now, but where we gradually follow a monitored trend. In a fast-moving consumer goods business, one such trend is demography.

Low-likelihood, fast-changing issues are the ones we need to **P**repare for. The implicit thinking that because the issue is fast-moving, we need to be ready to act fast if it materializes (which we do not expect it to). These "prepare" issues are often some of the strategic risks we will be facing in our strategy, which may materialize if and when the world changes in a different way than what we plan for.

High-likelihood, fast-moving issues are **A**ct issues, and this is where the content ownership becomes strong. The leadership team picked the key uncertainties and defined the scenarios that inspired the issues, which they have now decided are important, fast-moving and very likely.

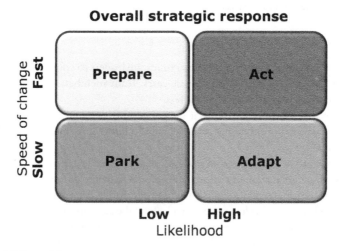

Figure 11.9 PAPA model

Now is not the time to ignore them. Essentially, addressing these is management rather than not risk management – but let that just be an added "gift" from the process. If a management team decide to ignore these, they have almost certainly designed their strategy to fail – assuming their own assessments are valid.

This step of the process may take as much as an hour to go through.

STEP 5: ADDRESSING "ACT" ISSUES

The last hour was originally added and recommended by some of the leadership team, where we went through the Prepare for Uncertainty process. This process was considered so valuable that we formally added it to the process.

Normally, a team will have around a handful of "act" issues. The purpose of the fifth and final hour of the workshop is to agree on exactly "Who," "What," and "When" – and "How" do we follow-up on this?

Naturally – adequate resources and focus has to be assigned to:

- Deploy the actions decided on the "act" issues
- Define the monitoring metric and course of action on "adapt" issues
- Define the potential early warnings and mitigating actions for "prepare" issues.

This is presumed done subsequently to the Prepare for Uncertainty process. However, as risk professionals and hence professionally paranoid, we do follow up on what is being done to the different issues when the process is being used.

Even with this scenario-based process, there are no guarantees that the strategy will be successful, but it is believed that doing this will add to the resilience of the strategies deployed to such an extent that the process is well worth while.

Today, at the LEGO Group, the Prepare for Uncertainty process as described is a mandatory element of business planning, and frequently used in connection with defining long-term or new strategic initiatives.

Bridging strategic risk management

Combining the foregoing, the LEGO Group has developed and deployed systematic risk management processes for strategy development, implementation and execution. Furthermore, we explicitly link the processes.

Prepare for Uncertainty (PfU) naturally feeds both the AROPs created in connection with implementation projects (each strategy may invoke a number of explicit business projects) as well as risks directly to the ERM.

On some occasions AROP might create risks, which are subsequently embedded in the ERM – and the overall exposure of active projects is a defined strategic risk in itself.

The cost/benefit of the PfU is naturally better than that of the AROP, which is better than that of the ERM. Nevertheless, the "license to operate" moves upstream. No management team will be interested in risk-managing strategic development if deployment and execution is not adequately controlled.

Now what?

So – the LEGO Group "has it all" and is "home safe" – alas, no. We have a comprehensive, yet reasonably intuitive strategic risk management apparatus, which we believe works, but there are still plenty of enhancements and improvements to make. Just to mention a few – in no particular order:

- Validation and assurance that defined risk mitigations are truly and effectively deployed is based on self-assessment only. We are currently in the process of enhancing the monitoring and validation part of risk management, where we no longer base our assurance solely on leaders statements about expected handling, but rather qualify through interviews and documentation that defined processes are indeed executed upon.
- Assessment validity is most often, especially for strategic risks, based on the "gut feeling" and experience of (knowledgeable) individuals. Fact-based insights would be much preferred to ensure assessment validity – especially on impact.
- Proactive risk-taking, where a more deliberate utilization of a higher share of the provided risk tolerance may well create more value to the company – but is not currently a matter of discussion at present due to the significant success of the LEGO Group without taking further chances – but these days will not last forever.
- In the ERM process, everything is monetized. We are working on introducing parallel scales (as we do in the AROP process) to enable a more nuanced risk discussion based on impacts (e.g. financial, reputational or other).
- There might be managers who do this based on demand rather than belief. Being able to prove value and convince leaders of the value will help further risk management.

Plus, all the smaller things where this or that particular risk is potentially not adequately catered for or another one may be severely overmanaged. On top of that is the rollout and cross-organizational deployment, training of project managers and other relevant employees, establishing a risk-taking culture, collection and spread of cumulated learnings and so forth.

Closing

Over the past 7–8 years at the LEGO Group, we have developed and deployed the risk management processes discussed in this chapter, and a journey like this takes time. We have extracted a number of key learnings related to implementation of risk management:

- Risk management is about managing risks rather than a relentless focus on fixed processes. Hence the facilitating/driving team can allow itself to be quite flexible to match business needs and sentiment as long as risks are identified and prudently addressed.
- Essentially, risk management is about explicitly responding to three questions:
  o What can hit you?
  o How serious is it?
  o What are you going to do about it?
- To quote Albert Einstein: "Simplify as much as possible" – but not further. In the end it is about managerial behavior.
- Focus your effort and pick the low-hanging fruit.
- Drive and use all of your imagination. Real life is often more fantastic than any one of us expects.
- Ensure agreed mitigations are actually done; poor risk management can be more dangerous than no risk management.
- To our knowledge, nobody (yet) has the perfect way of doing risk management. Risk

management must be content dependent, and hence do not worry about creating and deploying your own tailor-made processes.

A final comment quoting Nike: "Just do it."

Notes

1   Hans Læssøe, Head of Strategic Risk Management, The LEGO Group.
2   Analysis made by the corporate executive board.

12

The enterprise risk management (ERM) story

Experiences from Nestlé

Markus Schädeli[1]

Abstract

In my professional career, I have been involved in risk management since 1987. The following ERM story describes my journey since then, and highlights the key learning made during this period. Hereafter you get a comprehensive list of these points:

- A small issue (a weak point in a supply chain) can create a big disruption.
- You need to be proactive, and management commitment is a must.
- Cross-functional networking is very helpful.
- Make sure that you always share the relevant learning within your organisation.
- You need to be transparent and create a high level of awareness around the relevant risks.
- Initiate a systematic approach; do not wait for major events to initiate the discussion!
- Keep the process simple and adapted to the culture of the organisation.
- Use colleagues and your own employees to promote the process internally.
- Loss prevention and/or business continuity are at the core of managing risks.
- Capturing opportunities with the same process can make the process more attractive.
- Use the same process in all entities to be compliant with new legal requirements (easier to implement).
- Keep the process as pragmatic as possible; do not overengineer the process; do not simply believe the numbers; and be prepared for the unexpected.
- The ERM process should not be seen as 'on top of' or 'in addition to' something.
- Use whenever possible existing tools/processes and align ERM with them.
- Apply an integrated approach to become a more performant organisation.

To make a long story short, it's worthwhile to put some efforts into ERM. Common sense and pragmatism should help you to find the necessary balance between risk taking and risk management, while providing the necessary transparency within the management team. Simply do it!

The initial trigger

I graduated as a food science engineer from the Eidgenösische Technische Hochschule (ETH) in Zurich in 1986. I started my professional career at the Forschunganstalt für Milchwissenschaft (FAM) in Bern-Liebefeld, working as a consultant for smaller local producers of Gruyère and Vacherin Mont d'Or cheese in the French part of Switzerland. My role was to provide technical support, mainly to improve the quality of cheese. In 1987, the Centre Hospitalier Universitaire Vaudois (CHUV) – the university hospital in Lausanne – documented an outbreak of listeria. Most of the affected persons were living in the area around Lausanne. This is why the CHUV was confronted with all these patients. Over a period of 2 years, the CHUV tried to find the origin of the outbreak. In November 1987, the source of the infection was found. It was identified as the Vacherin Mont d'Or cheese, a specialty produced in small cheese-dairies in the Jura Vaudois. This was actually the starting point of an amazing risk management journey, which led me, over the next 2 decades, to my current position as head of group risk management at Nestlé. In this chapter I will describe my journey and highlight the evolution of risk management since 1987 in my personal context.

The Vacherin Mont d'Or case – a first very operational case study

From the position I occupied at FAM in November 1987, I was nominated as a member of the task force in charge of resolving the issue with the outbreak of listeria in the Vacherin Mont d'Or cheese. Doctors, food safety and hygiene specialists, technical advisors and members of the Vacherin Mont d'Or cheese-making community were part of the multifunctional task force. The main objectives of this task force were to resolve this food safety issue and ensure that this cheese could again be produced and sold under safe conditions. The root cause analysis highlighted a number of weaknesses in the very traditional manufacturing process of this cheese. The production was done exclusively in winter in small cheese-dairies. In the past, the cheese was manufactured in small villages; once matured, it was sold 15–20 days later in the same region. When the cheese became more popular, the marketing organisation of the Vacherin Mont d'Or and the maturation of the cheese were centralised. The *affineurs* (as the companies in charge of the maturation of the cheese are called) were collecting cheeses from different cheese-dairies and organised the maturation of the cheese in very traditional cellars. The marketing of the cheese was so successful that you could buy Vacherin Mont d'Or all over Europe and in the US before the outbreak in 1987. The commercial success was impressive. Nevertheless, the production and maturation processes were never adapted to this commercial evolution. A number of factors (consistency, humidity, etc.) made it easy for the *Listeria monocytogenes* bacterium to grow on the surface of this cheese. Once the bacterium found its way from the environment (where this microorganism is widely spread) to the maturation cellars, it found the perfect environment to grow without other predators around. This situation led to the outbreak. The root cause analysis finally identified the most critical process step which seems to be at the origin of the entire disaster: a simple elastic band which holds the wood around the cheese during the maturation!

How can it be that an elastic band costing almost nothing was at the origin of such an outbreak? These elastic bands were commonly used in all the maturation centres. The cellars recycled these elastic bands without real cleaning and/or disinfection. These elastic bands were then distributed back to all the cheese-dairies and reused there for the next productions. Unfortunately, the elastic bands were not only sent back to the cheese-dairies; they were also shared between the different maturation centres. This is the way *Listeria monocytogenes* spread over time to most of the cheese-dairies and maturation centres.

The key learning I took from this event was that the *weakest point* in a process can actually create a *big disruption*. This point can also easily be avoided, but you need to identify it well in advance. In the case of the Vacherin Mont d'Or, the full production restarted in 1989, 2 years after the production had been stopped by the authorities.

The Nestlé journey starts

This was the beginning of an exciting journey for me. I remained a member of the task force until the cheese manufacturing could finally restart in 1989, even after I left FAM in 1988 and started to work for Nestlé. When I started to work at Nestlé, my first job was to audit the cheese factories of Nestlé in Europe and ensure that they had adequate processes in place to avoid that a listeria contamination could occur. The experience and learning from the Vacherin Mont d'Or helped me to identify weaknesses, even in an industrial manufacturing setup. A zoning concept, which has since been replicated in a number of other manufacturing setups at Nestlé, was implemented to reduce the probability that *Listeria monocytogenes* could contaminate the areas in the factories where the cheese manufacturing / maturation took place.

A *proactive behaviour* and the *necessary management commitment* helped ensure that robust processes were put in place to avoid such contaminations.

The Nestlé journey continues

Once all cheese factories had been visited, I believed that I would start my induction programme to become an 'expat' in one of the nice places Nestlé had around the world at that time. I managed to do a 5-week stage in Konolfingen at one of the Nestlé milk factories in Switzerland. Then I was called back to the headquarters of Nestlé in Vevey. I would never have guessed that my next assignment at Nestlé would lead me from cheese to meat, as an outbreak of listeria in a meat factory of Nestlé in Belgium crossed my induction programme. I became a member of a Nestlé internal task force, trying to bring this 'pâté' factory back to normal operations after its products had been found contaminated with *Listeria monocytogenes* and the production was stopped by the local health authorities. The task force was also requested to audit the other Nestlé meat factories in the world, to ensure that all these sites had adequate procedures in place to avoid a listeria contamination that would disturb the regular operations. Working in a *cross-functional network* was a great experience for me, and was also very helpful for the concerned operations. It helped *share the relevant learning* in an efficient way with all involved stakeholders. It also reduced the likelihood that a similar event could happen in one of the other Nestlé meat factories.

Ten-year sabbatical from Nestlé – moving into a more strategic role

Between 1991 and 2001, I took an extended sabbatical from Nestlé. I worked in a small start-up company, providing consumer research consulting to large food and beverage companies (like Nestlé!). My role was to organise and conduct consumer preference tests for strategic product innovation and important renovation projects. Specific project risks such as inadequate timing, continuous changes in project briefs/resources, insufficient networking and so forth appeared to be major bottlenecks for the successful implementation of new products. With my inside-out view of the food and beverage industry, I was able not only to perform my consumer research consulting role, but also to support the customers in managing their project specific problems. It was also the first time that I was in contact with other business functions, for example commercial, marketing and sales or business management. I saw large differences in perceptions and/or unconscious bias in a number of these organisations, especially between operational functions (manufacturing, logistics, supply chain, procurement, etc.) and strategic positions (commercial, finance, strategic planning, etc.). Insufficient transparency and a low level of awareness for the most critical issues and/or hurdles for project implementation were a fact in most companies. Insufficient communication between these different functions was also a weakness.

From my activities in this start-up company, I acquired further knowledge in developing business plans and managing risks associated with these plans.

Later in my sabbatical I worked as a qualified risk engineer for Zurich Insurance, one of the largest insurance companies in Switzerland. At that time, I was for the first time in my career directly confronted with the concept of risk management. I was trained to perform risk assessments on behalf of the insurance companies, as well as at the request of customers wanting to identify and quantify specific business and/or project risks. A systematic approach towards risk management was helping insurance carriers and customers to create a competitive advantage. Creating *higher transparency, higher level of awareness and communication* around risks was essential for all these organisations. A *systematic approach* to regularly assess risks was seen as a real added value.

Back to the roots

In 2000, the chief financial officer of Nestlé, returning from his previous assignment in the US, initiated an internal discussion related to risk management and the way Nestlé should approach this in future within its organisation. After numerous exchanges and contacts with different consultants, a proposal to create a corporate risk management function at Nestlé was prepared and submitted to general management. This proposal was approved and I was contacted by Nestlé and asked if I would be interested to build up this new corporate role. My specific experience as well as my good knowledge of the Nestlé organisation made me an ideal candidate for this position. I started in my new role on 1 September 2001. In the course of my first month in Vevey, several major events occurred:

- A large Nestlé warehouse was set on fire in Venezuela (arson, insufficient protection)
- The 9/11 terrorist attack occurred in the US
- An even larger Nestlé warehouse burned down to the ground in Brazil (poor fire prevention)
- An attack on the Swiss Parliament, resulting in 14 deaths and several injuries
- The grounding of Swissair
- A fire in the Gotthard tunnel in Switzerland, resulting in several fatalities; the road tunnel was subsequently blocked for several months.

It was very unfortunate that all these events occurred, but they prepared the ground for me to get more attention from management when speaking about risk management. At that time, there was no big discussion about 'why it would be important for Nestlé to have a systematic process in place to identify and quantify its risks'. It was already accepted that well managing risks along the supply chain – from farm to fork – for business or other project risks, was essential for Nestlé.

Internal or external events can trigger a lot of attention and can be helpful when deciding upon change management in an organisation, but *you should not wait for such events to initiate the discussion!* It is much easier if you can follow your own agenda to implement such changes than if you are under the scrutiny of external stakeholders and have to implement changes under big time pressures and external constraints.

Operational risk management: initial implementation and learning

At the end of 2001, I started to propagate at Nestlé the concept of risk management/risk assessments that I had already been using in the insurance industry. Feedback was positive, but it was also obvious that the time required for these assessments was considered to be much too long. I scheduled the assessments as if I was still a consultant. It took me 2–3 days to perform one risk assessment. I also involved 10–20 participants in the assessments. A number of people were very sceptical regarding the usefulness of this process, but once they had participated in such a session, they found the process very interesting and the outcome pretty good and useful. One of my colleagues, who had been working 40 years for Nestlé, was fairly reluctant to accept this process until he joined such an assessment for the first time. This colleague became my best and most credible promoter within the organisation. All of this led me to further adapt the risk management process to the Nestlé culture: 2–3 hours' workshop with some mandatory individual prework and 5–10 participants representing the different functions involved in the business/project. I also invited a number of senior managers to such assessments with the aim to convince them about the process and gain them as internal promoters.

Keep the process simple, adapt it to the *culture of the organisation* and *use your own colleagues/ employees to promote* the process internally for you were key learnings which helped to position risk management the way it is still organised today at Nestlé.

Loss prevention and business continuity management as additional pillars

Early 2002, together with my colleagues from the insurance department, I realised that Nestlé was spending a significant amount of money for loss prevention visits of the factories and other sites around the world. These visits were made by insurance carriers for their own purposes and more than 10 different service providers were involved in these visits. Nestlé decided to develop a Global Loss Prevention Programme (GLPP) and requested Zurich Risk Engineering to perform these visits, using a unique framework to assess the premises and share all relevant data with Nestlé. A GLPP dashboard was developed over time to share the key outcomes with internal and external stakeholders. This initiative resulted in an increased visibility of prevention gaps as well as significant improvement of the fire prevention and protection status on Nestlé premises. This programme is still working, and around 250 Nestlé locations are (re) visited each year. It has also led to a significant reduction of the number of annual claims for property damage as well as a better loss ratio in the internal captive reinsurance company of Nestlé. This was a perfect win–win situation for both risk management and insurance as well as local management.

In the course of 2006, Nestlé decided to extend its insurance coverage to include business interruption coverage to all locations insured in the global property insurance programme. In line with this additional insurance coverage, Nestlé general management approved a proposal to establish a corporate business continuity management (BCM) position at Nestlé. The purpose of this position was to develop a BCM framework for the Nestlé organisation and coordinate the different BCM activities within the group. Initially, this position reported to me and provided direct support to local entities to assess potential business impacts and develop adequate business continuity plans against the most important impacts. Since then, the role has expanded to also include the development of training material and programmes and conduct BCM workshops in different parts of the world.

The house of risks is built on four different pillars: anticipation (identification and quantification of risks), prevention, planning/BCM and risk financing. You should manage the risks in a holistic way; therefore you should not forget that *loss prevention and/or business continuity* are key pillars to mitigate risks within your organisation.

Risk (and opportunity) management

Very early in the process of adapting the risk management to Nestlé's culture, I identified the possibility to address not only events which could have a negative impact on Nestlé, but also document events – not yet fully captured in the objectives/targets – which contribute positively to the business and/or project objectives/targets. Using the same process to capture threat (negative impact) and opportunities (positive impact) made the risk management process more attractive, especially for participants coming from the financial, commercial, marketing and sales backgrounds. *Capturing opportunities with the same process* opens the floor for a more holistic approach to manage risks.

The first mandatory risk assessments

After 4 years in my job, I was called to perform its first mandatory risk assessment in a business. Nestlé India – being a locally listed company – had to fulfil a legal requirement. I facilitated the initial risk assessment process to comply with the local legislation. The participants were all the local general managers. The outcome of this assessment was later presented to the board of directors of Nestlé India and used to provide evidence to the local legislators that a strong risk management process was in place and that relevant risks were identified and quantified as well as adequately managed with Nestlé India. The process used for this assessment was identical to the one developed and continuously improved since 2001. Other local requests followed from Japan, Mexico and Brazil.

In 2008, 7 years after initializing the risk management process, Nestlé general management approved a proposal requiring from each local market to perform an annual risk assessment. This proposal was submitted in view of complying with a new legal requirement in Switzerland, requesting from each company domiciled in Switzerland evidence that a risk management process was in place and the most relevant risks were adequately managed.

The risk management process developed in 2001 and continuously updated could be used for this purpose without having to make any significant modifications. The initial risk assessments were all facilitated internally; no external support was requested. The full rollout was scheduled over a period of 18 months. At the end of 2010, all markets had at least conducted their initial risk assessment, using the corporate risk management process.

Introducing a *well-adapted process in all markets* could be done very smoothly and *compliance with new legal requirement achieved, using existing processes.*

Financial crisis and initial group consolidation and reporting

As of mid-2008, the world of risks has fundamentally changed. If risk management was only known in specialised areas or in the financial industry before then, it is now broadly known. But risk management is not always perceived as positive, especially in the finance industry, where risk management was now part of the problem and not really providing a solution! Never before seen volatilities in the commodity area, for assets under investment, for counterparty exposure or more recently for regulatory/political/social events have materialised in the last 6 years. And it seems that every time the end of a given pick is announced, another pick pops up, creating additional volatilities in the marketplace. In this period, the chief financial officer asked me to focus on the negative impact of the risks/downside of the equation, as there were more than enough persons trying to capture all these nice opportunities in the world! I managed to keep the opportunities side in the ERM process, but had to rename the process in order to address his concern. This was also the time when Nestlé started to develop its initial consolidation of the most relevant risks for the group. Developing this consolidation took some time and it is actually still on the move. The initial feedback from general management and the board of directors was very positive, but I was regularly reminded to avoid process overengineering. Presenting a trend was considered to be sufficient as numbers (e.g., value-at-risk or more complex simulations / risk-based financial models) are anyway wrong! The last few years were very stimulating due to the tremendous tumults, never before seen volatilities and/or sequential occurrence of '100-year'/black-swan type events in a very short period of time. Regulatory requirements or good governance practices have put more emphasis upon risk management and the way it should be integrated into the day-to-day activities in the organisations. On the other hand, the world has also seen more than once the limitations of the system. The world is changing fast; it's therefore good to regularly shake the crystal ball to see what could be the next sandstorm building up. But do not expect to get all the answers from risk management; you need to remain flexible and be prepared for the unexpected.

You have to remain *pragmatic*, you should *not overengineer* your processes, and do *not simply believe the numbers* you get out of your systems, but *be prepared for the unexpected*.

Long-term risks (LTR) integrated into risk management

In 2010, the risk management organisation at Nestlé was extended to include a longer-term perspective into the normal risk management process. The aim was to develop and to maintain a methodology to identify long-term risks. A number of scenarios are analysed and assessments are performed on a regular basis to explore the future and identify major exposures for the organisations.

The collection of internally and externally information, from people and available databases and documents, the consolidation of those information to monitor long-term trends and the oversight and/or deeper investigation of them are part of this process. A number of data sets and databases have been developed and have been made available for this purpose.

Developing and managing *adequate knowledge databases* and perform analysis, preparing synthesis/reports and present them to relevant stakeholders is another activity related to LTR. A number of reports and relevant dashboards have been developed since.

Anticipating and mastering effects of long-term risks on today's impacted innovation strategies and project management are also essential to reduce major surprises. For this purpose, we regularly follow the evolution of a number of long-term risks.

Another activity is to *leverage internal and external existing knowledge* in developing horizontal network (inter-silo bridges) and share best practices as well as establish adequate lobbying and communicate throughout the value chain. All necessary media and tools are used to stay aware of new trends and tendencies in areas like technology, human behaviour, marketing, finance, research and development, nutrition and so forth. Research is therefore performed, information channels are accessed and/or conferences are attended.

This new role reports to me and provides support to corporate and local entities. This function has also been instrumental in helping ERM to further expand in the strategic planning.

Move towards strategic planning and integration into monthly business review

Since 2013, Nestlé resources have been focused on better aligning the ERM process with the existing strategic planning process. Nestlé has a well-established market business and strategies (MBS) framework. The integration of the ERM process into this MBS framework was deemed necessary to bring ERM to a higher level of credibility at Nestlé. It increased transparency around strategic risk-taking. ERM also gained additional attention from the management teams as it is well known that the key MBS outcomes are shared with general management! The question was not anymore 'Why shall we do it' but 'Is the content adequately addressing all relevant risks, and is it good enough to be shared with general management?'

Another identified weakness of the ERM process was that the mitigation actions follow-up was not done in a systematic way in all management teams. Another existing process – Nestlé Continuous Excellence (NCE) – was used this time to integrate the monitoring and follow-up into the monthly operational review (MOR) meeting. The key benefit was that without any additional resources, it was possible to establish consistent and systematic monitoring and follow-up in all parts of the organisation.

Risk management has to be an integral part of the way a business works. It *should not be seen as 'on top off' / 'in addition to'*. You should therefore *use – whenever possible – existing tools / processes and integrate / align ERM into / with them.*

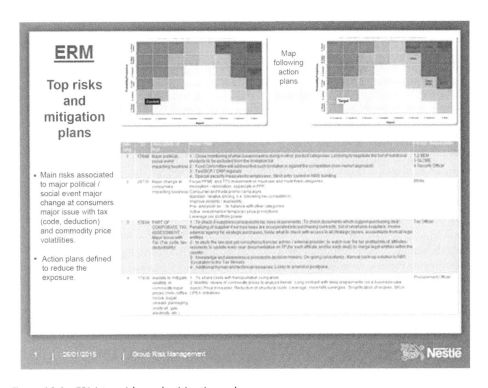

Figure 12.1   ERM top risks and mitigations plans

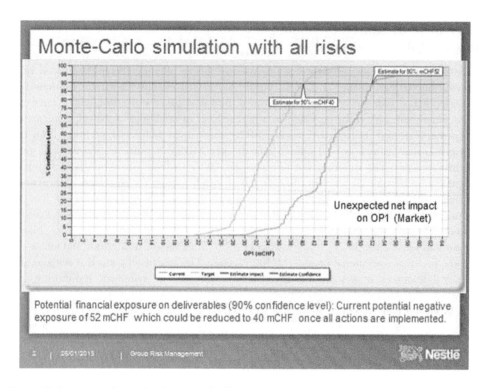

Figure 12.2 Monte Carlo simulation with all risks

What's next? Integrated approach to create true governance, risk management and compliance (GRC) model

Where will ERM evolve at Nestlé? Where will ERM evolve in the world? In my opinion, these are fascinating topics, but yet fully open questions. We see the need to further increase performance within the organisation. Can ERM help in this respect? I believe that it can. If the true concept of risk management is applied, it should help to reduce overlaps and redundancies within the organisation as, for example, only risk-based controls should be maintained in the organisation. If in addition, all functions involved in the risk management and internal control activities are truly aligned and working together, this will further reduce redundancies and increase the overall performance of the organisation. Can risk management be the answer to all our expectations? Maybe not. But risk management can certainly help us to achieve our objectives and protect the company's value through proactive risk mapping. And by setting up mitigating actions we can support the organisation in becoming even more performant and aligned. The ERM process helps by raising risk awareness, anticipating risks early and making sound business decisions.

A *more integrated approach to become more performant* is one of the next key milestones of Nestlé. Risk management is a fascinating journey. Every day I discover 'unplanned and unexpected' issues which could impact the business. It's not always easy to be ahead of this game, and it's not always possible to justify the time and resources invested into it, but it's certainly worthwhile to do!

Note

1   Markus Schädeli, Head of Group *Risk Management Nestlé.*

13

Strategic risk management in Suncorp Personal Insurance

Kirsten Dunlop and Mark Milliner

Abstract

Suncorp is the leading general insurer in Australia. In 2012 Mark Milliner, CEO of Suncorp Personal Insurance (PI), created an internal division to manage strategic risk, applying a framework developed by Dr. Luca Gatti and Dr. Kirsten Dunlop, and appointed Kirsten to lead the division. The journey that led to the creation of the PI Strategic Innovation division started with a program of work called Marco Polo, involving employees from all over Suncorp Personal Insurance. Marco Polo enabled PI to articulate a sense of its own identity (Business Rationale), and to identify 11 areas of strategic risk, emerging from relevant and possible systemic and long-term changes in the future market context. The Strategic Innovation division is charged with responsibility for monitoring, reporting and managing these Risks, as well as working on embedding a unique capability for strategic innovation as part of the solution to managing strategic risk. Three and half years on, in part because of its investment in this approach, Suncorp PI has successfully:

- Accelerated a vertical integration strategy for repair and restoration supply chain with sufficient benefit to the bottom line to enable Suncorp to maintain excellent margins through market downturn and increase customer satisfaction to world-class levels.
- Experimented with innovative approaches to employees working from home with extraordinary customer satisfaction results, unprecedentedly low levels of absenteeism and high sales performance.
- Partnered with start-ups to co-develop pioneering and disruptive business models for insurance.
- Achieved exceptional employee engagement scores for the SI division that are consistently higher than global high performing norms.
- Built an asset base of relationships globally with access to new business models, research ideas, thought leaders and regulators.
- Started to renew/adapt the model of the core insurance business to prepare for change.

In April 2011, Mark Milliner, CEO of Suncorp Personal Insurance, Australia's largest general insurer, met with a consultant who had recently relocated to Australia from Italy. Their conversation was about strategic risk. They would later understand that between them they shared the will and the ability to help an organisation think beyond the security of a market leading position, to understand and manage external change of a disruptive order and to equip its leaders with the courage and the capability to lean into change.

The consultant in question, Kirsten Dunlop, had been working for Generali Group, a global insurance conglomerate headquartered in Italy, leading a division called the Generali Group Innovation Academy. In response to a remit for leadership development and business innovation globally, Kirsten had introduced in Generali a C-suite program exploring external change, designed and facilitated by the director of Contextf, Luca Gatti, which had led to the identification of strategic risk as the key factor of concern in considering how to thrive and compete in a changing world. It had quickly become apparent in the course of the Generali Executive Forum that strategic risk was little understood, despite being identified as the responsibility of country and company CEOs in Generali's risk register, and despite representing the most significant cause for concern in terms of potential value destruction, a reality later borne out by the collapse of Lehman Brothers and the financial crisis. Through conversations with Generali executives over a period of 4 years, Kirsten and Luca, now husband and wife, experimented with better defining strategic risk and with forming a view on how best to manage strategic risk effectively (see Chapter 10 by Luca Gatti in this volume). This led to a full-year program focused exclusively on identifying strategic risks for Generali's core insurance businesses in the wake of the financial crisis, followed by a further year of exploring the notion of developing strategic innovation options as a means to hedge against exposure and build capability to adapt the business model ahead of change.

After a change of management, Kirsten left Generali at the end of 2010 and moved with her family to Australia. The encounter with Mark Milliner, which happened shortly after, proved to be life-changing for both. It led to the launch of a program for Suncorp Personal Insurance (PI) focused on exploration and management of strategic risk. Called Marco Polo, the initiative ran for 18 months and was so successful that Mark decided to create a permanent division in PI with responsibility for managing strategic risk through innovation. Now three years in, the Strategic Innovation division consists of a team of 24 people, part permanent, part rotational, furnishing the organisation with a robust framework for governance of Strategic Risk characterised by practical and effective practices of generating intelligence and insight into relevant and possible change in the future, access to alternative business models, and the means to understand why and how to adapt the business to achieve resilience and competitiveness over the long term. Flow of insight and exploration of alternative business models is now embedded in PI's strategic decision making and planning practices and has led to the organisation seizing and consolidating disruptive opportunities in the market, and determining to shift the centre of gravity of its core businesses as well as its relationships with customers.

The business: Suncorp Personal Insurance

Suncorp Group is of one of two large general insurers operating in the Australian market, each with about 30% market share. Grown primarily through acquisition and unlike its primary competitor, IAG, Suncorp Group is a financial services conglomerate, made up of leading general insurance, banking, life insurance and superannuation brands in Australia and New Zealand. The Group has 15,000 employees and relationships with nine million customers. It is a Top 20 ASX-listed company with $94 billion in assets. Suncorp has five core businesses: Personal Insurance, Commercial Insurance, Vero New Zealand, Suncorp Bank and Suncorp Life. It is the largest general insurer of Australians by Gross Written Premium (GWP) and largest provider of personal injury and Compulsory Third Party (CTP) insurance. The portfolio of personal and commercial insurance brands sells motor, home and contents, travel, boat, motorbike, caravan, business, workers' compensation and CTP insurances. A multibrand portfolio reaches 92% of Australians.

Unlike European and American insurance businesses, the Suncorp personal insurance model is primarily direct: 98% of insurance products and services are sold direct to the consumer through online platforms and call centres. Suncorp is therefore amongst the biggest e-retailers in Australia. Furthermore, insurance claims fulfilment is also delivered in a direct and material way through an end-to-end vertically integrated claims supply chain which supports the repair of cars and homes and replacement of lost or damaged items – leveraging Australia's largest repair network – unless customers specifically request cash settlement. Claims fulfilment includes full end-to-end service in motor repair, home repair and contents replacement with market disrupting supply chain innovation in both.

In 2009 Suncorp Group took on a new CEO in the wake of the global financial crisis which had seriously tested the Group's business model and culture, based on individual brands and siloed business units that had never been fully integrated. One of the first things Patrick Snowball and the executive team outlined was a business model built around the concept of One Company Many Brands, designed to demonstrate that the value of the whole was greater than the sum of the parts. Each executive took on end-to-end accountability for delivering outcomes in their business units working to a plan based on immediate priorities and supported by creating what Patrick called "building blocks for success". These building blocks consisted of consolidating a single view across key operating platforms: pricing and claims in General Insurance, customers, finance and terms and conditions for Suncorp's people, part of a rollout of a refocused strategy targeting simplified corporate and operational structures.

For Mark Milliner and his team, running the Personal Insurance business, that meant a focus on implementing an operating model known as the 'peg model' designed to pull 17 brands off legacy systems and onto one common operating platform for risk assessment, pricing and claims settlement. In a remarkably short space of time, the PI business was delivering on the implementation of the Legacy Simplification Program (LSP) and seeing positive results in terms of better customer experience and lower costs, along with higher levels of employee engagement and pride in the company. Amid this success, however, Mark was conscious that the PI leadership team had necessarily become inwardly focused. He was also increasingly aware of the susceptibility of traditional industries to disruption by major change in external conditions. For Mark, this highlighted the need to balance out the short-term operational focus by developing long-term thinking capabilities.

It was about this time that Mark met with Kirsten and heard about her experience of developing a process for managing strategic risk in Generali Group. He realised that PI could build on a program with a proven pedigree and capitalise on the learning it had produced. As a result, in 2011, PI embarked on the Marco Polo journey – a program of work designed to explore possible future contexts of business, evolutions in the market and structural changes that would affect the personal insurance business and the industry as a whole. The intent was to identify strategic risks for personal lines insurance and for Suncorp PI in particular, and to introduce to the organisation and its leadership a distinctive practice for managing those risks through strategic innovation. The program would also aim to develop and extend strategic thinking capability within the PI leadership team and the organisation as a whole. As part of the program, Mark wanted to establish a shared strategic language and conceptual knowledge amongst all PI leaders, unite teams around a common purpose and produce valuable collective intelligence about the future. He also wanted Suncorp's people to develop the methods and the mind-set to continue to build that intelligence over time, with a view to eventually engaging with these issues on a Group-wide scale.

> *The things that had been keeping me up at night were no longer operational issues but the "invisible forces" of change that threaten the status quo, fundamental changes not only reshaping the insurance industry of the future but our world of the future, things like changing technology, changing lifestyles and the very evolution of human society. Our business and our success in this business depend on how well we adjust to these currents and tides of change. The Marco Polo process came about not because of a crisis or a reaction to the latest management fad but because of my growing, nagging sense that the number one risk to our business could be the status quo. The risk that we could wake up one day after a long winning streak and realise we were irrelevant.*
>
> Mark Milliner

The initial program: Marco Polo 2011

The Marco Polo program was the first leg of Suncorp PI's journey towards investing in long-term competitiveness and resilience. The program was built around the definition and framework that Kirsten and Luca had developed for understanding and managing strategic risk, with adjustments for a specific application designed to engage the PI leadership team directly in the process, help lift its horizons and start to build and stretch vision and strategic leadership capabilities following a long and challenging period of postmerger reorganisation and streamlining.

Running from mid-2011 through mid-2012, Marco Polo comprised four phases of work that brought together external thought leaders and people from all areas of Suncorp PI. The program was launched with two declared objectives:

1. Identify Strategic Risks for the PI business and develop Strategic Options to manage them in order to ensure long-term competitiveness and resilience.
2. Build and stretch the vision and capabilities of our people, specifically:
   - share strategic language and concepts amongst key decision makers;
   - produce collective intelligence about the future, as well as the methods and the mindset to continue to build that intelligence over time;
   - hone the strategic thinking, systemic thinking and competitive thinking of the leadership team and of the organisation as a whole;
   - cohere teams around a common purpose;
   - complement and extend individual leadership development initiatives currently underway.

More than 160 people across Suncorp contributed to Marco Polo. Participation in some phases of work was extended to people at every level of the business through a top-down/bottom-up mechanism in order to enrich the conversation and the thinking in that phase, and to ensure that the organisation at large became involved in thinking about the sustainability and resilience of the business and became energised around a strategic innovation agenda. The commitment to involve people at multiple levels of the organisation was designed to engender shared thinking about the sustainability and resilience of the business and generate a widespread open-mindedness and creativity.

The program's four phases of work consisted of:

1. Articulation of a Business Rationale for Suncorp PI.
2. Research and imagination of possible alternative future contexts of business.
3. Investigation of the relationship between the business rationale and the future contexts to uncover strategic risks for the PI business.
4. Creation of a portfolio of strategic options with which to hedge against those risks: test, learn and build agility and adaptability in PI's business and its people.

1. Business Rationale – Why are we in business?

The Marco Polo journey started with the PI Executive General Manager (EGM) team and an exploration of Suncorp PI's Business Rationale (business identity). The Business Rationale shows the business as a system arranged around need in the market. This drove a challenging initial conversation about underlying assumptions and about evolutions in current, latent and future need, with respect to which other elements of business identity may or may not have been in tension. The workshop focused reflection on the nature of insurance as a business that emerges from the individual and social experience of time, being finite, unpredictable and uncertain. This level of reflectiveness was driven by the questions, "Why are we in business? What human need explains the existence of this industry in the market?"

Work on the Business Rationale produced a rich and significant reframing in understanding of the business. It produced strategic value in and of itself by identifying opportunity spaces in the market and by examining, in terms of need and relevance, what really made PI distinctive. Attention focused on changing expectations of customer experience and on shifts in perception of protecting what is valued. The conversation led to a collective representation of the nature of the business, uncovering differences of perspective and experience in the leadership team. Following the workshop, the EGMs and other contributors maintained a dialogue about the evolving Business Rationale, resulting in further updates to its visual representation. In the end, this achieved greater alignment and a deeper, shared understanding of the system of value creation that the team was called to lead.

> *Truly understanding the reason for your business, the true "why," is hard work and is critical to a successful business.*
>
> Mark Milliner

2. Futures – What is possible and relevant in the future?

The second stage of Marco Polo imagined possible future contexts of the business, working from the premise introduced to the leadership team by Luca that the principal concern of strategy is the future state of the relationship between a business identity and its context. Collective exploration of possible future contexts of the business was to enable the team to test the sustainability and competitiveness of PI's Business Rationale over time. Imagining the future called for substantial diversity of views, so PI widened involvement for this phase to include contributors outside the EGM team. Their participation was prepared by training in the conceptual underpinnings of the Strategic Risk framework to ensure that all participants started the process with a shared understanding of how imagining and exploring future worlds would bring strategic intelligence to PI.

Participants then created 16 alternative future states (Futures), covering a broad spectrum of individual and social needs to which personal insurance connects, as identified in the Business Rationale. Major areas of change were sought out by looking through four lenses: economy, environment, technology and social dynamics. Within each of these areas, groups focused on relevant drivers of structural change such as domotics, longevity, mobility, trust, data, climate, health, cities, networks and resources. Participants used a specially designed activity template to guide them in imagining future context and ensure a rich, multiperspectival representation of their Future. The template prompted people to articulate both micro and macro perspectives on the future to ensure richness and depth of exploration. This also served the purpose of engaging different thinking styles as people zoomed in and out of global systems and individual experience.

The future worlds that emerged from this process were evocative snapshots, rich in detail and anecdote and underpinned by extensive exploration of possible evolutions in society, technology, environment and the economy. Each Future reconfigured the world around the exponential effects of one significant structural change, looking for the possible rather than the probable. It did so as an act of imagination and representation, not prediction, anticipating that everything could be possible, in order to achieve greater range and richness and hence produce a more meaningful and more prudent test of the Business Rationale.

For PI, the Futures proved to be especially meaningful and effective because they were created by people from within the business. Involving employees directly in this process leveraged the fact that people engaged with the future with an embodied knowledge and understanding of what might be relevant to them. As a consequence, they imagined possibilities that proved to be insightful and revealing. The process also raised general levels of awareness with respect to emerging trends, which drove home an understanding of the relative proximity of dynamics that would significantly affect PI's context of business. This, and the opportunity to think differently about PI's business, galvanised energy and interest. As a result, the organisation continues to benefit from an informal network of people who are on the lookout for new trends in broad domains – not only staying aware of what is happening in the world, but also understanding it and delivering intelligence back about its significance for PI.

3. *Strategic risks* – Would we be relevant? If not, why not?

The third stage of the Marco Polo journey brought together PI's Business Rationale and the 16 Futures to look for tension or potential incoherence between the terms of each, on the premise that incoherence signals strategic risk. The participant group widened again: people from all areas and all levels of the PI business, as well as people from the broader Suncorp Group, contributed to this part of the process. As in earlier phases of the program, newcomers were trained in the conceptual framework of Marco Polo to enable them to understand the Business Rationale and orient them to their task of identifying strategic risks. Strategic Risk emerges from changes, mostly external, that an organisation will experience and that would impact survival and performance. Strategic Risk is a function of incoherence between the current business identity and future systemic and long-term evolutions of the external environment.

The activity for this phase took place over a series of four workshops. Participants were asked to become 'citizens of the future', exploring what it would be like to live in the particular world they were given. To be 'good citizens', they had to get a handle on the structural change their Future embodied and explore further what life might be like for individuals, workers, children, companies, societies, nations, families and regulators. They then considered whether PI's Business Rationale would be competitive in that context, applying a mechanism of virtual 'wind-tunnelling', enquiring, for example, "What is different in this future? What aspects of our business model would struggle or simply not survive? What conditions, that we rely on, would no longer be in place?"

The strategic intelligence each group developed was unique in that only one group explored each Future. This permitted deep reflection and immersion into each Future and drove robust arguments for areas of risk. Insights gained through this process were then shared back with the groups exploring other futures. A number of common themes of incoherence emerged, even across very different futures, suggesting that these themes were reliable indicators of a threat to the competitiveness and sustainability of the business, should the change identified by those futures manifest itself in a significant way. Following the workshops, the consulting team worked with the EGMs to refine and consolidate the outputs in order to identify a set of strategic risks that wove together the multiple threads of structural change explored across the 16 Futures. At the conclusion of this process the team identified 11 Strategic Risks for Suncorp PI.

Thinking about strategic risk in these terms equipped the organisation with a robust understanding of relevant change, and a dynamic point of view for navigating evolving future contexts. The Strategic Risks identified for Suncorp PI are structured in terms of a tension between current identity and future context, with each Risk captured on a single page. The Risks focus on the juxtaposition of specific elements of the current Business Rationale with aspects of emerging external forces of change that would challenge the sustainability and/or competitive advantage of those elements of the business identity. This visual representation emphasises the fact that it is potential incoherence that represents the risk, not external change in and of itself. The structural simplicity of the representation captures potential incoherence in such a way that it can become the object of decision making and action and equips the leadership team with a sense of what matters for the purposes of monitoring and decision making. At the same time the Risks encourage a focus on the dynamic and evolving nature of a relationship between identity and context which requires intelligence and learning to occur over time rather than a sudden commitment to the prediction of one outcome or another.

PI's experience of the Strategic Risk workshops was rich with challenge, energy and confronting realisations about the risks facing Suncorp PI. The process of identifying Strategic Risks brought people together from many different brands, cultures and operating principles into a conversation that was bigger than all of them. The process maximised the time they spent together, helping to drive collaboration and cross-fertilisation of ideas. This diverse group also further enriched and refined the articulation of Suncorp PI's Business Rationale, building a common understanding of PI's business identity while testing it through exposure to diverse perspectives. For Mark and the EGMs, it was both encouraging and thought-provoking to see strong common themes in the risks coming out of each workshop. At the time, reflection on that experience prompted a decision to reshape the PI strategy so that it explicitly directed attention at the need to future proof the business.

At this point PI started actively discussing the Marco Polo program internally, including a presentation from Luca and Mark at the PI Senior Leadership Team Conference in October 2011, which raised awareness and generated a broader understanding of the Marco Polo process. The incoming chairman of the board, Zygmunt Switkowski, spent time reviewing all the outputs of the process with Mark and PI EGM team. Suncorp Bank took an interest and eventually set up its own version of Marco Polo, entitled Project Cookie, with Luca's help. Insights from the Marco Polo process served to encourage and shape an international study tour for Mark and several PI EGMs with access to global thought leaders to continue the dialogue about structural changes and the future context of business. Mark also took the opportunity to raise awareness in the local industry, delivering a rousing speech at an industry conference on the future of insurance. This was republished as an article in *InsuranceNEWS* magazine titled

"Insurance in 2030". Editors of the magazine received substantial positive feedback on Mark's speech and hailed it as one of the most forward-thinking editorials they published in the last 20 years.

> *Having a Nobel Prize winner fly all the way from Europe just to speak to us was an amazing experience. My informal conversations with John [Schellnhuber] were profound for me. He gave me a new appreciation of the importance of climate change, not just for insurance but for our whole social system. I can now speak with much greater confidence and authority about climate change with regulators and government. I know what needs to be said and what matters (or should matter) to decision makers. As an executive, I now really have something to bring to the table on this that gives me stature and credibility.*
>
> Mark Milliner

4. Strategic options – Where to from here?

In Generali Group, Luca and Kirsten had experimented with a hypothesis that the most prudent and effective hedge against strategic risk is targeted innovation in the form of strategic options. Options are a hedge against disruptive change. They take a learning position with respect to change that provides experience, and hence intelligence, encouraging experimentation with different forms or concepts of the business necessary to evolve the business identity. By definition they do not entail a commitment of significant resources. Each strategic option needs to be an innovation to the existing business model that addresses a possible future structural change in the market context. An option renews, transforms or enriches an element in the current Business Rationale to help the business become relevant in that context and potentially deliver significant competitive advantage. An option then becomes a possible action that an organisation might choose to execute at an opportune moment in the future.

So in the fourth stage of the Marco Polo journey, PI started on the work of building strategic options to manage the Strategic Risks that had been identified. Once again, a diverse group of people from all divisions came together to produce ideas for options and refine them into compelling strategic arguments. More than 70 people took part in this part of the process, working in teams, each focused on one Strategic Risk. The teams brainstormed a range of ideas regarding how each Strategic Risk could be managed, clustered these ideas and picked those that managed the relevant risk best. They then outlined strategic arguments for each of these ideas using a business model canvas to demonstrate how these ideas could help manage the Strategic Risk in question. The ideation process culminated in the presentation of ideas for strategic options at an 'Options Fair' in early 2012. This event was the highlight of Marco Polo, marked by enormous energy and excitement.

The Options teams had conceived over 50 ideas to help Suncorp PI manage its Strategic Risks. These ideas were grouped and consolidated into briefs for developing portfolios of strategic options. In a review of the outputs, the PI EGMs agreed that the majority of strategic option briefs should be developed further. They also acknowledged numerous areas of overlap between some of the briefs, and called for consolidation. Many options stood out noticeably as opportunities or quick wins, rather than being firmly rooted in the future context. In the period that followed, one of the key areas of reflection and learning was around the need for focused and sustained work on strategic options, given the challenges associated with imagining alternative business models whilst stepping in and out of business as usual. Continual reference back to the Strategic Risk framework emerged as a key success factor in order to distinguish between strategic options and immediate business opportunities, and that was proving increasingly difficult to hold on to. Opportunities precipitate naturally and quickly from the process of thinking about evolving customer need or emerging technologies and are inherently attractive. What became evident was that they were not going to serve the purpose of managing PI's Strategic Risks to the extent that they were coherent with the current Business Rationale.

After 6 months, Mark's reflection with Luca was that in an execution-focused culture, it is instinctual and tempting to move towards thinking in terms of opportunities. Staying in the space of strategic options requires discipline in recognising the differences, and methodology and process for staying focused on options and on management of strategic risk. And that requires a mandate.

The Marco Polo program was so successful in terms of its benefits, immediate flow-on effects and impact on participants that Mark determined to transform it into an embedded organisational capability and driver of value. Guided by conversations with Luca, Mark reviewed the learnings from the experience of experimenting with strategic options and explored what might be possible if he were to internalise the strategic risk and innovation framework within PI. In August 2012, he asked Kirsten, now at KPMG, if she would be interested in joining Suncorp to design and lead a function called Strategic Innovation within PI, reporting to him.

> *This transformative journey has shown us how shifting collective focus to the future can unlock energy, passion and talent; it has shown us how powerful it can be when we bring our diverse talent and intelligence together to bear on uncertainty; and it has shown us how great our future can be if we dare to think differently. In taking this decision, I reflected back on how it all started and how much the outcomes have far surpassed my original expectations, both personally and professionally.*
>
> Mark Milliner

They agreed to start with three building blocks: documentation of the process so far; presentation to the Board for endorsement of intent and direction; and organisational design, to be agreed with the PI executive team. Kirsten started work on all three, supported by a colleague from the PI HR Business Partner team, Briana Van Strijp, who had requested to be assigned to the division after her experience of Marco Polo. Within two months, the new division had a proposal for an distinctive organisational design, a 250-page publication entitled *Managing Strategic Risk in Suncorp Personal Insurance*, which captured PI's Marco Polo journey alongside the conceptual framework of strategic risk and strategic innovation that Suncorp had adopted, and a paper prepared for the Board Strategy Retreat laying out the objectives, approach and direction of PI's Strategic Innovation division.

Engaging the Board

The paper to the Board described the primary accountabilities of the Strategic Innovation function as follows:

1. Develop strategic intelligence about global trends, possible structural changes of the business context in the future and future market opportunities.
2. Develop strategic relational capital as part of an innovation ecosystem for Suncorp that facilitates information gathering, identification of relevant structural changes and generation of Strategic Options.
3. Embed a Strategic Risk framework in the PI business supported by a cyclical, participative approach to refreshing the Risks.
4. Build and manage a portfolio of Strategic Options to manage PI's Strategic Risks.

5. Hone the competitive thinking of leadership teams and the organisation as a whole to think about the future and its impact to our business.
6. Enable Suncorp PI to evolve its business models to remain relevant and resilient over time and to deliver a constant supply of capability with which to be competitive in the market.

The paper recognised that the most important outcome of the Marco Polo program for PI had been the identification of Strategic Risks for the business together with a means of understanding them and managing them dynamically over time in order to adapt and compete. It pointed out the link between that outcome and the PI Three-Year Business Plan that, following Marco Polo, explicitly called out the need to future-proof the business through its strategy and forward agenda. Marco Polo had also produced a significant number of positive flow-on effects across the full spectrum of PI's core competencies, from data and underwriting to brand, culture and business support, which was expressed in the following quotes from different process participants:

> We can see signals that we were blind to before. This includes understanding the impact of multiple systems that are not disruptive in their own right but are highly disruptive collectively.

> We are accelerating new ways of connecting with customers. We are shaping our thinking around brands and brand portfolio management differently.

> We have restored the confidence to act without fearing failure and demonstrated to ourselves that we have the potential not just to respond to disruption, but also perhaps to generate disruption to capture value.

> We can see new value pools. Our view of being a "personal insurance business" has changed. We have a broader view of our role in society that opens up new opportunities to understand and satisfy new needs and stay relevant as these needs change. Marco Polo has stretched our capacity to think and to learn and produced an effect of exhilaration, unlocking energy, passion and talent.

Discussion of the new Strategic Innovation function with the Board in November 2012 went well. Mark, Luca and Kirsten embarked upon the implementation of the division, encouraged by a lively and curious debate and warm words of encouragement and endorsement. The first step was to finalise the design of work and organisation for the division and recruit.

Organisational design

To facilitate the development of the skills needed to think in terms of Strategic Risk and Strategic Options and with them, importantly, strategic leadership capabilities to support the quality of decision making that would be required for strategic innovation. Hence, a distinctive organisational structure for the new division was designed based on the principle of a complex adaptive ecosystem. This design was intended to enable SI to leverage internal business experience and capabilities through the rotation of leaders on secondment from other divisions in PI and to learn from external perspectives by engaging with global experts, thought leaders and entrepreneurs. The design was also intended to accelerate growth in the mind-set and capabilities of team members through emphasis on interdisciplinary learning, learning how to learn, self-organisation and on deliberately development work practices and collaboration.

The Strategic Innovation function was designed with a flat structure – all team members report to the EGM Strategic Innovation. The function consists of a small core team that facilitates, guides and leads the execution of the SI program of work, and a number of secondment roles (Strategic Innovation Principals) available to leaders from the business on 12-month rotations. Secondments start and finish every quarter in groups of three or four. The design of the rotational model is now a key consideration in career progression to business leader and strategic leader levels. Over time, as more leaders and talented professionals have been seconded to SI and have moved to their next role in the business, carrying new capabilities and mind-set with them, PI is building a broader organisational ability to lead through ambiguity, adapt to change and leverage disruptive innovation for competitive advantage.

The Strategic Innovation core team consists of full-time roles offering a diverse mix of specialist skills and strong interdisciplinary capabilities designed to 'power' capability building, provide thought leadership, quality assurance, support and acceleration for activities across the division's core streams of work. These roles were designed to bring together a diverse set of epistemological and disciplinary 'DNA' strands: hermeneutics, semiotics and semantics, cultural history, design thinking and human-centred design practice, network design and theory, project and program management, theories of strategy, military intelligence and foresight, portfolio theory, human resources and organisational design, scenario thinking, complexity theory and systems thinking, visualisation and marketing.

Role design for the rotational roles emphasised responsibility for strategic options activation and management, inductive and associative sense-making and strategic learning, presentation of strategic learning, distributed leadership and carriage of an ambassador function with other divisions in the organisation. Collaboration between the two teams enriches the skills and perspectives of both and maximises the effectiveness of the function.

The founding plans for PI Strategic Innovation also encompassed design of a broader Strategic Innovation System that included an Advisory Board, internal and external ecosystems. The purpose of a deliberately fostered internal ecosystem was to provide a close interface with leaders and innovation communities within Suncorp to add value and relevance to the Strategic Innovation work. The external ecosystem anticipated the relational capital and value to be exchanged through partnership in capability building and resourcing, sense making and ideation, networking and investment. The Advisory Board is made up of global thought leaders and subject matter experts whose role is to challenge the division's thinking and facilitate access to sources of information and intelligence. Working together, these different layers of the Strategic Innovation System enable focused management of PI's Strategic Risks while exposing the business to new thinking and evolution in Suncorp's external context. As a whole, the Strategic Innovation System was designed to unite and leverage the benefits of dedicated time and energy, cross-fertilisation from people actively engaged with customers and current business problems and collective intelligence from networks within and outside PI.

> One of the critical success factors has been the whole concept of networks. We have been able to create relationships with start-ups and with influential individuals all over the world. All business gets done through relationships and conversations. We have created the possibility to punch above our weight because we've had something interesting to talk about – not necessarily SI per se, but the process we have been through and what we are trying to achieve and do through the SI process – and through the SI approach to building and participating in networks.
>
> Mark Milliner

Once recruitment of the core team was complete, and the first secondees commenced, the Strategic Innovation division turned its attention to the eleven areas of strategic risk for the PI business identified during Marco Polo and to the problem of developing a portfolio of Strategic Options to manage those Risks. The division was charged with responsibility for monitoring, reporting and managing these risks, and as well as working on embedding a unique capability for strategic innovation as part of the solution to managing strategic risk. Over the course of the first eighteen months, Kirsten, Luca and the team focused on four building blocks:

1. A portfolio of strategic options – designing a robust process for option development, selection and activation.
2. Strategic leadership capability – investing in our people to think differently, be comfortable with uncertainty, learn to look for and look at assumptions; think critically and systemically; supporting people through the full cycle of secondment.
3. A strategic risk reporting system – creating a unique framework to help decision makers understand and engage with PI's strategic risks.
4. A strategic intelligence system – developing a proprietary information system to capture and manage knowledge and strategic intelligence generated by the work of the division.

In addition, learning from the experience of Marco Polo, the SI team addressed the need for an effective means of separating out and capturing ideas for immediate opportunities that could enhance or extend the value proposition of the existing business. Very quickly opportunities began to emerge. A practice of identification and meaning-making was developed to ensure a timely feed into business-as-usual development, providing support where necessary and appropriate. One of the responsibilities of the Strategic Innovation System has now become to leverage the intelligence it attracts and produces to capture ideas for market opportunities where they present themselves and deliver insights, ideas and proposals to those areas of the business that can best develop and implement competitive products and services. This feeds back to the organisation intelligence and distributed strategic leadership capabilities as well as commercial advantage.

> My thinking about SI has now evolved to appreciate that we can also use this work to create innovative opportunities for our business.
>
> Mark Milliner

Strategic options to manage strategic risks

The creation of a more robust process for developing Strategic Options started with the definition of strategic risk that PI had adopted with Marco Polo and the principle of structural change – complex, systemic, long-term evolutions. At the core of Luca and Kirsten's approach to strategic risk was the notion of managing exposure by establishing a diverse portfolio of strategic options from which to learn about future business environments, uncover drivers of structural change, identify opportunities, explore alternative business models, acquire capabilities and support decision makers with a strategic argument for business model renewal.

Each strategic option needed to allow Suncorp to take a specific learning and capability building position with respect to a dynamic of change that would represent a threat to the competitiveness of the business. An Option is a position we are in with respect to a future action that we may and can execute at an opportune moment in Time. Luca designed a 20-day process for developing Strategic Options to the point of being a blueprint for action. He presented it to the newly formed team who built upon it, documented it, tested it and refined it through parallel iterations and trial variations over the course of the next 12 months to the point where it is now: one of the most thoughtful and robust components of the SI division's work, and the starting point for every new secondee to the division.

Options development

The Options Development Process works through three phases – argument, choice and design – with the objective of developing a strategic argument for why PI should invest in an option. It does so by revisiting a strategic risk; making a choice about what the SI team will pay attention to in the present with this option that will enable it to learn about a particular structural change and hence manage strategic risk; designing a blueprint that would set the business up to get into option quickly; and crafting a brief that gathers all the elements into a compelling and coherent document. The SI process establishes strategic options as learning hypotheses: positions *through* which to experience and reflect on the dynamics of change in the environment, develop insights and capabilities with which to modify the business identity, and thus enhance resilience and competitiveness.

What makes an option 'strategic' is its capability to sustain or develop coherence with a future context. Exercising the option, that is making an option 'active' at the opportune moment, offers the possibility of extending or improving coherence and of delivering significant competitive advantage. The 'solution' that particular options present can be anything that delivers the value of being prepared for future strategic action. SI Options have included the design and prototyping of a new service or new product, taking part in external projects, conducting, commissioning or participating in research, hiring or developing or partnering with a certain capability, framing a venture or project in the current business to learn about change, taking a new position in the market, investing time or sponsorship in an appropriate start-up or joint venture. Counterintuitively for many within the core business, options are not intended to be pilots of PI's next business model. On the contrary they are a lens, a point of view (literally) as well as a potential asset: they are learning positions that generate experience and insight to inform decision makers about the nature and dynamics of change and provide PI with the means to adapt its business, often through partnership and goodwill (relational capital).

The development of a dynamic portfolio

In the first 18 months, the new SI division generated arguments and blueprints for 23 Strategic Options and successfully activated 16 as the first step in composing a robust, diversified portfolio. The division soon arrived at an inflexion point: in need of a set of criteria and a process for composing a portfolio of strategic options. Options on their own are interesting learning positions, but they are not sufficient to deliver actionable intelligence. A portfolio approach maximises opportunity and minimises downside of risk. It ascertains a spread of possible actions that hedge against loss of value, it supports competitiveness by developing distinctiveness, it opens new markets, and increases shares or rates of return in current markets by enhancing strategic flexibility and providing a rationale to identify areas of possible innovation.

Working together with SI core team members, Luca and Kirsten developed a draft portfolio composition process that the team then tested and refined for robustness and effectiveness. Portfolio composition is now a weeklong activity carried out on a quarterly rhythm. The first 3 days consist of a full 'stock take' of what the SI team has available to it (active options, options that have just been built, options that are still in the early stages of activation, options that are 'on the shelf', previously active options). The stock take involves the whole team initially, followed by the core team examining and discussing in detail newly built option blueprints so that they can be compared effectively with already active options. The last 2 days of the process involve selecting options to activate, looking at the composition of the portfolio and designing adjustments so that the options within the portfolio function as a set, assuming the broadest possible spread across the Risks, and translating the portfolio into a program of work for the next quarter. This part of the process includes Mark as a key, interested stakeholder whereas the initial stock take often includes other stakeholders in the internal ecosystem with an interest in the work of the division. At the conclusion of the process the whole team comes together again to review the new portfolio and its implications.

> *The SI portfolio enables strategic innovation by building knowledge and insight of the underlying changes generating strategic risks and by providing us with resources, capabilities and new business models we can leverage to change. This portfolio generates invaluable human and organisational networks, know-how and reveals alternatives available to us. Importantly, we are not investing in a suite of start-ups hoping that something pays off, nor are we hoping that disruption will go away if we seek to influence it. We are creating the time, space and information to make more informed decisions.*
>
> Mark Milliner

The portfolio process is designed to balance many competing tensions: sufficient breadth of coverage to inform PI of structural changes taking place; sufficient depth to equip the business with the relationships and resources to begin to change our business if it decides to. The portfolio also takes into consideration how resources can be allocated (funds, people, time), the unique combination of option typologies, third-party relationships, and the likely effectiveness of that particular learning position to give the SI team what it needs. The team appreciated over time the extent to which a networked suite of options, complete with intended diversity and tensions, provides much greater value and a more robust mechanism for detecting contextual changes, ensuring a diversified spread of active options across all the PI strategic risks, balanced with a concentration of options managing those risks judged to be of most concern.

Managing active options

Given a quarterly process of decision making and portfolio composition, getting in and out of options smoothly, and ensuring that SI captures the value of each learning position, is critical to the success of the Strategic Options portfolio and the extent to which it manages PI's strategic risk successfully. As a consequence, the division developed a framework for managing active options that provides methodology, tools and processes for entering into, experiencing and reflecting upon experience to learn, and for exiting option learning positions. Like the process for Developing Strategic Options and Portfolio Composition, Managing Active Options is documented in a detailed manual that opens with a statement of intent and explanation designed to teach and remind team members of the necessarily tight connection with the purpose of each Strategic Option and of the whole portfolio. Managing an active option is a deliberate experience over time, focusing on what matters (Position > structural change). It is a framed learning journey taking into account the relationship between self (identity: individual or business) and the environment (context). Deliberate design and management of an Option experience is necessary to maximise the quality and value of our insights and learning. We need to ensure that the experience allows us to reflect on our Position (is it the right Position? Is this the right way to take this Position? What are we learning from our Position?) and what it is telling us about a structural change. . . . Learning within this context is a philosophical concept, a conceptual mechanism. A paradigm where learning is used to acquire the resources to be different (and is not just about collecting information). An Option is not a point of finality; it is designed to contribute to a strategic argument.

In addition to methods and disciplines of structured observation, reflection, sense-making, documentation and knowledge management, the process includes considerations such as legal requirements, compliance, procurement and effective operational risk management, so as not to pose unnecessary enterprise risk. As the options usually involve third-party relationships, care is also taken to nurture and support relationships so that they remain positive should an option position be deactivated. The SI Managing Active Options process is also used as a wiki to document and capture the accumulated experience and lessons learned of the team over time as to how to set up Options to generate valuable insights and maximise learning.

Strategic learning from a portfolio of options

Once the first portfolio was activated, and now on a rolling basis, a significant part of the focus of the SI team is on learning from options: learning from individual options, from combinations both logical and random (serendipity works) and above all from the perspective that the portfolio provides. The intelligence and insights that the SI division derives from the whole set of strategic options informs strategic conversations within the PI business on a quarterly basis, as a minimum. These are conversations focused on three primary questions: 'What is the portfolio telling us about uncertainty relevant to our business? What is our portfolio giving us in terms of resources and capabilities to enable us to change our business? Should we change?' They are conversations that support strategic learning with respect to whether and how to change PI's business model.

Sense-making

A year into the creation of the division, the SI team began to transition out of a purely start-up phase of building and testing methodology and process into the first steps towards systematic strategic learning for the business. This began with implementation of a process for managing and making sense of the learning from active options, part of the broader Managing Active Options process. The critical component in managing an active option, and the principal source of the value SI delivers to the business, is sense-making: learning from options. Sense-making is an activity of preparing for and having experiences, generating observations, and making sense of those observations ('So what?') in a way that builds insights and intelligence about the learning position. Sense-making in SI happens within teams working on single options, and then amongst multiple teams working on options, both related and unrelated to common areas of strategic risk, so that over time sense can be made of the strategic intelligence being generated for PI by the full option portfolio. Portfolio-level sense-making takes place on a quarterly basis, following the completion of each portfolio composition and timed to lead into strategic conversation with the PI EGM and key Group stakeholders. Sense-making at every level is documented and captured within the division's Strategic Intelligence System, designed to tag and organise the intelligence emerging over time so that patterns become more easily apparent and so that knowledge is transferable within SI's rotational model.

As the SI division has turned its attention to a deeper exploration of, reflection on and formalisation of processes of sense-making, it became apparent that the division's capability building framework and program of leadership development was remarkably well placed to contribute and build appropriate mind-set and skills, given its basis in theories and practice of adult forms of mind and subject/object perspectives as well as sense-making frameworks like *Cynefin*. Working with Jennifer Garvey-Berger of Cultivating Leadership, the team has internalised a practice of deep listening through questions that open rather than solve, listening for structure, taking multiple perspectives and thinking in systems, the last reinforced and further stretched by collaboration with Alain Wouters. Reflection, experimentation and continuous improvement in sense-making process, approaches and capabilities are ongoing in the Strategic Innovation division. Increasingly the team has been experimenting with sense-making partnerships (such as an agreement with WIRED) and with criteria for selecting Options that include an assessment of the likely quality of sense-making.

Supporting strategic conversation

As an accumulation of sense-making within and across multiple options and as a perspective on patterns and triggers in its own right, portfolio level sense-making generates insights and questions and strategic arguments for PI. It is this intelligence that provides the input for Quarterly Strategy Sessions (QSS) with the PI EGM team, followed by strategy sessions with the next level of management down (PI Executive Managers) across all principal office sites immediately following the QSS.

PI's QSS, structured as a series of strategic conversations, are at the core of the PI business's strategy-making process under Mark's leadership. Suncorp Group's official strategy process is an exercise in rolling 3-year financial planning, managed by the chief financial office, and informed by the Group's Risk Appetite. PI's approach to strategy and planning supplements that with a social process of divisional strategy formation and strategic thinking through conversation. When Marco Polo was launched, PI's QSS sessions were used to introduce the objectives of the program, explore and refine the Business Rationale, present the outcomes from the Futures' workshops and debate the Strategic Risks produced by the process. Once the Strategic Innovation division was established, it became apparent that the existing management framework of business planning and operational discussions about the activities of PI divisions was not well suited to the material and questions that SI started to bring to the table. So the formula of the quarterly strategy sessions was extended to 2 days, with the first dedicated to learnings and challenges to existing business assumptions from the SI portfolio, and the second focused on decision making relevant to the frame of the rolling 3-year business planning period.

Over time, these two decision spaces have become increasingly interwoven as conversation about if, when and how the PI business needs to become different have opened up more self-critical perspectives on current market dynamics and built greater preparedness, decision space and confidence in PI's understanding of the future context. In turn, this has led to leadership resolve and interest in the competitive advantages and resilience offered by systematic experimentation. It has given rise to greater appreciation for and receptiveness to nurturing strategic alliance partnerships with small and disruptive start-up businesses. Suncorp PI's growing maturity in this respect has in large part been made possible by an unusual level of access to start-ups and thought leaders globally, and above all by the quality of relationships with them – based on creative commons, mutual exchange, goodwill and high trust – both of which have come with the SI approach to strategic learning and to strategic innovation.

> *By working together with this framework I think we have helped our partners to go in a better direction that may well help them to be more successful businesses regardless of their arrangements with us.*
>
> Mark Milliner

Facilitating action

Acting on the implications of strategic risk has happened over an extended time frame for PI and as an experience of growing understanding, informed first by the ground-breaking experience of Marco Polo and then by the portfolio of strategic innovation options. PI's strategy decisions have gradually, increasingly been informed by learning from the SI portfolio and have become more and more explicit in making a strategic argument for renewal and evolution of the PI business model with reference to the landscape of strategic risk and strategic innovation. Between 2011 and 2015, for example, three initiatives have respectively derived resolve, inspiration and facilitation from strategic risk management insights as means of anticipating and hedging systemic long-term external change: PI's innovative approach to vertical supply chain integration in motor and home repair managed by a Suncorp Insurance Ventures (SIV) division; its commitment to experimenting with alternative ways of arranging flexible working based on enabling people who would not normally have access to the workforce to arrange work around their lives (Work@Home hub); and its willingness to co-create a new business platforms with an early stage start-up that has the potential to significantly disrupt the traditional business model of insurance (Trōv). In May 2015, for the first time, the PI EGM presented to the Suncorp Board a 3-year business plan for PI that makes an explicit acknowledgement of PI's understanding of the possibility of significant structural disruption to its highly successful core businesses in the future, as a result of its considered approach to managing strategic risk. The plan presents an argument for transforming those core businesses ahead of that change, citing benefits of resilience and competitiveness through creating a timely foothold in emerging markets (new sources of value). Furthermore, as intelligence about changing market contexts has come into play, the PI EGM team have also started to debate the shape of a more deliberate, 'antifragile' approach to implementing business model renewal through bigger commitments and ventures – deploying 'real options' – by leveraging the assets that the SI portfolio represents and mashing up design and innovation capabilities within the SI division with execution and governance capabilities in the core business.

> *Building options around the notion of strategic risk is giving us the ability to innovate in a "pinpoint" way as opposed to a "shotgun" way, meaning that everything we do has some value. The SI approach has taught us to change processes and business model within reason as fast as possible. It has pushed us to be change fit rather than change fatigued. You could argue that we are spending our limited resources more wisely to adapt to the changes going on externally.*
>
> Mark Milliner

The benefit that PI has been able to realise from embedding a structured and systematic approach to managing strategic risk in the organisation, has also manifested itself in the engagement of leaders and employees more broadly throughout the organisation in strategic conversation. PI's employee engagement scores are well above global high-performing norms and have been rising steadily since 2011. The design of the Strategic Innovation core team includes a 'Networking and Facilitation Lead' whose job is to build a lymphatic system: ensure access, connectivity and 'resilience building' in the exchange of insights between SI and other divisions. This has resulted in SI team members contributing to more than 100 engagements in the course of each year – presentations, workshops, seminars, conferences, sales performance rewards, bespoke events – as well as the SI division hosting career days, a newsletter on relevant signals of change and the most subscribed Yammer feed in the organisation.

> It was the highlight of my career to be involved in Marco Polo with so many amazing people – our people. Through their intelligence, imagination and intuition, we saw that we can bring the future forward. For me, one of the important achievements of our investment in SI has been that people feel they want to work here. It has helped us build a business where people perceive that we care. And that has leveraged itself back into better customer service . . .
>
> Mark Milliner

Two years into the creation of the division, the PI EGM team agreed that conversation about the future of the business and about strategic uncertainty should be extended in a systematic way to include EGM direct reports and executive managers in order to build capability and achieve a more systemic engagement in preparing for and leading change. In November 2014, SI launched a quarterly series of workshops across three locations for PI executive managers immediately following each QSS to talk through the insights and questions discussed by the PI EGMs. In January 2015, as an outcome of a QSS conversation about becoming more deliberately antifragile, the PI EGM team voted to improve the extent of everyday exchange and integration between SI thinking and business-as-usual decision making by introducing a business partner model for SI, whereby members of the SI core team participate in divisional leadership meetings with other EGM direct reports. This model is proving to be particularly successful as a means of enabling access to tacit as well as explicit knowledge and granular moments of reflection and longer-term thinking.

Finally, once a year PI Strategic Innovation provides a direct contribution to the content and focus of the Suncorp Board Annual Strategy Retreat, in association with the Group Strategy function, with the Group Head of Marketing and the Chief Risk Officer. Over the last 3 years, the Board's growing interest in PI's approach to strategic risk and strategic innovation has created a groundswell of curiosity and concern in the conglomerate's other lines of business, many of which are now reaching out to partner with PI.

Reporting on governance of strategic risk

As an extension of PI's approach to enterprise risk management, the implementation of Strategic Innovation has allowed Suncorp to bring more structure and substance to management consideration of strategic risk. This has supported the Board and the executive in the exercising of their duty of care with respect to an area of governance responsibility that is of increasing interest to regulators and financial services institutions. The approach PI has adopted anticipates calls from regulators for a more robust approach to management of strategic risk and therefore represents a potential opportunity for the Group. Suncorp is now well positioned to respond to calls from international financial services regulators (such as the Financial Stability Board) for best practice approaches to management of strategic risk.

In 2013, the Strategic Innovation team introduced a Strategic Risk Dynamic Reporting System (SRDRS) to support conversation about PI's strategic risks and good governance of them. Designed by Luca, together with Kirsten and an SI team member, Gina Belle, with outstanding capabilities in systemic thinking through visualisation, the reporting system functions as a tablet application that provides access to information about the SI portfolio of strategic options in the context of the risks they are addressing. More importantly it is intended to make available strategic intelligence and solutions derived from the portfolio of options to inform decision making.

Strategic risk does not fit established protocols of risk reporting. Quantifiable data about the nature and dynamics of the changes that are significant within the frame of strategic risk is either not available or not reliable. As a result the SRDRS had to be purpose-designed to enable reporting on and engaging with strategic risk in a way that allows for representation of the problem to evolve over time, frame uncertainty and explain its relevance to the business. The SRDRS is designed to:

- identify relevant possibilities of change, each of which is a critical uncertainty.
- make visible the process of dynamically managing a portfolio of strategic options which transforms information about those uncertainties into strategic intelligence.
- capture the intelligence and solutions that the options are maturing for the purposes of effective decision making.
- enable and support qualitative judgement across the strategic risk decision making cycle.
- be visually appealing and easy to use.

The system was presented to the Board in November 2013 at the Annual Strategy Retreat and was made available to Board members. The PI EGM team and the PI Strategic Innovation team went on to use the system to document progress and to start to express qualitative judgements with respect to the level of incoherence that each team associates with each of the PI strategic risks.

While visually appealing and effective, the original SRDRS was built in open-source, interactive pdf software, making it onerous to update with new content and material. Over the summer of 2014–15, Gina and Kirsten commissioned and co-designed with an external software partner a purpose-built tablet application that allows for dynamic interaction, adjournment and user profiling. In this new iteration, entitled Kairos, users are able to access the app for strategic intelligence updates and time-stamped records of insights and strategic risk management questions tabled at every PI QSS; comprehend the overall governance of strategic risks through options and the extent of risk management coverage of individual risks; explore the system of structural change, elements of PI's business rationale at risk, individual options and their purpose, intent and forthcoming activities; and configure a preference for any one of those views as their landing page. Every month the SI team updates Kairos with strategic intelligence reports and once a quarter, following the portfolio composition process, the system is refreshed with the full set of options it tracks. Kairos is now poised to become the primary interface for communication and documentation of strategic risk management within PI and between PI and other stakeholders.

Building strategic leadership capability

One of the critical success factors in the work that Strategic Innovation does for Suncorp PI is its ability to stretch and challenge the thinking of individuals and the PI business as a whole. At the heart of the division's purpose and value to the organisation, and its value for Mark, is its commitment to building strategic leadership capabilities in talented people across PI. In turn, the effectiveness of Strategic Innovation depends on being able to draw on the experience and talent of people from across the business as they participate in and contribute to thinking about assumptions at risk and business model renewal.

SI applies a paradigm of learning to strategy. This assumes that adapting to external change comes through experience of a changing context which leads to reflection and eventually to a reconceptualisation of oneself – whether as an individual or as a business. At both of these levels, embedding the SI function within an incumbent business is an exercise in learning how to operate with confidence in a context where there are no right and wrong answers. The design of SI is predicated on a belief, born of Kirsten's experience in Generali, that no amount of robust and clever thinking about managing strategic risk will help an established business if, at the same time, it doesn't grow the capabilities of its own people to make sense of that and do something with it – engage in strategic conversation about uncertainty, respond to it, and ideally lead change in the market. So a significant component of the work that Strategic Innovation does is to build strategic leadership capability.

> One of the main functions of SI is to help develop the capabilities we need our leaders to have around dealing with the complexity and ambiguity of the external environment.
>
> Mark Milliner

The principal concern of strategic leadership is managing the relationship between business identity and context. This means learning to identify and represent meaning across a constantly shifting, ambiguous and volatile exchange. It means thinking in systems, suspending judgement, considering possibilities and contradictions at the same time as certainties and priorities. It is about generating reflections, inducing insight, shaping purpose in a human system, understanding and assuming the risk of that position and taking decisions to realise it and to keep it moving. It is the combining of science and art, interpretation and representation.

Early on in the development of the division, Kirsten drew on two powerful influences for her own thinking – Jennifer Garvey-Berger of Cultivating Leadership and Isobel Kirk of Executive Voice. Jennifer's work on adult forms of mind, ways of seeing and making sense of the world and ways of leading in complexity have assisted the team to explore a deliberately developmental approach to interpretation through self-reflection, collaboration with others in the team, exchange with internal and external stakeholders and focus on understanding transformation. Isobel's role has been to challenge the team to turn its work into a powerful play, representing in every moment and for different audiences, a compelling and enticing story for what the division is seeing and for how that might be useful to an already successful business.

Developing strategic leadership capabilities is a fractal of the work that the SI division is doing to develop strategic innovation capabilities for the PI business: in both cases it requires the ability to make a difference in the self on an ongoing basis. Learning to make a difference in the self at an individual level helps to understand what it takes to do so at an organisational level. As a result, in addition to specific program of learning with Jennifer and Isobel, much of what SI team members are engaged in is threaded through with a theme of personal leadership development. A significant component of the developmental program of the division is to help people unlearn personal or organisational habits, biases and defaults for the purposes of developing and deriving value from strategic options. For example, defaulting to a solution mode before understanding problems; seeking to simplify processes and problems which limits insight; prioritising activity to a few big bets which in the case of strategic risk makes for greater risk exposure.

A major contributor to learning and insight has been the diversity of the team and of the perspectives gained through SI's external ecosystem. Diversity is critical to the robustness of strategic innovation. Extracting value from diversity by developing the capability to take different perspectives requires deep self-awareness, collaborative thinking and sense-making. Internal diversity has been achieved through the secondment process that has selected people from functions across the business at very different levels of seniority. Selection for secondment is a combination of self-candidature and nomination through PI's talent management process.

The organisational design of the division has also been a significant catalyst for the development of individuals as well as for the development of robust strategic options. The Strategic Innovation division was deliberately designed to be flat structure operating as a self-organising system and designed to promote complex adaptive leadership. By taking the form of an ecosystem and working together, the internal and external layers of the Strategic Innovation System have enabled focused management of Strategic Risks, and at the same time have exposed PI's leaders to new thinking. Strategic Innovation Principals learn how to lead from within a team without positional power and how to transfer skills and capabilities to others in the PI business. The flat structure has facilitated team collaboration and self-organisation in a way that is particularly flexible and responsive to change and complexity. Diffused leadership demands and develops initiative, influence and skills in collaboration and communication, which do not always come naturally. If there is one thing that SI has proved, it is that being in and of the business, thinking about the future in terms of relevant possibilities rather than probabilities, requires a great degree of ambidexterity.

Coming full circle

When we began the Strategic Innovation (SI) journey three years ago through the Marco Polo project, ideas like 3D printers and self-driving cars seemed like science fiction or at the very least seemed so far off that they would not become a reality we would have to consider within our lifetime. In the time since Marco Polo, many of these ideas have indeed become reality. I'm incredibly proud of the fact we have identified relevant changes and invested in understanding what they might mean for our business model through the work of the Strategic Innovation team. We are essentially exploring the future of what matters to people. It's imperative that we continue to evolve our understanding of what our customers, shareholders and community value in order to protect what matters to them well into the future.

Mark Milliner

A strategic risk decision making cycle starts with the identification of relevant strategic risks followed by the development of a portfolio of strategic options. Options provide information, intelligence and the capabilities to mitigate, adapt and innovate. Where opportune, they will enable Suncorp PI to commit to new business models, based on a new understanding of the business identity. At this point the cycle begins again.

In 2014 the SI division worked with the PI EGMs to refresh their understanding of PI's business identity. The team revisited assumptions about individual and community needs that explain why the industry exists; they looked at the structural elements of PI's business model in relationship to one another and to the needs it serves in light of the significant differences that PI had made in itself in the course of 3 years; and they discussed the necessary external conditions that enable a listed commercial business in Australia and New Zealand to meet those needs. In 2015, armed with that refreshed understanding of the business at risk, SI launched another Marco Polo process in order to ensure that PI's mapping of strategic risk remains current. This process has another 300 or so people involved, some of whom were contributors in the first instance; most of whom are not. Excitement, enthusiasm and pride in the organisation is running high.

> *I have a new appreciation for the company's commitment to its staff, customers and the industry in which it operates. I also left the workshop with a new view and appreciation of my imagination and of the "possibilities" out there. And to top it all off, I felt like a valued employee.*
>
> Participant in Marco Polo 2015

14

Risk taking for the modern risk leader

A fresh perspective of trust, transparency, and social media

Kathleen Edmond, Michelle D. Rovang, and Douglas J. Jondle[1]

Abstract

In today's modern business environment the roles and confluence of ethics, compliance, corporate responsibility, and risk management are all in play. It remains to be seen who at the end of the day will own the domain of values-based, ethical risk management and wear the Risk Leader hat. While the answer clearly is up for debate, one thing remains clear – social media will play a pivotal role and be a powerful vehicle for change. It is all the more important that trust and transparency pervade all transactions and communications, becoming essential elements in fostering a healthy risk environment. Risk Leaders will need to take risks, embrace transparency, and make themselves vulnerable and current.

Risk Leaders need stakeholders' trust to successfully address organizational risks. Aside from growing cynicism, warp-speed changes in technologies and communication modes compound the challenges risk managers face in securing constituents' trust. To combat these impediments, today's risk managers need to venture into unchartered territory and try untested methods. Risk Leaders need to cultivate open, direct dialogue, practice unprecedented transparency, and embrace newly minted communication methods. Balancing these riskier activities with solid risk management strategies and robust audit protocols allows businesses to cultivate, maintain and, if necessary, restore the trust and loyalty of its key stakeholders.

It is not a revelation to anyone – practitioner or academic – that good and bad companies will have failures. The difference between the two is the path chosen to correct the situation and make things right by their stakeholders. If the error is corrected with transparency and honesty, the misstep can be viewed as a badge of honor and resilience. Risk Leaders must learn to embrace the risk of transparency and not be afraid of it. Obviously, the Risk Leader must take intelligent risks, but there are many times action must be taken, even if it is uncomfortable and the outcome uncertain. As much as one might like to think otherwise, there really is no such thing as "no risk," as not making a decision is often the biggest risk of all.

We take the position that the roles of the Ethics Leader and the Risk Leader are similar, and in fact may be even more closely aligned in the future. Both roles must deal with risks of all kind, and handle risks ethically in accordance with the company's organizational values. To carry out their responsibilities, both the Ethics Leader and the Risk Leader act as facilitators and sometimes enforcers. These roles often serve simultaneously as the embodiment of the corporate conscience and a lightning rod for gnarly ethical conversations. The most effective Risk Leaders actively participate in establishing processes, controls, training, and remediation strategies. Although execution is owned by the business operators, the risk/ethics role is charged with providing the strategy, blueprint, and assuring ongoing corporate support. Ultimately the Risk Leader must create, keep, and protect trust.

Be real

To be trustworthy, the Risk Leader needs to be real. Your constituents will be less likely to value or comply with your policies, programs, and messages if they do not believe you are authentic. Whenever business leaders distance themselves from their employees and other stakeholders essential to the organization's mission, the separation can be demotivating to the very base that leadership wants to inspire. Personalizing an organization's senior leaders goes a long way to creating a culture of trust and ethics. For those charged with managing the business's risk, securing the trust of those acting on its behalf is equally, if not more, important.

To gain this trust, risk managers must let their constituents know who they are personally. Gil Dennis, Senior Director in Human Resources at Best Buy, understood the need for open communication and transparency. In a conversation with Kathleen Edmond, he said,

> This generation [Millennials] needs to know who you are personally. They don't need your title, they don't need your degrees, they don't need all that – they need to know who you are. When they do, what will happen is they will feel like they know you and they will call you and you will get information you wouldn't get otherwise.

With frank interactions comes a level of comfort and, as a result, a greater willingness for employees and others to receive and provide valuable communications. Establishing this open dialogue is essential to effectively manage the company's risk. This includes being open and honest when mistakes occur, taking responsibility when appropriate. While putting yourself "out there," may feel risky, the resulting trust and flow of information are well worth it.

Be proactive

Proactive, positive messaging from an organization's leaders, including its risk managers, also enhances stakeholders' trust in the enterprise. As the Risk Leader, ensure that your presence is not associated only with bad news. Get in front of your constituents frequently and integrate ethics and compliance messages into all other aspects of the business. This includes constant reinforcement of the corporation's values and how those values lead to key decision-making within the organization.

Risk is a reality; there will be business decisions that go awry or are poorly executed and employee behavior that falls outside the range of acceptability. In order to establish an effective "after event" plan, the Risk Leader needs to foster strong pre-event relationships and action plans. They need to understand the business, the organization's culture, and risk tolerance. It's vital they learn how corporate culture is built, sustained, mended, repaired, and rebuilt. The Risk Leader must arrange for regular critique and review of the ethics and compliance program, as well as set the tone for difficult discussions.

If the Risk Leader fails to lead the conversation within the organization, the conversation will either occur elsewhere in the organization without her or not at all. Neither of these options is optimal. It is important for the Risk Leader to facilitate difficult discussions with respect and persistence, as well as work through discomfort and angst in discussing missteps and mistakes. This is usually much easier within a healthy organizational structure and with solid working relationships among key constituents: the Risk Leader, Chief Executive Officer, General Counsel, Internal Audit, Chief Financial Officer, and Human Resource Executive. In creating an organization that honors and encourages open communication, the Risk Leader is creating a learning organization that has established criteria and forums for examining ethics failures. If the Risk Leader is unskilled or uncomfortable carrying out any of these duties, the Risk Leader role may be a poor fit for the individual.

Be uncomfortable

While positive messaging is crucial, the Risk Leader also needs to be adept at talking about subjects that make employees and businesses squirm. They have to be comfortable leading and participating in dialogue involving uncomfortable and sensitive subjects. Stakeholders expect these disclosures and reward them with their trust and loyalty.

It is imperative that Risk Leaders show others in their organizations that they are not afraid to hear about or discuss significant lapses and mistakes. This is accomplished by Risk Leaders modeling the behavior they seek to invoke. They must be direct and not evade or sidestep sensitive topics. Stakeholders expect and appreciate this honesty and transparency. The more the Risk Leader encourages frequent and frank conversations within an organization, the more likely they will learn about issues when the organization still has an opportunity to mitigate or remedy them. As a Risk Leader, your role is to explicitly honor and encourage these types of exchanges. It is imperative that as the Risk Leader encourages employees and key stakeholders to speak openly, they also promote the organization's nonretaliation and whistleblower policies.

Embrace stakeholders' communication methods

Using key stakeholders' communication vehicles creates comfort, promotes productive dialogue, and fosters trust. The stakeholders gain confidence that their organization understands and values them. Talking to stakeholders through their means of communication maximizes the business's ability to connect and relate. No matter how great the message, if sent through the wrong vehicle, it is unlikely to be valued or taken seriously. In communicating mission-critical information about protocols or other risk management issues to employees, would you use snail mail? Likely not. Using the preferred communication method of the target audience makes sense.

Case in point by Kathleen Edmond:

Early in my Best Buy tenure, I was the lone ethics professional in a company with roughly 140,000 employees. A board member expressed concern over recurring ethical issues among the employees. While these incidents were quite typical in the retail industry with employees new to the workforce, the board member expressed the need for me to get out, train these employees, and really talk to them in an effort to stop the infractions.

In my head, I questioned the viability of managing that task alone. Given the sheer number of employees and an annual turnover rate of 60–70 percent (which is actually low for the retail industry), it seemed an enormous task. Even as I knew the only way to mitigate risks and identify similar mistakes was to educate the employee base around the country, I questioned how I could do that effectively.

I needed to figure out a means for reaching these tens of thousands of technically savvy employees in a meaningful way. I needed them to trust me; they needed to know who I was as a person. A company newsletter was not their means of communicating. Nor was it an effective forum for revealing true personal character. Just like any stakeholder, I knew I had to meet these employees where they were. These employees were on social media, an area generally seen by risk management as a frightening vulnerability, not a useful risk management tool. I knew that if I wanted to meaningfully reach this demographic, I too had to go to social media, a momentous task almost ten years ago. With the support from the CEO and the General Counsel, I created a blog.

I used the blog to educate employees about very basic ethical decision-making skills. *How do I make an in-the-moment decision when I am unsure of the right course? What do I do when I am in front of a customer and my supervisor is telling me one thing and the store manager is telling me another? How do I make these decisions?* As a result of the blog, employees received concrete, situation-specific training aimed directly at minimizing recurring transgressions.

The blog's intended purpose was to communicate a single, consistent message to all employees about decision-making. The unintended consequence was that it allowed others outside the company to take risks in promoting organizational ethics and compliance. Industry colleagues told me how our social media use allowed them to push the envelope in their own corporations. They would point to our blog to convince their general counsel to take communication risks. In many ways, we pushed the boundaries, making movement safer for others and their internal, less conventional communications vehicles. Several companies now include authentic ethics lessons in their internal newsletters and say that is their most-read column.

What many people do not realize is that the beginning of the blog was really meant to be risk mitigation. Similar to other "founder" companies, Best Buy had an Ethics Office before it had either Compliance or Risk functions because the focus was about brand, reputation, and the founder's strongly held values. At some level, there is often a concern in an entrepreneurial start-up that compliance and regulation will "slow down" the process, a process that needs to move fast to effectively compete in the marketplace. There was an ethics hotline before I arrived, but it was solely for human resources matters. Neither vendors nor non-customer community members had a single designated access point. When we expanded the scope of the hotline to ethics, employee relations issues remained with Human Resources, while conflicts of interest, corporate fraud, gifts, and vendor issues were directed to the Ethics Office.

In another effort to promote transparency and open communication using fresh methods, I adopted using texts for the Best Buy ethics hotline. I actually saw the idea used with the Los Angeles Police Department (LAPD). The LAPD has been using secure and anonymous texts for several years, referred to as Text-a-tip (Los Angeles Police Department, 2015). At the time that I read about it, almost half of their calls were coming through texts. About two years before I left Best Buy, we implemented texts as another avenue for people to file complaints anonymously and be more responsive. Obviously, this generation (and the Best Buy employee base) has extreme comfort with this instant communication form. By letting employees relay information using a means completely natural to them, Best Buy maximized its opportunities to solicit anonymous comments, complaints, and reports.

Leverage transparency

Transparently advertising your flaws, or worse, your outright failures, seems risky. Thoughts of diminished reputation, stakeholder defection, or public scorn come to mind. Yet, disclosing your organizational mistakes and misfortunes can provide numerous benefits, most significantly the trust of the organization's stakeholders. While there are many benefits to disclosure, obviously circumstances exist when it is wholly inappropriate. Risk Leaders should conduct individualized analyses, weighing and testing the benefits and risks of transparency prior to disclosure. Brave and strategic transparency can demonstrate honesty, integrity, and a willingness to learn from mistakes. It also provides a valuable educational tool instructing others to avoid the same pitfalls.

Transparency avoided: an opportunity lost

In the early 2000s Best Buy embarked on a touchy investigation around Thanksgiving – a critical time for retailers. The snafu implicated the rollout of a new product and confusion around the selling strategy. Employees found the holiday rollout missteps, combined with the subsequent investigation, extremely distracting.

At the conclusion of an extensive investigation, there was diminished appetite to keep the matter open longer to communicate the lessons learned from the investigation findings. Thus, key learnings were never widely communicated. According to Kathleen Edmond:

> I failed to take advantage of a real and important opportunity to teach managers and employees about what went wrong. These lessons would have guided decision-makers when they encountered the same predicament down the road, as well as provided valuable learning on a variety of related subjects.

In the midst of this investigation, a different, unexpected, but valuable lesson was learned. In an effort to reduce stress and encourage productivity a Best Buy executive emailed a one-page memo to all employees. He reminded employees to stay calm during the investigation, cooperate, and focus on the real work of serving customers. Within 8 hours, the memo showed up in its entirety on a UK gaming site, moving the discussion of a local risk on to a global stage. The fundamental learning from this was that the safeguards of a firewall can be defeated by human behavior. This valuable lesson was key to the design and accessibility of the soon-to-be launched ethics blog.

Transparency embraced: opportunities capitalized

Several years later, another unfortunate opportunity presented itself – one of the biggest corporate fraud cases in Minnesota history, the Chip Factory scam. This time the occasion was leveraged, with the company using it to educate employees and restore the trust of its key stakeholders.

In 2003, Best Buy set up an online reverse auction to procure parts to repair laptops, appliances, and other consumer electronics sold in its stores (Federal Bureau of Investigation, 2010). Vendors bid through a third party. One of these vendors, Chip Factory, would routinely win orders with bids as low as $1, and then bill Best Buy exponentially more. When Best Buy repair centers complained about pricing, Chip Factory and a Best Buy employee in on the scam said it was a mistake and would not take further action. Chip Factory continued to pay the Best Buy employee cash and gifts to conceal the fraud.

Through the course of the ensuing prosecution, the government showed Chip Factory duped Best Buy from the beginning of their relationship. At the onset, the company overstated revenues and falsified its organization chart. When Best Buy visited the Chip Factory warehouse, family members and friends pretended to be workers in the warehouse that actually belonged to another supplier. All forms of media touted the case and the underlying facts, further adding to the confusion and stress of the Best Buy employees and management. In all, Chip Factory swindled Best Buy out of tens of millions of dollars.

From Kathleen Edmond:

The day after the federal judge announced the verdict, I reserved the Best Buy auditorium. Recalling the earlier missed learning opportunity, I was determined not to make the same mistake managing this situation. I messaged the employees that we were holding an open forum to discuss the Chip Factory matter, assembled a panel, including the whistleblower, an officer from the affected group, asset protection, outside counsel, and others. We held open phone lines across the country so all employees could listen and call with questions.

While I presumed all of the listeners in the auditorium and on the phone lines were employees, I was forthright when I announced that could not be guaranteed. I reminded attendees to not share confidential information in this setting, knowing that the inherent risk is truly unavoidable. The learning opportunities Chip Factory presented outweighed the risk of transparency.

Over 400 employees attended, filling the auditorium, the aisles, and the overflow conference rooms. A frank, difficult discussion and question and answer session ensued. We talked about what happened, what went wrong, and what we could all do differently next time.

After the session, one of Best Buy's most long tenured employees came up to me and said, "This was the best goddamn thing I've seen. – Do it again." I did. Following the sentencing, I held a second forum. We secured the Assistant U.S. Attorney who prosecuted the case to sit on the panel. Following the event, the attorney said that she had never seen a company try so hard to learn from a failure.

The U.S. Department of Defense (DOD) provides another bold example of an organization leveraging its blunders by disclosing them. Its online publication *Encyclopedia of Ethical Failures* reveals actual examples of DOD travel miscues, kickbacks, and other failures (U.S. Department of Defense, 2014). The substantial document reads easily with short, individual case summaries that are forthright and accessible. The DOD's efforts provide a great example of an established institution finding novel ways to be transparent and approachable. By using more current forms of purposeful and functional communication, the DOD increases the odds that the hard lessons of others will serve as an effective teaching tool for its employees. In the document, the DOD strongly encourages management and others to reproduce the scenarios to provide guideposts for all federal employees.

Balance transparency pros and cons

While transparency is a key component to gaining, recovering, and maintaining trust, if not used judiciously it can backfire. Avoiding transparency can be equally risky. Walking this fine line successfully is essential to effective risk management. Reasonable minds disagree over this controversial topic. An organization's many constituents will fall on several different points of the spectrum, further complicating the analysis.

Ultimately, the unique needs of the specific organization dictate the more strategic path. To discern these needs, the Risk Leader must determine the organization's risk tolerance. The organization's appetite for risk is part of its culture. While transparency in the Chip Factory matter served Best Buy's interests, it is important to note that this occurred in the context of a competitive, information-sharing employee population, and not a highly regulated industry. The conversation needs to be focused on the organization's audience, industry, and risk tolerance as well as its culture.

The organization's constituents' expectations and demands also are important elements of this discussion. In the current climate, often employees, customers, clients, and other relevant constituents expect a degree of transparency following a challenging event. Deciding not to disclose can create distrust and public relations headaches.

Another important question to ask when deciding this issue is how public was the event? How much visibility did the organization's respective stakeholders have to the event? If specific key constituents lacked any awareness of the issues, analyze the benefits of bringing them up to speed. Also, determine whether the situation implicates regulatory requirements. A heavily regulated environment may dictate a position very different from that in a much less regulated industry. For example, in financial services or healthcare, sharing even unidentified or perceived personal information can thrust an organization into the danger zone.

Once the organization agrees to transparency, the question of how and where to publish the information requires equal strategizing. Both the message and the means of communicating must be current, real, and relevant to the intended recipients. Organizations need to use the communication vehicles used by the constituents it intends to reach. Often this means going beyond your current understanding of the media landscape. A 40-year-old risk manager may not intuitively know how and where employees in their twenties access information. It is not enough to know that social media plays a huge role (see Appendix 14.1). Do the homework to determine what networks, platforms, and devices represent the current communication vehicles. Involve focus groups and your internal communications team in the process.

The ultimate decision whether or not to disclose information may face resistance, so the Risk Leader's course of action should be based on pre-event communication patterns and shared values. Obtain the buy-in of senior leadership to provide a united front. The Risk Leader also need to conduct a risk assessment of the organization's postevent strategy. Relevant internal stakeholders should be included in this plan testing and decision-making. Include pros and cons, time frame, and purpose in the analysis. To cover all bases, prepare a Plan B to leverage learning and close out the event if, in the end, thoughtful consensus suggests disclosure would not serve the company's best interest.

Checks and balances

Despite a stellar risk management program, business crises will still occur. These challenges can wreak havoc on the coveted asset of stakeholder trust. Conversely, if handled properly, organizational crises can present an opportunity to actually build and solidify the trust of key constituents; educate and protect against further lapses; and improve the strength and resilience of the company.

Establish a rock solid pre-event strategy

The first step to effectively implementing a successful crisis plan is a firmly rooted, robust pre-event risk management strategy. While every crisis looks different, some standard questions should be hard-wired into every risk management handbook. When thoughtfully examined and answered *prior* to a crisis, these inquiries will insure a consistent, thorough, and objective approach at a time when cool heads must prevail. As the Risk Leader, these general questions need to be asked:

- Have you previously vetted and engaged an independent investigator?
- Do you have established criteria to determine when the investigation is in-house?
- Which department should oversee the investigation?
- Have you coordinated interested internal departments and communications?
- Have you established escalation criteria to inform the board of an issue?

Established protocol on each of these points will make managing through difficult situations more seamless. Asking these questions in the relative calm of ordinary business allows an organization to prioritize and make value judgments when not under fire. Further, parsing responsibilities, engaging key partners, and making key decisions ahead of a crisis minimize confusion, turf battles, skipped steps, and real or perceived conflicts.

Engage in hard, honest postevent reflection

Once an investigation takes place, the remediation begins, incorporating critical conversations and a hard look in the mirror. The organization must examine the ethics and compliance controls to understand if they worked as intended. Did management or others miss or ignore red flags? Chances are that if a crisis occurred, ethics or compliance gaps exist. Identifying and addressing these vulnerabilities is a crucial part of an organization's recovery.

When an ethical infraction takes place, cracks may appear in the corporate culture. As the Risk Leader, you should work with the appropriate internal partner to understand how the organization builds, sustains, repairs, and rebuilds its culture. Carefully reflect on and design specific efforts to reengage employees in the organization's mission and values.

These infractions take a toll on stakeholders' trust. Depending on the size, scale, and nature of the occurrence, the organization will need to earn back the trust of its employees, managers, vendors, and customers. Given the nature of the organization and reporting structures, the Risk Leader may lead, follow, or partner in this process. While this varies by organization, the Risk Leader should always have a seat at the table, and should clarify the roles of various other culture leaders, such as the CEO, Human Resources, and Public Relations.

Risk Leaders must install strong processes to regularly review and audit the efficacy of the risk management programs. These processes should include clear criteria and specified forums for examining failures. These leaders also must encourage honest, at times difficult, observations about the programs' strengths, vulnerabilities, and impediments. Most importantly, to successfully recover, it is incumbent upon the organization to take extensive action to prevent the same mistake from reoccurring. Hard, postevent reflection and analysis is vital to this assurance.

Further, it is important to keep in mind when developing an effective postevent strategy that the organization may reach a point where continued analysis and review no longer adds value. Constantly monitor the process to determine when and if the business reaches this inflexion point.

Conclusion

In the course of my career and in my current role working with different industries and different departments, I have had the opportunity to see the evolution of the role ethics, compliance, corporate responsibility, and risk management play. The question of the day seems to be what is next and who will own it. While the answer clearly is up for debate, one thing remains clear. Trust continues to be an essential element of risk management. To get, keep, and restore this valuable asset, Risk Leaders need to take risks, embrace transparency, and make themselves vulnerable and current.

Kathleen Edmond

Kathleen Edmond is a Partner at Robins Kaplan LLP. Prior to private practice, she spent 10 years as the chief ethics officer for Best Buy, building and subsequently leading the company's ethics department. She has spent the majority of her career in corporate ethics, compliance, and risk management. In 2015, she was selected as the recipient of the 2015 Women in Compliance Lifetime Achievement Award. Edmond received the award based on her early use of social media and transparency as chief ethics officer of Best Buy, as well as her broad, positive impact on the field of ethics and corporate compliance.

Note

1 Kathleen Edmond, Partner, Robins Kaplan LLP (formerly Chief Ethics Officer, Best Buy); Michelle Rovang, Director, Veritas Institute; Douglas J. Jondle, Research Director, Center for Ethical Business Cultures.

References

Edmond, K. (2010). Kathleen Edmond's Blog. Retrieved from http://www.kathleenedmond.com/2010/07/05/good-intentions-but-wrong-message/

Federal Bureau of Investigation. (2010). Illinois Couple, Company Insider Sentenced for Defrauding Best Buy. Retrieved from http://www.fbi.gov/minneapolis/press-releases/2010/mp122010.htm

Los Angeles Police Department. (2015). Los Angeles Police Department Anonymous Crime Tip Program. Retrieved from Public Fact Sheet, http://assets.lapdonline.org/assets/pdf/lapd-crimetip.pdf

U.S. Department of Defense. (2014). Encyclopedia of Ethical Failure. Retrieved from http://www.dod.mil/dodgc/defense_ethics/resource_library/guidance.htm

Appendix 14.1

Kathleen Edmond's ethics blog (excerpt)

By making ethics a completely transparent dialogue, Best Buy can be a leader in ethical standards for our employees, our customers, and our shareholders. Please feel free to join the conversation.

Good Intentions but Wrong Message

Best Buy Ethics, by Kathleen Edmond (July 5, 2010)

One of Best Buy's senior executives recently asked a colleague in the company's Merchandising department for their honest opinion regarding various brands of home appliances he was considering for personal purchase. As an unrequested, surprise "favor" to the senior executive and a "good deed" for a great vendor partner, someone on the Merchandising team arranged for the senior executive to receive free appliances in exchange for him blogging about his experience with the products.

The vendor was a willing partner – eager for the PR value of the blog – and the executive would benefit from free use of the new appliances. No one would have been harmed. What ethical challenges, if any, do you see in this scenario?

1) Is it OK for a Best Buy employee to exchange favors in this manner with a company vendor? Why or why not?
2) Does it matter that the employee was an executive of the company? If so, how?
3) What about the blog itself? Could the executive's comments be compromised in any way by his underlying relationship with the vendor?

The outcome

This turned out to be an excellent learning opportunity for all. The preceding scenario was well into the planning stages until a flag was raised by a departmental Administrative Assistant. Somehow, the situation did not "feel" right to this employee and the issue was brought to the Ethics Office for their opinion. Upon reviewing the situation, the Ethics Office recommended that the Merchandising team and vendor not proceed with the plan. The Ethics Office also reached out to the senior executive who was completely unaware of the activity being taken as a "favor" to him. What were the concerns?

- Regardless of the good intentions of all involved, such a scenario could potentially create the perception that Best Buy's leaders are "for sale" to the highest bidder. As noted in Best Buy's Code of Business Ethics, employees are to avoid any activity that places – or gives the *appearance* of placing – personal interests ahead of the company's interests.
- The FTC requires that bloggers involved in product marketing clearly state whether the merchandise in question was obtained for free and/or if any compensation was received. Without such a disclosure, public comments on the blog could have violated the required transparency.

Broader questions for thought and discussion

- Do leaders underestimate the potential for subordinates to "over interpret" casual inquiries/requests – and then take action without being asked, that they think will please the executive?
- Do individuals at any level try too often to please or be helpful, without asking the uncomfortable questions or following their own internal compass?
- Note the courage of the administrative assistant to listen to her inner voice and ask whether this was really in the best interest of the company. Would you have spotted the risk – and then asked the question?

This was a situation in which none of the players had any bad intent, and several did not have full context, yet it could have been badly misinterpreted both internally and externally.

As Chief Ethics Officer I am proud of our folks – from the admin who asked the question, to the senior exec who wanted to be sure that he was playing by all the rules.

This is a great reminder for all of us: ethical behavior does not mean that we never make mistakes – it is about quickly and transparently correcting a course of action when needed, and sharing the learning.

Source: Kathleen Edmond's Blog, Accessed February 23, 2012. www.kathleenedmond.com/2010/07/05/good-intentions-but-wrong-message/

Part IV

The managerial impact on risk outcomes

15

Reflections on "How psychological pitfalls generated the global financial crisis"

Hersh Shefrin

Reviewing what I wrote over five years ago about the contribution of psychological pitfalls to generating the financial crisis has led me to some additional thoughts.

My first thought is to note that my contribution appeared alongside a most insightful piece by Paul McCulley titled "The Shadow Banking System and Hyman Minsky's Economic Journey." To McCulley belongs the credit for having coined the term "shadow banking." He was also among the minority of those who appreciated the perspective of economist Hyman Minsky, whose writings in the aftermath of the financial crisis read like those of a true prophet. During the Asian currency crisis of the late 1990s, McCulley coined another term – "Minsky moment" – to describe that crisis, because it captured many of the features about which Minsky had warned. That crisis erupted in 1997, a year after Minsky's death. A decade would elapse before the eruption of the global financial crisis, which was perhaps the epitome of a "Minsky moment." What McCulley called "shadow banking" Minsky called "fringe finance."

My second thought is that after reading McCulley's contribution, I came to see that while my piece focused on micro-prudential issues associated with financial institutions and regulators, Minsky's perspective provided the macro-prudential perspective. Minsky characterized the macro-system dynamic that houses the actions comprising the micro-perspective. For Minsky, the underlying psychology was encapsulated in one concept: euphoria. To be sure, euphoria is a genuine psychological state. However, the explosion of research in psychology in the last half century has provided us with a much deeper understanding of cognitive and emotional features that make up human psychology. In this respect, my contribution complements Minsky's euphoria-based explanation by providing a deep dive into the multifaceted character of the psychological pitfalls that generated the global financial crisis.

My third thought is to note that reading Minsky carefully has led me to conclude that avoiding financial crises is much more challenging, if not impossible, than I had thought back in 2009. This perspective is in line with Daniel Kahneman, who writes in *Thinking: Fast and Slow* about why it is so difficult to overcome psychological pitfalls at the individual level.[1] This is not to say that people cannot learn. Certainly, in the wake of the stock market crashes of 1907 and 1929, and of course the Great Depression, financial regulations were put in place that addressed many of the structural weaknesses at the time. However, regulatory change is endogenous and subject to what Meir Statman and I call a "tug of war" over time, which leads them to be weakened during euphoric times.[2] Minsky forcefully pointed out that the forces of regulation would be outgunned by forces representing the financial sector. The lesson to take away from this is the importance of preparation to mitigate the extent of crises when they occur, by instituting appropriate 'stimulating' fiscal and monetary policies. Otherwise, the aftereffects of a financial crisis will be deeper and long lasting than necessary. Anemic economic growth in Europe, and to a lesser extent the U.S. and Asia, during the half decade after the global financial crisis are cases in point.

Notes

1   Kahneman, D. (2011). *Thinking, Fast and Slow*, New York: Farrar, Straus, and Giroux.
2   Shefrin, H. and Statman, M. (2009). *Striking Regulatory Irons While Hot*. SCU Leavey School of Business Research Paper (10-07).

How psychological pitfalls generated the global financial crisis[1]

Hersh Shefrin[2]

Abstract

The root cause of the financial crisis that erupted in 2008 is psychological. In the events which led up to the crisis, heuristics, biases, and framing effects strongly influenced the judgments and decisions of financial firms, rating agencies, elected officials, government regulators, and institutional investors. Among the many lessons to be learned from the crisis is the importance of focusing on the behavioral aspects of organizational process.

In this article, I present evidence that psychological pitfalls played a crucial role in generating the global financial crisis that began in September 2008. The evidence indicates that specific psychological phenomena – reference point–induced risk seeking, excessive optimism, overconfidence, and categorization – were at work. I am not saying that fundamental factors, such as shifts in housing demand, changes in global net savings rates, and rises in oil prices, were not relevant. They most certainly were relevant. I suggest that specific psychological reactions to these fundamentals, however, rather than the fundamentals themselves, took the global financial system to the brink of collapse.

To what extent did analysts see the crisis coming? In late 2007, four analysts (among others) forecasted that the financial sector would experience severe difficulties. They were Meredith Whitney, then at Oppenheimer; Dick Bove, then at Punk Ziegel & Company; Michael Mayo, then at Deutsche Bank; and Charles Peabody at Portales Partners (see Berman 2009). For example, in October 2007, Mayo issued a sell recommendation on Citigroup stock. Two weeks later, Whitney issued a research report on Citigroup stating that its survival would require it to raise $30 billion, either by cutting its dividend or by selling assets. More than any other analyst, Whitney raised concerns about the risks posed by the subprime mortgage market – and by the attendant threat to overall economic activity.

How timely were analysts in raising the alarm? As it happens, public markets had begun to signal concerns early in 2007. At that time, the VIX was fluctuating in the range 9.5 to 20, having fallen from its 2001–2002 20 to 50 range. On 27 February 2007, an 8.8 percent decline in the Chinese stock market set off a cascade in the global financial markets. In the United States, the S&P 500 Index declined by 3.5 percent, which was unusual during a period of relatively

269

low volatility. Among the explanations that surfaced in the financial press for the decline in U.S. stocks was concern about weakness in the market for subprime mortgages.

In a book published in 2008, I argued that psychological pitfalls have three impacts that analysts should be aware of (Shefrin 2008b): First is the impact on the pricing of assets, particularly the securities of firms followed by analysts. Second is the impact on decisions by corporate managers that are germane to companies' operational risks. Third is the impact on the judgments of analysts themselves.

The financial crisis contains illustrations of all three impacts. I use five specific cases to explain how psychological pitfalls affected judgments and decisions at various points along the supply chain for financial products, particularly home mortgages, in the crisis. The cases involve (1) UBS, a bank; (2) Standard & Poor's (S&P), a rating firm; (3) American International Group (AIG), an insurance company; (4) the investment committee for the town of Narvik, Norway, an institutional investor; and (5) the U.S. SEC, a regulatory agency.

I use these cases to make two points. First, common threads link the psychological pitfalls that affected the judgments and decisions of the various participants along the supply chain. In this respect, a relatively small set of psychological pitfalls were especially germane to the creation of the crisis. The key mistakes made were not the product of random stupidity but of specific phenomena lying at the heart of behavioral finance.

Second, the major psychological lessons to be learned from the financial crisis pertain to *behavioral corporate finance* (Shefrin 2005). Many readers think of behavioral finance as focusing on mistakes made by *investors*, but issuers (corporations, governments, and so on) are people too and are just as prone to mistakes; behavioral corporate finance focuses on their side of the equation. Specifically, behavioral corporate finance focuses on how psychology affects the financial decisions of corporate managers, especially those in markets that feature mispricing.

The key decisions that precipitated the crisis need to be understood in the context of behavioral corporate finance. Moreover, behavioral corporate finance offers guidelines about what to do differently in the future. For analysts, the general lesson to be learned is the importance of including a behavioral corporate perspective in their toolbox.

The five cases are intended to be representative. For example, UBS is hardly unique among investment banks, as the fates of Lehman Brothers, Merrill Lynch, and Bear Stearns illustrate. As discussed later in the paper, Citigroup engaged in strategies similar to those pursued by the investment banks. Indeed, in April 2009, the *Washington Post* reported that banks relied on intuition instead of quantitative models to assess their exposure to a severe downturn in the economy. This statement was based on interviews with staff at the Federal Reserve Bank of New York and the U.S. Government Accountability Office.

The source material for the five cases is varied. For UBS, the main source is an internal document from the firm itself. For the SEC, the main source material is an audio transcript from an SEC meeting. For the other three cases, the main source material is press coverage. Material from press coverage features both strengths and weaknesses. One of the key strengths is that information comes from the level of the individual decision maker, as revealed in interviews with decision makers and their colleagues. From a behavioral perspective, this level of detail is invaluable. One of the key weaknesses is that press coverage is less than fully comprehensive and is prone to distortion. In this regard, I discuss an example illustrating a case of distorted coverage.

Fundamentals and controversy

Mohamed El-Erian (2008) described a broad set of fundamentals related to the financial crisis. He identified the following three structural factors associated with changes in the global economy during the current decade: (1) a realignment of global power and influence from developed economies to developing economies, (2) the accumulation of wealth by countries that in the past were borrowers and that have now become lenders, and (3) the proliferation of new financial instruments, such as collateralized debt obligations (CDOs) and credit default swaps (CDS). El-Erian described how these structural factors worked in combination. Developing countries' external accounts, which had been in deficit before 2000, switched to being in surplus after 2000, with the current account surplus rising to more than $600 billion in 2007. In contrast, the United States ran an external deficit of almost $800 billion in 2007. El-Erian explained that these imbalances permitted U.S. consumers to sustain consumption in excess of their incomes.

He pointed out that U.S. financial markets facilitated this pattern by providing a way for U.S. consumers to monetize their home equity. And, he added, emerging economies purchased U.S. Treasury instruments, mortgages, and corporate bonds as they converted their trade surpluses into long-term investment accounts.

El-Erian described how these structural elements have affected financial markets. For instance, in 2004, the U.S. Federal Reserve Board increased short-term interest rates with the expectation that long-term rates would also rise. Instead, long-term rates fell – to the point where, in November 2006, the yield curve inverted. This phenomenon puzzled many investors at the time.[3] El-Erian suggested that the inversion might have been caused by emerging economies purchasing long-term T-bonds in an attempt to invest their growing trade surpluses at favorable (high) interest rates. Those purchases drove prices up and yields down. During the 2005–06 period, the yield spread of 10-year over 2-year T-bonds fell from +125 bps to more than −25 bps.

Typically, yield-curve inversions are precursors of recessions. The U.S. stock market was robust in 2005 and 2006, however, with the S&P 500 rising from 1,200 to 1,400, which hardly signaled recession. Moreover, perceptions of future volatility, as measured by the Chicago Board Options Exchange Volatility Index, were at very low levels. As a result, El-Erian concluded that the bond market, stock market, and options market were providing mixed signals during a period he characterized as exhibiting "large systemic uncertainty."

The biggest puzzle for El-Erian is what he called "the ability *and* willingness of the financial system to overconsume and overproduce risky products in the context of such large systemic uncertainty" (p. 20). He suggested that as risk premiums declined from 2004 on, investors used leverage in a determined effort "to squeeze out additional returns" (p. 21). This behavior created a feedback loop that further depressed risk premiums, which, in turn, induced additional leverage. He went on to say:

> Think of it: At a time when the world's economies seemed more difficult to understand . . . and multilateral financial regulation mechanisms were failing us, the marketplace ended up taking on greater risk exposures through the alchemy of new structured products, off-balance sheet conduits, and other vehicles that lie outside the purview of sophisticated oversight bodies. . . . More generally, the pressure to assume greater risk, especially through complex structured finance instruments and buyout loan commitments, combined with overconfidence in a "just in time" risk management paradigm led to the trio that would (and should) keep any trustee, shareholder, or policy maker awake at night: a set of institutions taking risk beyond what they can comfortably tolerate; another set of institutions taking risk beyond what they can understand and process; and a third set of institutions doing both!
>
> *(pp. 51–53)*

Is the institutional behavior that El-Erian described (1) rational risk taking in which the outcomes simply turned out to be unfavorable, (2) rational risk taking responding to problematic incentives, or (3) irrational risk taking? I argue that the phrases "beyond what they can comfortably tolerate" and "beyond what they can understand and process" suggest that the answer is irrational risk taking. In this regard, it seems to me that El-Erian laid out the market fundamentals that preceded the crisis and then described behavioral patterns that represent *irrational* responses to those fundamentals: Rather than responding to a riskier environment by cutting back on risk, institutions took more risk.

Akerlof and Shiller (2009) argued that irrational decisions associated with the subprime housing market were central to the financial crisis. In this respect, consider some history. From 1997 to 2006, U.S. home prices rose by about 85 percent, even after adjustment for inflation, making this period a time of the biggest national housing boom in U.S. history. The rate of increase was five times the historical rate of 1.4 percent a year. As a result, the authors suggested, the sentiment of many people at the time was that housing prices would continue to increase at well above their historical growth rates. This belief supported a dramatic increase in the volume of subprime mortgages, especially mortgages requiring no documentation and little or no down payment. Later in this article, I discuss the time-series properties of loan-to-value ratios (LTVs), limited documentation, and 100 percent financing in the mortgage market.

Housing prices peaked in December 2006, when the Federal Reserve was raising short-term interest rates, and then declined by 30 percent over the subsequent 26 months. During the decline, many new homeowners (and some old ones who had engaged in repeated cash-out refinancing) found that the values of their mortgages exceeded the values of their homes. Some in this situation chose to default on their mortgages. Some homeowners had taken out adjustable rate mortgages with low initial rates that would reset after a period of time to rates that were much higher. These homeowners were planning on refinancing before rates reset. Once housing prices began to decline, however, they did not qualify for refinancing. Many were unable to afford the higher rates and had to default.[4]

The mortgage product supply chain began with mortgage initiation by financial institutions such as Indy Mac, Countrywide, and Washington Mutual. It continued with such firms as Fannie Mae and Freddie Mac, which purchased and "securitized" mortgages, thus creating mortgage-backed securities (MBS). Next in the chain were investment banks, such as Lehman Brothers, Merrill Lynch, Citigroup, and UBS, which created and sold CDOs backed by the MBS. The supply chain also included financial firms such as AIG, which insured against the risk of default by selling CDS. The risks of both the products and the financial firms were rated by rating agencies, such as Moody's Investors Service and S&P. At the end of the supply chain were the end investors, such as foreign banks, pension funds, and municipal governments, who ultimately held the claims to cash flows generated by the mortgages. Along the way, the supply chain was subject to regulation by various bodies, such as the SEC, the Board of Governors of the Federal Reserve, the Federal Reserve Bank of New York, and the Office of Thrift Supervision.

Taken together, the viewpoints expressed by El-Erian and Akerlof–Shiller suggest that financial institutions exhibited behavior inconsistent with the predictions of the Akerlof adverse selection "lemons" model, in which all agents use the information at their disposal to make rational decisions. The lemons model predicts the collapse of trade, resulting in, for example, a credit freeze when rational agents who perceive themselves to be at an information disadvantage assume the worst (e.g., all cars are lemons) when forming their expectations. In contrast to this model, despite the opaqueness of securitized asset pools, CDOs, and CDS – with their attendant information asymmetries – the subprime mortgage market did not collapse; it proceeded as if no cars could be lemons and thrived.

Whether financial institutions behaved irrationally and whether the associated market movements reflected market inefficiency are the subject of controversy. Posner (2009a) maintained that institutions behaved rationally in light of the incentives they faced. He wrote, "At no stage need irrationality be posited to explain" the collapse of financial markets in 2008 and the deep recession in 2009. In an interview, Eugene Fama contended that past market movements are consistent with the notion of market efficiency.[5]

In his critique of Akerlof and Shiller's 2009 book, Posner (2009b) stated, "But mistakes and ignorance are not symptoms of irrationality. They usually are the result of limited information." This line of reasoning leads him to conclude that the stock market increases of the late 1920s and late 1990s did not reflect mispricing and that in 2005 and 2006, people did not overpay for their houses in an *ex ante* sense.

Of Akerlof and Shiller's (2009) contention that irrational decisions in the subprime housing market were central to the financial crisis, Posner (2009b) wrote, "They think that mortgage fraud was a major cause of the present crisis. How all this relates to animal spirits is unclear, but in any event they are wrong about the causality." Posner then provided his own list of what caused the crisis:

> The underlying causes were the deregulation of financial services; lax enforcement of the remaining regulations; unsound decisions on interest rates by the Federal Reserve; huge budget deficits; the globalization of the finance industry; the financial rewards of risky lending, and competitive pressures to engage in it, in the absence of effective regulation; the overconfidence of economists inside and outside government; and the government's erratic, confidence-destroying improvisational responses to the banking collapse. Some of these mistakes of commission and omission had emotional components. The overconfidence of economists might even be thought a manifestation of animal spirits. But the career and reward structures, and the ideological preconceptions, of macroeconomists are likelier explanations than emotion for the economics profession's failure to foresee or respond effectively to the crisis.
>
> *(Posner, 2009b)*

Posner might well be correct in identifying problematic decisions in the regulatory process. Whether he is correct in his view that institutions acted rationally is another matter. One way of dealing with this issue is to examine decision making on a case-by-case basis, as I will do in this article, to identify the nature of the decision processes within financial institutions.[6]

This discussion needs to be based on a well-defined notion of rationality. In financial economics, rationality is typically understood in the neoclassical sense. Neoclassical rationality has two parts: rationality of judgments and rationality of choice. People make rational judgments when they make efficient use of the information at their disposal and form beliefs that are free from bias. People make rational choices when they have well-defined preferences that express the trade-offs they are willing to make and choose the best means to meet their objectives. In financial economics, rationality is typically said to prevail when decision makers act as Bayesian expected-utility maximizers who are averse to risk.

Behavioral corporate finance

Behavioral corporate finance highlights the psychological errors and biases associated with major corporate tasks – capital budgeting, capital structure, payout policy, valuation, mergers and acquisitions, risk management, and corporate governance. In my 2008 book, I suggested that suboptimal corporate financial decisions can largely be traced to the impact of psychological errors and biases on specific organizational processes (Shefrin 2008b). These processes involve planning, the setting of standards, the sharing of information, and incentives.

Planning includes the development of strategy and the preparation of *pro forma* financial statements. Standards involve the establishment of goals and performance metrics. Information sharing results from the nature of organizational design. Incentives stem from the compensation system and are a major aspect of corporate governance. Sullivan (2009) emphasized the importance of governance failures in generating the crisis.

Among the main psychological pitfalls at the center of behavioral finance are the following:

- reference point–induced risk seeking
- narrow framing
- opaque framing
- excessive optimism
- overconfidence
- extrapolation bias
- confirmation bias
- conservatism
- the "affect heuristic"
- "groupthink"
- hindsight bias, and
- categorization bias.

I suggest that these pitfalls figured prominently in the decisions that precipitated the financial crisis. For this reason, I provide here a brief description of each.

Psychologically based theories of risk taking emphasize that people measure outcomes relative to reference points. A reference point might be a purchase price used to define gains and losses, as suggested by Shefrin and Statman (1985), building on Kahneman and Tversky (1979), or a level of aspiration, as suggested by Lopes (1987). *Reference point–induced risk seeking* is the tendency of people to behave in a risk-seeking fashion to avoid an outcome that lies below the reference point. As an illustration, consider El-Erian's comment that as risk premiums declined from 2004 on, investors used leverage in a determined effort "to squeeze out additional returns." This comment is consistent with the idea that investors had fixed aspirations and became more tolerant of risk as risk premiums declined.

Narrow framing is the practice of simplifying a multidimensional decision problem by decomposing it into several smaller subtasks and ignoring the interaction between these subtasks. The term "silo" is sometimes used to describe the impact of narrow framing because subtasks are assigned to silos.

Opaque framing versus transparent framing involves the level of clarity in the description of the decision task and associated consequences. For illustration, consider El-Erian's comment about institutions taking risk beyond what they can understand and process. This comment suggests opaque, or nontransparent, framing.

Excessive optimism leads people to look at the world through rose-colored glasses.

Overconfidence leads people to be too sure of their opinions, a tendency that frequently results in their underestimating risk. Although excessive optimism and overconfidence sound related, they are really quite different psychological shortcomings in a decision maker. For example, somebody might be an overconfident pessimist – one who has too much conviction that the future will be gloomy.

Extrapolation bias leads people to forecast that recent changes will continue into the future. A pertinent example of extrapolation bias is the belief that housing prices will continue to grow at the same above-average rates that have prevailed in the recent past.

Confirmation bias leads people to overweight information that confirms their prior views and to underweight information that disconfirms those views.

Conservatism is the tendency to overweight base-rate information relative to new (or singular) information. This phenomenon is sometimes called "under reaction."

The *affect heuristic* refers to the making of judgments on the basis of positive or negative feelings rather than underlying fundamentals. Reliance on the affect heuristic is often described as using "gut feel" or intuition.

Groupthink leads people in groups to act as if they value conformity over quality when making decisions. Groupthink typically occurs because group members value cohesiveness and do not want to appear uncooperative so they tend to support the positions advocated by group leaders rather than playing devil's advocate. Group members may also be afraid of looking foolish or poorly informed if they vocally disagree with a leader whom the majority of the group regards as wise.

Hindsight bias is the tendency to view outcomes in hindsight and judge that these outcomes were more likely to have occurred than they appeared in foresight. That is, *ex post*, the *ex ante* probability of the event that actually occurred is judged to be higher than the *ex ante* estimate of that *ex ante* probability. Consider Posner's (2009b) comment about equities being efficiently priced in the late 1990s or houses being efficiently priced in the first six years of this decade. In making this claim, he effectively charges Akerlof and Shiller (2009) with succumbing to hindsight bias in that he suggests that the subsequent price decline is nothing more than an unfavorable outcome that is being viewed as more likely in hindsight than it was in foresight.

Categorization bias is the act of partitioning objects into general categories and ignoring the differences among members of the same category. Categorization bias may produce unintended side effects if the members of the same category are different from each other in meaningful ways.

In the remainder of this article, I use the behavioral corporate finance framework to analyze each of five cases. One way to think about this framework is in terms of the interaction of psychological biases with business processes, as illustrated in Exhibit 1. (Exhibit 1 is merely for illustration; only the first five pitfalls discussed in this section are displayed.) The intersections of the rows showing organizational processes with the columns depicting psychological pitfalls are shown as question marks to prompt questions for those using such a framework about whether a specific pitfall occurred as part of the business process. This perspective helps to show how psychological pitfalls affect the decisions made in connection with each process.

UBS

At the end of 2007, UBS announced that it would write off $18 billion of failed investments involving the subprime housing market in the United States. In 2008, the write-offs increased to more than $50 billion. In October 2008, the Swiss central bank announced its intention to take $60 billion of toxic assets off UBS's balance sheet and to inject $6 billion of equity capital.

In April 2008, UBS published a report (2008) detailing the reasons for its losses. In this section, I quote extensively from the report to let UBS management speak for itself. The report states, "UBS's retrospective review focused on root causes of these losses with the view toward improving UBS's processes" (p. 28). That is, the write-offs were the result of having ineffective processes in place, a statement that, I argue, failed to address psychological biases. In the following discussion, I view the UBS report through the prism of the four specific processes shown in Exhibit 1: planning, standards, information sharing, and incentives. As readers will see, biases permeated many of the decisions UBS made in connection with subprime mortgages and financial derivatives.

Planning at UBS

The report states, "[T]he 5 year strategic focus articulated for 2006–2010 was to aim for significant revenue increases whilst also allowing for more cost expansion. However the Group's risk profile in 2006 was not predicted to change substantially ..." (p. 8). In retrospect, the firm's risk profile did increase dramatically, which raises the question of whether UBS's management team displayed overconfidence.

UBS says that in 2005 it engaged the services of an external consultant, who compared UBS's past performance with that of its chief competitors.[7] Notably, UBS's performance trailed those of its competitors. To close the competitive gap, the consultant recommended the following:

> [S]trategic and tactical initiatives were required to address these gaps and recommended that UBS selectively invest in developing certain areas of its business to close key product gaps, including in Credit, Rates, MBS Subprime and Adjustable Rate Mortgage products ("ARMs"), Commodities and Emerging Markets. ABS (asset backed securities), MBS, and ARMs (in each case including underlying assets of Subprime nature) were specifically identified as significant revenue growth opportunities. The consultant's review did not consider the risk capacity (e.g. stress risk and market risk) associated with the recommended product expansion.
>
> (p. 11)

Notice that, although subprime was specifically identified as providing significant revenue growth opportunities, the consultant's review did not consider the implications for UBS's risk capacity. Given that risk and return lie at the heart of finance and that subprime mortgages feature more default risk than higher rated mortgages, the absence of an analysis of risk is striking.[8]

Standards for risk at UBS

Standards for risk management include targets and goals that relate to accounting controls and include position limits and other risk-control mechanisms. The report tells how UBS reacted to the consulting firm's failure to address the implications of its recommendations for risk:

> There were not however any Operational Limits on the CDO Warehouse, nor was there an umbrella Operational Limit across the IB [the investment banking unit] (or the combination of IB and DRCM [the hedge fund subsidiary Dillon Read Capital Management]) that limited overall exposure to the Subprime sector (securities, derivatives and loans).
>
> (p. 20)

That is, UBS did not develop any operational limits that would restrict the firm's overall exposure to subprime loans, securities, and derivatives. Was this behavior rational, or did UBS irrationally ignore risk for psychological reasons? One possibility is that by virtue of being behind the competition, UBS set a high reference point for itself and exhibited reference point–induced risk-seeking behavior. Perhaps this attitude is why it did not question the consulting firm's failure to address the risk implications of its recommendations and did not develop risk standards for itself. Its psychological profile led it to act as if it implicitly attached little or no value to avoiding risk.

UBS's internal report does indeed suggest that the reference point for the company corresponded to the superior performance of its competitors. The report states:

> It was recognized in 2005 that, of all the businesses conducted by the IB, the biggest competitive gap was in Fixed Income, and that UBS's Fixed Income positioning had declined vis-à-vis leading competitors since 2002. In particular, the IB's Fixed Income, Rates & Currencies ("FIRC") revenues decreased since 2004, and accordingly, FIRC moved down in competitor league tables by revenue. According to an external consultant, the IB Fixed Income business grew its revenue at a slower rate than its peers.
>
> *(p. 10)*

CDOs are akin to families of mutual funds that hold bonds instead of stocks. Each member of the fund family, or tranche, holds bonds with a different degree of priority in the event of default from the priority of other tranches in the family. Investors pay lower prices for riskier tranches. Holders of the equity (riskiest) tranche absorb the first losses stemming from default. If at some point the holders of the equity tranche receive zero cash flows from the underlying assets, holders of the next tranche begin to absorb losses. Holders of the senior tranche are the most protected, but the existence of a "super senior" tranche is also possible. If the CDO contains leverage, meaning that the issuer of the CDO borrowed money to purchase assets for the CDO, then some party must stand ready to absorb the losses once the holders of even the senior tranche receive no cash flows. Holders of the super senior tranche must play this role. Instead of paying to participate in the CDO, they receive payments that are analogous to insurance premiums.

UBS's investment banking unit did hold super senior positions, and that unit did consider the risk of those positions. Moody's and S&P both rated various CDO tranches. The report states:

> MRC [Market Risk Control] VaR [value-at-risk] methodologies relied on the AAA rating of the Super Senior positions. The AAA rating determined the relevant product-type time series to be used in calculating VaR. In turn, the product-type time series determined the volatility sensitivities to be applied to Super Senior positions. Until Q3 [third quarter] 2007, the 5-year time series had demonstrated very low levels of volatility sensitivities. As a consequence, even unhedged Super Senior positions contributed little to VaR utilisation.
>
> *(p. 20)*

Piskorski, Seru, and Vig (2009) found, conditional on a loan becoming seriously delinquent, a significantly lower foreclosure rate for loans held by banks than for similar loans that were securitized. Indeed, Eggert (2009) takes the position that securitization *caused* the subprime meltdown. In this regard, UBS's behavior provides examples of key psychological pitfalls related to securitization. For instance, in relying solely on risk ratings, UBS's risk management group did no independent analysis. The report states:

> In analyzing the retained positions, MRC generally did not "look through" the CDO structure to analyse the risks of the underlying collateral. In addition, the CDO desk does not appear to have conducted such "look through" analysis and the static data maintained in the front-office systems did not capture several important dimensions of the underlying collateral types. For example, the static data did not capture FICO [credit] scores, 1st/2nd

lien status, collateral vintage (which term relates to the year in which the assets backing the securities had been sourced), and did not distinguish a CDO from an ABS. MRC did not examine or analyze such information on a regular or systematic basis.

(p. 20)

In a similar vein, it appears that no attempt was made to develop an RFL [risk factor loss] structure that captured more meaningful attributes related to the U.S. housing market generally, such as defaults, loan to value ratios, or other similar attributes to statistically shock the existing portfolio.

(p. 38)

Was it rational for UBS to ignore the underlying fundamentals of the U.S. mortgage market? Was it rational for UBS to make no attempt to investigate key statistics related to the U.S. housing market, such as LTVs, percentage of loans that featured 100 percent financing, limited-documentation loans, and default rates? Between 2001 and 2006, the following occurred: The LTVs of newly originated mortgages rose from 80 percent to 90 percent; the percentage of loans that were 100 percent financed climbed from 3 percent to 33 percent; and limited documentation loans almost doubled – rising from 27 percent to 46 percent. In terms of increasing risk, these trends are akin to powder kegs waiting for a match.[9]

As for defaults, the insufficient focus on fundamentals, in combination with an overattention to historical default rates – a strong illustration of conservatism bias (i.e., the tendency to overweight base-rate information) – gave rise to the "risk-free illusion." UBS's CDO desk considered a super senior position to be fully hedged if 2–4 percent of the position was protected. They referred to such super seniors as AMPS (amplified mortgage protected trades).

In this regard, UBS erroneously judged that it had hedged its AMPS positions sufficiently and that the associated VaR was effectively zero. Was this judgment rational? Not in my opinion, as UBS assumed that historical default rates would continue to apply, despite the changed fundamentals in the U.S. housing market. The UBS report indicates in respect to AMPS that

Amplified Mortgage Portfolio: . . . at the end of 2007, losses on these trades contributed approximately 63% of total Super Senior losses.

Unhedged Super Senior positions: Positions retained by UBS in anticipation of executing AMPS trades which did not materialise. . . . at the end of 2007, losses on these trades contributed approximately 27% of total Super Senior losses.

(p. 14)

Information sharing at UBS

Narrow framing and opaque framing are two of the psychological pitfalls described previously. UBS's report criticizes its risk managers for *opaquely* presenting information about risks to be managed and decisions to be taken. The report states:

Complex and incomplete risk reporting: . . . Risks were siloed within the risk functions, without presenting a holistic picture of the risk situation of a particular business.

Lack of substantive assessment: MRC did not routinely put numbers into the broader economic context or the fundamentals of the market when presenting to Senior Management.

(p. 39)

When risk managers eventually recognized the deteriorating values of their subprime positions, they mistakenly assumed that the problem was restricted to subprime and would not affect the values of their other ABS positions.

As a general matter, risk managers did not properly share information with those who needed the information at UBS, and the information they did share was overly complex and often out of date. Examples of what went wrong are that risk managers often netted long and short positions, which obscured the manner in which positions were structured, and they did not make the inventory of super senior positions clear.

Information sharing takes place as part of the deliberations about which decisions to take. UBS managers exhibited groupthink in these deliberations by not challenging each other about the ways their various businesses were developing. The report states:

> Members of the IB Senior Management apparently did not sufficiently challenge each other in relation to the development of their various businesses. The Fixed Income strategy does not appear to have been subject to critical challenge, for instance in view of the substantial investments in systems, people and financial resources that the growth plans entailed.
>
> *(p. 36)*

UBS's risk managers also appeared vulnerable to confirmation bias. As the firm began to experience losses on its inventories of MBS in the first and second quarters of 2007, the risk management team did not implement additional risk methodologies. Then, matters got worse. In a subsection titled "Absence of risk management," the report states:

> In Q2 2007, the CDO desk was giving a relatively pessimistic outlook in relation to certain aspects of the Subprime market generally in response to questions from Group and IB Senior Management about UBS's Subprime exposures. Notwithstanding this assessment, the MBS CDO business acquired further substantial Mezz RMBS [mezzanine residential MBS] holdings and the CDO desk prepared a paper to support the significant limit increase requests. The increase was ultimately not pursued.
>
> *(p. 29)*

Incentives and governance at UBS

In theory, compensation provides managers with incentives to maximize the value of their firms. Incentive compensation frameworks (beyond the base salary) often rely on a combination of (1) a bonus plan that relates to the short term and (2) equity-based compensation that relates to the long term.

In practice, UBS's compensation system was plagued by at least three serious flaws. The first flaw was that UBS's incentive structure did not take risk properly into account. The report states, "The compensation structure generally made little recognition of risk issues or adjustment for risk/other qualitative indicators" (p. 42). Did this amount to rational governance? Keep in mind that fundamental value is based on discounted cash flow, where the discount rate reflects risk as well as the time value of money.

Higher risk leads to a higher discount rate and, therefore, to lower discounted cash flows. UBS's compensation structure barely took risk issues into consideration and made little to no adjustment for risk. Therefore, employees had no direct incentive to focus on risk when making decisions, including decisions about positions involving subprime mortgages and their associated derivatives.

The second flaw concerned undue emphasis on short-term profit and loss (P&L) in overall employee compensation – specifically, bonuses – and insufficient attention to the implications of decisions about positions for long-term value. The report states, "Day1 P&L treatment of many of the transactions meant that employee remuneration (including bonuses) was not directly affected by the longer term development of positions created" (p. 42). To be sure, the compensation structure featured an equity component which could have provided UBS employees with an indirect incentive to avoid risks that were detrimental to long-term value. The bonus focus, however, dominated. Bonus payments for successful and senior fixed-income traders, including those in businesses holding subprime positions, were significant. Particularly noteworthy is that UBS based bonuses on gross revenue after personnel costs but did not take formal account of the quality or sustainability of earnings.

The third flaw was that UBS's incentives did not differentiate between skill-based returns and returns attributable to cost advantages. The report states:

> [E]mployee incentivisation arrangements did not differentiate between return generated by skill in creating additional returns versus returns made from exploiting UBS's comparatively low cost of funding in what were essentially carry trades. There are no findings that special arrangements were made for employees in the businesses holding Subprime positions.
>
> *(p. 42)*

Are these reward systems, policies, and practices consistent with rational governance? The authors of the UBS report suggest not, and I concur.

Standard and Poor's

One of the major elements of the financial crisis was the fact that rating agencies assigned AAA ratings to mortgage-related securities that were very risky. As a result, many investors purchased these securities under the impression that they were safe, and they found out otherwise only when housing prices declined and default rates rose. Financial intermediaries such as UBS also paid a steep price when the securities they held in inventory declined in value and became illiquid.

In this section, I discuss the psychological issues that affected the judgments and decisions made by rating agencies. The processes of planning, standards, and information sharing were the most germane processes; also important were agency issues.

Planning and standards at S&P

Consider some background. In August 2004, Moody's unveiled a new credit-rating model that enabled securities firms to increase their sales of top-rated subprime mortgage-backed bonds. The new model eliminated a non-diversification penalty that was present in the prior model, a penalty that applied to concentrated mortgage risk. According to Douglas Lucas, head of CDO research at UBS Securities in New York City, Moody's was pressured to make the change. He was quoted by Smith (2008) as having stated, "I know people lobbied Moody's to accommodate more concentrated residential mortgage risk in CDOs, and Moody's obliged."[10] Notably, Moody's competitor, S&P, revised its own methods one week after Moody's did. In important ways, S&P shared traits with UBS at this time. Both firms found themselves behind their respective industry leaders and were thus susceptible to reference point–induced risk-seeking behavior.

The *Wall Street Journal* reported that in August 2004, S&P commercial mortgage analyst Gale Scott sent the following message to colleagues: "We are meeting with your group this week to discuss adjusting criteria for rating CDOs of real-estate assets . . . because of the ongoing threat of losing deals" (see Lucchetti 2008b). Richard Gugliada, a former S&P executive who oversaw CDOs from the late 1990s until 2005, replied to the e-mail, "OK with me to revise criteria" (see Smith 2008). The criteria for rating commercial mortgages were changed after several meetings. According to an S&P report that Scott co-wrote in May 2008, the change in criteria directly preceded "aggressive underwriting and lower credit support" (Smith 2008) in the market for commercial MBS from 2005 to 2007. The report went on to say that this change led to growing delinquencies, defaults, and losses.

Consider S&P against the backdrop of its parent organization, McGraw-Hill Companies. According to reports that appeared in the *Wall Street Journal*, CEO and Chairman Harold McGraw established unrealistic profit goals for his organization (Lucchetti 2008a). I suggest that these goals induced risk-seeking behavior in the rating of mortgage-related products. The *Wall Street Journal* reported that because McGraw-Hill had been suffering financially in other areas, it exerted pressure on S&P to expand 15–20 percent a year. McGraw-Hill's financial services unit, which includes S&P, generated 75 percent of McGraw-Hill's total operating profit in 2007, up from 42 percent in 2000. In 2007, the ratings business generated a third of McGraw-Hill's revenue.

Goal setting is the basis for establishing standards and planning, through which goals are folded into strategy. S&P's efforts to achieve its goals focused on increasing its revenues from rating mortgage-related products while keeping its costs down. In regard to the latter, Gugliada told *Bloomberg* that he was given tough budget targets (see Smith 2008).

According to Lucchetti (2008a), the combination of high revenue goals and low cost goals led understaffed analytical teams to underestimate the default risk associated with mortgage-related products. Before the collapse in housing prices, S&P and Moody's earned approximately three times more from grading CDOs than from grading corporate bonds.

Consider how the ratings on mortgage-related securities came to be lowered over time. Once housing prices began to decline and homeowners began to default, raters eventually downgraded most of the AAA rated CDO bonds that had been issued in the prior three years. On 10 July 2008, Moody's reduced its ratings on $5.2 billion in subprime-backed CDOs. The same day, S&P said it was considering reductions on $12 billion of residential MBS. By August 2007, Moody's had downgraded 90 percent of all asset-backed CDO investments issued in 2006 and 2007, including 85 percent of the debt originally rated Aaa. S&P reduced 84 percent of the CDO tranches it had rated, including 76 percent of all those rated AAA.[11]

Information sharing at S&P

Former employees at S&P have provided insights into the ways that information used for rating CDOs was shared. Kai Gilkes is a former S&P quantitative analyst in London. The following comments in Smith (2008) recreate the tenor of the discussion about the sharing of information and points of view:

> "Look, I know you're not comfortable with such and such [an] assumption, but apparently Moody's are even lower, and, if that's the only thing that is standing between rating this deal and not rating this deal, are we really hung up on that assumption?" You don't have infinite data. Nothing is perfect. So the line in the sand shifts and shifts, and can shift quite a bit.

Gilkes' remark about shifting sands needs to be understood in the context of group processes. The behavioral decision literature emphasizes that working in a group tends to reduce the biases of the group's members when the tasks feature clearly correct solutions, which everyone can confirm once the solution has been presented. For judgmental tasks that have no clearly correct solution, however, working in groups actually exacerbates the biases of the group members. Gilkes' remark about "shifting sands" effectively points to the judgmental character of the ratings decision.

Additional insight about the sharing of information and exchange of viewpoints has come from Gugliada, who told *Bloomberg* that when a proposal to tighten S&P's criteria was considered, the codirector of CDO ratings, David Tesher, responded: "Don't kill the golden goose."

Was groupthink an issue here, or were managers behaving rationally? The answer might depend on their personal ethics. In retrospect, Gugliada stated, competition with Moody's amounted to a "market-share war where criteria were relaxed. . . . I knew it was wrong at the time. It was either that or skip the business. That wasn't my mandate. My mandate was to find a way" (see Smith 2008). In this regard, Griffin and Tang (2009) find that ratings by both firms were higher than what their models implied. They conclude that tranches that were rated AAA actually corresponded to BBB when rated according to the firms' models and default standards.

To be sure, analysts at S&P were not oblivious to the possibility of a housing bubble. In 2005, S&P staff observed that the housing market was in a bubble, the bursting of which might lead housing prices to decline by 30 percent at some stage. The vague "at some stage" could have meant, however, next month or 10 years hence. The timing of the bursting of a bubble is highly uncertain. The report, including its implications for ratings, was discussed internally, but the discussion did not alter the rating methodology.

S&P had been telling investors that their ratings were but one piece of information about securities and that ratings were not a perfect substitute for being diligent about acquiring additional information to assess security risk. S&P's protocol was to accept the documentation as presented and to issue a rating conditional on that information. The firm's practice was not to verify the documentation. If S&P rated a security on the basis of limited-documentation mortgages, it did not seek to verify whether or not the information was correct. Just as UBS did, however, the investment bank treated AAA ratings on mortgage-related securities as unconditional ratings. Moreover, the same was true for many other investors, especially end investors, who were much less sophisticated than investment bankers.

As it happens, some of the analysts engaged in rating CDOs were highly skeptical of their assignments, and they shared this skepticism with colleagues. Lucchetti (2008b) reports that one S&P analytical staffer e-mailed another saying that a mortgage or structured-finance deal was "ridiculous" and that "we should not be rating it." The recipient of the e-mail famously responded, "We rate every deal," and added that, "it could be structured by cows and we would rate it." An analytical manager in the CDO group at S&P told a senior analytical manager in a separate e-mail that "rating agencies continue to create" an "even bigger monster – the CDO market. Let's hope we are all wealthy and retired by the time this house of cards falters" [Lucchetti 2008b].

AIG

AIG is an insurance company with a financial products division (AIGFP).[12] Because of AIGFP's involvement in the market for subprime mortgages, AIG required a $182 billion bailout from the U.S. government. In September 2008, the decision to bail out AIG was a defining moment in the unfolding of the global financial crisis. To understand the decisions that led to this event, consider some background.

AIGFP was created in 1987; it generated income by assuming various parties' counterparty risks in such transactions as interest rate swaps. It was able to do so because its parent, AIG, had an AAA rating and a large balance sheet. AIGFP was highly profitable during its first 15 years and, by 2001, was generating 15 percent of AIG's profit.

AIGFP's main role in the global financial crisis involved its trades in the market for CDS associated with subprime mortgages. Effectively, AIG provided insurance against defaults by homeowners who had taken out subprime mortgages.

AIGFP entered the market for CDS in 1998 by insuring against the default risk of corporate bonds issued by investment-grade public corporations. The default risk associated with these bonds as a group was relatively low. Although insuring corporate debt remained AIGFP's key business, over time the company also began to insure risks associated with credit card debt, student loans, auto loans, pools of prime mortgages, and eventually, pools of subprime mortgages.

Planning and risk standards at AIGFP

The need for a bailout of AIG stemmed from AIGFP having underestimated its risk exposure to subprime mortgages. The psychological pitfalls underlying the underestimation were categorization, overconfidence, and groupthink.

When the Federal Reserve began to increase short-term interest rates in June 2004, the volume of prime mortgage lending fell by 50 percent. At the same time, however, the volume of subprime mortgage lending increased dramatically.[13] Lewis (2009) related that, as a result, the composition of mortgage pools that AIGFP was insuring shifted over the next 18 months; the proportion of mortgages that were subprime increased from 2 percent to 95 percent of the total over that period. Yet, AIGFP's decisions were invariant to the change. The decision makers succumbed to categorization; that is, they treated a pool with 2 percent subprime mortgages as equivalent to a pool with 95 percent subprime mortgages.

Recall the failure of the rational lemons paradigm. A major reason the subprime market thrived instead of collapsed is that during 2004 and 2005, AIGFP assumed the default risk of subprime mortgages apparently unknowingly. AIGFP failed to assume the worst, as rational behavior in the lemons framework requires.

In addition to categorization, overconfidence and groupthink played key roles. AIGFP was headed by Joseph Cassano. His predecessor at the helm of AIGFP was Tom Savage, a trained mathematician who understood the models used by AIGFP traders to price the risks they were assuming. Savage encouraged debates about the models AIGFP was using and the trades being made. According to Lewis (2009), in contrast to Savage, Cassano stifled debate and intimidated those who expressed views he did not share. Cassano was not a trained mathematician. His academic background was in political science, and he spent most of his career in the back office doing operations. Lewis reports that his reputation at AIGFP was someone who had a crude feel for financial risk and a strong tendency to bully people who challenged him. One of his colleagues said of him, "The way you dealt with Joe was to start everything by saying, 'You're right, Joe.'" When the issue of a shift toward taking more subprime mortgage risk eventually made its way onto a formal agenda, Cassano, pointing to the AAA ratings from Moody's and S&P, dismissed any concerns as overblown.

Eventually, Cassano did change his mind. It happened when he was persuaded to meet with a series of AIGFP's Wall Street trading partners to discuss the premises underlying the rating of CDO tranches based on subprime mortgages. Cassano learned that the main premise was that the historical default rate for the U.S. housing market would continue to apply in the future, a judgment consistent with conservatism bias. To his credit, Cassano did not accept the premise, and at the end of 2005, AIGFP ceased its CDS trades.

AIGFP's decision to stop insuring mortgage defaults did not stop Wall Street firms from continuing to create CDOs based on subprime mortgages. It did force Wall Street firms to bear some of the default risk however, that AIGFP had previously borne. That outcome is a major reason Merrill Lynch, Morgan Stanley, Lehman Brothers, and Bear Stearns took the losses they did.

In August 2007, in a conference call to investors, Cassano made the following statement: "It is hard for us, without being flippant, to even see a scenario within any kind of realm of reason that would see us losing $1 on any of those transactions." Major surprises are the hallmark of overconfidence. Cassano apparently based his statement on the fact that the subprime mortgages that were beginning to default had originated in 2006 and 2007, which were riskier years for mortgage issuance than 2004 and 2005, the years in which AIGFP had taken its CDS positions. The CDS contracts on which Cassano had signed off stipulated however, that AIG would post collateral if its credit rating were downgraded. As it happens, AIG's credit rating did come to be downgraded, in September 2008 from AA to A, thereby triggering calls for collateral that AIG was unable to meet.

Incentives and governance at AIGFP

Poor incentives were not the problem at AIGFP, which balanced long-term against short-term results. To its credit, AIGFP required that employees leave 50 percent of their bonuses in the firm, a policy that skewed their incentive toward the long run.[14] As for Cassano, in 2007, he was paid $38 million in total, but he left almost all that amount ($36.75 million) in the firm. Clearly, he had a strong financial incentive to maximize the long-term value of AIG. His decisions destroyed value at AIG, however, and nearly brought down the firm. Why did Cassano behave in ways that seem highly irrational? The reason is that when it comes to behaving rationally, psychological pitfalls can trump incentives. Good governance involves more than structuring good incentives.

A host of additional governance questions can be raised about AIG. Why did AIGFP's board of directors agree to appoint someone with Cassano's temperament to head the division? How thoroughly did the executives at the parent firm monitor Cassano's actions? To what extent did the resignation of AIG CEO Hank Greenberg in March 2005 make a difference to the risks assumed by the firm as a whole?

Most of these questions are difficult to answer. We do know that Greenberg, who had run AIG since 1968, was known for being a diligent monitor. His successor, Edward Liddy, lacked Greenberg's deep understanding of the company. For the six-month period preceding the bailout, the firm had neither a full-time chief financial officer nor a chief risk assessment officer and was engaged in a search for both. As a result, in the period leading up to the bailout, the executives of the 18th-largest firm in the world had no clear sense of their firm's exposure to subprime mortgage risk.

Narvik

At the end of the supply chain for the financial products in this story are the investors who purchased and held the complex securities at the heart of the tale. Narvik, Norway, population 17,000 and located above the Arctic Circle, is just such an investor. It was featured in a February 2009 CNBC documentary titled "House of Cards," which explored issues surrounding the financial crisis.[15] Narvik had been losing population and its tax base. To address the issue, its local council invested $200 million in a series of complex securities that included CDOs. The purchase of the CDOs was part of a larger strategy in which the town took out a loan, using as collateral future revenues from its hydroelectric plant, and invested the proceeds in complex securities with the intent of capturing the spread. Narvik ended up losing $35 million, roughly a quarter of its annual budget.

Two main psychological features tie the situation in Narvik to the discussion in previous sections. First, given the decline in population and tax revenues, the council members in Narvik quite plausibly exhibited reference point–induced risk-seeking behavior. They were fiduciary managers of cash flows derived from their hydroelectric plant, but because money and population were higher in the past, they swapped those monies for what they hoped would be higher cash flows from U.S. mortgages and municipal bond payments.

Second, the mayor of Narvik at the time, Karen Kuvaas, insists that the council members were not naive, but in this respect, she might have been overconfident; she also admits that she did not read the prospectus before signing off on the deal and was not aware that if some of the securities declined in value, Narvik would have to post payments. In defense of the council, Kuvaas indicated that the securities they purchased were represented to them as AAA rated and, therefore, as very safe. The lesson here is that fiduciaries or other agents who may be knowledgeable enough in one set of circumstances may be way over their heads in another. One should always be on the lookout to see if one is falling prey to overconfidence.

The SEC

The SEC came under intense criticism for its lax oversight of investment banking practices and for failing to detect a large hedge fund Ponzi scheme run by Bernard Madoff. A focal point of the criticism of investment bank oversight involved a meeting that took place at the SEC on 28 April 2004, when the commission was chaired by William Donaldson. That meeting established the Consolidated Supervised Entities (CSE) program, a voluntary regulatory program that allowed the SEC to review the capital structure and risk management procedures of participating financial institutions. Five investment banks joined the CSE program, as did two bank holding companies. The investment banks were Bear Stearns, Goldman Sachs, Lehman Brothers, Merrill Lynch, and Morgan Stanley, and the bank holding companies were Citigroup and JPMorgan Chase.

As part of the CSE program, the SEC agreed to a change in elements of the net capital rule, which limited the leverage of broker/dealer subsidiaries. Some analysts have suggested that this change led the CSE participants to increase their leverage – from approximately 12 to 1 to ratios exceeding 30 to 1 – thereby greatly magnifying the losses these institutions later incurred on their subprime mortgage positions (Labaton 2008; Coffee 2008).

Prior to 2004, the SEC had limited authority to oversee investment banks. In 2004, the European Union passed a rule permitting the SEC's European counterpart to oversee the risk of both broker/dealers and their parent holding companies. This change could have meant that the European divisions of U.S. financial institutions would be regulated by European agencies, but the European Union agreed to waive regulatory oversight by its own agencies if equivalent oversight was provided by the host countries' agencies. This policy is what led the SEC to institute the CSE program, although the SEC required that the entities be large firms, firms with capital of at least $5 billion. Indeed, U.S investment banks, anxious to avoid European oversight, lobbied the SEC for the change.

The change to the net capital rule made it consistent with the Basel II standards. The key feature of the change was an alteration in the way net capital is measured. Prior to the change, net capital was measured by financial statement variables and was subject to formulaic discounts ("haircuts") to adjust for risk. The main change to the rule replaced the formulaic approach with discounts derived from the risk management models in use at the financial institutions.

Controversy surrounds the impact associated with the change to the net capital rule. The *New York Times* first reported the change to the rule (Labaton (2008), and this report was subsequently echoed by academics (e.g., Coffee 2008). The coverage by the *New York Times* might have been misleading, however, in that it suggested that this change allowed the leverage levels at parent holding companies to grow from 15 to above 30, thereby exacerbating faulty decisions about subprime mortgages. The SEC maintains that the change in provisions of the net capital rule applied to broker/dealer subsidiaries and had no discernible impact on the degree of leverage of the parent holding companies. Sirri (2009) argued that the change in the net capital rule left the same leverage limits in place and changed only the manner in which net capital is measured.[16]

Perhaps the most important feature of the CSE program was the SEC's failure to provide effective oversight of the risk profiles at the financial institutions in question. Consider the following remarks by Coffee (2008):

> Basel II contemplated close monitoring and supervision by regulators. Thus, the Federal Reserve assigns members of its staff to maintain an office within a regulated bank holding company in order to provide constant oversight. In the case of the SEC, a team of only three SEC staffers were [sic] assigned to each CSE firm (and a total of only 13 individuals comprised the SEC's Office of Prudential Supervision and Risk Analysis that oversaw and conducted this monitoring effort). From the start, it was a mismatch: three SEC staffers to oversee an investment bank the size of Merrill Lynch, which could easily afford to hire scores of highly quantitative economists and financial analysts, implied that the SEC was simply outgunned.

Planning at the SEC

Did the SEC display overconfidence in its planning process for the CSE program? Perhaps. Evidence suggesting overconfidence can be observed in the following two excerpts from the transcript of the 28 April 2004 meeting. In the excerpt, Harvey Goldschmid, who was an SEC commissioner at the time, directs a question to an SEC staffer:[17]

> HARVEY GOLDSCHMID: We've talked a lot about this. This is going to be much more complicated – compliance, inspection, understanding of risk – than we've ever had to do. Mike, I trust you no end. But I take it you think we can do this?
>
> GROUP: [Laughter.]
>
> MIKE: Well we've hired Matt Eichler and other folks as well who are skilled in quantitative analysis. They're both PhDs right now. And we've hired other people as well who are quantitatively skilled. So we're going to continue to develop that staff. And then we have a good accounting staff as well. And then our auditors in New York, as well as in Washington will be useful in this process.
>
> I mean, so we're going to have to depend on the firms, obviously. They're frontline. They're going to have to develop their entire risk framework. We'll be reading that first. And they'll have to explain that to us in a way that makes sense. And then we'll do the examinations of that process. In addition to approving their models and their risk control systems.
>
> It's a large undertaking. I'm not going to try to do it alone.
>
> GROUP: [Laughter.]

The two instances of group laughter in the above excerpt mark points at which "Mike" might have exhibited overconfidence about his ability to oversee risk management at seven major financial institutions with combined assets of about $4 trillion with the help of only two PhDs, some additional quantitatively oriented personnel, and agency accountants and auditors.[18]

Consider a second excerpt involving Goldschmid and Annette Nazareth, who at the time was the SEC director of the Division of Market Regulation. Their interchange is particularly interesting in light of the later collapse of Bear Stearns, Lehman Brothers, and Merrill Lynch:

> GOLDSCHMID: We've said these are the big guys but that means if anything goes wrong, it's going to be an awfully big mess.
> GROUP: [Laughter.]
> ANNETTE NAZARETH: Again, we have very broad discretionary. . . . As we mentioned, we're going to be meeting with these firms on a monthly basis. And hopefully from month to month you don't see wild swings. Among other things, we can require firms to put in additional capital, to keep additional capital against the risks. We can actually – the commission has the authority to limit their ability to engage in certain businesses, just as any prudent regulator would. We have hopefully a lot of early warnings and the ability to constrict activity that we think is problematic.
> GOLDSCHMID: I think you've been very good at thinking this through carefully and working this through with skill.

The deliberations to establish the CSE program lasted less than an hour. The vote by the SEC was unanimous. Little probing for weaknesses in such a far-reaching proposal occurred. I suggest that overconfidence and confirmation bias were high. This kind of setting is where groupthink thrives.

Goldschmid left the commission in 2005. In an October 2008 interview with the *New York Times*, he reflected: "In retrospect, the tragedy is that the 2004 rule making gave us the ability to get information that would have been critical to sensible monitoring, and yet the SEC didn't oversee well enough" (Labaton 2008). I suggest that this recollection indicates that Goldschmid was overconfident in 2004.

Although Goldschmid was apparently overconfident at that time, other forces that led to weak oversight were also at work. In April 2004, when Goldschmid was serving as one of the commissioners, the SEC was chaired by Donaldson, but in 2005, Christopher Cox replaced Donaldson. Cox was generally regarded as favoring weaker regulations, which might explain why so few resources were allocated to the CSE program. In February 2009, Linda Thomsen, the director of enforcement at the SEC, resigned under pressure. It was on her watch that Wall Street investment banks took disastrous risk management decisions and the Ponzi scheme conducted by Madoff went undetected. In describing her resignation, the press noted that she should not have to bear the entire blame for these failures because Cox set the tone, including public criticism of SEC staff, for weak regulatory oversight.

Madoff and behavioral pitfalls at the SEC

According to an internal report by the SEC (2009), between 1992 and 2008, the agency received six distinct complaints about Madoff's operations, one of which involved three versions. Several of the complaints suggested that Madoff was running a Ponzi scheme. The report reveals that the SEC conducted investigations and examinations related to Madoff's investment advisory business but failed to uncover the fraud.

I suggest that confirmation bias lay at the heart of the SEC's failure to detect Madoff's Ponzi scheme. An excerpt from the SEC's internal report follows.[19] As you read through the excerpt, keep in mind that a person exhibits confirmation bias when he or she overweighs information that confirms a view or hypothesis and underweights information that disconfirms the view or hypothesis. The report states:

> The OIG investigation found the SEC conducted two investigations and three examinations related to Madoff's investment advisory business based upon the detailed and credible complaints that raised the possibility that Madoff was misrepresenting his trading and could have been operating a Ponzi scheme. Yet, at no time did the SEC ever verify Madoff's trading through an independent third party, and in fact, never actually conducted a Ponzi scheme examination or investigation of Madoff.
>
> In the examination of Madoff, the SEC did not seek Depository Trust Company (DTC) (an independent third-party) records, but sought copies of such records from Madoff himself. Had they sought records from DTC, there is an excellent chance that they would have uncovered Madoff's Ponzi scheme in 1992.
>
> The teams assembled were relatively inexperienced, and there was insufficient planning for the examinations. The scopes of the examination were in both cases too narrowly focused on the possibility of front-running, with no significant attempts made to analyze the numerous red flags about Madoff's trading and returns . . .
>
> The investigation that arose from the most detailed complaint provided to the SEC, which explicitly stated it was "highly likely" that "Madoff was operating a Ponzi scheme," never really investigated the possibility of a Ponzi scheme. The relatively inexperienced Enforcement staff failed to appreciate the significance of the analysis in the complaint, and almost immediately expressed skepticism and disbelief. Most of their investigation was directed at determining whether Madoff should register as an investment adviser or whether Madoff's hedge fund investors' disclosures were adequate.
>
> As with the examinations, the Enforcement staff almost immediately caught Madoff in lies and misrepresentations, but failed to follow up on inconsistencies. They rebuffed offers of additional evidence from the complainant, and were confused about certain critical and fundamental aspects of Madoff's operations. When Madoff provided evasive or contradictory answers to important questions in testimony, they simply accepted as plausible his explanations.
>
> Although the Enforcement staff made attempts to seek information from independent third-parties, they failed to follow up on these requests. They reached out to the NASD [now, FINRA, the Financial Industry Regulatory Authority] and asked for information on whether Madoff had options positions on a certain date, but when they received a report that there were in fact no options positions on that date, they did not take any further steps. An Enforcement staff attorney made several attempts to obtain documentation from European counterparties (another independent third-party), and although a letter was drafted, the Enforcement staff decided not to send it. Had any of these efforts been fully executed, they would have led to Madoff's Ponzi scheme being uncovered.
>
> *(pp. 23–25)*

People who succumb to confirmation bias test hypotheses by searching for information that confirms the hypothesis they are testing. The antidote to confirmation bias is to search for information that *disconfirms* the hypothesis, to ask whether the hypothesis is untrue, a lie. What the

SEC report strongly indicates is that its staff actively avoided seeking disconfirming information to their view that Madoff was innocent of running a Ponzi scheme. Confirmation bias was not the only psychological pitfall afflicting the SEC in connection with its investigations of Madoff. An incentive issue was also involved in respect to the way the SEC rewarded investigators. Nocera (2009) pointed out that the SEC bases its success on quantitative measures, such as the number of actions it brings and the number of cases it settles.

He suggests that through its choice of standards and incentives, the SEC tends to pursue small cases, cases in which those being investigated will prefer to settle and pay a fine even if they are innocent. Madoff was not a small case.

Reference point–induced risk seeking was also a factor. Nocera indicated that the SEC finds it difficult to shut cases down once they have been initiated. Such behavior is throwing good money after bad, a phenomenon technically known as "escalation of commitment." Nocera stated:

> Even if the facts start to look shaky, the internal dynamics of the agency push its lawyers to either settle or go to trial, but never to abandon it. [quoting] "The staff has a real problem persuading the commission to cut off a case once it has begun."[20]

Given the SEC's limited resources, the costs of escalation of commitment can be very high. In addition to confirmation bias and escalation of commitment, the SEC also exhibited poor information sharing. In this regard, the SEC report relates that the agency was unaware that it was running separate examinations out of two offices. The report states:

> Astoundingly, both examinations were open at the same time in different offices without either knowing the other one was conducting an identical examination. In fact, it was Madoff himself who informed one of the examination teams that the other examination team had already received the information they were seeking from him.

(p. 24)

Discussion and conclusion

Opinions about the root cause of the financial crisis differ. Some argue that the root lies with a weak regulatory structure, within which private-sector decisions were largely rational. Others argue that the root lies with irrational decisions associated with the occurrence of a housing market bubble, a surge in subprime mortgage lending, and the breakdown of the rational lemons paradigm. Still others blame poor corporate governance, explicit corruption, and unwise governmental mandates and guarantees. Differentiating among these various views requires a search for the devil in the details. The details considered here involve five cases, all of which highlight (to a greater or lesser degree) irrational decision making at key points in the financial product supply chain. Consider decisions made at AIG. AIG facilitated the explosive growth in subprime mortgage lending in 2004 and 2005 by selling CDS that insured against default. AIG's financial product division irrationally failed to track the proportion of subprime mortgages in the pools being insured, thereby misgauging the risk of those assets and causing the associated CDS to be mispriced. Interestingly, this failure occurred despite incentives that balanced long-term performance against short-term performance. Moreover, conversations that AIG had with its trading partners indicate the presence of a widespread conservatism bias regarding the assumption that historical mortgage default rates would continue to apply.

Similarly, the UBS investment banking division admitted to misgauging subprime mortgage risk by not "looking through" the CDO structures and by assuming that historical default rates would continue to apply. UBS's underperformance relative to competitors led them to exhibit reference point–induced risk seeking. This behavior was compounded by poor incentive structures at UBS that emphasized short-term performance over long-term performance.

Recall that UBS placed no operational limits on the size of its CDO warehouse. It was not alone. Investment banks are typically intermediaries, not end investors planning to hold large positions in subprime mortgages. Some hold the equity tranches of CDOs as a signal to the buyers of the less risky tranches. What created many of the losses for investment banks, however, was inventory risk – risk stemming from warehousing the subprime positions that underlay CDOs. As the housing market fell into decline, many investment banks found that they could not find buyers for the CDOs and, as a result, inadvertently became end investors.

The rating agencies and investors' reliance on them played a huge role in the financial crisis. Both (supposedly) sophisticated investors, such as the investment bankers at UBS, and naive end investors, such as the Narvik town council, relied on the risk assessments of rating agencies. The rating agencies, however, explicitly indicated that their ratings were premised on accepting the information they received as accurate, even if the mortgages featured limited documentation. For this reason, the agencies suggested that their ratings be treated as only one piece of information when assessing risk. By this argument, users who accepted their ratings at face value behaved irrationally.

Did the rating agencies exhibit irrational behavior by weakening their risk assessment criteria to cultivate more business? This question is different from asking whether the ratings agencies behaved ethically. The major problem with the behavior of rating agencies might arise more from a conflict of interests (the principal–agent conflict) than irrationality, in the sense that the issuers of securities, not the end investors in the securities, pay for ratings. Still, the evidence suggests that reference point–induced risk seeking and groupthink were issues at S&P.

In addition to the five entities highlighted here, many others participated in the financial product supply chain. For example, press coverage suggests that the value-destructive dynamics at UBS were also at work at other financial institutions active in initiating subprime mortgages and in creating CDOs that included subprime mortgages (see Shefrin 2009).

In 2004 and 2005, the activities of these financial institutions might have been rational because they were able to shift default risk to AIG by purchasing CDS. Lewis (2009) quoted AIG employees as stating that their firm's willingness to sell CDS allowed the CDO market to grow at a rapid rate. After AIG stopped selling CDS, however, many financial firms took on the risk themselves, apparently under the illusion that housing prices would continue to rise and that default rates would not be affected by the increased ratio of subprime to prime mortgages. At one point, Merrill Lynch used CDS to create synthetic CDOs because the number of subprime mortgages available to create traditional CDOs was insufficient relative to the firm's aspirations.

The financial crisis also raises issues involving being "too big to fail" and moral hazard. Some might argue that the root of the financial crisis was a rational response by executives of large financial institutions to the perception that they could take on excessive risk because the U.S. government would intervene should those risks prove disastrous. To be sure, the executives must have been aware of such a possibility. The management failures at these institutions bore the telltale signs, however, of psychological pitfalls. In addition, a sign that intervention was not guaranteed came with the government's choice to let Lehman Brothers fail.

Not only was the SEC subject to confirmation bias, but I believe overconfidence might have pervaded the entire regulatory landscape. Consider the comments of Alan Greenspan, who chaired the Federal Reserve during the key years in which the seeds of the crisis were sown. In June 2005, Greenspan testified before Congress that some local housing markets exhibited "froth." He pointed to the use of risky financing by some homeowners and suggested that the price increases in those local markets were unsustainable. He concluded, however, that there was no national housing bubble and that the economy was not at risk.[21] In the same vein, Greenspan's successor at the Fed, Ben Bernanke, gave a speech on 17 May 2007 in which he stated, "[W]e do not expect significant spillovers from the subprime market to the rest of the economy or to the financial system."[22]

In 2008, Greenspan testified before the House of Representatives Committee on Oversight and Government Reform as follows:

> [T]his crisis, however, has turned out to be much broader than anything I could have imagined. . . . Those of us who have looked to the self-interest of lending institutions to protect shareholders' equity – myself especially – are in a state of shocked disbelief.
>
> *(Felsenthal 2008)*

Consider the behavioral issues raised by Greenspan's comment about self-interest. Lending institutions are not masochists. The behavioral point is that psychological pitfalls created a gap between perceived self-interest and objective self-interest, thereby inducing irrational decisions. Most parties involved in the financial crisis are asking what they can learn from the experience. Under the leadership of the SEC's new enforcement chief, Robert Khuzami, the SEC is instituting a series of new procedures, such as providing senior enforcement officers the power to issue subpoenas without requesting permission from commissioners. UBS has created a presentation titled "Risk Management and Controls at UBS." The presentation emphasizes that managers must pay explicit attention to a series of behavioral issues, such as irrational exuberance in asset pricing.

These steps are in the right direction. A body of academic literature describes how organizations can take steps to avoid behavioral pitfalls (see Heath, Larrick, and Klayman 1998), but dealing with psychological pitfalls is not easy. The application of behavioral corporate finance and behavioral asset-pricing theory is not yet widespread. Moreover, little evidence indicates that organizations have developed systematic procedures along these lines.

The most useful behavioral lessons we can learn from the crisis are how to restructure processes to incorporate the explicit elements of behavioral corporate finance that this article has discussed. I have suggested that to avoid the kinds of process weaknesses exemplified by the five cases described here, systematic procedures within organizations should focus on the four key organizational processes listed in Exhibit 1: planning, standards, information sharing, and incentives (Shefrin 2008b).[23] Checklists are no panacea, but they do make the issue of vulnerability an explicit agenda item.

Still, the removal of psychological biases is not easy. Psychological pitfalls are likely to persist and to continue to affect decisions. For this reason, managers, analysts, investors and regulators would be well advised to keep three main points in mind. First, sentiment can affect asset pricing, particularly pricing of the securities of companies followed by analysts. Second, corporate managers are vulnerable to psychological biases (as we all are); therefore, these pitfalls are germane to companies' operational risks. Third, analysts themselves are vulnerable to psychological pitfalls and need to be mindful of how these pitfalls affect their own processes and decisions.

For example, consider what analysts might have missed about Citigroup before October 2007. Were Citigroup and AIG connected? In this regard, consider the CDS deals that AIGFP did in 2004 and 2005. Lewis (2009) quoted an AIGFP trader as saying, "We were doing every single deal with every single Wall Street firm, except Citigroup. Citigroup decided it liked the risk and kept it on their books. We took all the rest" (p. 1).

This remark should hold a lesson for analysts about applying tools from behavioral corporate finance. For example, analysts might use the framework encapsulated by Exhibit 1 to focus on the combination of process and psychological pitfalls in a situation. In the case of Citigroup, analysts could have focused on Citigroup's planning process in late 2004 and early 2005, when it was dealing with flagging profit growth. In that situation, Citigroup would have been especially vulnerable to reference point–based risk seeking. Indeed, Citigroup's board did decide to increase the firm's risk exposure after a presentation from a consultant, thereby taking a path similar to that of UBS.

Although analysts have no direct access to boardroom discussions, keeping the quality of governance in mind can be worthwhile. Consider whether Citigroup's board exhibited group-think. In a *Wall Street Journal* article about Citigroup board member Robert Rubin, Brown and Enrich (2008) stated, "Colleagues deferred to him, as the only board member with experience as a trader or risk manager. 'I knew what a CDO was,' Mr. Rubin said" (p. 1).

As the cases discussed in this chapter attest, assuming that financial institutions will make intelligent, bias-free risk–reward decisions is a mistake. Looking back after the crisis unfolded, Brown and Enrich (2008) quoted Rubin as saying about Citigroup's decision to take on more risk, "It gave room to do more, assuming you're doing intelligent risk–reward decisions" (p. 1). Learning that decision makers have psychological biases is an important lesson, not just for analysts but for everyone. Moreover, the lesson applies at all times, a point to keep in mind even as economic conditions improve and the financial crisis that erupted in 2007–2008 fades into memory.

Acknowledgements

I thank Mark Lawrence for his insightful comments about UBS; Marc Heerkens from UBS; participants at seminars I gave at the University of Lugano and at the University of California, Los Angeles; and participants in the Executive Master of Science in Risk Management program at the Amsterdam Institute of Finance, a program cosponsored with New York University. I also express my appreciation to Rodney Sullivan and Larry Siegel for their comments on previous drafts.

Notes

1 The bulk of this article is extracted from Mind | Work: Research News, Santa Clara University, SCU Leavey School of Business, Research Paper No. 10–04.

2 Hersh Shefrin, Mario L. Belotti Professor of Finance, Santa Clara University, Santa Clara, CA.

3 For example, in an 18-month period beginning in January 2007, crude oil prices tripled – from $50 a barrel to $150 a barrel – and as the financial crisis unfolded in 2008, several sovereign wealth funds in Middle Eastern countries took positions in U.S. financial institutions that were in need of additional equity capital.

4 The proportion of all mortgage originations that were subprime increased from near zero in the early 1980s to 20.1 percent in 2006, although not monotonically. Chomsisengphet and Pennington-Cross (2006) described the history of subprime mortgage lending in the United States beginning in 1980 as follows: "Many factors have contributed to the growth of subprime lending. Most fundamentally, it became legal. The ability to charge high rates and fees to borrowers was not possible until the Depository Institutions Deregulation and Monetary Control Act . . . was adopted in 1980. It preempted state interest rate caps. The Alternative Mortgage Transaction Parity Act . . . in 1982 permitted the use of variable interest rates and balloon payments. These laws opened the door for the development of a subprime market, but subprime lending would not become a viable large-scale lending alternative until

the Tax Reform Act of 1986 (TRA). The TRA increased the demand for mortgage debt because it prohibited the deduction of interest on consumer loans, yet allowed interest deductions on mortgages for a primary residence as well as one additional home." (p. 38)

5 As an example of foreign banks in the supply chain, consider that the Industrial and Commercial Bank of China bought $1.23 billion in securities backed by mortgages.

6 The five case studies are not intended to provide a comprehensive analysis of decision making in the financial crisis. Rather, the case studies are intended to provide examples of behavior that can be classified as rational or irrational. To deal with the issues raised by Posner (2009b), the focus is on financial institutions and government agencies, not on the behavior of individual homeowners. Nevertheless, many homeowners used subprime mortgages to purchase homes with the unfounded expectation that housing prices would continue to increase and that the homeowners would be able to refinance adjustable-rate mortgages in which the future interest rates would reset to a much higher rate.

7 UBS relied on McKinsey & Company for consulting services. Peter Wuffli, who was UBS Investment Bank CEO at the time, had previously been a principal with McKinsey

8 The nature of the consultant's recommendation provides an interesting illustration of how a "follow the leader" approach results in herding. UBS followed a leader in its peer group, plausibly Lehman Brothers although they do not say so explicitly. As I report later, a consultant advised Citigroup also to increase its risk exposure. Shefrin (2009) discussed how Merrill Lynch sought to emulate the subprime strategy of the industry leader (at the time, Lehman Brothers).

9 In this regard, the President's Working Group on Financial Markets (2008) concluded, "The turmoil in financial markets was triggered by *a dramatic weakening of underwriting standards for U.S. subprime mortgages, beginning in late 2004, and extending into early 2007.*" In contrast, studies by Bhardwaj and Sengupta (2008a, 2008b) from the Federal Reserve Bank of St. Louis suggest that subprime mortgage quality did not deteriorate after 2004 because FICO scores improved at the same time that the other indicators of credit quality worsened. The authors also pointed out that adjustable-rate subprime mortgages are designed as bridge loans, with the view that they be prepaid when interest rates reset as homeowners refinance. They attributed the subprime meltdown to the decline in housing prices that began at the end of 2006 rather than to a lowering of lending standards.

10 Interestingly, Lucas had been an analyst at Moody's and claims to have invented the diversity score in the late 1980s.

11 Still, in the last week of August 2007, Moody's assigned Aaa grades for at least $12.7 billion of new CDOs, which would be downgraded within six months.

12 The source material for AIG is Lewis (2009).

13 In 2003, the volume of subprime mortgages was less than $100 billion. Between June 2004 and June 2007, the volume of subprime loans increased to $1.6 trillion and Alt-A loans (limited-documentation loans) increased to $1.2 trillion.

14 When AIG collapsed, employees lost more than $500 million of their own money.

15 A video of the program is available at www.cnbc.com/id/28892719.

16 The purpose of the net capital rule is not to limit overall leverage at financial institutions, so the rule did not impose leverage restrictions on parent holding companies. The rule's purpose was to provide protection of such assets as consumer receivables in case of liquidation by a broker/dealer. Indeed, leverage ratios for the major investment banks during the late 1990s averaged 27, well above the maximum ratio associated with the net capital rule.

17 An audio file of the relevant portion of the SEC meeting is available at www.nytimes.com/2008/10/03/business/03sec.html. Transcripts of open meetings of the SEC can be accessed at www.sec.gov/news/openmeetings.shtml.

18 The audio contains information (especially about what the laughter signifies) that does not come across in the written transcript. In the first instance, the laughter comes as a response to the contrast between Goldschmid's remark about trusting staff and his question, including tone of voice, about the staff being capable of performing the task. The second instance of laughter comes in response to Mike's humorous statement that he will not be doing the task alone. Notably, he is serious when he describes the resources he envisages being allocated to the task. In my view, the group laughter in the second instance does not reflect doubt that the SEC staff was capable of performing the task or doubt that the resources described were woefully inadequate.

19 The SEC's internal report rejects the possibility that political influence played a part in the SEC's failure to detect the Madoff fraud. Rather, it focuses the blame squarely on the judgment calls of agency investigators and staff.

20 The person Nocera quoted is John A. Sten, a former SEC lawyer who represented a former Morgan Stanley broker whom the SEC prosecuted unsuccessfully for almost a decade.

21 Under Greenspan, in the recession that followed the bursting of the dot-com bubble, the Federal Reserve cut interest rates to 1 percent. Some have criticized the Fed for keeping interest rates too low for too long, thereby encouraging the dramatic increase in mortgage volume. See http://www.federalreserve.gov/BOARDDOCS/TESTIMONY/2005/200506092/default.htm

22 The speech was given at the Federal Reserve Bank of Chicago's 43rd Annual Conference on Bank Structure and Competition held in Chicago. See http://www.federalreserve.gov/newsevents/speech/bernanke20070517a.htm

23 Only a thumbnail sketch of the approach can be provided here; for the detailed approach, see Shefrin (2008b).

References

Akerlof, George, and Robert Shiller. 2009. *Animal Spirits: How Human Psychology Drives the Economy, and Why It Matters for Global Capitalism*. Princeton, NJ: Princeton University Press.

Berman, David. 2009. "In Defence of a 'Sell' Analyst." *Globe and Mail* (10 April): http://pulse.alacra.com/analyst-comments/Portales_Partners-F594.

Bhardwaj, Geetesh, and Rajdeep Sengupta. 2008a. "Where's the Smoking Gun? A Study of Underwriting Standards for US Subprime Mortgages." Federal Reserve Bank of St. Louis, Working Paper 2008–036B.

Bhardwaj, Geetesh, and Rajdeep Sengupta. 2008b. "Did Prepayments Sustain the Subprime Market?" Federal Reserve Bank of St. Louis, Working Paper 2008–039B.

Brown, Ken, and David Enrich. 2008. "Rubin, under Fire, Defends His Role at Citi – 'Nobody Was Prepared' for Crisis of '08." *Wall Street Journal* (29 November): http://online.wsj.com/article/SB122791795940965645.html.

Chomsisengphet, Souphala, and Anthony Pennington-Cross. 2006. "The Evolution of the Subprime Mortgage Market." *Federal Reserve Bank of St. Louis Review*, vol. 88, no. 1 (January/February):31–56.

Coffee, John C., Jr. 2008. "Analyzing the Credit Crisis: Was the SEC Missing in Action?" *New York Law Journal* (5 December): www.law.com/jsp/ihc/PubArticleIHC.jsp?id=1202426495544.

Eggert, Kurt. 2009. "The Great Collapse: How Securitization Caused the Subprime Meltdown." *Connecticut Law Review*, vol. 41, no. 4 (May):1257–1312.

El-Erian, Mohamed. 2008. *When Markets Collide: Investment Strategies for the Age of Global Economic Change*. New York: McGraw-Hill.

Felsenthal, Mark. "Moment of Crisis Could Test Fed's Independence." Reuters (23 October 2008): www.reuters.com/article/companyNewsAndPR/idUSN2338704220081023.

Griffin, John and Dragon Yongjun Tang, 2009. "Did Subjectivity Play a Role in CDO Credit Ratings?" Working paper, the University of Texas at Austin.

Heath, Chip, Richard P. Larrick, and Joshua Klayman. 1998. "Cognitive Repairs: How Organizational Practices Can Compensate for Individual Shortcomings." *Research in Organizational Behavior*, vol. 20:1–37.

Kahneman, Daniel, and Amos Tversky. 1979. "Prospect Theory: An Analysis of Decision Making under Risk." *Econometrica*, vol. 47, no. 2 (March):263–291.

Labaton, Stephen. 2008. "The Reckoning: Agency's '04 Rule Let Banks Pile Up New Debt." *New York Times* (2 October): www.nytimes.com/2008/10/03/business/03sec.html.

Lewis, Michael. 2009. "The Man Who Crashed the World." *Vanity Fair* (August):98–103.

Lopes, Lola. 1987. "Between Hope and Fear: The Psychology of Risk." *Advances in Experimental Social Psychology*, vol. 20:255–295.

Lucchetti, Aaron. 2008a, "McGraw Scion Grapples With S&P's Woes – Chairman Helped Set Tone in Profit Push as Ratings Firms Feasted on New Products." *Wall Street Journal* (2 August).

Lucchetti, Aaron. 2008b. "S&P Email: 'We Should Not Be Rating It'." *Wall Street Journal* (2 August):B1.

Nocera, Joe. 2009. "Chasing Small Fry, S.E.C. Let Madoff Get Away." *New York Times* (26 June): www.nytimes.com/2009/06/27/business/27nocera.html.

Piskorski, Tomasz, Amit Seru, and Vikrant Vig. 2009. "Securitization and Distressed Loan Renegotiation: Evidence from the Subprime Mortgage Crisis." Working paper, Columbia University.

Posner, Richard A. 2009a. *A Failure of Capitalism: The Crisis of '08 and the Descent into Depression*. Cambridge, MA: Harvard University Press.

Posner, Richard A. 2009b. "Shorting Reason." *New Republic* vol. 240, no. 6 (15 April):30–33.

President's Working Group on Financial Markets. 2008. (March): www.ustreas.gov/press/releases/reports/pwgpolicystatemktturmoil_03122008.pdf.

SEC. 2004. Audio Transcript of Meeting Minutes, Item 3. Securities and Exchange Commission (28 April): www.nytimes.com/2008/10/03/business/03sec.html.

SEC. 2009. Office of Investigations. "Investigation of Failure of the SEC to Uncover Bernard Madoff's Ponzi Scheme: Public Version," Report No. OIG-509, Securities and Exchange Commission (31 August).

Shefrin, Hersh. 2005. *Behavioral Corporate Finance*. Burr Ridge, IL: McGraw-Hill/Irwin.

Shefrin, Hersh. 2008a. *A Behavioral Approach to Asset Pricing*: Boston: Elsevier.

Shefrin, Hersh. 2008b. *Ending the Management Illusion*. New York: McGraw-Hill.

Shefrin, Hersh. 2009. "Ending the Management Illusion: Preventing Another Financial Crisis." *Ivey Business Journal*, vol. 73, no. 1 (January/February).

Shefrin, Hersh, and Meir Statman. 1985. "The Disposition to Sell Winners Too Early and Ride Losers Too Long: Theory and Evidence." *Journal of Finance*, vol. 40, no. 3 (July):777–790.

Sirri, Erik. 2009. "Securities Markets and Regulatory Reform." Speech given at the National Economists Club, Washington, DC (9 April).

Smith, Elliot Blair. 2008. "'Race to Bottom' at Moody's, S&P Secured Subprime's Boom, Bust." *Bloomberg* (25 September): http://www.bloomberg.com/apps/news?pid=20601109&sid=ax3vfya_Vtdo.

Sullivan, Rodney. 2009. "Governance: Travel and Destinations." *Financial Analysts Journal*, vol. 65, no. 4 (July/August):6–10.

Tversky, Amos, and Daniel Kahneman. 1986. "Rational Choice and the Framing of Decisions." *Journal of Business*, vol. 59, no. 4 (October):251–278.

UBS. 2008. "Shareholder Report on UBS Writedowns." Accessed at www.ubs.com/1/ShowMedia/investors/agm?contentId=140333&name=080418ShareholderReport.pdf on July 16, 2008.

16

Risk as feeling in risk taking and risk management in organizations

Laurel C. Austin

Abstract

When faced with a risk that threatens something they value, peoples' risk perceptions and assessments of the risk's acceptability are typically influenced first by *affective* reactions (*risk as feelings*). These reactions may be followed by considered application of logic and reasoning to the situation (*risk as analysis*), but this subsequent consideration may follow a path biased in favour of confirmation of affectively formed hypotheses. Such reactions are important within the context of organizational decision making and risk management because they may cause managers and employees to act in ways inconsistent with organizational effectiveness. In this chapter, I discuss how such biased decision processes unfold, two categories of harm that can result, and, especially, how an organization's definitions of risk influence the process. I examine, in particular, how organizations sometimes convey definitions of risk and values relevant to risk management through formal systems, e.g., performance management systems, often without intending to or even realizing it; and also how such definitions and messages may interact with employees' and managers' affective reactions to risk. In organizational settings, people may *over*-perceive or *over*-react to risk, causing misallocation of limited resources, or they may *under*-estimate or *under*-react to risk, which can lead to disaster. I argue that risks defined, valued, and communicated about, and thus socially amplified by formal systems, are more likely to be perceived and assessed as unacceptable and worthy of attention. Risks not defined or communicated about are seemingly not valued and thus socially attenuated by formal systems, are more likely to not be perceived at all, or to be assessed as acceptable and ignored. Managers who take the time to consider these broad effects on risk management will be better equipped to help their organizations get risk management more right more often.

Individuals' perceptions of risk, and also their assessments of its acceptability, affect how they behave in risk situations. This is, of course, entirely reasonable. But, it applies as well to *mis*perceptions and *mistaken* assessments.[1] When the individuals in question are managers and employees in an organization, inclinations toward misperception or mistaken assessment can be determinants of how well the organization functions as it pursues its objectives. In general, we can characterize misperceptions and mistaken assessments as happening in two directions, each presenting different perils to an organization's ability to function.

First, people may *over*-perceive or *over*-react to risks, thereby causing an organization to misallocate limited resources away from real concerns or opportunities. For example, during a time of immense budget shortfalls following the 2008 financial crisis, the University of California at San Diego (UCSD) invested large sums of money in renovations to its Literature Building to address employee worries about health risks, even though studies found the worries to be unfounded. Despite strong evidence to the contrary, beliefs that the work environment contained health hazards persisted and forced the university to act (Austin, 2015a, 2015b; UCSD, 2009).[2]

Situations in which risk is over-estimated, or in which people over-react to a possible risk, are hard to detect as such, either at the time they are perceived or after the fact. Those who want to take action, or do take action, believe they are mitigating or avoiding *real* problems. And unless risk mitigation efforts lead to other observable problems, the fact that feared outcomes never materialize is usually taken as evidence that mitigation actions were successful – whether or not those actions were actually ever needed at all (which often cannot be known). At a societal level, some authors (e.g., Gawande, 1999) have argued that the vast majority of concerns about some risks – cancer clusters, for example, such as those that drove the situation at UCSD – are misplaced and cause misallocation of societal resources on a grand scale.

An analogy to medicine helps highlight just how high the stakes might be in instances of over-estimation or over-reaction. In medicine, diagnosing and treating a problem that does not exist, or that would never progress enough to cause symptomatic problems, is referred to as *over-diagnosis* and *over-treatment*. These problems relate especially to early disease screening and preventive treatment (Austin, Reventlow, Sandøe, & Brodersen, 2013; Moynihan, Doust, & Henry, 2012). Sometimes early-stage disease that has only a very small probability of progressing enough to ever cause harm is, nevertheless, diagnosed and treated. When this happens, most people who are treated receive no benefit (because they would not have experienced harm from the disease without treatment), but may suffer diagnosis and treatment harms, such as discomfort, being labelled as ill and forgoing activities restricted to those who are well, reduced quality of life from unneeded surgery, risk from subsequent complications of treatment, and so forth.[3] These consequences of over-diagnosis and over-treatment are experienced by individuals, but there are also, of course, societal costs. Medical researchers look at long-term aggregate data, summarized across many individuals and over time, to determine the societal value of preventive practices in net benefit and harm terms (see e.g., Brodersen, Jørgensen, & Gøtzsche, 2010). Over-treatment of large numbers of people increases the possibility that at the aggregate level treatment harm outweighs benefit, meaning treatment funds have been allocated inefficiently (i.e., there were better uses for the money). Unfortunately, aggregate data is generally not available for organizational risk management efforts, but potential costs to organizations of over-diagnosis and over-treatment are no less real just because they are harder to detect.

The second category of peril for managers, which is more widely recognized and addressed in organizational risk management research and practice, arises when risk is *under*-estimated, or judged 'acceptable' when it should be judged 'not acceptable.' In these cases, people take risks they otherwise, on the basis of better estimates or judgments, would not take. Or, they fail to engage in preventive or risk mitigation behaviours that they otherwise would. When people in organizations take risks and fail to take appropriate preventive or risk mitigation actions, losses may be incurred by individuals or the organization. When compounded across many individuals and over time, failure to adequately perceive, properly assess, and appropriately react to possible risk increases the likelihood that events will spiral into large-scale problems, even outright disaster. Returning to the medical analogy, problems that are not diagnosed and not treated are said to be *under-diagnosed* and *under-treated*, which represents a high-stakes failure to take beneficial action that was readily available.

When large-scale disasters happen in organizational settings, subsequent investigation often examine contextual and behavioural factors to understand the most fundamental causes of the problem. This is important so that the organization in question, and other similar organizations, can learn from the events. Some disasters are found to have been due to technical error, such as the explosion on Apollo 13 (Cortright et al., 1970). Some are attributed to errors by one or a few individuals (Shappell et al., 2007). Others are attributed to poor managerial decision making and risk management processes that lead to systemic under-diagnosis or under-treatment of risk in the organization. For example: "Better management by BP, Halliburton, and Transocean would almost certainly have prevented the [oil platform] blowout by improving the ability of individuals involved to identify the risks they faced, and to properly evaluate, communicate, and address them" (National Commission on the BP Deepwater Horizon Oil Spill and Offshore Drilling, 2011). Regarding the Fukushima Daiichi Nuclear Power Plant disaster: "The accident was clearly 'manmade.' We believe that the root causes were the organizational and regulatory systems that supported faulty rationales for decisions and actions, rather than issues relating to the competency of any specific individual" (Kurokawa et al., 2012, p. 16). And,

> The [financial] crisis was the result of human action and inaction, not of Mother Nature or computer models gone haywire. The captains of finance and the public stewards of our financial system ignored warnings and failed to question, understand, and manage evolving risks within a system essential to the well-being of the American public.
>
> *(Financial Crisis Inquiry Commission, 2011)*

Just as there are high stakes trade-offs between under-diagnosis/under-treatment or over-diagnosis/over-treatment in medicine, there are similar trade-offs in organizational risk management. There is the potential in organizations to over-estimate risk (over-diagnose), or over-react and introduce preventive activities that are not really needed (over-treat). This may result in diverting limited resources away for more pressing concerns or opportunities. If an organization suffers routinely from under-estimation of risk (under-diagnosis), too much acceptance of risk, or too little risk mitigation effort (under-treatment), the resulting behaviours can compound over time and across individuals, possibly leading to more spectacular and obvious problems than those associated with organizational over-treatment of risk. This greater potential for spectacular (negative) outcomes suggests to many that organizations need to be more concerned about systematic under-treatment of risk than about systematic over-treatment. Both directions, however, can be sources of significant problems, as an organization that too often misallocates its resources may eventually find its objectives threatened as well.

Thankfully, most failures to accurately perceive, assess, and behave appropriately with respect to risks in organizations do not lead to disasters. However, systematic mismanagement of risk, in whichever direction, generally causes harm eventually. Small organizations have less ability to absorb the costs and harms of poor risk management than large organizations like BP, Tokyo Electric Power Company, or large US banks. Clearly, it is important for all organizations, large and small, to get risk perceptions, assessment, and risk management as 'right' as possible throughout the organization.

Given all this, here are three broad questions that we might take as a starting point for balancing trade-offs between being overly cautious and not cautious enough in managing risk in organizations:

- What affects how people perceive risks around them in organizations?
- What affects how people in organizations judge risk acceptability?
- What can we do to improve people's ability to appropriately perceive and assess risk, and therefore their risk taking and risk management behaviours in organizational contexts?

In this chapter, I discuss some of the common ways our intuitive, automatic thinking systematically affects how we perceive risk in organizations. My focus will be on some ways people are inclined to selectively think about information in ways that lead to biased risk perceptions or faulty conclusions, especially those related to affective responses – perceptions of risk that manifest in *feelings*. I'll discuss factors that affect how people judge acceptability of a risk, including how organizational risk definitions, values, and pay-for-performance systems can impact risk perceptions and behaviours. Finally, I will discuss some things managers and leaders in organizations can do to try to improve the balance between over- and under-diagnosis and treatment of risk in organizations.

What kinds of factors affect risk perceptions?

'Risk' can be defined in many ways. In this chapter, I adopt Fischhoff and Kadvany's definition: a risk is something that threatens things people value (Fischhoff & Kadvany, 2011). When people perceive risk, which is to say a threat, they tend to experience automatic reactions that are largely *affective* (*risk as feelings*); they may or may not also apply logic and reasoning to the situation (*risk as analysis*) (Loewenstein, Weber, Hsee, & Welch, 2001; Slovic, Finucane, Peters, & MacGregor, 2004). Automatic, unconscious thinking processes have been referred to as *System 1 thinking* or *experiential thinking*, while deliberate, analytic thinking is referred to as *System 2 thinking* or *analytic thinking* (Slovic et al., 2004; Stanovich, 1999). System 1 thinking involves unconscious application of *heuristics*, or rules-of-thumb, that facilitate fast decision making (Kahneman, 2011). System 1 thinking is not bad in and of itself, and often serves us well, especially when decisions are of small consequence; after all, we cannot deliberate over every decision. At other times, however, biased risk perceptions and decision making based solely in System 1 thinking can lead us to wrong conclusions and bad decisions in situations that really matter to us or others.

Research shows that when we perceive a situation that presents risk, we typically have automatic, intuitive, System 1 reactions to elements within the situation. We might immediately feel, for example, that "I like option A," or "I don't like option B." Or we might feel that "this explanation of what is happening is most likely," or that "I don't want to think that is happening." At times our immediate response is even more emotional: "this situation scares me" or "that makes me angry." Such strong emotions have been shown to affect risk perceptions; for example, fear amplifies perceived risk and anger reduces it (Slovic & Peters, 2006).

When we form an intuitive hypothesis about what is happening, or about what the best course of action might be, via System 1 thinking, our brains are wired to search for evidence that confirms those beliefs. Accordingly, we tend to ignore disconfirming evidence, and we may even interpret what would otherwise seem to be disconfirming evidence as confirmation of what we already believe. This kind of biased thinking is called the confirmation heuristic, or 'confirmation trap' (see Bazerman & Moore, 2013, pp. 46–57). Put simply, we become trapped by early hunches and impressions and by our natural tendency (often unconscious) to seek and perceive additional information that confirms those early conclusions or suspicions. Options we intuitively/affectively like, we perceive to be less risky, with more benefits and fewer costs or harms; options we don't like, we perceive to be more risky, with fewer benefits and with more costs or harms (Alhakami & Slovic, 1994; Zajonc, 1980). What this all means is that the perceptions and assessments of risk that result when emotional, System 1 thinking starts us down a particular path are likely to be biased relative to what we might have concluded if we had taken the time to search for additional information and hypotheses and engaged in unemotional analysis.

How we intuitively perceive and process information from the world around us can lead to other biases in risk perceptions. Consider a person who judges a risk situation and decides to engage in a behaviour that presents a small probability of something bad happening – for example an injury. Someone who, say, decides to press down on the gas and continue through the yellow light. Since the probability of injury is small, in all likelihood she will avoid being injured. From that experience, she 'learns' she can successfully engage in this behaviour. The more she repeats the behaviour and is not harmed, the lower she assesses the probability of injury to be (Barron & Erev, 2003). She is likely to observe that some others who engage in the behaviour are injured (because the probability that some person who engages in the behaviour will be injured is much higher than the probability that any particular individual will be injured). But research shows that people generally tend to consider themselves to be less likely than others to experience bad outcomes; this is known as an *optimism bias* (Weinstein & Klein, 1996). Similarly, we tend to feel we are better able than others of similar ability to control a risk situation; that is, we maintain an unrealistic *illusion of control* (Langer, 1975).

Another human tendency that has a potential basis in affect and can bias risk perceptions in organizations is our tendency to focus on 'events of interest,' while ignoring instances when the event does not occur. Focusing on a subset of data because it has some salient characteristic is called focalism (Bazerman & Moore, 2013). This kind of thinking has several problems. First, a data set that has been selected based on having some salient characteristic is inherently biased (because every observation has that characteristic) and incomplete (because data without the characteristic is ignored). Often, however, we try to use that biased, incomplete dataset to understand how two things are related, in order to understand what is causing something we are concerned about. The problem with this is that understanding the relationship between two variables requires observations of how each of the variables change. If we watch one thing change while another factor stays the same, we haven't learned very much about their relationship, because we have not seen what happens when the second variable changes. But that doesn't keep us from thinking that we understand more than we do. Furthermore, a presumed relationship between two variables, even if it is not arrived at erroneously, may not imply causation, although we often act as though it does.[4]

Focalism was found to be a factor in the decision making that led to the fatal launch of the space shuttle Challenger in 1986 (Vaughan, 1997). The night before the launch, contractor engineers who were responsible for the solid rocket booster were concerned that an O-ring would not perform adequately in the cold temperatures predicted for launch the next day. They provided NASA with a graph of temperature versus 'number of incidents,' but for only the seven launches in which there had been problems associated with the O-rings. No relationship between temperature and number of incidents could be seen on this graph. Subsequent investigation into the explosion considered all previous launches, including the 17 that had experienced no incidents. With the data set complete, a relationship became visible: launches at lower temperatures were more likely to have problems; only 1 of 10 launches above 70 degrees Fahrenheit had a problem, versus 6 of the 14 launches at temperatures of 70 degrees or less. Had the engineers not focused on only the launches that had experienced problems, their intuitive understanding would have been more visible in the graphs they constructed.

The 'Texas Sharpshooter Fallacy' provides an illustration of the problem with focalism (Gawande, 1999). According to this fallacy, a Texan wanting to lay claim to being a sharpshooter aims at the side of a barn and fires several bullets into its side in rapid succession. He then puts down his gun, takes up a can of paint, and proceeds to draw a bulls-eye target around the just created cluster of bullet holes. Later, he points to the cluster of bullet holes at the centre of the target as evidence of his ability to shoot accurately. In this story, the focus is on events that share a given characteristic defined by place.

The tendency in our thinking to focus on a subset of events that shares some salient characteristic is so strong that even highly trained experts can succumb to this bias. For example, the epidemiologist at UCSD who conducted the first study in response to employee concerns about health risks from the building noted that there had been nine breast cancer cases since 1991, but chose to focus his analysis investigation on the eight breast cancer cases between 2000 and 2006. In essence, he drew a target around a cluster of cases that already existed (though in an interval of time, rather than on the side of a barn). Because he did this, the rate of breast cancer appeared higher than it was, leading him to conclude there *was* a cancer cluster, thereby fuelling employee concerns (Austin, 2015a). A second investigation considered the longer time frame (there was no valid reason to ignore years when there were mostly no cases) and found the rate to be closer to that in the general population, although still somewhat higher than average (Kheifets & Sudan, 2009; it is, of course, quite normal that some outcomes will be higher than the average outcome, due purely to chance effects). Those authors noted that what had been done in the first study is a common problem when investigating cancer clusters. Such errors are often a result of System 1 thinking that leads people, even experts, to unconsciously focus on elements of a situation that have characteristics we can easily perceive and emotionally associate with a problem or opportunity of interest.[5]

What affects how people in organizations judge risk acceptability?

Whether a person assesses a risk as acceptable or not will also influence her or his behaviours with respect to that risk. Risks found to be acceptable are likely to be tolerated and ignored, or perhaps monitored. Risks found to be unacceptable are more likely to be met with preventive or risk mitigation efforts, contingent upon resource and other constraints. Employees and students at UCSD who perceived an unacceptable breast cancer risk in the Literature Building reacted by holding a protest, refusing to hold courses and meetings in the building, and demanding that the university replace the elevator that they believed caused electromagnetic surges that caused breast cancer (Austin 2015a). These were the methods they used in attempts to mitigate the perceived unacceptable risk.

One individual level factor that affects the assessment of whether a risk is acceptable is the decision maker's values. For example, Slimak and Dietz (2006) had people rank a number of environmental risks and found that rankings were correlated with personal values, spiritual beliefs, and worldviews. Peoples' personal values and worldviews are shaped the culture they are immersed in, because within that culture will be shared narratives and understanding of what does or does not constitute a problem that deserves attention, or shared narratives and understanding of the trade-offs between risks, and so forth. These culturally shared belief systems impact individuals' interpretations of risk situations and their reactions to those situations (Dake, 1992).

It is important, then, to organizational risk managers, to understand that the communications and culture that create shared beliefs and values within an organization do influence how individuals in the organization interpret and react to risk. Research on the 'social amplification of risk' and 'social attenuation of risk' finds that the social and cultural contexts in which people operate significantly affect how a risk situation is perceived, assessments of risk acceptability, and beliefs about which behaviours are appropriate in which situations (Kasperson, Kasperson, Pidgeon, & Slovic, 2003; Kasperson et al., 1988). Communication plays a central role in establishing a shared culture and understanding of how to interpret, assess, and react to risk. This means that organizational culture and communication can cause specific risks, or risks generally, to become amplified (perceived as larger, less acceptable, more in need of mitigation) or attenuated (seen as smaller, more acceptable, something that can be tolerated). Socially amplified risks will receive attention; socially attenuated risks will not.

Another factor that influences individuals' values in organizations is how the organization *defines* risk. Fischhoff and Kadvany (2011) suggest that how risk is defined conveys, and perhaps even specifies, what is valued by those who have defined it. This has implications that may not be obvious. It is useful to look at alternative definitions of a given risk to see how different values are conveyed by different definitions.

Public health authorities who want to develop policies to preserve life might define risk as 'death' and then look at the major causes of death to determine where to focus preventive health efforts. Developed countries would place high value on preventing cancer and heart disease; accidental injury, which causes fewer deaths, is unlikely to be a major focus. If the same authorities define the risk as 'potential years of life lost,' then accidental injury comes more into focus. For example, auto and other injury accounted for only about 15% of lives lost in 1974 in Canada, but accounted for about 30% of years of life lost because of the disproportionate number of young deaths (Romeder & McWhinnie, 1977). If risk is defined as quality years-of-life lost (discounting the value of life after some age when quality of life tends to be low) or as economically productive years-of-life lost (e.g., by not counting years after some age), then deaths to younger people would again be weighted more heavily, and accidental injury would likely be prioritized even higher. Each of these risk definitions conveys different values and will differentially affect where efforts are focused, how money will be invested or spent, and what kinds of policies or interventions will be developed.

These examples make it easy to see that risk definitions are inherently value-laden, so we can imagine the kind of debates that might ensue when deciding which basis for a definition to choose. Is the life of someone young really worth more than that of someone older? Can we really measure someone else's quality of life? At what age are most people nonproductive? It seems likely that when we define risk by first thinking hard about what we value, then the risk definition and our values have the best chance of being closely aligned. But sometimes we might define a risk because we always have defined it that way, or because we don't give it a lot of thought and define risk in a way that seems superficially obvious, or in a way that comes first or most easily to mind. When we do that, we may not realize the values that are conveyed with a given definition, and we may not consider how those values will be understood and adopted by others, affecting their choices, behaviours, and resulting outcomes.

One way that organizations, whether consciously or not, define risk and socially amplify specific risks is through their development and use of performance measurement systems. Many organizations implement performance metrics or pay-for-performance systems as a way to measure and reward performance believed to improve organizational outcomes. Few statements elicit more agreement from managers than the classic "you can't manage what you can't measure."

When an organization rewards achievement based on performance as determined by known metrics, employees internalize a desire to excel on those dimensions. Often incentives (e.g., bonuses) are offered to managers, who then establish lower-level metrics and goals throughout the organization. It has long been realized that management implemented in this manner can lead to dysfunctional behaviours that cause more harm than good to the organization (see, e.g., Austin, 1996; Kerr, 1975; Ridgway, 1956). Using game-theoretic models, Austin (1996) shows that in conditions where some but not *all* performance dimensions are measured (which will generally be the case), behaviours are likely to give the appearance of improving performance up until the moment when these appearances can no longer be maintained and performance is discovered to have declined sharply (Holmstrom & Milgrom, 1991, develop a similar but narrower claim). This happens because employees expend more effort toward measured objectives, which are rewarded, by diverting effort from activities that enhance objectives but are not measured or rewarded.

An early example in the research literature was reported by Blau (1963), who found that when employment agency employees were rewarded for the number of job seekers interviewed, they interviewed many job seekers. However, they did not expend effort on placing those job seekers into jobs (they were not rewarded for doing so). Eventually, it became obvious service quality had decreased, even though performance had improved according to the chosen performance metric. The agency then tried a variety of things (e.g., adding various additional measures). But no matter what they did, employees found ways to game the system and achieve rewards, without improving overall service quality. Similar problems commonly afflict organizational efforts across a range of business and governmental contexts (see Austin, 1996, for many more examples).

When managers design and implement performance measurement systems, they may not sufficiently appreciate that they are also implicitly conveying organizational values and information about how an organization defines risks to employees. In simplest terms, performance management systems convey to employees what managers consider more important and less important. In the process, these systems socially amplify some risks (those that are reflected in the measurement system in some way, and which are associated with rewards or penalties), and attenuate others (those that do not find their way into the measurement system, possibly because they are difficult to measure, or because they have not been thought of). There is no necessary relationship between what is most important to an organization, in determining appropriate risk trade-offs, and what is measurable.

This fact becomes even more important if we take into account research findings that suggest that extrinsic motivators, like pay-for-performance systems, crowd out intrinsic motivators, like the worries of an individual close to a potentially hazardous situation. Extrinsic motivators remove the 'locus of control' of organizational action from an internal position within the responsibilities of individual workers and move it to an external position within a system of organizational incentives. They substitute organizational values for individual values and direct attention and authority to the former. The more closely rewards and performance measures are related, the more intrinsic motivations are crowded out (Austin, 1996; Osterloch & Frey, 2002).

When organizational values conveyed by managers are accepted by employees, System 1 thinking will lead to positive feelings about choices consistent with organizational values and negative feelings about choices inconsistent with those values. Put simply, employees like to please their supervisors by taking actions that demonstrate alignment with the values formally defined within systems of performance. This System 1 thinking can, however, lead to the cascade of initial hypothesis formation followed by a search for confirming evidence that I discussed earlier. System 2 thinking, if it kicks in, will likely take into account the fact that the formal performance systems explicitly associate rewards with certain choices, possibly reinforcing the System 1 cascade of actions. That is, even if an employee engaged in System 1 analysis has a vague sense that a choice doesn't make sense from a risk trade-off standpoint, the fact that the choice seems consistent with rewards from a performance system might cause the employee to set aside such concerns and give in to System 1 temptations.

Finally, research shows that peoples' determinations of whether a risk is acceptable can be predicted by fairly simple measures of whether the risk is 'dreaded' and by whether it is perceived to be 'unknown' (Fischhoff, Slovic, Lichtenstein, Read, & Combs, 1978). The dreaded dimension seems to reflect risk as feeling, while the unknown dimension seems to reflect risk as analysis. Dreaded risks are perceived to have fatal or catastrophic consequences and are perceived as out of the decision maker's control; nondreaded risks affect one or few people and tend to be voluntary. Whether a risk is unknown depends on how well the decision maker feels it is understood by experts and/or by the decision maker himself. Observable risks and risks with immediate consequences are more known, unobservable risks or those with consequences in the distant future are less known. Fischhoff, Nadaï, and Fischhoff (2001) looked at technologies ranging from bicycles to nuclear power. 'Dreaded' and 'unknown' technologies were least acceptable, while those 'not dreaded' and 'known' were most acceptable. Thus, risks that are perceived to be known by experts and self, voluntary, controllable, and with immediate and noncatastrophic outcomes are most acceptable; skiing fell into this category. Those judged to be not known, imposed by others, out of personal control, with future, possibly catastrophic consequences were least acceptable, including nuclear power and pesticides. Later research showed that technologies that fell into the least acceptable category were the ones most likely to be boycotted by consumers or local communities (Fischhoff, Nadaï, & Fischhoff, 2001).

Given all of this, the following is suggested: when organizations define, communicate, and establish policies about the risks they care about, including performance measurement and reward policies, this becomes an important part of the organizational culture that includes a shared understanding of what is valued. Managers or other employees who internalize those values and encounter a decision situation where one alternative is associated with what is valued, while the other option is not, will intuitively, unconsciously, automatically prefer the first. If they search for additional information, unconsciously they will selectively perceive information that confirms that the first alternative is the best, and they will tend to perceive new information as confirming that the first option is better than the second. These automatic preferences and selective perceptions manifest because of their automated System 1 thinking.

Consider an organization that has defined risk primarily in terms of minimizing maintenance costs, offering financial incentives to employees for reducing them. In other words, the organization wants to reduce maintenance costs which threaten organizational finances, and implements this via impacts on employee salaries, seemingly aligning individual desires for higher salaries with managers' desires for lower costs. Consequently, maintenance cost reductions become highly valued. Imagine a manager faced with a situation where he or she can have employees either (1) perform routine maintenance that will increase maintenance costs and may make equipment safer, or (2) not do the maintenance and so accrue no maintenance costs *and* no improvement to equipment safety. If the value within the edict 'reduce maintenance costs' has been internalized, and there is no equally compelling, offsetting value related to maximizing equipment safety, the manager is likely to have an immediate System 1 preference for the no-maintenance option. Henceforth, the manager is likely to perceive information that confirms this is the best choice, and ignore or not even perceive disconfirming information. Further, he or she is likely to be cognizant of the benefits of not doing the maintenance (good for performance measures and valued by company), and of the harms of doing it (higher maintenance costs; against company values; bad for performance measures). The manager might then simply act on these beliefs and instruct employees not to do the maintenance. If he or she takes time to analytically think through whether or not to do the maintenance, his or her perceptions will have been started down a biased path in a manner that may influence the analysis toward a conclusion not to.

Of course, that System 2, risk-as-analysis thinking could lead to a conclusion to do the maintenance, even given the initial negative response toward that option. The important point here is that it takes extra cognitive effort and extra convincing evidence to overcome early, inappropriate conclusions that our risk-as-feelings, System 1 thinking has led us to. It easier to achieve good risk management practices in an organization if people have automatic intuitive preferences for the 'correct' risk taking and risk management behaviours in the first instant. But this would only happen reliably if there were an offsetting statement of values, related to safety, also expressed within formal risk definitions and performance systems.

Applying these ideas: British Petroleum Texas City oil refinery explosion

Let's consider these ideas with respect to the British Petroleum (BP) Texas City oil refinery explosion of March 23, 2005. The explosion caused 15 deaths, 180 injuries, and financial losses of over $1.5 billion. It occurred in a facility where there had been 23 work-related deaths in the preceding 30 years, although BP had only owned the facility since 1999 (US Chemical Safety Board, 2007). The director of the refinery had earlier commented to investigators investigating a previous incident: "Killing somebody every 18 months seems to be acceptable at this site . . . Why would people take the risk, based on the risk of not going home?" (Clark & Macalister, 2006).

We might surmise that as BP employees were repeatedly exposed to their risky work environment (by virtue of accepting a job and coming to work repeatedly), and that generally individuals did not personally experience bad outcomes (because they were low-probability events). They probably, however, observed or heard of others who were injured (because a few of the many others facing the same risks would experience low-probability outcomes). What we have learned from risk research is that we would expect them to unconsciously 'learn,' and go on to confirm, that they are able to successfully manage the risks and furthermore that they control the situation better than others. Through experience they will come to 'know' the risks they face. In voluntarily choosing to be in this setting, and with perceptions of mounting evidence that the low-probability risks are known and controllable, employees will increasingly find it the situation acceptable and thus be more likely to passively accept those risks.

Furthermore, willingness to passively accept risky situations will be even greater in organizations with a culture that tolerates a lot of risk taking or that conveys that preventive or risk management efforts are not valued. According to reports, such seems to have been the case at Texas City. Concerns about risk definitions, organizational values and organizational culture were highlighted by a Chemical Safety Board (CSB) investigation of the context and events that led up to the explosion:

> Simply targeting the mistakes of BP's operators and supervisors misses the underlying and significant cultural, human factors, and organizational causes of the disaster that have a greater preventative impact. . . . [T]he overall safety culture and process safety management program had serious deficiencies.
>
> *(US Chemical Safety Board 2007, p. 19)*[6]

> BP Texas City lacked a reporting and learning culture. Personnel were not encouraged to report safety problems and some feared retaliation for doing so. The lessons from incidents and near-misses, therefore, were generally not captured or acted upon.
>
> *(US Chemical Safety Board 2007, p. 26)*

The CSB was so concerned about BP's organizational culture that it issued an "urgent safety recommendation" that BP "convene an independent panel of experts to examine BP's corporate safety management systems, safety culture, and oversight of the North American refineries" (US Chemical Safety Board, 2007, p. 27). BP authorized such an investigation which found:

> BP has not provided effective process safety leadership and has not adequately established process safety as a core value across all its five U.S. refineries. While BP has an aspirational goal of "no accidents, no harm to people," BP has not provided effective leadership in making certain its management and U.S. refining workforce understand what is expected of them regarding process safety performance. BP has emphasized personal safety in recent years and has achieved significant improvement in personal safety performance, but BP did not emphasize process safety.
>
> *(Baker, Leveson, Bowman, & Priest, 2007, p. xii)*

In fact, BP went further than simply defining risk in terms of personal safety and forgetting or omitting to define risk also as process safety. The company instituted extrinsic monetary incentives through a pay-for-performance system that focused on reducing costs and, to a much smaller extent, personal safety measures:

> BP Group implemented an incentive program based on performance metrics, the Variable Pay Plan (VPP), which was in place at the Texas City refinery for several years prior to the ISOM incident. Payouts under the VPP were approved by the refining executive managers in London. "Cost leadership" categories accounted for 50 percent and safety metrics for 10 percent of the total bonus. For the 2003–2004 period, the single safety metric for the VPP bonus was the OSHA Recordable Injury Rate.
>
> *(US Chemical Safety Board, 2007, p. 153)*[7]

The measures defined by BP prioritized 'cost leadership' (i.e., reducing costs) conveying to management that operational costs were a threat to something of value (i.e., costs were a risk to be mitigated). Low costs were valued. Budget cuts over several years would have confirmed the perception that reducing costs was highly valued. And so it would not be surprising to find that managers at Texas City routinely did not perceive or did not act upon evidence of needed process safety maintenance and improvements. Of course, by cutting personnel and equipment maintenance, process safety, not measured or rewarded, was negatively impacted, leading to deteriorated process safety conditions which ultimately culminated in the explosion:

> BP Group and Texas City managers were working to make safety changes in the year prior to the ISOM incident, but the focus was largely on personal rather than process safety. As personal injury safety statistics improved, BP Group executives stated that they thought safety performance was headed in the right direction. At the same time, process safety performance continued to deteriorate at Texas City. This decline, combined with a legacy of safety and maintenance budget cuts from prior years, led to major problems with mechanical integrity, training, and safety leadership.
>
> *(US Chemical Safety Board, pp. 143–144)*

Here we clearly see the causes and results of dysfunction as predicted by Austin's treatment of performance measurement systems. BP measured safety via injury statistics, and had no measures of process safety. Management and employees focused their efforts on reducing injuries, while process safety, unmeasured and thus ignored, spiraled downward. The refinery had been improving on the safety measure, and in fact contractors on the day of the accident had over lunch celebrated a month with zero injuries. While the observed quality measure seemed to improve, real quality was declining drastically. The communication of values embedded in the performance systems led to a human tendency toward under-estimation of risk and unwarranted acceptance of risk.

Performance systems are intended to produce focus on certain dimensions of performance. In this case, those systems prompted a kind of focalism that resulted, ultimately, in disaster. Focus on some measures defined and valued by the organization led to observable 'improvements' in quality as measured by those indicators (cost and personal safety), while overall quality severely suffered. Implicit risk definitions established what was valued in the organization, and those played a role in shaping behaviour that was compounded over many people and over time, leading to the disaster. BP had defined safety risk in terms of personal safety risk when it should have defined it in terms of both personal and process safety risks. More than that, they prioritized cost risks over safety risks. With respect to safety, throughout the company efforts had been made to change things that minimized things like trips and falls by focusing on personal safety behaviours, consistent with the high value placed on personal safety. With respect to cost risks, budgets were cut by 25% in 1999 and again in 2004. Maintenance was ignored, and even simple, low-cost maintenance tasks such repairing leaky pipes did not take place (Clark & Macalister, 2006). Yet the performance measures showed that safety and costs risks, as defined and valued by BP, were improving. As those measures of risk improved, measures of process safety risk declined – process safety was not defined as a risk to be concerned about, was not measured, was therefore not valued, and the declines seemingly not noticed or ignored until something that could not go unnoticed happened.

What can organizations do to improve risk taking and risk management behaviours?

A central concern in managing risk in organizations is people's natural and well-developed tendency to learn in ways that lead them to confirm their initial hunches (confirmation bias), to be over-confident of their ability to control risks they routinely face (over-confidence bias), and to learn that they are better than others when facing those routine risks (invulnerability bias). To date, some organizations simply try to encourage awareness of over-confidence and confirmation biases; this is done in the security sector for training of intelligence analysts (Mandel, 2015). Kasperson and Kasperson (2005) argue that in organizations where technical risks are routinely faced on a daily basis (so a very different context than security intelligence risks), the need is for *organizations*, not *individuals*, to learn. Organizational learning requires gathering evidence at the aggregate level (across many people or groups over time), using that evidence to inform development of routines, training for use of the routines, and then continuing to gather data in order to understand whether there has been improvement.

For biases related to focalism, where people have a tendency to focus on a subset of available data or events when trying to discern associations between two or more variables, or to discern the probability of something happening, the problem is with people's intuitive statistical reasoning. There is ample evidence that people just are not very good at this, and as seen in the UCSD and NASA cases, this problem afflicts even technical experts. One solution would seem to be statistical reasoning training. With respect to overcoming focalism when interpreting data in the real world, a key goal in such education is to train people to reason, "if I want to understand the causes of this event (or problem or opportunity), I need to consider the times it has happened, as well as times it did not," and "I need to avoid drawing an inappropriate boundary around the information I do and do not consider." Organizations need to train people to be consciously aware that all data is relevant, not simply data with some salient characteristic. Some guidelines for statistical reasoning training include using real (or realistic) data; using graphics and other visual aids; using situated and workshop-based learning where projects simulate the context in which people will actually be working and where the learning takes place in settings that encourage trial-and-error; asking questions; and active participation (Bradstreet, 1996). Many people tend to be afraid of the word 'statistics,' so training in 'reasoning skills' might appear more accessible to a broad range of managers and employees.

It would seem wise, as well, for managers to recognize that the organizational systems that formally define performance, also implicitly define risk and thus influence risk trade-off behaviours. Austin (1996) and others (Osterloch & Frey, 2002) point to a role that can be played by facilitating intrinsic motivation, empowering employees to make their own judgments about whether the organization is achieving its objectives, rather than ceding control to an extrinsically based performance system. Austin suggests also emphasizing the informational, as opposed to motivational, uses of measurement information. Asking questions like "What does our performance measurement system say if we interpret it as a statement of our values?" might lead managers to an understanding of the need to make other, complementary statements in order to prompt better risk management trade-offs throughout an organization.

Increasingly, research suggests that risk as feeling drives a lot of behaviour (at all levels) in organizations (as well as in other settings). As we encounter a risk situation and perceive possible responses to it, our brains are well tuned to immediately assess which responses we like, and which we do not, and then our analytical brain is geared to confirm the preferences we already have. The choices we prefer intuitively and automatically are those that our brain unconsciously associates with outcomes we value. What people value is, to some extent (perhaps a large extent), malleable, dependent upon not only their personal values, world outlook, and spiritual beliefs, but also upon the culture in which they operate, including their work culture. Perhaps organizations need to put more thought into deriving risk definitions from carefully considered organizational values. Further, creating an organizational culture that amplifies those values-based risks should lead more people to be attentive to them, and to have intuitive, emotive reactions to them that lead to behaviours and risk management that is most in line with organizational goals. Organizations need to develop a culture and create risk definitions that instil values that are most likely to lead members of the organization to have immediate affective responses in risk situations that are consistent with the responses the organization would most like them to have.

Summing this all up

While we all like to think of ourselves as rational, considerable evidence suggests that we are often not deserving of this label. Our capacity to focus and get work done can be a blessing because it can make us efficient and effective. But it can also be a curse, because when focusing on something, our brains are very well adapted *not* to perceive other information in the world around us, meaning sometimes we miss important information that we will later regret having missed. Other common biases lead us to systematically over-estimate risk in some situations, causing us to misdirect limited resources toward unnecessarily mitigating those risks, and to under-estimate risk in other situations. When we under-estimate risk we feel unrealistically in control of our situation, and we are less likely to take appropriate preventive measures. In organizational settings, under-estimating and under-reacting to risk seems to many to be the greater evil, because when these problems are endemic, they can spiral into disaster for the organization, and maybe for other stakeholders as well.

All of this is made more complicated by the fact that risk perceptions have both an automatic, affective component (risk as feelings) that leads us to intuitively prefer one available option over others, as well as a more analytical component (risk as analysis) that allows us to deliberately consider and assess a risk situation. However, that deliberate thinking can itself be biased, unconsciously, toward confirming choices that we have already felt we prefer. Whether a risk is deemed acceptable (so not needing attention) or not acceptable (so needing attention), depends on a number of factors: how risk is defined, and thus what is valued; on whether the situation evokes feelings of dread; on how known the risk is. These factors are influenced by personal experience as well as by organizational culture. Risks defined, valued and communicated about by the organization, and thus socially amplified, are more likely to perceived and assessed as unacceptable and worthy of attention; those that are 'socially attenuated,' perhaps by not being defined or communicated about, are more likely to not be perceived at all, or to be analytically assessed as acceptable and ignored. Organizational pay-for-performance systems, by definition, amplify specific risks (those that are measured, as well as salary and status) and attenuate others (those not explicitly defined). Time and again, we see that such systems lead to dysfunctional behaviours, which when compounded over many people lead to trouble. However, we are not helpless in the face of these difficulties. Managers who take the time to consider how values, expressed in many ways, especially in formal systems, and who convey definitions and information about risk taking, will be better equipped to help their organizations get this more often right. As in most things, this is a matter of inclinations that manifest in probabilities in the end.

Notes

1   Throughout this chapter, when I use descriptors such as misperception, mistaken assessment, over-estimation and under-estimation, and over-reaction and under-reaction, I mean perceptions and assessments that differ significantly from normative estimates arrived at by the best scientific methods currently available, in which there is confidence according a well-established scientific consensus. It is possible, of course, that such a consensus might be contested. Indeed, there has been healthy debate about the appropriateness of efforts to separate allegedly reasonable analysis from irrational fear, and whether attempts to minimize the influence of "risk panics" (Sunstein, 2005) are antidemocratic (see, e.g., Kahan, Slovic, Braman, & Gastil, 2006). These debates fall well outside the scope of the current chapter, however. Since the issue at hand here is how risk management impacts organizational functioning, I adopt the assumption that in many situations commonly faced by managers the basis of consensus used to arrive at scientific estimates is not widely contested, and that there are valid normative estimates that would, if used, lead to practical outcomes more preferred by those making decisions.
2   A cancer cluster is defined as "a greater-than-expected number of cancer cases that occurs within a group of people in a geographic area over a period of time" (Centers for Disease Control and Prevention, available at http://www.cdc.gov/nceh/clusters/).
3   See for example, Johansson, Hansson, and Brodersen (2015) regarding over-diagnosis and over-treatment concerns regarding abdominal aortic aneurysm screening as an example of this in medicine.
4   For an easily understood discussion of this see Plous (1993). In a hypothetical example, shown in a two-by-two table (p. 162), 160 people have dizziness and a brain tumor; 40 have dizziness but no brain tumor; 40 have no dizziness and have brain tumor; and 10 have no dizziness and no brain tumor. Plous notes that many people report an association between the two factors because the 'present-present cell' has the largest number. However, careful consideration of the data shows that the ratio of tumor-present to tumor-absent is 4 to 1 whether dizziness is present or absent. Similarly, the ratio of dizziness present to dizziness absent is 4 to 1 whether a tumor is present or absent. In other words, there is absolutely no relationship, although many people perceive that there is. Plous concludes, "Decision makers should focus on more than the positive and confirming cases of a relationship. In judgments of contingency, what did *not* take place is often as significant as what did."
5   Research in several fields shows that the human brain is well developed to focus on what is perceived to be important, and to not perceive 'unneeded' information. (Simons & Chabris, 1999) conducted a now

well-known study of whether people would see a black gorilla walk through a basketball game when they were told to focus on players wearing white. Many do not see it. Perhaps similarly, the human brain is designed to automatically filter out light waves as needed in order to see color accurately in different lighting contexts (see Rogers, 2015, for a nontechnical discussion).

6 Process safety management refers to actions taken to prevent major accidents; personal safety management refers to actions taken to prevent worker occupational health and safety problems.

7 OSHA recordable injury rate at the time excluded fatalities. In 2004 the refinery had its lowest recordable injury rate ever, which was only one-third of the oil refinery sector average. There were three fatalities that year (US Chemical Safety Board, 2007, p. 306).

References

Acton, J.M., & Hibbs, M. (2012). *Why Fukushima was preventable*. The Carnegie Papers. Retrieved from http://carnegieendowment.org/files/fukushima.pdf

Alhakami, A.S., & Slovic, P. (1994). A psychological study of the inverse relationship between perceived risk and perceived benefit. *Risk Analysis, 14*, 1085–1096.

Austin, L.C. (2015a). *UCSD: A Cancer Cluster in the Literature Building?* (A Case). Cranfield, UK: Case Centre.

Austin, L.C. (2015b). *UCSD: A Cancer Cluster in the Literature Building?* (B Case). Cranfield, UK: Case Centre.

Austin, L.C., Reventlow, S., Sandøe, P., & Brodersen, J. (2013). The structure of medical decisions: Uncertainty, probability and risk in five common choice situations. *Health, Risk & Society, 15*(April), 37–41.

Austin, R.D. (1996). *Measuring and Managing Performance in Oorganizations*. New York: Dorset House.

Baker, J., Bowman, F.L., Erwin, G., Gorton, S., Hendershot, D., Leveson, N., . . . Wilson, L.D. (2007). *The Report of the BP US Refineries Independent Safety Review Panel*. Retrieved from http://scholar.google.com/scholar?hl=en&btnG=Search&q=intitle:The+report+of+the+BP+U.S.+Refineries+Independent+Safety+Review+Panel#0

Baker, J.A., Leveson, N., Bowman, F.L., Priest, S., Erwin, G., Rosenthal, I., et al. (2007). The report of the BP US refineries independent safety review panel. Retrieved from http://www.propublica.org/documents/item/the-bp-us-refineries-independent-safety-review-panel-report

Barron, G., & Erev, I. (2003). Small feedback-based decisions and their limited correspondence to description-based decisions. *Journal of Behavioral Decision Making, 16*(May), 215–233. doi:10.1002/bdm.443

Bazerman, M.H., & Moore, D.A. (2013). *Judgment in Managerial Decision Making* (8th ed.). Danvers, UK: John Wiley & Sons.

Blau, P.M. (1963). *The Dynamics of Bureaucracy: A Study of Interpersonal Relations in Two Government Agencies* (2nd ed.). Chicago: University of Chicago Press.

Bradstreet, T.E. (1996). Teaching introductory statistics courses so that nonstatisticians experience statistical reasoning. *American Statistician, 50*(1), 69–78. doi:10.2307/2685047

Brodersen, J., Jørgensen, K., & Gøtzsche, P.C. (2010). The benefits and harms of screening for cancer with a focus on breast screening. *IPOLSKIE ARCHIWUM MEDYCYNY WEWNĘTRZNEJ, 120*(3), 89–92. doi:10.1093/ije/dyh014

Clark, A., & Macalister, T. (2006, December 8). BP disaster site "held together with band aids." *Guardian*. Retrieved from http://www.theguardian.com/business/2006/dec/08/oilandpetrol.news

Cortright, E., Allnutt, R., Armstrong, N., Clark, J.F., Hedrick, W., Johnson, V., . . . Mark, H. (1970). *Report of the Apollo 13 Review Board*. Washington, DC: National Aeronautics and Space Administration.

Dake, K. (1992). Myths of nature: Culture and the social construction of risk. *Journal of Social Issues, 48*(4), 21–37. doi:10.1111/j.1540–4560.1992.tb01943.x

Financial Crisis Inquiry Commission. (2011). *The Financial Crisis Inquiry Report: Final Report of the National Commission on the Causes of the Financial and Economic Crisis in the United States*. Washington, DC: U.S. Government Printing Office.

Fischhoff, B., & Kadvany, J. (2011). *Risk: A Very Short Introduction*. Oxford: Oxford University Press.

Fischhoff, B., Nadaï, A., & Fischhoff, I. (2001). Investing in frankenfirms: Predicting socially unacceptable risks. *Journal of Psychology and Financial Markets, 2*(2), 100–111.

Fischhoff, B., Slovic, P., Lichtenstein, S., Read, S., & Combs, B. (1978). How safe is safe enough? A psychometric study of attitudes towards technological risks and benefits. *Policy Sciences, 9*, 127–152. doi:10.1007/BF00143739

Gawande, A. (1999, August 2). The cancer-cluster myth. *New Yorker*, pp. 34–37.

Holmstrom, B., & Milgrom, P. (1991). Multitask principal-agent analyses: Incentive contracts, asset ownership, and job design. *Journal of Law, Economics, & Organization, 7*(Spring), 24–52. doi:10.2307/764957

Johansson, M., Hansson, A., & Brodersen, J. (2015). Estimating overdiagnosis in screening for abdominal aortic aneurysm: Could a change in smoking habits and lowered aortic diameter tip the balance of screening towards harm? *BMJ, 350*(March), h825. doi:10.1136/bmj.h825

Kahan, D. Slovic, P. Braman, D., & Gastil, J. (2006). Fear of democracy: A cultural evaluation of Sunstein on risk laws of fear: Beyond the precautionary principle. *Harvard Law Review, 119*(4), 1071–1109. doi:10.2139/ssrn.801964

Kahneman, D. (2011). *Thinking, Fast and Slow*. London: Penguin Books.

Kasperson, J.X., & Kasperson, R.E. (2005). Corporate culture and technology transfer. In J.X. Kasperson (Ed.), *The Social Contours of Risk. Volume II: Risk Analysis, Corporations & the Globalizaton of Risk* (pp. 118–143). London: Earthscan.

Kasperson, J.X., Kasperson, R.E., Pidgeon, N., & Slovic, P. (2003). The social amplification of risk: Assessing fifteen years of research and theory. In N. Pidgeon, R.E. Kasperson, & P. Slovic (Eds.), *The Social Amplification of Risk* (pp. 13–46). Cambridge: Cambridge University Press.

Kasperson, R.E., Renn, O., Slovic, P., Brown, H.S., Emel, J., Goble, R., . . . Ratick, S. (1988). The social amplification of risk: A conceptual framework. *Risk Analysis, 8*(2), 177–187. doi:10.1111/j.1539-6924.1988.tb01168.x

Kerr, S. (1975). On the folly of rewarding A, while hoping for B. *Academy of Management Journal, 18*(4), 769–783. doi:10.1109/EMR.1978.4306645

Kheifets, L., & Sudan, M. (2009). *Report Prepared for Chancellor Marye Anne Fox on the Investigated Cancer Cluster in the Literature Building at UCSD*. Retrieved from http://www-ehs.ucsd.edu/LBCI/Kheifets_Final_Report_LB_7–2009.pdf

Kurokawa, K., Ishibashi, K., Oshima, K., Sakiyama, H., Sakurai, M., Tanaka, K., . . . Yokoyama, Y. (2012). *The Official Report of the Fukushima Nuclear Accident Independent Investigation Commission*. The National Diet of Japan. Retrieved from http://www.nirs.org/fukushima/naiic_report.pdf

Langer, E.J. (1975). The illusion of control. *Journal of Personality and Social Psychology, 32*, 311–328. doi:10.1037/0022–3514.32.2.311

Loewenstein, G.F., Weber, E.U., Hsee, C.K., & Welch, N. (2001). Risk as feelings. *Psychological Bulletin, 127*(2), 267–286. Retrieved from http://www.ncbi.nlm.nih.gov/pubmed/11316014

Mandel, D.R. (2015). Instruction in information structuring improves Bayesian judgment in intelligence analysts. *Frontiers in Psychology, 6*(387). doi:10.3389/fpsyg.2015.00387

Moynihan, R., Doust, J., & Henry, D. (2012). Preventing overdiagnosis: How to stop harming the healthy. *BMJ, 344*, e3502. doi:10.1136/bmj.e3502

National Commission on the BP Deepwater Horizon Oil Spill and Offshore Drilling. (2011). *Deep Water: The Gulf Oil Disaster and the Future of Offshore Drilling*. Retrieved from http://digital.library.unt.edu/ark:/67531/metadc132999/

Osterloch, M., & Frey, B. (2002). Does pay for performance really motivate employees? In A. Neely (Ed.), *Business Performance Measurement: Theory and Practice* (pp. 107–122). Cambridge: Cambridge Univeristy Press.

Plous, S. (1993). *The Psychology of Judgment and Decision Making*. New York: McGraw-Hill.

Ridgway, V.F. (1956). Dysfunctional consequences of performance measurements. *Administrative Science Quarterly, 1*, 240–247. doi:10.2307/2390989

Rogers, A. (2015, February 26). The science of why no one agrees on the color of this dress. *Wired*. Retrieved from http://www.wired.com/2015/02/science-one-agrees-color-dress/

Romeder, J.M., & McWhinnie, J.R. (1977). Potential years of life lost between ages 1 and 70: An indicator of premature mortality for health planning. *International Journal of Epidemiology, 6*(2), 143–151.

Shappell, S., Detwiler, C., Holcomb, K., Hackworth, C., Boquet, A., & Wiegmann, D. A. (2007). Human error and commercial aviation accidents: an analysis using the human factors analysis and classification system. *Human Factors, 49*(2), 227–242. doi:10.1518/001872007X312469

Simons, D.J., & Chabris, C.F. (1999). Gorillas in our midst: Sustained inattentional blindness for dynamic events. *Perception, 28*, 1059–1074.

Slimak, M.W., & Dietz, T. (2006). Personal values, beliefs, and ecological risk perception. *Risk Analysis, 26*(6), 1689–1705. doi:10.1111/j.1539–6924.2006.00832.x

Slovic, P., Finucane, M.L., Peters, E., & MacGregor, D.G. (2004). Risk as analysis and risk as feelings. *Risk Analysis, 24*(2), 311–322. Retrieved from papers2://publication/uuid/F4B3EA59-C2F7–4F62–9223–701C27F152C2

Slovic, P., & Peters, E. (2006). Risk perception and affect. *Current Directions in Psychological Science, 15*(6), 322–325. doi:10.1111/j.1467–8721.2006.00461.x

Stanovich, K.E. (1999). *Who Is Rational? Studies of Individual Differences in Reasoning.* Mahwah, NJ: Lawrence Erlbaum Associates.

Sunstein, C.R. (2005). *Laws of Fear: Beyond the Precautionary Principle* (Vol. 6). Cambridge: Cambridge University Press.

UCSD. (2009). *UC San Diego Literature Building Update.* Retrieved from http://www-ehs.ucsd.edu/LBCI/litbldg_update_9–18–09.pdf

US Chemical Safety Board. (2007). *Investigation Report Refinery Explosion and Fire. BP Texas City.* Retrieved from http://www.csb.gov/bp-america-refinery-explosion/

Vaughan, D. (1997). *The Challenger Launch Decision: Risky Technology, Culture, and Deviance at NASA.* Chicago: University of Chicago Press.

Weinstein, N.D., & Klein, W.M. (1996). Unrealistic optimism: Present and future. *Journal of Social and Clinical Psychology, 15*(1), 1–8. doi:10.1521/jscp.1996.15.1.1

Zajonc, R.B. (1980). Feeling and thinking. *American Psychologist, 35*, 151–175.

17

Diagrams for strategic risk management

Baruch Fischhoff[1]

Successful management requires having the right people focused on the right topics at the right times. In many settings, those goals can be achieved by trial and error. Such incremental learning from experience is less possible with strategic management, where feedback may come slowly and have ambiguous lessons when it arrives. It may be impossible with strategic risk management, where clear lessons are even harder to come by. As a result, strategic risk management requires acts of faith, adopting procedures trusted to recruit and coordinate the essential people and topics in a timely fashion.

One obvious goal in addressing these tasks is comprehensiveness. If critical people or topics are missing, then it is pointless to belabor those that are included. Conducting elaborate sensitivity analyses on incomplete models (e.g., with only readily quantified factors) would represent misplaced imprecision. Conducting sustained consultations with only some stakeholders (e.g., just lobbyists) would foster distrust. Both could create an illusion of thoroughness, until the omissions become apparent.

However, the desire for comprehensiveness can lead to consultations that are too unwieldy for participants to be heard properly and to analyses that are too complex to review or update. In such cases, an organization might be better off abandoning strategic risk management altogether and just taking things as they come and muddling through. If its attention is naturally drawn to critical people and topics, then better strategies might emerge from treating them in depth, rather than trying to consider everything (Lindblom, 1968; Long and Fischhoff, 2000).

The following sections offer two approaches designed to balance the strategic risk managers' desire for comprehensiveness with the limits to the attention. The first offers a process for engaging internal and external stakeholders. The second offers a procedure for identifying integrating topics relevant to their concerns. In combination, they offer some hope of bringing together the right people and topics. A feature shared by the two approaches is using a graphic representation intended to be simple enough to show participants where they are in the risk management process and explicit enough to direct their work within it.

Managing the process

Figure 17.1 embodies principles echoed in many reports on risk management (e.g., National Research Council, 1996; Presidential/Congressional Commission on Risk Assessment and Risk

Management, 1997). It views that process as coordinating *risk analysis*, charged with estimating the expected size of potentially valued outcomes, and *risk assessment*, charged with determining the values of those outcomes. It includes roles for an organization's internal stakeholders, in its central column, and its external stakeholders, in *risk communication*. It is *iterative*, as seen in the three-headed arrows connecting its stages, and *interactive*, as seen in the two-headed arrows connecting the columns.

One distinctive feature of Figure 17.1 is how strongly it endorses those two principles. Two-way interaction with stakeholders is required at each step of the process. Thus, risk managers must both inform stakeholders when they initiate a process and be willing to initiate one at stakeholders' behest. They must consult with stakeholders on the problem's framing, so that the Preliminary Analysis does not set off in unexpected or unacceptable directions. And so on

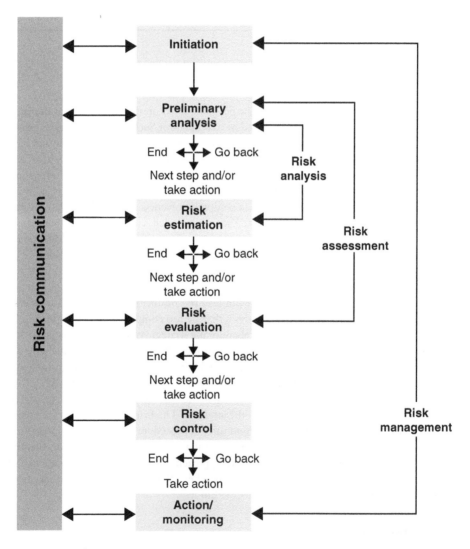

Figure 17.1 Risk communication

through the stages, until (at bottom) the parties create a social contract for how to implement and monitor the resulting risk management plan. The more strategic the context, the more important these commitments become. With great changes come great opportunities for the parties to misunderstand one another and great value for communication itself, by showing respect and creating human ties, in addition to sharing information and concerns.

The strength of Figure 17.1's commitment to an iterative process is seen in its recognition that the transition between two stages may require revisiting earlier ones (Go back) or even abandoning the process (End). For example, the first transition might lead to repeating the Initiation stage if the Preliminary Analysis reveals problems with the problem formulation (e.g., if new issues have arisen or seemingly important ones have proven less so). It might lead to ending the process if internal or external agreement unravels, once a problem's dimensions or uncertainties become clearer.

In their important analysis "Why a Diagram Is (Sometimes) Worth Ten Thousand Words," Larkin and Simon (1987) propose that the value of a diagram depends on how well it facilitates three functions: search, recognition, and inference. In the context of a strategic risk management process, *search* is locating management tasks in it; *recognition* is characterizing situations in its terms; *inference* is understanding the implications of that characterization. For example, Figure 17.1 would have value for dealing with stakeholder discontent, if it helped risk managers to locate its origins in the Risk Estimation (search), see that it reflects poor communication of those estimates (recognition), and identify ways to address the problem (inference).

Figure 17.2 offers another depiction of strategic risk management. Its elements roughly parallel those in Figure 17.1 and its structure expresses roughly the same two organizing principles. The arrows seem to show an iterative process (although it does not explicitly call for repeating the process, should the Evaluation be disappointing). The central circle shows continuing interactive stakeholder engagement.

If both figures express the same underlying philosophy, then the risk managers should prefer the one that is more helpful for performing the three functions of search, recognition, and inference. One test of that success is how useful each is in diagnosing problems, such as stakeholder

Figure 17.2 A depiction of strategic risk management

discontent. A second is how well each guides risk managers to research relevant to their task. For example, *Understanding Risk* (National Research Council, 1996) provides guidance on using analytical-deliberative processes for setting the terms of analyses. Is its relevance more readily seen and its details more readily applied with the appropriate sections of Figure 17.1 (Initiation) or Figure 17.2 (Problem/Context)? Dietz and Stern (2008) summarize the evidence on public participation. Which figure makes the need for that evidence and its application more obvious?

A strong guidance document might still have a weak summary diagram, if an attractive design were adopted without testing its usefulness. Yet, without a strong diagram, users will be hard-pressed to access the document's contents or keep its organizing principles in mind. As Larkin and Simon (1987) note, with a good diagram,

> information is organized by location, and often much of the information needed to make an inference is present and explicit at a single location. In addition, cues to the next logical step in the problem may be present at an adjacent location. Therefore problem solving ... may require very little search or computation of elements that had been implicit.

(p. 65)

Without such a diagram, users might wonder whether there is a useful "program" latent in the "sentential" text (to use Larkin and Simon's terms).

Managing the content

Figure 17.3 illustrates a cognitively tractable approach to organizing the topics relevant to a strategic risk management process. Its formalisms are adapted from influence diagrams

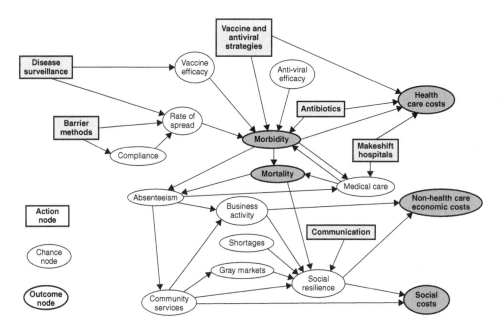

Figure 17.3 A computable influence diagram for strategic risk management of pandemic diseases using behavioral interventions

(Howard, 1989; Howard and Matheson, 2005). The nodes represent variables and the links influences, in the sense that knowing the value of the variable at the tail of an arrow should influence estimates of the value of the variable at its head. A causal connection could, but need not, underlie a link (which could be just diagnostic). The elements are chosen for their value in predicting outcome variables (e.g., social costs).

A formal influence diagram would quantify the variables and relationships, and then compute estimates of the outcome variables, along with the uncertainties captured by sensitivity analyses (seeing how the outcomes vary with alternative values for the variables and relationships). As strategic risk management tools, these diagrams were meant to be *computable* models, in the sense that the variables and relationships are sufficiently well defined that the outcomes and uncertainties could be computed were the data available. However, actual computation is secondary to creating a shared understanding of the problem. In this view, computing is a tactic, useful when precise numbers matter to decision makers or can inform analysts' intuitions. Deciding what to compute is strategic, by establishing which outcomes have standing and what expertise is needed.

A vital feature of influence diagrams is that, as applications of Bayesian decision theory, they can accommodate any form of evidence, including expert judgment, while capturing uncertainties and disagreements in relatively transparent form. As such, they are well suited to strategic risk management, which brings together people with diverse perspectives and takes them into semi-charted territory. Risk managers can use established elicitation procedures for helping participants to articulate their concerns (Fischhoff, 2005; Morgan and Henrion, 1990; O'Hagan et al., 2006) and communication procedures for helping them to understand analyses' assumptions and results (Fischhoff, 2013; Fischhoff and Davis, 2014; Keisler and Noonan, 2012).

In principle, influence diagrams are natural centerpieces of risk management processes. In practice, though, the natural course of formal analyses may undermine that potential. Analysts are often eager to get on to the computing rather than spend time on the iterative interactions needed to create shared problem definitions. Once that computing begins, it typically proceeds outside the public eye (and on the analysts' computers), undermining the continuing consultation needed to make its results relevant and credible. Moreover, the culture of computation may favor readily quantified variables, especially if analysts have difficulty recruit the relevant experts and convincing them to summarize their beliefs in quantitative terms. "Hard" data, even with known flaws, may just feel more scientific than expert judgments, however carefully elicited (Morgan, 2014).

The example in Figure 17.3 was created for Pandefense 1.0, a strategic risk management initiative launched in late summer 2006, prior to the threatened avian flu pandemic. Its initial drafts drew on the knowledge of a subset of experts. They were refined with input from a structure survey of participants prior to an expert workshop (Bruine de Bruin et al., 2006). Further refinement followed from interactions at that meeting, whose richness was also captured in a "mess map" summarizing participants' reflection (Horn, 2006) and scenarios used to tests the diagram's inclusiveness.

As the threat of pandemic waned, so did Pandefense 1.0. Had it continued, completing the Initiation stage would have required securing agreement over the terms of the analysis. As Pauker and Wong (2005) discuss in the context of medical decision making, even analytically trained individuals may be slow to adopt a formalism unless they feel comfortable with it. Table 17.1 has instructions created to structure that process for participants unfamiliar with the formalisms.

The success of such an analytical process is an empirical question, answered by seeing how well users of an influence diagram can perform the Larkin and Simon functions. In one test, Bruine de Bruin et al. (2009) found better performance with a diagram than with narratives (or

Table 17.1 Guide to creating a computable influence diagram for strategic risk management

---

Node review

Complete the following for each node:

1. Name of variable (or vector of related variables)
2. Possible values of the variable(s)
3. Possible procedures for measuring variable
4. Methods for measuring variables

Single link review

Complete the following for each link:

1. Names of nodes involved.
2. Simple statement of the link (e.g., X causes Y because; X is a good indicator of Y because).
3. If there are multiple variables at a node, does this simple statement hold for each combination of variables? (If not, consider partitioning the variables into separate nodes.)
4. Source and strength of claim for link. (Use dashed lines for speculative links or ones whose existence is in dispute.)
5. (optional) Strategies for studying link.
6. (optional) Strategies for affecting link.

Multiple link review

Complete for each link:

1. Does it go into a node that also has only one link going out? (If so, the intermediate note could be eliminated, unless having it provides a useful reminder of the connection between the nodes that it separates.)
2. Does it have the same input and output arrows as another link? (If so, consider combining them or representing that area in the influence diagram as a single topic in a higher-order [simpler] model.)
3. Is it part of a circular chain of links? (If so, identify the time dependency among the links – or group the chain in a single node, with its own internal dynamics.)

Overall model review

1. Are critical endpoints easily identifiable?
2. Would connecting any pair of unconnected nodes add predictive value?
3. Is there feedback from the endpoints to the initial conditions (indicating temporal dynamics)?
4. Are there important "index variables" that affect many model values, within the basic structure (e.g., gender: for a disease with different expressions for men and women)?

Source: Fischhoff et al. (2006).

scenarios) representing the same material. If this result is robust, it might reflect the benefits that a good diagram has for refining users' mental models of a domain – and with it, their capabilities for search, recognition, and inference (Bruine de Bruin and Bostrom, 2013).

Conclusion: the sciences of strategic risk management

Strategic risk management has many moving parts. Diagrams offer a way to keep the relevant people and topics in view, with implicit prompts regarding how to proceed. In order to realize that potential, diagrams need to be precise enough for their elements to have clear implications, yet simple enough to be readily grasped and kept in mind. The Canadian Standards Association's risk management guide offers an approach for managing the people, and computable influence diagrams offer an approach for managing the topics. Each reflects and invites contributions from the multiple disciplines needed to inform strategic risk management (Fischhoff and Kadvany, 2011).

Note

1   Baruch Fischhoff, Department of Engineering and Public Policy, Department of Social and Decision Sciences, Carnegie Mellon University.

References

Bruine de Bruin, W., and Bostrom, A. (2013). Assessing what to address in science communication. *Proceedings of the National Academy of Sciences, 110*, 14062–14068.

Bruine de Bruin, W., Fischhoff, B., Brilliant, L., and Caruso, D. (2006). Expert judgments of pandemic influenza. *Global Public Health, 1*(2), 178–193.

Bruine de Bruin, W., Güvenç, Ü., Fischhoff, B., Armstrong, C.M., and Caruso, D. (2009). Communicating about xenotransplantation: Models and scenarios. *Risk Analysis, 29*, 1105–1115.

Canadian Standards Association. (1997, affirmed 2002). *Risk management: Guidelines for decision makers* (Q850). Ottawa: Author.

Dietz, T., and Stern, P. (Eds.). (2008). *Public participation in environmental assessment and decision making*. Washington, DC: National Academy Press.

Fischhoff, B. (2005). Cognitive processes in stated preference methods. In K.-G. Mäler and J. Vincent (Eds.), *Handbook of Environmental Economics* (pp. 937–968). Amsterdam: Elsevier.

Fischhoff, B. (2012). Good decisions require good communication. *Drug Safety, 35*, 983–993.

Fischhoff, B. (2013). The sciences of science communication. *Proceedings of the National Academy of Sciences, 110*(Supplement 3), 14033–14039.

Fischhoff, B., Bruine de Bruin, W., Guvenc, U., Caruso, D., and Brilliant, L. (2006). Analyzing disaster risks and plans: An avian flu example. *Journal of Risk and Uncertainty, 33*, 133–151.

Fischhoff, B., and Davis, A.L. (2014). Communicating scientific uncertainty. *Proceedings of the National Academy of Sciences, 111*(Supplement 4), 13664–13671.

Fischhoff, B., and Kadvany, J. (2011). *Risk: A very short introduction*. Oxford: Oxford University Press.

Fischhoff, M.E. (2007). Electricity company managers' views of environmental issues. *Energy Policy, 35*, 3868–3878.

Horn, R. (2006). Pandemic scenario. http://web.stanford.edu/~rhorn/a/recent/AvianFluMuralIntro.html (accessed April 21, 2015).

Howard, R.A. (1989). Knowledge maps. *Management Science, 35*, 903–922.

Howard, R.A., and Matheson, J.E. (2005). Influence diagrams. *Decision Analysis, 2*(3), 127–143.

Keisler, J.M., and Noonan, P.S. (2012). Communicating analytic results. *Decision Analysis, 9*(3), 274–292.

Larkin, J.H., and Simon, H.A. (1987). Why a diagram is (sometimes) worth ten thousand words. *Cognitive Science, 11*, 65–99.

Lindblom, C. E. (1968). *The policy-making process*. Englewood Cliffs, NJ: Prentice-Hall.

Long, J., and Fischhoff, B. (2000). Setting risk priorities: A formal model. *Risk Analysis, 20*, 339–351.

Morgan, M.G. (2014). The used (and abuse) of expert elicitation in support of decision making for public policy. *Proceedings of the National Academy of Sciences, 110*, 7176–7184.

Morgan, M.G., and Henrion, M. (1990). *Uncertainty*. New York: Cambridge University Press.

National Research Council. (1996). *Understanding risk*. Washington, DC: Author.

National Research Council. (2011). *Intelligence analysis for the future*. Washington, DC: Author.

O'Hagan, A., Buck, C.E., Daneshkhah, A., Eiser, J.R., Garthwaite, P.H., Jenkinson, D.J., . . . Rakow, T. (2006). *Uncertain judgments: Eliciting expert probabilities*. Chichester: Wiley.

Pauker, S.G., and Wong, J.B. (2005). The influence of influence diagrams in medicine. *Decision Analysis, 2*(4), 238–244.

Presidential/Congressional Commission on Risk Assessment and Risk Management. (1997). *Risk Management*. Washington, DC: Author.

18

Capital structure, environmental dynamism, innovation strategy, and strategic risk management

Torben Juul Andersen[1]

Abstract

Previous research found capital structure effects on performance when it is adapted to the level of environmental dynamism and pursuit of an innovation strategy. The current study reproduces some of these relationships in a recent dataset and identifies significant nuances across industrial environments. Analyses of a large cross-sectional sample with various industry subsamples suggest that other factors influence capital structure effects including flexibilities in multinational organization and effective strategic risk management capabilities.

Recent strategy research on capital structure effects (Simerly and Li, 2000) found empirical evidence of interactive performance relationships between environmental dynamism and financial leverage. A subsequent study demonstrated that capital structure has a comparable influence on the performance of innovation strategy (O'Brien, 2003). These findings are highly relevant in the context of the 'hypercompetitive' conditions that seem to permeate contemporary business environments (D'Aveni, 1994; Thomas, 1996). To pursue these issues further, this chapter presents the results of a study based on more recent data covering the period 1996–2000 across firms operating in different industrial environments.

The study replicates some of the effects of dynamism and innovation found in the previous studies but also identifies differences across subsamples of specific industry segments where expected effects are subdued or even show inverse relationships. This has urged the consideration of other potential influencers on the strategic effects of capital structure deriving from the firm's ability to respond to changes in environmental conditions. Given the considerable emphasis on potential advantages from flexibilities embedded in multinational organizations (Kogut and Kulatilaka, 1994) and risk management capabilities (Miller, 1998), this research considered potential confounding effects from these factors in addition to dynamism and innovation on the relationship between capital structure and performance.

The chapter is structured as follows. First, there is a brief overview of the basic finance and strategic management literatures on the choice of capital structure. Then aspects of agency theory, transaction cost economics, the resource-based view, and real options theory are incorporated in the development of hypotheses. Following this, the chapter describes an empirical study performed to test the hypotheses and the results of the study are presented. Finally, the chapter offers a discussion of the findings and provides tentative conclusions.

Literature and theory

The seminal study by Modigliani and Miller (1958) argued that the value of the firm is independent of capital structure under certain conditions. One important condition was perfect capital markets, i.e., no taxes, no transaction costs, and no bankruptcy costs. Another condition was information symmetry, i.e., investors and managers have equal information about the firm's investment potential. In a subsequent paper, Modigliani and Miller (1963) eased the conditions and showed that under a capital market imperfection where interest expenses are tax deductible, firm value will increase with higher financial leverage. In this situation, the optimal capital structure will be determined by a trade-off between increased bankruptcy risk from a higher debt load and the tax advantage associated with debt.

Myers and Majluf (1984) analyzed the effects of asymmetric information where internal managers know more about the firm's prospective investments than investors in the market. In this situation, the capital structure may be determined in accordance with a 'pecking order' approach, whereby firms prefer internal sources to fund good projects and only assume debt when there is a need for additional funds to finance less attractive projects. The two perspectives on optimal capital structure reach different conclusions. The 'trade-off' perspective argues for a proportional relationship between economic performance and leverage due to the tax advantage of debt. In contrast, the pecking order perspective, if anything, is more likely to cause an inverse relationship between performance and leverage, as internal funds are reserved for projects with the highest return potentials.

The agency costs associated with equity financing relate to management's potential divergence of productive resources toward employment benefits with no or limited returns to the shareholders (Jensen and Meckling, 1976). This discrepancy between management and shareholder interests may have implications for the firm's investment decisions. Management could obtain financing through issuance of new equity to gain flexibility in pursuit of their own objectives and engage in questionable investments, some of which might represent negative net present values (Jensen, 1986; Stulz, 1990) – that is, it could lead to an 'overinvestment' problem. Assuming more debt might arguably solve this problem. On the other hand, excessive financial leverage can create an 'underinvestment' problem, as high debt service commitments limit the discretion to engage in new business propositions and thereby discourage investment in positive net present value (NPV) projects (Myers, 1977).

In an analysis of capital structure decisions, Ward (1993) draws a distinction between business risk and financial risk. Business risk is associated with managing the uncertainty of the firm's business environment, whereas financial risk relates to the trade-offs between providers of funds (lenders, investors, and shareholders) and the users of funds (firm management). Here, debt is considered riskier to firm management because the regular repayment claims can be enforced. Conversely, equity is considered riskier to the investing shareholders because it constitutes residual claims that serve as a buffer to ensure the servicing of senior debt obligations in case of bankruptcy. Hence, from the perspective of firm management, the lower financial risk associated with equity should be a better way to fund ventures with high business risk because the underlying financial buffer to cope with uncertainties in the business environment is larger. Conversely, the higher financial risk associated with debt instruments would be better suited to fund more stable business activities where the need for a financial buffer is considerably lower. This analysis would argue for an inverse relationship between business risk and financial leverage, a phenomenon that has been confirmed in some empirical studies using different conceptualizations of business risk, such as variance in sales growth (Thies and Klock, 1992) and volatility of demand (Chung, 1993).

The choice of the firm's capital structure is generally considered a central strategic issue, and Balakrishnan and Fox (1993) argue that strategic management can improve our understanding of the capital structure decisions. In this spirit, the following sections provide a brief overview of strategy analyses aimed at developing these insights.

Environmental dynamism

Simerly and Li (2000) integrate agency theory, transaction cost economics, and the resource-based view in strategic management to explain the environmental contingencies of capital structure and provide a comprehensive overview of the related literatures. From a resource-based view, sustainable competitive advantage reflected in excess rents or Shumpeterian returns can be achieved through deployment of valuable, rare, unsubstitutable, inimitable, firm-specific assets (Barney, 1991). This implies that firms operating in environments characterized by dynamic competition must engage in innovative ventures and consider more risky actions to create superior performance. This in turn will impose a higher level of business risk on organizational activities, which argues for lower financial leverage.

From the perspective of transaction cost economics, transaction costs are lower when they are carried out on the basis of standardized assets with low specificity, whereas transaction costs are higher in the case of firm-specific assets. Therefore, the higher the asset specificity, the more economical internal hierarchical coordination should be compared to market clearance of transactions. A higher equity base supports internal hierarchical control, whereas a higher debt load imposes more market discipline on organizational activities. That is, equity should be the preferred source of financing when asset specificity is high (Harris, 1991). Since dynamic environments arguably are associated with deployment of assets with high specificity, equity funding will tend to lower the firm's transaction costs in this situation and, therefore, should constitute a more suitable funding alternative. Conversely, debt should be more appropriate to fund assets with a low degree of specificity as they pertain to relatively stable environmental conditions.

From the perspective of agency theory, debt can be used as a disciplinary tool to ensure that managers give preference to wealth creation for the equity holders (Jensen, 1986, 1989). In this setup, lenders are the prime governance constituents because debt payment obligations and restrictive covenants make it more difficult for indebted firms to engage in peripheral and riskier business ventures. Conversely, it will also reduce the number of strategic options available to the firm and hence make it more difficult for management to maneuver in a dynamic market environment. In other words, debt can become too restrictive for firms operating in rapidly changing industries that require a high degree of strategic responsiveness. Together, these arguments imply that the appropriate financial strategy for firms operating in dynamic industries is to reduce leverage to economize on transaction cost and ensure sufficient flexibility to respond to environmental change and higher levels of business risk.

Innovation strategy

The resource-based view can be extended to argue that contemporary hypercompetitive environments characterized by ongoing innovation require a strategy driven by idiosyncratic and firm-specific assets and processes (Barney, 1991). A transaction cost perspective further argues that the higher specificity of assets employed in research and development (R&D) activities makes equity financing more economical and constitutes a better market signal (Santarelli,

1991; Banerjee and Wihlborg, 2003). Since information asymmetry between firm managers and external investors is higher in R&D intensive organizations, the level of financial slack will also tend to increase (Opler and Titman, 1994; Opler, Pinkowitz, Stulz and Williamson, 1999). Hence, to succeed with an innovation strategy it is necessary for the firm to maintain a certain level of financial slack to ensure sufficient and uninterrupted funding sources for R&D investment, new product launches, and ongoing knowledge expansion (O'Brien, 2003). Therefore, a certain level of equity funding that provides a financial buffer will be critical for firms following an innovation strategy, and if the firms assume too high financial leverage they are expected to perform relatively poorly. The empirical evidence seems to confirm the existence of an inverse relationship between above industry average R&D intensity and leverage (Titman and Wessels, 1988; Opler and Titman, 1994; Hovakimian, Opler and Titman, 2001; O'Brien, 2003).

Multinational organization

The wider array of business opportunities across many different national markets should provide flexibility to firms that maintain a multinational organization and thereby increase the ability to respond to changing environmental conditions. It has specifically been argued that operational flexibilities can allow the corporation to restructure in response to changes in international price relations by shifting activities between national entities controlled by the multinational enterprise (Kogut, 1985; Rangan, 1998). The ability to switch business activities across international assets can be conceived as a particular real option structure where the value of the implied flexibility can be determined on the basis of option pricing theory (Kogut and Kulatilaka, 1994). The flexibility of a multinational organization should allow the corporation to mitigate effects of major economic exposures, e.g., associated with changes in relative demand conditions and factor costs across national environments (Allen and Pantzalis, 1996; Kogut and Chang, 1996).

Furthermore, a multinational organization may also provide opportunities to exchange diverse knowledge between national environments where different insights and perspectives enhance the ability to innovate and develop new growth options (Kogut and Zander, 1992, 1993; Grant, 1996). So, multinationality might be linked to the innovative capacity of multinational diversity that forms the basis for strategic opportunities that can increase maneuverability in an uncertain global environment (e.g., Mang, 1998; Foss and Pedersen, 2002; Desouza and Evaristo, 2003). This particular view of multinationality has some resemblance to innovation strategy as the firm expends resources towards the creation of a more innovative multinational organization. In either case, the multinational organization should increase flexibility and strategic responsiveness and thereby improve economic performance.

Risk management

Strategic risk management practices have evolved in conjunction with the rapid growth of derivative instruments traded in financial markets (Rawls and Smithson, 1990) and new product enhancements bridging the conventional insurance and capital markets (Shimpi, 1999).[2] These instruments cover a wide array of financial markets that allow users to hedge against fluctuations in foreign exchange rates, interest rates, commodity prices, credit exposures, commercial risk, etc. At the same time, new types of performance related insurance contracts and contingent capital instruments have emerged that serve to reduce the expected cost of financial distress beyond the cushion provided by the firm's equity position (e.g., Colarossi, 2000). Many of the new risk management techniques have been developed within the financial industry, which by definition is engaged in the risk management business (e.g., Saunders, 2003).

Effective risk management practices should reduce the volatility of the firm's earnings and thereby reduce the costs associated with potential financial distress. Another effect of improved risk management capabilities would be to reduce underinvestment in the firm caused by debt overhang because better risk management will reduce the need for a financial buffer. If the volatility of the firm's cash flows is reduced and the firm maintains a certain financial cushion in the form liquid financial assets and committed credit facilities, then funding should always be available for positive NPV projects, all the while the lower performance volatility will reduce the firm's average cost of funding. To the extent an organization is able to manage the uncertainties imposed by dynamic environmental conditions that expose business activities and reduce variability in firm earnings, the underinvestment problem could be reduced, which provides a basic argument for financial hedging (Froot, Scharfstein and Stein, 1993, 1994).

By introducing an 'insurative model' that incorporates both insurance contracts and equity funding as residual claims on the firm, Shimpi (1999) shows that capital management and risk management are two sides of the same coin. A firm needs equity capital to fund its operations and establish a certain financial cushion against adverse economic performance, and thereby assure different stakeholders about the stability, strength, and soundness of the firm as a going concern. Insurance contracts and financial derivatives serve the same purpose by transferring risk exposures that are beyond the discretionary control of firm management. Hence, insurance contracts and alternative risk-transfer instruments constitute important sources of financial capital for the firm (Culp, 2002).

Miller (1998) argues that a general strategic management perspective requires that all risk factors exposing the firm be considered, such as competition, sourcing, customers, demand conditions, etc. In other words, the risk management perspective should be extended well beyond a focus on foreign exchange and other price risks in the financial markets. Furthermore, it can be important to improve risk management capabilities relating to firm-specific strategic exposures because many stakeholders are unable to diversify investments that are geared specifically to cater to the firm, e.g., buyer and supplier relationships, business partnerships, and management and employment contracts, etc. (Miller, 1998). Since competitive exposures often require strategic responses that are unique to the firm, there is a limit to how far traded financial derivatives can accomplish this task. Financial derivatives exist for many fairly standardized and hence tradable asset classes, but do not extend to firm-specific competitive factors including environmental contingencies in technology, sourcing, distribution, etc. To deal with these risk factors, a firm may try to invest in the creation of real options that can enhance the firm's ability to respond to competitive risk exposures. Hence, strategic risk management can be extended to include a real options perspective where firms are able to develop opportunities and claims on the future that can be evaluated based on assumptions about the underlying risk factors (Leiblein, 2003). The real options differ from financial options in the way the option value is tied to idiosyncratic conditions in the firm (McGrath, 1997) as well as firm-specific strategy processes may differ in unique ways that influence the firm's ability to exploit the options. Hence, the presence of real options can enhance sustainable value creation since they are based on firm-specific assets and processes not readily available in the market (Barney, 1991).

Hypotheses

Environmental dynamism imposes higher business risk on organizational activities, and therefore firm management will impose a higher equity ratio to create a financial buffer of sufficient size to absorb the associated performance volatility (Ward, 1993). Furthermore, firms need a stronger equity position to deal with the higher specificity of firm assets required to create excess rents in dynamic environments (Harris, 1991; Simerly and Li, 2000); all the while excessive leverage can cause underinvestment problems (Myers, 1977). These arguments lead to the following hypothesis:

Hypothesis 1: Firms operating in dynamic environments (a) have lower financial leverage and (b) if they assume a high level of financial leverage it is associated with lower economic performance.

Firms pursuing an innovation strategy require a certain level of equity that provide a financial buffer to ensure stability and availability of funds for research efforts, new product launches, and ongoing development of knowledge based capabilities (O'Brien, 2003). Innovation is associated with the creation of new growth options for the firm including potential process improvements and product introductions (Myers, 1984). The implied real options give the firm flexibilities that can be exploited through a wider choice of alternative actions and better timing of responsive strategic moves to the firm's economic advantage. This argues for the following hypothesis:

Hypothesis 2: Firms pursuing an innovation strategy are (a) associated with higher economic performance and (b) lower financial leverage, and (c) if they assume a high level of financial leverage it is associated with lower economic performance.

The multinational organization can create flexibilities, e.g., in the form of switching options that enable the firm to respond to and manage risks associated with changes in international demand and price relations (Kogut and Kulatilaka, 1994). Within a flexible multinational structure the enhanced risk management capabilities should reduce the need for an equity funded financial buffer. On the other hand, building a multinational organization across diverse national settings can often be costly (Christophe, 1996) and associated with incremental business risk (Reeb, Kwok and Baek, 1998), which argues for equity financing. Multinationality can also be conceived as a form of innovation strategy where international diversity is used to create new growth options that extend the strategic opportunities available in different national markets (Grant, 1996; Foss and Pedersen, 2002). In this case, the associated strategic opportunities can be exploited to the firm's economic advantage, but development of innovative growth options requires a certain level of organizational slack, as does the ability to exercise them when conditions are favorable. This reasoning leads to the following hypothesis:

Hypothesis 3: Firms with a multinational organization are (a) associated with higher economic performance and (b) lower financial leverage, and (c) if they assume a high level of financial leverage it is associated with lower economic performance.

A firm displaying effective risk management capabilities has lower cash flow volatility, which should reduce potential underinvestment problems (Froot, Scharfstein and Stein, 1993, 1994) and hence improve the firm's economic performance. Effective risk management capabilities reduce the need for an equity-based financial buffer and therefore should increase the debt capacity of the firm because the cash flow volatility associated with a given business environment is reduced (Ward, 1993). To the extent that real options constitute an element of the firm's risk management processes, there might be a need to maintain some financial slack to ensure that option structures continue to be developed and that funding is available for underlying projects if and when the real options are exercised. However, risk management capabilities may also derive from use of traded financial derivatives, insurance contracts, and contingent capital arrangements as well as more process-related flexibilities as opposed to relatively asset intensive real option structures. In this case, the need for a financial buffer is reduced and effective risk management should result in higher financial leverage. If financial derivatives and other traded risk-transfer instruments are correctly priced they should not generate excess returns to firms that acquire them for hedging purposes. In contrast, real options have the potential to shield against downside risk and exploit upside potential and thereby generate excess returns. However, there is a need to maintain a certain level of financial slack to exploit the potential economic advantages associated with real options (Miller, 1998; Leiblein, 2003) and ensure that the underlying business opportunities can be realized. These arguments lead to the following hypothesis:

Hypothesis 4: Firms with effective risk management capabilities are (a) associated with higher economic performance and (b) higher financial leverage, but (c) if they assume a high level of financial leverage it is associated with lower economic performance.

The next section describes an empirical study devised to test the hypotheses.

Methods

Sources

The empirical study is based on a sample consisting of large US firms operating across industries identified by their four-digit SIC codes. The sample includes the Fortune 500 companies, the Stern-Stewart Performance Top 1000 companies, and the 1,000 largest companies in Compustat selected on the basis of their market capitalization reported as of May 2001. These three sources produced a total sample of 1,357 companies with financial information available from Compustat. Data on overseas establishments was obtained from America's Corporate Families and International Affiliates (Dun & Bradstreet), Vol. III, 2001.

Variables

Organizational performance

Performance was measured by two financial ratios, return on assets and return on investment. Return on assets (ROA) was calculated as income before extraordinary items divided by total assets (including current assets, net property, plant and equipment, and other noncurrent assets). Return on investment (ROI) was calculated as income before extraordinary items divided by total invested capital (including total long-term debt, preferred stock, minority interest, and total common equity). The financial ratios were averaged over the 5-year period 1996–2000 to assess longer-term relations as opposed to short-term effects and avoid influences by potential spurious events. This approach is consistent with Simerly and Li (2000) and updates their study, which used data for the period 1989–1993. The analysis defined performance as reported economic results as opposed to indicative markets returns, e.g., reflected in market to book value. Market returns are influenced by investor behaviors and therefore could lead to skewed performance indicators in the inflated market of the late 1990s (Schleifer, 2000).

Financial leverage

The firm's financial leverage was measured as the ratio of debt to equity calculated as all fixed charge debt obligations and preferred stock divided by common equity. The debt to equity ratio was averaged over the 5-year period 1996–2000 to control for spurious effects (Simerly and Li, 2000). The study assessed leverage based on realized economic performance rather than the market value of equity, which is influenced by investor expectations about the firm's future financial performance and general market prospects.

Environmental dynamism

Environmental dynamism was measured by an instability index calculated as the standard error of the regression coefficient in the regression of total industry sales over the 5-year period 1996–2000 against a time variable divided by the average value of industry sales to reach a standardized indicator of dynamism (Dess and Beard, 1984; Keats and Hitt, 1988; Simerly and Li, 2000). To get more consistent measures of environmental dynamism, the instability indexes were calculated on the basis of aggregate industry data identified by the two-digit SIC codes from the complete Compustat database and were not limited to the sampled firms.

Innovation strategy

Innovation was measured by R&D intensity calculated as all costs incurred by the firm to develop new products and services divided by total sales. The firm's R&D intensity was then compared to its industry peers to capture a distinct strategy dimension indicating the importance the firm assigns to innovation (O'Brien, 2003). Hence, we calculated the R&D intensity for each firm in the sample, averaged the ratio over the 5-year period 1996–2000, and standardized the firm measures within the industries identified by their two-digit SIC codes. This procedure captured the relative emphasis the firms put on innovation as a strategic approach compared to peers within their own industries.

Multinational organization

Multinationality was measured on the basis of the number of foreign subsidiaries and the number of foreign countries in which the firm's subsidiaries are situated (Kogut and Singh, 1988; Reuer and Leiblein, 2000). The measure was calculated as the natural logarithm of one plus the number of foreign subsidiaries the firm has and the natural logarithm of one plus the number of countries with subsidiaries. The two numbers were added to indicate diversity in term of national environments as well as operational knowledge. The natural logarithm was applied to adjust for skewness and ensure normality.

Risk management

Risk management was conceived as the extent to which the firm was able to cope with uncertainties in the external environment and stabilize the earnings development. Hence, the firm's adherence to risk management was calculated in two ways. First, we calculated the standard deviation of the firm's net sales during 1996–2000, which reflects the level of uncertainty in the firm's business environment, and divided it by the standard deviation of the firm's ROA during the same period. Second, we calculated the standard deviation of net sales divided by the standard deviation of ROI during the same period. The ratios provide direct indications of the firm's ability to adapt to the influence of environmental risk factors and manage the associated exposures so as to reduce variability in economic performance.

Analyses

The hypotheses were tested in multiple regression analyses. One set of regressions used the economic performance measures, i.e., the 5-year average ROA and 5-year average ROI, as dependent variables and measures of environmental dynamism, innovation strategy, multinational organization, risk management, and their interaction terms with financial leverage as independent variables. Another set of regressions used financial leverage as dependent variable and dynamism, innovation, multinationality, and risk management as independent variables. This approach is comparable to previous strategic capital structure studies (Simerly and Li, 2000; O'Brien, 2003).

The relative R&D intensity was used as a measure of the extent to which the firms pursue an innovation strategy (O'Brien, 2003), which can be looked upon as the firm's ability to create future growth options (Myers, 1977). As discussed, the same real options perspective can be adopted to the multinational organization (Grant, 1996) and strategic risk management (Miller, 1998). To assess this, two indicators were developed as the natural logarithm of one plus the number of announced product introductions made by the firms during the 5-year period and the number of patents registered by the firms at the US Patent Office, which have been used to measure real options (McGrath and Nerkar, 2004). The correlation coefficient between the innovation and multinationality measures and the two options indicators calculated on the total sample were statistically significant and ranged between 0.35 and 0.45, and hence provided some credence to the real options perspective applied on these two measures. The risk management measure did not show high correlations with the real options indicators, which seems to indicate that the risk management construct captured here reflects the use of traded financial derivatives, alternative risk-transfer instruments, and supportive management processes as much as potential flexibilities associated with real options.

The regressions considered a number of control variables. The size of the firm reflects past success and hence may represent resource availability that could affect the choice of capital structure (Aldrich and Auster, 1986; Aldrich, 2000). Hence, firm size was included in the regressions (measured as the natural logarithm of total assets to correct for positive skew in the data). Consistent with Simerly and Li (2000) we included two variables reflecting potential exposures to agency and transaction cost problems. Firm dummy 1 indicated firms with average annual returns on capital ranging between −2.5 and +2.5 percent and growth in capital below 25 percent during the 5-year period, with return on capital calculated as operating profit after tax divided by outstanding capital at the beginning of the year. Firm dummy 2 indicated firms with returns on capital below −2.5 percent and capital growth below 25 percent. The dummy variables were assigned a value of 1 for firms belonging to the specific subgroup while all other firms were given a value of 0. Firms belonging to these subgroups have not been able to create returns in excess of the cost of capital during the period of study and, therefore, are likely to have agency or transaction cost problems that could affect the choice of capital structure. The market to book ratio reflects the potential issue price of new equity in the firm, which might influence capital structure decisions (Hovakimian, Opler and Titman, 2001). The market to book ratio has also been identified as a potential predictor of market returns (Fama and French, 1992, 1993) and hence could influence the economic performance measures used as dependent variables in the regressions.

The regression analyses were tested for possible outlier effects and multicollinearity. Data sets causing excessive prediction errors were excluded from the sample in a sequential manner to observe potential changes in regression coefficients. The final sample excluded 34 observations where prediction errors exceeded three times the standard deviation, but no material changes were observed in regression coefficients compared to calculations based on the full sample. No multicollinearity problems were registered and variance inflation factors (VIF) did not exceed 3.4 in any of the reported regressions, i.e., well below the level indicating potential multicollinearity problems (Kleinbaum, Kupper, Muller and Nizam, 1998; Lomax, 1992).

Results

Statistics and correlation coefficients on the full sample are reported in Tables 18.1 and 18.2.

Average leverage showed a negative association with performance and vice versa (Table 18.3) and seemed to indicate a prevalence for the pecking order model in the choice of capital structure. Dynamism had a significant positive association with leverage in contradiction with Hypothesis 1a (Table 18.3). That is, firms operating in dynamic environments do not seem to reduce financial leverage. The interaction term between dynamism and leverage indicated a negative relationship to performance and showed statistical significance in the case of 5-year average ROI. This provides support for Hypothesis 1b. Hence, when firms in dynamic environments assume high financial leverage it seems to be associated with lower economic performance.

Innovation had a positive relationship to performance and showed statistical significance against 5-year average ROA. This provides support for Hypothesis 2a, i.e., firms pursuing an innovation strategy appear associated with higher economic performance. Innovation had a negative relationship to leverage and showed statistical significance against 5-year average ROI. This provides support for Hypothesis 2b, i.e., firms pursuing an innovation strategy seem to be associated with lower financial leverage. The interaction term between innovation and leverage did not seem to have any discernible relationship to performance, i.e., there is no support for Hypothesis 2c.

Multinational organization had a significant positive relationship to both performance measures, which supports Hypothesis 3a, i.e., multinationality seems to be associated with higher economic performance. A multinational organization indicated a negative relationship to leverage but the regression coefficients were not statistically significant, so there is no support for Hypothesis 3b. The interaction term between multinational organization and leverage had a negative relationship to performance and showed statistical significance against 5-year ROA, i.e., there is some support for Hypothesis 3c. Hence, multinational firms with a relatively high level of financial leverage may be associated with lower economic performance.

Risk management had significant positive relationships to both performance measures, which supports Hypothesis 4a. Hence, firms with effective risk management capabilities are associated with higher economic performance. Risk management had a positive relationship to leverage. This provides support for Hypothesis 4b, i.e., it seems like effective risk management increases the debt capacity of the firm and reduces the need for an equity-based financial buffer. The interaction term between risk management and leverage had a significant negative relationship to performance, which supports Hypothesis 4c. Therefore, if firms with effective risk management capabilities assume a relatively high level of financial leverage it appears associated with lower economic performance.

We performed the same regression analyses on different industry subsamples to investigate potential discrepancies across industrial settings. In manufacturing industries (SIC: 2000–3999) we found that dynamism is negatively associated with financial leverage (Table 18.4), i.e., in this subsample Hypothesis 1a is supported. However, the interaction between dynamism and leverage indicated a positive performance relationship, i.e., there is no support for Hypothesis 1b in this subsample.

Table 18.1 Descriptive statistics and correlation coefficients[a]

	Mean	S.D.	1	2	3	4	5	6	7	8	9	10	11	12	13
1 Average 5-year ROA	4.254	5.687													
2 Average leverage	113.237	207.858	-0.144**												
3 Dynamism	0.007	0.021	-0.033	0.045*											
4 Firm dummy 1	0.081	0.273	-0.015	0.031+	-0.004										
5 Firm dummy 2	0.108	0.311	-0.110**	-0.111**	0.024	-0.107**									
6 Size (in assets)	7.847	1.599	-0.020	0.236**	-0.103**	0.005	-0.075**								
7 Market/book	1.821	1.576	0.083**	-0.151**	-0.092**	-0.037+	-0.038+	-0.405**							
8 Innovation	1.707	2.441	0.111**	-0.100**	-0.070**	-0.004	-0.054*	-0.053*	0.252**						
9 Multinational	0.861	1.059	0.165**	0.039+	-0.103**	-0.001	-0.050*	0.204**	0.213**	0.307**					
10 Risk management	5.449	1.946	0.074**	0.223**	-0.083**	-0.028	-0.142**	0.735**	-0.358**	-0.189**	0.105**				
11 Dynamism*leverage	0.202	6.279	-0.040+	-0.043	0.374**	0.021	-0.005	-0.046*	0.040	-0.021	-0.024	-0.056*			
12 Innovation*leverage	52.223	518.215	0.015	-0.045+	-0.039	-0.006	0.016	-0.056*	0.006	-0.023	-0.021	-0.062*	-0.100**		
13 Multinational*leverage	-7.546	211.945	-0.033	0.118**	-0.033	0.006	0.015	0.004	-0.010	-0.026	0.035+	0.024	-0.080**	-0.033	
14 Risk mgt.*leverage	90.775	494.287	-0.098**	0.2869**	-0.059*	0.017	0.018	0.205**	-0.062*	-0.051*	-0.008	0.196**	-0.109**	-0.258**	0.252**

[a] N = 1,323; + p < 0.10; * p < 0.05; ** p < 0.01.

Table 18.2 Descriptive statistics and correlation coefficients[a]

	Mean	S.D.	1	2	3	4	5	6	7	8	9	10	11	12	13
1 **Average 5-year ROI**	7.547	8.735													
2 **Average leverage**	113.237	207.858	−0.098**												
3 **Dynamism**	0.007	0.021	−0.038*	0.045*											
4 **Firm dummy 1**	0.081	0.273	−0.035+	0.031+	−0.004										
5 **Firm dummy 2**	0.108	0.311	−0.128**	−0.111**	0.024	−0.107**									
6 **Size (in assets)**	7.847	1.599	0.095**	0.236**	−0.103**	0.005	−0.075**								
7 **Market/book**	1.821	1.576	0.061*	−0.151**	−0.092**	−0.037+	−0.038+	−0.405**							
8 **Innovation**	1.707	2.441	0.075**	−0.100**	−0.070**	−0.004	−0.054*	−0.053*	0.252**						
9 **Multinational**	0.861	1.059	.170**	0.039+	−0.103**	−0.001	−0.050*	0.204**	0.213**	0.307**					
10 **Risk management**	4.795	1.750	.170**	0.166**	−0.076**	0.015	−0.141**	0.653**	−0.286**	−0.155**	0.122**				
11 **Dynamism*leverage**	0.202	6.279	−0.061+	−0.043	0.374**	0.021	−0.005	−0.046*	0.040	−0.021	−0.024	−0.056+			
12 **Innovation*leverage**	−52.223	518.215	0.011	−0.045+	−0.039	−0.006	0.016	−0.056*	0.006	−0.023	−0.021	−0.062*	−0.100**		
13 **Multinational*leverage**	−7.546	211.945	−0.019	−0.118**	−0.033	0.006	0.015	0.004	−0.010	−0.026	0.035+	0.024	−0.080**	−0.033	
14 **Risk mgt.*leverage**	61.816	376.713	−0.051*	0.219**	−0.043+	0.030	0.024	0.166**	−0.041+	−0.038+	0.001	0.086**	−0.114**	−0.203**	0.274**

[a] N = 1,323; + $p < 0.10$; * $p < 0.05$; ** $p < 0.01$.

Table 18.3 Analyses – cross-sectional sample[a] [standardized regression coefficients]

Dependent variable	5-year average ROA					Leverage	5-year average ROI					Leverage
Average leverage	-0.153**	-0.146**	-0.119**	-0.141**	-0.137**	–	-0.131**	-0.128**	-0.121**	-0.122**	-0.118**	–
Dynamism	0.000	0.002	-0.004	0.002	0.008	0.058*	0.019	0.020	0.022	0.021	0.025**	0.059*
Dynamism*leverage	-0.035	-0.033	-0.038	-0.040	-0.037	–	-0.059*	-0.057+	-0.060*	-0.064*	-0.063*	–
Firm Dummy 1	-0.020	-0.020	-0.021	-0.014	-0.015	0.017	-0.041	-0.041	-0.042	-0.039	-0.049+	0.012
Firm Dummy 2	-0.125**	-0.121**	-0.122**	-0.102**	-0.094**	-0.106**	-0.132**	-0.130**	-0.130**	-0.112**	-0.108**	-0.114**
Size (ln assets)	0.034	0.029	-0.020	-0.094*	-0.170**	0.157**	0.150**	0.154**	0.112**	0.054+	0.024	0.236**
Market/Book	0.070*	0.049	0.015	0.090**	0.023	-0.020	0.103**	0.092**	0.059+	0.112**	0.062*	-0.019
Performance	–	–	–	–	–	-0.145**	–	–	–	–	–	-0.121**
Innovation	–	0.079**	–	–	0.075*	-0.041	–	0.041	–	–	0.033	-0.060*
Innovation*leverage	–	0.010	–	–	0.000	–	–	0.011	–	–	0.004	–
Multinational	–	–	0.156**	–	0.138**	-0.040	–	–	0.126**	–	0.115**	-0.046
Multinational*leverage	–	–	-0.057*	–	-0.038	–	–	–	-0.040	–	-0.031	–
Risk management	–	–	–	0.215**	0.233**	0.097**	–	–	–	0.174**	0.123**	0.010
Risk mgt*leverage	–	–	–	-0.075**	-0.053+	–	–	–	–	-0.047+	-0.031	–
Multiple R2	0.206	0.220	0.257	0.255	0.303	0.321	0.234	0.238	0.264	0.273	0.299	0.309
Adjusted R2	0.038	0.042	0.059	0.059	0.083	0.097	0.053	0.050	0.063	0.068	0.080	0.089
F-significance	0.000	0.000	0.000	0.000	0.000	0.000	0.000	0.000	0.000	0.000	0.000	0.000

[a] N = 1323; + p < 0.10; * p < 0.05; ** p < 0.01.

Table 18.4 Regression analyses – industry subsamples [standardized regression coefficients]

Dependent variable	Manufacturing industries[a]				Financial institutions[b]			
	5-year avg. ROA		Leverage		5-year avg. ROI		Leverage	
Average leverage	-0.102+	-0.082	-0.109+	–	-0.172**	-0.721**	-0.147*	-0.271*
Dynamism	-0.001	-0.028	-0.025	-0.057*	-0.164+	-0.105	-0.196+	-0.176+
Dynamism*leverage	0.059	0.067	0.092	–	0.008	0.153*	0.027	0.051
Firm Dummy 1	-0.052	-0.058	-0.059	-0.008	0.118**	0.065	-0.011	-0.037
Firm Dummy 2	-0.212**	-0.216**	-0.190**	-0.122**	-0.011	-0.090	-0.159*	-0.204**
Size (ln assets)	0.080+	0.182**	-0.030	0.130+	-0.326**	-0.170+	0.125	0.033
Market/Book	0.088+	0.065	0.076	-0.014	0.354**	0.203*	0.062	0.053
Performance	–	–	–	-0.142**	–	–	–	–
Innovation	–	0.042	–	-0.026	–	–	–	–
Innovation*leverage	–	0.043	–	0.077	–	–	–	–
Multinational	–	0.080+	–	-0.104+	–	0.011	–	0.049
Multinational*leverage	–	-0.041	–	-0.049	–	0.063	–	0.084
Risk management	–	0.324**	–	0.246**	–	-0.320**	–	-0.251*
Risk mgt*leverage	–	-0.040	–	-0.063	–	0.720**	–	0.200
Multiple R2	0.276	0.372	0.388	0.228	0.603	0.680	0.296	0.343
Adjusted R2	0.063	0.116	0.129	0.035	0.341	0.437	0.055	0.076
F-significance	0.000	0.000	0.000	0.000	0.000	0.000	0.000	0.000

[a] N = 509 (SIC: 2000–3999); [b] N = 203 (SIC: 6000–6999); + p < 0.10; * p < 0.05; ** p < 0.01.

The multinational organization and risk management relationships were largely reproduced in the manufacturing industries, but risk management showed inverse relationships in the financial institutions subsample (Table 18.4). Among financial institutions risk management showed a negative relationship to performance and was enhanced only in firms with higher financial leverage.

Discussion

Whereas the regressions on the full sample provide support for most of the hypotheses and thereby give some credence to the underlying theoretical reasoning, the analyses of specific industry subsamples indicate that there are some discrepancies across industrial settings. The study fails to show that firms operating in dynamic environments pursue lower financial leverage possibly because there is a certain reliance on venture capital in emerging industries. Firms pursuing an innovation strategy do seem to perform better and maintain lower financial leverage, but the study cannot demonstrate that innovation strategy combined with leverage has adverse effects on economic performance. Again, these findings could relate to a situation where innovative ventures are financed as levered investments. In general, a multinational organization is associated with superior economic performance, although this finding cannot be reproduced in the manufacturing industry by itself. There are no significant indications that multinationality is associated with lower financial leverage or that a multinational organization with high financial leverage is associated with poorer economic performance. Risk management is associated with higher economic performance, lower financial leverage, and the combination of risk management and high financial leverage is associated with lower economic performance. However, among the credit intermediating financial institutions the positive performance effect only materializes when effective risk management capabilities are used to increase the financial leverage, which provides a basis to expand the credit multiplier.

Whereas Simerly and Li (2000) consistently found strong adverse economic effects from higher financial leverage in dynamic environments during the period 1989–1993, the results in this study are not as apparent, and in certain industry subsamples, e.g., manufacturing industries, the effect actually turns out to be positive, if anything. The study also fails to show adverse performance effects when innovation strategy is debt financed, which is inconsistent with O'Brien's (2003) results covering the period 1980–1999. O'Brien's (2003) study used annual firm observations and performance measures based on market capitalization as opposed to reported economic results, which could partially explain the inconsistent results. Another reason could relate to changes in the managerial imperatives from the 1980s to the second half of the 1990s, which is the period covered by the current study. Firms have continued to compete in increasingly open global markets often by establishing a multinational organization (e.g., Govingarajan and Gupta, 2001). The emphasis on strategic risk management has also increased considerably throughout this period (e.g., Rawls and Smithson, 1990; Froot, Scharfstein and Stein, 1993). Hence, it is not inconceivable that firms have been able to utilize financial derivatives and alternative risk-transfer instruments as well as real options–related flexibilities to better cope with the uncertainties surrounding business activities in dynamic environments (Miller, 1998). Hence, the results from this study seem to confirm that both multinational organization and risk management have had significant influences on the choice of capital structure in recent years.

The dramatic increase in the use of derivative instruments and the recognition of real options, e.g., embedded in new business opportunities and multinational organization, reflect increased attention to strategic risk management issues. The proliferation of financial derivatives, insurance contracts, alternative risk-transfer instruments, and real options should enhance the firm's ability to increase its responsiveness to environmental change and thereby reduce variability in its economic performance (Froot, Scharfstein and Stein, 1993, 1994; Miller, 1998; Culp, 2002). However, there seems to be two opposing effects at play that need further scrutiny in future research. The 'slack resources' argument for pursuing an innovation strategy (O'Brien, 2003) was adopted in this study to explain the capital structure rationale in conjunction with exploitation of real options embedded in innovations, multinational organization, and strategic risk management. On the other hand, effective use of real option structures to manage risk exposures should reduce the need for an equity-based financial buffer.

We argued that the firm needs slack resources in the form of an equity-based financial buffer, to ensure that real options are continuously developed and to make sure they can be executed effectively when market circumstances warrant it. The ability to develop real options will usually require a certain amount of slack resources and the existence of real options is, therefore, likely to have an inverse relationship to financial leverage. Furthermore, the eventual exercise of real options implies that the firm invests in the project that represents the growth option as the investment constitutes the 'exercise price' in the options jargon (e.g., Dixit and Pindyck, 1994; Leuhrman, 1998). Hence, to fully exploit the flexibilities embedded in real options, the firm must have a certain level of financial slack that allows it to execute the underlying business propositions in response to changing conditions. This is in contrast to the use of traded financial derivatives that often are used to hedge and smooth cash flows from underlying positions and where the premium typically is paid up front and, therefore, constitutes a 'sunk cost' at the time of exercise.

The fact that multinational organization and effective risk management seem to matter in the choice of optimal capital structure may be partially explained by a real options perspective as the associated flexibilities increases the firms' maneuverability and strategic responsiveness (Bettis and Hitt, 1995; Miller, 1998). In contrast, real options seem less important among financial institutions where major risk factors relate to the price volatility of financial assets and credit exposures that can be hedged in the market through trading in derivative instruments. However, more research is needed to investigate how the strategic risk management effects spill over into improved economic performance, and how an explanation based on firm-specific real options relate to conventional perspectives of innovation strategy and multinational opportunities.

Conclusions

The results of this study based on analyses of a large cross-sectional sample of firms operating in different industries demonstrate that innovation, multinationality, and risk management all have positive associations with economic performance. However, the evidence does not clarify what the optimal capital structure is for each of these strategic approaches, although it seems pretty clear that effective risk management practices outside the financial industry requires some financial slack. Hence, to achieve economic performance effects from effective risk management, financial leverage should not be excessive. One reason presumably is that that it takes a financial buffer to develop real options that underpin effective management of firm-specific risk exposures as well as financial resources are needed to exercise the options when conditions suggest it is opportune to do so. The study also finds differences between the capital structure decisions in specific industrial settings, e.g., manufacturing companies and financial institutions, partially affected by differences in financing practices, regulatory constraints, and use of traded financial derivatives in the risk management process.

Notes

1   Torben Juul Andersen, Copenhagen Business School.
2   According to data assembled by the Bank for International Settlement (BIS), the use of derivative instruments has been growing exponentially over the past decade.

References

Aldrich HE. 2000. *Organizations evolving*. Newbury Park, CA, Sage.

Aldrich HE, Auster E. 1986. Even dwarfs started small: Liabilities of age and size and their strategic implications, in Staw B, Cummings, LL (eds.). *Research in Organizational Behavior, VIII*. Greenwich, CT, JAI Press.

Allen L, Pantzalis C. 1996. Valuation of the operating flexibility of multinational corporations. *Journal of International Business Studies* 27, 633–653.

Balakrishnan S, Fox I. 1993. Asset specificity, firm heterogeneity and capital structure. *Strategic Management Journal* 14, 3–16.

Banerjee S, Wihlborg C. 2003. *Irreversibilities, assets specificity and capital structure*. Working paper, Copenhagen Business School.

Barney JB. 1991. Firm resources and sustained competitive advantage. *Journal of Management* 17, 99–120.

Barton SL, Gordon PJ. 1987. Corporate strategy: Useful perspectives for the study of capital structure. *Academy of Management Review* 12, 67–75.

Barton SL, Gordon PJ. 1988. Corporate strategy and capital structure. *Strategic Management Journal* 9, 623–632.

Berger P, Ofek E, Yermack D. 1997. Managerial entrenchment and capital structure decisions. *Journal of Finance* 52, 1411–1438.

Bettis RA, Hitt MA. 1995. The new competitive landscape. *Strategic Management Journal* 16, 7–19.

Bowman EH, Hurry D. 1993. Strategy through the option lens: an integrated view of resource investments and the incremental-choice process. *Academy of Management Review* 18, 760–782.

Bradley M, Jarrell GA, Kim EH. 1984. On the existence of an optimal capital structure: Theory and evidence. *Journal of Finance* 39, 857–878.

Christophe SE. 1996. Hysteresis and the value of the U.S. multinational corporation, *Journal of Business* 75, 67–93.

Chung KH. 1993. Asset characteristics and corporate debt policy: An empirical test. *Journal of Business Finance* 20, 83–98.

Colarossi, D. (2000). Capitalizing on innovation in the use of contingent capital. New York, Swiss Re New Markets.

Culp CL. 2002. *The ART of risk management: Alternative risk transfer, capital structure, and the convergence of insurance and capital markets*. New York, Wiley.

D'Aveni R. 1994. *Hypercompetition*. New York, Free Press.

Davis R, Duhaime IM. 1992. Diversification, vertical integration, and industry analysis: New perspectives and measurement. *Strategic Management Journal* 13, 511–524.

DeAngelo H, Masulis R. 1980. Optimal capital structure under corporate and personal taxation. *Journal of Financial Economics* 8, 3–29.

Dess GG, Beard DW. 1984. Dimensions of organizational task environments. *Administrative Science Quarterly* 29, 52–73.

Desouza K, Evaristo R. 2003. Global knowledge management strategies. *European Management Journal* 21, 62–67.

Dierickx I, Cool K. 1989. Asset stock accumulation and sustainability of competitive advantage. *Management Science* 35, 1504–1511.

Dixit A, Pindyck RS. 1994. *Investment under uncertainty*. Princeton, NJ, Princeton University Press.

Fama EF, French KR. 1992. The cross-section of expected stock returns. *Journal of Finance* 47, 427–465.

Fama EF, French KR. 1993. Common risk factors in returns on stocks and bonds. *Journal of Financial Economics* 33, 3–56.

Foss NJ, Pedersen T. 2002. Transferring knowledge in MNCs: The role of subsidiary knowledge and organizational context. *Journal of International Management* 8, 49–67.

Froot KA, Scharfstein DS, Stein JC. 1993. Risk management: Coordinating corporate investment and financing policies. *Journal of Finance* 48, 1629–1658.

Froot KA, Scharfstein DS, Stein JC. 1994. A framework for risk management. *Harvard Business Review* 72(6), 91–102.

Gardner JC, Trzcinka CA. 1992. All-equity firms and the balancing theory of capital structure. *Journal of Financial Research* 15, 77–90.

Ghosh DK. 1992. Optimum capital structure redefined. *Financial Review* 27, 411–429.

Govingarajan V, Gupta AK. 2001. The quest for global dominance: Transforming global presence into global competitive advantage. San Francisco, Jossey-Bass.

Grant RM. 1996. Toward a knowledge-based theory of the firm. *Strategic Management Journal* 17, 109–122.

Harris M, Raviv A. 1991. The theory of capital structure. *Journal of Finance* 46, 297–355.

Hovakimian A, Opler T, Titman S. 2001. The debt-equity choice. *Journal of Financial and Quantitative Analysis* 36, 1–24.

Jensen MC. 1986. Agency costs of free cash flow, corporate finance, and takeovers. *American Economic Review* 76, 323–329.

Jensen MC. 1989. Eclipse of the public corporation. *Harvard Business Review* 67(5), 61–74.

Jensen MC, Meckling WH. 1976. Theory of the firm: Managerial behavior, agency costs and ownership structure. *Journal of Financial Economics* 76, 323–329.

Keats BW, Hitt MA. 1988. A causal model of linkages among environmental dimensions, macro organizational characteristics, and performance. *Academy of Management Journal* 31, 570–598.

Kleinbaum DG, Kupper LK, Mullerm KE, Nizam A. 1998. *Applied regression analysis and other multivariate methods* (3rd ed.). Pacific Grove, CA, Duxbury Press.

Kochar R. 1996. Explaining firm capital structure: The role of agency theory vs. transaction cost economics. *Strategic Management Journal* 17, 713–728.

Kochar R, Hitt MA. 1998. Linking corporate strategy to capital structure: diversification strategy, type and source of financing. *Strategic Management Journal* 19, 601–610.

Kogut B. 1985. Designing global strategies: Profiting from operational flexibility. *MIT Sloan Management Review* 27(4), 27–38.

Kogut B, Chang SJ. 1996. Platform investments and volatile exchange rates: Direct investment in the U.S. by Japanese electronic companies. *Review of Economics and Statistics* 78, 221–231.

Kogut B, Kulatilaka N. 1994. Operating flexibility, global manufacturing and the option value of a multinational network. *Management Science* 40, 123–138.

Kogut B, Singh H. 1988. The effect of national culture on the choice of entry mode. *Journal of International Business Studies* 19, 411–432.

Kogut B, Zander U. 1992. Knowledge of the firm, combinative capabilities, and the replication of technology. *Organization Science* 3, 383–397.

Kogut B, Zander U. 1993. Knowledge of the firm and the evolutionary theory of the multinational corporation. *Journal of International Business Studies* 15, 151–168.

Leiblein MJ. 2003. The choice of organizational governance form and performance: Predictions from transaction cost, resource-based, and real options theories. *Journal of Management* 29, 937–961.

Leuhrman TA. 1998. Investment opportunities as real options: Getting started on the numbers. *Harvard Business Review*, July–August, 51–67.

Lomax RG. 1992. *Statistical concepts: A second course for education and the behavioral sciences*. New York: Longman.

Mang PL. 1998. Exploiting innovation options: An empirical analysis of R&D intensive firms. *Journal of Economic Behavior and Organization* 35, 229–242.

McGrath RG. 1997. A real options logic for initiating technology positioning investments. *Academy of Management Review* 22, 974–996.

McGrath RG, Nerkar A. 2004. Real options reasoning and a new look at the R&D investment strategies of pharmaceutical firms. *Strategic Management Journal* 25, 1–21.

Miller KD. 1998. Economic exposure and integrated risk management. *Strategic Management Journal* 19, 497–514.

Modigliani F, Miller MH. 1958. The cost of capital, corporate finance and the theory of investment. *American Economic Review* 48, 261–297.

Modigliani F, Miller MH. 1963. Corporate income taxes and the cost of capital: A correction. *American Economic Review* 53, 433–443.

Myers SC. 1977. Determinants of corporate borrowing. *Journal of Financial Economics* 5, 147–175.

Myers SC. 1984. The capital structure puzzle. *Journal of Finance* 39, 575–592.

Myers SC, Majluf NS. 1984. Corporate financing and investment decisions when firms have information that investors do not have. *Journal of Financial Economics* 13, 187–221.

O'Brien JP. 2003. The capital structure implications of pursuing a strategy of innovation. *Strategic Management Journal* 24, 415–432.

Opler TC, Pinkowitz L, Stulz R, Williamson R. 1999. The determinants and implications of corporate cash holdings. *Journal of Financial Economics* 52, 3–46.

Opler TC, Titman S. 1994. Financial distress and corporate performance. *Journal of Finance* 49, 1015–1040.

Rangan S. 1998. Do multinationals operate flexibly? Theory and evidence. *Journal of International Business Studies* 29, 217–237.

Rawls SW, Smithson CW. 1990. Strategic risk management. *Journal of Applied Corporate Finance* 2(2), 6–18.

Reeb DM, Kwok CCY, Baek HY. 1998. Systematic risk of the multinational corporation. *Journal of International Business Studies* 29, 263–279.

Reuer JJ, Leiblein MJ. 2000. Downside risk implications of multinationality and international joint ventures. *Academy of Management Journal* 43, 203–214.

Sandberg CM, Lewellen WG, Stanley KL. 1987. Financial strategy: Planning and managing the corporate leverage position. *Strategic Management Journal* 8, 15–24.

Santarelli E. 1991. Asset specificity, R&D financing, and the signaling properties of the firm's financial structure. *Economics of Innovation and New Technology* 1(4), 279–294.

Saunders A, Cornett MM. 2003. *Financial institutions management: Risk management approach.* New York, McGraw-Hill Irwin.

Schleifer, A. (2000). *Inefficient markets: An introduction to behavioral finance.* Oxford: Oxford University Press.

Shimpi PA. 1999. Integrating risk management and capital management, in Shimpi PA (ed.). *Integrating corporate risk management.* New York, Swiss Re New Markets.

Simerly RL, Li M. 2000. Environmental dynamism, capital structure and performance: a theoretical integration and an empirical test. *Strategic Management Journal* 21, 31–50.

Stulz R. 1990. Managerial discretion and optimal financing policies. *Journal of Financial Economics* 26, 3–27.

Taylor P, Lowe J. 1995. A note on corporate strategy and capital structure. *Strategic Management Journal* 16, 411–414.

Thies CF, Klock MS. 1992. Determinants of capital structure. *Review of Financial Economics* 1, 40–52.

Thomas LG. 1996. Dynamic resourcefulness and the hypercompetitive shift. *Organization Science* 7, 221–242.

Titman S, Wessels R. 1988. The determinants of capital structure choice. *Journal of Finance* 43, 1–19.

Ward K. 1993. *Corporate financial strategy,* Oxford, Butterworth Heinemann.

Williamson O. 1988. Corporate finance and corporate governance. *Journal of Finance* 43, 567–591

19

Effective risk management

Do we have the right management skills and employee competences?

Simon Torp

Abstract

This study analyses the risk performance effects of organisations that combine formalised enterprise risk management (ERM) with a decentralised risk management system (DRM) that allow low-level managers and employees to engage in risk-reducing and opportunity exploiting activities without prior approval from top management. Based on survey responses from 295 of the 500 largest Danish companies, the study develops measures of ERM and DRM to be applied in empirical analysis finding that the combination of ERM and DRM enhances risk management effectiveness. The study further reveals that employee and low-level managerial risk management competences strengthens the positive risk management effects of DRM and without these risk competences, DRM may significantly impede risk effectiveness. Finally, the study shows how a participative leadership style in support of involvement creates a risk effective culture where risk management processes integrate all levels of the organisation as a vital feature of effective risk management.

The interest in enterprise risk management (ERM) has increased rapidly over the last decades (Choi, Ye, Zhao and Luo, 2015) due to more dynamic business environments that enhance the need to measure and hedge risks across the entire organisation and at the same time decentralise decisions to allow different departments rapid reactions to new threats and opportunities (McMullen and Shepherd, 2006). As risk is an inevitable part of the business environment, the capability to effectively hedge downside risks while at the same time quickly exploit opportunities has become an important means to achieve competitive advantages.

The concept of ERM was developed during the 1990s based on a need for a more holistic and strategic approach to risk management. As opposed to traditional risk management, which is scattered around specialist functions in the company, with financial risks hedged in the finance department, operational risks in the production, sales or purchase departments, and strategic risks addressed (if at all) only in the top management team, ERM focuses on identifying, measuring and addressing risks across departments using a holistic approach. ERM takes a systematic approach to risk management across the entire organisation "for identifying, assessing, deciding on responses to, and reporting on opportunities and threats that affect the achievement of its objectives" (Institute of Internal Auditors, 2009). The purpose of ERM is to handle the total risks that firms face in an integrated manner (Barton, Shenkir and Walker, 2002).

While an increasing amount of research in ERM has dealt with methods to identify and measure different kinds of risk or how to implement ERM, some scholars still see the research field as largely unproven and emerging (Mikes and Kaplan, 2014). A number of practitioners have called for more applicable frameworks and empirical evidence on the effectiveness of the proposed frameworks (Beasley, Branson and Hancock, 2010), while other scholars claim that formal ERM is too narrow and only captures traditional and measurable risks, while unforeseeable risks and uncertainty business conditions are neglected, despite the potential significant impact on company performance (Andersen, 2009, 2010). Andersen (2009) finds that effective risk management needs to combine a centrally structured holistic risk management system, which systematically identifies, measures and addresses risks across the company, with a decentralised dynamic organisation of empowered employees that increase responsiveness, adaptability and speed. This emphasises the need for more research into the effects of different types of ERM on risk effectiveness and the combined effect of a central ERM system and different organisational approaches that can support empowerment, decentralisation and, eventually, a responsive and dynamic risk management culture in the entire organisation.

The creation of a dynamic company culture that involves all employees in the identification and assessment of threats and opportunities has been at the core of strategy research for a number of decades. Teece (2007) proposes that the creation of dynamic capabilities, as a construct based on distinct skills, processes, procedures, organisational structures, decision rules and specific disciplines, enables the company to more rapidly sense changes in the business environment, seize opportunities and reconstruct the company. Similarly, the concept of strategic responsiveness highlights the company's ability to "assess the environment, identify firm resources, and mobilize them in effective response actions" (Andersen, Denrell and Bettis, 2007). While the main interest in the strategy literature has been the effect on company performance, the insights can also be used to understand how dynamic capabilities or strategic responsiveness creates a company that can address threats and exploit opportunities more rapidly and effectively to eventually reduce earnings volatility and thereby achieve lower corporate performance risk.

The scope of the current research on ERM focuses on the development of systems to systematise and measure a number of different risks, like climate risk, tax-related risks, IT risk, and so forth, and create scorecards, computer systems and measurement models that, in a standardised way, can be applied by a central risk management department headed by a chief risk officer, or CRO (Choi et al., 2015). This is contrasted by the research on dynamic capabilities and strategic responsiveness, which is embedded in organisational studies, motivation theory, psychology and strategic management (Helfat and Peteraf, 2014; Teece, 2007). The combination of systematic centralised ERM practices and decentralised, empowering organisational processes might, on the one hand, support each other in a more effective risk management system, but might, on the other, crowd out the individual positive risk effects. While the two approaches have been analysed separately, more research into the combined effects is warranted. The current study aims at unfolding some of the individual and combined effects of ERM in a decentralised organization structure. Decentralisation of identification and decisions of risk-reducing action has been argued to enhance risk performance (Andersen, 2010), but empirical tests of the effects are limited, and a discussion of whether or not the employees have the necessary competences to effectively use this autonomy has, to our knowledge, never been tested. Based on a survey among the top 500 Danish companies, the current study tests the individual and combined effects of ERM, decentralised risk management and a supportive leadership style on risk performance. The findings support earlier findings by Paape and Speklé (2012) indicating that ERM enhances risk performance, thus underpinning the importance of ERM as a path to effective risk management. Additionally, a leadership style that supports the involvement of employees, thereby creating a more dynamic company, is also found to enhance risk performance. The importance of management and the conducted leadership style in supporting employee involvement, empowering employee initiatives and creating a dynamic company has been highlighted in a number of studies (Mantera and Vaara, 2008; Torp and Linder, 2014), and emphasise that risk management is not something that can be stored in a lower-level department or can be expected to automatically develop in the organisation. A responsive organisation is initiated by the management and imposed by its leadership style. Furthermore, the paper finds that decentralisation by itself is not enough to ensure effective risk performance; on the contrary, decentralisation by itself is negatively associated with risk effectiveness, unless the employees have the necessary competences. Hence, the study extends our knowledge about how a dynamic company might support effective risk management practices by empirically testing the effect of ERM and decentralisation and showing that positive effects also need employee competencies for identifying and addressing new opportunities and threats. The study finds that decentralisation and ERM combined enhance overall risk performance when the ERM system develops risk awareness and engagement across the entire organisation. As Senge (1990) writes: To survive and excel in environments with rapid changes, organisations must "discover how to tap people's commitment and capacity to learn at *all* levels" (p. 4). This indicates that formalising ERM and decentralising risk management put the company in a position where it can benefit from the best of two worlds. It can identify, measure and address foreseeable risks in a systematic way using a number of ERM techniques and at the same time develop a dynamic organization with risk-aware employees with autonomy to quickly address these risks and opportunities. Consequently, the chapter expands our knowledge of how to combine ERM with strategic responsiveness and highlights the need for more research to elaborate on how the two fields can be combined effectively and how to ensure that employees acquire the necessary risk management competences. Effective risk management is not only essential to reduce adverse risk outcomes but also to enhance competitive advantage and increase company value (Choi et al., 2015; Gordon, Loeb and Tseng, 2009; Teece, 2007).

Literature review and hypothesis development

The Committee of Sponsoring Organizations of the Treadway Commission (COSO) defines ERM as

> a process, effected by an entity's board of directors, management and other personnel, applied in strategy setting and across the enterprise, designed to identify potential events that may affect the entity, and manage risks to be within its risk appetite, to provide reasonable assurance regarding the achievement of entity objectives.
>
> *(COSO, 2004, p. 6)*

The focus is mainly procedural in the form of identifying, assessing and evaluating potential outcomes (Choi et al., 2015), thereby indicating that structural or organisational changes lie outside the purpose of ERM. Due to the procedural focus of ERM, the majority of research on ERM focuses on developing tools to create risk maps and balanced scorecards, stress tests or scenario analyses in the pursuit of foreseeing future events, assessments of potential implications and actions to address the potential risk. Despite up to 1,600 different articles per year related to ERM over the years 2009–2014 (Choi et al., 2015), both scholars and practitioners have stated that the field is still largely unproven and emerging (Mikes and Kaplan, 2014) and that the existing frameworks are dissatisfactory (Beasley et al., 2010). Mikes and Kaplan (2014) argue that ERM research generally treats the field as self-evident and "fails to answer if its usefulness can be proven by more than its apparent popularity" (Mikes and Kaplan, 2014, p. 3). To test the usefulness of ERM, scholars have highlighted that more research is needed to more directly measure the level of ERM implementation based on a number of systematic and procedural characteristics of ERM and the effect of ERM on risk management effectiveness. When measuring ERM, the majority of research so far has used a binary proxy in the form of the presence of a CRO (Beasley, Pagach and Warr, 2008; Lienenberg and Hoyt, 2003; Pagach and Warr, 2011), SEC filings (Hoyt and Liebenberg, 2011) or Standard & Poor's (S&P) Ratings (Baxter et al., 2012; McShane, Nair and Rustambekov, 2011; Mikes and Kaplan, 2014). Using CRO as a proxy for ERM has been criticised for capturing neither the level of implementation of an ERM programme (Beasley et al., 2008) nor the quality of the different processes applied in the ERM system (Kaplan and Mikes, 2013). Additionally, Kaplan and Mikes (2013) emphasise that formal ERM is implemented in a number of different ways, with or without a formal CRO, and that it is "deployed at different levels, for different purposes, by different staff groups in different organizations" (p. 8). This calls for a measure of ERM that captures the complexity and diversity of how ERM is implemented in different organisations.

The outcome of ERM has been tested in a number of studies. Gordon et al. (2009) find a positive relationship between ERM and company performance moderated by environmental uncertainty, industry competition, firm size, firm complexity and monitoring by the board of directors. Similarly, Hoyt and Liebenberg (2011) find a positive effect of ERM on company performance. Others studies find no effect (e.g., McShane, Nair and Rustambekov, 2011; Sekerci, Chapter 22 in this volume), and in a study by Lin, Wen and Yu (2011), ERM is even shown to reduce company value. While the effect of ERM on company performance and value is relevant, the most direct outcome of ERM would be in terms of risk effectiveness in the form of lower volatility in performance and reduced negative impacts from risk events. Despite these expected effects of ERM, only a limited number of studies have actually tested if ERM reduces company risk. Paape and Speklé (2012) found that the frequency of risk assessment and reporting and the use of quantitative risk assessment techniques are associated with higher perceived risk management effectiveness. Their study, however, raises a number of concerns about the effect of applying the COSO framework and it posits that the mechanistic view on risk management proposed by the COSO recommendations seems not to improve risk effectiveness. This suggests that, even though we still would expect ERM to improve risk effectiveness, the traditional measures of ERM may not fully capture what constitutes an effective ERM system. More research on the ERM measure to capture the many facets of ERM seems warranted to advance the academic and practical implications of the field. Despite the lack of empirical support, it seems logical that by applying a structured, systematic and holistic approach to risk management, the overall risk effectiveness should increase as a consequence of adopting ERM practices. This leads to the following hypothesis:

Hypothesis 1: Implementation of ERM enhances risk effectiveness.

The management literature has for several decades emphasised lower-level employee behaviour in complex and fast-changing environments where locally held knowledge is important for risk recognition and evaluation (Burgelman and Grove, 2006; Dodgson, Gann and Salter, 2008; Meeus and Edquist, 2006). Allowing lower-level employees to be heard widens the scope of input and increases the speed at which top management can receive information on new risks, opportunities and emerging trends (Dutton, Ashford, Neill, Hayes, and Wierba, 1997). The literature suggests that top management needs to create an atmosphere where employees feel their opinions are valued and where open-minded discussions of opposing positions are acknowledged (Galanou, 2010). To create such a culture, top management should support the involvement of employees in decision-making, soliciting and considering their ideas (Kaufman, 2001; Somech, 2006). Furthermore, top management should signal that individuals are allowed to express themselves, challenge the status quo and ask questions without fear of negative consequences (Scully, Kirkpatrick and Locke, 1995). Such a participative leadership style can be an important factor to stimulate an organizational climate where risk ideas are openly proposed, discussed, evaluated and reflected on (Torp and Linder, 2014).

The conceptual literature and case study evidence point out that top management can play a decisive role in encouraging such behaviour by facilitating experimentation and risk-taking through organisational systems, informal processes and their own behaviour at both individual and team levels (e.g., Burgelman, 1983; Lumpkin, Cogliser, and Schneider, 2009). Leadership has been defined in many different ways, but common for most definitions is that it involves an influence process concerned with facilitating the performance of a collective task by others. Moreover, a supportive leadership style is characterised by clearly signalling support of bottom-up initiatives and experimentation and readiness for active engagement discussing ideas in an honest, serious and interested manner (Burgelman, 1983; Choi, 2004; Kuratko, Ireland, Covin and Hornsby, 2005). Likewise, Simons (2005) emphasises the role of how top managers interact with their subordinates when discussing performance and the strategic uncertainties as important for fostering bottom-up driven innovation and strategic renewal. Such leadership also acknowledges the inherent risks of experimentation, that is, that many – if not most – initiatives will not turn out to be very successful (Burgelman, 1983; Kuratko et al., 2005). By adopting a supportive leadership style, the leaders express confidence in the abilities of organizational members to perform effectively and succeed in working on challenging issues and projects (Carless, Wearing and Mann, 2000). Such behaviour has been shown in studies to enhance the creativity and innovative behaviour of individuals, which should also have a positive effect on risk effectiveness through more rapid risk identification and development of solutions that improve the ability to respond in a timely and effective manner. This leads to the following hypothesis:

Hypothesis 2: A participative leadership style enhances risk effectiveness.

Despite the expected positive effect of a central, holistic and systematic risk management process on risk effectiveness, a number of scholars emphasise that companies also face a number of unforeseeable risks that are hard to quantify and even predict (Andersen, 2009; Bettis and Hitt, 1995). Andersen (2010) emphasises that, since strategic risks often are highly uncertain while constituting some of the biggest corporate exposures, the development of a risk management system capable of dealing with these risks remains a fundamental challenge (Andersen, 2010; Slywotzky and Drzik, 2005). This calls for the creation of dynamic capabilities through decentralisation of risk identification and risk-reducing initiatives, since traditional ERM, due to its often centralised, formal and bureaucratic character, is unable to capture the intricacies of a dynamic and unforeseeable business environment (Henriksen and Uhlenfeldt, 2006; Power, 2007). Teece (2007) finds the creation of dynamic capabilities to be based on distinct skills, processes, procedures, organisational structures, decision rules and specific disciplines that enable the company to more rapidly sense changes in the business environment, seize opportunities and reconstruct the company. This is in line with the concept of strategic responsiveness that highlights the company's ability to "assess the environment, identify firm resources, and mobilize them in effective response actions" (Andersen et al., 2007). While the strategy literature's main interest often has been the creation of enhanced company performance, these insights might also be used to understand how dynamic capabilities or strategic responsiveness creates a company that more rapidly can address threats and exploit opportunities, eventually reducing volatility in performance and thereby reducing company risks.

Decentralised risk management allows lower-level managers located closer to the actual business transactions, and who also possess the knowledge and information necessary to develop an effective and appropriate response, to identify signals of environmental change (Daft, 1992). Hence, companies with a more decentralised decision structure, where managers are able to respond without the prior approval of higher organisational levels, may react faster and more effectively to unforeseeable environmental changes. Andersen (2010) finds that, in companies with many unknowns and a high risk interrelation, a combination of a central risk handling system and decentralised risk responses allows the company to most effectively benefit from the systematic holistic effects of ERM while also satisfying the need for rapid and appropriate responses to unforeseeable changes in a dynamic business environment. This supports the following hypothesis:

Hypothesis 3: *Decentralised* risk management enhances risk effectiveness.

While an extensive amount of research has discussed the potential positive effects of decentralisation, only limited attention has been given to whether or not the employees and the organisation possess the right competences to engage into a decentralised risk management system. Competences can be seen both at the individual level as comprised by a set of knowledge, abilities and attitudes that supports superior performance (Gray, 1999; Spencer and Spencer, 1993) and at the organisational level as describing the organisation's ability to combine, mix and integrate resources in products or services, thereby creating benefits to the customer (Prahalad and Hamel, 1990). In the literature on competences, it is highlighted that, while knowledge or qualifications are linked to the individual or the organisation, competences are related to the task that needs to be completed. A competence is to act responsibly and knowing how to mobilise, integrate and transfer knowledge, resources and capabilities in a given professional context (Fleury, Fleury and Fleury, 2007). This means that competences are constituted by applied knowledge and capabilities. To develop competences, the effect must be aligned with the company strategy and the tasks at hand. In a risk management setting, this implies the capability to identify important opportunities and threats and knowing how to support information sharing vertically and horizontally in the organisation, while allocating attention, resources and knowledge to actions taken locally and when and how to escalate to higher-level decisions when needed.

At the organisational level, Mills, Platte, Bourne and Richards (2002) make a distinction between core competences (central to the strategy), distinctive competences (recognised by customers), business competences (related to business units), supportive competences (supporting other activities) and dynamic capabilities (resources important for change). Especially the dynamic capabilities are important when the organization is faced with unforeseen changes in the business environment. Here, the organisation needs to have the necessary knowledge and information available to identify and react to ongoing changes, paired with a culture where information is easily shared and discussed among members of the organisation and across section boundaries to allow for rapid combination, mix and integration of resources in support of appropriate actions. In sum, an effective decentralised risk management system is essentially formed by an organisation, where individual members hold the necessary competences related to risk identification, evaluation and response. It is an organisation with dynamic capabilities in the form of relevant information and knowledge, a culture of information sharing and discussion, and allocation of decision power that allows the organisation to react fast and effectively. This leads to the following hypothesis:

Hypothesis 4: The effect of a decentralised risk management system is *mediated* by the level of risk management competences in the organisation

Methods

The use of multiple data sources makes it possible to overcome the dangers of common method bias that could arise if the use of a single data source creates spurious covariance between variables (Podsakoff, MacKenzie and Lee, 2003). Our predictor and mediator variables, in turn, were collected through a double-respondent survey of senior executives. Responses from the firms' chief financial officers (CFOs) provided information on some predictors: formalised ERM, decentralised risk management, risk competences and – our dependent variable – risk performance. In contrast, information on leadership style was provided by the heads of marketing or sales. Since this setup does not fully exclude common method bias, as some predictors and the dependent variable are based on information provided by the same source (the firms' CFOs), we implemented both procedural and statistical means to minimise common method variance as recommended in literature (Podsakoff et al., 2003). Procedural remedies included embedding the targeted scales in a larger set of scales dealing with quite diverse topics, thereby reducing the likelihood that CFOs would associate the two constructs of interest. In addition, items were pretested among 87 managers from 57 firms not included in the final sample to reduce ambiguity of questions as much as possible. Finally, respondents were assured that responses would be confidential. As a statistical remedy, we applied Harman's one-factor test on the CFOs' responses where items load on multiple factors lending further credence to the validity of responses and constructs (Podsakoff et al., 2003).

Data

Data for the study were collected from a cross-sectional mail survey. The 500 largest companies in Denmark measured by the number of employees were approached by a two-page questionnaire in April 2013. The companies covered a broad set of industries and had at least 300 full-time employees. The questionnaire was initially tested on three managers to obtain an impression of how the questions were perceived and to clarify any ambiguity. Subsequently, the questionnaire was tested on 45 managers from 45 different firms (not part of the main dataset) to test the robustness of the constructs. The pretests raised no concerns.

In a first step, the accounting managers and sales/marketing managers were approached by a personalised cover letter and a two-page questionnaire. Three weeks later, a second letter was sent to those who had not yet responded. These letters produced a total of 248 responses (141 from CFOs and 107 from marketing managers). In June 2013, a marketing agency was assigned to contact the remaining managers by phone, resulting in 345 extra responses and producing a total of 593 responses (298 from CFOs and 295 from marketing managers) – a response rate of 59.3%. After careful inspection, 295 double responses from the top 500 companies were included in the analysis. Using multiple sources allows us to reduce the risk of common method bias, which may arise if the use of a single data source creates spurious covariance between variables (Podsakoff et al., 2003).

A test for nonresponse bias was conducted on sector, size, turnover and a number of other financial data comparing the responding companies with the population of the 500 largest companies in Denmark. None of the tests gave any cause for concern.

Measures

Formal enterprise risk management: The items were developed from the risk management process described in the ERM frameworks COSO (2004) and ISO 31000 (2009). The items explore the extent to which the company during the last three years has assigned priority to (1) having standard procedures for identifying major risks and opportunities, (2) analysing risks and opportunities as a basis for determining how they should be managed, (3) having standard procedures in place for launching risk-reducing activities, (4) preparing regularly risk reports for top management and (5) having standard procedures in place for monitoring the development in major risks and the risk-reducing activities launched. The respondents were asked to rate each of the items on a 7-point Likert scale. The construct was tested in a factor model, which showed only one factor with an eigenvalue above 1 (eigenvalue = 3.935).

Participative leadership style: Assessment of top management's leadership style was based on Choi (2004). The instrument focuses specifically on the participatory leadership style, leaving out other aspects of a more broadly defined concept, such as individual work effort, work duration and the like. The instrument is derived from Choi's (2004) construct of supportive leadership. The resulting four-item measure asked managers to rate the degree to which top management was open to middle managers' (MM's) ideas and willing to let middle managers experiment with new concepts or products on a 7-point Likert scale (1 = fully disagree; 7 = fully agree). The construct was tested in a factor model, showing only one factor with an eigenvalue above 1 (eigenvalue = 2.754).

Decentralised risk management: Decentralised risk management is measured by three items based on 7-point Likert scale (1 = fully disagree; 7 = fully agree) measuring the delegation of tasks as well as responsibilities. The three items were (1) identification of risks and opportunities is delegated to the different business units, their managers and employees, (2) decisions on risk-reducing measures and exploitation of opportunities are delegated to the individual business units and (3) each single business unit is responsible for identifying and assessing risks and opportunities. The construct was tested in a factor model, with only one factor showing an eigenvalue above 1 (eigenvalue = 2.439).

Risk competences: The measure of risk competences, on both the individual and organisational level, is based on three items using a 7-point Likert scale (1 = fully disagree; 7 = fully agree). The items were (1) the managers and employees of the business units have the necessary competences and knowledge to identify relevant risks and opportunities, (2) the individual business unit has the necessary information and knowledge to decide how to handle risks and opportunities and (3) the new risks and opportunities observed in the different business units are discussed among employees and managers. The construct was tested in a factor model, and only one factor showed an eigenvalue above 1 (eigenvalue =2.349).

Risk effectiveness: The risk effectiveness was measured by three items designed to uncover the relative risk management performance over the last 3 years compared to the sector in general. The respondents were asked to rate on a 7-point Likert scale (1 = significantly worse; 7 = significantly better) how the company had performed compared to the sector in general in its (1) ability to hedge important known risks and uncertainties, (2) ability to react to and reduce unforeseen risks and (3) ability to exploit new opportunities. The construct was tested in a factor model, which showed only one factor with an eigenvalue above 1 (eigenvalue =2.349).

Analysis

All latent constructs were measured with multiple items, thereby increasing construct validity. Moreover, we ensured a match between the level of theory and analysis (Nielsen, 2013), as all items and constructs were designed to measure organisational-level phenomena. Internal consistency and reliability were assessed by Cronbach's alpha, factor loadings, composite reliability and average variance extracted for all latent constructs, as shown in Table 19.1.

Table 19.1 Factor loadings and reliabilities

Dimensions and variables	n	Cronbach's alpha	Construct reliability	AVE	Factor loadings	Indicator reliability
Leadership style	295	0.85	0.85	0.59		
Top management actively seeks MM opinions and ideas on strategic issues					0.83	0.69
Top management are open to new ideas and initiatives from all employees					0.81	0.66
Top management appreciate that MM experiments with new ideas and products					0.81	0.66
Top management ensure that the interest of MM are considered when making strategic decisions					0.87	0.75
Decentralised risk management	295	0.88	0.89	0.72		
Identification of risks and opportunities is delegated to the different business units, their managers and employees					0.89	0.79
Decisions on risk-reducing measures and exploitation of opportunities are delegated to the individual business units					0.92	0.84
Each single business unit is responsible for identifying and assessing risks and opportunities					0.90	0.80
Risk competences	295	0.86	0.87	0.69		
The managers and employees of the business units have the necessary competences and knowledge to identify relevant risks and opportunities					0.90	0.81
The individual business unit have the necessary information and knowledge to decide how to handle risks and opportunities					0.92	0.85

(*Continued*)

Table 19.1 Continued

Dimensions and variables	n	Cronbach's alpha	Construct reliability	AVE	Factor loadings	Indicator reliability
The new risks and opportunities observed in the different business units are discussed among employees and managers					0.83	0.69
Enterprise risk management	295	0.93	0.93	0.73		
In our firm we have standard procedures in place for identifying major risks and opportunities					0.89	0.80
Risks and opportunities are analysed as a basis for determining how they should be managed					0.88	0.77
We apply risk analysis for determining risk-reducing measures					0.90	0.81
We regularly prepare risk reports for the top management and the board of directors					0.87	0.76
We have standard procedures in place for monitoring the developments in major risks and the risk-reducing measures launched					0.89	0.79
Strategic risk management performance (performed in the last 3 years compared to the sector in general)	295	0.80	0.82	0.62		
Ability to hedge important known risks and uncertainties					0.90	0.81
Ability to react to and reduce unforeseen risks					0.92	0.85
Ability to exploit new opportunities					0.83	0.69

As reported in Table 19.1, the constructs display high levels of reliability, as indicated by composite reliabilities (CR) above 0.82 and average variance extracted (AVE) ranging from 0.59 to 0.73 (Fornell and Larcker, 1981). The latent constructs meet the convergent criteria with each loading being significantly related to its underlying factor. Likewise, a series of chi-square difference tests on the factor correlations showed that discriminant validity (the degree to which the constructs differ from each other) is achieved (Anderson and Gerbing, 1988). Finally, a test of normality was conducted, as recommended by Hult et al. (2006). Using the Kolmogorov-Smirnov test of normality, both variables were significantly normally distributed within the 0.001 level.

Common method issues

We employed a number of ex ante procedural and ex post statistical steps in order to examine the potential for common method bias in our data. First, in the survey instrument, we varied anchors and scales of items related to the various constructs. In addition, we interspersed open-ended questions throughout the survey, reversed several items and physically separated related constructs from each other. Together, these steps minimise the effects of consistency artefacts (Chang, Witteloostuijn and Eden, 2010). Second, a Harman's one-factor test was conducted on all items underlying the latent factors with variance explained between 6.192% and 35.794%, confirming the validity of the constructs. Since no single factor accounted for the majority of the covariance in the independent and criterion variables, and items related to perceptual measures all loaded on distinct factors with eigenvalues exceeding one, we find no evidence of common method variance (Podsakoff, MacKenzie and Podsakoff, 2012). Third, the nature of our theorisation, which includes moderation, helps alleviate common method bias concerns since such complex relationships are "in all likelihood not part of the respondents' theory-in-use" (Chang, van Witteloostuijn and Eden, 2010, p. 180). There is no reason to believe that common method bias would create an artificial interaction effect (Podsakoff et al., 2012).

Analytical procedure

The proposed theoretical model necessitates simultaneous estimation of multiple relationships between observed and latent constructs, and the survey data are subject to potential measurement error. As a result, the hypotheses were tested in a structural equation model using AMOS 22 SEM (structural equation modelling) software in a two-stage procedure recommended by Anderson and Gerbing (1988). The first stage involved estimation of the measurement model by the use of confirmatory factor analysis (CFA) to determine convergent and discriminant validity. The second stage compared the theoretical model with the measurement model. Based on the results of the test, the structural model was used to provide path coefficients for hypothesis testing. Additional fit measures like the goodness-of-fit index (GFI) and the root mean square residual (RMSEA) were calculated to test the model fit, as recommended by Gerbing and Anderson (1992). A sequence of nested structural models (competing models) were evaluated in order to determine the model representing the best fit between the hypothesised relationships and the observed variance in the data.

Results

Table 19.2 shows the means, the standard deviations and the correlations of all items. All correlations between items representing different latent variables are well below 0.6, indicating no concern for multicollinearity. Furthermore, tests for variance inflation factors (VIF) on all items were below 1.5.

The chi-square test of the measurement model was significant; however, the test is well known and criticised for its sensitivity to sample size (Kline, 2005). Thus, it is recommended to rely on multiple fit indices rather than on the chi-square test alone, and we proceeded to inspect a number of comparative goodness-of-fit indices that measure the proportional improvement of the model fit by comparing the hypothesised model with a restricted baseline model. As recommended by Hult et al. (2006) and Gerbing and Anderson (1992), the fit of the models was tested using the RMSEA and the global comparative fit index (CFI) in addition to the normed fit index (NFI) and the Tucker-Lewis index (TLI). The CFI (Bentler, 1980) takes into

Table 19.2 Descriptive statistics and correlations

Variable	Mean	SD	1	2	3	4	5	6	7	8	9	10	11	12	13	14	15	16
1 ERM1	4.72	1.63	1															
2 ERM2	4.95	1.45	.76 ***	1														
3 ERM3	4.32	1.67	.75 ***	.73 ***	1													
4 ERM4	4.21	1.73	.69 ***	.68 ***	.75 ***	1												
5 ERM5	4.08	1.72	.76 ***	.70 ***	.73 ***	.75 ***	1											
6 DRM1	4.26	1.66	.20 ***	.20 ***	.24 ***	.18 **	.23 ***	1										
7 DRM2	3.85	1.47	.15 **	.14 *	.19 ***	.15 **	.19 ***	.73 ***	1									
8 DRM3	4.06	1.52	.21 ***	.20 ***	.24 ***	.15 *	.21 ***	.68 ***	.75 ***	1								
9 Competences1	4.17	1.49	.47 ***	.45 ***	.46 ***	.43 ***	.48 ***	.54 ***	.47 ***	0.55 ***	1							
10 Competences2	3.97	1.38	.51 ***	.48 ***	.50 ***	.47 ***	.52 ***	54 ***	.48 ***	0.53 ***	.78 ***	1						
11 Competences3	4.15	1.54	.43 ***	.46 ***	.44 ***	.47 ***	.52 ***	.43 ***	.31 ***	0.37 ***	.59 ***	.65 ***	1					
12 Leadership1	5.51	1.39	.03	.01	.06	.09	.02	.03	.05	0.00	.04	.01	.00	1				
13 Leadership2	5.80	1.23	.00	.01	.06	.10	.07	.00	.05	0.04	.03	.03	.03	0.57 ***	1			
14 Leadership3	5.31	1.42	-.01	-.05	.03	.03	.02	.03	.01	0.02	.05	.04	-.01	0.51 ***	0.57 ***	1		
15 Leadership4	5.35	1.36	.01	-.02	.02	.07	.03	.07	.09	-0.03	.02	-.02	-.02	0.67 ***	0.57 ***	0.62 ***	1	
16 Risk eff. 1	4.56	1.13	.51 ***	.50 ***	.48 ***	.51 ***	.54 ***	.01 *	.08	0.08	.34 ***	.39 ***	.42 ***	0.10	0.14	0.10	0.09	
17 Risk eff. 2	4.58	1.19	.45 ***	.46 ***	.44 ***	.45 ***	.51 ***	.16 **	0.11 *	0.07	.31 ***	.39 ***	.40 ***	0.16 *	0.17 *	0.13	0.16 *	0
18 Risk eff. 3	4.72	1.10	.22 ***	.23 ***	.21 ***	.24 ***	.26 ***	.03	.07	0.04	.01 *	.15 *	.19 ***	0.13	0.21 **	0.17 *	0.13	0

n = 295. Significance of correlations: *** p < .001; p < 0.1; *p < .05 (two-tailed test).

consideration sample size, and values of 0.90 or better indicate a model with a good fit. The RMSEA is sensitive to the number of estimated parameters in the model, as it considers the error of approximation in the population where values below 0.08 indicate a good fit. The fit characteristics of the measurement model indicated a model that fits the data very well (NFI = 0.95, Delta2 = 0.99, TLI = 0.98, CFI = 0.99, RMSEA = 0.03).

The causal structures among the latent variables suggested by our theoretical model were assessed in the structural model (Table 19.3). In accordance with theory (Andersen, 2010; Mantera and Vaara, 2008; Paape and Speklé, 2012), we started with a model testing the direct relationships between DRM, ERM, participative leadership style and risk competences, respectively, and risk performance. This model fits the data, but some fits are below the recommended levels (NFI = 0.88, Delta2 = 0.91, TLI = 0.89, CFI = 0.91, RMSEA = 0.07 and $\chi2$ = 428.99, df = 131, $p < 0.001$). We then added risk competences as a mediating factor between DRM and risk effectiveness. It can be argued that, by allowing lower-level departments and managers to autonomously take risk mitigating actions, these departments and managers might develop the right competences to effectively perform risk mitigating actions. This path was significant (β = 0.643, $p < 0.001$), and the fit statistics improved compared to model 1 (CFI = 0.92, Delta2 = 0.95, TLI = 0.93, CFI = 0.95, RMSEA = 0.05) with a significant chi-square difference test ($\Delta\chi2_1 df$ = +128.32, $p < 0.001$). An enterprise-wide approach to risk management promotes risk awareness and risk understanding to all managers and employees throughout the corporate structure. It recognises the value of the information and suggestions from people at all levels of the firm (COSO, 2004). As Senge (1990, p. 4) argues organisations must "discover how to tap people's commitment and capacity to learn at all levels" to survive and excel in environments with rapid changes. This indicates that, when implementing ERM, companies try to create a risk understanding and awareness throughout the entire organisation. This might also impose the wish and/or the need for distributed risk decision authority. Hence, it is expected that ERM can enhance DRM. Accordingly, we added a mediation effect from ERM to DRM in model 3. This path was also significant (β = 0.332, $p < 0.001$), and the fit statistics improved compared to model 2 (CFI = 0.92, Delta2 = 0.96, TLI = 0.94, CFI = 0.96, RMSEA = 0.05) with a significant chi-square difference test ($\Delta\chi2_1 df$ = +26.62, $p < 0.001$). Companies conducting a participative leadership style support employee involvement, for which reason the level of DRM is expected to increase if management supports involvement in their leadership style. In model 4, a mediation effect from participative leadership style to DRM was added. Despite the expected relationship, the path turned out to be insignificant, and the chi-square test was also

Table 19.3 Structural equation models (AMOS)

Model and description	x2	A%2	df	NFI	Delta2	TLI	CFI	RMSEA
0 Measurement model	**163.61**		**125**	**95.40**	**98.90**	**984.00**	**98.90**	**0.025**
1 Direct effects	**428.99**	kkk	**131**	**87.90**	**91.30**	**88.50**	**91.20**	**0.067**
2 DRM mediated by risk competences	**300.67**	kkk	**130**	**91.50**	**95.00**	**93.30**	**94.90**	**0.051**
3 ERM mediated by DRM	**274.05**	kkk	**129**	**92.30**	**95.80**	**94.30**	**95.70**	**0.047**
4 Leadership style mediated DRM	**273.67**		**128**	**92.30**	**95.70**	**94.20**	**95.70**	**0.048**
5 DRM moderates ERM	**295.04**		**146**	**91.70**	**95.70**	**94.30**	**95.60**	**0.045**

Significance levels: *** $p < .001$; ** $p < .01$; * $p < .05$ (two-tailed test).

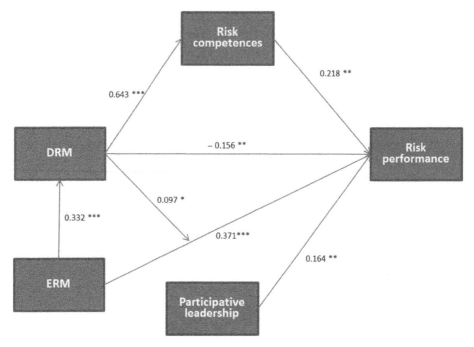

Significance levels: *** $p < 0.001$; ** $p < 0.01$; * $p < 0.05$ (two-tailed test)

Figure 19.1 Structural equation model

insignificant. Andersen (2010) argues that the combination of ERM and DRM is a viable path to improved risk performance and that the two methods might reinforce each other. In model 5, we therefore test a moderation effect between ERM and DRM. While the improvements of the fits turned out insignificant, the moderation effect based on the chi-square test was significant. Since the theoretical arguments support the moderation effect and the chi-square test is significant when compared with model 1, we prefer model 5 to model 3. Model 5 is depicted in Figure 19.1.

Hypothesis testing

Based on the nested models presented earlier, we continued to test our hypotheses considering the unstandardised parameter estimates. Hypothesis 1, suggesting a positive effect of ERM on risk effectiveness, had a significant path ($\beta = 0.371, p < 0.001$), which supports the theoretical argument that ERM enhances risk performance and extends the findings of Paape and Speklé (2012). Hypothesis 2 argues that management needs to practice a participative leadership style to support decentralised organisation-wide risk awareness. Consequently, we expect that a participative leadership style will have a positive effect on risk effectiveness. This hypothesis is supported ($\beta = 0.164, p < 0.01$), thus highlighting the importance of integrating management style and organisational settings when crafting an effective risk management system. These organisational settings support the creation of dynamic capabilities that allow the organisation to rapidly identify and address potential threats and opportunities. Andersen (2010) argues that a decentralised risk management system enhances risk performance. The model only partly supports Hypothesis 3, since it is shown that decentralised risk management only enhances risk performance if mediated by risk competences, as argued in Hypothesis 4. It is found that decentralised risk management by itself seems to have a significant, negative effect on risk effectiveness, which highlights the importance of ensuring that employees and lower-level managers have the proper competences to ensure risk effectiveness.

Discussion

Consistent with recent calls for more research on ERM and analyses of how organisational and managerial settings affect risk performance (Andersen, 2010; Beasley et al., 2010; Mikes and Kaplan, 2014), the current study conducts empirical tests that extend this theoretical insight and knowledge. While ERM has attracted considerable attention since the 1990s, there still is a lack of solid empirical testing of ERM effects on risk effectiveness based on appropriate measures of ERM that captures the different procedural aspects of ERM. While earlier studies have used a binary proxy in the form of the presence of a CRO (Beasley et al., 2008; Lienbenberg and Hoyt, 2003; Pagach and Warr, 2011), SEC filings (Hoyt and Liebenberg, 2011), S&R ERM Ratings (Baxter et al., 2013; McShane et al., 2011; Mikes and Kaplan, 2014) and the like, the present study applies a five-item measure of ERM. Using CRO as a proxy for ERM has been criticised for not capturing the level of ERM implementation (Beasley et al., 2008) or the application of different processes in the ERM system (Kaplan and Mikes, 2013). The measure of ERM introduced in this study includes standard procedures for identifying and measuring risks, allocating resources, reporting risks, engaging in risk-reducing activities and systematic monitoring of the risk-reducing actions. The empirical tests suggest that implementation of ERM does enhance risk effectiveness. Despite this seemingly logical outcome of ERM, only few scholars have actually tested this relationship (Paape and Speklé, 2012). The study thereby demonstrates the importance of ERM as a path to improved risk effectiveness while addressing the challenge articulated by Mikes and Kaplan (2014) that "much academic research treats ERM as self-evident and fails to answer if its usefulness can be proven by more than its apparent popularity" (p. 3).

While significant research has addressed how ERM can be implemented and how risks can be quantified, measured and registered in an appropriate IT system, a number of scholars have recently argued that, to ensure a more effective risk management system, organisations also need to create a more decentralised risk management organisation. Andersen (2010) poses that, while a number of foreseeable risks like financial, customer and supplier risks can be adequately identified, measured and hedged, a number of more strategic and unforeseen risks need to be dealt with in different ways. Andersen (2010) emphasises that, since strategic risks are often highly uncertain while constituting some of the biggest corporate exposures, the development of a risk management system to deal with these risks remains a fundamental challenge (Andersen, 2010; Slywotzky and Drzik, 2005). This calls for the creation of dynamic capabilities in the form of decentralised risk identification and risk-reducing initiatives, as traditional ERM, due to its often centralised, formal and bureaucratic characteristics, is unable to capture the intricacies of a dynamic and unforeseeable business environment (Henriksen and Uhlenfeldt, 2006; Power, 2007). Teece (2007) finds that the creation of dynamic capabilities, as a construct based on distinct skills, processes, procedures, organisational structures, decision rules and specific disciplines, enables the company to more rapidly sense changes in the business environment, seize opportunities and reconstruct the company. This is in line with the concept of strategic responsiveness, which highlights the company's ability to assess environmental changes and identify and mobilize firm resources in effective response actions (Andersen et al., 2007). The current study empirically tests whether a decentralised risk management system that allows managers and lower-level departments to identify risks and opportunities without prior approval of higher-level management and independently allocate resources to circumvent risks or exploit opportunities is an effective path to improved risk effectiveness. The findings highlight that even though decentralisation of risk actions might create dynamic capabilities and strategic responsiveness, there is an urgent need to ensure that employees and lower-level managers possess the necessary competences. An opposite effect may occur if a company implements a decentralised risk management system without developing adequate employee competences to identify relevant risks and opportunities with relevant information and knowledge at the organisational level to address risks and exploit opportunities. The study finds a significant, negative direct effect of DRM on risk effectiveness if it is not mediated by sufficient risk competences. If the company, on the other hand, creates adequate competences among employees and lower-level managers, the study results are consistent with the findings that an effective risk management systems needs to apply a central holistic ERM system and at the same time decentralise delegation of risk competences. These results highlight the need for more research into the combined applications of ERM and DRM systems in the context of organisation structure and strategic processes. The relevance of this focus is highlighted by the significant moderation effect of DRM on ERM, which indicates that the combination of ERM and DRM not only creates more effective risk management outcomes but that the two systems together support each other where the total effect exceeds the sum of the individual parts.

While much risk management research has addressed the importance of systems, processes and structure, the current study emphasises that effective risk management also depends on an appropriate leadership style. Top management needs to support involvement and empowerment through a participative leadership style. The empirical evidence shows that participative leadership, often defined as joint decision-making, or at least shared influence in decision-making, by a superior and his or her employees (Koopman and Wierdsma, 1998) tends to transmit its effects to work performance through psychological empowerment. For instance, Koberg, Boss, Senjem and Goodman (1999) find the participative style of management (leader approachability) positively related to psychological empowerment, which leads to increased self-rated productivity. By the same token, in their meta-analysis, Eby, Freeman, Rush and Lance (1999) found intrinsic motivation to mediate the link between participative management behaviour and employee organisational commitment. Hence, it seems vital that top management ensures motivation and a willingness to engage organizational members in risk management activities. It is equally important that top management takes measures to ensure that lower-level departments both feel supported in their autonomous activities and that a participative leadership style creates a culture, where it is considered natural that risk identification and opportunity exploitation are tasks that involve all parts of and people in the organisation.

Limitations and future research

Like most research, the present study suffers from a number of limitations. With respect to the empirical data, it is important to stress that we rely on cross-sectional data collected from a survey. As a consequence, the study does not allow us to identify the direction of relationships between variables, as the structural equation modelling approach suggests. SEM analysis tests for associations and only assumes a certain direction of the relations based on theoretical reasoning. Further testing with longitudinal or lagged data is therefore necessary to corroborate our findings.

Collecting longitudinal and/or lagged data may also provide an opportunity to address a second empirical limitation of our data, the exclusive focus on Danish companies. Whereas the open Danish economy and the flat hierarchies in most companies support the introduction of involvement and open discussion, cross-cultural research indicates that individuals from low-power distance cultures such as Denmark and the US may react and voice their ideas differently than their counterparts in high-power distance cultures such as China (Brockner et al., 2001; Hofstede, 2011). Thus, the power distance and cultural dimensions in general may moderate the impact of participation and top management support on innovativeness and risk management behaviour. Individuals in low-power distance cultures are likely to react more negatively to a lack of participation and management support. This, in turn, could imply that studies conducted in high-power distance cultures would find a positive impact of a participative leadership style to be smaller or even nonexistent. More research to explore the moderating role of cultural and national market factors, for example, a country's legal and economic environment, seems highly warranted.

Furthermore, as the study finds that risk management competences are essential to ensure the effectiveness of the risk management system, more research is needed to pry into the black box of how these competences work to uncover the necessary antecedents for developing effective competences. In general, the study pinpoints that more research is needed to better understand the combined interfaces between ERM and DRM.

Conclusion

The present study extends our knowledge about the combined effect of ERM and DRM. It demonstrates that companies must combine a systematic ERM system to identify measure and address risks across departments using holistic and structured methods with a more decentralised risk management system that allows lower-level managers and departments to identify and respond to threats and opportunities without prior approval from higher-level managers. The study introduces a more sophisticated measure of ERM to capture the different processes in an effective ERM and thereby enhances our theoretical knowledge about effective applications of ERM while demonstrating empirically that ERM can enhance risk effectiveness as suggested by Paape and Speklé (2012).

The findings show the importance of combining ERM with DRM, as suggested by Andersen (2010), and enhance our knowledge by underlining the importance of creating adequate competences among employees and lower-level departments for this to work, since DRM by itself can impede risk effectiveness, whereas DRM mediated by risk competences is a viable path to improved risk performance. While the combination of ERM and DRM might be embedded in the organisation as a "system," the study finds that management must adopt a leadership style that supports involvement and empowerment within a culture that ensures risk identification and opportunity exploitation supported by top management as a task that involves employees and departments at all levels in the organisation.

References

Andersen, T.J. (2009). Effective risk management outcomes: Exploring effects of innovation and capital structure. *Journal of Strategy and Management* 2, 352–379.

Andersen, T.J. (2010). Combining central planning and decentralization to enhance effective risk management outcomes. *Risk Management* 12(2), 101–115.

Andersen, T. J., Denrell, J., and Bettis, R. A. (2007). Strategic responsiveness and Bowman's risk-return paradox. *Strategic Management Journal* 28, 407–429.

Anderson, J., and Gerbing, D. (1988). An updated paradigm for scale development incorporating unidimensionality and its assessment. *Journal of Marketing Research* 25, 186–192.

Barton, T.L., Shenkir, W.G., and Walker, P.L. (2002). *Making enterprise risk management pay off*. Upper Saddle River, NJ: Financial Times/Prentice Hall.

Baxter, R., Bedard, J.C., Hoitash, R., and Yezegel, A. (2012). Enterprise risk management program quality: Determinants, value relevance, and the financial crisis. *Contemporary Accounting Research* 30(4), 1264–1295.

Beasley, M.S., Branson, B.C., and Hancock, B.V. (2010). Are you identifying your most significant risks? *Strategic Finance* 92(5), 29–35.

Beasley, M., Pagach, D., and Warr, R. (2008). Information conveyed in hiring announcements of senior executives overseeing enterprise-wide risk management processes. *Journal of Accounting, Auditing and Finance* 28(3), 311–332.

Bentler, P.M. (1980). Multivariate analysis with latent variables: Causal modeling. *Annual Review of Psychology* 31, 419–456.

Bettis, R.A., and Hitt, M.A. (1995). The new competitive landscape. *Strategic Management Journal* 16, 7–19.

Brockner, J., Ackerman, G., Greenberg, J., Gelfand, M.J., Francesco, A.M., Chen, Z.X., . . . Shapiro, D. (2001). Culture and procedural justice: The influence of power distance on reactions to voice. *Journal of Experimental Social Psychology* 37, 300–315.

Burgelman, R. (1983). Corporate entrepreneurship and strategic management: Insights from a process study. *Management Science* 29, 1349–1364.

Burgelman, R., and Grove, A.S. (2006). *Strategic dynamics: Concepts and cases*. Boston: McGraw-Hill.

Carless, S.A., Wearing, A.J., and Mann, L. (2000). A short measure of transformational leadership. *Journal of Business and Psychology* 14, 389–405.

Chang, S.J., van Witteloostuijn, A., and Eden, L. (2010). From the editors: Common method variance in international business research. *Journal of International Business Studies* 41, 178–184.

Choi, J.N. (2004). Individual and contextual predictors of creative performance: The mediating role of psychological processes. *Creativity Research Journal* 16, 187–199.

Choi, Y., Ye, X., Zhao, L., and Luo, A.C. (2015). Optimizing enterprise risk management: A literature review and critical analysis of the work of Wu and Olson. *Annals of Operations Research*. doi:10.1007/s10479-015-1789-5

COSO. (2004). *Enterprise risk management – integrated framework*. New York. Retrieved from http://www.coso.org

Daft, R. L. (1992). *Organization theory and design*. St. Paul, MN: West.

Dodgson, M., Gann, D., and Salter, A. (2008). *The management of technological innovation*. Oxford: Oxford University Press.

Dutton, J. E., Ashford, S.J., Neill, R.M.O., Hayes, E., and Wierba, E.E. (1997). Reading the wind: How middle managers assess the context for selling issues to top managers. *Strategic Management Journal* 18(5), 407–425.

Eby, L.T., Freeman, D.M., Rush, M.C., and Lance, C.E. (1999). Motivational bases of affective organizational commitment: A partial test of an integrative theoretical model. *Journal of Occupational and Organizational Psychology* 72, 463–483.

Fleury, M.T.L., Fleury, A.C.C., and Fleury, A.C.C. (2007). In search of competence: Aligning strategy and competences in the telecommunications industry. *International Journal of Human Resource Management* 16, 1640–1655.

Fornell, C., and Larcker, D.F. (1981). Evaluating structural equation models with unobservable variables and measurement error. *Journal of Marketing Research* 18, 39–50.

Galanou, E. (2010). The impact of leadership styles on four variables of executives workforce. *International Journal of Business and Management* 5(6), 3–16.

Gerbing, D., and Anderson, J. (1992). Monte Carlo evaluation of goodness of fit indices for structural equation models. *Sociological Methods and Research* 2, 132–160.

Gordon, L.A., Loeb, M.P., and Tseng, C. (2009). Enterprise risk management and firm performance: A contingency perspective. *Journal of Accounting and Public Policy* 28(4), 301–327.

Gray, L. (1999). New Zealand HRD practitioner competencies: Application of the ASTD competency model. *International Journal of Human Resource Management* 10, 1046–1059.

Helfat, C.E., and Peteraf, M.A. (2014). Managerial cognitive capabilities and the microfoundations of dynamic capabilities. *Strategic Management Journal* 36(6), 831–850. doi:10.1002/smj.2247

Henriksen, P., and Uhlenfeldt, T. (2006). Contemporary enterprise-wide risk management frameworks: A comparative analysis in a strategic perspective. In T.J. Andersen (Ed.), *Perspectives on strategic risk management* (pp. 107–130). Copenhagen: CBS Press.

Hofstede, G. (2011). Dimensionalizing cultures: The Hofstede model in context. *Online Readings in Psychology and Culture* 2(1). doi:10.9707/2307–0919.1014

Hoyt, R.E., and Liebenberg, A.P. (2011). The value of enterprise risk management. *Journal of Risk and Insurance* 78(4), 795–822.

Hult, T., Ketchen, D., Cui, A., Prud'homme, A., Seggie, S., Stanko, M., . . . Cavusgil, S. (2006). An assessment of the use of structural equation modelling in international business research. *Research Methodology in Strategy and Management* 3, 385–415.

Institute of Internal Auditors. (2009). *The role of internal auditing in enterprise-wide risk management.* Retrieved from https://na.theiia.org/Pages/IIAHome.aspx

Kaplan, R., and Mikes, A. (2013). *Towards a contingency theory of enterprise risk management.* Working paper, Harvard Business School, Cambridge, MA.

Kaufman, B.E. (2001). The theory and practice of strategic HRM and participative management antecedents in early industrial relations. *Human Resource Management Review* 11, 505–533.

Kline, R.B. (2005). *Principles and practice of structural equation modelling.* New York: Guilford.

Koberg, C.S., Boss, R.W., and Senjem, J.S. (1999). Antecedents and outcomes of empowerment. Empirical evidence from the health care industry. *Group & Organization Management* 24, 71–91.

Koopman, P.L., and Wierdsma, A.F.M. (1998). Participative management. In P.J.D. Doentu, H. Thierry and C.J. de-Wolf (Eds.), *Personnel psychology: Handbook of work and organizational psychology* (Vol. 3, 297–324). Hove: Psychology Press.

Kuratko, D.F., Ireland, R.D., Covin, J.G., and J.S. Hornsby (2005). A model of middle-level managers' entrepreneurial behavior. *Entrepreneurship Theory & Practice* 29, 699–716.

Liebenberg, A.P., and Hoyt, R.E. (2003). The determinants of enterprise risk management: Evidence from the appointment of chief risk officers. *Risk Management and Insurance Review* 6(1), 37–52.

Lin, Y., Wen, M., and Yu, J. (2012). Enterprise risk management: Strategic antecedents, risk integration and performance. *North American Actuarial Journal* 16(1), 1–28.

Lumpkin, G. T., Cogliser, C. C., and Schneider, D. R. (2009). Understanding and measuring autonomy: An entrepreneurial orientation perspective. *Entrepreneurship Theory and Practice* 33(1), 47–69.

Mantere, S., and Vaara, E. (2008). On the problem of participation in strategy: A critical discursive perspective. *Organizational Science* 19, 341–358.

McMullen, J.S., and Shepherd, D.A. (2006). Entrepreneurial action and the role of uncertainty in the theory of the entrepreneur. *Academy of Management Review* 32(1), 132–152.

McShane, M.K., Nair, A., and Rustambekov, E. (2011). Does enterprise risk management increase firm value? *Journal of Accounting, Auditing & Finance* 26(4), 641–658.

Meeus, M., and Edquist, C. (2006). Introduction to part I. In J. Hage and M. Meeus (Eds.), *Innovation, science, and institutional change* (pp. 1–37). New York: Oxford University Press.

Mikes, A., and Kaplan, R.S. (2014). *Towards a contingency theory of enterprise risk management.* AAA 2014 Management Accounting Section (MAS) Meeting Paper. Available at SSRN: http://ssrn.com/abstract=2311293

Mills, J., Platts, K., Bourne, M., and Richards, H. (2002). *Strategy and performance: Competing through competences.* New York: Cambridge University Press.

Nielsen, B.B. 2013. Construct measurement in management research: The importance of match between levels of theory and measurement, *Journal of Business Research* 67(3), 403–406. doi:10.1016/j.jbusres.2012.12.020

Paape, L., and Speklé, R.F. (2012). The adoption and design of enterprise risk management practices: An empirical study. *European Accounting Review* 21(3), 533–564.

Pagach, D., and Warr, R. (2011). The characteristics of firms that hire chief risk officers. *Journal of Risk and Insurance* 78(1), 185–211.

Podsakoff, P.M., MacKenzie, S.B., and Lee, J. (2003). Common method biases in behavioral research: A critical review of the literature and recommended remedies. *Journal of Applied Psychology* 88, 879–903.

Podsakoff, P.M., MacKenzie, S.B., and Podsakoff, N.P. (2012). Sources of methods bias in social science research and recommendations on how to control it. *Annual Review of Psychology* 63, 539–569.

Power, M. (2007). *Organized uncertainty: Designing a world of risk management.* Oxford: Oxford University Press.

Prahalad, C.K., and Hamel, G. (1990). The core competence of the corporation. *Harvard Business Review* 68, 79–91.

Scully, J.A., Kirkpatrick, S.A., and Locke, E.A. (1995). Locus of knowledge as a determinant of the effects of participation on performance, affect, and perceptions. *Organizational Behavior and Human Decision Processes* 61(3), 276–288.

Senge, P. (1990). *The fifth discipline*. New York: Doubleday.

Simons, R. (2005). *Levers of organization design*. Boston: Harvard Business Review Press.

Slywotzky, A.J., and Drzig, J. (2005). Countering the biggest risk of all. *Harvard Business Review* 83(4), 78–88.

Somech, A. (2006). The effects of leadership style and team process on performance and innovation in functionally heterogeneous teams. *Journal of Management* 32(1), 132–157.

Spencer, L.M., and Spencer, S.M. (1993). *Competence at work: Models for superior performance*. New York: John Wiley.

Teece, D.J. (2007). Explicating dynamic capabilities: The nature and microfoundations of (sustainable) enterprise performance. *Strategic Management Journal* 28, 1319–1350.

Torp, S.S., and Linder, S. (2014). The "soft" side of strategic risk manage.ment: How top managers' leadership style affects volatility in performance. In T.J. Andersen (Ed.), *Contemporary challenges in risk management: Dealing with risk, uncertainty and the unknown*. New York: Palgrave Macmillan.

Part V

Effects on enterprise risk management

20

The effects of enterprise risk management on firm performance

Don Pagach and Richard Warr[1]

Abstract

We study the effect of adoption of enterprise risk management (ERM) principles on firms' long-term performance by examining how financial, asset and market characteristics change around the time of ERM adoption. Using a sample of 106 firms that announce the hiring of a chief risk officer (an event frequently accompanied by adoption of enterprise risk management), we find that some firms adopting ERM experience a reduction in earnings volatility. In general, however, we find little impact from ERM adoption on a wide range of firm variables. While our results could be due to lower power tests, they also raise the question of whether ERM is achieving its stated goals. Overall, our results fail to find support for the proposition that ERM is value creating, although further study is called for, in particular the study of how ERM success can be measured.

Enterprise risk management (ERM) is an increasingly popular strategy that attempts to holistically evaluate and manage all of the risks faced by the firm. In doing so, ERM uses the firm's risk appetite to determine which risks should be accepted and which should be mitigated or avoided. While there has been a considerable increase in practitioner attention on ERM in recent years, little academic research exists about ERM, and in particular about the consequences of ERM on firm performance. This is true even though the Conference Board has found that a large number of companies are now starting to use ERM as a strategic management tool (Gates and Hexter, 2005). In addition, Standard and Poor's introduced ERM analysis into its global corporate credit rating process starting in the third quarter of 2008 (S&P Ratings Direct, 2008).

This purpose of this chapter is to examine the effect of ERM implementation and to establish whether firms adopting ERM actually achieve observable results consistent with the claimed benefits of ERM. Put another way, we seek to establish whether ERM works in increasing firm value and performance. We believe that our work is important and timely because although many surveys have stated the benefits of adopting ERM (Marsh and McLennan Companies, 2005), there has been little empirical evidence on how ERM affects firms. We argue that the primary goal of ERM is to reduce the probability of financial distress and allow firms to continue their investment strategies by reducing the effect lower-tail outcomes, whether earnings or cash flow, cause by unexpected events. Having smoother, steadier earnings and cash flow performance allows the firm to increase leverage, pursue more growth options and perhaps be more profitable. However, these changes are potential consequences of a successful ERM program, and not necessarily evidence of the program itself.

Our research focuses on the following questions. First, do firms experience a change in earnings volatility around ERM adoption? This research question examines the proactive nature of ERM and whether companies adopting ERM are able to protect themselves from severe earnings events and generate smoothed earnings. The COSO (Committee of Sponsoring Organizations of the Treadway Commission) ERM framework states that ERM aids in reducing operational surprises and losses by allowing managers to better identify potential events that cause such surprises. Firms can then establish responses to reduce the effects of these surprises (COSO, 2004).

Second, do firms adopting ERM improve financial performance relative to past performance and after controlling for industry performance? This research question provides evidence on the view that ERM has value creating ability, captured in the following statement: "There is clearly a heightened awareness of the need to manage risks more strategically in order to achieve expected shareholder value" (The Conference Board, July 2005). Under this view ERM creates value by identifying and proactively addressing risks.

Third, do firms' financial characteristics, such as leverage, growth and asset opacity, change after ERM implementation? This research question examines the effect that ERM has on the firm and whether ERM processes change-critical risk interdependencies. Proponents argue that an additional benefit of initiating ERM is that it allows firms to seize opportunities by allowing managers to better identify and more effectively assess capital needs and improve capital allocation (COSO, 2004).

Understanding whether or not ERM is achieving its stated goals is an important question. First, significant resources, both corporate and governmental, are being expended on understanding, developing and implementing ERM programs. Second, even if ERM provides a consistent process for risk identification it is possible that the benefits are not significant enough to become evident in the firm's financial performance. ERM is not a costless activity, and as such, if it fails to deliver observable benefits, its implementation may be called into question.

As a preview of our results we find that very little evidence that ERM results in many significant changes in the sample firms. However, when we examine a subset of firms for whom the market perceived ERM adoption in a positive light, we find some evidence of risk reduction.

This chapter proceeds as follows: first hypotheses are developed based on a review of the literature, then method and data are described, results are presented and analyzed, and conclusions and limitations are offered.

Hypothesis development

In a frictionless capital market with no asymmetric information, risk management at the firm level should be a negative net present value (NPV) project. However, Stulz (1996, 2003) and Nocco and Stulz (2006) present arguments under which risk management activities could be value-increasing for shareholders when agency costs, market imperfections and information asymmetries interfere with the operation of perfect capital markets.[2]

Although risk is generally considered to be the possibility of outcomes that deviate from what was expected, it is primarily negative outcomes that are of most concern to firms. Stulz (1996, 2003) argues that any potential value creation role for risk management is in the reduction or elimination of "costly lower-tail outcomes." Lower-tail outcomes are primarily negative earnings and cash flow shocks and can have both direct and indirect costs. Direct costs are incurred in events such as bankruptcy and financial distress when the firm must make outlays to creditors, lawyers and courts. Indirect costs associated with negative earnings and cash flow shocks include the loss of reputation that may affect customer and vendor relationships.

In addition, indirect costs hamper the ability to pursue profitable growth options and the ability to realize the full value of intangible assets upon liquidation. A decline in debt ratings and the resulting increase in borrowing costs can also be costly for shareholders in that previously positive NPV projects may now have to be forgone. Direct costs also include the costs associated with missing earnings targets and violating debt covenants.[3] Stulz (1996, 2003) argues that risk management can be value-creating if it is able to reduce the likelihood of these negative earnings shocks and, in turn, help the firm avoid the direct and indirect costs associated with financial distress. Risk management in the traditional sense usually implies offsetting known risks by purchasing derivatives.[4]

ERM takes a holistic view of risk management and attempts to reduce the probability of large negative earnings and cash flows by coordinating and controlling offsetting risks across the enterprise. For example, The COSO framework defines ERM as follows:

> Enterprise risk management is a process, effected by an entity's board of directors, management and other personnel, applied in strategy setting and across the enterprise, designed to identify potential events that may affect the entity, and manage risk to be within its risk appetite, to provide reasonable assurance regarding the achievement of entity objectives.[5]

COSO summarizes ERM as "help(ing) an entity get to where it wants to go and avoid pitfalls and surprises along the way."[6]

Although there are many variations in the definition of ERM, the basic theme is that ERM is primarily as a way of measuring understanding and controlling the risks facing the firm. In some cases ERM is also viewed as a management tool that can identify profitable opportunities to enhance shareholder wealth. ERM does not necessarily necessitate usage of derivatives, as for most operational risks, no appropriate traded derivative contract is available. Risk management in this manner can ensure that no single project risk has an adverse effect on the overall firm. Thus ERM provides the potential benefit of reducing the direct and indirect costs associated with financial distress.[7] ERM will have its greatest effect on earnings by reducing their variability through controls on the risk of cost centers and revenue sources.

Consistent with this view of ERM, Standard and Poor's states that evaluations of firms' enterprise risk management structures will focus on ensuring that firms are addressing all of their risks, setting proper expectations about which risks are and are not taken and setting methods that ensure that firms avoid losses outside tolerance levels.[8] Standard and Poor's also states that ERM is not a process to ensure that a firm eliminates all risks or a guarantee that losses will be avoided or a replacement for internal controls. ERM analysis by Standard and Poor's will be incorporated into regular credit reviews and will be part of the analysis of risk management culture, which will also include governance, accounting policies and issues and derivatives.

Previous research has sought to understand the benefits of ERM by examining the stock market reaction to ERM adoption, as proxied by the appointment of a chief risk officer (CRO) or equivalent. Examining a sample of 120 companies appointing CROs, Beasley, Pagach and Warr (2008) find no significant stock price reaction (positive or negative) to ERM adoption. However, a cross-sectional analysis finds that firms in nonfinancial industries that are more likely to experience costly lower-tail outcomes have a positive stock price reaction around the adoption of ERM. These results are consistent with Stulz (1996, 2003), who points out that it is only firms that face these lower-tail outcomes that will benefit from ERM, while other firms will see no benefit and could destroy value by spending corporate resources on risk management.[9]

In this chapter, we seek to examine whether ERM adoption has a material change on a range of observable financial measures. We fully recognize that ERM may be working very effectively, but observable financial measures are unaffected. This unobservability could be a result of ERM working properly and mitigating problems such that the firm's performance is better than if it had not used ERM. In addition, we may not be able to observe changes in financial performance because the firm has not had any earnings or operating shocks in the recent past and has none after ERM adoption. This is analogous to a firm having insurance but not needing to draw on it. However, in both cases, even though we may not observe a direct reduction in risk, through smoother earnings we might expect changes in capital structure, profitability and asset composition, consistent with the firm being more confident in its management of risks.

To specifically examine the effect of ERM on the firm, we look at a range of characteristics. We group these characteristics in four broad categories: risk characteristics, financial characteristics, asset characteristics and market characteristics. We compare changes in a sample of ERM adopters to a carefully selected control group. In addition, because the adoption of ERM is more advanced in the financial industry we examine a subsample of banks using industry-specific characteristics.

Risk characteristics

As a goal of ERM is to reduce operational surprises and particularly losses, we should expect ERM-adopting firms to see a reduction in earnings and stock price volatility. This reduced volatility is the expected result of a successful implementation of ERM which should lead to smoother earnings and a reduced probability of experiencing a lower-tail outcome.

Financial characteristics

The financial characteristics we examine are related to the likelihood of the firm experiencing a costly lower-tail outcome. The first financial characteristic is leverage. Firms with higher leverage are more likely to suffer financial distress. Excessive leverage may also limit a firm's flexibility when pursuing additional profitable investment projects. The effect of ERM adoption on leverage is dependent upon whether the firm decides that it needs to lower its risk exposure in these areas, or whether the firm decides that because of ERM it can afford to bear more financial risk. Thus the impact of ERM adoption on leverage is unclear, however, for firms that were previously at their target leverage level, greater control of operational risks would suggest that the firm could increase its debt capacity.

Cash availability or financial slack provides a measure of a company's ability to persist during a period of operating cash shortfall. Slack measures the amount of highly liquid assets that the firm has on hand that could be used to make up a shortfall in operating cash flows. Firms adopting ERM may decide to increase financial slack to provide a greater cushion against financial distress, or like leverage, may feel less financial slack is needed given that they are managing risks more thoroughly.

We examine various profitability measures, as some argue that ERM adoption results in a better overall management of the firm. Alternatively, profitability could suffer if ERM results in increased operational costs. As with leverage, the effect of ERM adoption on profitability is ambiguous. More coordinated management and loss avoidance may boost profits by reducing avoidable losses. However, greater emphasis on risk management may lead to a reduction in upper-tail outcomes. Profitability may also be endogenously determined with ERM adoption. For example, ERM may be adopted if the firm has experienced a decline in profitability due to some losses, and ERM is implemented to prevent a future reoccurrence.

Asset characteristics

The asset characteristics used provide information about the degree to which a firm's assets are likely to be impaired in financial distress. The first asset characteristic we examine is opacity. In a period of financial distress brought on by a operating shortfall, firms that derive much of their operating income from opaque assets may have difficulty quickly liquidating these assets at fair market value in order to raise capital to avert financial distress. This is due to the information asymmetries normally associated with opaque assets and the relative lack of marketability for such assets.

The second asset characteristic we examine is growth options. Firms with growth options have much of the firm's value tied to future and as yet unrealized cash flows. Because of the uncertain nature of the payoff from such assets, the value of these investments is unlikely to be fully realized in bankruptcy. If, after adopting ERM, the firm considers financial distress to be less likely (through a reduction in lower-tail outcomes), we expect to observe greater investment in opaque assets and assets with growth options.

Market characteristics

Market characteristics provide information about the degree to which a firm's equity benefits from a reduction in the expected costs associated with financial distress. Previous work has examined the market reaction to ERM adoption, and consequently, we do not include an event study style analysis in this chapter.[10] However, we examine the stock price return volatility to see if ERM reduces operational surprises and subsequently stock price volatility. If ERM reduces the likelihood of lower-tail outcomes, we should see a more stable stock price as the firm's idiosyncratic risk is reduced. The firm's market risk (or nondiversifiability) cannot be affected by ERM unless the firm changes its fundamental business lines. We also examine the valuation of the firm to see whether ERM adoption has an effect on firm value (either positive or negative).

Bank characteristics

The unique financial characteristics of banks limits the usefulness of traditional financial measures and therefore we compute specific measures such as tier 1 capital levels, loan loss reserves and duration gap. The effect of ERM on these measures is potentially ambiguous as they all measure, in some ways, the risk tolerance of the firm. For example, greater risk management may allow the firm to increase leverage or risk weighted assets and thus reduce its tier 1 capital. Conversely, the firm may determine that given its level of operational risk, a greater amount of capital would be prudent. Loan loss reserves measure the extent to which the bank has or is engaged in risky lending activities. Duration gap measures the sensitivity of the bank's earnings to adverse fluctuations in interest rates – again another form of risk exposure.

Data and method

The primary objective of our study is to examine the changes in financial characteristics around the firm's adoption of ERM. Unfortunately, firms usually do not publicly announce the adoption of ERM, and in addition tend to disclose only minimal details of their risk management programs (Tufano, 1996). We therefore focus on hiring announcements of enterprise-level officers or CROs as a signal of a firm's adoption of an ERM process. There are good reasons to believe that CRO hiring coincides with the decision to follow an ERM program. For example, the Economist Intelligence Unit (2005) reports that many organizations appoint a member of the senior executive team, often referred to as the CRO, to oversee the enterprise's risk management process. Walker, Shenkir, and Barton (2002) note that because of its scope and impact ERM requires strong support from senior management. Beasley, Clune and Hermanson (2005) show that the presence of a CRO is associated with a greater stage of ERM adoption. Finally, Liebenberg and Hoyt (2003) argue that the CRO appointment signals the initiation of ERM because CROs are generally appointed to implement and manage ERM programs.

We therefore start our study with 138 announcements of senior risk officer appointments made from 1992–2004 for which we are able to obtain all the necessary data for our tests. Announcements are obtained by searching the business library of LexisNexis for announcements containing the words "announced," "named," or "appointed," in conjunction with position descriptions such as "chief risk officer" or "director of risk management."[11] Only announcements for publicly traded companies are retained, and in the case of multiple announcements for the same company we select only the first announcement on the assumption that this represented the initiation of the enterprise risk management program. By starting our search in 1992, we hope to capture the first appointment of a CRO; however, it is possible that some appointments, although being the first announcements, are not actually the first appointments. These announcements will add noise to our sample and reduce the power of our tests. We require that firms have 5 years of continuous data in order to be in our tests (2 years prior to and 2 years after the appointment year). After imposing this restriction, our sample is reduced to 106 firms. We do not search for appointments beyond 2004, because of the 2-year post appointment data requirement.

We collect data for all firms listed in Compustat and we supplement the data with stock price data from the Center for Research in Security Prices (CRSP). Table 20.1 presents the distribution of the announcements through time as well as the distribution across industries. Most CRO hires tend to be in the later part of the sample period, clustered from 1999 through 2002. A substantial portion of the appointments is located in the financial and utility industries. These are defined in our sample as having SIC codes in the 6000s for financial firms and in the 4900s for utilities.

To test whether CRO appointments are associated with changes in key financial variables, our basic approach is to measure changes in these variables in the years after a CRO appointment relative to the years before. In multivariate tests, we employ a matched sample and logit model to determine if there are differences between the CRO sample and the industry matched sample (which has no CRO appointments). The following are the variables used in the analysis (Compustat data item numbers d# are reported where available). The motivation for using these variables is discussed in more detail in the earlier hypothesis section.

Risk characteristics

We measure earnings volatility (SD(E)) as the standard deviation of the error term from a regression of the firm's quarterly earnings on the prior quarter's earnings. We use Compustat quarterly data item 19 – basic EPS excluding extraordinary items as a measure of quarterly earnings. This regression is run for eight quarters. Stock price volatility (SD(RET)) is the standard deviation of the firm's daily returns over the year prior to the hiring of the CRO.

Table 20.1 Sample firms by year

Sample firms are firms with CRO announcements reported in LexisNexis. Firms have to have 5 years of continuous data, 2 years before the announcement and 2 years after, to be in the sample. The totals are broken out by financial firms (SICC: 6000–6999) and utilities (SICC: 4900–4999).

Year	All firms	Financial firms	Utilities
1992	5	3	0
1993	5	1	0
1994	4	0	0
1995	9	3	1
1996	9	5	3
1997	4	2	1
1998	5	3	0
1999	7	4	0
2000	9	4	1
2001	20	12	5
2002	10	5	3
2003	12	9	1
2004	7	5	0
Total	106	56	15

Financial characteristics

We measure leverage as total liabilities to assets:

$$\text{Leverage} = \text{Total liabilities} / \text{Total Assets} = (d6 - d60) / d6 \tag{1}$$

To measure accounting return we use return on equity:

$$\text{ROE} = \text{Net Income} / \text{Book Equity} = d18 / d60 \tag{2}$$

We measure financial slack as the proportion of the firm's assets that are cash or cash equivalents:

$$\text{Slack} = \text{Cash and marketable securities} / \text{Total Assets} = d1 / d6 \tag{3}$$

Asset characteristics

Opacity is the ratio of intangibles to total assets:

$$\text{Opacity} = \text{Intangibles} / \text{Total Assets} = d33 / d6 \tag{4}$$

We proxy for growth options using the market-to-book (MB) ratio and research and development intensity (RD) compounded as:

$$\text{MB} = \text{Market Value of Equity} / \text{Book Value of Equity} = (d199 \times d25) / d60 \tag{5}$$

$$\text{RD} = \text{Research and Development Expense} / \text{Total Assets} = d46 / d6 \tag{6}$$

Market-to-book also proxies for firm valuation, as higher market-to-book indicates that the investors perceive that the firm is more valuable.

Bank variables

To measure the unique financial risks faced by banks we include three measures of risk commonly used in the banking industry. Our measurement of these measures is simplified to accommodate the use of Compustat data.

Duration Ratio = [Change in interest income-change in interest expense]/Total Assets

$$= [(d321_t - d321_{t-1}) - (d339_t - d339_{t-1})] / d6 \tag{7}$$

Loan Loss Provision = Provision for Loan & Asset Losses / Total Assets

$$= d342 / d6 \tag{8}$$

Tier 1 Risk Adjusted Capital Ratio = d337 \hspace{4em} (9)

Results and analysis

Table 20.2 presents summary statistics for the sample of ERM adopting firms. The average firm is quite highly leveraged, consistent with the large number of financial and utility firms in the sample. Most carry some slack on their balance sheet, with the average of cash and marketable securities being 7.72% of total assets. The average firm has a market value of nearly $8.6 billion, but the distribution of firm size is quite skewed. The average firm in the sample is moderately profitable with an average return on equity (ROE) of 7.24%. The sample firms have an average of 5% opaque assets. Panel B of Table 20.2 provides industry specific data for our sample of banks. Tier 1 capital is the core measure of a bank's financial stability from a regulator's perspective and is measured as a percentage of weighted risk assets. The Federal Deposit Insurance Corporation (FDIC) requires a minimum level of 3.6% tier 1 capital to weighted risk assets.

Table 20.2 Summary statistics for CRO firms

Panel A. All firms [n = 104]	Mean	Median	Std. dev
Leverage [%]	77.35	83.2	19.83
Slack [%]	7.72	4.66	9.32
Size [$ millions]	8637	4225	10946
Opacity [%]	5.11	1.31	9.99
R&D [%]	0.22	0.00	0.88
Market to book	2.25	1.90	2.95
ROE [%]	7.24	12.65	21.93
SD(RET) [%]	2.38	2.00	1.45
SD(E)	0.88	0.30	1.33
Panel B. Banks [n = 37]	Mean	Median	Std. dev
Duration ratio [%]	0.4	0.24	0.42
Loan loss provision [%]	0.42	0.27	0.42
Tier 1 capital [%]	9.5	8.8	3.3

In Table 20.3 we examine whether there are any changes in the key variables before and after the CRO appointment. For each variable of interest we test that the change in the two year average before the CRO appointment compared to the two year average after the CRO appointment is equal to zero. The only exception to this approach is for the earnings volatility, SD(E), variable and for the Duration Ratio variable which are computed over eight quarters. For these variables we measure the change from the eight quarters prior to the CRO appointment to the eight quarters after the CRO appointment.

Looking first at the risk measures in Panel A, we find a significant decline in the standard deviation of stock returns, SD(RET), for the CRO firms. This decline is consistent with the firm becoming less risky, following the appointment of the CRO and the adoption of ERM. Of course, we cannot rule out market-wide effects as well. We do not observe any significant change in the earnings volatility SD(E).

We do not find a significant leverage increase after the CRO appointment relative to the period prior to the appointment, although the change is positive. Unsurprisingly, size increases, but we believe that this is more a function of the rising stock market during the period, rather than any direct effect of ERM. No other variables show a significant change.

Table 20.3 Before and after CRO appointment t-tests

Variables are measured as averages over the 2 years prior to and the 2 years after the CRO appointment. The exception is the SD(E) and Duration Ratio which are the ratios of the value in the second year after the CRO appointment to the year prior to the CRO appointment. Panel A presents data for all CRO appointing firms. Panel B presents data for Banks only (SICC 6000–6099). Leverage = Total liabilities / Total Assets = (data6 – data60)/data6, Slack = Cash and marketable securities / Total Assets = data1 / data6. Size is market value of equity. Opacity = Intangibles / Total Assets = data33 / data6. R&D = Research and Development Expense / Total Assets = data46 / data6. Market to Book = Market Value of Equity / Book Value of Equity = (data199 × data25) / data60. ROE is Net Income divided by equity (data12 / data60). SD(RET) is the standard deviation of the firm's daily returns over the year prior to the hiring of the CRO. SD(E) is the standard deviation of the error term from a regression of the firm's quarterly earnings on the prior quarter's earnings. This regression is run for eight quarters. Duration ratio is the annual change in interest income (data321) – the annual change interest expense (data33) divided by assets (data6). Loan loss provision is data342 / data6. Tier 1 capital is data337. *, **, *** indicates significance at the 10%, 5%, and 1% levels respectively.

Panel A. All firms	Before	After	Change	t-stat
Leverage	76.13	77.32	1.19	1.33
Slack	7.89	7.90	0.01	0.01
Size	7,806.08	9,567.48	1,761.42***	3.01
Opacity	5.16	5.74	0.58	1.25
R&D	0.21	0.19	−0.02	−1.59
Market to book	2.41	2.50	0.93	0.32
ROE	6.21	12.04	5.83	0.96
SD(RET)	2.35	2.10	−0.25**	−2.14
SD(E)	0.82	0.72	−0.99	−0.84
Panel B: Banks	Before	After	Change	t-stat
Duration ratio	0.41	0.31	−0.10	−1.40
Loan loss provision	0.42	0.29	−0.13	−1.23
Tier 1 capital	9.77	9.76	−0.01	−0.02

In Panel B we observe no significant changes in the bank specific variables. We do observe a decrease in the duration ratio, which is consistent with a bank reducing its interest rate exposure, but this decrease is not significant in a two-sided test.

It is possible that market or industry wide changes are adding noise to the tests and reducing our ability to find firm specific changes. To attempt to control for this possibility, we scale each variable by the three digit SIC industry average for the variable for that specific year. We then repeat the analysis from Table 20.3 using these industry adjusted variables. These results are presented in Table 20.4. Looking first at Panel A, we observe a statistically significant increase in the relative leverage of the sample firms, compared to the industry as a whole. However, the magnitude of this change is not very large and it would be reaching to try and assign some economic significance to this result. For the remainder of Table 20.4, all the changes are insignificant, consistent with the results from Table 20.3.[12]

At this stage in our analysis we have found essentially no effect on firm characteristics from ERM adoption. A possible explanation for the lack of significant change is that out of the firms adopting ERM, not all of them are positioned to actually benefit from adoption. Beasley et al. (2008) find that while the overall stock market response to the announcement of a CRO appointment is close to zero, there is significant cross-sectional variation in the announcement

Table 20.4 Before and after CRO appointment t-tests – industry adjusted

Variables are measured as averages over the 2 years prior to and the 2 years after the CRO appointment. The exception is the SD(E) and Duration Ratio which are the ratios of the value in the second year after the CRO appointment to the year prior to the CRO appointment. Panel A presents data for all CRO appointing firms. Panel B presents data for Banks only (SICC 6000–6099). Leverage = Total liabilities / Total Assets = (data6 – data60) / data6, Slack = Cash and marketable securities / Total Assets = data1 / data6. Size is market value of equity. Opacity = Intangibles / Total Assets = data33 / data6. R&D = Research and Development Expense / Total Assets = data46 / data6. Market to Book = Market Value of Equity / Book Value of Equity = (data199 × data25) / data60. ROE is Net Income divided by equity (data12 / data60). SD(RET) is the standard deviation of the firm's daily returns over the year prior to the hiring of the CRO. SD(E) is the standard deviation of the error term from a regression of the firm's quarterly earnings on the prior quarter's earnings. This regression is run for eight quarters. Duration ratio is the annual change in interest income (data321) – the annual change interest expense (data33) divided by assets (data6). Loan loss provision is data342 / data6. Tier 1 capital is data337. *, **, *** indicates significance at the 10%, 5%, and 1% levels respectively.

Panel A. All firms	Before	After	Change	t-stat
Leverage	1.06	1.09	0.03*	1.97
Slack	0.89	0.83	−0.06	−0.52
Size	4.23	4.09	−0.15	−0.54
Opacity	1.42	1.36	−0.07	−0.37
R&D	0.78	0.99	0.21	1.02
Market to book	1.13	1.11	−0.02	−0.14
ROE	4.1	1.04	−3.07	−1.29
SD(RET)	0.77	0.78	0	0.07
SD(E)	1.06	1.39	−0.21	−0.81
Panel B: Banks	Before	After	Change	t-stat
Duration ratio	0.92	0.72	−0.2	1.24
Loan loss provision	1.19	1.15	−0.04	−0.2
Tier 1 capital	0.81	0.82	0	0.1

returns. Further, the variations in the announcement returns are correlated with variables that Beasley et al. hypothesize would be indicators of the potential benefit of an integrated risk management program. To incorporate Beasley et al.'s finding in to our tests, we bifurcate the sample based on the 1-day abnormal stock return recorded on the CRO announcement date. If firms that received positive announcements are viewed as being potential beneficiaries of ERM, we may expect to see some changes in these firm's characteristics once they adopt the program. The results for these tests are presented in Table 20.5 where we rerun the prior tests on the subset of firms that had a positive announcement returns.

In the Table 20.5, Panel A we observe a statistically significant increase in ROE and statistically significant decrease in the standard deviation of earnings. We also observe a statistically significant increase in leverage. It is very possible that the increase in ROE is related to the increase in leverage. An increase in leverage is consistent with a firm bearing more financial risk once it has a better understanding of operating risks. The decline in the standard deviation of earnings is perhaps the only evidence so far that firms are managing risk in a manner in which earnings volatility is targeted.

Table 20.5 Before and after CRO appointment t-tests – positive announcement CAR only

This table repeats the tests in Table 20.3 for the subset of firms that had positive cumulative abnormal returns around the announcement of the CRO appointment. Variables are measured as averages over the 2 years prior to and the 2 years after the CRO appointment. The exception is the SD(E) and Duration Ratio which are the ratios of the value in the second year after the CRO appointment to the year prior to the CRO appointment. Panel A presents data for all CRO appointing firms. Panel B presents data for Banks only (SICC 6000–6099). Leverage = Total liabilities / Total Assets = (data6 – data60) / data6, Slack = Cash and marketable securities / Total Assets = data1 / data6. Size is market value of equity. Opacity = Intangibles / Total Assets = data33 / data6. R&D = Research and Development Expense / Total Assets = data46 / data6. Market to Book = Market Value of Equity / Book Value of Equity = (data199 × data25) / data60. ROE is Net Income divided by equity (data12 / data60). SD(RET) is the standard deviation of the firm's daily returns over the year prior to the hiring of the CRO. SD(E) is the standard deviation of the error term from a regression of the firm's quarterly earnings on the prior quarter's earnings. This regression is run for eight quarters. Duration ratio is the annual change in interest income (data321) – the annual change interest expense (data33) divided by assets (data6). Loan loss provision is data342 / data6. Tier 1 capital is data337. *, **, *** indicates significance at the 10%, 5%, and 1% levels respectively.

Panel A. All firms	Before	After	Change	t-stat
Leverage	77.35	77.95	0.6	0.41
Slack	8.59	9.38	0.8	0.62
Size	9275.03	11352.64	2077.61	2.13**
Opacity	7.26	7.96	0.7	0.84
R&D	0.28	0.24	−0.04	−1.75*
Market to book	2.53	3.01	0.48	0.93
ROE	4.86	21.41	16.55	1.74*
SD(RET)	1.05	0.76	−0.28	−1.42
SD(E)	2.56	2.15	−0.41	−2.09**
Panel B: Banks	Before	After	Change	t-stat
Duration ratio	0.41	0.28	−0.13	−1.55
Loan loss provision	0.39	0.34	−0.05	−0.53
Tier 1 capital	8.87	9.72	0.85	2.22**

In Panel B we also observe an increase in tier 1 capital, which actually goes against the leverage result in Panel A, but is consistent with banks increasing equity capital and reducing financial risk. The decline in the duration is still insignificant but closer to the 10% level than before.

Conclusion and discussion

To our knowledge this is the first study to examine the change in financial performance as a result of adopting ERM. Our results are unimpressive. We find little evidence in our sample of ERM adopters for any significant changes in various key firm variables. When we look at firms that might be expected to benefit more from ERM (as proxied for by a positive CRO abnormal announcement return), we find limited evidence of risk reduction in the firm's earnings.

Our results or lack of results could be due to attributed to a variety of causes. First, our data may be too noisy or our tests too weak for us to pick up the changes. In this case failing to find a result does not mean that the result is not there. Second, it could be that ERM takes a lot longer to implement and reap benefits from. While this is possible, constructing a balanced sample that tracks firms relatively unmolested by mergers, divestitures and other corporate events is quite difficult. Furthermore, with many of the adoptions occurring in recent years, we just do not have the time series of data to study the long run effects of ERM adoption. The third and perhaps most disconcerting cause for our lack of results is that ERM is not having any significant effect on firm performance, or at least no effect that can be measured from the outside. If this is the case, then the efficacy of ERM is in question. The burden on ERM proponents must be therefore not only to provide systems for implementing the program, but also to provide key metrics against which the program's performance can be measured.

The recent mandates from both public and private entities for ERM means that more and more firms are adopting ERM and expending corporate resources on implementation. There must be a way of establishing whether or not ERM is working for a particular firm in order for outsiders to establish whether that firm is actually doing ERM correctly, and more broadly, whether ERM is working at all.

We consider this work a first step in the important area of examining the effects of ERM adoption. Given the widespread adoption of ERM, and the nontrivial cost of implementing a fully functioning ERM program, the question of whether it is worthwhile is of great importance. Our results here suggest that for the sample we study, there are still important questions as to the long-term value creation of ERM. Additional research is needed on enterprise risk management.

Notes

1 Don Pagach is professor of accounting, phone: 919–515–4447, email: don@ncsu.edu; Richard Warr is professor of finance, 919–513–4646, rswarr@ncsu.edu. Jenkins Graduate School of Management, North Carolina State University, Raleigh, NC 27695. The authors gratefully acknowledge the support of the Global Association of Risk Professionals (http://www.garp.com).
2 See Tufano (1996) and Smith and Stulz (1985) for additional motivations, such as the convexity of the tax schedule, for corporate risk management.
3 Smith and Stulz (1985) argue that reducing earnings volatility in the presence of a convex income tax schedule would also provide a motivation for risk management.
4 While our study focuses on the costs associated with financial distress and costly external financing, taxes and managerial risk aversion also are areas in which risk management are value increasing activities.
5 COSO (2004), p. 2.
6 Ibid., p. 1.

7 See Liebenberg and Hoyt (2003), Beasley et al. (2005), and Slywotzky and Drzik (2005) for discussions of the development and adoption of ERM.
8 S&P Ratings Direct (2008).
9 In related work, Pagach and Warr (2011) examine the determinants of firms that adopt ERM.
10 See Beasley et al. (2008).
11 In our initial sample search we included the following "title" terms in order to capture firms engaging in ERM: chief, director, vice president, president, head, managing director, manager, general manager.
12 In unreported tests we also scale the firm variables using a matched sample matched on SICC, market value and market-to-book. The results are qualitatively the same as the industry adjusted results.

References

Beasley, M.S., R. Clune, and D.R. Hermanson. (2005). Enterprise risk management: An empirical analysis of factors associated with the extent of implementation. *Journal of Accounting and Public Policy* 24(6), 521–531.

Beasley, M., D. Pagach, and R. Warr (2008). The information conveyed in hiring announcements of senior executives overseeing enterprise-wide risk management processes. *Journal of Accounting, Auditing and Finance* 23(3), 311–332.

COSO (Committee of Sponsoring Organizations of the Treadway Commission). (2004, September). *Enterprise risk management – integrated framework.* New York.

Economist Intelligence Unit. (2005, May). *The evolving role of the CRO.* London: Author.

Gates, S., and E. Hexter. (2005, June). *From risk management to risk strategy.* New York: The Conference Board.

Liebenberg, A., and R. Hoyt. (2003). The determinants of enterprise risk management: Evidence from the appointment of chief risk officers. *Risk Management and Insurance Review* 6(1), 37–52.

Marsh and McLennan Companies. (2005). *A qualitative survey of enterprise risk management programs.* New York.

Nocco., B.W., and R. Stulz. (2006). Enterprise risk management: Theory and practice. *Journal of Applied Corporate Finance* 18(4), 8–20.

Pagach, D., and R. Warr. (2011). An empirical investigation of the characteristics of firms hiring chief risk officers. *Journal of Risk and Insurance* 78(1), 185–211.

S&P Ratings Direct. (2008, May). *Standard and Poor's to apply enterprise risk analysis to corporate ratings.* New York: Standard and Poor's.

Slywotzky, A. J., and J. Drzik. (2005). Countering the biggest risk of all. *Harvard Business Review* 82(4), 78–88.

Smith, C. W., and R. M. Stulz. (1985). The determinants of firms' hedging policies. *Journal of financial and quantitative analysis* 20(4), 391–405.

Stulz, R. (1996). Rethinking risk management. *Journal of Applied Corporate Finance* 9(3), 8–24.

Stulz, R.M. (2003). Rethinking risk management. In Stern, J.M. and Chew, D. (eds.), *The revolution in corporate finance* (4th ed., pp. 367–384). Oxford: Blackwell.

Tufano, P. (1996). Who manages risk? An empirical examination of risk management practices in the gold mining industry. *Journal of Finance* 51(4), 1097–1137.

Walker, P.L. (2003, August). ERM in practice. *Internal Auditor*, 51–55.

Walker, P. L., W. G. Shenkir, and T. Barton. (2002). *Enterprise risk management: Pulling it all together.* Altamonte Springs, FL: Institute of Internal Auditors Research Foundation.

21

An empirical examination of risk management effectiveness

Leen Paape and Roland F. Speklé[1]

Abstract

Using data from 596 organizations located in the Netherlands, we examine contemporary risk management practices and their association with perceived risk management system quality. Working from the COSO ERM framework as our main point of reference, we identify the major design choices organizations encounter when configuring their risk management systems, and then proceed to explore these choices empirically. The results indicate that organizations generally subscribe to the key ERM idea that risk management should be broad and inclusive, and that strategic, operational, reporting and compliance risks should be addressed simultaneously rather than separately. We find no support, however, for the premise that risk management should start from an explicit and objectified assessment of the organization's risk appetite and tolerance. Furthermore, the analysis underscores the importance of risk reporting and monitoring. These findings may help managers to make evidence-based decisions when designing their risk management processes and systems.

Research in risk management has moved beyond the specialized fields of health and safety, insurance, investment management and treasury, and has started to address more inclusive issues of how risk-based controls help organizations deal with risks and opportunities in the pursuit of organizational objectives (Soin and Collier, 2013). Examples of such research include Arena et al. (2010), Collier et al. (2007), Mikes (2008; 2009), Paape and Speklé (2012), Wahlström (2009), and Woods (2009). This incipient literature, however, has only just begun to scratch the surface of risk management design choices, and we still know very little about these choices and their effects on organizational effectiveness (Kaplan, 2011; Paape and Speklé, 2012; Speklé and Kruis, 2014). In this chapter, we seek to add some empirical insights into this matter. Using survey data from 596 organizations located in the Netherlands, we examine current risk management practices and their association with perceived risk management system quality. Because the field of risk management lacks sound theory (Power, 2009; Schiller and Prpich, 2014), our approach is explicitly exploratory. Instead of testing theory-based hypotheses, we propose a series of research questions and seek empirical answers to these questions. The COSO ERM framework (COSO, 2004) serves as an important point of reference in developing these research questions, which include truly fundamental choices as to the scope and objectives of risk management, but also more technical issues in the area of risk identification and risk reporting. We also look at the organizational position of the risk management function, covering the major design parameters organizations need to address when configuring their risk management systems.

This chapter is closely connected to an earlier study of risk management effectiveness, on which we reported in Paape and Speklé (2012). The empirical model we estimate in the current chapter is very similar to the one we analyse in Paape and Speklé (2012), and the data come from the same source. However, whereas we restricted the earlier examination to organizations that adopted enterprise risk management (ERM), we now also include organizations that rely on more traditional forms of risk management. This inclusion acknowledges that the distinction between ERM and traditional risk management may be a difference in degree rather than in kind, and that the organizational effects of specific design choices may be similar, irrespective of whether they have been made in an ERM context or whether they are part of a more traditional risk management system. Furthermore, it acknowledges that the decision whether or not to adopt ERM is a design choice itself, and that – normative claims by for instance COSO notwithstanding – some firms may be better of with a well-designed traditional system than with a full-fledged ERM system (McShane et al., 2011). The inclusion of non-ERM organizations, thus, allows a broader examination of the relevant issues. Moreover, it increases sample size from 193 responses included in the effectiveness analysis in Paape and Speklé (2012) to 596 observations in the current study, considerably strengthening the empirical basis underlying our findings and inferences.

The analysis broadly confirms the earlier findings. The results indicate that organizations generally prefer ERM over traditional forms of risk management, supporting a key idea underlying regulatory frameworks such as COSO ERM. Also consistent with Paape and Speklé (2012) is that we find no support for the premise commonly found in these normative frameworks that risk management should start from an explicit and objectified assessment of the organization's risk appetite and tolerance, thus suggesting that a heuristic approach to risk control is also feasible. Furthermore, the analysis underscores the importance of risk reporting and monitoring. These findings have important implications for risk management practice, and may help managers to make evidence-based decisions when designing their risk management processes and systems.

The remainder of this chapter is structured as follows. First, we review the literature and derive the research questions that drive the analysis. Then, we discuss data collection and variable measurement and present the analysis. Finally, we conclude and offer a discussion of the findings.

Risk management design

In designing risk management systems, organizations encounter various choices they need to address. A first and very fundamental choice is about the scope of the risk management system. Traditional risk management systems have been limited in scope, but more recent trends emphasize integrative and comprehensive approaches. For instance, COSO ERM as the leading normative framework (Power, 2009; Schiller and Prpich, 2014) takes an enterprise-spanning perspective and urges organizations to include all risks that affect the entity's strategic, operational, reporting, and compliance objectives (COSO, 2004). Equally fundamental is the choice of an overall risk management goal. How much risk is the organization prepared to accept? Is this something that can be quantified? Or is risk tolerance a subjective, "soft" target that guides behaviour in more implicit ways? Other potentially consequential design choices include risk identification and assessment practices, and the selection of tools, techniques, and processes to support risk reporting and monitoring. A final important design parameter is the organizational position of the risk management function. Would it be wise to appoint a chief risk officer, or is it better not to make risk management a dedicated responsibility, to ensure that risk management remains a joint organizational responsibility? We use these general themes to structure our analysis.

The scope of risk management

A first and very basic design choice relates to the scope of risk management, i.e. to the kind of risks to include in the risk management system and processes. The COSO ERM framework advocates a comprehensive approach in which organizations include all risks that affect the organization's strategic, operational, reporting, and compliance objectives. Some studies provide evidence to indicate that such a broad ERM approach improves firm performance (e.g. Beasley et al., 2008; Gordon et al., 2009). Other studies, however, suggest that firms may be better off with a well-developed traditional risk management system without the holistic, entity-spanning ambitions of ERM (McShane et al., 2011). Therefore:

Q1: Is the extent of ERM implementation associated with risk management effectiveness?

Risk tolerance

A central notion in the COSO ERM framework is the idea of the organization's risk appetite. Risk appetite refers to "the amount of risk, on a broad level, an entity is willing to accept in pursuit of value" (COSO, 2004: 19), and expresses the organization's risk attitude at the level of the organization as a whole. Risk appetite is the starting point of COSO-type risk management, and may be expressed either in qualitative or quantitative terms. According to the COSO framework, the next step is to disaggregate this broad notion of acceptable risk, specifying the organization's risk attitude at the level of specific objectives, i.e. its risk tolerance. Risk tolerance is defined by COSO as "the acceptable level of variation relative to achievement of a specific objective" (COSO, 2004: 20), and this level should be quantified: "risk tolerances can be measured, and often are best measured in the same units as the related objectives" (COSO, 2004: 40).

In these recommendations on risk appetite and tolerance, COSO espouses a mechanistic and technocratic view on risk management (Paape and Speklé, 2012; Schiller and Prpich, 2014). This technocratic perspective has been criticized quite heavily in the literature, both from an empirical and a theoretical point of view. For instance, Collier et al. (2007) find that subjective, heuristic methods of risk management are much more common than the systems-based approach advocated by COSO. Power (2009) dismisses the idea of organization-wide risk appetite and risk tolerance as reductive, simplistic, potentially misleading, and ill-aligned with accumulated knowledge from behavioural research. Given this critique, it is important to see what our data tell us in this respect. Therefore:

Q2: Does explication and quantification of risk tolerance improve risk management effectiveness?

Risk identification and assessment

Risk exposure is a dynamic phenomenon, and organizations need to review their risk positions periodically. But what is the frequency with which this should be done? A plausible assumption is that the frequency of risk assessment should keep pace with changes in the organization's environment. Additionally, some minimum level of frequency may be required to ensure that risk management becomes ingrained sufficiently deeply in the functioning of the organization so as to prevent it from becoming a purely ceremonial compliance exercise (Arena et al., 2010). The COSO framework provides no specific guidance, but the question is important nonetheless:

Q3: Is the frequency of risk assessment associated with risk management effectiveness?

Another choice organizations must make involves the number of hierarchical levels to include in the risk identification and assessment process. Should risk assessment be centralized at the senior management level or is a decentralized approach more appropriate? There is a relatively well-developed literature in the field of organization and accounting that argues that decentralization arises in response to problems of information and knowledge (e.g. Abernethy et al., 2004; Jensen and Meckling, 1992). Application of the insights of this literature to the current question would suggest that it makes sense to engage middle managers in risk identification and assessment if they enjoy an information advantage regarding the details of their businesses (cf. Nocco and Stulz, 2006):

Q4: Does engagement of lower levels of management in risk assessment contribute to risk management effectiveness?

The COSO ERM framework recommends that organizations apply a combination of qualitative and quantitative risk assessment techniques. Paape and Speklé (2012) suggest that in the context of COSO's overall preference for quantification, this provision should be taken to mean that organizations should not rely on qualitative methods alone, and should apply quantitative techniques wherever possible. This preference, however, is debatable. For instance, one could surmise that methods should match the organization's culture, and that quantitative methods may be less effective in a culture of "quantitative scepticism" (Mikes, 2008; 2009). In addition, it may be true that a strong focus on quantification may lead one to gloss over fundamental differences in risks, failing to see incommensurable trade-offs (Schiller and Prpich, 2014). Therefore:

Q5: Is the use of quantitative risk assessment techniques positively associated with risk management effectiveness?

Risk reporting and monitoring

Because risks are not static, their management requires relevant, timely and reliable information to act upon. The COSO ERM framework acknowledges this need, and argues that monitoring should ideally proceed on an ongoing basis (cf. COSO, 2004: 75–76). This suggests that high-frequency risk reporting may enhance the quality of risk management:

Q6: Does the frequency of risk reporting positively affect risk management effectiveness?

The COSO framework emphasizes the need to report all identified risk management deficiencies (COSO, 2004: 80). Internal risk reporting, however, will typically be broader, and will include retrospective diagnostic data on current risk profiles and ongoing risk management processes to support monitoring, as well as prospective information to allow a timely response to internal or external changes that may affect future risk exposure and risk control. It seems plausible to assume that risk management effectiveness is affected by the richness of both this retrospective and prospective information:

Q7: Does the richness of retrospective (Q7a) and prospective (Q7b) risk reporting enhance risk management effectiveness?

The locus of risk management responsibility

Some firms choose to assign risk management responsibility to a specialized senior executive, usually referred to as the chief risk officer or the CRO (Nocco and Stulz, 2006). The appointment of a CRO is often interpreted as an indicator of the organization's commitment to risk management (Beasley et al., 2008; Liebenberg and Hoyt, 2003). However, COSO ERM suggests that even though an organization's top management should assume ultimate responsibility for risk management, one should nevertheless ensure that a risk management orientation is spread throughout the organization (COSO, 2004: 88), and that lower-level business managers take the relevant risk–return trade-offs into account in their decisions (Nocco and Stulz, 2006). It could be the case that the appointment of a CRO helps to support such a broad risk awareness throughout the organization, increasing risk management effectiveness. But it is also possible that the presence of a CRO actually erodes a shared risk management orientation, because the presence of a specialized risk management office makes it possible for middle managers to neglect risk management issues as somebody else's problems, just referring them to the dedicated office to find a solution. Thus:

Q8: Does the presence of a CRO contribute to risk management effectiveness?

Control variables

In the analysis, we control for size and possible industry effects. There is good reason to expect that both the perceived quality of the risk management system and many of the individual structural design choices are correlated with the size of the organization, for instance because of economies of scale associated with the operation of a risk management system (e.g. Beasley et al., 2005; Kleffner et al., 2003) or because of size-dependent differences in the ability to absorb formal administrative practices like risk management.

There is also good reason to expect industry effects. Particularly, we will control for the special position of financial services firms and public sector and not-for-profit organizations. Banks have strong incentives to adopt sound risk management systems because these may help them to reduce Basel II capital requirements (Liebenberg and Hoyt, 2003; Mikes, 2009; Wahlström, 2009). However, it is also likely that in this sector, aspiration levels as to the quality of these systems are higher here as well. This would imply that perceived effectiveness is lower in the financial services sector, ceteris paribus (Paape and Speklé, 2012).

The reason to control for potential public sector effects is that it is commonly believed that the adoption of risk management in the public sector lags behind the private sector (Schiller and Prpich, 2014), and that the available risk management apparatus does not fit very well with the dominant culture and management style in the public and not-for-profit sector (Bhimani, 2003; Mikes, 2009). This would suggest that risk management effectiveness is generally lower in the public sector, but also that the contribution of various design choices to perceived effectiveness may be different in this sector.

Data, analysis, and results

Data collection and sample

The data for this chapter have been provided by a research team with participants from PricewaterhouseCoopers, Royal NIVRA (the Dutch Institute of Chartered Public Accountants), the University of Groningen, and Nyenrode Business University.[2] Based on information from public

Table 21.1 The dataset

	Mean	Std. dev.	Min	Median	Max
Revenue (€ millions)	1,059	6,113	11	70	85,000
Number of employees	1,416	5,609	31	270	80,000

Industry	Number	%
Wholesale and retail	66	11.1
Transportation	29	4.9
Manufacturing	98	16.4
Financial services	41	6.9
Business services	64	10.7
Telecom and IT	26	4.4
Energy and utilities	19	3.2
Public sector and not-for-profit	248	41.6
Unknown	5	0.8
Total	596	100.0

databases, the team identified organizations located in the Netherlands with annual revenues of more than €10 million and with more than 30 employees. Of these, 9,579 organizations appeared to fit these criteria. The survey was mailed to the board of these organizations in May 2009. Of the questionnaires, 240 were undeliverable. Of the remaining 9,339 surveys, 928 were returned, resulting in an overall response rate of 9.9%. Of the responses, 103 were found not to match the initial selection criteria after all, leaving 825 useable observations. This initial sample, however, includes a significant number of organizations that do not apply any systematic risk management systems and processes, but just respond reactively and ad hoc to risks as and when they become manifest. Because our interest is in the perceived quality of risk management systems and their components, we exclude these nonusers from the analysis, and base our examination only on data from organizations that engage in some form of periodic risk identification and assessment. This costs us 229 observations, leaving a final sample of 596 organizations that are engaged in some form of systematic risk management practices, either of the traditional, silo-based kind or of the ERM type.

Respondents were board members, chief financial officers (CFOs), or senior staff members. Although we do not have the data formally to examine representativeness, the sample is relatively large and heterogeneous qua organizational size and industry, and there are no obvious selection or response biases. Table 21.1 gives further information about the respondents and the dataset.

Measurement of variables

In Table 21.2, we describe variable measurement. Most variables are based on factual information. An important exception is risk management effectiveness as the dependent variable. The score on this variable is based on a survey question asking respondents to grade the quality of their risk management system on a 10-point scale. The question does not really define the notion of a risk management system, nor the dimensions that should be included in the quality assessment. Thus, we measure an intrinsically complex construct with a single survey item. However, the survey contains additional information to support this metric. Respondents were also asked to indicate whether they believe that their risk management system has helped them to cope with the effects of the financial crisis. The scores on this additional question can be interpreted as a somewhat narrow but nevertheless informative alternative proxy for the perceived quality of the risk management system. This alternative proxy correlates significantly with the effectiveness metric on which we rely ($r = 0.196; p = 0.000$), thus supporting our measure.

Table 21.2 Measurement of variables

Dependent variable:

Risk management effectiveness (EFFECTIVENESS) expresses respondents' assessment of the quality of their risk management systems (1 = deeply insufficient, 6 = adequate, 10 = excellent).

Research questions	*Measurement*
The scope of risk management • extent of ERM implementation (STAGE)	The scale for STAGE is adapted from Beasley et al. (2005): 1 = risk management is mainly incident-driven; no plans exist to implement ERM; 2 = we actively control risk in specific areas (e.g. health and safety, financial risk), and we are considering to implement a complete ERM; 3 = we identify, assess, and control risk in specific areas, and we are planning to implement a complete ERM; 4 = we identify, assess, and control strategic, financial, operational, and compliance risks, and we are in the process of implementing a complete ERM; 5 = we identify, assess, and control strategic, financial, operational, and compliance risks, and ERM is an integral part of the (strategic) planning and control cycle.
Risk tolerance • explication/quantification of risk tolerance (TOLERANCE)	TOLERANCE is measured using an ordinal scale: 1 = no explication of risk tolerance; 2 = risk tolerance is explicated in qualitative terms; 3 = risk tolerance is quantified.
Risk identification and assessment • frequency of risk assessment (ASSESSFREQ) • engagement of lower management levels (LEVEL) • quantitative risk assessment (QUANTMETHODS)	ASSESSFREQ expresses the frequency of the entity-wide risk identification/assessment exercise (1 = yearly, 2 = quarterly, 3 = monthly, 4 = weekly). LEVEL counts the number of management levels involved in risk identification/assessment. A score of 1 means that only the board is involved, 2 means that the exercise includes the board and the management level just below the board, etc. QUANTMETHODS is a dummy that takes on a value of 1 if the organizations uses one or more of the following four techniques: scenario analysis, sensitivity analysis, simulation, and stress testing.
Risk reporting and monitoring • reporting frequency (REPORTFREQ) • richness of reporting: retrospective (RETROSPECT) and prospective (PROSPECT) information	REPORTFREQ indicates the frequency with which the organization reports on risks to internal constituencies (1 = never, 2 = ad hoc, 3 = yearly, 4 = quarterly, 5 = monthly, 6 = weekly). Both RETROSPECT and PROSPECT count the number of items from a four-item list that the organization includes in its standard risk reporting format. The list for RETROSPECT includes general information on risks, the status of risk control activities, critical risk indicators, and incidents. The PROSPECT list consists of developments in risk profile, significant internal changes, significant external changes, and risk control improvements.

Research questions	Measurement
Locus of risk management responsibility • presence of a chief risk officer (CRO)	CRO is a dummy variable with a value of 1 if a CRO is present and 0 otherwise.
Control variables • size (SIZE) • industry effects (FINSERV and PUBSEC)	SIZE is calculated as the natural log of revenue (or the size of the budget in case of public sector organizations). FINSERV and PUBSEC are industry dummies that take on a value of 1 if the organization belongs to the financial services industry or the public or not-for-profit sector, respectively.

Another variable that requires additional discussion is STAGE. STAGE expresses the extent of ERM implementation, and is measured using a scale based on Beasley et al. (2005). However, the team that constructed the survey made some changes to this instrument. Specifically, whereas the original scale of Beasley et al. was based on statements regarding (intentional) ERM implementation,[3] the survey items that we work from contain additional information on actual ERM practices. These alterations could be problematic because they lead to double-barrelled questions. That is, the added description of manifest practices in a particular answer category does not necessarily coincide with the ERM intentions expressed in that same category. For instance, it is possible that an organization actively controls risk in specific areas (which should lead to a score of 2 or 3 on STAGE; see Table 21.2), yet has no intentions to implement full-scale ERM (which should lead to a score of 1). However, although this problem is quite serious in principle, it does not appear to be so in fact. Respondents could have checked more than one of the relevant categories in order to express the nuances of their situation, but none of them did so. We take this as an indication that respondents had no real trouble scoring their organizations on the scale, and that the answer categories were felt to be sufficiently clear. Furthermore, the questionnaire holds additional information to support the measurement of the extent of ERM adoption. Respondents were asked to provide information on the scope of their periodic risk identification and assessment efforts by indicating whether or not they include each of the categories strategic, financial, operational, reporting, and compliance risks in the exercise. Because ERM is characterized by its broadness and its comprehensive ambitions, the scope of risk assessment is a very relevant indicator of the extent of ERM implementation, and we expect a significant correlation between the scope of risk assessment (measured by the number of risk categories included in periodic risk assessment) and the STAGE metric. In support of our implementation proxy, the data corroborate this expectation ($r = 0.396$; $p = 0.000$).

A description of current ERM practices

Table 21.3 presents descriptive statistics on risk management effectiveness and the various design choices.

The descriptive statistics give interesting insights in contemporary risk management practices. The mean score on STAGE is 3, indicating that the average organization has fully implemented traditional risk management, and is planning to move towards an integrated ERM approach. Organizations appear to be quite content with their risk management system, grading it with an average of 6.7 on a 10-point scale. Untabulated results, however, indicate that 13% of the respondents rate their system as insufficient (score below 5.5), suggesting that there is still room for improvement. Another noteworthy fact is that that the mean score on TOLERANCE

Table 21.3 Descriptive statistics

Ordinal and ratio variables

	Mean	Std. Dev.	Scale	Min	Median	Max
EFFECTIVENESS	6.71	1.270	1–10	1	7	10
STAGE	2.99	1.182	1–5	1	3	5
TOLERANCE	1.61	0.856	1–3	1	1	3
ASSESSFREQ	1.37	0.706	1–4	1	1	4
LEVEL	2.46	1.160	1–5	1	2	5
REPORTFREQ	3.88	1.091	1–6	1	4	6
RETROSPECT	1.95	0.962	0–4	0	2	4
PROSPECT	1.59	1.240	0–4–	0	1	4
SIZE	4.58	1.571		2.35	4.25	11.35

Nominal variables

	Yes (= 1)	No (= 0)
CRO	144 (24.3%)	449 (75.7%)
QUANTMETHODS	325 (54.6%)	270 (45.4%)

is only 1.61, indicating that quantification of risk appetite and tolerance is rather uncommon. Further (untabulated) analysis reveals that only 25% of the respondents express risk tolerance in quantitative terms. Of the organizations, 64% convey that they do not explicate risk tolerance at all; not even in qualitative terms. Finally, it is worth noting that CROs are still relatively rare: only about one-quarter of the respondents have appointed one.

The relationship between ERM design and effectiveness

The correlation matrix is presented in Table 21.4. This matrix shows that perceived risk management quality is associated with all design choices we consider in this chapter. Public sector and not-for-profit organizations experience lower levels of effectiveness. Judging from the negative correlations we find, these organizations also report lower levels of ERM implementation, lower risk assessment frequencies, a lower reliance on quantitative risk assessment methods, and less extensive risk reporting than their private sector counterparts. Table 21.4 indicates that many design choices are to some extent interrelated. The correlations between the independent variables are, however, low enough not to signal multicollinearity issues.[4]

We further examine the contribution of the various design choices on risk management effectiveness in a OLS regression analysis. Due to missing values, we lose 95 observations in this analysis, and we run the model using data from 501 organizations. Table 21.5 reports the results.

The model explains 26% of the variance in risk management effectiveness. The results show that perceived risk management effectiveness is affected by the extent of ERM implementation (Q1). This finding is consistent with COSO's integrative and comprehensive ambitions, and suggests that organizations generally subscribe to the idea that ERM is to be preferred over traditional, silo-based approaches to risk management. COSO's belief in the importance of risk tolerance specification (Q2), however, finds no support in the data. Regarding the more technical issues of risk identification/assessment and risk reporting/monitoring, we find that the frequency of risk assessment (Q3), the frequency of risk reporting (Q6), and both the richness

Table 21.4 Spearman correlation matrix

	1	2	3	4	5	6	7	8	9	10	11	12
1: EFFECTIVENESS	1											
2: STAGE	.425***	1										
3: TOLERANCE	.166***	.217***	1									
4: ASSESSFREQ	.191***	.127***	0.054	1								
5: LEVEL	.099**	.233***	.126***	.017	1							
6: QUANTMETHODS	.185***	.153***	.171***	.100**	-.060	1						
7: REPORTFREQ	.260***	.262***	.089**	.225***	.044	.151***	1					
8: RETROSPECT	.174***	.214***	.068	-.003	.138***	.036	.108***	1				
9: PROSPECT	.105**	.119***	-.029	.068	.027	.159***	.035	.165***	1			
10: CRO	.121***	.183***	.134****	.034	.113***	.030	.091**	.100**	-.064	1		
11: SIZE	.097**	.214***	.137***	.005	.223***	.026	.051	.115***	.003	-.003	1	
12: FINSERV	.030	.145***	.142***	.006	.064	.059	.165***	.227***	.066	.064	.148***	1
13: PUBSEC	-.298***	-.112***	-.082*	-.107***	.040	-.122***	-.195***	-.081*	-.007	-.091**	-.096**	-.232***

* $p < 0.10$; ** $p < 0.05$; *** $p < 0.01$ (2-tailed)

Table 21.5 OLS regression results

Dependent variable: *EFFECTIVENESS*
Sample: 596; included observations: 501

	Beta	Std. error	t	p (2-tailed)
STAGE	0.297	0.046	6.829	0.000
TOLERANCE	0.057	0.059	1.400	0.162
ASSESSFREQ	0.116	0.073	2.888	0.004
LEVEL	−0.012	0.044	−0.301	0.764
QUANTMETHODS	0.061	0.101	1.513	0.131
REPORTFREQ	0.133	0.051	3.213	0.001
RETROSPECT	0.084	0.053	2.032	0.043
PROSPECT	0.086	0.040	2.139	0.033
CRO	−0.013	0.114	−0.326	0.745
SIZE	0.027	0.032	0.637	0.524
FINSERV	−0.118	0.194	−2.843	0.005
PUBSEC	−0.168	0.102	−4.107	0.000

$F = 15.608$; $p = 0.000$
$R^2 = 0.277$; adjusted $R^2 = 0.260$

of retrospective and prospective risk reporting (Q7a and Q7b) contribute to perceived risk management effectiveness. We do not find that the engagement of lower levels of management (Q4) affects effectiveness. Neither do we find that the use of quantitative risk assessment techniques (Q5) helps to advance the quality of ERM, nor that the appointment of a dedicated risk officer (Q8) has a significant effect. The influence of organizational size appears to be insignificant, but there are industry effects. Both firms in the financial services industry and organizations from the public and not-for-profit sector appear to be less satisfied with the quality of their risk management practices.

Additional analyses

There is some evidence in the literature to suggest that the optimal level of risk management sophistication is not a full-fledged ERM system, but rather a mature, well-developed traditional risk management system. In their study of 82 publicly traded US life insurance companies, McShane et al. (2011) find a positive relationship between increasing levels of traditional risk management capabilities and firm value, but they do not find an additional value effect for firms achieving a higher risk management level beyond the highest traditional risk management score. To test whether such curvilinear effects are also present in our data, we rerun the model, now including $STAGE^2$ in the analysis. The (untabulated) results show that the quadratic term is not significant, while all other results are qualitatively similar to the original model. Thus, we conclude that there is no evidence for a parabolic relationship, and that the effects of increasing risk management sophistication are strictly positive, at least over the empirical range we observe in our data.

A relatively large part of our sample consists of public sector and not-for-profit organizations, and it may be the case that some of our results are driven by this particular composition of our dataset. To examine this, we split our sample in a private sector ($n = 343$) and a public/non-profit subset ($n = 248$) and rerun the analysis in both samples. We report on these regressions in Table 21.6. The results for the private sector sample (Panel A, Table 21.6) are qualitatively

Table 21.6 Additional analyses

Panel A: sample excluding (semi)public sector and not-for-profit organizations

Dependent variable: EFFECTIVENESS
Sample: 343; included observations: 292

	Beta	Std. Error	t	p (2-tailed)
STAGE	0.249	0.060	4.039	0.000
TOLERANCE	0.022	0.078	0.395	0.693
ASSESSFREQ	0.138	0.087	2.502	0.013
LEVEL	0.066	0.059	1.137	0.257
QUANTMETHODS	0.093	0.138	1.638	0.103
REPORTFREQ	0.117	0.063	2.074	0.039
RETROSPECT	0.088	0.068	1.540	0.125
PROSPECT	0.060	0.055	1.070	0.285
CRO	0.015	0.144	0.278	0.781
SIZE	0.069	0.037	1.211	0.227
FINSERV	−0.149	0.199	−2.623	0.009

$F = 7.153; p = 0.000$
$R^2 = 0.219$; adjusted $R^2 = 0.189$

Panel B: (Semi)public sector and not-for-profit organizations only

Dependent variable: EFFECTIVENESS
Sample: 248; included observations: 209

	Beta	Std. Error	t	p (2-tailed)
STAGE	0.370	0.074	5.690	0.000
TOLERANCE	0.121	0.091	1.920	0.056
ASSESSFREQ	0.083	0.137	1.328	0.186
LEVEL	−0.085	0.068	−1.324	0.187
QUANTMETHODS	0.033	0.152	0.528	0.598
REPORTFREQ	0.172	0.088	2.717	0.007
RETROSPECT	0.070	0.090	1.039	0.300
PROSPECT	0.103	0.060	1.622	0.106
CRO	0.005	0.188	0.085	0.932
SIZE	−0.038	0.062	−0.593	0.554

$F = 7.884; p = 0.000$
$R^2 = 0.285$; adjusted $R^2 = 0.249$

similar to the original findings and lead to the same overall conclusions and inferences, except that we no longer find any effects for the richness of risk reporting – probably due to sample size issues. The public and not-for-profit regression, however, provide some different results (Panel B, Table 21.6). Somewhat surprisingly, we find that in this subsample, explication and quantification of risk tolerance does seem to contribute to perceived risk management effectiveness. This result, however, appears to be unstable, and is driven by a few "outliers"[5] in the sample. If we remove these from the analysis, the coefficient for TOLERANCE becomes insignificant again.

Conclusions and discussion

The findings of our study are generally in line with prior literature (Paape and Speklé, 2012) and support the key tenet of normative risk management frameworks like COSO (2004) ERM that risk management should be broad and inclusive, encompassing strategic and operational risks, as well as compliance and reporting risks. Apparently, such a comprehensive ERM approach is to be preferred over a more traditional, silo-based approach to risk management. Furthermore, it appears important to invest in the technical sophistication of the risk management system. That is, our results indicate that the frequency of risk assessment, together with the quality of risk reporting (including reporting frequency and broadness) are positively associated with risk management effectiveness. We find, however, no support for the highly systematic, "calculative" (Mikes, 2009) perspective on effective risk management that can be found in the COSO framework. Only one-quarter of our respondents quantify risk tolerances. Almost two-thirds of them indicate that they do not explicate risk tolerances at all, not even in qualitative terms. Moreover, the regression results suggest that quantification of risk tolerances does not contribute to perceived risk management effectiveness. In addition, the use of quantitative risk assessment techniques does not seem to affect risk management quality.[6] In conjunction, these findings may be taken to suggest that organizations generally see risk management as a way of thinking rather than as a hard and measureable process, and that a less objectified, more heuristic and exploratory approach to risk management is in fact feasible without loss of effectiveness (cf. Collier et al., 2007; Mikes, 2009; Paape and Speklé, 2012).

Another interesting null finding is that an appointment of a CRO does not appear to influence risk management effectiveness. One interpretation of this finding is that although the appointment of a risk management "champion" may help to ensure a solid position of risk management on the organizational agenda, it comes at a price as well, for instance through a reduced sense of risk management as a joint responsibility throughout the organization. An alternative explanation, however, is that it is not the absence nor the presence per se of a CRO that affect the quality of risk management, but rather the mechanisms and instruments he or she brings to manage risks. In support of this alternative explanation, the correlation table (Table 21.4) shows that the presence of a CRO is positively associated with the scope of risk management, the frequency of risk assessment, and with the frequency and richness of risk reporting–design variables that are in fact related to perceived risk management effectiveness in the multivariate model.

The findings of this study should be interpreted with care. We rely on cross-sectional survey data and, consequently, are unable to make strong claims regarding causality. In addition, the data reflect respondents' perceptions rather than hard facts, and some of our measurement instruments are somewhat naïve. However, as one of the first larger scale empirical studies of risk management design, the analysis may be an interesting step towards a more rigorous, evidence-based understanding of successful risk management practices. Such an understanding is valuable for organizations in their efforts to advance risk management. Our findings should also speak to regulators and standard-setters. In many countries, regulators are pressing firms to improve risk management and risk reporting (Collier et al., 2006; Kleffner et al., 2003). The natural response for many organizations is to fall back on normative frameworks like COSO ERM. Given the limited support we find for this framework's technocratic approach to risk management, it might well be the case that the effort to standardize and codify risk management practices is premature (Kaplan, 2011), and that regulators should allow room for experimentation and innovation (Paape and Speklé, 2012).

Notes

1 Leen Paape and Roland F. Speklé, Nyenrode Business University, Breukelen, the Netherlands.
2 One of the authors of the current chapter was part of this team.
3 The original Beasley scale is as follows: (1) no plans exist to implement ERM; (2) investigating ERM, but no decision made yet; (3) planning to implement ERM; (4) partial ERM is in place; and (5) complete ERM is in place (Beasley et al., 2005).
4 A diagnosis of the variance inflation factors (VIF) in the OLS regressions confirms this; the highest VIF we find is only 1.277, well below the threshold values of 6 or 10 recommended by Cohen et al. (2003) and Hair et al. (2010), respectively.
5 This refers to a total of seven observations. A further analysis of these observations does not make clear why they are so different from the rest.
6 This finding differs from Paape and Speklé (2012) who in a sample of ERM adopters do find that the use of quantitative methods contributes to risk management effectiveness. To reconcile this difference, one could perhaps conjecture that the benefits of quantitative methods can only be reaped in a setting of relatively high levels of risk management sophistication. If this tentative explanation holds, the upshot would be that there are complementarities between components of the risk management system. Future studies could seek to address this idea.

References

Abernethy, M.A., Bouwens, J., and Van Lent, L. 2004. Determinants of control system design in divisionalized firms. *Accounting Review*, 79: 545–570.
Arena, M., Arnaboldi, M., and Azzone, G. 2010. The organizational dynamics of enterprise risk management. *Accounting, Organizations and Society*, 35: 659–675.
Beasley, M.S., Clune, R., and Hermanson, D.R. 2005. Enterprise risk management: an empirical analysis of factors associated with the extent of implementation. *Journal of Accounting and Public Policy*, 24: 521–531.
Beasley, M., Pagach, D., and Warr, R. 2008. Information conveyed in hiring announcements of senior executives overseeing enterprise-wide risk management processes. *Journal of Accounting, Auditing & Finance*, 23: 311–332.
Bhimani, A. 2003. A study of the emergence of management accounting system ethos and its influence on perceived system success. *Accounting, Organizations and Society*, 28: 523–548.
Cohen, J., Cohen, P., West, S.G., and Aiken, L.S. 2003. *Applied multiple regression/correlation analysis for the behavioral sciences* (3rd ed.). Mahwah, NJ: Lawrence Erlbaum Associates.
Collier, P.M., Berry, A.J., and Burke, G.T. 2006. Risk and management accounting: best practice guidelines for enterprise-wide internal control procedures. *CIMA Research Executive Summary Series*, 2(11).
Collier, P.M., Berry, A.J., and Burke, G.T. 2007. *Risk and management accounting: best practice guidelines for enterprise-wide internal control procedures*. Oxford: CIMA/Elsevier.
COSO. 2004. *Enterprise risk management – integrated framework. Executive summary & framework*. Committee of Sponsoring Organizations of the Treadway Commission.
Gordon, L.A., Loeb, M.P., and Tseng, C. 2009. Enterprise risk management and firm performance: a contingency perspective. *Journal of Accounting and Public Policy*, 28: 301–327.
Hair, J.F., Black, W.C., Babin, B.J., and Anderson, R.E. 2010. *Multivariate data analysis. A global perspective* (7th ed.). Upper Saddle River, NJ: Pearson Prentice Hall.
Jensen, M.C., and Meckling, W.H. 1992. Specific and general knowledge, and organization structure. In L. Werin and H. Wijkander (Eds.), *Contract economics* (pp. 251–274). Oxford: Basil Blackwell.
Kaplan, R.S. 2011. Accounting scholarship that advances professional knowledge and practice. *Accounting Review*, 86: 367–383.
Kleffner, A.E., Lee, R.B., and McGannon, B. 2003. The effect of corporate governance on the use of enterprise risk management: evidence from Canada. *Risk Management and Insurance Review*, 6: 53–73.
Liebenberg, A.P., and Hoyt, R.E. 2003. The determinants of enterprise risk management: evidence from the appointment of chief risk officers. *Risk Management and Insurance Review*, 6: 37–52.
McShane, M.K., Nair, A., and Rustambekov, E. 2011. Does enterprise risk management increase firm value? *Journal of Accounting, Auditing & Finance*, 26: 641–658.
Mikes, A. 2008. Chief risk officers at crunch time: compliance champions of business partners? *Journal of Risk Management in Financial Institutions*, 2: 7–25.

Mikes, A. 2009. Risk management and calculative cultures. *Management Accounting Research*, 20: 18–40.

Nocco, B.W., and Stulz, R.M. 2006. Enterprise risk management: theory and practice. *Journal of Applied Corporate Finance*, 18(4): 8–20.

Paape, L., and Speklé, R.F. 2012. The adoption and design of enterprise risk management practices: an empirical study. *European Accounting Review*, 21: 533–564.

Power, M. 2009. The risk management of nothing. *Accounting, Organizations and Society*, 34: 849–855. Schiller, F., and Prpich, G. 2014. Learning to organise risk management in organisations: what future for enterprise risk management? *Journal of Risk Research*, 17: 999–1017.

Soin, K., and Collier, P. 2013. Risk and risk management in management accounting and control. *Management Accounting Research*, 24: 82–87.

Speklé, R.F., and Kruis, A. 2014. Management control research: a review of current developments. In D.T. Otley and K. Soin (Eds.), *Management control and uncertainty*. Houndmills: Palgrave Macmillan, forthcoming.

Wahlström, G. 2009. Risk management versus operational action: Basel II in a Swedish context. *Management Accounting Research*, 20: 53–68.

Woods, M. 2009. A contingency perspective on the risk management control system within Birmingham City Council. *Management Accounting Research*, 20: 69–81.

22

Does enterprise risk management create value for firms?

Evidence from Nordic countries

Naciye Sekerci[1]

Abstract

Risk management has grabbed more attention due to the recent financial crisis. Firms have started investing significant amount of money in implementing enterprise-wide (integrated) risk management programs. Despite increased attention on enterprise risk management (ERM) and its wide usage, we know very little if ERM is value adding to firms. This chapter provides evidence from listed Nordic firms on value relevance of ERM by investigating the impact of ERM adoption on firm value. It also advances prior studies by introducing a new, sound measure for ERM process. ERM is measured by using a unique dataset which is constructed by a survey conducted on how listed Nordic firms organize their risk management programs. Accordingly, we are able to introduce more dimensions into ERM measurement, as well as capture its complexity and distinguishing features – thanks to valuable inside information on firms' risk management programs, most of which otherwise would not be obtainable through publicly available information. The main finding of the chapter is that value creation of ERM is not supported after controlling for other determinants of firm value and endogeneity bias. The findings are highly consistent over different specifications.

A well-known definition of enterprise risk management (ERM) is provided in ERM framework of Committee of Sponsoring Organizations of the Treadway Commission (COSO, 2004):

> A process, affected by an entity's board of directors, management and other personnel, applied in strategy setting and across the enterprise, designed to identify potential events that may affect the entity, and manage risk to be within its risk appetite, to provide reasonable assurance regarding the achievement of entity objectives.
>
> *(COSO, 2004, p. 2)*

Another definition of ERM is stated in the following way by Casualty Actuarial Society (CAS) Committee:

> ERM is the discipline by which an organization in any industry assesses, controls, exploits, finances, and monitors risks from all sources for the purpose of increasing the organization's short- and long-term value to its stakeholders.
>
> *(CAS, 2003, p. 8)*

ERM process or discipline[2] is a centralized and integrated approach suggesting a high level of oversight of risks on a portfolio basis. It has been developed as an alternative approach to traditional silo-based (disintegrated or fragmentized) risk management where various types of risks are managed in different units in a firm.[3] Implementation of an enterprise-wide approach to risk management has risen recently (Hoyt and Liebenberg, 2011) due to great emphasis put on robust risk management by external corporate governance mechanisms (country-level),[4] stock exchange regulations,[5] internal (firm-level) corporate governance structures,[6] as well as rating agencies.[7]

It is argued in the literature – and is elaborated on later – that ERM could be a value-creating activity for firms thanks to enabling objective capital allocation as a result of risk–return trade-off assessments, as well as thanks to mitigating financial risks and facilitating to exploit business risks which in turn leads to gaining and/or maintaining competitive advantage (Lam, 2001; Meulbroek, 2002; Nocco and Stulz, 2006; Hoyt and Liebenberg, 2011). However, these argued benefits of ERM would come at a cost. Implementing an ERM program potentially has (high) costs since it requires a substantial change in how the company organizes their risk management process and deals with risks; such as appointing a chief risk officer (CRO), establishing a risk committee at the board level, establishing a centralized risk management department, developing a formal statement on the firm's risk appetite and so on.

Given these cost-benefits considerations, we know little if ERM creates value for firms. Only a few empirical studies have been conducted on value relevance of ERM, and the evidence provided by those studies is inconclusive. Two papers find that ERM is value-creating (Hoyt and Liebenberg, 2011; Baxter, Bedard, Hoitash and Yezegel, 2013) while Lin, Wen and Yu (2012) show that it is value-destroying for firms. The remaining four articles either suggest that the benefit of an ERM program is firm-specific or find no support for value creation of ERM (Beasley, Pagach and Warr, 2008; Gordon, Loeb and Tseng, 2009; Pagach and Warr, 2010; McShane, Nair and Rustambekov, 2011).

In addition to this inconclusive evidence, the methods used in those studies to measure ERM have some drawbacks. Most of them are unable to capture the complexity of an ERM *process*;[8] instead they use very simplistic measures. For example, most of the previous studies use CRO hiring announcements as a proxy for ERM. However, some firms may not have ERM, yet have the position due to its popularity. Or, firms might have ERM in place but have another position with the same responsibilities as a CRO has.

The objective of this chapter is to provide evidence on value relevance of ERM. The chapter investigates if ERM increases firm value by introducing a well-developed measure for ERM process than those used by the prior studies. ERM is measured by exploiting a unique dataset which is constructed by using survey responses on how firms organize their risk management programs. Thanks to the survey, we are able to introduce more dimensions into ERM measurement – compared to the prior studies – enabling us to capture the complexity and distinguishing features of an ERM process. The survey, directed to firms' chief executive officers (CEOs), chief financial officers (CFOs) or any other equivalent person who has adequate knowledge about risk management process in the firm, provides valuable inside information on risk management programs of the firms, most of which otherwise would not be obtainable through publicly available information. For example, information about "risk appetite" (which is one of the elements of ERM[9] included in this chapter) of a firm is not publicly available for many firms.

Overall, this chapter contributes to the literature in two ways. First, it provides evidence on value relevance of ERM by testing the hypothesis that ERM is value-creating for firms with a new dataset formed by listed Nordic firms. Second, we attempt to develop a new, sound measure for ERM process that could be further used in the ERM literature – with possible adjustments and improvements.

The unique dataset just mentioned comes from a survey conducted to all listed Nordic firms. Our results from such a broad sample is relatively more generalizable compared to industry-based samples, such as those in Hoyt and Liebenberg (2011), McShane et al. (2011) and Lin et al. (2012), who focus on insurance companies; and Baxter et al. (2013) who focus on banks and insurance companies. Despite the fact that the survey is directed to senior executives, the total response rate is 23%, which is better than the comparable study by Beasley, Clune and Hermanson (2005) (10.3%). To estimate the impact of ERM on firm value, as our main estimation technique we employ instrumental variables estimation where endogeneity between ERM and firm value is taken into account. The main finding of the chapter is that ERM does not increase firm value, which is in line with McShane et al. (2011) and Pagach and Warr (2010) while conflicting with Hoyt and Liebenberg (2011) and Baxter et al. (2013). Our insignificant finding suggests that ERM is an investment with zero net present value (NPV). Investors value ERM implementation neither positively nor negatively. This finding is consistent with Beasley et al. (2008), who find no significant market reaction to ERM implementation.

The chapter proceeds as follows. First, we review the literature, develop our hypotheses, and discuss theoretical arguments on how ERM increases firm value in comparison to traditional risk management approaches. Then we present our sample, data and methodology and discuss the empirical results. Finally, we draw concluding remarks, and mention the limitations of the study and give some suggestions for future research.

Literature review and hypotheses development

Firms engage in risk management activities for several reasons. Some of these theoretical motives are managerial risk aversion, reducing financial distress costs, mitigating agency cost of free cash flow, lowering expected tax payments, mitigating underinvestment problem, and reducing cost of external financing for new investment (Myers, 1977; Stulz, 1984; Smith and Stulz, 1985; Jensen, 1986; Mayers and Smith, 1990; Froot, Scharfstein and Stein, 1993).

The studies investigating the impact of risk management, in particular hedging, on firm value or performance form the basis for value relevance studies on ERM. The results from this particular literature are mostly conclusive and show that risk management is associated with higher firm valuation. For example, an early study, Cassidy, Constand and Corbett (1990) find that shareholders value the use of risk management by conducting an event analysis. Smithson and Simkins (2005) provide a review of empirical studies on value relevance of risk management. As a proxy for firm value, 9 of the 10 studies that Smithson and Simkins look into use Tobin's Q. They separate these 10 papers into four groups. In the first two groups, there are studies investigating the impact of managing interest rate and foreign exchange risk on firm value. All the papers in the first two groups find a positive relation between the use of risk management and value of the firm. The last two categories are formed by studies examining the relationship between commodity price risk management and firm value. While this specific form of hedging increases firm value for commodity users, the results for commodity producers are mixed. Mackay and Moeller (2007) also provide empirical evidence that risk management is value adding. A recent study by Zou (2010) shows that while hedging with property insurance increases firm value to a certain level, overhedging could be value-reducing. Overall, most of the findings from this literature support the argument that risk management is a value-creating activity.

These studies provide empirical evidence on the value relevance of risk management by focusing mostly on hedging. However, investigating only hedging activities may not be enough to give the big picture of a firm's risk management, since hedging could only be a part of the risk management process. For example, there are mainly two types of risks that a firm's risk management program has to deal with: financial and business risks. The former can be transferred through use of derivatives with low transaction costs, while the latter cannot always be transferred easily due to the scarcity of hedging tools available for them. In other words, risk management is more than just hedging. Thus, this chapter investigates value of ERM which is an *integrated* and *overarching* approach to risk management where all types of risks are taken into account in a systematic way.

The findings in the value relevance of ERM literature are rather mixed. Hoyt and Liebenberg (2011) show that ERM firms in the insurance industry are awarded with approximately 20% value premium. Baxter et al. (2013) also find that ERM quality is positively associated with firm value for banks and insurance companies. On the contrary, Lin et al. (2012) provide the evidence that ERM is value-destroying for firms (with around 11% discount in firm value). The following two papers fail to support the argument that ERM creates value for firms. McShane et al. (2011) find that ERM adoption does not increase firm value whereas a more traditional (fragmentized) risk management approach creates value for insurers. In a similar vein, Pagach and Warr (2010), who analyze how financial performance of the firm changes after ERM adoption, fail to find that ERM is value-creating in general. The two remaining papers suggest that advantages a firm could obtain from ERM adoption is firm-specific, which is consistent with the argument by Meulbroek (2002). First, Beasley et al. (2008), who investigate shareholders' valuation of ERM, find that on average there is no significant market reaction to ERM adoption by investors. However, their full sample results suggest that firms that are larger and have limited cash on hand value ERM implementation. Second, Gordon et al. (2009) find that the relationship between ERM and firm performance is contingent upon the appropriate match between ERM and the following firm characteristics: environmental uncertainty, industry competition, firm size, firm complexity and monitoring by the board.

To sum up, while traditional risk management literature shows consistent evidence that hedging increases firm value, findings in the ERM literature are inconclusive, calling for further investigation on the issue.

Theoretical arguments on how ERM increases firm value additionally

How does ERM create value for firms additionally? More specifically, is there some additional benefit of ERM which are different from those provided by traditional risk management, such as managerial risk aversion, reducing financial distress costs, mitigating agency cost of free cash flow, lowering expected tax payments, mitigating underinvestment problems and reducing cost of external financing for new investment?

Nocco and Stulz's (2006) study is the one which attempts to develop the underlying theory of ERM. According to them, ERM, as additional to traditional risk management, brings two main advantages to a firm, which are at macro and micro level. The *macro* benefits refer to long-run competitive advantage that a firm can gain through ERM. This becomes possible with ERM since it enables firms to transfer its noncore risks, that is, financial risks which can be transferred effectively thanks to the presence of liquid derivatives market. By reducing exposure to these noncore risks, the firm can take up more core risks, that is, business risks which the firm has competitive advantage in bearing. In other words, companies do business in order to take strategic and business risks; hence by increasing the ability to bear more business risk, thanks to ERM, firms can create competitive advantage in long run.

The *micro* benefits of ERM come from assigning carefully how and by whom risk is owned, as well as from allocating capital based on risk–return trade-off analyses. Risk is "owned" by business unit managers, meaning that investment and operational decisions are taken at business unit level since centralizing such decisions could cause congestion in the firm. The CRO is, on the other hand, responsible for providing information and incentives for the business managers. In such a framework, business unit managers are expected to do a risk–return trade-off for new projects, which could potentially increase the firm's total risk. In other words, they evaluate the returns of each project with respect to the risk that the project adds to the firm's total risk. Then, capital is allocated to the units based on these risk–return analyses. To make sure that unit managers do a good job, their performance is evaluated based on their trade-off analyses. As a result, they are forced to take into account all material risks which can have a detrimental effect on the projects, and accordingly on the firm's total risk. In sum, when risk–return allocation is combined with performance evaluation of business managers, business managers are forced to consider risk in their investment and operating decisions. This would in turn improve capital allocation.

In sum, according to Nocco and Stulz (2006), ERM increases firm value (1) by mitigating financial risks, and hence, enabling the firm to exploit its business risks, which in turn leads to remain and/or improve firm's competitive advantage; and (2) through careful risk–return trade-offs on projects for improved capital allocation.

In addition, there are several other arguments which are in line with micro benefits stated in Nocco and Stulz (2006). Similarly, Lam (2001) argues that the CRO, who is in charge of the ERM process, can help improve return on equity and shareholder value by allocating capital to the business activities which have the highest risk-adjusted return. Moreover, Meulbroek (2002) and Hoyt and Liebenberg (2011) argue that the holistic dimension of the ERM approach enables firms to understand risks across business units well; accordingly, this leads to an objective resource allocation, improving return on equity and capital efficiency.

Sample, data and methodology survey, data and motivation to conduct a survey

We conducted a survey to identify ERM firms. There are mainly four methods used in the literature to measure ERM process. One of them is using CRO hiring announcements, as the majority of ERM studies do (Liebenberg and Hoyt, 2003; Beasley et al., 2008; Pagach and Warr, 2011). However, since the CRO position is popular, firms could just have the position without having ERM in place. One explanation for that could be a *catering approach*, which suggests that managers would take actions in order to boost share prices above fundamental value (Baker and Wurgler, 2011). In our case, a firm basically could try to increase short-run firm value by appointing a CRO, signaling about how sound their risk management is. Even if a firm has a CRO, it does not necessarily mean that the firm implements ERM. Moreover, firms might have ERM in place, but have another position with the same responsibilities as the CRO has. However, these other positions are not fully taken into account by these studies.

The second way to identify ERM firms, as in the works of Hoyt and Liebenberg (2011) and Lin et al. (2012), is to search for evidence of ERM (through databases such as LexisNexis and Dow Jones) by entering key words like "chief risk officer", "enterprise risk management" and "risk committee". However, reporting on formations such as risk committee is not mandatory for firms. Hence, this method would not give us a sound measure.

Third, ERM ratings provided by Standard & Poor's are used as a proxy for degree of ERM adoption (McShane et al., 2011; Baxter et al., 2013). However, these ratings are available only for insurance firms.

The last option is to survey firms to determine to what degree they have ERM adoption, as Beasley et al. (2005) do, by *asking* firms to score level of their ERM implementation. However, asking firms to score the level of their ERM program can potentially lead to biased results, since managers might tend to overstate the level of ERM programs that they are in charge of due to several reasons, which might include the popularity of ERM, being seen strong in risk management in a post–financial crisis and so on.

In this study, we also employ a survey which provides detailed information on risk management programs of firms, most of which otherwise would not be obtained by publicly available information. For example, information about "risk appetite" of a firm is not publicly available for a majority of firms. In that sense, the data collected through the survey becomes unique, which enables us to calculate ERM by using a rich set of organizational characteristics related to risk management. Our survey also advances Beasley et al. (2005)'s work, in that it is not subject to the bias that they might have. Our respondents were not informed that they were filling in a survey on ERM. At the beginning of the survey, firms were told that the survey would be on risk management in general. In this way, we try to minimize the potential response bias that would result from the possibility that managers exaggerate the level of ERM programs in place.[10]

As seen in Appendix 22.2, the survey questions are straightforward, mainly searching for existence of the key elements of ERM that are discussed later in the section "Key Components of ERM." The survey was directed to CEOs, CFOs or any other senior level position that has adequate knowledge about firm's risk management. They were asked to reply to the questions based on firm's activities in 2010.

The final sample is formed by 150 Nordic firms that are listed on Stockholm, Copenhagen, Oslo and Helsinki stock exchanges with headquarters located within Sweden, Denmark, Norway and Finland, respectively. Firms domiciled in foreign countries are excluded in order to increase comparability. Some basic characteristics of Nordic countries are that they have advance market economies. Their capital markets are also well developed and integrated. Except Norway (Oslo Stock Exchange), the stock exchanges of the others are operated under Nasdaq OMX, creating harmonization in terms of rules and regulations among the exchanges.

Large, medium and small cap listed firms on the Stockholm, Copenhagen, Oslo and Helsinki stock exchanges were included in the survey as of January 21, 2011. In total, 676 Nordic firms were surveyed. The survey was conducted in cooperation with the Swedish survey company, Sinitor, during the period March 14–May 13, 2011. The biggest motivation for us to collaborate with Sinitor was to be able get a high response rate by utilizing their experience in multilingual surveys. Sinitor translated the survey, which was prepared in English into the official languages of the four countries. Sinitor's staff, who could speak those four languages, called all 676 firms and asked them for participation in the survey. The staff's being multilingual brought standardization to the whole survey. In this way, ambiguity related to language skills was eliminated to a great extent. The firms who accepted to fill in the survey were directed to a web-based survey. After several reminder calls, the final response rate for the whole sample was nearly 23%, which is better, in terms of sample representativeness, than the comparable study by Beasley et al. (2005) (10.3% out of 1,770 electronic surveys to the members of the Institute of Internal Auditor's [IIA] Global Audit Information Network [GAIN]. Their survey process was operated by IIA). Our country-based response rates are 18.5% (32 firms out of 173), 21% (26 out of 123), 25% (37 out of 147) and 25% (58 out of 233) for Denmark, Finland, Norway and Sweden, respectively.

In sum, the data used in this chapter consists of survey data and secondary data.[11] The sources of the secondary data, as well as how the variables are constructed, are presented in Appendix 22.1.

Out of 153 respondent firms, one firm had relatively high missing values in the survey and therefore was omitted from the sample. Two firms were also removed from the sample due to the fact that they were delisted after they filled in the survey, since their data could not be obtained fully. As a result, the final sample to be included for the empirical analyses was 150.

Drop-out analysis

The possibility that the firms who filled in the survey might show some similar patterns could create bias to the sample. Hence, an analysis is conducted to examine if the firms who participated in the survey are statistically different in some key firm characteristics (in terms of size and leverage) than those who rejected filling in the survey. As shown in Table 22.1, the respondent firms are not statistically different from nonrespondents. This indicates that our sample is an unbiased representation of the population.

Key components of ERM

There are some organizational aspects which make ERM different from traditional risk management approaches. These key aspects of ERM compiled in this chapter constitute the major part of the questions in the survey, and are used in constructing our ERM measurement.[12] First, ERM suggests having a *formal report* which is submitted to the board at least annually on the current state of, and effectiveness of the risk management program. In ERM there is also a senior level position usually called the *chief risk officer (CRO)*,[13] who has the highest responsibility for overseeing the centralized risk management function and who is independent of risk taking activities and decisions. The CRO assumes ownership of the risk management program and reports directly to the top of the organization. Moreover, a *board level committee* with pure responsibility for risk management oversight is another key element in an ERM process. Furthermore, ERM has a *formal written risk management philosophy (policy)* which refers to a set of shared

Table 22.1 Univariate differences between respondents and nonrespondents

	Respondents (n = 150)			Nonrespondents (n = 523)			All sample (n = 673)			Difference	
	Mean	Median	SD	Mean	Median	SD	Mean	Median	SD	Mean	Mean
Ln(Total Assets '000)	12.773	12.665	2.144	12.763	12.601	2.089	12.766	12.602	2.100	−0.050	0.020
Leverage	0.291	0.281	0.198	0.301	0.254	0.500	0.299	0.263	0.448	0.250	1.416

Note: Leverage is calculated as Total Debt / Total Assets. All values are in thousands of US dollars, and are 2009 year-end or the year-end values of the fiscal year 2009–2010. Total assets are in natural logarithm form. ***, **, * denote statistical significance at the 1, 5 and 10% levels, respectively. *t*-test is used for testing statistical significance of difference in means of respondent and nonrespondent firms while the median test is a Wilcoxon rank sum test with *Z* statistic reported.

Table 22.2 Descriptive statistics on scores given by respondents on ERM components

ERM component	Mean	Median	Std. dev.	Max	Min	Observation
Formal risk management report	2.287	3	0.901	3	0	146
CRO	0.182	0	0.387	3	0	148
Board level risk committee	1.462	2	1.274	3	0	145
Risk management philosophy	1.783	2	1.007	3	0	148
Formal written statement of the firm's risk appetite	1.398	1	1.086	3	0	148
Centralized department or staff function	1.080	0	1.255	3	0	150
Risk owners	1.568	2	1.185	3	0	146
Centralized technology-enabled process	1.120	1	1.098	3	0	141

Note: See the section "Key Components of ERM" for the definition of ERM components. The statistics belong to the scores that the respondent firms give on each ERM component. The maximum score that they can give per component is 3 and the minimum is 0; the exception is that CRO is a Yes or No question since it is not logical to create scorings for that ERM component. Accordingly, the score for the CRO question is as follows: Yes = 1 and No = 0 (zero).

beliefs and attitudes characterizing how firm considers risk in everything it does and delineates responsibility of management and board. A *formal written statement of the firm's risk appetite*, which is the amount of risk specified at board level that firm is willing to accept in pursuit of value, is also considered to be essential in ERM implementation. A *centralized department or staff function* dedicated to risk management is another component of ERM. ERM also suggests allocating *risk owners* who have primary responsibility and accountability for managing risk within their respective areas. Lastly, a *centralized technology-enabled process* to obtain risk-related information has importance in an ERM process.

Table 22.2 presents descriptive statistics on scores given by respondent firms on each ERM component in order to give further information about the ERM components. The ERM component which has the highest level of implementation, on average, among the others is "formal risk management report" (2.287 out of the maximum score, 3), while "CRO" is the least popular ERM element (0.182). The average scores of each of the remaining six ERM elements are around 1.400. The table briefly tells us that, among all ERM components, formal risk management report is the one that appears most frequently in firms while CRO position is, surprisingly, not observed very commonly.

Measuring ERM

To be used in the econometric analyses, we use five different measures of ERM which are constructed based on the survey data: *ERM-dummy* (main variable), *ERM15, ERM20, ERM-raw score* and *ERM-ordinal*. Calculations of the variables are explained in this section. In the survey in Appendix 22.2, questions 1–3 investigate existence of ERM in a firm while questions 4–7 are follow-up queries. The first 10 questions (Q1.1–Q3.3) are considered to represent the key elements of ERM. Q3 explores existence of CRO, as well as characteristics of this position. We also ask if there is any other equivalent position to CRO; however, with a difference from the literature that in our chapter this alternative position is supposed to have the same responsibilities as a CRO does. Hence, Q3.1a and Q3.1b are treated as one question in ERM score calculation resulting in 10 key component questions (Q1.1–Q3.3). Firms that replied to Q3.1a with "Yes" were not able to see Q3.1b since these two questions were set as conditional upon each other on the web-based survey.

When it comes to scoring by the respondents, each of the first seven subquestions (Q1.1–Q2.3) has a possible score between 0 and 3 which represent the following: 0 = "does not exist" (does not count in ERM scoring), 1 = "ad hoc implementation", 2 = "implemented but improvements needed" and 3 = "robustly implemented". Further, the three subquestions of Q3 (3.1a, 3.2 and 3.3) are Yes or No questions since it is not logical to create scorings for them. Accordingly, the scores of Q3 are as follows: Yes = 3 and No = 0 (zero).

Regarding missing values, we treat them as zero in ERM scoring. Only one firm was removed from the sample due to having exceptionally high missing values (6 out of 10 component questions).

The final ERM score is calculated by summing the scores of each of the 10 questions (as discussed before, Q3.1a and Q3.1b are treated as one question). Our main *ERM-dummy* variable is constructed based on these ERM scores; it takes the value of 1 if the firm has an ERM score in the top 50% and 0 otherwise.

The mean value of the ERM score is 12.72, out of 30. The mean value of the ERM score in the top 50% ERM firms is 19.36 while in the lowest 50% ERM firms it is 6.08, indicating a large difference between the two groups. Moreover, before conducting our analysis, we give a rough idea about the relationship between ERM and TQ: the mean value of TQ for the top 50% ERM firms is 1.142 while for the lowest 50% ERM firms it is 1.481, suggesting a negative relationship between ERM and firm value.

We also have two other ERM dummy variables with two different cut-off points to be used in robustness checks compared to our main top 50% ERM dummy variable.

(1) *ERM15*: ERM takes the value of 1 if the firm has an ERM score above 15 ($n = 54$), and 0 otherwise ($n = 96$);
(2) *ERM20*: ERM takes the value of 1 if the firm has an ERM score above 20 ($n = 31$), and 0 otherwise ($n = 119$).

ERM15 reflects the case where, for example, a firm scores 2 (out of 3) on half of the components, while 1 on the other half of the components. ERM20 reflects the case where a firm scores at least 2 (out of 3) on each ERM component.

The last two ERM proxies are as follows. The *ERM-raw score* variable is the score before being converted into a dummy. Here we make the basic assumption that the intervals between each scores are the same so that we could use OLS for the estimation. The last one, *ERM-ordinal* variable, is constructed based on this ERM-raw score variable by creating categories from 1 to 5 in the following way:

$$
ERM_i = \begin{cases}
1 \text{ if } ERM \text{ score} \le 6 \\
2 \text{ if } 7 < ERM \text{ score} \le 12 \\
3 \text{ if } 13 < ERM \text{ score} \le 18 \\
4 \text{ if } 19 < ERM \text{ score} \le 24 \\
5 \text{ if } 25 < ERM \text{ score} \le 30.
\end{cases}
$$

Econometric model

The relationship between firm value and ERM is likely to be subject to endogeneity bias resulting from the endogenous nature of ERM in the firm value equation. One source of endogeneity could be that the ERM independent variable can be simultaneously determined with the Tobin's Q (TQ) dependent variable. For example, highly valued firms can also be more likely to adopt ERM, for example, in order to reduce cash flow volatility if they have growth opportunities (Froot et al., 1993). Or another source could be that there can be some unobserved factors that affect both ERM adoption and firm value, such as good managerial skills. For example, managers with superior skills might be more likely to engage in ERM since they would be aware of benefits of ERM and would believe in themselves to undertake such a huge and costly investment compared to less-equipped managers with narrower vision. In parallel, good managerial skills would lead to success and ultimately higher firm value. Hoyt and Liebenberg (2011) also emphasize the endogenous nature of ERM in firm value equation by arguing that firms might self-select to have ERM programs. Hence, they use a treatment effect model to control for this selection bias.

In the presence of any potential endogeneity, OLS should not be used since it would yield inconsistent coefficients as well as standard errors. One solution is to use instrumental variable (IV) regression (two-stage least square – 2SLS) where the endogeneity between ERM and TQ is taken into account. In an IV regression, the IV(s) is (are) correlated with ERM adoption (instrument relevance: partial correlation between the IV and ERM is not zero) while not with the error term of the TQ equation (instrument exogeneity: cov (IV, u) = 0). The instrument relevance and instrument exogeneity are two conditions to be satisfied to be a valid instrument. In this chapter, one IV is used which is the Big 4[14] variable.[15] The motivations why Big 4 is expected to be a valid IV are as follows.

Instrument relevance condition can be tested while there is no possibility to test *instrument exogeneity* as we discuss shortly. First, we check if our IV fulfills the instrument relevance requirement. To check this, a Wald test is conducted on the IV coefficient in the reduced form of the ERM equation (Equation 1). The IV coefficient needs to be statistically different from zero. This is the key identification assumption after assuming that the IV is exogenous to TQ (Wooldridge, 2002). The TQ equation is not identified if the IV coefficient is equal to zero. In the unreported results, the t-statistic of this Wald test shows that the IV (Big 4) has a coefficient different from zero (rejection is at 5% significance level). Accordingly, we conclude that the Big 4 variable fulfills the instrument relevance condition.

Moreover, the following studies support the instrument relevance condition for our IV choice. It is expected that firms engaging Big 4 is more likely to be committed to advanced risk management practices due to high standards asked by Big 4 firms in terms of risk management. Beasley et al. (2005), Desender (2010) and Desender and Lafuente (2009) provide the evidence that Big 4 is positively associated with ERM.

Second, when it comes to the instrument exogeneity condition, together with the instrument relevance, cov (Big 4, u) = 0 implies that Big 4 affects firm value only through its effect on ERM. In order to support this implication, we can ask if the IV has any impact on the dependent variable (firm value): either its observed part (TQ) or its unobserved part (u) (Roberts and Whited, 2012). Cov (Big 4, u) = 0 is not testable since the error term is unobservable. However, based on economic reasoning, we can argue that Big 4 is a suitable IV based on the very low correlation between Big 4 and firm value, which is 0.061 (see Table 22.5). Moreover, to our knowledge, there is no evidence in the literature showing that Big 4 explains firm value.

The 2SLS regression, where our primary interest is in the second equation, is demonstrated as follows:

$$ERM_i = \beta_0 + \beta_1 Big\ 4_{i} + \beta_2 X_{Control\,Variables,i} + e_i \tag{1}$$

$$TQ_i = \delta_0 + \delta_1 E\hat{R}M_i + \delta_2 X_{Control\,Varialbles.i} + u_i \tag{2}$$

In the first stage, *ERM* is our ERM-dummy variable[16] while explanatory variables are a set of both continuous and dummy variables (Big 4 (IV) and control variables), and *e* is the residuals. In the second stage, TQ is the dependent variable explained by $\hat{ERM}$ (instrumented with Big 4) where the model also includes control variables (the same firm characteristics as in Equation 1), and *u* the error term.

The majority of the value relevance of ERM and hedging literature analyze the impact of ERM and hedging on firm value where firm value is proxied by TQ. (ERM literature: Hoyt and Liebenberg, 2011; McShane et al., 2011; Lin et al., 2012; Baxter et al., 2013. Hedging Literature: Smithson and Simkins [2005] review 10 hedging papers, nine of which use Tobin's Q.) For comparability reasons, we also use Tobin's Q (TQ) in this study as our dependent variable. It is measured in two ways:

(1) *Tobin's Q*[17] which is equal to (Market Value of Equity 2010 + Total Liabilities 2010) / Book Value of Total Assets 2010.
(2) *Industry Adjusted Tobin's Q* which is calculated for each firm by subtracting the median TQ value of the industry from the TQ of the firm.

The 2SLS regression should not be performed separately since the standard errors and test statistics become invalid. The reason for this is that the second stage (the TQ equation) includes the error terms of *both* the ERM and TQ equations; however, the standard errors reported for the second stage (if estimated separately) involve only the error term of the TQ equation (Wooldridge, 2002).

Control variables in the firm value equation (second stage)

Size: The evidence regarding the impact of firm size on firm value is mixed. In the literature, it is commonly argued that larger firms are more likely to suffer from agency problems,[18] which in turn has a detrimental effect on firm value. On the other hand, the value of large firms can increase through economies of scale which is brought by being large. Most prior studies find that size is negatively associated with firm value (Lang and Stulz, 1994; Allayannis and Weston, 2001; Carter, Rogers and Simkins, 2006), while Jin and Jorion (2006) and Zou (2010) find a positive relationship between size and firm value. Therefore, we control for the effect of firm size. Size is calculated as the natural logarithm of total assets of 2009 by following Zou (2010), Hoyt and Liebenberg (2011) and Carter et al. (2006).

Leverage: The capital structure of a firm is shown to have an impact on firm value. According to Jensen's "control hypothesis," debt can mitigate agency cost of free cash flow by reducing the cash flow available to managers (Jensen, 1986). Hence, debt increases firm value to the extent that this free cash flow is reduced.[19] On the other hand, debt can have a negative influence on firm value since high debt prevents firms from taking on investment opportunities with positive net present value (underinvestment problem – Myers, 1977). Allayannis and Weston (2001) presents both positive and negative findings for the leverage variable depending on how they calculate Tobin's Q. Jin and Jorion (2006), Carter et al. (2006) and Zou (2010) find that leverage is positively related to firm value. Thus, leverage measured as the ratio of total debt of 2009 to total assets of 2009, as in Zou (2010) and Pagach and Warr (2011), is included in the model as a control variable.

Profitability: Profitable firms are expected to be valued higher by investors than less profitable ones. Allayannis and Weston (2001) and Zou (2010) provide evidence of a positive relation between profitability and firm value. Hence, return on assets (ROA), calculated as net income in

2009 divided by total assets in 2009 (following Allayannis and Weston, 2001; Carter et al., 2006; Jin and Jorion, 2006; Hoyt and Liebenberg, 2011), is included to control for profitability.

Growth opportunities: The market value of a firm incorporates the present value of its future investment opportunities. Thus, firms with high growth prospects have higher firm value. Jin and Jorion (2006) find that investment growth is positively related to firm value (their finding is robust to all different specifications of Tobin's Q measurement). Therefore, we control for the effect of investment opportunities measured as capital expenditures (as additions to fixed assets) in 2009 divided by total assets in 2009 as in Allayannis and Weston (2001), Zou (2010), Jin and Jorion (2006) and Carter et al. (2006).

Dividends: Allayannis and Weston (2001), Lang and Stulz (1994) and Fazzari, Hubbard and Petersen (1988) argue that firms who are financially constrained might need to forgo growth opportunities available to them. However, their Tobin's Q ratio may still be high because of being more careful in evaluating available options by undertaking projects only with positive NPV. Therefore, dividend payout, which is a proxy for ability to access to financial markets, is expected to be negatively related to firm value. On the other hand, dividend payment, which is a sign of being financially unconstrained, can be viewed as a positive signal from management which would result in higher firm valuation (Carter et al., 2006). Another possible argument is that to the extent to which dividend payments can reduce free cash available to managers, firm value increases (Hoyt and Liebenberg, 2011). Zou (2010) and Allayannis and Weston (2001) show that dividend payment is negatively related to firm value, while Carter et al. (2006) and Hoyt and Liebenberg (2011) find evidence of a positive association between firm value and dividend payment. Hence, dividend payout ratio (following Berkman and Bradbury, 1996), measured as dividend per share in 2009 divided by earnings per share in 2009, is included in the model.

Geographic diversification: International diversification (multinationality) might increase firm value through diverse markets offered to the firm. However, it is also argued that being multinational can increase agency costs as a result of weaker controls due to size-related concerns, which in turn causes value reduction (Allayannis and Weston, 2001). Following Allayannis and Weston (2001), geographic diversification is included in the model as the ratio[20] of foreign sales in 2009 to net sales in 2009, unlike Hoyt and Liebenberg (2011)'s dummy proxy, which takes the value of 1 if the firm has sales abroad and 0 otherwise.

Industrial diversification: Similar to geographic diversification, Allayannis and Weston (2001) discuss two counter arguments regarding the relation between firm value and industrial diversification. Most empirical evidence support the claim that diversification decreases firm value due to possible agency problems (Lang and Stulz, 1994; Berger and Ofek, 1995). Hence, an industrial diversification variable is included to control for its effect on firm value. Unlike Allayannis and Weston (2001) and Zou (2010), whose industrial diversification variable is just a dummy which takes the value of 1 if the firm operates in more than one business segments, we use the number of business segments as a proxy for industrial diversification.

Industry: Some firms could be highly valued because of the industries that they are operating in. To control for the effects of industry, a dummy variable is included based on the first 2 digits of the 8-digit Global Industry Classification System Codes (GICS).[21] GICS classifies 10 sectors which are as follows: Energy, Materials, Industrial, Consumer Discretionary, Consumer Staples, Health Care, Financials, Information Technology, Telecommunication Services, and Utilities.[22] In the sample, the Telecommunications Services and Utilities sectors had only two and one observations, respectively. Thus, these observations were moved to the categories Information Technology and Energy, respectively. Consumer Staples is the omitted industry dummy.

Two remaining control variables of Allayannis and Weston (2001), *credit rating (quality)* and *time effects*, are excluded in this study due to the following reasons. An insufficient number of firms in the sample have credit ratings to be included in the regressions. The data in this study does not have a time dimension.

Control variables in the ERM equation (first stage)

The following variables are included in the ERM equation as control variables for ERM adoption: size, leverage, profitability, growth opportunities, dividends, geographic and industrial diversification, and industry. The variables are decided by following the literature on determinants of ERM (Smith and Stulz, 1985; Froot et al., 1993; Berkman and Bradbury, 1996; Liebenberg and Hoyt, 2003; Beasley et al., 2005; Beasley et al., 2008; Desender and Lafuente, 2009; Gordon et al., 2009; Desender, 2010; Desender and Lafuente, 2011; Hoyt and Liebenberg, 2011; Jankensgård, 2011; Pagach and Warr, 2011; Sekerci, 2011; Lin et al., 2012; Baxter et al., 2013).

In addition to them, we include Big 4 to account for ERM in the 2SLS estimation:

Engaging Big 4: External auditors report their opinions on the quality of the internal control of a firm. More specifically, they examine and express their views on annual accounts, consolidated financial statements, as well as the administration of the board of directors and the CEO. Extensive audit quality research suggests that Big 4 audit firms have high quality auditors (Beasley et al., 2005). Hence, working with one of these firms is expected to increase commitment to risk management. Beasley et al. (2005) find a significant and positive relation between level of ERM adoption and engaging one of the Big 4 firms. Desender (2010) and Desender and Lafuente (2009) also provide evidence in line with Beasley et al. (2005). It is a dummy variable which takes the value of 1 if the firm engages one of the Big 4 firms in 2009 and 0 otherwise.

Results

Descriptive statistics and univariate analyses

Table 22.3 presents the descriptive statistics for the variables. Some of the items are noteworthy. The descriptives of TQ (mean value: 1.311, std. dev.: 0.985) are comparable to prior studies by Allayannis and Weston (2001), Hoyt and Liebenberg (2011), Jin and Jorion (2006), Zou (2010) and Lin et al. (2012). The average ERM score is 12.720 out of 30, indicating not a very high level of ERM implementation among listed Nordic firms. We observe firms which do not implement ERM at all. The unreported results show that there are four firms with no ERM at all, while two firms have the highest level of ERM implementation. Most of the firms engage one of the Big 4 auditing companies (mean value for Big 4 is 88%). This 88% mean statistic is similar to that of Beasley et al. (2005) while higher than that of Desender (2010). Another item to point out is leverage. Nordic firms are found to have less leverage than US firms. Nordic firms in our sample have, on average, 30% leverage, while in Pagach and Warr (2011) – who give evidence from the US – the mean value of leverage is 64% for firms which hire a CRO and 48% for those which do not. The statistics of the other control variables are more or less comparable to prior studies.

We also present descriptive statistics of the variables on country level. As seen in Table 22.4, Finnish firms have the highest valuation (1.583) while Danish counterparts have the lowest (1.125). ERM scores on a country basis suggest that listed Danish firms have more advanced risk management programs than the rest of the sample. The scores are as follows in decreasing order: Denmark (14.781), Finland (14.192), Norway (12.555) and lastly Sweden (10.964). Since financial firms are in general more advanced in risk management than nonfinancial firms, these descriptives on ERM could be due to relatively high number of Danish financial firms in the

Table 22.3 Summary statistics of the variables

	Mean	Median	Std. dev.	Max	Min	Observation
Tobin's Q	1.311	0.996	0.985	5.693	0.016	150
Industry adjusted TQ	0.280	0.000	0.889	4.062	−1.614	143
Test variable						
ERM-dummy	0.500	0.500	0.501	1.000	0.000	150
ERM-ordinal	2.560	2.000	1.287	5.000	1.000	150
ERM-raw score	12.720	11.000	7.998	30.000	0.000	150
Control variables						
Size	12.773	12.665	2.144	19.510	8.267	150
Leverage	0.291	0.281	0.198	0.832	0.001	150
Profitability	−0.034	0.009	0.227	0.434	−1.816	149
Growth opportunities	0.040	0.021	0.059	0.439	0.000	148
Dividends	22.043	0.000	29.812	100.000	0.000	124
Geographic diversification	58.791	58.791	24.296	100.000	0.000	150
Industrial diversification	3.482	3.000	2.409	15.000	0.000	145
Big 4	0.880	1.000	0.326	1.000	0.000	150

Note: TQ has two different measures: (1) Tobin's Q = (Market Value of Equity 2010 + Total Liabilities 2010) / Book Value of Total Assets 2010. (2) Industry Adjusted Tobin's Q calculated for each firm by subtracting the median TQ value of the industry from the TQ of the firm. Other variables are as follows: ERM has three different measures (see the section "Measuring ERM" for their calculations). Size = natural logarithm of Total Assets 2009. Leverage = Total Debt 2009 / Total Assets 2009. Profitability = ROA (= Net Income 2009 / Total Assets 2009). Growth Opportunities = Capital Expenditures (as additions to fixed assets) 2009 / Total Assets 2009. Dividends = Dividend Payout Ratio (= Dividend per Share 2009 / Earnings per Share in 2009). Geographic Diversification = (Foreign Sales 2009 / Net Sales 2009) × 100. Industrial Diversification = number of business segments. Big 4 = 1 if the firm engages one of the Big 4 and 0 otherwise.

sample. Moreover, Norwegian firms are, on average, more leveraged than the others (0.346). Profitability in all four countries is negative except Finland (ROA: 0.018). The average dividend payout ratio in Finnish firms is rather higher than the sample mean (45.019) while the ratio is relatively low for Norwegian firms (11.960). In addition to these, the following firm-specific characteristics are more or less the same for all four countries: size, growth opportunities, geographic and industrial diversification, and Big 4.

The correlation matrix of the variables included in the baseline regression is reported in Table 22.5. Pearson correlation coefficients can be found below the diagonal while Spearman correlations are presented above the diagonal. As seen, multicollinearity is not a problem in the model since none of the explanatory variables are highly correlated with another. However, there are two remarkable items that are the correlations between size and ERM (0.378), and between size and profitability (0.384).

Multivariate analyses dealing with endogeneity

In this section we report the results from the baseline regressions where ERM is our ERM-dummy variable. We first present the results where the endogeneity between ERM and firm value is not taken into account, and compare them to the 2SLS estimations with which the endogeneity bias is controlled for. Model 1 in Table 22.6 reports the results from this OLS regression. As seen, there is no significant relationship between ERM and firm value.

Next, we move on to the 2SLS estimations. At the first stage, ERM determinants are estimated, and at the second stage—main interest equation, the impact of ERM on firm value is

Table 22.4 Summary statistics of the variables on country level

	Denmark			Finland			Norway			Sweden		
	Mean	Std. dev.	Observation	Mean	Std. dev.	Observation	Mean	Std. dev.	Observation	Mean	Std. dev.	Observation
Tobin's Q	1.125	1.181	32	1.583	1.038	26	1.134	0.706	36	1.404	0.975	56
Industry adj. TQ	0.083	0.970	30	0.543	1.006	25	0.109	0.579	34	0.375	0.924	54
Test variable												
ERM-dummy	0.526	0.504	32	0.615	0.496	26	0.472	0.506	36	0.428	0.499	56
ERM-ordinal	2.968	1.402	32	2.730	1.185	26	2.583	1.401	36	2.232	1.128	56
ERM-raw score	14.781	8.746	32	14.192	7.874	26	12.555	8.261	36	10.964	7.205	56
Control variables												
Size	12.683	2.023	32	13.045	2.096	26	12.891	2.124	36	12.623	2.283	56
Leverage	0.268	0.192	32	0.268	0.177	26	0.346	0.228	36	0.278	0.187	56
Profitability	-0.049	0.199	31	0.018	0.082	26	-0.105	0.390	36	-0.005	0.106	56
Growth opport.	0.031	0.051	30	0.030	0.025	26	0.059	0.068	36	0.037	0.066	56
Dividends	14.774	26.780	28	45.019	35.916	16	11.960	24.848	33	25.631	28.345	47
Geographic divers.	58.267	27.376	32	56.433	22.635	26	60.802	18.930	36	58.894	26.654	56
Industrial divers.	3.142	1.994	28	3.884	3.024	26	3.694	2.278	36	3.327	2.388	55
Big 4	0.884	0.325	26	0.884	0.325	26	0.805	0.401	36	0.988	0.133	56

Note: TQ has two different measures: (1) Tobin's Q = (Market Value of Equity 2010 + Total Liabilities 2010) / Book Value of Total Assets 2010. (2) Industry Adjusted Tobin's Q calculated for each firm by subtracting the median TQ value of the industry from the TQ of the firm. Other variables are as follows: ERM has three different measures (see the section "Measuring ERM" for their calculations). Size = natural logarithm of Total Assets 2009. Leverage = Total Debt 2009 / Total Assets 2009. Profitability = ROA (= Net Income 2009 / Total Assets 2009). Growth Opportunities = Capital Expenditures (as additions to fixed assets) 2009 / Total Assets 2009. Dividends = Dividend Payout Ratio (= Dividend per Share 2009 / Earnings per Share in 2009). Geographic Diversification = (Foreign Sales 2009 / Net Sales 2009) × 100. Industrial Diversification = number of business segments. Big 4 = 1 if the firm engages one of the Big 4 and 0 otherwise.

Table 22.5 Pearson and Spearman rank-order correlations between variables

	Tobin's Q	ERM	Size	Leverage	Profitability	Growth opport.	Dividends	Geographic divers.	Industrial divers.	Big 4
Tobin's Q	1	-0.125	-0.258***	-0.010	0.304***	0.099	0.290***	0.130	-0.148*	0.095
ERM	-0.118	1	0.378***	-0.144	0.141	0.041	0.104	-0.079	0.050	0.251***
Size	-0.283***	0.378***	1	0.249***	0.276***	0.252***	0.269***	0.094	0.293***	0.251***
Leverage	-0.013	-0.162*	0.186**	1	-0.162*	0.285***	-0.190**	0.049	-0.084	0.132
Profitability	0.065	0.128	0.384***	0.041	1	0.226***	0.638***	0.124	0.052	0.153*
Growth opport.	-0.072	0.099	0.176**	0.216***	0.172*	1	0.116	0.124	0.205**	0.042
Dividends	0.278***	0.063	0.195**	-0.171*	0.330***	-0.063	1	0.063	0.070	0.097
Geographic divers.	0.126	-0.057	0.089	-0.018	0.063	-0.021	0.039	1	0.064	0.014
Industrial divers.	-0.133	0.085	0.295***	-0.125	0.006	0.085	0.076	0.050	1	-0.120
Big 4	0.061	0.251***	0.246***	0.140	0.294***	0.059	0.068	0.040	-0.095	1

Note: Tobin's Q = (Market Value of Equity 2010 + Total Liabilities 2010) / Book Value of Total Assets 2010. Other variables are as follows: ERM is a dummy variable which takes the value of 1 if the firm has an ERM score in the top 50% and 0 otherwise (see the section "Measuring ERM" for ERM score calculation). Size = natural logarithm of Total Assets 2009. Leverage = Total Debt 2009 / Total Assets 2009. Profitability = ROA (= Net Income 2009 / Total Assets 2009). Growth Opportunities = Capital Expenditures (as additions to fixed assets) 2009 / Total Assets 2009. Dividends = Dividend Payout Ratio (= Dividend per Share 2009 / Earnings per Share in 2009). Geographic Diversification = (Foreign Sales 2009 / Net Sales 2009) × 100. Industrial Diversification = number of business segments. Big 4 = 1 if the firm engages one of the Big 4 and 0 otherwise. Pearson correlation coefficients can be found below the diagonal while Spearman correlations are presented above. ***, **, * denote statistical significance at the 1, 5 and 10% levels, respectively.

analyzed. The findings are shown in Models 2 and 3 in Table 22.6. In Model 2, industry dummy variables are included to control for industry effects. In Model 3, industry adjusted TQ is used, and hence we do not include industry dummies any more. Both models give the same results failing to support that ERM increases firm value[23] which is consistent with McShane et al. (2011) and Pagach and Warr (2010); however it contradicts Hoyt and Liebenberg (2011), who find a 20% valuation premium by ERM adoption, and Baxter et al. (2013).

Our findings suggest that ERM implementation seems to be neither a positive nor a negative NPV project. That could mean that benefits of ERM are offset by high costs related to the investment. Yet, there might still be some advantages in having an ERM program such as having improved management accountability (Gates, 2006), and new insights gained from keeping track on the interaction of different kinds of risks facing the firm (Meulbroek, 2002). However, these benefits are not directly reflected in firm value, and that could be the reason why we do not find any significant relationship between ERM and firm value.

When it comes to the control variables in the TQ equation, the finding regarding dividend payout ratio supports the argument that dividend payment is a signal to the market that the firm is financially unconstrained. And this signaling is valued positively by shareholders. Or, the finding could be interpreted in the way that dividend payments can increase firm value to the extent that free cash available to managers is reduced.

Robustness checks

In this section, first we conduct robustness analyses in Models 4–10 (in Tables 22.7, 22.8 and 22.9) by proxying ERM with different ERM measurements to analyze if the findings are sensitive to how we measure our ERM-dummy variable. Second, unreported tests investigate if the relation between ERM and TQ could be nonlinear.

In the first four robustness checks (Models 4–7 in Tables 22.7 and 22.8), we conduct our baseline analyses by using ERM-ordinal and ERM-raw score variables instead of our main ERM-dummy. In Models 4 and 5, the ERM-ordinal variable is used, and in Models 6 and 7 the ERM variable is our ERM-raw score variable. In these specifications, we also use industry adjusted TQ. The findings that we get are similar to those of the baseline regressions. We fail to find a significant association between ERM and firm value while the only significant control variable in the main interest equation remains as the dividend payout variable.

More robustness checks are performed by using different cut-off points for the ERM-dummy variable. In Models 8 and 9 (Table 22.9), ERM15 and ERM20 are used respectively. Model 8 and 9 are presented in comparison to the baseline regression (the very left column in Table 22.9). The results show that ERM does not have any statistically significant impact on firm value.

After trying different cut-off points, we conduct some more robustness checks by using one of the ERM components (one at a time) to proxy for ERM process – instead of the main ERM-dummy variable which is constructed *based on* ERM components. The aim is to analyze if any of the ERM components can explain the change in TQ. For example, maybe the presence of a CRO, which is also the proxy that the literature uses most commonly, can increase firm value. In Table 22.9, Model 10 presents the results from the analysis which is conducted by using the CRO component, which is a dummy variable, instead of the ERM-dummy in order to also compare our study with those that use the CRO variable as a proxy for ERM. While CRO fails to explain firm value, the R-squared of Model 10 is even lower than our baseline regression. The unreported results from regressions each run by the remaining ERM components,[24] as the independent variable instead of the ERM-dummy, also show that ERM does not have a significant effect on firm valuation.

Table 22.6 ERM and firm value – baseline regressions

		Model 1	Model 2		Model 3	
		OLS	2SLS		2SLS	
			ERM (1st stage) – logit	TQ (2nd stage)	ERM (1st stage) – logit	Industry adj. TQ (2nd stage)
Test variable	ERM-dummy	0.007 (0.183)		0.282 (0.873)		0.464 (0.843)
Controls variables	Size	-0.087 (0.063)	0.106 (0.033)***	-0.120 (0.119)	0.106 (0.025)***	-0.182 (0.107)*
	Leverage	1.034 (0.498)**	-0.813 (0.261)***	1.242 (0.801)	-0.760 (0.234)***	1.173 (0.743)
	Profitability	0.335 (0.371)	-0.186 (0.204)	0.365 (0.360)	-0.191 (0.200)	0.422 (0.368)
	Growth opportunities	0.380 (1.630)	0.257 (0.883)	0.307 (1.544)	0.707 (0.714)	-0.339 (1.424)
	Dividends	0.012 (0.003)***	-0.001 (0.001)	0.012 (0.003)***	-0.001 (0.001)	0.011 (0.003)***
	Geographic diversification	0.003 (0.003)	-0.003 (0.002)*	0.005 (0.004)	-0.002 (0.001)	0.005 (0.003)
	Industrial diversification	-0.004 (0.046)	-0.018 (0.025)	0.003 (0.049)	-0.018 (0.022)	-0.001 (0.045)
	Industry dummy	Yes (2)	No	Yes (2)		
	Big 4		0.297 (0.150)**		0.311 (0.144)**	
	Constant	1.039 (0.830)	-0.806 (0.447)*	1.236 (0.991)	-0.746 (0.321)**	1.442 (0.738)**
	Obs.	113	113	113	113	113
	Pseudo R-sq./R-sq.	0.354	0.278	0.339	0.245	0.141
	F-statistic	3.549***	2.50***		4.23***	
	Wald Chi-sq.			60.72***		24.63***
	Root MSE		0.458	0.791	0.452	0.823

Note: TQ has two different measures: (1) Tobin's Q = (Market Value of Equity 2010 + Total Liabilities 2010) / Book Value of Total Assets 2010. (2) Industry Adjusted Tobin's Q calculated for each firm by subtracting the median TQ value of the industry from the TQ of the firm. Other variables are as follows: ERM-dummy is a dummy variable which takes the value of 1 if the firm has an ERM score in the top 50% and 0 otherwise (see the section "Measuring ERM" for ERM score calculation). Size = natural logarithm of Total Assets 2009. Leverage = Total Debt 2009 / Total Assets 2009. Profitability = ROA (= Net Income 2009 / Total Assets 2009). Growth Opportunities = Capital Expenditures (as additions to fixed assets) 2009 / Total Assets 2009. Dividends = Dividend Payout Ratio (= Dividend per Share 2009 / Earnings per Share in 2009). Geographic Diversification = (Foreign Sales 2009 / Net Sales 2009) x 100. Industrial Diversification = number of business segments. Big 4 = 1 if the firm engages one of the Big 4 and 0 otherwise. Standard errors are in parenthesis. ***, **, * denote statistical significance at the 1, 5 and 10% levels, respectively. The figures in parentheses refer to the number of industry dummies that are significant at least at the 10% confidence level. Root MSE represents the standard error of the regressions.

Table 22.7 Robustness checks – ERM and firm value

		Model 4		Model 5	
		2SLS		2SLS	
		ERM (1st stage) – ordered	TQ (2nd stage)	ERM (1st stage) – ordered	Industry adj. TQ (2nd stage)
Test variable	ERM-ordinal		0.106 (0.332)		0.210 (0.391)
Controls variables	Size	0.263 (0.080)***	-0.118 (0.114)	0.338 (0.064)***	-0.204 (0.147)
	Leverage	-2.170 (0.637)***	1.244 (0.810)	-1.921 (0.586)***	1.226 (0.840)
	Profitability	-0.177 (0.500)	0.331 (0.349)	-0.158 (0.499)	0.367 (0.365)
	Growth opportunities	1.003 (2.156)	0.272 (1.573)	1.788 (1.783)	-0.388 (1.493)
	Dividends	-0.003 (0.004)	0.012 (0.003)***	-0.005 (0.004)	0.012 (0.003)***
	Geographic diversification	-0.003 (0.005)	0.004 (0.003)	-0.004 (0.004)	0.004 (0.003)
	Industrial diversification	-0.007 (0.062)	-0.001 (0.044)	-0.038 (0.055)	-0.002 (0.046)
	Industry dummy	Yes (2)	Yes (2)		
	Big 4	0.786 (0.366)**		0.686 (0.360)*	
	Constant	-1.316 (1.091)	1.149 (0.852)	-1.375 (0.801)*	1.386 (0.691)**
	Obs.	113	113	113	113
	R-square	0.368	0.331	0.308	0.104
	F-statistic	3.77***		5.80***	
	Wald Chi-sq.		60.00***		23.61***
	Root MSE	1.117	0.796	1.129	0.841

Note: TQ has two different measures: (1) Tobin's Q = (Market Value of Equity 2010 + Total Liabilities 2010) / Book Value of Total Assets 2010. (2) Industry Adjusted Tobin's Q calculated for each firm by subtracting the median TQ value of the industry from the TQ value of the firm. Other variables are as follows: ERM-ordinal (see the section "Measuring ERM" for its calculation). Size = natural logarithm of Total Assets 2009. Leverage = Total Debt 2009 / Total Assets 2009. Profitability = ROA (= Net Income 2009 / Total Assets 2009). Growth Opportunities = Capital Expenditures (as additions to fixed assets) 2009 / Total Assets 2009. Dividends = Dividend Payout Ratio (= Dividend per Share 2009 / Earnings per Share in 2009). Geographic Diversification = (Foreign Sales 2009 / Net Sales 2009) × 100. Industrial Diversification = number of business segments. Big 4 = 1 if the firm engages one of the Big 4 and 0 otherwise. Standard errors are in parenthesis. ***, **, * denote statistical significance at the 1, 5 and 10% levels, respectively. The figures in parentheses refer to the number of industry dummies that are significant at least at the 10% confidence level. Root MSE represents the standard error of the regressions.

Table 22.8 Robustness checks – ERM and firm value

		Model 6		Model 7	
		2SLS		2SLS	
		ERM (1st stage) – OLS	TQ (2nd stage)	ERM (1st stage) – OLS	Industry adj. TQ (2nd stage)
Test variable	ERM-raw score		0.019 (0.061)		0.038 (0.073)
Controls variables	Size	1.839 (0.481)***	-0.126 (0.137)	2.253 (0.381)***	-0.220 (0.178)
	Leverage	-14.338 (3.791)***	1.294 (0.947)	-12.873 (3.67)***	1.321 (1.008)
	Profitability	-1.555 (2.974)	0.342 (0.352)	-1.549 (2.958)	0.394 (0.371)
	Growth opportunities	2.464 (12.826)	0.331 (1.552)	8.255 (10.550)	-0.332 (1.468)
	Dividends	-0.019 (0.025)	0.012 (0.003)***	-0.031 (0.024)	0.012 (0.003)***
	Geographic diversification	-0.029 (0.030)	0.004 (0.004)	-0.033 (0.026)	0.005 (0.004)
	Industrial diversification	-0.152 (0.368)	0.001 (0.047)	-0.366 (0.326)	0.003 (0.053)
	Industry dummy	Yes (2)	Yes (2)		
	Big 4	4.281 (2.180)**		3.723 (2.133)*	
	Constant	-11.340 (6.490)*	1.230 (0.991)	-12.076 (4.741)***	1.565 (0.929)*
	Obs.	113	113	113	113
	R-square	0.391	0.324	0.340	0.080
	F-statistic	4.16***		6.71***	
	Wald Chi-sq.		59.36***		23.01***
	Root MSE	6.648	0.800	6.683	0.852

Note: TQ has two different measures: (1) Tobin's Q = (Market Value of Equity 2010 + Total Liabilities 2010) / Book Value of Total Assets 2010. (2) Industry Adjusted Tobin's Q calculated for each firm by subtracting the median TQ value of the industry from the TQ of the firm. Other variables are as follows: ERM-raw score (see the section "Measuring ERM" for its calculation). Size = natural logarithm of Total Assets 2009. Leverage = Total Debt 2009 / Total Assets 2009. Profitability = ROA (= Net Income 2009 / Total Assets 2009). Growth Opportunities = Capital Expenditures (as additions to fixed assets) 2009 / Total Assets 2009. Dividends = Dividend Payout Ratio (= Dividend per Share 2009 / Earnings per Share in 2009). Geographic Diversification = (Foreign Sales 2009 / Net Sales 2009) × 100. Industrial Diversification = number of business segments. Big 4 = 1 if the firm engages one of the Big 4 and 0 otherwise. Standard errors are in parenthesis. ***, **, * denote statistical significance at the 1, 5 and 10% levels, respectively. The figures in parentheses refer to the number of industry dummies that are significant at least at the 10% confidence level. Root MSE represents the standard error of the regressions.

Table 22.9 Robustness checks – ERM and firm value

		Baseline regression		Model 8		Model 9		Model 10	
		2SLS		2SLS		2SLS		2SLS	
		TQ (2nd stage)		TQ (2nd stage)		TQ (2nd stage)		TQ (2nd stage)	
Test variable	ERM/CRO	0.282	(0.873)	0.453	(1.513)	0.604	(2.067)	1.576	(5.531)
Controls variables	Size	−0.120	(0.119)	−0.136	(0.177)	−0.118	(0.124)	−0.203	(0.384)
	Leverage	1.242	(0.801)	1.301	(1.030)	1.446	(1.515)	1.366	(1.433)
	Profitability	0.365	(0.360)	0.288	(0.404)	0.321	(0.387)	0.426	(0.521)
	Growth opportunities	0.307	(1.544)	0.257	(1.698)	0.203	(1.799)	−0.184	(2.722)
	Dividends	0.012	(0.003)***	0.012	(0.003)***	0.012	(0.003)***	0.013	(0.005)***
	Geographic diversification	0.005	(0.004)	0.004	(0.004)	0.004	(0.004)	0.003	(0.004)
	Industrial diversification	0.003	(0.049)	−0.007	(0.047)	−0.005	(0.047)	−0.024	(0.073)
	Industry dummy	Yes (2)		Yes (2)		Yes (2)		No	
	Constant	1.236	(0.991)	1.530	(1.851)	1.220	(1.063)	2.558	(4.883)
	Obs.	113		113		113		111	
	R-squared	0.339		0.341		0.304		0.137	
	F-statistic	3.475***		3.483***		3.298***		2.585***	

Note: TQ has two different measures: (1) Tobin's Q = (Market Value of Equity 2010 + Total Liabilities 2010) / Book Value of Total Assets 2010. (2) Industry Adjusted Tobin's Q calculated for each firm by subtracting the median TQ value of the industry from the TQ of the firm. Other variables are as follows: ERM-dummy is used in the baseline regression while ERM15 and ERM20 dummy variables are used in Model 8 and 9, respectively (see the section "Measuring ERM" for the calculations). In Model 10, CRO dummy variable is used (see Q3.1a in the survey). Size = natural logarithm of Total Assets 2009. Leverage = Total Debt 2009 / Total Assets 2009. Profitability = ROA (= Net Income 2009 / Total Assets 2009). Growth Opportunities = Capital Expenditures (as additions to fixed assets) 2009 / Total Assets 2009. Dividends = Dividend Payout Ratio (= Dividend per Share 2009 / Earnings per Share in 2009). Geographic Diversification = (Foreign Sales 2009 / Net Sales 2009) × 100. Industrial Diversification = number of business segments. Big 4 = 1 if the firm engages one of the Big 4 and 0 otherwise. Standard errors are in parenthesis. ***, **, * denote statistical significance at the 1, 5 and 10% levels, respectively. The figures in parentheses refer to the number of industry dummies that are significant at least at the 10% confidence level.

Lastly, we check if the relation between ERM and TQ can be nonlinear. To address a potential nonlinearity, we estimate a regression where (1 / ERM-raw score) is used instead of the ERM-dummy variable in the baseline regression. The unreported results from this regression[25] also show an insignificant relation between ERM and TQ.

Overall, the results from all the models up to now show that the findings are highly stable over different specifications.

Further and subsample analyses

In this section, we first conduct a further analysis to analyze if the relationship between ERM and firm value is conditional on some certain firm characteristics (Model 11 in Table 22.10). Second, we estimate our model by splitting the sample into two based on TQ values (Models 12 and 13 in Table 22.10).

The first analysis (Model 11) focuses on a possible conditional relationship between ERM and firm value. The valuation premium for ERM may differ across firms. For example, the effect of ERM on firm value can be higher for larger firms. Large firms might be in need of more advanced risk management due to a wide range of and complex risks that threaten them (Liebenberg and Hoyt, 2003; Beasley et al., 2005; Beasley et al., 2008). Larger firms can gain more from ERM implementation by being able to manage those risks thanks to economies of scale. Accordingly, the value of ERM could be expected to be higher in these firms.

The instrumented variable in this model is ERM×Size, and the second stage of the IV model discussed earlier looks as follows:

$$TQ_i = \delta_0 + \delta_1 ERM_i \times Size_i + \delta_2 X_{\text{Control Variables,i}} + u_i \qquad (3)$$

where TQ is the dependent variable explained by ERM×Size (instrumented with Big 4×Size) where the model also includes a set of control variables (the same firm characteristics as in Equation 2), and u the error term. The IV, Big 4×Size, is a valid IV for ERM×Size as long as Big 4 is a valid one for ERM (Becker, 2007). The insignificant test results show that value of ERM does not change across firms with different sizes. Overall, we get similar results to those of our main model.

As the second analysis, in Models 12 and 13 (Table 22.10), we conduct the baseline analysis by creating two subsamples based on the TQ variable (TQ-low and TQ-high) since ERM values show interesting figures in subsamples: mean ERM in TQ-low firms is 14.893 while it is 10.546 in TQ-high firms. TQ-low represents the first 75 firms with the lowest TQ value, while TQ-high are the remaining 75 firms with the highest TQ value among total 150 firms in the sample. Table 22.10 presents the findings of this analysis in comparison to the baseline regression (on the very right column in Table 22.10). In both subsamples, we fail to find that ERM affects firm value. In sum, all the results from this section as well suggest that ERM has no impact on firm value. As one final remark regarding the control variables, another control variable also shows a significant relation with firm value in Model 12. We find that leverage and firm value are positively related to each other, supporting Jensen (1986)'s control hypothesis; that is, high debt increases firm value due to its ability to control managerial actions on the free cash flow available to them.

Summary and concluding remarks

This chapter investigates the impact of ERM adoption on firm value. We do not find a statistically significant relationship between ERM and firm value after controlling for other determinants of

Table 22.10 Further and subsample analyses – ERM and firm value

		Model 11		Model 12		Model 13		Baseline regression	
		2SLS		2SLS		2SLS		2SLS	
		TQ (2nd stage)		TQ-low (2nd stage)		TQ-high (2nd stage)		TQ (2nd stage)	
Test variable	ERM-dummy×Size / ERM-dummy	0.018	(0.110)	0.028	(0.184)	-3.508	(16.695)	0.282	(0.873)
Controls variables	Size	-0.125	(0.241)	-0.016	(0.023)	0.304	(2.233)	-0.120	(0.119)
	Leverage	1.214	(1.215)	0.751	(0.196)***	-1.856	(16.831)	1.242	(0.801)
	Profitability	0.367	(0.422)	0.331	(0.216)	0.833	(2.305)	0.365	(0.360)
	Growth opportunities	0.324	(1.675)	0.599	(0.631)	-3.409	(16.557)	0.307	(1.544)
	Dividends	0.012	(0.003)***	0.002	(0.001)***	0.010	(0.013)	0.012	(0.003)***
	Geographic diversification	0.004	(0.007)	-0.001	(0.001)	-0.005	(0.063)	0.005	(0.004)
	Industrial diversification	0.001	(0.059)	0.004	(0.018)	-0.067	(0.502)	0.003	(0.049)
	Industry dummy	Yes (2)		No (0)		No (0)		Yes (2)	
	Constant	1.323	(1.921)	0.661	(0.248)***	-0.551	(12.664)	1.236	(0.991)
	Obs.	113		62		51		113	
	R-squared	0.347		0.573		0.269		0.339	
	F-statistic	3.511***		4.160***				3.475***	

Note: TQ has two different measures: (1) Tobin's Q = (Market Value of Equity 2010 + Total Liabilities 2010) / Book Value of Total Assets 2010. (2) Industry Adjusted Tobin's Q calculated for each firm by subtracting the median TQ value of the industry from the TQ of the firm. Other variables are as follows: ERM-dummy is a variable which takes the value of 1 if the firm has an ERM score in the top 50% and 0 otherwise (see the section "Measuring ERM" for ERM score calculation). ERM-dummy×Size is used in Model 11 while ERM-dummy is used in Model 12 and 13. Size = natural logarithm of Total Assets 2009. Leverage = Total Debt 2009 / Total Assets 2009. Profitability = ROA (= Net Income 2009 / Total Assets 2009). Growth Opportunities = Capital Expenditures (as additions to fixed assets) 2009 / Total Assets 2009. Dividends = Dividend Payout Ratio (= Dividend per Share 2009 / Earnings per Share in 2009). Geographic Diversification = (Foreign Sales 2009 / Net Sales 2009) × 100. Industrial Diversification = number of business segments. Big 4 = 1 if the firm engages one of the Big 4 and 0 otherwise. Standard errors are in parenthesis. ***, **, * denote statistical significance at the 1, 5 and 10% levels, respectively. The figures in parentheses refer to the number of industry dummies that are significant at least at the 10% confidence level.

firm value and endogeneity bias. Our finding is robust across a number of model specifications we run, and in line with McShane et al. (2011) and Pagach and Warr (2010) while in contrast to Hoyt and Liebenberg (2011) and Baxter et al. (2013).

Our insignificant results might indicate that shareholders are not really concerned much about ERM adoption. For example, our survey findings show that "shareholder pressure" is the least cited factor as a driver of ERM (see Question 5 in Appendix 22.2). Similarly, Beasley et al. (2008) fail to find a significant positive market reaction to ERM implementation, on average. On the other hand, we do not find any discount in firm value either, unlike Lin et al. (2012). That might imply that ERM could be regarded as a zero NPV investment by investors. In other words, benefits of ERM could be offset by high costs associated with the implementation. However, that does not necessarily mean that ERM does not bring any benefits to a firm. For example, benefits such as improved management accountability (Gates, 2006), and new insights gained from the high level of oversight of the interplay between different kinds of risks (Meulbroek, 2002), are those that are not incorporated in firm value directly. However, they potentially provide some advantages to the firm.

More reflection could be on our sample type. Evidence of value creation by ERM comes from the samples of firms which are from financial sector (in particular the insurance and banking industries) (Hoyt and Liebenberg, 2011; Baxter et al., 2013). On the other hand, the value creation evidence from nonfinancial firms is firm specific and is as follows: Beasley et al. (2008) show that firms that are larger and have limited cash on hand value ERM implementation. In sum, it could be interpreted that ERM is beneficial, however in only some certain industries.

This chapter has both academic and policy implications. Although there has been growing interest in ERM by both professionals and academics, we have limited knowledge as to whether ERM creates value for firms. Regarding academic implications, first, this chapter increases our knowledge on value relevance of ERM by showing no support for the argument that ERM increases firm value. Second, we attempt to develop a new, sound measure for ERM process which overcomes drawbacks of the previous measurements. Since the survey conducted to measure ERM is in Appendix 22.2 and the secondary data used in this study is publicly available, this new measure could be used in the ERM literature – with possible adjustments and improvements – and foster future research.

This chapter has some policy implications as well. Firms might hesitate to commit to ERM without having much empirical evidence on the value creation of ERM. Thus, managers and boards of directors, who are the key actors in giving the decision of initiating an ERM program, could take the findings of this chapter into account in their decision-making.

We fail to find support that ERM contributes to firm valuation in listed Nordic firms by using a relatively small sample. Therefore, future research should test the same hypothesis in different and larger samples in order to broaden our knowledge on the topic. Future research should also focus on the channels through which ERM possibly creates value.

Acknowledgements

I am grateful for comments made by Lars Oxelheim, Niclas Andrén, Anders Vilhelmsson, Jens Forssbaeck, Håkan Jankensgård, Sara Lundqvist, Claes Wihlborg, Niels Hermes, Kristoffer Milonas and the participants at the following conferences: 11th Infiniti Conference on International Finance, June 2013, Aix-en-Provence, France; 7th Nordic Econometric Meeting, June 2013, Bergen, Norway; 15th Annual SNEE European Integration Conference, May 2013, Mölle, Sweden; as well as those at the KWC finance seminar series at Lund University. This paper is financed by the scholarship provided by the Jan Wallander and Tom Hedelius Foundation while the survey is financed by NASDAQOMX Nordic Foundation.

Notes

1 Naciye Sekerci, School of Economics and Management, Knut Wicksell Centre (KWC) for Financial Studies, Lund University, PO-BOX 7080, SE-220 07, Lund, Sweden.

2 It is also possible to find other definitions of ERM in the literature. However, for the moment we give a broad definition of ERM, and later on we elaborate on it more when discussing our ERM measure.

3 Apart from ERM, there are other similar centralized approaches to risk management. For example, see MUST (Macroeconomic Uncertainty Strategy) analysis developed in Oxelheim and Whilborg (2008).

4 That is, the Codes of Corporate Governance in Sweden, Denmark, Norway and Finland.

5 For example, Sarens and Christopher (2010) show that weaker focus of Belgian corporate governance guidelines on risk management is associated with less developed risk management practices in Belgium compared to the examples in Australia. Kleffner, Lee and McGannon (2003) also find that 37% of the 118 firms in their sample state that the Toronto Stock Exchange (TSE) guidelines influence their decision to adopt ERM.

6 Internal codes, policies and guidelines within the firm.

7 For example, Standard and Poor's has already taken ERM into account as part of their credit rating assessments (Standard and Poor's, 2008, 2010).

8 There is one study by Gordon et al. (2010) who construct an ERM index based on a firm's ability to achieve the four objectives stated in COSO (2004). Their ERM index stands for *effectiveness* of an ERM program rather than ERM *implementation* itself.

9 These key elements of ERM are compiled by the author as a result of careful and intense work: first, from reading COSO (2004) whose ERM discussions are taken as a base for this study; second, from thoroughly reviewing ERM literature; third, from searching through annual reports and websites of the firms who claim that they have ERM in place.

10 The first explicit question about ERM (Question 4 in Appendix 22.2) is only asked after the questions whose answers are used to measure ERM (Questions 1.1–3.3). And the respondents were not allowed to turn back to the previous questions on the web-based survey.

11 After collecting secondary data, there were missing values for some firms. They were missing at random, that is, there was no systematic pattern for any firm for having missing data. Therefore, we leave these firms with their missing values in the analysis. Methods such as mean and regression substitution are not used due to their suspicious ability to improve the quality of the analysis. For example, by employing mean substitution, we reduce standard errors by increasing sample size; however we do not add much information to the sample. For similar reasons, complex solutions such as Maximum Likelihood, Multiple Imputation (EM Algorithm), Complete Case Analysis are not preferred, either. Although our ignoring the missing observations causes the estimators to be less precise, it does not introduce any bias to the model (Wooldridge, 2009).

12 See the survey in Appendix 22.2. Questions 1.1–3.3 refer to those key components of ERM.

13 For the origins of the CRO position, see Fraser and Simkins (2010).

14 The Big 4 audit firms are PricewaterhouseCoopers, Deloitte, KPMG and Ernst & Young.

15 Since we have only one endogenous regressor (ERM), in order to have the coefficients identified, we need at least one IV. We have only one IV, therefore there is no overidentification problem in the 2SLS (Roberts and Whited, 2012).

16 According to Wooldridge (2002), there are no special requirements while estimating the parameters in the second stage by 2SLS when the endogenous variable is a binary choice.

17 When we take natural logarithm of TQ, it is still nonnormally distributed. In addition, when we run the baseline regression by using both raw-TQ and lnTQ, we get higher R^2 for the estimation with raw TQ. Therefore, we choose to use raw TQ which is also in line with Hoyt and Liebenberg (2011), Lin et al. (2012) and Baxter et al. (2013).

18 Jensen (1986) argues that managers might have incentives to grow the firm more than necessary only for the sake of their own reputation and compensation tied to firm growth.

19 Debt has this "control" ability mostly in firms that have more cash on hand and less investment opportunities (Jensen, 1986).

20 Among all the other variables included in the regressions, only the geographic diversification variable has relatively high missing values, hence the mean value replacement method is used for this particular variable in order not to lose observations in the regressions.

21 GICS is based on an "economic sector" classification which further is divided into industry groups (four-digit), industries (six-digit) and subindustries (eight-digit). Given the sample size of this study, two-digit economic sector codes are used instead of four or more digit industry codes (see http://www.standardandpoors.com/indices/gics/en/us for further information).

22 When we look at the industry dummies in our sample, we see that we have firms from the Industrials sector as most (n = 32) while the least common sector in the sample is Consumer Staples (n = 7).

23 Since ERM has positive correlations with "profitability" and "growth opportunities," we also run the analysis by excluding one of profitability and growth opportunities variables at a time (as well as excluding both at the same time) to check if these variables take some of ERM's effect away. However, we get qualitatively similar results. When we run the same analysis with ROA instead of TQ, we get qualitatively similar results.

24 All the remaining ERM components are ordered variables that take values between 1 and 3. Therefore, the first-stage regressions are ordered models.

25 The results are available upon request.

References

Allayannis, G., & Weston, J. (2001). The use of foreign currency derivatives and firm market value. *Review of Financial Studies, 14*(1), 243–276.

Baker, M., & Wurgler, J. (2011). Behavioral corporate finance: An undated survey (No. w17333). Cambridge, MA: National Bureau of Economic Research.

Baxter, R., Bedard, J.C., Hoitash, R., & Yezegel, A. (2013). Enterprise risk management program quality: Determinants, value relevance, and the financial crisis. *Contemporary Accounting Research, 30*(4), 1264–1295.

Beasley, M.S., Clune, R., & Hermanson, D.R. (2005). Enterprise risk management: An empirical analysis of factors associated with the extent of implementation. *Journal of Accounting and Public Policy, 24*(6), 521–531.

Beasley, M., Pagach, D., & Warr, R. (2008). Information conveyed in hiring announcements of senior executives overseeing enterprise-wide risk management processes. *Journal of Accounting, Auditing & Finance, 23*(3), 311–332.

Becker, B. (2007). Geographical segmentation of US capital markets. *Journal of Financial Economics, 85*(1), 151–178.

Berger, P.G., & Ofek, E. (1995). Diversification's effect on firm value. *Journal of Financial Economics, 37*(1), 39–65.

Berkman, H., & Bradbury, M.E. (1996). Empirical evidence on the corporate use of derivatives. *Financial Management*, 25(2), 5–13.

Carter, D.A., Rogers, D.A., & Simkins, B.J. (2006). Does hedging affect firm value? Evidence from the US airline industry. *Financial Management, 35*(1), 53–86.

CAS. (2003). *Overview of enterprise risk management.* Arlington, VA: Casualty Actuarial Society (CAS), Enterprise Risk Management Committee.

Cassidy, S.M., Constand, R.L., & Corbett, R.B. (1990). The market value of the corporate risk management function. *Journal of Risk and Insurance, 57*(4), 664–670.

COSO (Committee of Sponsoring Organizations of the Treadway Commission). (2004). Enterprise Risk Management – Integrated Framework: Executive Summary. New York: Author.

Desender, K. (2010). On the determinants of enterprise risk management implementation. In S.S.N. Si & G. Silvius (Eds.), *Handbook of Research on Enterprise, IT Governance, Business Value and Performance Measurement* (pp. 87–100). Singapore: IGI Global.

Desender, K.A., & Lafuente, E. (2009). *The influence of board composition, audit fees and ownership concentration on enterprise risk management.* SSRN Working Paper Series.

Desender, K.A., & Lafuente, E. (2011). The relationship between enterprise risk management and external audit fees: Are they complements or substitutes? In J. Abolhassan (Ed.), *Risk management and corporate governance.* London: Routledge.

Fazzari, S., Hubbard, R.G., & Petersen, B.C. (1988). Financing constraints and corporate investment. *Brookings Papers on Economic Activity, 1*, 141–195.

Fraser, J.R.S., & Simkins, B.J. (2007). Ten common misconceptions about enterprise risk management. *Journal of Applied Corporate Finance, 19*(4), 75–81.

Fraser, J.R.S., & Simkins, B.J. (2010). *Enterprise risk management.* Hoboken, NJ: Wiley.

Froot, K.A., Scharfstein, D.S., & Stein, J.C. (1993). Risk management: Coordinating corporate investment and financing policies. *Journal of Finance, 48*(5), 1629–1658.

Gates, S. (2006). Incorporating strategic risk into enterprise risk management: A survey of current corporate practice. *Journal of Applied Corporate Finance, 18*(4), 81–90.

Gordon, L.A., Loeb, M.P., & Tseng, C.Y. (2009). Enterprise risk management and firm performance: A contingency perspective. *Journal of Accounting and Public Policy, 28*(4), 301–327.

Hausman, J.A. (1978). Specification tests in econometrics. *Econometrica: Journal of the Econometric Society, 46*(6), 1251–1271.

Hoyt, R.E., & Liebenberg, A.P. (2011). The value of enterprise risk management. *Journal of Risk and Insurance, 78*(4), 795–822.

Jankensgård, H. (2011). *Essays on corporate risk management* (Dissertation, Lund University).

Jensen, M.C. (1986). Agency costs of free cash flow, corporate finance, and takeovers. *American Economic Review, 76*(2), 323–329.

Jin, Y., & Jorion, P. (2006). Firm value and hedging: Evidence from US oil and gas producers. *Journal of Finance, 61*(2), 893–919.

Kleffner, A.E., Lee, R.B., & McGannon, B. (2003). The effect of corporate governance on the use of enterprise risk management: Evidence from Canada. *Risk Management and Insurance Review, 6*(1), 53–73.

Lam, J. (2001), The CRO is here to stay. *Risk Management, 48*(4), 16–20.

Lang, L.H.P., & Stulz, R.M. (1994). Tobin's Q, corporate diversification, and firm performance. *Journal of Political Economy, 102*(6), 1248–1280.

Liebenberg, A.P., & Hoyt, R.E. (2003). The determinants of enterprise risk management: Evidence from the appointment of chief risk officers. *Risk Management and Insurance Review, 6*(1), 37–52.

Lin, Y., Wen, M.M., & Yu, J. (2012). Enterprise risk management: Strategic antecedents, risk integration, and performance. *North American Actuarial Journal, 16*(1), 1–28.

MacKay, P., & Moeller, S.B. (2007). The value of corporate risk management. *Journal of Finance, 62*(3), 1379–1419.

Mayers, D., & Smith, C.W., Jr. (1990). On the corporate demand for insurance: Evidence from the reinsurance market. *Journal of Business, 63*, 19–40.

McShane, M.K., Nair, A., & Rustambekov, E. (2011). Does enterprise risk management increase firm value? *Journal of Accounting, Auditing & Finance, 26*(4), 641–658.

Meulbroek, L.K. (2002). A senior manager's guide to integrated risk management. *Journal of Applied Corporate Finance, 14*(4), 56–70.

Myers, S.C. (1977). Determinants of corporate borrowing. *Journal of Financial Economics, 5*(2), 147–175.

Nocco, B.W., & Stulz, R.M. (2006). Enterprise risk management: Theory and practice. *Journal of Applied Corporate Finance, 18*(4), 8–20.

Oxelheim, L., & Whilborg, C. (2008). *Corporate decision-making with macroeconomic uncertainty*. Oxford: Oxford University Press.

Pagach, D., & Warr, R. (2010). *The effects of enterprise risk management on firm performance*. Retrieved from http://papers.ssrn.com/sol3/papers.cfm?abstract_id=1155218

Pagach, D., & Warr, R. (2011). The characteristics of firms that hire chief risk officers. *Journal of Risk and Insurance, 78*(1), 185–211.

Roberts, M.R., & Whited, T.M. (2012). *Endogeneity in empirical corporate finance*. Retrieved from http://papers.ssrn.com/sol3/papers.cfm?abstract_id=1748604

Sarens, G., & Christopher, J. (2010). The association between corporate governance guidelines and risk management and internal control practices: Evidence from a comparative study. *Managerial Auditing Journal, 25*(4), 288–308.

Sekerci, N. (2011). *Is enterprise risk management a corporate governance tool? Evidence from Nordic countries* (PhD thesis, Lund University).

Smith, C.W., & Stulz, R.M. (1985). The determinants of firms' hedging policies. *Journal of Financial and Quantitative Analysis, 20*(4), 391–405.

Smithson, C., & Simkins, B.J. (2005). Does risk management add value? A survey of the evidence. *Journal of Applied Corporate Finance, 17*(3), 8–17.

Standard & Poor's. (2008, May). *Enterprise risk management: Standard & Poor's to apply enterprise risk analysis to corporate ratings*. Retrieved from http://www.nyu.edu/intercep/ERM%20for%20Non-Financial%20Companies%205.7.08.pdf

Standard & Poor's. (2010, June). *Credit FAQ: Standard and Poor's looks further into how nonfinancial companies manage risk*. Retrieved from http://www.qsp.org.br/pdf/Corporates_ERM_FAQ_06_24_10.pdf

Stulz, R.M. (1984). Optimal hedging policies. *Journal of Financial and Quantitative Analysis, 19*(2), 127–140.

Stulz, R.M. (1996). Rethinking risk management. *Journal of Applied Corporate Finance, 9*(3), 8–25.

Wooldridge, J.M. (2002). *Econometrics analysis of cross section and panel data*. Cambridge, MA: MIT Press.

Wooldridge, J.M. (2009). *Introductory econometrics – A modern approach*. Mason, OH: South-Western Cengage Learning.

Zou, H. (2010). Hedging affecting firm value via financing and investment: Evidence from property insurance use. *Financial Management, 39*(3), 965–996.

Appendix 22.1

Variable definitions

Variable Name	Definition	Source
Tobin's Q	2 measures: (1) Tobin's Q is equal to ((Market Value of Equity 2010 + Total Liabilities 2010) / Book Value of Total Assets 2010). (2) Industry Adjusted Tobin's Q calculated for each firm by subtracting the median TQ of the industry from the TQ of the firm	Datastream
ERM	See the section "Measuring ERM"	The survey
Size	Natural logarithm of Total Assets 2009	Datastream, Osiris and annual reports
Leverage	Total Debt 2009 / Total Assets 2009	Datastream, Osiris and annual reports
Profitability	ROA, calculated as Net Income 2009 / Total Assets 2009	Datastream
Growth opportunities	Capital Expenditures (as additions to fixed assets) 2009 / Total Assets 2009	Datastream
Dividends	Dividend Payout Ratio, calculated as Dividend per Share 2009 / Earnings per Share in 2009	Datastream
Geographic diversification	(Foreign Sales 2009 / Net Sales 2009) × 100	Datastream
Industrial diversification	Number of business segments	Osiris
Industry dummy	Dummy variable which takes the value of 1 if the 8-digit GICS starts with 40, and 0 otherwise	Osiris
Big 4	Dummy variable which takes the value of 1 if the firm engages one of the Big 4 in 2009, and 0 otherwise	Annual reports

Note: The accounting values are in thousands of US dollars and are lagged data, collected as of December 2009. In the case where firms have their fiscal year as 2009–2010, the fiscal year-end values stated in their 2009–2010 annual reports are taken. All the other data apart from those accounting data are 2010 year-end values since 2010 is the year to which firms referred while filling in the survey. In the case where firms have their fiscal year as 2009–2010, the fiscal year-end values stated in their 2009–2010 annual reports are taken.

Appendix 22.2

The survey

Risk management, organization, and value creation

Directions:

Please read each question carefully and choose from the answers provided or fill in the blanks for open-ended questions. Please answer based on the firm's activities in 2010.

Please provide us with some identification information on the individual filling out this survey.

Your title/position

To what degree are you familiar with the organization of risk management and risk management activities at the firm?

	Not at all	Some familiarity	Working knowledge	Very familiar
	☐	☐	☐	☐

1. To what degree are the following risk management dimensions implemented throughout the firm?

	Does not exist	Ad hoc implementation	Implemented but improvements needed	Robustly implemented	Don't know
1.1 Formal report submitted to the board at least annually on the current state of risk and effectiveness of risk management	☐	☐	☐	☐	☐
1.2 Centralized technology-enabled process to obtain risk-related information	☐	☐	☐	☐	☐
1.3 Formal written risk management philosophy (policy) (a set of shared beliefs and attitudes characterizing how the firm considers risk in everything it does and delineates the responsibility of management and the board)	☐	☐	☐	☐	☐
1.4 Formal written statement of the firm's risk appetite (the amount of risk specified at the board level that the firm is willing to accept in pursuit of value)	☐	☐	☐	☐	☐

(Continued)

Risk management, organization, and value creation

2. To what degree are the following risk management organizational dimensions implemented throughout the firm?

	Does not exist	Ad hoc implementation	Implemented but improvements needed	Robustly implemented	Don't know
2.1 Board level committee with responsibility for risk management oversight	☐	☐	☐	☐	☐
2.2 Centralized department or staff function dedicated to risk management	☐	☐	☐	☐	☐
2.3 Allocated risk owners who have primary responsibility and accountability for managing risk within their respective areas	☐	☐	☐	☐	☐

3. Please answer the following Yes/No questions about the firm's risk management organization.

	Yes	No	Don't know
3.1a Does anyone at the firm hold the title Chief Risk Officer (CRO)?	☐	☐	☐
3.2 Does the Chief Risk Officer (CRO) have the highest responsibility for overseeing the centralized risk management (CRM) function?		☐	☐
3.1b If the firm does not have a CRO, but has a (CRM) function, please specify what the title of the person in charge of that function is.			
3.3 Is the CRO (or equivalent position) independent of risk taking activities and decisions?		☐	

4. Please answer the following questions about the firm's risk management practices.

A frequently cited definition of Enterprise Risk Management (ERM) is "a process, affected by an entity's board of directors, management and other personnel, applied in strategy setting and across the enterprise, designed to identify potential events that may affect the entity, and manage risk to be within its risk appetite, to provide reasonable assurance regarding the achievement of entity objectives."

	Not at all	Ad hoc implementation	Implemented but improvements needed	Robustly implemented	Implement ERM but only according to other definition	Don't know
To what degree does the firm implement ERM according to the above definition?	☐	☐	☐	☐	☐	☐

5. What led the firm to implement ERM (mark those which apply)?

- ☐ Encouragement from the Board of Directors
- ☐ Encouragement from executive management
- ☐ Competition or other industry-related pressures
- ☐ Shareholder pressure
- ☐ Regulation compliance
- ☐ Compliance with stock exchange guidelines
- ☐ The need for more effective internal audit control
- ☐ The recent financial crisis
- ☐ Other:

6. Does the firm have any plans to implement ERM?

Yes	No	Don't know
☐	☐	☐

(Continued)

Risk management, organization, and value creation

7a. What are the main challenges the firm has faced in implementing ERM (mark those which apply)?

7b. What has held the firm back from implementing ERM (mark those which apply)?

Resistance from the Board of Directors ☐

Need for internal control and review systems ☐

Embedding risk management within company culture ☐

Difficulty in quantifying risks ☐

Timeliness and quality of information ☐

Difficulty in integrating risk management with other business processes ☐

Lack of necessary knowledge and skills within the organization ☐

Corporate priorities are often conflicting ☐

Availability of information ☐

Unclear who is responsible for managing risk ☐

Organizational culture which is resistant to change ☐

Other: ☐ ☐

Notes: Questions represented here are in the same order as those in the web-based survey. Some are conditional, i.e., Question 7 is conditional upon Question 4. If the firm answered anything besides "not at all" to Question 4, Question 7a appears on the screen. If the answer is "not at all" to Question 4, then Question 7b appears on the screen of the web-based survey.

23

Strategic risk management and corporate value creation[1]

Oliviero Roggi and Torben Juul Andersen[2]

Abstract

Major corporate failures and volatile market conditions have intensified the focus on corporate risk management as the means to deal with turbulent business conditions where the ability to respond effectively to often dramatic environmental changes is considered an important source of competitive advantage. However, surprisingly little research has analyzed the presumed advantages of effective risk management or assessed important antecedents of the underlying risk management capabilities. Here we present a comprehensive study of risk management effectiveness and the relationship to corporate performance based on panel data for more than 3,400 firms with over 33,500 annual observations during the turbulent period 1991–2010. Determining effective risk management as the ability to reduce earnings and cash flow volatility, we find significant positive relationships to lagged performance measures after controlling for industry effects and company size. We also find that availability of slack resources and investment commitments affect the risk management capabilities and their relationship to performance.

Strategic risk management has become a mantra in executive board rooms following the corporate scandals and financial crises of recent years. There is general awareness that the ability to deal effectively with major risk events is an important aspect of strategic management (e.g., Miller, 1998; Wang, Barney and Reuer, 2003). However, we are not sure whether the adopted risk management practices truly lead to superior outcomes and, if so, what the essential drivers of effective risk handling are (e.g., Beasly, Pagach and Warr, 2008; Liebenberg and Hoyt, 2003; Pagach and Warr, 2011). In reality, there is limited evidence on the proposed benefits from effective risk management capabilities and it is unclear what the implications are for governance, management practice, and strategy conduct in general (Power, 2009; Smithson and Simkins, 2005). So, while risk management has assumed a central executive focus, little is known about the strategic effects and how potential effects may be derived.

The ability to adapt to changing conditions is considered beneficial for organizations and has a long tradition in social science (e.g., Levinthal and March, 1981; March, 1988). Strategic response capabilities allow firms to adjust to abrupt environmental changes, and strategic renewal facilitates organizational adaptation (Agarwal and Helfat, 2009; Bettis and Hitt, 1995). The dynamic capabilities construct suggests that observant and innovative organizations respond better to changing conditions (Teece, 2007; Teece, Pisano and Shuen, 1997) where knowledge exploration identifies opportunities that can adapt the way the firm operates (Damodaran, 2008). That is, maintaining sufficient slack for investing in opportunities can enhance responsiveness and thus support effective risk management (Andersen, 2009). However, these rationales are fairly unexplored and represent a promising area for empirical studies. To this end, we investigate the performance outcomes of effective risk management and its antecedents drawing on panel data from more than 3,400 firms with over 33,500 data points during the turbulent period 1991–2010.

In the following we first review literature streams related to strategic risk management and provide an overview of the few empirical studies conducted to date. Then we develop a model of risk management effectiveness linked to investment intensity and available slack and conduct a number of preliminary empirical tests. We find initial support for positive value creation effects from effective risk management capabilities and indications that these effects are associated with availability of slack resources and investment in opportunities. These findings are presented and implications for future research enhancements are discussed.

Theory and hypotheses

Risk management and strategic responsiveness

One argument for risk management is that lower cash flow volatility reduces the likelihood of liquidity shortfalls so funds are more readily available for good investments (Froot, Scharfstein and Stein, 1993; Myers, 1977; Nocco and Stulz, 2006). The associated earnings stability reduces bankruptcy risk and provides access to external funding at more favorable rates (e.g., Minton and Schrand, 1999; Smithson and Simkin, 2005). Hence, effective risk management can help the firm obtain better access to capital markets and other resources in support of the implementation of business plans (Nocco and Stulz, 2006). Lower cash flow volatility reduces the need for liquidity buffers, and a lower level of cash reserves will release funds for alternative business investment with higher returns (Merton, 2005). That is, incremental value can accrue from the ability to finance more profitable projects and at lower funding cost. The lower bankruptcy risk can also reduce the transaction costs associated with the firm's interactions with essential stakeholders that offer less than favorable business conditions in their dealings with vulnerable counterparts (e.g., Miller and Chen, 2003; Wang, Barney and Reuer, 2003).

This reasoning is consistent with the valuation principles where the value of the firm (VOF) is determined as the present value (PV) of future cash generation (C) minus bankruptcy costs as reflected in transaction and funding charges: VOF = PV(C – bankruptcy costs) (e.g., Stulz, 2003: 57). So, value from effective risk management can derive either from a reduction in the bankruptcy costs or through an increase in future cash flows from profitable projects or from both of these sources. In addition to this, we argue that there is an incremental value-creating potential associated with the ability to develop innovative opportunities that can be implemented if and when abrupt changes in the competitive environment call for it. The availability of these optional responses improves the strategic maneuverability of the firm and the execution of the new business initiatives will enhance future cash flow generation that creates corporate value.

The resulting capacity to adapt the organization and pursue strategic renewal should enable the firm to modify the way things are done in response to major changes in the environment so it can maintain a reasonable fit with current customer needs and operational practices. Strategic reference point theory and considerations about strategic fit suggest that there is potential value associated with the firm's ability to better match the requirements imposed by the strategic context at any given time (Fiegenbaum, Hart and Schendel, 1996; Porter, 1996). If the firm is able to fulfill changing customer needs then total revenues should remain high, and if the firm is able to implement state-of the-art operating practices then costs should remain low, and as a consequence of both hence performance and ongoing value creation should be high.

However, many important risk factors are exogenous to the firm and imposed by socioeconomic conditions in the macro environment that are beyond managerial control. This may comprise events that are identical under similar circumstances and allow prediction of probable outcomes as well as events that must be assessed without a valid basis for classification reflecting the well-known distinction between risk and uncertainty (Knight, 1921/2006: 224). It may also relate to factors that are impossible to foresee in advance sometimes referred to as "unknown unknowns" (e.g., Loch, DeMeyer and Pich, 2006). Strategic risk factors including competitor moves, technology shifts, changing industry paradigms, etc., are hard to quantify and difficult to predict because the underlying events are irregular and may arise from complex nonlinear conditions (Bettis and Hitt, 1995). That is, strategic risks are typically in the unknown end of the risk scale. Furthermore, the related risk exposures arise from the unique structures and market positions assumed by the individual firms. Hence, the response capabilities required to deal effectively with the strategic risks must also be of a firm-specific nature (Helfat et al., 2007; Teece, Pisano and Shuen, 1997; Zollo and Winter, 2002). The ability to develop new business opportunities and execute them as responsive initiatives in view of environmental changes constitutes one such form of firm-specific response capability.

The ability to adapt to changing conditions has been referred to as "dynamic capabilities" formally described as the firm's ability to integrate, build, and reconfigure internal and external competences in rapidly changing environments (Teece, Pisano and Shuen, 1997). They are formed by distinct skills, processes, and procedures embedded in the organizational structures in ways that enable the firm to sense change, seize opportunities, and reconfigure in the face of change (Teece, 2007). Like "strategic responsiveness" this requires an ability to assess environmental change and mobilize firm resources around responsive actions taken to adapt the firm to new challenges in the environment (Andersen, Denrell and Bettis, 2007). These response capabilities are affected by the decision structure, information and communication systems, coordination mechanisms, incentives, and corporate values applied in the organization (Teece, 2007). Hence, we conceive of effective risk management (ERM) capabilities as the firm's ability to observe, react, and adapt to major risk events so the variation in corporate cash flows and earnings are reduced compared to industry peers.

H1: Firms that demonstrate effective risk management capabilities are associated with higher value creation potentials.

Slack resources and investment intensity

The conventional view on risk evolved from insurance and financial hedging perspectives where the aim is to obtain economic cover against excessive loss situations. However, variability in cash flows and returns implies that outcomes go both up and down over time, and suggests that we must assume a broader view when we deal with strategic risk management to consider the potential for positive upside gains as well as negative downside losses (Andersen, 2012; Damodaran, 2008; Slywotzky, 2007). Nocco and Stulz (2006) discuss the ERM approach where top management prioritizes corporate risk-taking and decentralized decision makers evaluate local risk–return tradeoff. However, many important responsive initiatives can be taken at dispersed decision nodes where exogenous influences are observed first and where a certain excess of resources, or slack, may facilitate the underpinning innovative opportunity development.

Slack can be conceived as the means to smooth performance against environmental shocks thereby avoiding disruptive layoffs, so value-creating capital investments in promising business opportunities can be retained. However, we are particularly interested in the way slack resources may enhance responsive initiatives and corporate adaptability in the face of exogenous risk events and the literature implicitly speaks to this. For example, Thompson (1967) recognizes that slack can allow the firm to take advantage of opportunities afforded by the environment in which it operates. Bromiley (1991) argues that firms in possession of many resources have more strategic options than firms with fewer resources. The presence of slack resources argu-ably leads to a range of strategic options and alternative profit-yielding activities (Amit and Schoemaker, 1993). Slack may facilitate product innovation and experimentation that enable endogenous corporate growth (Greve, 2003; Lawson, 2001; Penrose, 1959/1995; Pitelis, 2007). Hence, there are arguments for positive relationships between slack and innovation (Nohria and Gulati, 1996), risk-taking (Singh, 1986), and adaptation (Kraatz and Zajac, 2001). That is, slack resources can provide funding for initiatives with strong subunit support that otherwise might fail in the formal approval procedures. These activities relate to process, technology and product improvements rather than problem-oriented innovations typically imposed through more for-mal managerial interventions (Cyert and March, 1963).

Hence, innovative risk-taking behavior is more likely in the presence of organizational slack where resources can be released for experimentation without formalized controls and mana-gerial scrutiny. That is, slack thrives under economic affluence and is associated with decentral-ized structures whereas poor performance may lead to tighter controls and more centralization (Bourgeois and Singh, 1983; Singh, 1986). Organizational search may often be induced by failure to reach targeted performance aspirations (March and Shapira, 1987, 1992), but it may also unintentionally be stimulated by organizational slack and managers' illusions about their ability to overcome risks (March, 1995). Experimentation with new ideas, technologies, and market offerings often thrives on risk-taking, loose discipline, poor controls, and even on mad-ness and serendipity (March, 1995), all conditions that may derive from the availability of slack resources. Innovation is fostered by individuals in the organization as they generate, discuss, promote, and realize new ideas (Damanpour, 1991; Scott and Bruce, 1994; Van de Ven, 1986) and slack resources induce experimentation, risk-taking, and proactive strategic choices (Greve, 2003; Judge, Fryxell and Dooley, 1997; Keegan and Turner, 2002). In short, slack should induce strategic responsiveness and there is some evidence that slack is associated with lower downside risk (Miller and Leiblein, 1996).

The key to dealing effectively with strategic risks that are hard to predict and foresee depends on the organization's ability to sense impending changes and seize ways to respond to them (Teece, 2007). Hence, a responsive organization is one where new suggestions about how things can be done differently are allowed to flourish. So, organizational adaptation is reflected in an ability to innovate and apply new ideas, devices, systems, policies, programs, processes, products, services, and markets in ways that make firm operations more compliant with current condi-tions (Damanpour, 1991; Nohria and Gulati, 1996; Scott and Bruce, 1994). Finding new ways of doing things can also be conceptualized as a type of experimentation where the organization explores the effects of different combinations of technical and organizational elements (Kogut and Kulatilaka, 2001). The innovations can relate to product development, use of new technol-ogies, new market entry, etc., but may also include changes in organizational processes, admin-istrative practices, management approaches, etc. (Bourgeois, 1981; Damanpour and Evan, 1984). These responsive behaviors can be seen to drive exploratory actions that make it possible for the firm to modify business activities and accommodate changes in customer needs, technologies, economic conditions, etc. Accordingly, the associated strategic responsiveness, or dynamic capabilities, are considered a fundamental source of competitive advantage (Bettis and Hitt, 1995; Teece et al., 1997). Hence, the extent to which investment and slack resources are made available to drive these business opportunities and innovative initiatives can be important moderators of effective risk management capabilities.

H2: The level of slack resources positively moderates the performance effect of the firm's effective risk management capabilities

The availability of investment and slack resources can build up in various ways, e.g., as low financial leverage, strong cash flow generation, extraordinary dividends, high liquidity reserves, excess salaries, incremental service fees, room for budgeted expenses, perks, and prerequisites. Hence, slack can comprise excess payments to organizational members above what is required to perform current activities and it may comprise excess payments from customers for individual services. It may reflect additional financial means from internal self-generation or through access to external capital markets. It can also manifest itself in physical things including extra people, additional cash, more time, excess capacity, etc., and thereby constitutes a mechanism that can absorb fluctuations in the business environment (Bromiley, 2005; Cyert and March, 1963; Singh, 1986).

Recoverable slack is made up by excessive payments for various factor inputs and excess operating capacity. This kind of slack can be recovered fairly easily through internal budget reallocations at the business unit level and constitutes a resource buffer that allows pursuit of development projects despite environmental disruptions (Cyert and March, 1963; Sharfman, Wolf, Chase and Tansik, 1988). While this kind of absorbed slack has discretionary limitations it does provide room for ongoing collaborative learning activities and can fund immediate initiatives with strong subunit support that otherwise might fail in formal approval procedures (Cyert and March, 1963; Keegan and Turner, 2002; Wayne and Rubinstein, 1992). Hence, these generic absorbed resources provide sufficient discretion to reallocate resources for local purposes to facilitate innovation, experimentation, responsive initiatives, and adaptive moves (Greve, 2003; Kraatz and Zajac, 2001; Lawson, 2001; Nohria and Gulati, 1996; Pitelis, 2007). As a consequence recoverable slack is likely to facilitate experimentation that generates innovation around alternative ways to conduct business that increases the organization's ability to adapt to changing environmental conditions despite formalized controls.

Available slack constitutes unabsorbed resources that are readily available from the firm's cash position and consists of bank balances, marketable securities, short term receivables, etc. It is argued that this provides a higher level of managerial discretion and furnish financial means that otherwise might be hard to get approved (Cyert and March, 1963; Nohria and Gulati, 1996). However, these generic unabsorbed resources are monitored by the treasury function that requires more formal approvals and leaves less discretion to local entities (Voss, Sirdeshmukh and Voss, 2008). Nonetheless, this type of slack allows for relatively quick access to resources in support of development projects even though the release of financial means is expected to undergo some type of formal approval. Everything else being equal, the availability of these additional resources should furnish more alternative business propositions and strategic options (Amit and Schoemaker, 1993; Bromiley, 1991). This ability to generate more viable strategic alternatives should increase corporate maneuverability and thereby enhance the ability to adapt to strategic risk events caused by environmental changes.

Potential slack constitutes the ability to access external funding, such as bank borrowing and securities issues, and thus makes up part of the generic unabsorbed resources in the firm that would need formal approval and more extensive preparations to be released (Bourgeois and Singh, 1983; Voss et al., 2008). These financing sources constitute the funding reservoir discussed in much of the finance literature as the means to support investment in profitable business development projects (e.g., Froot et al. 1993; Smithson and Simkins, 2005). We can interpret this as a way to execute the firm's strategic options that will require an initial investment layout to be set in motion (McGrath and Nerkar, 2004; O'Brien, 2003). Hence, the availability of additional capital resources from the market by maintaining relatively low financial leverage gives the firm more leeway to exercise strategic options, i.e., investment propositions, when environmental conditions suggest that it is advantageous to do so (Luehrman, 1998; Miller, 1998). Hence, the availability of potential slack makes it possible to execute alternative business propositions once they have been developed and thereby enhance adaptability to changes in the environment.

Recoverable slack provides more discretion to reallocate resources for new innovative purposes by reshuffling internal budget allocations at the local business unit level (Cyert and March, 1963; Sharfman et al., 1988; Voss et al., 2008). Hence, it can provide room to take immediate initiatives in response to changing conditions, experiment, and learn from these activities (Keegan and Turner, 2002; Wayne and Rubinstein, 1992). Available slack is made up by cash and liquid assets that can fund more extensive or expansive business activities. However, access to these resources is typically monitored by the treasurer and thus requires formal approval to be deployed (Nohria and Gulati, 1996; Voss et al., 2008). Potential slack represents the firm's borrowing capacity in the bank and capital markets as the means to implement larger business propositions. However, access to this funding typically requires substantial legal documentation, sign-off by corporate executives and may even require formal board approval, i.e., the deployment of such resources is more time consuming and demanding (Bourgeois and Singh, 1983; Voss et al., 2008). In short, recoverable slack are resources more readily accessible for grass roots initiatives responding to current changes, whereas available and potential slack are the potential funding sources that can help expand these initiatives as they evolve into larger and more important organizational activities.

H3: Higher levels of recoverable, available, and potential slack are positively related to the firm's effective risk management capabilities.

H4: Recoverable, available, and potential slack have positive interactive effects on the firm's effective risk management capabilities.

Availability of slack can shield the firm's operating core from exogenous changes in the environment but may thereby create complacency and ignorance among organizational actors that eliminate or reduce responsive behaviors (Bansal, 2003; Thompson, 1967; Yasai-Ardekani, 1986). So, slack can reduce managerial risk-taking and cause poor responsiveness, operational inefficiencies, and suboptimization (Palmer and Wiseman, 1999; Singh, 1986). Hence, excessive slack may induce risk aversion that reduces exploratory initiatives (Mishina, Pollock and Porac, 2004). Furthermore, slack may represent wasteful use of resources where organizational agents assume fringe benefits as they act in their own self-interest (Jensen and Meckling, 1976; Williamson, 1964). In short, the potential risk management effects of slack seem to have limitations.

H5: The positive relationships between recoverable, available, and potential slack resources and effective risk management capabilities are nonlinear.

In the following, we outline an empirical study devised to test the proposed hypotheses and present the results from the associated analyses.

Methodology

Data and measures

The data for the study was extracted from Compustat over the 20 years from 1991 to 2010 including companies across all industries but excluding firms in the regulated financial sector (6000 < SIC < 6999) and diverse conglomerates (SIC > 8800). The time period was chosen because it covers a decade (1991–2000) of economic growth and global expansion for which a number of empirical studies exist followed by a decade (2001–2010) of turbulence and two economic recessions. Given the implied volatility of the business environment, the 20-year period 1991–2010 is considered suitable for a study of potential risk management effects. We excluded firms with total sales below US$50 million, which is set as the limit for small to medium-sized enterprise firms (SMEs). Hence, the accessible dataset comprised 3,436 companies with an average of 7 years of panel data available on key variables. The proposed risk management relationships expressed in Hypotheses 1 and 2 were analyzed in multiple regressions using annual performance (PER_t) as the dependent variable and effective risk management (ERM_{t-5}) over the preceding five-year period and its interaction terms with slack variables from the current year ($ERM_{t-5} \times SLACK_t$) as independent variables. The regressions were controlled for industry performance in the current period ($PER_{industry, t}$) and included a number of other control variables ($CONTROL_t$) for the same year.

$$PER_t = \alpha + \beta_1 ERM_{t-5} + \beta_2 PER_{industry, t} + \beta_3 ERM_{t-5} \times SLACK_t + \beta_4 CONTROL_t \quad (1)$$

The potential antecedents to risk management as expressed in Hypotheses 3, 4 and 5 were analyzed in multiple regressions using effective risk management (ERM_{t-5}) as the dependent variable and different measures of slack ($SLACK_{t-5}$), interaction terms between different types of slack ($SLACK\{X\}_{t-5} * SLACK\{Y\}$), and slack measures to the second power ($\{SLACK_{t-5}\}^2$) as independent variables. The regressions included other control variables ($CONTROL_{t-5}$) and all variables were calculated across the same five-year periods.

$$ERM_{t-5} = \alpha + \beta_1 SLACK_{t-5} + \beta_2 SLACK\{X\}_{t-5} \times SLACK\{Y\}_{t-5}$$
$$+ \beta_3 \{SLACK_{t-5}\}^2 + \beta_4 CONTROL_{t-5} \quad (2)$$

Performance was measured as return on assets (ROA) for the full year calculated as the annual net income divided by average assets over the period determined as the simple mean of assets at the beginning of the year and at yearend. Tobin's q was included as an alternative performance measure and calculated as market value of equity divided by the book value of equity to indicate how the market values the company in relation to the replacement cost of the productive assets. The ERM measure was determined as the coefficient of variation in corporate sales divided by the standard deviation in corporate performance outcomes both calculated over consecutive 5-year periods. For this purpose corporate performance was defined as earnings and cash flow returns measured as ROA and cash flow return on invested capital (CFROI) respectively. ROA was determined as net profit divided by total assets and CFROI was determined as net cash flows for the year divided by total invested capital.

The variability in corporate sales over a given period will capture the direct influences of exogenous strategic risk factors, including things like economic shocks and abrupt competitor moves, whereas earnings and cash flow volatility reflects the firm's ability to dampen the impact of these events on performance outcomes during the same period. Hence, the ratio of variation in sales divided by the earnings volatility has been adopted as an indicator of risk management effectiveness (Andersen, 2008, 2009). Here, we used two measures for ERM, one based on the volatility in annual earnings development expressed as ROA and another based on cash flow volatility expressed as CFROI. This is broadly consistent with measures adopted in strategic management based on accounting returns, such as, standard deviation on return on equity (ROE), ROA, return on investment (ROI), etc. (e.g., Bromiley et al., 2006; Miller and Reuer, 1996) and the use of the standard deviation in cash flow returns in finance inspired studies (e.g., Miller and Chen, 2003; Minton and Schrand, 1999).

The risk management process implied by the ERM construct captures an organizational capacity to deal with all major risk events including environmental hazards, financial turmoil, operational disruptions, and strategic incidents like changes in competitive structure, technology shifts, new regulations, etc. The variability in realized returns, e.g., ROA, indicates performance after the firm has responded to the exogenous risk events and thus indicates the extent to which cash and earnings flows have been stabilized through the influence of good risk management capabilities. Incidentally, the risk measure will also capture adverse effects caused by endogenous risk events within the firm, such as operational disruptions, technological breakdowns, processing errors, human failures, administrative mistakes, fraud, etc. Since net profit, and thereby return on assets, is influenced by developments in total revenues and expenditures, the measure of the ERM variable indicates whether the firm has been able to adapt its current costs to changes in corporate sales.

The net profit is determined as total revenues minus total costs, i.e., Profit{P} = Revenues{R} − Cost{C}. So, the variance in net profits is affected by variations in the revenue generation and in the cost development. That is, the standard deviation in profitability is affected by the standard deviation in revenues, the standard deviation in costs, and their inverse covariation between the two.[3] Hence, the more revenues and costs covary over time the lower will be the variation in profits and by extension the variation in ROA. This means that a simple interpretation of the risk management process is the firm's ability to engage in cost-effective responses to dramatic changes in sales where new initiatives can be taken quickly without incurring excessive incremental costs as market demand expands and find alternative ways in a costless manner when the market contracts. This reflects effective strategic response capabilities under conditions of unpredictable changes in the competitive environment where the adaptation of internal processes that modify use of resources to accommodate responsive initiatives is done in cost-efficient ways (Bettis and Hitt, 1995).

ERM may be affected by a number of things, including the ability to innovate and search for new business opportunities within the organization that can be driven by the availability of slack resources and internal cash generation. Recoverable slack is determined as total expenses devoted to operational activities measured as sales, general, and administrative expenses divided by total sales (Bourgeois and Singh, 1983; Miller and Leiblein, 1996; Reuer and Leiblein, 2000). This is often referred to as the firm's SGA ratio. Available slack indicates the organization's ability to meet short-term resource commitments and is measured by the current ratio equal to current assets divided by current liabilities (Bourgeois and Singh, 1983). We also refer to this as the firm's liquidity reserves. Potential slack is captured by the debt-to-equity ratio measured as total long-term debt divided by shareholders' equity consisting of paid-in capital and retained earnings. The debt-equity ratio has been adopted in a variety of studies as a measure of financial slack (Bourgeois and Singh, 1983; Bromiley, 1991). To be more exact, we use the equity–debt ratio here to measure the firm's capital reserves because it is a positive indicator of the ability to obtain new funding from the external debt and capital markets.

We included a number of control variables in the regressions. The performance regressions included industry performance measured as average performance of peers within the firm's two-digit SIC code industry to control for systematic differences in industry performance. Organizational size reflects prior success and may provide the firm with additional leeway to cope with external shocks and periods of adverse conditions (Aldrich, 1999; Sharfman et al., 1988) and was measured as the natural logarithm of total sales to reduce effects of skewed data. Investment intensity reflects the level of capital expenditures assumed by the firm compared to the total assets and captures the firm's ongoing investment in business opportunities. Autonomous investments measure the free cash flows available to firm compared to total capital expenditures and thus reflects a certain leeway to make ongoing investment in responsive initiatives (Minton and Schrand, 1999; Opler, Pinkowitz, Stulz and Williamson, 1999). Finally, all the measures of performance, effective risk management, organizational slack and control variables were standardized across two-digit SIC code firms to eliminate industry specific effects (McGrath and Nerkar, 2004; O'Brien, 2003).

Analysis

The hypotheses were tested in stepwise regressions incorporating standardized interaction terms where one set of regressions analyzed risk management effects against performance and another set of regressions analyzed the antecedents to effective risk management (Aiken and West, 1991; Kleinbaum, Kupper, Mullerm and Nizam, 1998). A number of robustness checks were carried out to test the sensitivity of results to alternatives variable measures, different data trimming techniques, sample splits, and potential endogeneity problems that might cause biased parameter estimates. Hence, we also applied two-stage least square (2SLS) regressions to determine ERM variables as predictors in the performance equations, which is considered appropriate when the independent variables may be correlated with the error terms of the dependent variable (Theil, 1971).

Results

Descriptive statistics and correlation coefficients on key variables are reported in Table 23.1.

The initial results from the stepwise multiple regression analyses are presented in Table 23.2, where the regression coefficients against return on assets and Tobin's q as dependent variables are reported for comparative purposes. It is apparent from these results that ERM has a significant positive relationship to the lagged performance measures of ROA after controlling for industry performance, company size, financial leverage, and other influential factors. The same result prevails when Tobin's q is used as performance measure even though the sample size is somewhat smaller due to missing observations. These results are consistent with Hypothesis 1. Further analyses were conducted to test the robustness of results with different data trimming techniques applied. Hence, we first excluded observations with performance below and above the mean value plus and minus three times the standard deviation and subsequently Winsorized the data around 3 times the standard deviation. This did not alter the results.

We repeated the regressions using the alternative measure of ERM based on volatility of CFROI, but this did not change the findings. We conducted split-sample analysis based on data from the high growth decade 1991–2000 and the turbulent decade 2001–2010 with periodic

Table 23.1 Descriptive statistics and correlations

	Mean	S.D.	1	2	3	4	5	6	7	8
1 Return on assets	0.027	0.241	–	–	–	–	–	–	–	–
2 Tobin's q	1.821	2.078	0.426**	–	–	–	–	–	–	–
3 Effective risk management	4.153	7.816	0.178*	0.094	–	–	–	–	–	–
4 Organizational size	7.744	5.481	0.199*	0.239**	0.082	–	–	–	–	–
5 Capital reserves	0.350	0.476	0.020	0.085	0.080	0.038	–	–	–	–
6 Liquidity reserves	1.563	1.642	–0.036	0.139+	–0.088	0.007	0.024	–	–	–
7 Sales, general & adm.	0.046	0.437	0.067	0.086	0.044	0.008	0.333**	0.072	–	–
8 Investment intensity	0.096	0.544	0.008	0.162*	–0.052	0.006	0.006	–0.059	–0.050	–
9 Autonomous investment	0.567	0.859	0.112+	0.035	0.012	0.056	0.200**	0.285**	–0.056	–0.070

$+p < 0.10$; $*p < 0.05$; $**p < 0.01$.

Table 23.2 Regression analyses – performance effects of effective risk management

Dependent variable	Return on assets			Tobin's q		
Number of observations	32,313	6,067	6,067	21,095	4,658	4,658
Number of groups	3,378	897	897	2,625	737	737
Intercept	−.044***	.045*	.047*	.521***	3.955***	3.915***
	(−4.37)	(2.25)	(2.32)	(3.55)	(18.43)	(18.24)
Effective risk management (ERM)	.009***	.009***	.008***	.051***	.088***	.082***
	(16.39)	(6.01)	(5.36)	(7.02)	(6.33)	(5.73)
Industry performance	.923***	.984***	.981***	.875***	.896***	.892***
	(34.65)	(23.11)	(23.09)	(31.73)	(17.22)	(17.14)
Organizational size (ln[sales])	.007***	−.004	−.004	−.054*	−.328***	−.322***
	(4.78)	(−1.40)	(−1.36)	(−2.56)	(−10.56)	(−10.36)
Sales, general and adm. (SGA ratio)	–	−.065***	−.064***	–	−.344***	−.339***
		(−22.63)	(−22.25)		(−12.61)	(−12.33)
Liquidity reserves (Current ratio)	–	.014***	.013***	–	.018	.019
		(6.87)	(6.54)		(1.02)	(111)
Capital reserves (Equity–debt ratio)	.035***	.033***	.032***	.139***	.106***	.116***
	(22.81)	(16.42)	(2.05)	(10.45)	(5.41)	(5.72)
Investment intensity (Cap. exp./assets)	–	−.001 (− .49)	.001 (.67)	–	.150***	.156***
					(8.32)	(8.56)
Autonomous inv. (Cash flow/cap. exp.)	–	.006***	.010***	–	.095***	.106***
		(3.33)	(4.45)		(5.39)	(4.93)

Dependent variable	Return on assets			Tobin's q		
ERM*Sales, general & adm. costs	–	–	.006***(4.08)	–	–	–.009 (– .61)
ERM*Liquidity reserves	–	–	–.003 (–1.05)	–	–	.035* (2.51)
ERM*Capital reserves	–	–	–.001 (– .67)	–	–	.012 (.76)
ERM*Autonomous investment	–	–	.006** (3.15)	–	–	.042** (2.49)
R-squared within	.154	.231	.235	.159	.146	.149
R-squared between	.167	.130	.135	.134	.012	.009
R-squared overall	.171	.130	.135	.139	.000	.000
F-significance	.000	.000	.000	.000	.000	.000

recessions. Although there were some modifications in the regression coefficients the analytical results were not materially different from those reported in either of the two subperiods. It should be noted that the number of observations is significantly reduced as more variables are included in the regressions due to lack of complete data coverage, and this may call for more refined techniques to the analyses. Nonetheless, the general result remains robust in all the regressions.

The regression coefficients on the interaction terms between ERM and the different slack variables show mixed results. Hence, the interaction between ERM and sales, general and administrative costs (the SGA ratio) has a significant positive relationship to return on assets, and the interaction between ERM and liquidity reserves (the current ratio) has a significant positive relationship to Tobin's q. While this is not a clear cut result, it seems to indicate that some recoverable slack may support responsive initiatives and thereby enhance effective risk responses as well as some liquidity can help the execution of value-creating business opportunities as part of the effective risk responses. The interaction between ERM and autonomous investment as an indicator of incremental leeway for responsive investment has significant positive relationships to both performance measures, which provides some support for Hypothesis 2.

The results from the second regression analyzing potential antecedents to ERM are shown in Table 23.3. It should be noted that the number of observations is vastly reduced in these analyses due to incomplete data and because we apply the analysis to datasets across consecutive 5-year periods. The results show that resources available in the form of allocated sales, general and administrative expenses (the SGA ratio) have a negative first-order relationship to ERM and that only capital reserves (the equity–debt ratio) have a direct positive relationship to ERM as proposed by the conventional risk management literature (Moelbroek, 2002). This provides weak support for Hypothesis 3.

The interaction terms between sales, general and administrative expenses (the SGA ratio), and capital reserves (the equity–debt ratio) has a significant positive relationship to ERM thus indicating that initial development of responsive initiatives can enhance risk management effectiveness if there is potential slack available to fund implementation. This reasoning is supported by a positive interaction effect between capital reserves and autonomous investment as an indicator of leeway to invest in business opportunities. These results lend some support for Hypothesis 4.

Table 23.3 Regression analyses – risk management antecedents

Dependent variable	Effective risk management (ERM)	
Number of observations	4,112	3,203
Number of groups	694	576
Intercept	−.641**	−1.858***
	(−2.52)	(−5.62)
Organizational size (ln[sales])	.008*	.025***
	(2.39)	(5.63)
Sales, general and adm. (SGA ratio)	−.443***	−.352***
	(−7.69)	(−4.71)
Liquidity reserves (Current ratio)	.020	.101
	(0.43)	(1.57)
Capital reserves (Equity–debt ratio)	.205***	.162***
	(5.01)	(3.22)
Investment intensity (Cap. exp./assets)	−	−.059
		(1.06)
Autonomous inv. (Cash flow/cap. exp.)	−	.216***
		(3.18)
SGA ratio* SGA ratio	.131***	.125***
	(4.54)	(3.73)
Liquidity reserves* Liquidity reserves	−.042**	−.058***
	(−2.90)	(−3.59)
Capital reserves* Capital reserves	.011	.001 (.03)
	(0.60)	
Liquidity reserves* SGA ratio	−	−.020 (− .35)
Capital reserves* Liquidity reserves	−	.006
		(1.46)
SGA ratio* Capital reserves	−	.035*
		(2.51)
Investment intensity*Autonomous inv.	.0006	.019 (.38)
	(1.50)	
Capital reserves*Autonomous inv.	.064+	.121***
	(1.64)	(2.74)
R-squared within	.032	.041
R-squared between	.044	.059
R-squared overall	.029	.034
F-significance	.000	.000

+ $p < 0.10$; * $p < 0.05$; ** $p < 0.01$; *** $p < 0.001$.

Finally, we see that while the first-order direct effect of sales, general, and administrative costs (the SGA ratio) is negative, the second-order effect is significantly positive as a potential indicator that sufficient recoverable slack may drive innovation and responsive initiatives to enhance effective risk responses. However, the second-order effect of liquidity reserves (the current ratio) is significant and negative, which indicates a diminishing risk effect from excessive cash positions. There is no significant second-order effect of capital reserves (the equity–debt ratio) but only a significant positive direct first-order relationship to effective risk management. While these results may hint the potential contours of nonlinear relationships between slack and effective risk management, there is no clear support for Hypothesis 5.

Discussion and conclusion

The reported results based on analyses of a comprehensive updated dataset support the notion that an ability to dampen the impacts from exogenous risk events so the corporate cash flow and earnings volatility is reduced will be associated with higher performance outcomes. This study reports on effects related to a contemporary time period including the turbulent decade 2001–2010 that comprised two interim periods of economic recession and thus complements prior risk management studies. Based on a time-lagged effects analysis, the positive relationship between ERM and the economic value-creating potential of the firm is found to be robust against alternative performance and risk measures, different data trimming techniques and regression analytical approaches. More interestingly perhaps, the findings are also robust across two different economic subperiods the high growth globalization decade 1991–2000 and the subsequent recession and crisis ridden decade 2001–2010. Hence, we find consistency with risk management results reported in prior time periods (e.g., Andersen, 2008, 2009; Smithson and Simkin, 2005).

Prior studies investigating the direct effects of adopting formal enterprise risk management approaches have so far been inconclusive (e.g., Beasley, Pagach and Warr, 2008). However, here we report significant and robust relationships between effective risk management capabilities and economic returns in subsequent periods over a recent period of 20 years. That is, firms that responded effectively to exogenous risk events throughout this time period and thereby reduced the adverse downside effects were apparently able to extend their value creation potential. Yet, the analysis cannot say precisely what constituted the main drivers of the underlying strategic response capabilities. However, the study provides an initial search for important moderating influences from different forms of organizational slack on the effective risk management outcomes and reports on a preliminary investigation of related antecedents to effective risk management.

While this search is inconclusive at this stage, we find strong hints that some availability of slack resources provide the basis for innovation and responsive initiatives and that these can be important for the ability to create business opportunities that enhance corporate maneuverability. Furthermore, maintaining a certain level of self-generated cash flow and potential financial slack seem to provide leeway to execute business opportunities when changing environmental conditions call for these kinds of adaptive business responses. However, more detailed analysis is still required to uncover explicitly how this underlying dynamic operates.

These initial results seem to suggest that effective risk management capabilities relate to availability of sufficient resources to develop innovative opportunities that enable the firm to respond to changing conditions in the competitive environment. The findings uncover a potential tension between management control and corporate entrepreneurial perspectives where the availability of sufficient, although not excessive, slack resources is a prerequisite for effective risk management outcomes (Jensen, 1986, 1993). The incremental insights from this study suggest that these are not either or considerations. There is an urge for balanced solutions, which points to a need for more refined analyses into the intriguing and important relationships between resource availability, corporate entrepreneurship, risk management, performance, and corporate longevity.

It is argued that risk reduction allows the firm to reduce expensive equity capital needed to support operating risk exposures and where effective risk management is seen as a substitute for capital reserves (e.g., Nocco and Stulz, 2006). Hence, a major goal (and advantage) of risk management supposedly is that it can reduce waste and thereby save scarce capital resources and that this should be an important part of the job of a corporate risk officer (CRO) and top

433

management. Hence, a prior study found that the appointment of CROs is more likely in firms with high financial leverage and poor risk management outcomes (Liebenberg and Hoyt, 2003). Another study of CRO announcements found that a common antecedent includes volatile operating cash flows, high stock volatility, and CEOs with incentives based on stock options (Pagach and Warr, 2011). This may suggest that adoption of formal risk management practices often is driven by aggressive CEOs who (or possibly their boards) feel a need to contain potential excessive downside losses.

However, as this study suggests reducing capital buffers can have potential adverse risk management effects. That is, if potential slack is reduced to a very low level it may reduce the organization's ability to take autonomous initiatives and respond effectively to new risk events. The conventional risk management view is one-sided and inflexible with the aim to avoid downside risk and reduce resource waste. However, the key to enable effective responses to uncertain strategic risks is the availability of slack that induces learning from local responses and builds it into viable business opportunities in the changing business environment.

This means that firms need to take initial probing risks to create opportunities needed for strategic renewal and effective responses to unexpected and unpredictable competitive developments. So effective risk management is the process where individual decision makers assume calculated risk within areas of expertise and deep business insights in order to develop effective responses to future challenges (e.g., Culp, 2001). Hence, risk management in practice is not really conceived to reduce all risks but rather to assume the necessary risks that enable opportunistic responses to emerge (e.g., Adams, 1995). Hence, some slack must be invested in innovative efforts to create new strategic options and the availability of financial slack makes it possible to execute these strategic options when the competitive conditions change.

In short, effective risk management does seem to have a significant positive relationship to organizational performance outcomes and corporate value creation, and this result appears to be robust against alternative measures, data refinements, and time periods. Corporate risk management capabilities can be enhanced by availability of different types of slack resources in the form of recoverable, available, and potential slack as well as self-generating financial means. Slack resources can provide leverage for responsive initiatives and engage in needed development activities that provide strategic choices under environmental uncertainty. However, the limited data availability in the updated datasets calls for more refined studies to uncover the details of the dynamic risk management process that lies underneath.

Notes

1 An earlier version of this article was presented at the Strategic Management Society Annual International Conference in Prague, October 2012. Nominated as SMS Best Conference Paper for Practice Implications.
2 Oliviero Roggi, University of Florence and New York University, Leonard N. Stern School of Business; Torben Juul Andersen, Copenhagen Business School.
3 $\sigma_P = [(\omega_R \sigma_R)^2 + (\omega_C \sigma_C)^2 - 2(\rho_{R,C} \, \omega_R \, \omega_C \, \sigma_R \, \sigma_C)]^{1/2}$, where σ_P is the standard deviation in net profit (P), σ_R is the standard deviation in total revenues (R), σ_C is the standard deviation in total costs (C), $\rho_{R,C}$ is the correlation coefficient between revenues and costs, and ω_R and ω_C are the relative weights of revenues against costs. Ideally $\omega_R > \omega_C$ but they are often of almost equal size, which simplifies the equation to: $\sigma_P = [\sigma_R^2 + \sigma_C^2 - 2\rho_{R,C} \, \sigma_R \, \sigma_C)]^{1/2}$.

References

Adams J. 1995. *Risk*. Routledge, London.
Agarwal R, Helfat C. 2009. Strategic renewal of organizations. *Organization Science* 20, 281–293.

Aiken LS, West SG. 1991. *Multiple Regression: Testing and Interpreting Interactions.* Sage, Newbury Park, California.

Aldrich HE. 1999. *Organizations Evolving.* Sage, Newbury Park, California.

Amit R, Schoemaker PJH. 1993. Strategic assets and organizational rent. *Strategic Management Journal* 14, 33–46.

Andersen TJ. 2008. The performance relationship of effective risk management: Exploring the firm-specific investment rationale. *Long Range Planning* 41(2), 155–176.

Andersen TJ. 2009. Effective risk management: Exploring effects of innovation and capital structure. *Journal of Strategy and Management* 2(4), 352–379.

Andersen TJ. 2012. Multinational risk and performance outcomes: Effects of knowledge intensity and industry context. *International Business Review* 21(2), 139–152.

Andersen TJ, Denrell J, Bettis RA. 2007. Strategic responsiveness and Bowman's risk-return paradox. *Strategic Management Journal* 28, 407–429.

Bansal P. 2003. From issues to actions: The importance of individual concerns and organizational values in responding to natural environmental issues. *Organization Science* 14(5), 510–527.

Beasley MS, Pagach D, Warr R. 2008. The information conveyed in hiring announcements of senior executives overseeing enterprise-wide risk management processes. *Journal of Accounting, Auditing and Finance* 23(3), 311–332.

Bettis RA, Hitt MA. 1995. The new competitive landscape. *Strategic Management Journal* 16, 7–19.

Bourgeois LJ. 1981. On the measurement of organizational slack. *Academy of Management Review* 6, 29–39.

Bourgeois LJ, Singh JV. 1983. Organizational slack and political behavior within top management teams. *Academy of Management Proceedings* 43–47.

Bromiley P. 1991. Testing a causal model of corporate risk taking and performance. *Academy of Management Journal* 134, 37–59.

Bromiley P. 2005. *The Behavioral Foundations of Strategic Management.* Blackwell, Malden, MA.

Bromiley P, Miller K, Rau D. 2006. Risk in strategic management research. In Hitt MA, Freeman RE, Harrison JS. (Eds.), *The Blackwell Handbook of Strategic Management* (pp. 259–288). Malden, MA: Blackwell.

Chen CJ, Huang YF. 2010. Creative workforce density, organizational slack, and innovation performance. *Journal of Business Research* 63, 411–417.

Culp CL. 2001. *The Risk Management Process: Business Strategy and Tactics.* Wiley, New York.

Cyert RM, March JG. 1963. *A Behavioral Theory of the Firm.* Prentice Hall, Englewood Cliffs, NJ.

Damanpour F. 1991. Organizational innovation: A meta-analysis of effects of determinants and moderators. *Academy of Management Journal* 34, 555–590.

Damanpour F, Evan WM. 1984. Organizational innovation and performance: The problem of "organizational lag". *Administrative Science Quarterly* 29, 392–409.

Damodaran A. 2008. *Strategic Risk Taking: A Framework for Risk Management.* Wharton School, Upper Saddle River, NJ.

Fiegenbaum A, Hart S, Schendel D. 1996. Strategic reference point theory. *Strategic Management Journal* 17(2), 219–235.

Froot KA, Scharfstein DS, Stein JC. 1993. Risk management: Coordinating corporate investment and financing policies. *Journal of Finance* 48, 1629–1658.

Greve HR. 2003. A behavioral theory of R&D expenditures and innovations: Evidence from shipbuilding. *Academy of Management Journal* 46, 685–702.

Helfat CE, Finkelstein S, Mitchell W, Peteraf MA, Singh H, Teece DJ, Winter SG. 2007. *Dynamic Capabilities: Understanding Strategic Change in Organizations.* Blackwell, Malden, MA.

Jensen MC. 1986. Agency costs of free cash flow, corporate finance, and takeovers. *American Economic Review* 76, 323–329.

Jensen MC. 1993. The modern industrial revolution, exit, and the failure of internal control systems. *Journal of Finance* 48, 831–880.

Jensen MC, Meckling WH. 1976. Theory of the firm: Managerial behavior, agency cost, and ownership structure. *Journal of Financial Economics* 3, 305–360.

Judge WQ, Fryxell GE, Dooley RS. 1997. The new task of R&D management: Creating goal directed communities for innovation. *California Management Review* 39, 72–85.

Keegan A, Turner JR. 2002. The management of innovation in project-based firms. *Long Range Planning* 35, 367–388.

Kleinbaum DG, Kupper LK, Mullerm KE, Nizam A. 1998. *Applied Regression Analysis and Other Multivariate Methods* (3rd ed.). Duxbury Press, Pacific Grove, CA.

Knight FH. 2006. *Risk, Uncertainty and Profit*. Dover, Mineola, NY. (first published in 1921)

Kogut B, Kulatilaka N. 2001. Capabilities as real options. *Organization Science* 12, 744–758.

Kraatz MS, Zajac EJ. 2001. How organizational resources affect strategic change and performance in turbulent environments: Theory and evidence. *Organization Science* 12, 632–657.

Lawson MB. 2001. In praise of slack: Time is of the essence. *Academy of Management Executive* 15, 125–135.

Levinthal D, March JG. 1981. A model of adaptive organizational search. *Journal of Economic Behavior and Organization* 2, 307–333.

Liebenberg AP, Hoyt RE. 2003. The determinants of enterprise risk management: Evidence from the appointment of chief risk officers. *Risk Management and Insurance Review* 6, 37–52.

Loch CH, DeMeyer A, Pich MT. 2006. *Managing the Unknown: A New Approach to Managing High Uncertainty and Risk in Projects*. Wiley, Hoboken, NJ.

Luehrman TA. 1998. Strategy as a portfolio of real options. *Harvard Business Review* 76(6), 89–99.

March JG. 1988. Variable risk preferences and adaptive aspirations. *Journal of Economic Behavior and Organizations* 9, 5–24.

March JG. 1995. The future, disposable organizations and the rigidities of imagination. *Organization* 2, 427–440.

March JG, Shapira Z. 1987. Managerial perspectives on risk and risk taking. *Management Science* 33, 1404–1418.

March JG, Shapira Z. 1992. Variable risk preferences and the focus of attention. *Psychological Review* 99, 172–183.

McGrath RG, Nerkar A. 2004. Real options reasoning and a new look at the R&D investment strategies of pharmaceutical firms. *Strategic Management Journal* 25, 1–21.

Merton RC. 2005. You have more capital than you think. *Harvard Business Review* 83(11), 84–94.

Miller KD. 1998. Economic exposure and integrated risk management. *Strategic Management Journal* 19, 497–514.

Miller KD, Chen W. 2003. Risk and firms' costs. *Strategic Organization* 1, 355–382.

Miller KD, Leiblein M. 1996. Corporate risk-return relations: Returns variability versus downside risk. *Academy of Management Journal* 39, 91–122.

Miller KD, Reuer JJ. 1996. Measuring organizational downside risk. *Strategic Management Journal* 17, 671–691.

Minton B, Schrand C. 1999. The impact of cash flow volatility on discretionary investment and the costs of debt and equity financing. *Journal of Financial Economics* 54, 423–460.

Mishina Y, Pollock TG, Porac JF. 2004. Are more resources always better for growth? Resource stickiness in market and product expansion. *Strategic Management Journal* 25, 1179–1197.

Moelbroek L. 2002. The promise and challenge of integrated risk management. *Risk Management and Insurance Review* 5, 55–66.

Myers S. 1977. Determinants of corporate borrowing. *Journal of Financial Economics* 5, 147–175.

Nocco BW, Stulz RM. 2006. Enterprise risk management: Theory and practice. *Journal of Applied Corporate Finance* 18(4), 8–20.

Nohria N, Gulati R. 1996. Is slack good or bad for innovation? *Academy of Management Journal* 39, 1245–1264.

O'Brien JP. 2003. The capital structure implications of pursuing a strategy of innovation. *Strategic Management Journal* 24, 415–432.

Opler TC, Pinkowitz L, Stulz R, Williamson R. 1999. The determinants of and implications of corporate cash holdings. *Journal of Financial Economics* 52, 3–46.

Pagach D, Warr R. 2011. The characteristics of firms that hire chief risk officers. *Journal of Risk and Insurance* 78(1), 185–211.

Palmer T, Wiseman R. 1999. Decoupling risk taking from income stream uncertainty: A holistic model of risk. *Strategic Management Journal* 20, 1037–1062.

Penrose ET. 1995. *The Theory of the Growth of the Firm*. Oxford University Press, Oxford. (first published in 1959)

Pitelis CN. 2007. A behavioral resource-based view of the firm: The synergy of Cyert and March (1963) and Penrose (1959). *Organization Science* 18(3), 478–490.

Porter ME. 1996. What is strategy? *Harvard Business Review* 74(6), 61–78.

Power M. 2009. The risk management of nothing. *Accounting, Organizations and Society* 34, 849–855.

Reuer JJ, Leiblein MJ. 2000. Downside risk implications of multinationality and international joint ventures. *Academy of Management Journal* 43, 203–214.

Scott SG, Bruce RA. 1994. Determinants of innovative behavior: A path model of individual innovation in the workplace. *Academy of Management Journal* 37, 580–607.

Sharfman M, Wolf G, Chase R, Tansik D. 1988. Antecedents of organizational slack. *Academy of Management Review* 13, 601–614.

Singh JV. 1986. Performance, slack and risk-taking in organizational decision making. *Academy of Management Journal* 29, 562–585.

Slywotzky AJ. 2007. *The Upside: How to Turn Your Greatest Threat Into Your Biggest Growth Opportunity*. Capstone, Chichester.

Smithson C, Simkins BJ. 2005. Does risk management add value? A survey of the evidence. *Journal of Applied Corporate Finance* 17(3), 8–17.

Stulz RM. 1990. Managerial discretion and optimal financing policies. *Journal of Financial Economics* 26, 3–27.

Stulz RM. 2003. *Risk Management & Derivatives*. Thomson South-Western, Mason, OH.

Teece DJ. 2007. Explicating dynamic capabilities: The nature and microfoundations of (sustainable) enterprise performance. *Strategic Management Journal* 28, 1319–1350.

Teece DJ, Pisano G, Shuen O. 1997. Dynamic capabilities and strategic management. *Strategic Management Journal* 18, 509–533.

Theil H. 1971. *Principles of Econometrics*. North-Holland Publishing, Amsterdam.

Thompson JD. 1967. *Organizations in Action*. McGraw-Hill, New York.

Thompson JD. 2008. *Organizations in Action: Social Science Base of Administrative Theory* (6th printing). Transaction, New Brunswick, NJ. (first published in 1967)

Van de Ven A. 1986. Central problems in the management of innovation. *Management Science* 32, 590–607.

Voss GB, Sirdeshmukh D, Voss ZG. 2008. The effects of slack resources and environmental threat on product exploration and exploitation. *Academy of Management Journal* 51, 147–164.

Wang H, Barney JB, Reuer JJ. 2003. Stimulating firm-specific investment through risk management. *Long Range Planning* 36, 49–59.

Wayne SJ, Rubinstein D. 1992. Extending game theoretic propositions about slack and scarcity in managerial decision making. *Human Relations* 45, 525–536.

Williamson OE. 1964. *The Economics of Discretionary Behavior: Managerial Objectives in a Theory of the Firm*. Prentice Hall, Englewood Cliffs, NJ.

Yasai-Ardekani M. 1986. Structural adaptations to environments. *Academy of Management Review* 11, 9–21.

Zollo M, Winter SG. 2002. Deliberate learning and the evolution of dynamic capabilities. *Organization Science* 13, 339–351.

24

Creating value through strategic risk management

Kim B. Staking[1]

Abstract

Corporations expend considerable resources in establishing strategic risk management programs, establishing risk tolerance levels, developing risk cultures, and transferring risk. Practitioners view these as value enhancing, eliminating the impact of stochastic shocks. Notwithstanding, a widespread, naïve interpretation of modern portfolio theory considers such investments as costly attempts to reduce idiosyncratic risk, costlessly eliminated via shareholder diversification. This chapter notes some limitations inherent in Modern Portfolio Theory (MPT) analysis with respect to insurance and risk management expenditures and reviews efficiencies associated with risk management and risk transfer for midrange losses. Finally, the chapter focuses on the impact of significant losses (localized black swan events) on a corporation's cost of capital, noting increased information asymmetries, increased leverage and the weighted average cost of capital, and the associated increase in the cost of financial distress. Risk transfer/insurance is viewed as an option to reduce information asymmetries while providing immediate financial resources preventing major distortions in capital structure.

Key words: Corporate demand for insurance; localized black swan events; risk transfer; optimal capital structure; risk management culture; enterprise risk management.

This chapter explores the generation of firm value through strategic risk management. As the majority of the chapters in this book focus on financial risk management, the focus in this chapter is on what is commonly referred to as enterprise risk management,[2] the strategic plans that are established to manage risks associated with stochastic, unexpected events, especially those that have a negative impact on the value of assets, at times significantly. Stochastic risks are those that are largely beyond a firm's control. They include elements such as property and bodily injury risks (related to fire, windstorms, earth movement, flooding, etc.), business income, transportation risks including commercial auto, aviation, etc. Finally, they include losses from operational errors and liability risks (product liability, worker's compensation, employment practices liability, pollution, director's and officer's coverage, etc.). In recent years, transferring risks associated with terrorism, reputational, and cyber risks have figured more prominently in firm's risk management programs. Stochastic risks do not include normal business risk (managing operations, marketing, pricing, overall management, etc.). In the insurance literature, these are often referred to as pure risks as they have only downside potential.[3] They are the known unknowns, and at times, the unknowable unknowns discussed by Nassim Nicholas Taleb in *The Black Swan* (2007).

Pure risks can range from small events (minor glass breakage, business interruption of a few hours or a few days due to a small fire, or a minor worker's compensation claim) to large localized black swan events (major product liability claim, major cyber risks, or catastrophic disasters). In this chapter the latter will be referred to as "localized black swan events." These are not the black swan events that impact the nation or the world, but events that significantly impact a specific firm, potentially leading to severe financial distress or bankruptcy.

In a response to the potential for a localized black swan event, firms have relieved on risk management and risk transfer programs to deal with unforeseen risks as well as those risks that are within their experience. Insurers, with a greater knowledge of and expertise in managing risks have likewise responded in providing new forms of coverage while setting up reinsurance and capital markets instruments (e.g., cat bonds) to deal with some of the known unknowns. Governments have played an important role in reinsuring terrorism risk following 9/11 as the risk profile was in complete flux, stabilizing markets as unknowable unknowns created an insurance crisis.[4] As such, investment of resources in enterprise risk management (including the purchase of insurance where appropriate) is undertaken to create value for the firm. Value can be created directly, where the value is observed on a year-in year-out basis, or indirectly via reducing the cost of debt and/or equity for the firm changing the weighted average cost of capital. There is general agreement that enterprise risk management can serve to reduce or eliminate negative cash flows and/or to modify the frequency and severity distributions of stochastic risks. Sometimes the impact is minor. An investment in safety training programs can reduce injuries or death, thereby reducing related worker's compensation premiums. Others can have major impact on cash flows, such as reducing lawsuits against the firm, cyber attacks, environmental liability, etc.

Motivation

A common interpretation of Modern Portfolio Theory (which I will refer to as the naïve application of MPT) often results in a prescription that firms should not spend scarce resources to reduce idiosyncratic risks (and especially not purchase insurance at rates above the actuarially fair value) as this presumes to violate the stated goal of increasing shareholder value. As shown in Figure 24.1, the diversified investor is indifferent to idiosyncratic risks. Investors are only reward for market risks; thus the cost of capital applied to the firm is determined solely by nondiversifiable risk and not total risk (commonly measured by the standard deviation of portfolio returns). From a shareholder's perspective insurance directly reduces expected returns with no impact on risk. The expenditure of a considerable effort and firm resources in enterprise risk management is similarly viewed as a negative net present value investment from the onset, as idiosyncratic risk is costlessly diversified away.

In general, such criticisms do not take account of the underlying probability distribution of losses. Using the standard Gaussian analysis underlying modern portfolio theory (based on returns following a normal distribution) ignores skewness, kurtosis, and other higher moments of the probability distributions, especially those associated with highly skewed localized black swan events. What is particularly troublesome is not only that numerous academic financial economists teach this without questioning the validity of underlying assumptions, but that their

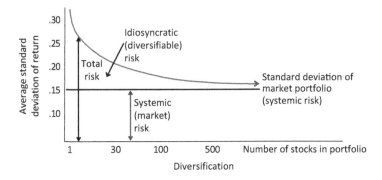

Figure 24.1 Idiosyncratic (diversifiable) vs. systemic risk in a diversified portfolio

undergraduates and MBAs unquestionably accept this naïve version of the MPT as they enter the workforce.

In exploring how strategic risk management creates value, this chapter will address how this naïve application of MPT, which seems to suggest that risk management activities can only reduce value, are fundamentally unsound.

When examined on a deeper level, it is shown that the impact of reducing stochastic risk through risk management and risk transfer mechanisms serves to manage most losses through a corporate-wide risk culture. In addition, for significantly high loss events, these can prevent a rupture in a firm's access to financial markets, a sudden in crease in the weighted average cost of capital (WAAC), while reducing the firm's cost of financial distress and probability of bankruptcy. In essence, the firm can be thought of as insuring its optimal capital structure. As such, insurance serves as a mechanism for providing access to funding at times when financial markets are most needed and least available, whether due to information asymmetry problems or the underinvestment problems associated with a firm's shareholders not being willing to add capital as a major portion of the new funds will benefit creditors (Mayers & Smith, 1987). Both hamper a firm's ability to take advantage of already identified positive net present value investment opportunities, so insurance can also assure firms are more able to invest and reap the associated increased value. Finally, some risk management investments, such as preventing cyber risk and the associated negative impact on a firm's reputation and competitiveness, can clearly be of unmeasured value. Between 2001 and 2014 the cost of reported cyber crime in the United States increased from US$17.8 million to just over US$800 million (Statista, n.d.).

A simple model

Financial economists often focus on understanding incentives and how these influence behavior. Following Leland and Pyle (1997), the problem of enterprise risk management is one of creating an optimal risk management culture within a firm.[5] In equation 1, the value of enterprise risk management (V_{RM}) is a function of a firm's risk management culture (γ) and the cost of enterprise risk management (C_{RM}) based on the selected risk management culture. V_{RM} is the expected (mean) discounted present value of the benefits associated with establishing a risk management culture at level γ. Adding to the Leland and Pyle approach, C_{RM} is the cost of implementing the selected risk culture. Both are observed by senior management. A one-period model would take the form specified in equations 1 and 2. This can easily be extended to a multi-period model.[6]

$$V_{RM} = \frac{1}{1+r}\mu(\gamma) - \lambda \tag{1}$$

$$C_{RM} = \nu(\gamma) \tag{2}$$

In this set of equations, the functions μ and ν are not independent, but depend on the selection of risk culture (γ). It can be assumed that the firm will jointly select a risk management culture and the associated costs to maximize the expected value of risk management. It is assumed that firm value is increasing with the creation of a risk management culture ($\delta\mu / \delta\gamma > 0$), but with a diminishing marginal return to the creation of a risk culture ($\delta^2\mu / \delta^2\nu < 0$). Intuitively, eliminating all risks (even if costless) will result in an expected return no greater than the risk free rate. Likewise, the cost of risk management increases with risk culture ($\delta C / \delta\gamma < 0$), with costs growing at an increasing rate ($\delta^2 C / \delta^2\gamma > 0$) as the marginal cost of eliminating risk increases. The optimal level of enterprise risk management is where the marginal increase in value associated with a risk culture is equal to the marginal cost of creating that value.

$$\delta V / \delta\gamma = \delta V / \delta C \tag{3}$$

Firm value can be expected to increase, reaching a maximum and then declining as the marginal return to risk management expenditures declines and costs increase. A sample solution is noted in Figure 24.2.

The value of enterprise risk management is not fully observable for outside investors and commitment of senior management to risk management goals is not transparent. However the culture of risk management is observable by specialists and will definitely impact the insurance costs as underwriters and brokers are able to observe the risk management culture. The logic is similar to the determination of optimal capital structure taking into account the tax shield of debt and the increasing cost of financial distress. It is an art as much of a science, requiring skill and a detailed understanding of the structure and operations of a firm. Similar to determining optimal capital structure, the result will differ among industries and between firms. It is particularly difficult for outside analysis to understand the structure and value of insurance purchases, let alone the impact of a strategic risk management strategy. A firm may report total insurance expenditures, but equally important is the structure of a firm's insurance program, which risks are covered, the deductibles, and the coinsurance requirements. The anticipated risk management culture and expenditures required to reach an optimal value is an internal decision of

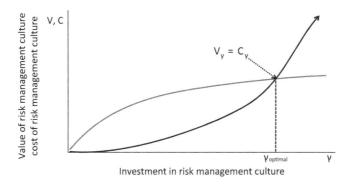

Figure 24.2 Optimal level of risk culture (marginal benefit = marginal cost)

management and owners. For this reason little empirical work has been undertaken regarding the impact of insurance and risk management on firm value.

Developing a risk management culture is multifaceted. It begins with the strategic decision by owners/board and the senior management to determine a risk tolerance level – the level of losses they considers the firm is able to absorb. Risk tolerance can be though of as an estimate of the maximum stochastic loss a firm could manage without seriously disrupting access to financial markets and/or relationships with customers, suppliers and other stakeholders. Beyond the determination of a firm's risk tolerance level is the concrete development of a risk management strategy to manage the frequency and severity of the sum of stochastic risks up to this risk tolerance level. In a simplified version, a risk management plan consists of:

- Evaluating risk exposures, including the values exposed to loss from property, income, liability exposures and providing protection for key personnel.
- Appraising risk management techniques, including risk avoidance, loss prevention (frequency), loss reduction (severity), and the contractual transfer of risk control activities.
- Risk financing of minor stochastic losses, ranging from paying out of pocket and charging to income, funded reserves (whether specific or shared liquidity pools), and accessing financial markets (credit or equity).
- Risk financing via risk transfers, including insurance, structured programs such as catastrophic bonds where risks are transferred to capital markets, and government insurance coverage for risks including flooding, earth movement, windstorm, and terrorism – often risk transfers are used to transferring those losses that exceed the firm's risk tolerance level.
- Diffusion of an appropriate risk management culture throughout the firm.

This is a continuous process, needing adjustments as new risks are undertaken or recognized. Over time, especially as a firm grows, the firm's risk tolerance can change substantially. The risk management strategy needs to be a living document.

The remainder of this chapter will address how the establishment of a strategically focused enterprise risk management program, including the purchase of insurance, can create value to multiple stakeholders, including shareholders. By doing so, the analysis enriches the literature related to the corporate demand for insurance and the creation of value by professional enterprise risk management. This is a result of a blend between financial theory and practitioner practices in evaluating the following:

- Determination of risk tolerance and demand for risk management investment
- Corporate demand for insurance and extensions to risk management activities
- Implicit measurement error underlying the testing of modern portfolio theory (as related to insurance and risk management activities)
- Impact of enterprise risk management and insurance on a firm's optimal capital structure determination, noting the likely change in the underlying parameters following catastrophic events.

These sections will be followed by a conclusion.

Determination of risk tolerance and demand for risk management investment

A mantra among the professional risk managers of medium to large corporations is the need to understand their firm's risk tolerance level. Crickette et al. (2012) provides an excellent discussion of the relationship between risk appetite and risk tolerance. Their definitions are useful in this discussion.

> **Risk Appetite** is the total exposed amount that an organization wishes to undertake on the basis of risk-return trade-offs for one or more desired and expected outcomes. As such, risk appetite is inextricably linked with – and may vary according to – expected returns.
>
> **Risk Tolerance** is the amount of uncertainty an organization is prepared to accept in total or more narrowly within a certain business unit, a particular risk category or for a specific initiative. Expressed in quantitative terms that can be monitored, risk tolerance often is communicated in terms of acceptable or unacceptable outcomes or as limited levels of risk. Risk tolerance statements identify the specific minimum and maximum levels beyond which the organization is unwilling to lose.
>
> **Risk Culture** consists of the norms and traditions of behavior of individuals and of groups within an organization that determine the way in which they identify, understand, discuss and act on the risk the organization confronts and takes. Organizations get in trouble when individuals, knowingly or unknowingly, act outside of the expected risk culture, or when the expected risk culture either is not well understood or enforced.
>
> *(Crickette et al., 2012, p. 3)*

Risk appetite is similar to the standard capital budgeting approach to the valuation of a firm's equity value based on the net present value of cash flows discounted by a risk-adjusted interest rate. In contrast, risk tolerance is the maximum willingness or ability to internally bear losses, that is, stochastic events with large loss exposures.[7] Finally, the risk culture underlies the organizational approach to the management of stochastic risk. This is not just the focus of the risk manager or the chief financial officers, but how risk management is communicated to and incorporated by all employees.

The selection of a risk tolerance levels is a strategic decision made at the board of directors level with considerable input from the chief executive, chief financial officer, and risk manager. The board sets a risk tolerance level (the losses that they are willing to absorb) based on the corporation's ability to generate cash, access to financial markets following a major setback, its preferred capital structure, and possibly the ability to quickly sell assets at market values in the event of a crisis, among other factors. Once the risk tolerance level is set, the risk manager is charged with investing corporate resources to create a risk management culture and manage risks below the risk tolerance level. The risk manager is also charged with developing programs to transfer risks, reducing the impact of loss severity.[8] In managing risk, there are many valid reasons for the corporate purchase of insurance, as covered in the following section. The remainder of this chapter addresses how implantation of a strategically focused enterprise risk management program, including insurance, creates value.

The corporate demand for insurance and extensions to risk management

In their seminal article, "On the Corporate Demand for Insurance" (1982), David Mayers and Clifford Smith ask the dual questions of why the finance literature pays little attention to the purchase of insurance by corporations, and why the insurance literature treated risk aversion as a justification for corporate insurance. They also note that the finance literature in 1982 assumed that insurance purchases at above an actuarially fair rate is by definition an investment in a negative net present value project – the naïve approach discussed in the Motivation section earlier in this chapter. More than 30 years later, this assumption continues. Yet, nonlife insurance premiums have grown tenfold since Mayer and Smith raised these questions, reaching approximately 6% of GDP, the highest by far in the Organisation for Economic Co-operation and Development (OECD). Over the past decade more than 50% are corporate purchases. Their second observation has undergone change. By 2015, the insurance academic literature no longer looks at risk aversion to describe corporate insurance purchase, other than small or family-held firms. Individuals can be assumed to be more or less risk averse. Risk aversion will depend on personality and wealth level, but one cannot judge the risk aversion of a corporation. Individual investors may be risk averse, but it is not possible to determine the risk aversion of a portfolio of well-diversified investors.

Mayers and Smith address a number of reasons why corporations with well-diversified shareholders might demand insurance. These include:

- Comparative advantage in risk bearing: Insurers have an expertise in measuring and pricing risk, along with ready access to international reinsurance markets. They may also bear an advantage in covering risks for stakeholders other than equity and debt holders (e.g., employees, supplies, customers, etc.).
- Avoiding transactions costs associated with bankruptcy: Insurers can provide critical funds following a major loss. These can protect against bankruptcy and the associated dead weight transactions costs. This will be discussed in more detail later in the section entitled Insurance Role in Preservation of Optimal Capital Structure.
- Real service efficiencies: Insurers that manage claims on a daily basis will be more transactionally efficient. If firms experience major property or liability losses infrequently, their expected costs of loss expenditures (including paying losses, identifying the underlying cause, dealing with claimants, legal fees and processes, subrogation, etc.) will be higher than the loading costs charged by insurers.
- Insurance and monitoring: The use of an outside party to evaluate risks and the firm's internal risk management program provides owners and senior management with a market means of monitoring loss exposures, similar to the role that banks play in delegated monitoring on behalf of depositors. Insurance can also help manage some of the agency conflict between shareholders and creditors and between shareholders and managers.
- Bonding: Insurance contracts can be used to guarantee debt holders and others that the firm is protecting assess from undue risk.
- Compulsory insurance requirements by law or regulation: Firms are required to provide coverage for some risk exposures. In the US, this includes worker's compensation insurance and minimum liability coverage for trucks and trailers.
- Taxation: The convexity of the tax code can provide some incentives towards purchasing tax-deductible insurance premiums versus creating a nondeductible liquidity fund to cover losses.

In addition to the points raised by Mayers and Smith, there are other reasons why a firm may demand insurance coverage, including:

- Management focus on core business: Managers are hired and rewarded for their ability or manage operations, financial management, marketing and sales, information technology, research and development, human resources, etc. These managers may not have the skills and knowledge to manage the impact of large, stochastic losses. Transferring these risks to an insurer that can step in and deal with losses and loss administration expenses and associated legal issues allows the management team to focus on its expertise on the core purpose of the corporation in rebuilding the franchise.

- Insurer's duty to defend: Under most property and liability contracts, the insurer's duty to defend the policyholder extends to all claims that fall under the policy, whether legitimate or not. This can be valuable for a corporation that can be exposed to meritless claims. Again, the insurance expertise in managing legal claims should allow them to perform this duty for less than the internal legal resources and without using ill-suited managerial resources.

- Outsourcing claims management – employee practices: Many corporations internally pool health or worker's compensation (often with stop-loss reinsurance). Outsourcing claims management to a third party provides a level of equality to employees while protecting the firm from employees asking for deviations from benefit limitations, based on their "unique situation." The external health care administrator will ensure benefits are paid for provided under the plan. This can avoid potential discrimination issues if "favored" employees get better coverage than everyone else.

Modern Portfolio Theory and the purchase of insurance

The naïve approach to MPT, described in the Motivation section of this chapter, is insufficient to determine the value creation (or value reduction) associated with corporate insurance purchases and risk management investments. First, corporations are observed to spend significant resources in enterprise risk management, including the purchase of insurance. The management and boards of directors apparently perceive value in these activities. We do not hear of firms announcing that they are reducing risk management and insurance expenditures to maximize firm value and to better match the goals of diversified investors. Second, the analytics underlying the measurement of the reduction of idiosyncratic risk as measured by standard deviation uses equity returns of firms that are actively engaged in enterprise risk management and purchasing insurance. If firms were not doing so, equity returns would undoubtedly be more volatile; and a far greater number of firms would have to be incorporated into random portfolios to eliminate risk. There would also be a greater degree of survivorship bias in historical returns (perverting returns or eliminating firms that experience localized black swan events). Excluding negative black swan events while including positive events will create an upward bias in the measure of historical returns. Likewise, the measure of variance will be understated. Third, firms will reject some positive net present value investments due to the potential for localized black swan events and/or creditors will balk at financing.

In many ways, the decision to insure against losses beyond a firm's risk tolerance level is akin to the decision of a corporation to hedge against price fluctuations using derivative instruments. An airline may hedge the cost of jet fuel; capital equipment suppliers may hedge exchange rate fluctuations when paid in one currency and expenses are in another currency. There has long been a consensus among finance practitioners and financial economists that such hedging operations can create value, but the academy continues to apply the naïve understanding of the role of diversification within modern portfolio theory with respect to risk management and insurance. In the naïve view, there is no reduction in the cost of capital as diversified investors only reward market risk, excluding any idiosyncratic or diversifiable risks.

Insurance role in preservation of optimal capital structure

A more nuanced approach looks at the impact of potentially severe losses on the corporate cost of capital, attempting to deal with the localized black swan events to which a firm individual is exposed. An understanding of the impact of a major stochastic event on a firm's movement away from its chosen (optimal) capital structure must be incorporated. Following a major loss, value is decreased by the amount of the loss resulting in an immediate increase in leverage and in the weighted average cost of capital. Not only is the cost of financial distress increased by leverage, all things being equal, but the increase in information asymmetry may move the firm to a steeper cost of financial distress curve through changes in the parameters used to measure the cost of financial distress and the likelihood of bearing the dead weight costs of bankruptcy. Liquidity will suffer. Firms will need to access financial markets at just the time when markets are closed or when the costs of raising financial resources (both equity and debt) increase sharply. The purchase of insurance for these large losses can be thought of as insuring capital structure – providing funds at just the time when other sources are not available at any price or may only be available at a price that destroys the claim of existing stakeholders (current shareholders, bond holders, suppliers, etc.). Thus, its treatment in financial modeling should be identical to hedging against price changes to protect the value of capital.

The Modigliani-Miller models demonstrate how minimizing the weighted average cost of capital correlates with maximizing firm value resulting 3in a firm's optimal capital structure. Figure 24.3 presents a standard approach. The line $V_U - V_L$ corresponds to the steady increase in firm value as leverage increases due to the cost of debt being lower than the cost of equity in addition to the value of the tax shield associated with debt. Note there are two implicit assumptions.

$$\delta r / \delta L = 0 \tag{4}$$

$$\delta \tau / \delta L = 0 \tag{5}$$

Equation 4 assumes that interest rates are constant with respect to changes in leverage while equation assumes that the tax rate is constant with respect to leverage. The curve $V_U - V_L$ (pre-loss) incorporates the increasing cost of financial distress (CFD) as leverage increases due to a

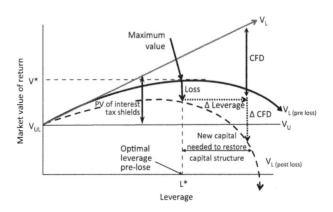

Figure 24.3 Impact of a major loss (localized black swan) on optimal capital structure given changed cost of financial distress

combination of increased interest rates as well as the increasing probability of bearing the deadweight costs associated with bankruptcy.

$$\delta CFD / \delta L > 0 \tag{6}$$

There is an optimal level of leverage (L$\star$) where the value of the firm is maximized. This is also the point where the WAAC is minimized. One of the important roles of the chief financial officer is keep the firm close to its optimal level of leverage, where value is maximized. This point fluctuates with profits (or the lack thereof), with changes in the perception of riskiness by creditors and perceptions of equity markets regarding the value of shares. While it may not be possible to stay right on the point (individual issues of debt or equity tend to be large due to flotation costs), there is a target for minimizing the weighted cost of capital. Further, we can expect that the cost of financial distress will increase after the loss. As shown in Figure 24.3, there will be a sudden decrease in firm value associated with a localized black swan event joined with a marked increase in the cost of financial distress. There will be considerable uncertainly regarding specific risks including the firm's chance of survival. It will be difficult for the firm to communicate any errors between the true and perceived valuation. Access to capital and debt markets will be limited (or nonexistent) given surrounding volatility.

$$\frac{\partial CFD}{\partial L} > 0 \tag{7}$$

$$[Post\ Loss]\ \frac{\delta^2 CFD}{\delta^2 L} >> \frac{\delta^2 CFD}{\delta^2 L}\ [Pre\ Loss] \tag{8}$$

Utilizing this analysis, it is easy to visualize the impact of a major loss on the optimal capital structure. As a first approximation, the value of the firm (and therefore equity) is reduced by the amount of the loss while there is no initial change in creditor claims. In addition to the cost of loss, Figure 24.3 shows the resulting (immediate) increase in leverage. It further shows a potential new relationship and the firm is subject to a new relationship between the value of an unlevered firm and the value of a levered firm $V_U - V_L$ (post loss). Until, the financial situation is resolved, the firm's WAAC shifts upward where the cost of financial distress is higher. Extrapolating backwards, a major deleveraging process will be required by selling assets or raising capital.

Notwithstanding, there will be compounding effects. Following a substantive loss, the level of market uncertainty surrounding the firm will increase dramatically. The parameters underlying the valuation of current debt and equity change due to enhanced levels of asymmetric information and the increased incentive towards risk-taking as this may be the only way to recover value for the shareholders who own an option on the assets of the firm with a strike price equal to the debt levels (Merton, 1998). With uncertainty regarding firm survival and even uncertainty regarding the true level of the loss, the cost and time of recovery must enter into analysis. Analysts may wonder if the enterprise risk management system in place was flawed and whether there are other potential losses lurking in the background. If the time to recover is long, customers and suppliers may develop closer relationships with competitors, while critical employees with other options may not stay around if the survival of the firm is in doubt. Reputational risk and the value of goodwill will be reduced. Credit markets will price risk by charging much higher interest rates, or credit markets may be closed altogether. The firm's optimal decision may be to issue equity, but the risk premium will be very high.

This is where insurance will be of great value. Insurance becomes the lowest cost source of financing. Investors and creditors will know that funds will be available on a timely fashion to cover a substantial portion of the loss. While there will be some damage to the value of the firm, the likelihood of recovery is substantially increased. As such, the purchase of insurance can be viewed as an option for protecting the firm's capital structure. Combined with the many justifications for a corporate demand for insurance noted earlier in this chapter, it is understandable why corporations purchase high levels of insurance in practice, if not in theory.

Conclusion

Corporations invest scarce resources in risk management activities to establish a risk culture and purchase high levels of insurance. They do so despite the predictions of the standard models of portfolio optimization which, based on expected return and the standard deviation of expected return, predict such investments and especially risk transfer (insurance) purchases are unnecessary as shareholders can costlessly diversify "idiosyncratic" risks. This naïve application of modern portfolio theory is flawed for a number of reasons. The models are tested on firms that have already expended considerable resources in risk management and risk transfer. Firms in practice establish levels of risk tolerance as a strategic undertaking to remove the risk of localized black swan events and then manage the risks below this level by creating a risk management culture, thereby reducing the frequency, and more importantly, the severity of losses. There are multiple justifications for the corporate demand for insurance based on risk expertise, operational efficiencies, and keeping the management's focus on the firm's core business, among others. To these, this chapter adds the impact of insurance purchases as an option for protecting the firm's selected capital structure following major losses (localized black swans) that would otherwise disrupt the firm's access to financial markets and damage relationships with customers, suppliers, and other stakeholders. Enterprise risk management deals with the same kind and scope of issues dealt with in price hedging transactions, which are supported in the finance literature as value-creating. The same value-creating concepts are applied by firms in practice for enterprise risks, dealing with stochastic shocks, must enter the larger discussion regarding value creation and value protection in their treatment in the modern portfolio theory and optimal capital structure literatures.

Notes

1   Kim B. Staking, assistant professor of finance, California State University, Sacramento.
2   While this chapter focuses on enterprise risk management, many of the concepts and tools are applicable to overall financial risk management. Likewise, enterprise and financial risk management need to be coordinated.
3   Pure risks in theory have only downside potential, although the risk management literature recognizes that there can be upside potential to some stochastic losses. A home in Jamestown, Virginia, may be destroyed in a fire that uncovers an archeological trove, or a fire at a chemical plant may result in a new plastic polymer of great value. However, these can be considered so rare that they can safely excluded from the discussion in this chapter.
4   Insurers were unwilling to extend terrorism coverage as coverage matured, but many corporations had loan covenants that required terrorism insurance. They could collectively be in technical default. Countries used various approaches, but most had to develop a backstop facility.
5   Leland and Pyle explored how investors select among multiple investment projects, where an entrepreneur's commitment level is uncertain. It is a problem of asymmetric information. They solve this problem by finding an observable measure of the entrepreneurial effort, the level of investment of the entrepreneur. The current focus is on how a firm selects a risk management strategy and a willingness to bear the cost. The resulting risk management culture is observable by the risk management team and reported to senior management.

6   For simplicity, it is assumed that all risk management costs are paid at the beginning of the period, while the increased value is observed at the end of the period (discounted by the interest rate *r*).

7   An example of the difference between risk appetite and risk tolerance could be the oil spill at the Deepwater Horizon offshore drilling platform owned by BP. They were drilling a deeper well where the engineering risks seemed mitigated. Their risk appetite would have been largely related to the amount and price of petroleum BP expected to recover. Risk tolerance would have been the maximum level of losses that BP could sustain without damaging their access to financial markets and reputation. It is doubtful that BP expected the cumulative claims of $14.2 billion (BP, 2015).

8   Larger firms may establish a captive insurer to access to reinsurance markets and take advantage of tax arbitrage.

References

Ashby, S. G., & Diacon, S. R. (1998). The corporate demand for insurance: A strategic perspective. *Geneva Papers on Risk and Insurance. Issues and Practice, 23(1)*, 34–51.

BP. (2015, April). *Gulf of Mexico oil spill claims and other payments*. Public report. Retrieved May 20, 2015, from http://www.bp.com/en/global/corporate/gulf-of-mexico-restoration/claims-information.html

Chen, J., & King, T.H.D. (2014). Corporate hedging and the cost of debt. *Journal of Corporate Finance, 29*, 221–245.

Cole, C. R., & McCullough, K.A. (2006). A reexamination of the corporate demand for reinsurance. *Journal of Risk and Insurance, 73(1)*, 169–192.

Crickette, G., Demian, R., Fox, C., Hach, J., Makomaski, J., Mazumdar, R., & McGuire, R. (2012). Exploring risk appetite and risk tolerance. *RIMS executive report: The risk perspective*. Retrieved April 13, 2015, from https://www.rims.org/resources/ERM/Documents/RIMS_Exploring_Risk_Appetite_Risk_Tolerance_0412.pdf

DeAngelo, H., & Stulz, R. M. (2014). Liquid-claim production, risk management, and bank capital structure: Why high leverage is optimal for banks. *Journal of Financial Economics*, forthcoming.

Diamond, D.W. (1984). Financial intermediation and delegated monitoring. *Review of Economic Studies, 51(3)*, 393–414.

Hoyt, R. E., & Khang, H. (2000). On the demand for corporate property insurance. *Journal of Risk and Insurance, 67(1)*, 91–107.

Kunreuther, H. C., & Michel-Kerjan, E. (2004). Challenges for terrorism risk insurance in the United States. *Journal of Economic Perspectives, 18(4)*, 201–214.

Leland, H.E., & Pyle, D. H. (1997). Informational asymmetries, financial structure, and financial intermediation. *Journal of Finance, 32(2)*, 371–387. http://www.jstor.org/stable/2326770

Mayers, D., & Smith, C. (1987). Corporate insurance and the underinvestment problem. *Journal of Risk and Insurance, 54(1)*, 45–54.

Mayers, D., & Smith, C. (1982). On the corporate demand for insurance. *Journal of Business, 55(2)*, 281–296.

Mayers, D., & Smith, C. (1990). On the corporate demand for insurance: Evidence from the reinsurance market. *Journal of Business, 66(1)*, 19–40.

Merton, R. C. (1998). Applications of option-pricing theory: Twenty-five years later. *American Economic Review, 88(3)*, 323–349.

Michel-Kerjan, E., Raschky, P., & Kunreuther, H. (2014). Corporate demand for insurance: New evidence from the US terrorism and property markets. *Journal of Risk and Insurance, 82(3)*, 505–530.

Modigliani, F., & Miller, M.H. (1958). The cost of capital, corporation finance and the theory of investment. *American Economic Review, 48(3)*, 261–297. http://www.jstor.org/stable/1809766

Myers, S.C. (1984). The capital structure puzzle. *Journal of Finance, 39(3)*, 574–592.

Myers, S.C., & Majluf, N. S. (1984). Corporate financing and investment decisions when firms have information that investors do not have. *Journal of Financial Economics, 13(2)*, 187–221.

Nance, D.R., Smith, C.W., & Smithson, C.W. (1993). On the determinants of corporate hedging. *Journal of Finance, 48(1)*, 267–284.

OECD. (2014). OECD Insurance Statistics 2014. Retrieved May 3, 2015, from http://www.oecd-ilibrary.org/finance-and-investment/oecd-insurance-statistics-2014/united-states_ins_stats-2014-40-en

Riley, J. G. (2002). Weak and strong signals. *Scandinavian Journal of Economics, 104(2)*, 213–236.

Statista. (n.d.). Amount of monetary damage caused by reported cyber crime to the IC3 from 2001 to 2014. Retrieved June 1, 2015, from http://www.statista.com/statistics/267132/total-damage-caused-by-by-cyber-crime-in-the-us/

Taleb, N.N. (2007). *The Black Swan*. New York: Random House.

Part VI

Other aspects of strategic risk management

25

Enterprise risk management

The need for distinguishing between task risk and enterprise risk management

Eyvind Aven and Terje Aven[1]

Abstract

This chapter discusses some fundamental issues related to enterprise risk management (ERM). A key issue is how to best structure and plan the ERM in situations involving risk and uncertainties. We argue that it is essential to make a distinction between three types of risk management: enterprise risk management, task risk management and personal risk management; and implement a structure where the enterprise risk management overrules both the task and personal risk management. The discussion is based on a "modern" perspective on risk highlighting knowledge and uncertainties beyond probabilities.

A common principal objective for a (profit-based) organization is to maximize the value but at the same time avoiding HSE (health, safety and environment) and integrity incidents. Often there is a weak link or no clear link between the principal objective and the subgoals in the organization. In addition, interdependencies between goals could generate inconsistencies and lower levels of performance than expected. Increasing the ambition set for the overall performance of the organization may lead to higher risk seen in relation to lower-level objectives. There is clearly a hierarchy of objectives, and concentrating on risk management in the sense of meeting objectives without understanding this hierarchy could lead to poor results, in the sense that the risk management on a lower organizational level shows excellent results, all goals met, but without having contributed to the main overall performance and objectives of the organization.

This chapter addresses this issue. We aim to bring new insights to the topic by making a distinction between three types of risk management: enterprise risk management, task risk management and personal risk management, and adopting a "modern" perspective on risk highlighting knowledge and uncertainties beyond probabilities. The chapter is to a large extent based on Aven and Aven (2015).

Fundamentals about risk and enterprise risk management

Risk management can be viewed as all measures and activities carried out to manage risk (Aven, 2012a). A main aim of risk management is to balance the need for exploring opportunities on the one hand, and avoiding losses, accidents and disasters on the other. The risk management measures and activities comprise the identification of threats/hazards, assessments of risk and risk-informed decision-making (including the management review and judgment), as well as more management-oriented measures and activities such as establishing objectives and strategies, establishing the risk management process (defining the overall structure of how to carry out the risk management, clarifying how to use various principles and methods), defining roles and responsibilities, implementing various assessment tools (in particular different types of risk assessments and cost-benefit type of analyses), training programmes and measures intended to improve the communication and culture in the organization in order to obtain a high level of performance and a drive for improvements in all type of activities.

There are many ways of describing the risk management process using risk assessment, but the steps are essentially the same (Ale, Aven and Jongejan, 2009):

1. Establish the context and set objectives. This step involves the definition of the entity's key objectives which could be defined in terms of profit, safety and so forth.
2. Identify threats/hazards/opportunities that could affect something that the entity values.
3. Assess associate risks.
4. Evaluate the risks. This step involves judgments as to whether the risks should be adjusted or not; for downside risks we talk about acceptable (tolerable) risk or not.
5. Risk control, risk treatment and risk response. When the risk is judged unacceptable we can abandon the (potential) activity, we can reduce the risk, or we can transfer it to third parties (e.g., insurance).

In addition, internal and external communication is also often included in this sequence. The process is iterative, not necessarily sequential. We also find these steps in most standards on risk management, including ISO 31000 (ISO, 2009) and enterprise risk management documents. They are relevant for all types of organizations, for example profit-maximizing enterprises, hospitals and NGOs (nongovernmental organizations). This chapter focuses on profit-maximizing enterprises, and for this type of organization the risk management process needs to be tailor-made in several ways, as discussed in the following.

In an enterprise context it is common to distinguish between strategic risk, financial risk and operational risk, where:

*   strategic risk is risk where the consequences for the enterprise are influenced by mergers and acquisitions, technology, competition, political conditions, laws and regulations, labour market and so forth;
*   financial risk is risk where the consequences for the enterprise are influenced by the market (associated with changes in the value of an investment due to movements in market factors: the stock prices, interest rates, foreign exchange rates and commodity prices), credit issues (associated with a debtor's failure to meet its obligations in accordance with agreed terms) and liquidity issues, reflecting lack of access to cash and the difficulty of selling an asset in a timely manner, that is, quickly enough to prevent a loss (or make the required profit);
*   operational risk is risk where the consequences for the enterprise are a result of safety or security related issues (accidental events, intentional acts, etc.).

An alternative way of approaching the enterprise risk is to focus on the value chain of the enterprise. Enterprise risk management (ERM) is about managing all of the organization's risks related to its activities in the value chain. In order to ensure completeness, the risks could be sorted in risk themes covering all activities in the whole value chain. These themes could cover, for example access, project maturation, project execution, operation and market. In addition, in order to capture specific risks going across the value chain, risk themes such as HSE, integrity and country-specific risks could be used. See Figure 25.1.

Formally, in this paper we define risk as deviation from a reference level (ideal states, planned values, expected values, objectives) and associated uncertainties (Aven and Aven, 2011; Aven, Baraldi, Flage and Zio, 2014). When describing risk, we specify potential deviations and use a measure of uncertainty (typically probability) to represent the uncertainties and express degrees of beliefs. In addition, the risk description needs to capture the background knowledge on which the measure is based as well as the strength of this knowledge (Aven, 2012a, 2012b). We may have two situations giving the same probability, but in one case the support could be strong, in the other case weak. This perspective to enterprise risk is new; compare, for example Cendrowski and Mair (2009), COSO (2004), Monahan (2008) and Olson and Wu (2010). The motivation for and the features of this risk perspective are well documented (Aven, 2012a, 2012b). The knowledge aspect as mentioned earlier is a key argument, so is the fact that there exist also other ways of describing the uncertainties than probability (interval probabilities, and measures based on possibility and evidence theory, as well as qualitative methods); see Aven, Baraldi, Flage and Zio, 2014. If risk is defined through probabilities as is commonly the case, the perspective is not sufficiently broad to allow for alternative uncertainty representations.

In more precise terms we can conceptualize risk in this way:

Risk is defined by the pair (C,U), where C is the consequences of the activity considered, and U expresses the associated uncertainties – that these consequences are not known. Here C is seen in relation to some reference values (planned values, objectives, etc.) and can be defined as the deviations from these reference values.

It is possible to define risk in different ways capturing basically the same ideas; see the list of alternatives in the Society of Risk Analysis (SRA) (Flage and Aven, 2009). ISO (2009) defines risk as the effect of uncertainty on objectives. It is possible to interpret this definition in different ways, also in line with the (C,U) definition, where the consequences are seen in relation to the defined objectives.

In general terms, risk is described by (C′,Q,K), where C′ are the specific consequences considered – here the specified deviations relative to defined references values; Q a measure of uncertainty (measure interpreted in a wide sense); and K the background knowledge on which C′ and Q are based. The most common method for measuring the uncertainties U is probability P, but other tools also exist, as mentioned earlier. When using probability we should also add judgment of the strength of knowledge supporting the probability judgments.

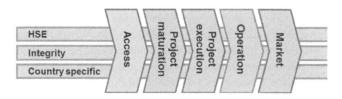

Figure 25.1 A model of the value chain of an enterprise, with risk themes (access, maturing, etc.) and specific risks crossing the value chain (HSE, etc.)

Such judgments can be based on qualitative assessment of aspects like Aven (2014) and Flage and Aven (2012):

- the degree to which the assumptions made are reasonable/realistic
- the degree to which data/information exist/s and are/is reliable/relevant
- the degree to which there is disagreement among experts
- the degree to which the phenomena involved are understood and accurate models exist.

Cost and the number of fatalities are examples of C'. Depending on what principles we adopt for representing C and the choice we make concerning Q, we obtain different ways of describing or measuring risk. Which measures to use will of course depend on the situation and the need for decision support.

Looking at the future operation (say next year) of a process plant, we are facing risk, for example economic loss due to some operational failures. The actual consequences we denote C, and they are unknown now. To describe the risk, we have to specify the types of consequences (deviations) we will address and how we are going to express the uncertainties about these consequences. We have to determine which measure Q to use.

We see that the (C,U) way of understanding and describing risk allows for all types of uncertainty representations, and it could consequently serve as a basis of a unified perspective on uncertainties in a risk assessment context. In the risk descriptions, various risk metrics can be used, for example based on expected values and probabilities, but the knowledge dimension (data, information, justified beliefs) and the strength of this knowledge need to be seen as an integral part. The risk descriptions may use modelling, for example probability models whenever they can be justified and are considered suitable for the analysis. If we use a probability model with a parameter p, this p is unknown and must be viewed as a component of C' in the general description of risk.

Enterprise risk, task risk and personal risk

For the purpose of the present study, we divide the risk into three categories: enterprise risk, task risk and personal risk; see Figure 25.2. For the enterprise risk, the deviation is explicitly expressed through the impact dimensions defined by the enterprise (change in monetary value, occurrence of incidents). For the task, the deviation is not directly expressed through these impact dimensions, but the deviation could for example be linked to delays in a project. For the personal risk, the deviation is linked to compensation and/or recognition. Distinguishing between these types of risk is essential in order to be able to understand the incentives behind the risk management.

In ERM the focus is the enterprise, and the impact dimensions are "change in monetary value" and/or "occurrence of incidents." The enterprise was established in order to create value, that is it seeks to increase the monetary value and avoid incidents consistent with the principal objectives. A number of tasks/projects are carried out in the enterprise, but the risks and related deviations are not explicitly linked to these impact dimensions. We speak about task risk management (TRM). The long-term aim of these tasks/projects could be to contribute to increasing the monetary value and avoiding incidents. However, it is not always a clear link between the task goals and these impacts. In some cases we may even experience the tasks having a negative influence on the principal objectives of the enterprise. We speak about goal-induced actions when the TRM induces actions aimed at satisfying the goals.

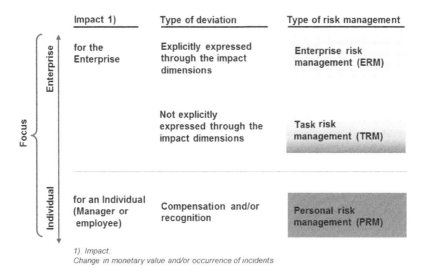

Figure 25.2 Types of risks and risk management

In addition, we use the concept of personal risk and personal risk management (PRM). A manager may for example have a goal of increasing his/her income by 50%, and the satisfaction of this goal is seen as dependent on meeting a specific task goal. It could also be that a bonus scheme is directly linked to the achievement of specific goals for which the manager is responsible.

The personal risk management is not a formal part of the management of an enterprise, but as it could strongly affect the TRM and ERM it needs to be given due attention. The challenge is to design the enterprise's incentive scheme to ensure consistency between the PRM and the TRM/ERM.

Often we see that ERM is juxtaposed with managing risk related to the achievement of goals and objectives. Such a perspective is, however, problematic as there is not a one-to-one relationship between the principal objectives and the lower-level goals. In line with our terminology, if you cannot explicitly express the goal through the impact dimensions of the enterprise, it is not ERM, but TRM.

In the hierarchy of risk management types, the ERM must always overrule both TRM and PRM in order to ensure fulfilment of the principal objectives.

Current thinking on performance and risk management does not capture these conflicts. Strategic objectives are set as desired future states, actions are put in place to move towards these objectives and the deliveries are often measured via KPIs only (key performance indicators). Based on the measured KPIs, actions are put into effect to increase the probability of meeting the objectives and increase performance. This approach is also supported by the ISO 31000 where risk is defined as the effect of uncertainty on objectives. Thus risk is linked to the achievement of objectives. An example may illustrate the point: company X states that their future desired state is to have a strong market position and actions have been put in place to increase the probability to reach the objective. The progress is measured by percentage market share (the KPI). The underlying principal objective is still to create value, but when actions are decided, the principal objective has little or no impact. To increase the market share becomes a goal in itself, and the risk management is about increasing the probability to achieve the goal. The typical question in this approach is, "What is threatening the goal fulfillment?"

In our approach a more holistic process is sought – the decisions have to be checked against the principal objectives, that is, higher market share is not necessarily good if it does not create value or if another mix of market shares of the products is more profitable. By this holistic approach the strategic objectives will have to be seen in relation to the principal objectives in order to reduce any conflicts of interests. The principal objectives are set at the highest level in the organization and will normally remain unchanged over time, while the strategic objectives will change over time.

The process is similar to the quality circle (Plan-Do-Check-Act) in quality management (Deming, 2000). When the Plan-Do-Check-Act process issues relate to enterprise risk, the performance management is also ERM. However, many performance management activities are not ERM, as shown earlier. The risk management process is, nevertheless, in line with ISO 31000. This interplay between the performance process and the risk management process is critical for the development of the enterprise. Disconnected processes will easily lead to KPIs which have weak links to the principal objectives. Figure 25.3 illustrates current practice versus the new approach on how we suggest ERM should be accomplished. In current practice the KPIs often become goals themselves and the risk management is about increasing the probability for achieving the targeted KPI. The link to the principal objectives is often weak or missing, but in the new approach the focus is on how actions can increase the probability for achieving the strategic objectives in a value creation perspective. Thus suboptimal risk management decisions can be avoided.

The strategic objectives are based on the ambition level, risk appetite and strategic considerations. Questions like "What does success look like?" and "Where are we going?" are important questions to answer when stating ambition level. It must also be assured that the concrete strategic objectives are in line with the principal objectives. The risk appetite expresses the amount of risk the enterprise intends to take in pursuing value creating opportunities (Aven, 2013). Running a business involves taking risks, thus the risk appetite is about risk/reward considerations.

Figure 25.3 Current versus proposed focus in ERM

A case showing why ERM must overrule TRM

We consider a case from the oil industry to illustrate some of the issues raised in the previous section. The executive committee and board of an international oil company are looking into how to create value for the shareholders, and alternative strategic objectives are being discussed and evaluated. Two formulations of strategic objectives are considered: "build a globally competitive oil company" and "create value as an upstream- and midstream-oriented and technology-based energy company." Let us assume that the latter strategic objective has been chosen and a portfolio of investment projects is planned to be executed in order to fulfil the objective. The Business Areas in the oil company assess investment proposals according to profitability criteria and relevance to strategic objectives. The entity in the company responsible for securing a good and consistent investment decision basis is defined as the Asset Owner.

A final decision has been made by the Asset Owner to realize an Investment project by performing detail design, construction and preparation for operations. The construction will be delivered by an in-house Delivery entity. The two main elements that need to be constructed are the facilities (platforms, subsea solutions, etc.) and the wells (drilling and well). We denote these as Facilities and D&W. In the overall plan a date for when the asset can produce oil and gas is set and a delivery agreement is signed between the suppliers (Delivery entities Facilities and D&W) and the Asset Owner. The main objectives of the Delivery entities are then to deliver on time, cost and quality (the task).

The Asset Owner represents the Enterprise which decided to realize an investment project as one element in the fulfillment of its strategic objectives. The Asset Owner has the overview on how the execution of this project creates value for the Enterprise and which risk management decisions that support it. The KPIs are set to reflect delivery on time, cost and quality (the task). The Enterprise has a portfolio of such projects going on all the time which aims at fulfill the strategic objectives and corresponding value creation.

In order to manage the risk related to the assigned task, the Delivery entity performs a task risk management where the impact dimensions are expressed as deviation from the task delivery (time, cost and quality) and not expressed through the enterprise' impact dimensions. The Asset owner manages the risk according to enterprise risk management principles, that is decide upon risk adjusting actions using a cost-benefit approach for creating value in monetary terms for the Enterprise, and paying due attention to relevant risks and uncertainties, in particular related to the major incidents. For this purpose the Asset Owner needs to get relevant risk information from the Delivery entities.

Let us assume that the Delivery entities shall execute their tasks by 1 January of Year 3 and both have to finish their tasks for the project to be able to start production from this date. During Year 1 the Facilities have new information and have realized that the schedule will be tight or almost impossible to meet – their risk assessment shows a high probability for not reaching the target (the Delivery entity's impact dimension). An updated estimate for delivery date without any further adjusting actions is 3 months' delay, that is 1 April of Year 3. We can simplify this situation for the Facilities by assuming that they face only two main decision alternatives:

(a) increase manpower significantly to accelerate progress to increase the probability for finalizing within original delivery date (increase cost considerably)
(b) focus strongly on critical lines and avoid any further delays.

The goals have already been set for the Facility management and a compensation scheme has been attached to it. The incentive for alternative (a) is then strong – both for fulfilment of the task and compensation to the Facility management. The risk management approaches here are Task risk management and Personal risk management.

In a narrow risk management context, that is where risk is related to meeting the objectives, the Facility management is doing exactly what it should do; it decides to go for alternative (a) since this alternative reduces the probability for not delivering according to the agreed task delivery.

However, in an Enterprise Risk management context the risk management incentives at project and project manager level could be in conflict with the interest of the Enterprise. The Asset Owner performs ERM and manages risk where the impact dimensions are seen relative to the Enterprise. The Asset Owner has to broaden up the considerations and take into account aspects not covered by the Task management. A key question to ask for the ERM is for example whether more costs should be incurred in order to increase the probability of meeting the planned production startup date. It turned out in this case that the D&W was also delayed (with an estimate of at least 6–9 months) and the Enterprise Risk management decision would then obviously be to go for alternative (b) (no need to accelerate Facilities when D&W is even more delayed) since this is in the interest of the Enterprise and its shareholders – as opposed to the "optimal" decision of the Task risk management and Personal risk management.

The KPIs from the D&W would show negative signs due to the delay and generate similar decision alternatives as (a) and (b). Since the focus of the Delivery entities is the agreed delivery and risks related to the task, they can only do TRM. However, it is crucial that important and relevant risk information flows from the Delivery entities to the Asset Owner enabling them to do ERM. The Asset Owner conducts then a risk assessment of the relevant activities in the context of the principal objectives, and based on a judgment of the overall performance and risk related to the delay and increased cost, it finds that case (a) is the preferred alternative. For oil projects, delays are often very costly in value terms due to the net present value (NPV) effect from the whole revenue stream being shifted in time. The ERM related to the D&W delay may thus imply costly actions being in the interest of the Enterprise.

The hierarchy of objectives is important in the risk management – the ERM has to overrule the TRM to ensure "optimal" risk management decisions. Managing the risk related to the tasks with their focus on meeting their "local" objectives must be executed with care. Reducing risk and uncertainties on the TRM level must always be seen in relation to the ERM objectives. This requires great flexibility and coordination in the organizations as decisions need to be made to simplify the management of complex activities. The key here is to highlight the different types of risk faced and acknowledge that the really important risk is the enterprise performance and risk, and not the task performance and risk. TRM is a just a tool in ERM. The effectiveness of the TRM is dependent on a well-functioning ERM to ensure parallel incentives since the Delivery entities only see the Task risk management dimension and cannot optimize on behalf of the Enterprise. To prevent "suboptimal" risk management the Delivery entities have to rely on relevant and updated delivery goals at all times from the ERM.

Discussion

Ideally, the aim is that every subgoal supports the principal objectives, but in real life the linkages could be indirect or even lacking completely if the subgoals have not been calibrated well enough. The statement "no goal, no risk" is a common misconception used in this context (Aven and Aven, 2011): if goals have not been formulated, there are no risks, as there is no reference for judging the degree of compliance. However, deviation needs not only to be considered in relation to goals. What we need is a reference value, and this could be delivery according to a specific project plan or just the normal or planned production level. If the risk is related to such a normal production level, we get focus on high and low values, and not only whether the production meets a specific target level.

For an enterprise, it is essential to be considered competitive, for example being cost-efficient, as this makes the company more attractive as a partner and increases its profit opportunities. The cost development over time can be measured using various performance indices and hopefully they will show a positive trend. Some of the cost-cutting could have a negative impact on principal objectives linked to safety and security, and thus care has to be shown in managing the activities to avoid unacceptable safety and security levels. To control the safety and security levels, risk studies have to be performed that see beyond the expected net present value calculations, and highlight the probabilities of occurrences of these events, the strength of knowledge of the probability assignments, as well as potential surprises (Aven, 2014), as briefly discussed in the previous sections.

As the example about drilling costs showed, the understanding of the drivers of the performance measures is an important element of the risk management. A reduction in the production unit cost does not necessarily support the principal objective of creating value, that is higher profits. If the focus is to reach a certain unit cost level this can be achieved by being more cost-efficient, and, everything else being equal, this would generate value. However, the goal could also be achieved by prioritizing fields with a low degree of complexity, for example low-cost production wells. The latter will certainly show a lower production cost per barrel produced, but this strategy need not be the best alternative when it comes to value creation. The strategy could mean lost opportunities compared to a strategy based on complex wells which could have a large potential for high rewards. A risk management approach focusing on uncertainty on nonprincipal objectives only (e.g., unit cost level) without considering the principal objectives of the Enterprise could easily imply suboptimization and value destruction. For example, the risk assessment would typically show lower downside probability for a strategy (i) going for plain vanilla wells compared with a strategy (ii) adopting complex wells. Combining this with a stronger background knowledge for the risk assessment in the (i) strategy, it is likely that this strategy will be chosen. However, as stressed earlier, such a perspective is too narrow – the principal ERM objectives need to be taken into account, both when it comes to risk and reward.

ERM and MBO (management by objectives) at the highest level, or MBO with a clear link to principal objectives, are consistent activities. Often MBO has no direct link to value creation, and risk management in this context is by definition TRM. An enhanced MBO approach can be developed by looking beyond the TRM results and focusing on holistic performance evaluation, as outlined for example by Bogsnes (2008). However, to ensure that the TRM is in line with the ERM, the key question to ask, as discussed and illustrated by this case, is "Does the TRM-induced action support the principal objectives of the Enterprise?" This is a question the top management in an enterprise must consider before the action is taken, and not in retrospect as part of a performance review. Processes need to be established where the TRM goals are seen in relation to the goals of the ERM. Top-level risk committees could play an important role here to discuss such questions and influence the enterprise to ensure consistency between MBOs and ERM.

Conclusions

This chapter has discussed risk in relation to strategic objectives and performance management in an enterprise risk setting. We have presented and discussed a setup and model for describing the links between performance and risk. To obtain clarity in communication about risk in the enterprise and to ensure the right approach in supporting the enterprise principal objectives, we recommend the use of the terms "enterprise risk management," "task risk management" and "personal risk management," defined earlier. The enterprise risk is defined by deviations from reference values expressed through the impact dimensions of the principal objectives (change in monetary value and occurrence of incidents) and associated uncertainties. The task risk management is to be seen as a tool supporting the enterprise risk management. The task risk management, as well as the personal risk management, must be carefully supervised to see that it leads to the desired results meeting the enterprise's principal objectives, that is, the ERM has to overrule both the TRM and PRM in the management of an enterprise.

Hierarchies and different types of management levels in an ERM context are not new. However, the ERM-TRM-PRM scheme here suggested with its risk conceptualization and characterizations based on deviations from relevant reference values, and associated uncertainties, represent a new way of thinking for the management of such organizations. Current risk management perspectives, for example based on ISO 31000 (ISO, 2009) and COSO (2004) have different building blocks and are not in the same way highlighting the "suboptimization risk" associated with the MBO thinking in an enterprise. Compared to the approach here presented, these standards and the current ERM practice give also less emphasis on the knowledge dimension. Probability is used to describe uncertainties without incorporating the strength of knowledge that these probabilities are based on.

Note

1   Eyvind Aven, Statoil ASA, Norway; Terje Aven, University of Stavanger, Norway.

References

Ale, B., Aven, T., & Jongejan, R.B. (2009). Review and discussion of basic concepts and principles in integrated risk management. In R. Bris, C.G. Soares, & S. Martorell (Eds.), *Reliability, risk and safety, theory and applications, ESREL* (pp. 421–427). London: CRC Press.

Aven, E., & Aven, T. (2011). On how to understand and express enterprise risk. *International Journal of Business Continuity and Risk Management*, 2(2): 20–34.

Aven, E., & Aven, T. (2015). On the need for rethinking current practice which highlights goal achievement risk in an enterprise context. *Risk Analysis* (published online 1 May 2015).

Aven T. (2012a). *Foundations of risk analysis* (2nd ed.). Chichester: Wiley.

Aven T. (2012b). The risk concept – historical and recent development trends. *Reliability Engineering and System Safety*, 99: 33–44.

Aven, T. (2013). On the meaning and use of the risk appetite concept. *Risk Analysis*, 33(3): 462–468.

Aven, T. (2014). *Risk, surprises and black swans*. London: Routledge.

Aven, T., Baraldi, P., Flage, R., & Zio, E. (2014). *Uncertainties in risk assessments*. Chichester: Wiley.

Bogsnes, B. (2008). *Implementing beyond budgeting: Unlocking the performance potential*. London: Wiley.

Cendrowski, H., & Mair, W.C. (2009). *Enterprise risk management and COSO*. Hoboken, NJ: Wiley. COSO (Committee of Sponsoring Organizations). (2004). *Enterprise risk management framework*. Hoboken, NJ: Committee of Sponsoring Organizations (COSO).

Deming, W.E. (2000). *The new economics* (2nd ed.). Cambridge, MA: MIT CAES.

Flage, R., & Aven, T. (2009). Expressing and communicating uncertainty in relation to quantitative risk analysis (QRA). *Reliability and Risk Analysis: Theory and Applications*, 2(13), 9–18.

ISO. (2009). *Risk management – principles and guidelines, ISO 31000*.

Monahan, G. (2008). *Enterprise risk management*. Hoboken, NJ: Wiley.

Olson, D.L., & Wu, D. (2010). *Enterprise risk management models*. London: Springer. SRA. (2015). *Draft glossary*. Society of Risk Analysis. http://www.sra.com/frasg

26

High reliability and the management of critical infrastructures

Paul Schulman, Emery Roe, Michel van Eeten, and Mark de Bruijne[1]

Abstract

Organization theorists and practitioners alike have become greatly interested in high reliability in the management of large hazardous technical systems and society's critical service infrastructures. But much of the reliability analysis is centered in particular organizations that have command and control over their technical cores. Many technical systems, including electricity generation, water, telecommunications, and other critical infrastructures, are not the exclusive domain of single organizations. Our chapter is organized around the following research question: How do organizations, many with competing if not conflicting goals and interests, provide highly reliable service in the absence of ongoing command and control and in the presence of rapidly changing task environments with highly consequential hazards? We analyze electricity restructuring in California as a specific case. Our conclusions have surprising and important implications both for high reliability theory and for the future management of critical infrastructures organized around large technical systems.

Interest among theorists in organizational reliability – the ability of organizations to manage hazardous technical systems safely and without serious error – has grown dramatically in recent years (LaPorte and Consolini, 1991; Roberts, 1993; Sagan, 1993; Schulman, 1993a; Rochlin and von Meier, 1994; Weick, Sutcliffe and Obstfeldt, 1999; Perrow, 1999; Sanne, 2000; Beamish, 2002; Evan and Manion, 2002). Interest has also heightened over "critical infrastructures" and their reliability in the face of potential terrorist attack. Assault on any of the critical infrastructures for power, water, telecommunications, and financial services entails great consequences for their users as well as the other interdependent critical infrastructures (Homer-Dixon, 2002; Mann, 2002).

A momentous debate has been taking place among policy and management experts over how best to protect critical infrastructures against attack. What are their key vulnerabilities? To what extent should the operation of critical services be centralized or decentralized? In a report released by the US National Academies of Science and Engineering and Institute of Medicine, it is argued that for a variety of infrastructures, including energy, transportation, information technology, and health care, the interconnectedness within and across systems makes the infrastructure vulnerable to local disruptions that could lead to catastrophic failure" (NRC, 2002).

The highly reliable management of large-scale critical service systems presents a major paradox: demands for ever higher reliability, and not only against terrorist assault, surround these services as we grow more dependent on them, yet at the same time, conventional organizational frameworks associated with high reliability are being dismantled. Deregulation in air traffic, electricity, and telecommunications has led to the unbundling and breakup of utilities and other organizations operating these systems. Increasing environmental requirements have brought new units and conflicting mandates into the management of large technical water systems (van Eeten and Roe, 2002). Dominant theories would predict that high reliability is unlikely or at great risk in the rapidly changing systems. In particular, high reliability in providing critical services has become a process that is achieved across organizations rather than a trait of any one organization. Critical infrastructures in communication, transportation, and water resources all display structurally and geographically diverse constituent elements. The inputs and disturbances to which they are subject are also diverse and place them under increasing pressure of fragmentation (e.g., deregulation and regulatory turmoil). Yet they are mandated to provide not just critical services to society, but reliably critical services, notwithstanding their turbulent task environments.

Examples of successful "high reliability management" continue to come forward: mobile telecom services are becoming more reliable across ever more complex hardware and service demands; the lights by and large stayed on during the California electricity crisis; Y2K passed without major incident; fairly rapid recovery in financial services from 9/11 was secured; and large hydropower systems reconcile hourly the conflicting reliability mandates across multiple uses of water.

How to explain such successful management under conditions where theory tells us to expect otherwise? By way of explanation we present a case study on how reliability of critical services was maintained in the restructured California electricity sector and the 2000–2001 electricity crisis.[2] This case study has been chosen for two reasons.

First, both Normal Accident Theory (NAT; Perrow, 1999) and most of the earlier High Reliability Organizations (HROs) research would predict that the restructuring of the California electricity sector should have demonstrably undermined the reliable provision of electricity. For its part, NAT would see the coupling of the state's two major electricity grids into a newly configured grid, with altogether novel and higher flows of energy, as an increase in the technology's tight coupling and complex interactivity. The probability of cascading failures would increase accordingly. For its part, the earlier HRO research would have concluded similarly. Since electricity HROs, especially at nuclear power plants, must stabilize both inputs and outputs, reliability would necessarily suffer to the extent that this stability was thrown into doubt (Schulman, 1993a). Indeed, subsequent events in California seemed to confirm both theories, as the chief feature of the California electricity crisis has been taken by many to be the *unreliability* of electricity provision.

Yet, notwithstanding the popular view of rolling blackouts sweeping California during its electricity crisis, in aggregate terms – both in hours and megawatts (MW) – blackouts were minimal. While no figures are available for the baseline before the crisis, it is important to note that rolling blackouts occurred on 6 days during 2001, accounting for no more than 30 hours. Load shedding ranged from 300 to 1000 MW in a state whose total daily load averaged in the upper 20,000 to lower 30,000 MW. The aggregate amount of megawatts that was actually shed during these rolling blackouts amounted to slightly more than 14,000 megawatt-hours (MWh), the rough equivalent of 10.5 million homes being out of power for 1 hour in a state having some 11.5 million households – with business and other nonresidential customers remaining unaffected. In short, the California electricity crisis had the effect of less than an hour's worth of outage for every household in the state in 2001. Why the lights by and large actually stayed on – and reliably stayed on – was due, we argue, to factors related to a special type of reliability management.

A second reason for focusing on the California case study is that it offers a challenge to the NAT notion of "complex interactivity and tight coupling" as an inevitable source of normal accidents in large technical systems. At least in the case of the electricity critical infrastructure, complexity and tight coupling can actually be important resources for high reliability management.

Reliable provision of electricity under the California restructuring: evidence from the 2000–2001 California electricity crisis

In 1996 California adopted a major restructuring of its system of electricity generation, transmission, and distribution. Through legislation, the state moved from a set of large, integrated utilities that owned and operated the generation facilities, the transmission lines, and the distribution and billing systems and set retail prices under a cost-based regulatory system to a market-based system consisting of independent generators who sold their power on wholesale markets to distributors who then sell it to retail customers. The major utilities were compelled to sell off their major generating capacity (except for nuclear and hydro sources) and to place their transmission lines under the control of a new organization, the California Independent System Operator (ISO), which assumed responsibility for managing a new statewide high voltage electrical grid formed by the merger of two separate grids formerly owned and managed by the two utilities Pacific Gas & Electric (PG&E) in the north and Southern California Edison (SCE) in the south.

The restructuring created a new set of institutions and relationships, many without precedent in the experience or culture of electric power provision. A fuller and more detailed history and description of these changes and relationships are beyond the scope of this paper and can be found in Roe and van Eeten (2002). Here we present the specific findings on the reliability of electricity provision under performance conditions arising out of California's electricity restructuring that relate most directly to the different organizations charged with the actual provision of reliable electricity under the restructured conditions – namely, the ISO, private generators, and distribution utilities, each with competing goals arising out of the deregulation-based restructuring.

Research methods. Our research team relied on multiple methods, documents and key informants to identify and crosscheck our findings. A two-phase study for this research was adopted. In early 1999, we reviewed the literature on deregulation of the energy sector, with special reference to California's electricity restructuring. During this initial phase, we identified the California ISO as the focal organization for primary research. We approached key officials there and received permission to interview staff in and around the ISO main control room. Key informant interviews proceeded by the snowballing technique, in which new interviewees were identified as "people we should talk to" by previous interviewees, until we reached a point where new interviewees were mentioning the same or similar problems and issues heard in previous interviews. An interview questionnaire was used throughout (allowing open-ended responses and follow up), with face-to-face interviews typically lasting an hour or more. A major portion of the research is from direct observation, watching what control room operators and engineers did in their jobs through many shifts in performance conditions.

We undertook the bulk of investigations between April and December 2001. Sixty inter-viewees were identified and interviewed: 33 in and around the main control room of the ISO; eight at PG&E (e.g., in and around their Transmission Operations Center and the Operations Engineering units); five with a large generation supplier (a senior generation official and control room operators in one of its large California plants) and a private market energy trading dot com; and 14 others located in the governor's office, California Public Utilities Commission, California Energy Commission, Electric Power Research Institute, Lawrence Berkeley National Laboratory, University of California, Berkeley, and Stanford. We were also able to observe con-trol room behavior at a high point of the electricity crisis in April–May 2001.

Our interviews and observations focused on control rooms. Earlier HRO research as well as more recent investigations (van Eeten and Roe, 2002) found control rooms to be the one place where HRO features were visible across a wide range of behavior, namely the technical compe-tence, complex activities, high performance at peak levels, search for improvements, teamwork, pressures for safety, multiple (redundant) sources of information and cross-checks, and a culture of reliability, all working through tightly coupled, sophisticated technologies and systems.

Our focus on the control rooms of the ISO, PG&E, and the unnamed private generator also allows us to address the issue of tight coupling and complex interactivity directly. The most remarkable feature we observed was that there was not one operator in the ISO control room who was not tightly linked to the outside through multiple communications and feedback systems. Everyone, all the time, uses the telephone; pagers were continually beeping; internal computers inside the control rooms "talked to" external computers outside; the AGC (Auto-matic Generation Control) system connects the ISO generation dispatcher directly to privately 4held generators; the ADS (Automatic Dispatch System) connected the dispatcher directly to the bidder of electricity; dynamic scheduling systems in the ISO controls out-of-state genera-tors; governors on generators automatically bring frequency back into line; the frequency and ACE (Area Control Error) measurements reflect real-time electricity usage across the grid; all kinds of telemetry measurements come back to the control room in real time; web pages used by the ISO, PG&E and private generators carried real-time prices and information; an operator in the ISO control room uses software to make the time error correction for the entire grid; and on and on.

We used this tight coupling and potential for complex interactions as the basis for our defi-nition of the "high reliability network" of control rooms in the ISO, distribution utilities, and private generators responsible for the direct provision of reliable electricity. "Network" means many things to many people, but for us California's "high reliability network" has a very spe-cific meaning: it is the control room operators and staff connected to each other through direct phone lines and speed dial monitors – those quintessential examples of "always on, always avail-able" communications with the greatest potential for operator and technological "error." For example, the ISO's generation dispatcher had a touch monitor speed dial that connected the operator directly to others in the distribution utilities and private generators. One connection was to the PG&E's control room for its own market trading activities. The PG&E control room operator, in turn, had speed dial contact with the ISO generation dispatcher. Some of the plants the PG&E control room used to contact directly are now owned by private energy suppliers. In our interview with plant operators in the one privately owned plant, an operator showed us his direct lines, particularly one to the company's trading floor and traders. These links come full circle, in that while the ISO generation dispatcher did not have a direct line to the plant we visited, that operator did have one to that supplier's trading floor just as does the operator in the plant's control room. In addition, we suspected that the ISO generation dispatcher might have been calling plant control operators informally during extreme peak demand days. Phone calls by operators who are wired to each other through the other sophisticated technologies and software just identified are the life blood of California's high reliability network for electricity provision.

Research framework. Figure 26.1 offers a closer view of the California high reliability network at the time of research (HRN) and as defined earlier.

Six nodes of activity in the HRN were unbundled as a result of electricity restructuring – from right to left in Figure 26.1: the three nodes of generation, transmission, and distribution and within each node both a market and technology subnode. The transmission node is run by the market and high-voltage grid transmission staff located in the ISO: its market desk coordinators and the generation dispatcher (GD) along with his or her grid support staff in the control room. The distribution node is represented by a utility, PG&E, in its market and lower-voltage grid distribution staff, particularly at the time of writing its trading unit (Electricity Portfolio and Operations Services or EPOS) and its distribution control room (Transmission Operations Center, TOC). There are also other distribution units, such as SCE. The generation node has both a market or trading floor and a plant generation or technology subnodes.

Restructuring coupled the three major nodes in two ways: through markets and through the grid and its support technology. In principle, markets were to be the main coordinative mechanism for grid operations – that is, market transactions result in the electricity schedules that are to be the basis of grid operations. In terms of Figure 26.1, PGE's TOC, the ISO's generation dispatcher, and the generation plant are organized around the grid, while PGE's EPOS, the ISO's markets, and private generator's trading floor were organized around market operations. Reflecting this functional interconnection, market people tended to talk to market people, just as grid people tend to talk to grid people across the HRN's three unbundled nodes.

Many relationships are possible between and among the three nodes and their market and grid subnodes. In practice, however, formal relations are circumscribed by objective, mandate, legislation and regulation. Within each node, market and grid operations are to be separate: PGE's EPOS was not meant to be in communication with TOC, generation plant staff were meant to have final authority over unscheduled outages, not the trading floor, and the ISO's ability to undertake outage coordination activities with the generators was highly restricted by what types of information either node can obtain from the other. Informal communications outside formally restricted channels, however, continued to be important for ensuring the reliability of electricity in volatile situations requiring a bridge between profit motive on the part of the generator or trading unit and the reliability mandate on the part of the transmission control room.

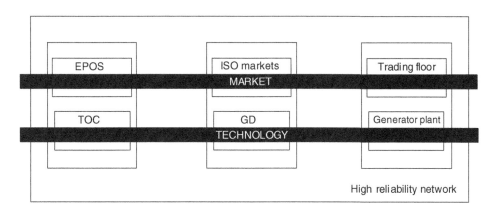

Figure 26.1 California's high reliability network for restructured electricity provision

Because unstable (that is, unpredictable or uncontrollable) situations increase the pressure to communicate between units, especially units within the same organization, an extensive set of support staff has grown up around the market and grid operations rooms of each unbundled node and its market and technology subnodes. We call this supporting staff the "wraparound" – in the ISO's case, the staff supporting market and grid operations are literally circled around the ISO's control room. We have found these wraparound supporting control room operations in other critical infrastructures as well, such as water and telecommunications. A wraparound is the site of formal and informal communication with counterparts in the other wraparounds, especially during crisis situations.

The respective control room and the wraparound form an organizational infrastructure around the market and the technology operations, which we term the market matrix and technology matrix. Each matrix connects the market or the technology subnodes across the three nodes of generation, transmission, and distribution. In Figure 26.1, the horizontal "market" bar represents the flow of market transactions; the horizontal "technology" bar represents the flow of electricity on the grid.

To a degree, the market and grid flows were also separated in the old utilities. The important difference between the California HRN and the older integrated utilities, however, is that the markets, under restructuring, were supposed to coordinate across the matrices, with the focal organization for coordination being the ISO. In reality, extensive organizational interactions between and among control rooms and wraparounds are needed in order that markets can operate, to connect market transactions to the physical properties of grid and, ultimately, to avoid grid collapse and decomposition or "islanding." Both the technology and market matrices are "opened" at their ends, as the California grid is itself part of the western grid, and the "California" electricity markets are themselves already globalized in important respects. For example, Mirant Energy Corporation was not only a California energy supplier at the time of our research, but also an international energy supplier. This openness, combined with the divergent interests of the generators, utilities, and the ISO, define the "open systems" feature of the HRN.

Research findings. Our research question was: How did this tightly coupled, highly interactive "network" of control rooms, which operated within organizations and systems having different mandates and interests, actually ensure the provision of reliable electricity during the California electricity crisis? Our answer: the focal organization, the ISO, balances load and generation in real time (that is, in the current hour or for the hour ahead) by developing and maintaining a repertoire of responses and options in the face of unpredictable or uncontrollable system instability produced either within the network (e.g., by generators acting in a strategic fashion) and from outside the network through its open system features (e.g., temperatures and climate change). "Load" is the demand for electricity and "generation" is the electricity to meet that load, both of which must be balanced (i.e., made equal to each other) within proscribed periods of time; otherwise service delivery is interrupted as the grid physically fails or collapses. We call this need to balance load and generation along with meeting other related limits the "reliability requirement" of the ISO control room operators.

In meeting the reliability requirement the ISO generation dispatcher, commonly known as the gen dispatcher, manages the grid in real time by estimating how much of an increase or decrease in energy is needed to control the ACE, which shows the relative balance between generation and load in California's grid. Maximum fluctuations in the ACE are set by the wider reliability criteria of the Western Electricity Coordinating Council (WECC), which sets standards of operation for that Western region. It is the task of the generation dispatchers to keep the imbalances of the ISO's grid within these bandwidths. How well the generation dispatcher does his or her work determines the number of violations of control performance standards

(CPS) and disturbance control standards (DCS) the ISO faces. Such control area reliability and performance standards are set by the WECC and the North American Electricity Reliability Council (NERC).

It is within these constraints that the generation dispatcher tries to control the grid. To keep the system within the parameters, the generation dispatcher closely watches the frequency and ACE trends, the output of all power plants, and some vital path indicators on his monitor to determine the stability state and "movement" of the grid on the ACE and frequency parameters. (The frequency standard within the US has been set to 60 Hertz and is an inherent characteristic of the stability of the grid.) To adjust frequency and ACE, the generation dispatcher can order contracted power plants to increase or decrease their electricity output. But it takes time before the actual dispatching order of the generation dispatcher and the effects of his or her orders can be noted in the grid behavior. Power plants increase or decrease their power output rather slowly, and it takes some time before the cumulative effects of these changes take effect in the ACE and frequency rate.

With that background in mind, our research led us to focus on the match between, on one hand, the options and strategies within the HRN to achieve its reliability requirement (namely, balancing load and generation, staying within standards set for key transmission lines or "paths," while meeting the other parameter constraints) and, on the other hand, the unpredictable or uncontrollable threats to fulfilling the reliability requirement. A match results from having at least one option sufficient to meet the requirement under given conditions. At any point, there is the possibility of a mismatch between the system variables that must be managed to achieve the reliability requirement and the options and strategies available for managing those variables.

The match between option and system requirements can be visualized in the following way. Within the HRN, the core reliability tasks are located in the focal organization, the ISO's main control room. It is the only unit that simultaneously has the two reliability mandates: keeping the flow and protecting the grid. Meeting the dual reliability mandate involves managing the options and strategies that coordinate actions of the independent generators, energy traders, and the distribution utilities in the HRN. As the focal organization, the options the ISO control room deploys are HRN-wide options; for example, outage coordination is the responsibility of the ISO, but involves the other partners in the high reliability network.

In other words, the ISO control management can be categorized in terms of the variety of HRN-based options it, the ISO, has available (high or low) and the instability of the California electricity system (high or low), as set out in Table 26.1.

Instability is the extent to which the focal control room in the ISO faces rapid, uncontrollable changes or unpredictable conditions that threaten the grid and service reliability of electricity supply, that is, that threaten the task of balancing load and generation. Some days are those of low instability, fondly called "normal days" in the past. A clear example of high instability are the days for which a large part of the forecasted load had not been scheduled through the day ahead

Table 26.1 Performance conditions for the focal ISO control room

		System instability	
		High	Low
Network options variety	High	Just-in-time performance	Just-in-case performance
	Low	Just-for-now performance	Just-this-way performance

market, which means that the ISO actual flows are unpredictable and congestion will have to be dealt with at the last minute. Additionally, any loss of transmission or generating capacity can introduce instability into the system.

Options variety is the amount of HRN resources, including strategies, available to the ISO control room to respond to events in the system in order to keep load and generation balanced at any specific point in time. It includes available operating reserves and other generation capacity, available transmission capacity, and the degree of congestion. High option variety means, for instance, that the ISO has available to it a range of resources and can operate well within required regulatory required conditions. Low options variety means the resources are below requirements and, ultimately, that very few resources are left and the ISO must operate close to, or even in violation of, some regulatory margins.

These two dimensions together set the conditions under which the ISO control room has to pursue its high reliability management. They demand, and we observed, four different performance modes for achieving reliability (i.e., balancing load and generation) which we term just-in-case, just-in-time, just-for-now, and just-this-way. "Low" and "high" are obviously imprecise terms, though they are the terms used and commonly recognized by many of our ISO interviewees. In practice, the system instability and options variety dimensions should be better thought of as continua without rigid high and low cut-off points. Let us turn now to a brief description of each performance mode.

Just-in-case performance, redundancy, and maximum equifinality. When options are high and instability low, just-in-case performance is dominant in the form of high redundancy. Reserves available to the ISO control room operators are large, excess plant capacity (the bête noire of so many deregulation economists) exists at the generator level, and the distribution lines are working with ample backups, all much as forecasted with little or no unpredictability and/or uncontrollability. More formally, redundancy is a state where the number of different but effective options to balance load and generation is high relative to the market and technology requirements for balancing load and generation. There are, in other words, a number of different options and strategies to achieve the same balance. The state of high redundancy is best summed up as one of maximum equifinality, that is, a multitude of means exist to meet the reliability requirement.

Just-in-time performance, real-time flexibility, and adaptive equifinality. When options and instability are both high, just-in-time performance is dominant. Option variety to maintain load and generation remains high, but so is the instability of system variables, in both markets (e.g., rapid price fluctuations leading to unexpected strategic behavior by market parties) and technology (e.g., sagging transmission lines during unexpectedly hot weather).

How does just-in-time performance work? Operators told us about days that started with major portions of the load still not scheduled and with the predictability of operations significantly diminished. Reliability becomes heavily dependent on the ISO control room's ability to pull resources and the balance together up to the last minute. Because of the time pressure this brings with it, operators cannot rely completely on their highly specialized tasks and procedures, but initiate a great deal of lateral communication to quickly and constantly relay and adapt all kinds of information. We call this "keeping the bubble" with respect to the variables that need to be managed given the performance conditions they face. They not only have to respond quickly to unpredictable and uncontrollable events. They also have to ensure that their responses are based on understanding variables so that these responses do not exacerbate the balance problem, especially as confusion over what is actually happening can be intense at these times as well as the risk of cascading variables. It is no longer possible to separate beforehand important and unimportant information. People from the wraparound are pulled into operations and real time to extend the capability to process information quickly and synthesize it into a "bubble" of understanding the many more variables and complex interactions possible in just-in-time performance.

This performance condition demands "real-time" flexibility, that is, the ability to utilize and develop different options and strategies quickly in order to balance load and generation. Since operators in the control room are in constant communication with each other and others in the HRN, options are reviewed and updated continually, and informal communications are much more frequent. Flexibility in real-time is the state where the operators are so focused on meeting the reliability requirement and the options to do so that more often than not they customize the match between them, that is, the options are just enough and just-in-time. The fact that the instability is high focuses operator attention on exactly what needs to be addressed and clarifies the search for adequate options and strategies. What needs to get done gets done with what is at hand as it is needed.

More formally, the state of real-time flexibility is best summed up as adaptive equifinality: there are effective alternative options, many of which are developed or assembled as required to meet the reliability requirement. The increased instability in system behavior is matched by the flexibility in the focal organization in using network options and strategies for keeping performance within reliability tolerances and bandwidths. Substitutability of options and strategies is high for "just-in-time" performance, an immensely important point to which we return at the paper's end. As one ISO control room shift manager put it, "in this [control room] situation, there are more variables and more chances to come up with solutions." "It's so dynamic," said one of the ISO's market resource coordinators, "and there are so many possibilities . . . Things are always changing."

Just-for-now performance and maximum potential for deviance amplification. When option variety is low but instability is high, just-for-now performance is dominant. Options to maintain load and generation have become visibly fewer and potentially insufficient relative to what is needed in order to balance load and generation. This state could result from various reasons related to the behavior of the open system that is the California energy sector. Unexpected outages can occur, load may increase to the physical limits of transmission capacity, and the use of some options can preclude or exhaust other options, for example, using stored hydro capacity now rather than later. In this case, unpredictability or uncontrollability has increased while the variety of effective options and strategies is diminished. Here, "crisis management" begins to come into play, for example, the ISO's declaration of "Stage 1" or "Stage 2" emergency (public alerts based upon reserve generation capacity falling below 7% and 5% of current load, respectively) may compel an ISO senior manager to go outside official channels and call his counterpart at a private generator, who agrees to keep the unit online "just for now."

More formally, just-for-now performance is a state summed up as one of maximum potential for "deviance amplification": even small deviations in elements of the market, technology or other factors in the system can ramify widely throughout the system (Maruyama, 1963). Marginal changes can have maximum impact in threatening the reliability requirement, that is, the loss of a low-megawatt generator can tip the system into blackouts. From the standpoint of reliability, this state is untenable. Here people have no delusions that they are in control. They understand how vulnerable the grid is, how limited the options are, and how precarious the balance; they are keeping communications lines open to monitor the state of the network; and they are busily engaged in developing options and strategies to move out of this state. They are not panicking and, indeed, by prior design, they still retain the crucial option to reconfigure the electricity system itself, by declaring a Stage 3 emergency (discussed later).

Just-for-now performance is also very fast-paced and best summed up as "firefighting." When options become few and room for maneuverability boxed in (e.g., when load continues to rise while new generation become much less assured and predictable), control operators become even more focused on the big threats to balancing load and generation. As options become depleted, wraparound staff in the control room come to have little more to add. There is less need for lateral, informal relations. Operators even walk away from their consoles and join the others in looking up at the big board on the side wall. "I'm all tapped out," said the gen dispatcher on the day we were there when the ISO just escaped issuing a Stage 3 declaration. Operators and support staff are waiting for new, vital information, because they are out of other options for controlling the ACE themselves.

Just-this-way performance, crisis management, and zero equifinality. In this last performance mode for balancing load and generation, system instability is lowered to match low options variety and just-this-way performance is dominant. This performance state occurs in the California electricity system as a short-term "emergency" solution. In an electricity crisis, the option is to tamp down instability directly with the hammer of crisis controls and forced network reconfigurations. The ultimate instrument of crisis management strategy is the Stage 3 declaration, which requires interruption of firm load in order to bring back the balance of load and generation from the brink of just-for-now performance. The effect of a Stage 3 declaration is to reconfigure the grid into a system under command and control management. Load reductions can be ordered from major wholesale electricity distributors.

More formally, just-this-way performance is a state best summed up as one of zero equifinality: whatever flexibility could be squeezed through the remaining option and strategies is forgone on behalf of maximum control of a single system variable, in this case load. The Stage 3 declaration has become both a necessary and sufficient condition for balancing load and generation, again by reducing load directly. This contrasts significantly with the other three performance conditions. There the options and strategies are sufficient, without being necessary. Under "just-this-way" performance conditions, the decision to shed load has been taken and now information is centered around compliance. The vertical relations and hierarchy of the control room extends into the HRN, even to the distribution utilities in their rotating outage blackouts. Formal rules and procedure move center stage, including the declaring and ending the Stage 3 declaration. Here the HRN looks most like the structure it was before restructuring, but only because of the exceptional vulnerability of grid reliability to threats. Interruptions to service become paramount. With Stage 3, operators reassume their responsibilities and roles. Wraparound staff remain ready to help and back up, if and when needed.

The operational differences we observed in the ISO control room and the larger HRN under these four performance modes are summarized in Table 26.2.

To conclude this section, note that one of the important features of the reliability management of the ISO within the HRN is the large proportion of that management that occurs in real-time, that is, under conditions of high system instability. Estimates given by ISO participants of time spent in just-in-time and just-for-now performance modes ranged from 75–85% in mid-2002, a year after the state's famous electricity "crisis". In April 2003, the percentage was some 60%, even after another year's stabilization efforts (including the must-offer requirements placed on generators and substantial new generation coming on line). This is a departure from the large preponderance of anticipatory, just-in-case management found in much of the earlier HRO research. Indeed, the California system cannot be reliable with respect to grid or service reliability without having the options to perform just-in-time or just-for-now. What this means is that the ISO control rooms and others in the HRN are engaged in a very different kind of reliability management from than found in much of earlier HROs.

Table 26.2 Features of high reliability performance modes

	Performance mode			
	Just-in-case	Just-in-time	Just-for-now	Just-this-way
Instability	low	high	high	low
Option variety	high	high	low	low
Principal feature	high redundancy	real-time flexibility	maximum potential for amplified deviance	command & control
Equifinality	maximum equifinality	adaptive equifinality	low equifinality	zero equifinality
Operational risks	risk of inattention & complacency	risk of misjudgment because of time & system constraints	risk of exhausted options & lack of maneuverability (most untenable mode)	risk of control failure over what needs to be controlled
Variables of attention	structural variables (e.g., operating reserves)	escalating variables (e.g., cascading accidents)	triggering variables (e.g., a single push over the edge)	control variables (e.g., enforcing load shedding requirements)
Information strategy	vigilant watchfulness	keeping the bubble	localized firefighting	compliance monitoring
Lateral communication	little lateral communication during routine operations	rich, lateral communication for complex system operations in real-time	lateral communication around focused issues and events	little lateral communication, during fixed protocol (closest to command & control)
Rules and procedures	performing according to wide-ranging established rules and procedures	performing in & outside analysis; many situations not covered by procedures	performing reactively, waiting for something to happen, i.e., "I'm all tapped out"	performing to very specific set of detailed procedures
Orientation toward area control error	having control	keeping control	losing control	forcing command & control

Reliability management revisited

Our interviewees told us that there was not one official reliability standard that has not been pushed to its limits and beyond in the California electricity crisis. The emerging reliability criteria, standards, and associated operational bandwidths had one common denominator: they reflect the effort by members of the HRN, particularly the ISO control room, to adapt reliability criteria to meet circumstances that they can actually manage, where those circumstances are increasingly real time in their urgency. What cannot be controlled "just-in-case" has to be managed "just-in-time"; if that does not work, performance has to be "just-for-now"; or, barring that, "just-this-way" by shedding load directly. In each instance, reliability becomes that bar that the operators can actually jump.

The standards at issue are many. Most important, operating reserve limits have not only been questioned, but the system has operated reliably – in particular, peak load demands have been met continuously and safely – at lower reserve levels than officially mandated in WECC standards. CPS criteria have been disputed and efforts are underway to change them. There has been mounting pressure to justify empirically standards that were formulated ex cathedra in earlier periods and have since become "best operating practices." One senior ISO engineer told us,

> Disturbance control standards (DCS) says that if I have a hit, a unit goes offline, ACE goes up, I have to recover within ten minutes. Theory was that during that time you were exposed to certain system problems. But who said 10 minutes? God? An engineering study? What are the odds that another unit will go offline? One in a million? So now with WECC we have turned the period into 15 minutes, because the chance of another [unit] going offline is low, as we know from study of historical records.

There is, in fact, a paradox between having reliability standards and having multiple ways to produce electricity reliably. On the one hand, the standards are operationalized (in terms of the WECC) and the fact that performance can be empirically gauged against these operational measures is the chief measuring stick of whether electricity is being provided reliably or not. On the other hand, the standards were everywhere being redefined in the crisis, when not questioned, because there are an increasing number of times when only by pushing the standards to their limits and sometimes beyond were the lights kept on. A senior manager in the ISO operations engineering unit, responsible for a large body of procedures, told us, "part of the [control room] experience is to know when not to follow procedures . . . there are bad days when a procedure doesn't cover it, and then you have to use your wits."

Perhaps the best way to understand the distinctiveness of this approach to reliability is to compare and contrast the principal features of traditional HROs (such as the Diablo Canyon nuclear power plant) with the approach taken in the California high reliability network, both of which seek and achieve high reliability in connection with electricity.

Table 26.3 can be seen as a multiple-dimensioned gradient in high reliability service provision between two approaches to reliability management of the tightly coupled, complexly interactive technologies in our electricity critical infrastructure. The dimensions that differ are telling. The differences between trial and error learning and redundancy are particularly important to understand.

The earlier literature on HROs found that they avoided anything like the large-scale experimentation we found in the California HRN. The improvisational and experimental are what we have summed up as "adaptive equifinality" in just-in-time performance. What was unacceptable in the HRO has become the sine qua non for service and grid reliability in the HRN – but only in real time.

First, there were experiments on the large scale – that is, on the scale of the California grid as a whole – which were grid-wide because the ISO could not do otherwise. They were undertaken involuntarily, that is, the ISO had little choice, for example, in introducing "proxy marketing" software over the whole grid. Over the course of the day it was introduced, complaints were made that price information was wrong, numbers were not showing up, and the information wasn't in real time.

Why experiment this way? Because the status quo had become untenable for the system operator, thanks to increased instabilities introduced into the electricity system through the restructuring-induced electricity crisis. Bids from market traders were not coming in and

Table 26.3 Comparison of selected features of HRO and HRN management

HRO management (vide HRO research on Diablo Canyon)	HRN management (vide research on California's HRN)
• high technical competence • constant search for improvement • often hazard-driven adaptation to ensure safety • often highly complex activities • reliability is nonfungible	• high technical competence • constant short-term search for improvement • often hazard-driven adaptation to ensure safety • often highly focused complex activities • reliability is nonfungible in real time, except when service reliability jeopardizes grid reliability
• limitations on trial & error learning • operation within anticipatory analysis • flexible authority patterns within HRO • positive, design-based redundancy to ensure stability of inputs and outputs	• real-time operations necessitating improvisation and experimentation • operations outside analysis • flexible authority patterns within focal organization and across HRN • maximum equifinality (positive redundancy), adaptive equifinality (not necessarily designed), and zero equifinality, all depending on network performance conditions

operators had to do something (i.e., we now know that some of the bids were being withheld for strategic reasons by the private energy traders). The "something" that the ISO did was to create proxy bids for the remainder of generation capacity not bid in by the energy traders. In such ways, real-time operations and experiments become synonyms. Moreover, even involuntary experiments can become occasions for learning, much as near misses are in other sectors. The real-time experiment, deliberate or inadvertent, became a design probe from which operators can learn more about the limits of service and grid reliability. "You don't learn as fast as you can, until you have to respond to something that requires fast response," argued a senior control room manager at PG&E's transmission operations center.

The traditional HRO nuclear power plant would never undertake (or in all likelihood be allowed to undertake by regulatory agencies) such experiments, as it seeks both stable inputs (for example, the predictable quality of parts and supplies through "nuclear grade" regulations, isolation from grid dispatch systems, even controlling its surrounding environment through guns and guards) as well as stable outcomes. In the HRN's case, there is no stable resting point for the grid and its demands, because there are few routines and operating procedures that can stabilize inputs (e.g., load, generation availability, or grid conditions) in order to facilitate highly reliable outputs. One reason why the operations-as-experimentation can continue is that shedding load is a live option for maintaining real-time reliability. If just-in-time performance fails, operators can always shift into just-for-now or just-this-way performance modes.

NAT revisited

What we see in the findings from the California HRN is that both complexity and tightly coupled interactions can serve, and often do serve, as positive sources of high reliability performance. The complexity actually allows adaptive equifinality in just-in-time performance because many variables are in play, such that some combination of options can be stitched together at the last minute. The tight coupling actually positions operators within the ISO where they can implement their reliability "solutions" as well as exercise the Stage 3 option of command and control.

An important aspect of this real-time reliability is *substitutability*. Substitutability is key for just-in-time performance, where system instabilities are compensated for by flexibility in responses. This view contrasts with that of Normal Accidents Theory (NAT). For NAT, the ability to substitute elements is a property of loosely coupled systems and linearly interactive ones. According to Perrow,

> what is true for buffers and redundancies is also true for substitutions of equipment, processes and personnel. Tightly coupled systems offer few occasions for such fortuitous substitutions; loosely coupled ones offer many.
>
> *(Perrow, 1999, 96)*

Yet we found that the same substitutability is key to just-in-time performance, when the technology of the grid remains as tightly coupled as it has always been.

The primary reason why tight coupling and complexity were found to serve as a resource or options in the HRN case study but not in the earlier Diablo Canyon case lies in the differing roles paid by causal analysis. Near-complete causal analysis is central to the high reliability performance of traditional HROs; not so for the HRN just described. In the HRN, pattern recognition in meeting the reliability requirement is especially important. The urgency of real time makes it crucial to "read" feedback in terms of signature events that can guide the balancing of load and generation, in the absence of operators having to have full causal knowledge of the system in the process. This substitutability of reliability-enhancing signature events for complete causal understanding of the system is particularly important, as the earlier HRO research found nearly complete causal understanding necessary for reliability, while its absence increases the risk of normal accidents.

None of this is to say that tight coupling and complex interactivity are not a problem for the electricity critical infrastructure as it currently exists. They are, but in a different way than NAT poses. There are indeed risks and dangers of errors arising because of misjudgment (important in just-in-time performance) and exhausting options without room to maneuver (important in just-for-now performance). We return to these situations in the concluding section of the paper.

The role of reliability professionals[3]

According to NAT, tightly coupled and complexly interactive technologies are particularly hazardous because each element summons up a contradictory management strategy. Tight coupling, according to Perrow, means that operators require centralization of authority and operations, with unquestioned obedience and immediate response capability. Complex interactivity, in contrast, requires decentralization of authority to cope with unplanned interactions on the ground by those closest to the system. What this description highlights is, in our terms, the trade-off between resistance and resilience in management.

The question is, who does this balancing between resistance and resilience? Who reconciles the need for anticipation and careful causal analysis with the need for flexibility and improvisation in the face of turbulent inputs into complex and tightly coupled systems? In our research we found a crucial, if neglected, role for middle level professionals – controllers, dispatchers, technical supervisors, and department heads – in doing the balancing act so necessary to the real-time reliability of these networked systems. We term them "reliability professionals" in recognition of their overriding commitment to the real-time reliability of their systems, and the unique set of skills they bring to their tasks.

The quest for high reliability in tightly coupled, highly interactive critical infrastructures can be characterized briefly along two dimensions: (1) the type of knowledge brought to bear on efforts to make an operation or system reliable, and (2) the focus of attention or scope of these reliability efforts. The knowledge base from which reliability is pursued can range from formal or representational knowledge, in which key activities are understood through abstract principles and deductive models based upon these principles, to experience, based on informal or tacit understanding, generally derived from trial and error. At the same time, the scope of attention can range from a purview which embraces reliability as an entire system output, encompassing many variables and elements of a process associated with producing a stream of reliable results; to a case-by-case focus in which each case is viewed as a particular event with distinct properties or characteristics. These two continua of knowledge and scope define a conceptual and perceptual space within which reliability can be pursued. Table 26.4 illustrates the point:

At the extreme of both scope and formal principles is the formal design approach to reliability. Here formal deductive principles are applied to understanding a wide variety of critical processes. It is considered inappropriate to operate beyond the design analysis, and that analysis is meant to cover an entire reliability system, including every last case to which that system can be subjected. The design in this sense is more than analysis; it is a major control instrument for the behavior of the system. This is the approach that dominates in a conventional HRO, such as a nuclear power plant, where operating "outside of analysis" is a major regulatory violation. At the other extreme is the activity of constant reactive behavior in the face of case-by-case challenges. Here reliability resides in the reaction time of control room operators rather than the anticipation of system designers.

Both positions are, however, extremes. Each alone is insufficient as an approach to providing grid and service reliability, though each is necessary. Designers cannot foresee everything, and the more "complete" a logic of design principles attempts to be, the more likely it is that the full set will contain two or more principles which contradict each other. On the other hand, case-by-case reactions by their very nature are likely to give the operator too specific and individualized a picture, losing sight of the proverbial forest for the trees. Experience can become a "trained incapacity" that leads to actions undermining reliability because operators may not be aware of the wider ramifications of what they are doing.

Table 26.4 Reliability space and key professional activities

		Scope of reliability focus	
		System-wide (All cases)	Specific event (Single case)
	Representational (Formal, deductive)	DESIGN	Contingency scenarios
Knowledge base		**Reliability professionals**	
	Experiential (Tacit; often trial and error)	Strategic adaptations	REACTIVE OPERATIONS

What to do? First, "moving horizontally" across the reliability space directly from one corner across to the opposite corner (i.e., upper left to upper right, lower right to lower left) is unlikely to be successful. A great deal of reliability research supports the findings to the effect that attempts to impose large-scale formal designs directly onto an individual case – to attempt to anticipate and fully deduce and determine the behavior of each instance – are fraught with risk (Turner, 1978; Perrow, 1983). Yet this is what system designers attempted at times to do to secure reliability in the California system – to, as one engineer described it, "design systems that are not only fool proof but damned fool proof."

At the same time, trying to account for an entire system on the basis of first-hand experiential knowledge can scarcely be successful either. Generalizations and some formalization are necessary in order to store, transmit, and apply the knowledge necessary to manage complex systems.

Instead of horizontal, corner-to-corner movements, Figure 26.3 indicates that reliability is enhanced when shifts in scope *are accompanied by shifts in the knowledge base*. Given the limitations of the extremes in this reliability space, it becomes important to operate in positions closer to a shared center by (1) moving from reactions to building pattern recognitions and strategic adaptations and (2) by moving from designs to contingency planning and scenario building. It is difficult to tack to this middle ground, to combine macro and micro perspectives on a complex system and to bring together logic and experience and (perhaps even more difficult) theory and practice. It is, however, in this middle ground where doctrine is tempered by experience, discretion added to design, and shared views reconciled with individualized perspectives. Here a high degree of improvisation and inventiveness is often in evidence.

The skill to pursue reliability from this center ground seems to derive less from disciplines than from professions, less from specialized training than from careers that span a variety of positions and perspectives. The middle ground, in a phrase, is the domain of the reliability professional. The importance of this middle-level reliability professional to the high reliability of complex technologies such as the California HRN could hardly be overstated. Yet they are typically neglected by system designers, regulators, and the public alike. It is with this group and their professionalism where we believe the greatest gains in grid and service reliability are to be found, both practical and conceptual. The next step in developing high reliability theory should be in better understanding these professionals, their work and the cognitive skills they bring to bear on it.

More to the point, the stakes have never been higher in getting the argument right. We raise one final issue to underscore this point: the reliability of critical infrastructures in the face of terrorist assault.

Potential security implications

At issue for *Making the Nation Safer* (National Research Council, 2002) and similar security analyses is the notion that critical infrastructures have discrete points of vulnerability or "choke points," which if subject to attack or failure threaten the performance of the entire infrastructure. Key transmission lines upon which an electrical grid depends, or single security screening portals for airline passengers, or a single financial audit on which countless investment decisions are predicated are points of vulnerability which can lead to cascading failures throughout the whole system. The more central the choke point to the operation of the complex system, so this logic goes, the more dependent and susceptible the system is to sabotage or failure.

Currently, the dominant recommendation is to redesign these systems by decentralizing them so as to render them less interdependent. Decentralize power grids and generators, making smaller, more self-contained transmission and distribution systems. A major assumption is that decentralization, looser coupling and reductions in the scale of critical systems will reduce their vulnerability to terrorist attack. Indeed the existence of choke points, it has been argued, signals the vulnerability of these systems, both inviting and guiding terrorist attack.

But our research suggests that this perspective on vulnerability to terrorists should be considered more carefully. In fact, redesigns undertaken from the current perspective might undermine some of the very features that ensure the operational reliability of these systems in the first place. As we have just seen, reliability has been rooted in the processes that take place within the tightly coupled complexly interactive infrastructure – the behaviors, adaptations, and innovations that take place when things do not go as anticipated. It is precisely this aspect of reliability – the skills, experience, and knowledge of reliability professionals – that could be lost in a preoccupation with design-focused perspectives on security.

While the current view sees choke points as the problem and decentralization or deconcentration as the answer, this is not at all clear from the perspective of reliability professionals. For them, tight coupling can be a system *resource* as well as a source of vulnerability. Choke points are the places where terrorists will likely direct their attention, but they are also, from an operational standpoint, the places to which reliability professionals, with their trained competencies in anticipation and recovery, are most attentive.

Furthermore, from an operational standpoint in relation to terrorism, our research suggests that the prevailing view of reliability could be stood on its head. Complex, tightly coupled systems convey reliability advantages to those trained professionals who seek to protect or restore them against terrorist assault. Their complexity allows for multiple strategies of resilience. Their tightly coupled choke points allow these professionals to see the same portion of the system as the terrorists, and positions them to see it *whole* against a backdrop of alternatives, options, improvisations, and counterstrategy.

In contrast, it is loosely coupled, decentralized systems which present many more independent targets to terrorists – they can strike anywhere and, while they may not bring down major portions of the grid, they can still score their points in the psychological game of terror and vulnerability. The local managers will probably not have a clear picture of what's happening overall, nor will they have as wide a range of alternatives and recovery options available.

Whatever their future vulnerability, it seems clear that more and more critical infrastructures in our society will consist of high performance interdependent systems, across which highly reliable performance is an ongoing requirement. These sets of highly interdependent organizations seem to be consistently pushed to the edge of their design envelopes, under pressure to maximize, if not optimize, their performance. They must subsist in unstable economic, political, and regulatory environments. Perhaps never before has our basic understanding – the "reliability" of reliability theory or the "normal" of normal accidents – been of such great social consequence.

Notes

1 Paul Schulman, Mills College; Emery Roe, University of California at Berkeley; Michel van Eeten and Mark de Bruijne, Delft University of Technology.

2 A fuller account of the California case study, covering more years and with an extension of the analytical framework presented here was subsequently published in Roe and Schulman (2008). In later research these same authors have extended our research and risk analysis to a wider variety of infrastructures including water systems, marine transport and navigation services, telecoms, dam and levee management organizations, railroads, and ports. For these findings see Roe and Schulman (forthcoming).

3 The material in this section on reliability professionals was substantially updated in Roe and Schulman (2008).

References

Beamish, T.D. 2002. *Silent Spill*. Cambridge, MA: MIT Press.

California Public Utilities Commission. 1993. *California's Electric Services Industry: Perspectives on the Past, Strategies for the Future ("The Yellow Book")*. Sacramento: Author.

California Public Utilities Commission. 1996. *Decision 95–12–063 as Modified by D.96–01–009 ("The Blue Book")*. Sacramento: Author.

Carroll, J.S. 1998. "Organizational Learning Activities in High-Hazard Industries." *Journal of Management Studies*, 35: 699–717.

Evan, W.M. and M. Manion. 2002. *Minding the Machines: Preventing Technological Disasters*. Upper Saddle River, NJ: Prentice-Hall.

Homer-Dixon, T. 2002. The rise of complex terrorism. *Foreign Policy*, 128: 52.

Langer, E. 1989. *Mindfulness*. New York: Addison-Wesley.

LaPorte, T. 1994. "A Strawman Speaks Up: Comments on Limits of Safety." *Journal of Contingencies and Crisis Management*, 2: 207–211.

LaPorte, T. 1996. "High Reliability Organizations: Unlikely, Demanding and At Risk." *Journal of Contingencies and Crisis Management*, 4: 60–71.

LaPorte, T. and P. Consolini. 1991. "Working in Practice But Not in Theory: Theoretical Challenges of High Reliability Organizations." *Public Administration Research and Theory*, 1: 19–47.

Mann, D. 2002. *Hands-On Systematic Innovation*. Leper, Belgium: CREAX Press.

Maruyama, M. 1963. The second cybernetics: Deviation-amplifying mutual causative processes. *American Scientist*, 51: 164–179.

Misumi, J., B. Wilpert and R. Miller. 1999. *Nuclear Safety: A Human Factors Perspective*. London: Taylor and Francis.

Morgan, G. 1997. *Images of Organization*. New York: Sage.

National Research Council. 2002. *Making The Nation Safer: The Role of Science and Technology in Countering Terrorism*. Washington, DC: National Academy Press.

Perrow, C. 1979. *Complex Organizations: A Critical Essay*. New York: Wadsworth.

Perrow, C. 1983. "The Organizational Context of Human Factors Engineering." *Administrative Science Quarterly*, 28: 521–541.

Perrow, C. 1994. "Review of S.D. Sagan, *Limits of Safety*." *Journal of Contingencies and Crisis Management*, 2: 212–220.

Perrow, C. 1999. *Normal Accidents*. Princeton, NJ: Princeton University Press.

Reason, J. 1972. *Human Error*. Cambridge: Cambridge University Press.

Rijpma, J.A. 1997. "Complexity, Tight Coupling and Reliability." *Journal of Contingencies and Crisis Management*, 5: 15–23.

Roberts, K. 1990. "Some Characteristics of One Type of High Reliability Organization." *Organization Science*, 1: 160–176.

Roberts, K. (ed.). 1993. *New Challenges To Understanding Organizations*. New York: Macmillan.

Rochlin, G.I. 1993. "Defining High Reliability Organizations in Practice." In K. Roberts (ed.), *New Challenges to Understanding Organizations* (pp. 11–32). New York: Macmillan.

Rochlin, G.I. and A. von Meier. 1994. "Nuclear Power Operations: A Cross Cultural Perspective." *Annual Review of Energy and Environment*, 19: 153–187.

Roe, E. and P. Schulman. (2008). *High Reliability Management*. Stanford, CA: Stanford University Press.

Roe, E. and P. Schulman. (forthcoming). *Reliability and Risk*. Stanford, CA: Stanford University Press.

Roe, E., P. Schulman and M.J.G. van Eeten. 2003. *Real-Time Reliability: Provision of Electricity Under Adverse Performance Conditions Arising from California's Electricity Restructuring and Crisis*. A report prepared for the California Energy Commission, Lawrence Berkeley National Laboratory, and the Electrical Power Research Institute. San Francisco: California Energy Commission.

Roe, E.P. and M.J.G. van Eeten. 2002. *Ecology, Engineering and Management: Reconciling Ecological Rehabilitation and Service Reliability*. New York: Oxford University Press.

Sagan, S. 1993. *The Limits of Safety*. Princeton, NJ: Princeton University Press.

Salvendy, G. 1997. *Handbook of Human Factors and Ergonomics*. New York: Wiley.

Sanne, J.M. 2000. *Creating Safety in Air Traffic Control*. Lund, Sweden: Arkiv Forlag.

Schulman, P.R. 1993a. "The Negotiated Order of Organizational Reliability." *Administration and Society*, 25: 353–372.

Schulman, P.R. 1993b. "The Analysis of High Reliability Organizations: A Comparative Framework." In K. Roberts (ed.), *New Challenges to Understanding Organizations* (pp. 33–54). New York: Macmillan.

Schulman, P.R. 2002. "Medical Errors: How Reliable Is Reliability Theory?" In M.M. Rosenthal and K.M. Sutcliffe (eds.), *Medical Error* (pp. 200–216). San Francisco: Jossey-Bass.

Turner, B.M. 1978. *Man-Made Disasters*. London: Wykeham.

Vaughn, D. 1996. *The Challenger Launch Decision*. Chicago: University of Chicago Press.

Wasserman, S., K. Faust and D. Iacobucci. 1994. *Social Network Analysis*. New York: Cambridge University Press.

Weick, K.E. 1987. "Organizational Culture as a Source of High Reliability." *California Management Review*, 29: 112–127.

Weick, K.E. 1993. "The Vulnerable System: An Analysis of the Tenerife Air Disaster." In K. Roberts (ed.), *New Challenges To Understanding Organizations* (pp. 173–197). New York: Macmillan.

Weick, K.E. and K.M. Sutcliffe. 2001. *Managing the Unexpected*. San Francisco: Jossey-Bass.

Weick, K.E., K.M. Sutcliffe and D. Obstfeld. 1999. "Organizing For High Reliability." *Research in Organizational Behavior*, 21: 81–123.

Wildavsky, A. 1988. *Searching for Safety*. New Brunswick, NJ: Transaction Books.

27

The opaque corners of ERM

S. Abraham (Avri) Ravid[1]

Abstract

The purpose of this chapter is to shed some preliminary light on some of the less obvious issues in enterprise risk management (ERM). Short of offering solutions, we suggest nevertheless that one of the reasons for some of the recent empirical findings may be that ERM is a complex process, which is very difficult to implement successfully.

ERM, frictions, and agency considerations

In markets without frictions, risk-neutral actors should not want to insure or hedge any risks if any insurance premium is charged and they should be indifferent to actuarially fair insurance. Furthermore, in general firms should assume appropriate business risks, since shareholders buy shares for risk exposure and can hedge more easily and cheaply by their own portfolio choices and in various derivative markets.[2] Therefore, it is important to identify the types of risks that a firm would want to assume and risks it would want to insure against. Enterprise risk management (ERM) is a fairly new concept; however, futures contracts date back for centuries (see Carlton, 1984), and the discussion of hedging, both in the academic literature and in the "real world," goes back several decades. The hedging literature proposes several motives for hedging, related to various market frictions, which can make hedging an optimal policy for an individual business entity and can apply to ERM as well.

Smith and Stulz (1985) suggest that taxes, bankruptcy costs, and managerial risk aversion may lead firms to optimally hedge. We will discuss the latter motive in detail later. Froot et al. (1993) justify hedging as a way of avoiding costly external financing, relaxing financial constraints and allowing firms to take advantage of potential future lucrative investment opportunities. Evidence regarding the financing constraint argument is mixed. Rampini et al. (2014) find that airlines with low net worth (i.e., more distressed firms) hedge less. However, Haushalter (2000), who studies the hedging behavior of oil and gas producers, finds a positive correlation between hedging and leverage-related variables. Tufano (1996) finds a positive relation between leverage (which is generally used as a proxy for distress) and the fraction of production hedged. More recently, Bartram et al. (2011) find that derivative users tend to have greater leverage than nonusers. Finally, Chernenko and Faulkender (2011), who study the decision to hedge interest-rate risk, find evidence supporting the theory in Froot et al. (1993).[3]

Many of these frictions relate to other ERM measures as well, although research in this area is less developed (see, e.g., McShane et al., 2011). Much of the theoretical and empirical hedging literature focuses on possibly suboptimal managerial hedging motives. Managers may want to hedge when they have too much of their wealth invested in their own companies. The same argument applies to ERM. Amihud and Lev (1981) suggest that managers diversify their own risky position via conglomerate mergers. The empirical testing of this argument has been somewhat difficult, but the most recent empirical study of that issue (Gormley and Matsa, 2015) supports this idea. DeMarzo and Duffie (1995) focus on another possible setup, which can lead managers to take too little risk, namely the presence of asymmetric information coupled with career concerns. Thus managers who are evaluated on the success of their projects may implement overly conservative policies. In addition to major steps, such as diversifying mergers, managers can lower the risk stemming from production uncertainty in two ways. One is by using hedging instruments (such as derivatives) and the other is by the suboptimal choice of projects. The latter is much more difficult to detect and monitor (who can tell which projects the manager might have taken but did not?). Similarly, while the decision to implement ERM may be publicly announced (see Chapter 22 by Sekerci in this volume), actual steps taken by the company may or may not be reported. Ravid and Basuroy (2004) use project data from the movie industry to show that executives choose suboptimal, low-risk projects (very violent films). Tufano (1996) assesses the motives of managers in the gold mining industry. He detects no correlation between hedging and measures of bankruptcy costs. However, he finds a significant relationship between hedging measures and proxies for risk exposure of executives. There is little support in Haushalter (2000) study for tax proxies and mixed support for managerial risk-aversion proxies, mainly the structure of compensation. Therefore, one may want to focus some more attention on managerial compensation and behavior in ERM as well. In particular, managerial agency issues can be particularly important for ERM – under new regulations firms need to report much of their hedging activity but they do not necessarily report ERM-related choices. It then may be true that agency issues can play an important role in suboptimal implementation of ERM strategies.

ERM and specific risks

An important article by Nocco and Stulz (2006) offers two key insights:

> A company that has no special ability to forecast market variables has no comparative advantage in bearing the risk associated with those variables. In contrast, the same company should have a comparative advantage in bearing information-intensive, firm-specific business risks because it knows more about these risks than anybody else.
>
> *(p. 9)*

Although the key principles that underlie the theory of ERM are well-established, it should be clear from this article that additional research is needed to help with the implementation of ERM. In particular, while much attention has been paid to measures of tail risk like VaR, it has become clear from attempts to implement ERM that a more complete understanding of the distribution of firm value is required. Though correlations between different types of risks are essential in measuring firm-wide risk, existing research provides little help in how to estimate these correlations. Companies also find that some of their most troubling risks – notably, reputational and strategic risks – are the most difficult to quantify.

(p. 20)

These insights focus on a portfolio approach to risks that the firm may want to use. However, in addition to the important insights from portfolio theory, even risks that are orthogonal to each other and where the firm has no particular advantage in bearing them may affect other risks, which the firm may want to bear and thus overall ERM policy. This suggests an overall policy which deviates from the portfolio approach. A good example would be a natural or manmade disaster's risks and fluctuations of market prices of either inputs or outputs. This is best illustrated with an example. Assume a firm that produces cars and uses energy as an input. It carries fire insurance for its plant and at the same time hedges input prices, say by having a forward contract for the delivery of oil at a pre-specified price and at a pre-specified time. There is no correlation between the fluctuations of oil prices and the risk of fire at the plant, therefore, one does not need to worry about the thorny question raised by Nocco and Stulz (2006) of evaluating correlations. Also, it is clear that the firm has no comparative advantage in either of these two risks, and according to Nocco and Stulz (2006) or De Angelis and Ravid (2015) should hedge them both. At the same time, it is clear that these two contracts should be evaluated simultaneously by a chief risk officer (CRO), because should the plant burn down the forward contracts will turn out to be detrimental rather than useful for the firm.

To provide an illustration, let us assume that we could quantify the value (benefit) of hedging oil prices at $10 (as Nocco and Stulz [2006] and many others suggest, it is very difficult to come up with such numbers unless you assume that the benefit to the firm is equal to the market price of the insurance). Let us further assume that there is a 10% chance of a fire that will close the plant. Then the expected value of hedging is only $0.9 \times \$10$ – that is, $9. It is not possible to my knowledge to insure hedging instruments themselves as part of a fire insurance policy, but this example suggests that the firm should consider even risks that are uncorrelated to each other and which it would want to insure as they do interact in the firm production process. Another way of putting it is that the value of the forward contract is lower than priced, since there are additional states of the world in which it will be useless.

Similarly, political risk which may cutoff supply or demand from different countries (in 2015 we may think in terms of Russian gas; in the 1970s, Middle Eastern oil) is uncorrelated to prices of inputs or outputs that are not embroiled in the crisis. However, such uninsurable political risks affect the value of any hedging the firm may engage in.

For example, think of a defense contractor using oil as an input in production of defense systems sold to a third country. The contractor hedges input risks and currency risks. In general one would expect international relations to be orthogonal to currency fluctuations and oil price changes (think a regional crisis in Yemen, not World War II). If defense exports are cut off, then the currency hedges and the oil price hedges will have been wasted.

Another example may be weather-related risks. Imagine an oil platform in the Caribbean. The producing company can hedge its production (see Haushalter, 2000), which may or may not be a good idea (see De Angelis and Ravid, 2015). Yet, such hedging may be of much lower value without weather insurance, since hurricanes can disrupt production and transport and thus render the hedged commodity worthless in additional states of the world.

Such risks and others, including labor unrest, are very different than financial risks that have been analyzed in the ERM literature. However, ERM requires an integrated approach to all of these risks in order to be effective.

The difficulties in implementing correctly such a complex policy and managerial agency issues which may be harder to detect in applying ERM may account for the mixed results in the empirical literature (see Chapter 22 by Sekerci in this volume). Most papers cannot assess the extent and precise implementation of risk management policies and have to rely on indirect indicators such as the nomination of a CRO or an announcement of the introduction of ERM (Liebenberg and Hoyt, 2003; Beasley et al., 2008; Pagach and Warr, 2010; Pagach and Warr, 2011). McShane et al. (2011) use Standard & Poor's risk strategy ratings. However, most of the studies including Pagach and Warr (2011), McShane et al. (2011), and the most recent study by Sekerci in this volume – which is survey based and uses a composite ERM score based on elements implemented and the quality of implementation – find no impact on firm value (Q).

Conclusion

It is mathematically clear that properly constructed ERM should be value enhancing to most firms. However, it is not clear that suboptimally implemented risk measures in the presence of agency issues can achieve a better outcome than partial hedging. For example, De Angelis and Ravid (2015) show that firms in noncompetitive industries with significant market power should not hedge output risks. Should such firms implement ERM by inappropriately hedging commodity risks such a policy can lower firm value. As argued before, since the process is complex, and overall empirical and theoretical modeling is difficult and not there yet, the lack of reaffirmation in empirical studies is not surprising.

Notes

1 S. Abraham (Avri) Ravid, Sy Syms Professor of Finance and Economics, Yeshiva University, Syms School of Business, Visiting Research Professor, NYU Stern School of Business, 500 W. 185th St., New York, NY 10033, Tel: (212) 960-0125. E-mail: ravid@yu.edu.
2 This can be easily understood by the following extreme example from De Angelis and Ravid (2014). Suppose that two firms produce the same product, and their revenue can be either $50 or $150 with equal probabilities. Suppose further that the revenue streams are perfectly negatively correlated. Each firm can pay an insurance company to guarantee $100 in all states by paying the $50 in the good state to cover the $50 shortfall in the bad state. Suppose the insurance company charges $3. Then investors are guaranteed $97. However, it should be obvious that just by buying the two stocks investors can guarantee $100 × 2 in all states on their own, without paying the $3. Or, of course, they can just buy treasuries. Thus, in a world without significant frictions, as long as investors can create portfolios relatively cheaply, firms should not hedge.
3 De Angelis and Ravid (2015) show that there is a marked difference between input and output hedging in particular for firms that have market power in output markets. The latter should and indeed do hedge less.

References

Adam, T., S. Dasgupta, and S. Titman. "Financial Constraints, Competition and Hedging in Industry Equilibrium." *Journal of Finance*, 62 (2007), 2445–2473.
Adam, T., C.S. Fernando, and J.S. Salas. "Why Do Firms Hedge Selectively? Evidence from the Gold Mining Industry." Working paper, University of Berlin, University of Oklahoma, and Lehigh University (2010).
Adam, T.R., and C.S. Fernando. "Hedging, Speculation, and Shareholder Value." *Journal of Financial Economics*, 81 (2006), 283–309.
Allayannis, G., and J.P. Weston. "The Use of Foreign Currency Derivatives and Firm Market Value." *Review of Financial Studies*, 14 (2001), 243–276.
Amihud, Y., and B. Lev. "Risk Reduction as a Managerial Motive for Conglomerate Mergers." *Bell Journal of Economics*, 12 (1981), 605–617.
Bartram, S. M., G. W. Brown, and J. Conrad. "The effects of derivatives on firm risk and value." *Journal of Financial and Quantitative Analysis*, 46 (2011), 967–999.

Beasley, M., J. Carcello, D. Hermanson, and T. Neal. "The audit committee oversight process." *Contemporary Accounting Research*, 26(1) (2009), 65–122.

Campello, M., C. Lin, Y. Ma, and H. Zou. "The Real and Financial Implications of Corporate Hedging." *Journal of Finance*, 66 (2011), 1615–1647.

Carlton, D.W. "Futures Markets: Their Purpose, Their History, Their Growth, Their Successes and Failures." *Journal of Futures Markets*, 4(3) (1984), 237–271.

Carter, D., D.A. Rogers, and B.J. Simkins. "Does Hedging Affect Firm Value? Evidence from the US Airline Industry." *Financial Management*, 35 (2006), 53–86.

Chernenko, S., and M. Faulkender. "The Two Sides of Derivatives Usage: Hedging and Speculating with Interest Rate Swaps." *Journal of Financial and Quantitative Analysis*, 46 (2011), 1727–1754.

De Angelis, D., and S.A. Ravid, "Hedging in an Input Industry, Hedging in an Output Industry and Market Power." Working Paper, Graduate School of Business, Rice University (2015).

DeMarzo, P.M., and D. Duffie. "Corporate Incentives for Hedging and Hedge Accounting." *Review of Financial Studies*, 8 (1995), 743–771.

Froot, K.A., D.S. Scharfstein, and J.C. Stein. "Risk Management: Coordinating Corporate Investment and Financing Policies." *Journal of Finance*, 48 (1993), 1629–1658.

Géczy, C., B.A. Minton, and C. Schrand. "Why Firms Use Currency Derivatives." *Journal of Finance*, 52 (1997), 1323–1354.

Gormley, T., and D. Matsa: "Playing it Safe? Managerial Preferences, Risk, and Agency Conflicts." (2015). http://papers.ssrn.com/sol3/papers.cfm?abstract_id=2465632

Graham, J.R., and D.A. Rogers. "Do Firms Hedge in Response to Tax Incentives?" *Journal of Finance*, 57 (2002), 815–839.

Haushalter, G.D. "Financing Policy, Basis Risk, and Corporate Hedging: Evidence from Oil and Gas Producers." *Journal of Finance*, 55 (2000), 107–152.

Jin, L. "CEO compensation, diversification, and incentives." *Journal of Financial Economics*, 66 (2002), 29–63.

Kedia, S., S.A. Ravid, and V. Pons. "When Do Vertical Mergers Create Value?" *Financial Management*, 40 (2011), 845–878.

Liebenberg, A.P., and R.E. Hoyt. "The Determinants of Enterprise Risk Management: Evidence from the Appointment of Chief Risk Officers". *Risk Management and Insurance Review*, 6(1) (2003), 37–52.

Loss, F. "Optimal Hedging Strategies and Interactions Between Firms." *Journal of Economics & Management Strategy*, 21 (2012), 79–129.

MacKay, P., and S.B. Moeller. "The Value of Corporate Risk Management." *Journal of Finance*, 62 (2007), 1379–1419.

McShane, M.K., A. Nair, and E. Rustambekov. "Does Enterprise Risk Management Increase Firm Value?" *Journal of Accounting, Auditing & Finance*, 26(4) (2011), 641–658.

Mian, S.L. "Evidence on Corporate Hedging Policy." *Journal of Financial and Quantitative Analysis*, 31 (1996), 419–439.

Nance, D.R., C.W. Smith, and C.W. Smithson. "On the Determinants of Corporate Hedging." *Journal of Finance*, 48 (1993), 267–284.

Nini, G., D.C. Smith, and A. Sufi. "Creditor Control Rights and Firm Investment Policy." *Journal of Financial Economics*, 92 (2009), 400–420.

Nocco, B. and R. Stulz. "Enterprise Risk Management: Theory and Practice." *Journal of Applied Corporate Finance*, 18(4) (2006), 8–20.

Pagach, D.P., and R.S. Warr. "The Effects of Enterprise Risk Management on Firm Performance." (2010). http://papers.ssrn.com/sol3/papers.cfm?abstract_id=1155218

Pagach, D., and R. Warr. "The Characteristics of Firms That Hire Chief Risk Officers." *Journal of Risk and Insurance*, 78(1) (2011), 185–211.

Raman, V., and C. Fernando. "Is Hedging Bad News? Evidence from Corporate Hedging Announcements." Working paper, University of Oklahoma (2010).

Rampini, A., A. Sufi, and S. Viswanathan. "Dynamic Risk Management." *Journal of Financial Economics*, 111 (2014), 271–296.

Ravid, S.A., and S. Basuroy. "Managerial Objectives, the R-Rating Puzzle, and the Production of Violent Films." *Journal of Business*, 77 (2004), 155–192.

Shavell, S. "On Liability and Insurance." *Bell Journal of Economics*, 13 (1982), 120–132.

Smith, C.W., and R. Stulz. "The Determinants of Firms' Hedging Policies." *Journal of Financial and Quantitative Analysis*, 20 (1985), 391–405.

Tufano, P. "Who Manages Risk? An Empirical Examination of Risk Management Practices in the Gold Mining Industry." *Journal of Finance*, 51 (1996), 1097–1137.

28

Aggregating predictions of operational uncertainties from the frontline

A new proactive risk management practice

Carina Antonia Hallin[1]

Abstract

This chapter introduces a new information aggregation method for enterprise risk management (ERM) developed from frontline employees' sensing and predictions of uncertainties in the firm's operational performance. Conventional enterprise risk management integrates the use of quantitative techniques based on historical data to provide effective deployment of common proactive risk practices throughout the firm. Yet, uncertainties are associated with events that cannot be easily predicted. Frontline employees acquire deep insights about operational uncertainties as they perform daily tasks and interact with internal and external stakeholders. Such experiential learning provides unique insights about operational uncertainties of strategic value, which are not otherwise available for proactive risk-taking by senior management. Drawing on a proactive risk-taking perspective, the chapter presents the relevance of sensing and leading predictions by frontline employees for capturing operational uncertainties. It presents the reader with the different steps of constructing an operational risk barometer (ORB) and provides a discussion of its use in practice. It outlines the implications of using sensing among frontline employees and other relevant stakeholders as a useful operational risk predictor and as an important information source in proactive risk-taking and dynamic strategic risk control processes.

Proactive risk management practices

Dealing with risks and uncertainties is an integral part of doing business in competitive environments. Risk and uncertainties are the foundations of creating entrepreneurial progress and corporate value (Andersen, Garvey, & Roggi, 2014). Enterprise risk management (ERM) is a formal framework that presents perspectives on the structure of proactive risk management practices incorporating various analytical tools and practices to identify, assess, treat, and monitor various types of risks. The framework entails the implicit assumption that good risk management can either reduce risks to achieve lower cost of capital or create new business opportunities through innovation search (Washburn & Bromiley, 2011). While a firm might make both innovative and cost reduction changes at the same time, research on budgeting indicates that organizations generally work on either additional funding schemes (where innovative suggestions may be considered) or cost reduction schemes (Behn, 1985; Crecine & Fischer, 1969; Fischer & Kamlet, 1984).

Proactive risk-taking practices are seen as an essential precondition for dealing effectively with uncertainty and unpredictable conditions, as a way of shaping corporate value for the future (Andersen et al., 2014). Various proactive risk-taking activities are outlined in the ERM framework, which is defined as "a comprehensive and integrated framework for managing credit risk, market risk, operational risks, and economic capital and risk transfer in order to maximize firm value" (Lam, 2003, p. 58). Other scholars point to proactive risk-taking practices being inherent in business activities as systematic processes (Monahan, 2008) and the processes whereby the enterprise methodically addresses its risk as a part of its strategic management (Andersen, 2010). Typically, proactive risk-taking practices are embedded in the general models of risk management and apply quantitative techniques integrating historical data to assess future risk such as the common ERM techniques "value-at-risk" (VaR) and "Monte Carlo" simulations (Roggi, 2014).

The need for new proactive risk-taking practices to better predict and understand how uncertain events influence firm performance is frequently emphasized among scholars. In a recent contribution, Bromiley and Rau (2014) call upon techniques that managers might use to develop strategies or generally apply as practices within the firm. They propose a practice-based view (PBV) of strategy scholarship to address this gap. They define practice as "an activity or set of activities that a variety of firms might execute" (Bromiley & Rau, 2014, p. 1249). Examples are setting goals, having clear performance measurement, working to attract talented people, rewarding high performance, and removing poor performers – all practices that are not technologically complex or require hard-to-transfer resources or capabilities, yet can influence firm performance significantly (Bloom, Dorgan, Dowdy, & Van Reenen, 2007; Bloom, Eifert, Mahajan, McKenzie, & Roberts, 2013; Bloom, Genakos, Sadun, & Van Reenen, 2012; Bloom & Van Reenen, 2006).

In the field of strategic management, risk has largely been studied using past firm performance and management incentives to explain firm-level risk behaviors and their effect on firm performance. Consequently, practical problems faced by managers are often overlooked in the strategy literature. As stated by Bromiley and Rau (2014, p. 1250), "Telling managers that low performance increases their tendency to take bad risks is helpful, but not central to strategic risk management. Managers want to know what to do (i.e., practices), and we have relatively little to tell them."

Recent perspectives on proactive risk-taking practice call upon the inclusion of engaged people throughout the enterprise to advance the ability to deal effectively with uncertainty and facilitate strategic responsiveness (Andersen et al., 2014). Different staff levels assume unique roles in the organization and contribute by dealing with strategic risk and adaptation in diverse ways. Top managers give directions to the strategy-making process, and middle managers typically identify emerging risks and opportunities and propose changes (Martens, Matthyssens, & Vandenbempt, 2012). The strategy literature suggests that the search for opportunities and risks is captured through the insights of lower-level employees located in the firm's operating entities (e.g., Bower, 1970; Burgelman, 1983). The operational frontline senses changes in operational conditions and develops intuitive judgments about their effectiveness (Hallin, Andersen, & Tveterås, 2013a, 2013b; Hallin, Tveterås, & Andersen, 2012; Hodgkinson & Healey, 2011). Involved as they are in the daily transactions of the firm, these frontline employees are well positioned to gather updated information about changes in the operating environment and their information should have strategic value. Frontline employees' sensing and leading predictions of uncertainties in operational conditions can serve as predictors of performance outcomes and indicate a potential need to change current action plans.

This chapter deals with predictions of operational uncertainties. It introduces a new proactive risk management practice derived from frontline employees' sensing of need for adaptation in operational conditions. It is proposed that the approach can be employed as a new information aggregation method for ERM practices across all types of firms and industries for assessing unknown operational uncertainties. The chapter presents various perspectives in ERM on risk, uncertainties, and strategies in terms of assessing risk versus true uncertainties. It explains operational uncertainties as an essential risk dimension. It then defines the importance of frontline employees' sensing of changes in operational performance for risk assessment and adaptation.

Capturing uncertainties

Considerable effort has been devoted to explaining the importance of uncertainty assessments (e.g., Aguilar, 1967; Ansoff, 1980; Bettis & Hitt, 1995; Teece, 2007), where local sensing of both external and operational environmental uncertainties are considered important for innovative opportunism (Teece, 2007). Yet, the approach of dealing with uncertainty as a measurable risk phenomenon is not commonly defined (Andersen et al., 2014). The concepts of risk and uncertainty have been described by Knight (1921), where he links risk to situations in which the probability distributions of outcomes are known, while in the case of uncertainties, probabilities and effects are unknown. That is, uncertainty is associated with events that cannot be quantified or at least are hard to specify. However, as argued by Bettis (1982, p. 22): "Almost all authors after noting this distinction ignore it and use risk and uncertainty interchangeably." As a consequence, uncertainty is also referred to as "true uncertainty" to remind us that we are in fact talking about uncertainty.

In this chapter, I will use the expressions interchangeably to refer to true uncertainty. Risk practitioners refer to "emergent risks," by which they mean risks "that have not yet occurred, but are at an early stage of becoming known and/or coming into being and expected to grow greatly in significance" (Richardson & Gerzon, 2004). So, risk professionals try to pay attention to the changing business conditions by gauging the future. Scholars have described this, for example, as continuous rule changes from ongoing innovation under "hypercompetition" (D'Aveni, 1994) or unpredictable shifts in technology and industry paradigms (Bettis & Hitt, 1995). This has urged the development of preparedness for the unexpected (Weick & Sutcliffe, 2007) and dealing with research about "unknowability" (Andersen & Schrøder, 2010).

Ansoff (1980) proposed a strategic issue management (SIM) system to capture uncertainties (weak signals) in "real time," that is, rapid uncertainties deriving from unexpected sources and that subsequently and quickly can exert a significant impact on the enterprise. A strategic issue is defined as "a forthcoming development, either internal or external of the organization, which is likely to have an important impact on the ability of the enterprise to meet its objectives" (p. 135). A strategic issue may be a positive uncertainty, which is an opportunity to be grabbed in the environment, or it may constitute an internal strength, which can be exploited for firm advantage. Yet, it may also be an unwelcome external threat or an internal weakness that can put the firm at risk for continuing survival. Frequently, external threats (uncertainties) can signal significant changes to come in the environment, and can possibly be converted into new opportunities through entrepreneurial management. Specifically, the combination of speed and novelty of strategic issues makes them too fast to permit timely perception and response within the conventional annual planning and budgeting systems. According to Ansoff, some of the most important issues may occur between the firm's periodic planning cycles, with impacts materializing so fast that intervention cannot be delayed to the next planning cycle. However, other strategic issues may coincide with the planning cycle and become part of the considerations used for the forthcoming planning period. Although strategic issue management was suggested in the early development of the strategic management field to deal with true environmental uncertainties, there is still a void in the theoretical and empirical foundations of these early warning systems, along with suggestions of effective aggregation of information for risk-taking initiatives. Nonetheless, the importance of management systems to capture uncertainties for effective decision making has been emphasized widely by several strategy scholars in discussing the contemporary challenges in strategic management related to the increasing turbulence in the business environment. This has, for example, identified a need for strategic response performance (Bettis & Hitt, 1995), dynamic capabilities (Helfat et al., 2007; Teece, 2007; Teece, Pisano, & Shuen, 1997), and dynamic managerial performance (Adner & Helfat, 2003; Helfat & Peteraf, 2014) to reconfigure organizational resources as environmental uncertainties change. The foregoing discussion has outlined perspectives on capturing uncertainties applicable for ERM, but in general these approaches lack an exact practical method to deal with unpredictable operational events.

Knowledge sources for emergent insights in operational uncertainties

Considerable effort has been devoted to explain the importance of uncertainty assessments (e.g., Aguilar, 1967; Ansoff, 1980; Bettis & Hitt, 1995; Teece, 2007) where local sensing of external and operational environmental uncertainties is considered important for innovative opportunism (Teece, 2007). A central idea of information aggregation is that dispersed individuals have diverse information and form expectations that can be aggregated and harnessed for organizational decision making (Deutsch & Madow, 1961; Felin & Zenger, 2011). The capacity to aggregate heterogeneous and dispersed information about the environment is acknowledged as a critical aspect for effective strategic decisions (Arrow, 1974; Bettis & Hitt, 1995).

In the microfoundations literature the aggregation of individual behaviors and performance is important for firm performance, but it constitutes an underresearched aspect of strategic organization (Felin & Foss, 2005; Felin & Zenger, 2011). That is, microfoundations infer a common understanding that aggregated locally held (and diverse) knowledge has a significant impact on firm performance (Felin & Zenger, 2011). Subsequently, the strategy field has paid increasingly attention to these microfoundations of the resource-based theory (RBT), suggesting a need to analyze and assess the firm's internal resource management processes (Barney, Ketchen, & Wright, 2011; Kraaijenbrink, Spender, & Groen, 2010). Gaining a better understanding of these cognitive structures and processes within organizations can provide corporate decision makers with access to important information for updating business strategies (Narayanan, Zane, & Kemmerer, 2011). Sensing is shaped through organizational interpretation systems (Daft & Weick, 1984); it is an essential part of the organization's sensemaking processes (Balogun & Johnson, 2004; Gioia & Chittipeddi, 1991; Weick, 1995); and recent contributions in strategic management have identified the psychological linkage between individual sensing and intuitions as essential firm performance (Hodgkinson & Healey, 2011).

Besides the literature on sensing and cognition mentioned earlier, other parts of strategic management have specifically examined the role of various employee groups as knowledge sources for environmental cognition and innovation search. Examples are studies of managerial schemas (Helfat & Peteraf, 2014; Walsh, 1995), and corporate venturing at different managerial levels in the organization (Burgelman, 1983), in strategy making (Regnér, 2003), and among middle managers in general (Wooldridge & Floyd, 1990). However, the sensing by frontline employees of the firm's operational performance as a knowledge source in proactive risk-taking initiatives has not yet been explicitly considered in the strategy literature.

Whereas management may have exclusive knowledge that influences operations, such as knowledge of investment decisions, governance practices, and organizational restructuring, operational employees tend to have hands-on knowledge about the operational conditions in their local work environments. The frontline employees involved in the daily execution of business transactions throughout the firm gather updated information about changes in the operating environment. They sense the effectiveness of the firm's operational performance based on experiences gained from their daily tasks where they interact with core stakeholders, such as customers, suppliers, managers, colleagues, and peers in competing businesses. The frontline employees engage with external and internal stakeholders and, therefore, are among the first to notice the subtle changes that may affect the way the firm operates. The individual ability to sense these changes is expressed as intuitions (Hodgkinson & Healey, 2011), and preliminary studies have indicated them to predict future operating conditions related to financial firm performance (Hallin, Andersen, & Tveterås, 2013a, 2013b; Hallin, Tveterås, & Andersen, 2012).

Conventionally, information in enterprises flows through different managerial hierarchical levels before it reaches strategic risk decision makers. As such, information about operational conditions that flows from lower-level employees to middle managers and to decision makers tends to be biased as it reaches the top management level, because middle managers tend to modify or withhold information as part of their job function (Thompson & Wildavsky, 1986). One of the rationales for this mechanism is power and control needs at various hierarchical levels. As lower levels filter and compress the data for the higher levels, details are removed and order added. The choices of which data is actually transmitted is formally found at the top but informally left to the lower managerial levels. Thus, if enterprise risk management shall capture (approximately) nonbiased information about changes in operational performance, it must be transferred directly to management, as depicted in Figure 28.1.

Consequently, an effective information aggregation mechanism that captures perceived operational uncertainties by frontline employees should be facilitated with information technologies that can transfer the information directly to the strategic decision making level, so top management receives a more precise and broader perspective on what is going on in operations.

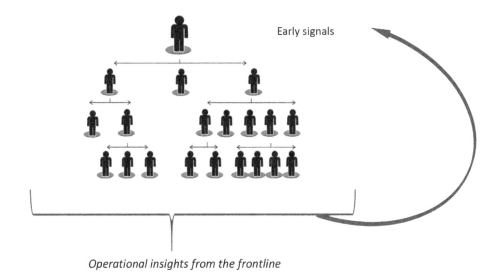

Operational insights from the frontline

Figure 28.1   Aggregating predictions about operational uncertainties from the frontline

Yet, this assumption is not new. For many years, scholars have foreseen that the integration of information technology (IT) in organizations will result in an overall reduction in the number of middle managers in enterprises (Child, 1984; Drucker, 1988; Leavitt & Whisler, 1958; Malone, Yates, & Benjamin, 1987). The rationale for this prediction is that middle managers have mostly provided an informational link between top managers and operations managers and that IT will now perform these functions. IT permits top managers to bypass middle managers in both upward and downward communication. IT has thus centralized organization structures: horizontally, by bringing business units together; and vertically, by bringing decision authority to the top of the hierarchy, but at the same time decentralizing information generation about environmental changes and innovation search from lower-level employees.

The application of information aggregation techniques in organizations fosters novel market-hierarchy hybrids with a variety of new practices and organizational forms (Felin & Zenger, 2011). These approaches include crowdsourcing (Howe, 2006, 2008) and prediction markets (Borison & Hamm, 2010; Graefe, Luckner, & Weinhardt, 2010; Wolfers & Zitzewitz, 2004), but can also take the form of employee surveys, voting, and opinion polls (Felin & Zenger, 2011). Survey information is relatively easy to handle and can feed naturally into the risk control process.

Development and implementation of operational risk performance indices

The sensing of the operational frontline about the firm's operational performance should help managers identify ongoing opportunities and risks. A dynamic assessment of risks in operations can be aggregated using computation of prediction indices that may also be applied to information aggregation from the firm's other important stakeholders, such as customers and suppliers. Detecting emergent risks in operational performance using indices can function as an ideation tool for continuous strategic control, decision making, and business innovation. The construction and testing of the ORB may consist of five phases, as depicted in Figure 28.2. Phase 1 is the

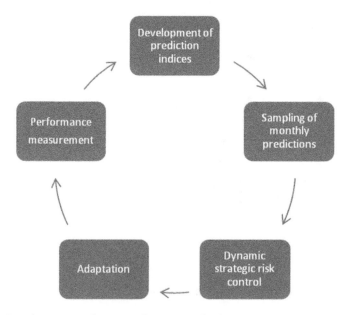

Figure 28.2 Development and testing of operational risk management indices

development of prediction indices; Phase 2 is the sampling of monthly quantitative and related qualitative prediction data; Phase 3 is a dynamic strategic risk control process; Phase 4 is the adaptation and implementation of solutions; and Phase 5 is performance measurement.

Phase 1 – Development of prediction indices

The first step in constructing prediction indices is to tailor the survey prediction instrument to the individual enterprise and assess the relevant indicators that drive operational performance. This can be done performing interviews with frontline employees and other relevant stakeholders. Content in prediction measures across the same types of firms tends to be similar. For example, a prediction instrument including measures of service efficiency used with frontline employees at a hotel chain should also be applicable across hotel chains to measure operational performance, but also be relevant in related service sectors such as the cruise industry (Hallin et al., 2013a).

The previous step support the construction of a final prediction survey, which is administered as a monthly time-series survey tapping into judgmental predictions by operational frontlines. The questions are framed as anticipatory questions (Katona, 1960); for example, "How would you predict the ability of top management to solve problems effectively in the next three months versus this month?" or "How would you predict the ability of your operational team to solve problems effectively in the next three months compared to this month?" Table 28.1 presents examples of variables. The response category is framed to indicate varying degrees of agreement with or endorsement of the statement. All indicators can be assessed on a 3-point scale, where a value of 1 indicates anticipations of negative development in operational performance over the next 3 months. This predicted development constitutes a risk to the operational performance. A value of 2 on the scale indicates expectations of no change over the next 3 months, and a value of 3 indicates a positive development compared to the present situation. For each quantitative prediction question, an open-ended question follows that asks respondents their

Table 28.1 Examples of operational risk barometer performance variables of enterprise X

Indicator	Feb	Mar	Apr	May	June	July
Revenue per available room	133.5	110.2	105.2	102.3	102.7	109.7
Teamwork in the department	111.7	97.8	96.6	89.5	104.5	111.8
Ability to adapt to changes in the market	132.5	109.7	102.3	102.5	101.8	109.7
Ability to meet customer expectations	101.0	95.1	85.7	94.7	91.8	87.1
Customers' perception of product quality	137.9	118.4	103	110.3	112.7	115.1
Collaboration between departments	94.7	93.0	85.9	91.7	100.0	103.2
How the customers will talk about the enterprise	95.6	80.6	81.1	86.5	86.4	95.7
Employees' desire to work for the company	101.9	96.8	79.0	78.9	101.9	107.5
Ability to develop new and creative services, systems, and processes	114.1	105.9	95.5	96.7	104.5	102.2
Ability of your immediate leader to solve problems	79.1	80.6	70.5	73.9	82.7	89.2
Ability of top management to solve problems	132.0	111.9	103.4	108.3	114.5	102.2
Ability to deliver service and products at the promised time	101.5	103. 2	100.2	100.8	103.6	102.2
Operational risk barometer	**100.0**	**90.10**	**83.00**	**85.07**	**90.41**	**92.52**

reason for choosing the particular ranking. This answer category makes it possible to tap into the underlying causes of the respondents' perceived development for each item. Thus, respondents' qualitative feedback for each quantitative prediction serves as a platform for opportunity search to deal with perceived risks.

Additionally, the survey instrument can include direct operational performance variables such as sales volume with the purpose of (1) predicting changes in observable actual firm performance, (2) measuring accuracy in predictions, (3) using it as a way to enhance the management of future service and product capacity, and (4) validating the information of the operational crowd for strategic decision making over time. For example, in the hotel industry common operational performance measures are guest arrivals, occupancy rate, and guest expenditures, all of which can be included in the survey as prediction items. Additionally, fluctuations in the firm's shares may be tested as a prediction item.

Constructing the ORB performance measures

To construct the prediction index from respondents' predictions, a diffusion measure for each of the questionnaire indicators is calculated (Curtin, 2006; Katona, 1960). The diffusion measure is calculated as the difference between the number of positive and negative responses in each time period divided by the total number of responses in that period. An operational performance barometer is then calculated by aggregating the diffusion measures for each of the indicators for each period and then dividing by the sum of the base period.

$$ORB_t = \frac{\sum_{i=1}^{13} ORB_{it}}{\sum_{i=1}^{13} ORB_{i0}} \times 100 \tag{1}$$

An operational financial enterprise performance measure needs to be identified that can be compared across firms within an industry to assess competiveness. For example, a common operational performance measure in the hotel industry is revenue per available room (REVPAR). So specifically, the percentage change in REVPAR from one period to the next for each hotel is compared with the percentage change in REVPAR in the relevant regional hotel industry. Formally, the relative performance measure of hotel i at time t ($Pfm_{i,}t$) can be calculated as:

$$Pfm_{i,t} = \ln(R_{\text{firm}})_{i,t} - \ln(R_{\text{industry}})_{i,t} \tag{2}$$

The prediction model estimation is as follows:

$$Pfm_{i,t} = \sum_{j=1}^{q} \delta_j \Delta \ln ORB_{i,t-j} + u_{i,t} \tag{3}$$

The models are tested against actual operational firm performance after several survey observations, say 15 time-series rounds, to test the validity of the prediction information. One may run prediction contests among enterprise units or collapse the data and test it against actual performance ($Pfm_{i,}t$) to validate the index (Hallin et al., 2012). Practitioners may alternatively use comparative performance data across similar units within a firm to isolate unit performance in comparison to other units.

Phase 2 – Sampling of monthly predictions

The ORB indicators are tested in monthly cross-sectional time-series surveys collected from the operational frontline (Hallin et al., 2012). The survey indicators can be monitored electronically each month. In some industries such as the hotel, airline, and cruise sectors, frontline employees work in shifts. Consequently, it is relevant to collect data during a longer period each month, such as a week. A survey app can be applied or a link to the survey can be sent directly to the respondents' e-mail accounts. In this manner, the researcher is able to identify the individuals and send reminders to those who have not responded, but still maintain confidentiality. Since newly hired operational frontlines have little experience about operations, it is relevant to let them accumulate some knowledge about operations before they are included in the prediction survey.

The sampling of monthly predictions involves initially communicating the incentive structure to the survey crowd to encourage participation among respondents over time. It can be argued that just involving employees and listening to them on a monthly basis will in itself increase motivation for participation as long as management communicates and takes action upon their survey responses.

In the prediction market literature, incentives are set up to create an efficient market for predefined situations with predictable outcomes by trading virtual stocks of uncertain events (Spann & Skiera, 2003). For example, in a public prediction market on a presidential election a contract can be structured as a binary variable ("Will a Republican win the next US presidential election?") and each share of virtual stock will receive a certain "cash dividend" (payoff), for example, $1 per share event bought, that is, according to a specific predetermined (market) outcome payable once the actual outcome is known. Yet, studies of employees' prediction behavior over time suggest that gift lotteries are effective to maintain motivation (Hallin et al., 2012). An example of a gift lottery is when employees and customers predict changes in operational performance; they may randomly win free gifts. Practitioners may choose to integrate a investment mechanisms in the time-series survey. This can be done by setting up by asking participants to invest in operational performance. The operational performance variables constituting the highest risk(s) or opportunity(ies) according to the employee sensing can identify potential problems and can also uncover suggestions on how the problems can be solved.

Participants may be given a sum of "fictive" money (e.g., US$100,000) for each survey month. They are encouraged to invest the money to enhance different operational performance they expect can respond the best way possible to operational challenges, for example, avoiding a risk or exploiting an opportunity within the prediction horizon of, say, the next 3 months. The prediction market literature suggests that when market participants prioritize items, they will tend to "trade" or allocate resources based on their personal preferences combined with their own expectations of what other people judge (Slamka, Jank, & Skiera, 2012). The identified problems that receive the highest accumulated bets, or allocated resources, will be selected as "the winning strategic issue" of the month, which needs a further analysis by management to assess how to deal with the problem.

Phase 3 – Dynamic strategic risk control

Each month a data file is sent to decision makers on the performance of the barometer. An index value well below 100 will flag potential risks, whereas an index value well above 100 indicates a positive development. This way, the ORB index might signal pending needs to engage into a dynamic strategic risk control process to deal with emerging risks and opportunities in a more proactive manner (Simons, 1991, 1994). As presented in Table 28.1, the shaded area represents "early warnings" of potential risks in operational performance. Based on this information, management may analyze relationships between various potential risks (shaded cells in Table 28.1) while searching for indicators in the qualitative prediction information from frontline employees for assessing opportunities to deal with the potential risks. The open-ended questions associated with the quantitative predictions of specific variables should generate ideas to solve potential risks.

A dynamic factor analysis may be performed to create insights in underlying latent variables of the ORB over time. Dynamic factor analysis (DFA) is a dimension-reduction technique especially designed for time-series data. Since the mid-1980s, DFA has been used in econometric (Harvey, 1989) and psychological fields (Molenaar, 1985; Molenaar, de Gooijer, & Schmitz, 1992). The DFA can be used to model short, nonstationary time-series in terms of common patterns and explanatory variables. For example, DFA can indicate whether there are some underlying common patterns in the N time series, whether there are interactions between the response variables, and what the effects of explanatory variables are.

Phase 4 – Adaptation and implementation

In this phase, management discusses and compiles a list of solutions, either based on survey results with a lottery as an incentive or with a prediction market mechanism. The number of qualitative comments suggested by participants for the particular variables can be filtered by management and issues for how to deal with winning strategic issues can be tested in a new prediction round for investment in particular strategic actions that are considered most relevant to deal with by the crowd. A dynamic and effective adaptation process requires that management is willing to listen to the stakeholder crowd and allocate resources for adjustments in operations (Malone, 2010).

Phase 5 – Performance measurement and adjustment

Finally, the implementation of the new initiatives to deal with identified risk and opportunities (Phases 1–4) can be evaluated in repeated prediction rounds. The implications of implemented solutions can have both short-term and long-term effects on organizational performance. Thus, it is essential to track the costs and benefits over time for each adjustment in operations.

Using the ORB as updated risk information

The importance of aggregating environmental information in support of ongoing strategic decisions about uncertainties has long been stressed in management research (e.g., Aguilar, 1967; Ansoff, 1980; Bettis & Hitt, 1995; Teece, 2007). In this chapter, I have outlined a new proactive risk management practice using operational frontlines' sensing and leading predictions as valuable information for assessing ongoing operational uncertainties. I outlined a mechanism, the operational risk barometer (ORB), to capture operational frontline employees' sensing and predictions and test the quality of operational performance over time. The ORB indicators, which are compiled from theory reviews and interviews with relevant frontlines, comprise various indicators of operational performance. The more positively frontline employees assess various ORB indicators in the future, the higher their scale responses and vice versa. An index value well below 100 will flag potential risks, whereas an index value well above 100 indicates great potential. This way, the ORB index might signal the pending needs for adaptation and to engage in an interactive dynamic strategic risk control process to deal with emerging risks and opportunities in a more proactive manner (Simons, 1991, 1994). Hence, the ORB represents how frontline employees' sensing of operational conditions may provide valuable information to the strategic control process. This implies that the ORB is not only a potential prediction tool, where information is validated against financial performance measures; the index can also signal the current state of operational conditions and give early warning signals about the need for proactive strategic risk initiatives. Dynamic factor modeling can be employed to explain the content of various operational performance as predictors of the ORB over time. Thus, it is possible to generate subindices of operational performance that allow for more detailed information about the development in various dimensions of operational conditions.

As such, the ORB should supply fully updated and validated information about operational performance on a monthly basis. This is useful for proactive risk management, enabling management to dynamically consider whether the current strategy conduct is sufficiently effective or there is a need to make strategic adjustments. Further advancements of the ORB index may include testing other groups of stakeholders, such as customers, suppliers, and the public, about updated signals of the current status of the firm's strategic conduct. Thus, the ORB represents a new method to capture both internal and external uncertainties that can inform considerations about the need for adaptive strategic moves.

However, developing an effective leading index of operational conditions as a predictor of firm performance entails continuing challenges. They are related to the development and increase in valid indicators with significant explanatory power that needs to be constructed for the instrument and tested against appropriate firm-specific performance measures. Validating and refining the instrument requires time-series analyses of large-scale samples across comparable business contexts. The analyses performed in initial studies (Hallin et al., 2013a, 2013b; Hallin et al., 2012) have identified a number of significant predictor indicators that can be tested and developed further in capital incentives service industries.

Future ORB studies should focus on examining the advancements and implications of the index on dynamic strategic risk control processes. That is, risk prediction studies should empirically assess the risk predictability power of the sensing by various stakeholder groups in the periphery of the business. Moreover, studies should investigate the implications of quantitative and qualitative predictions for strategic decision making. The quantitative predictions can serve as a new operational capacity management tool as well as being used to assess accuracy in predictions. The qualitative comments by participants could suggest ideas for innovations in the organizations. Thus, it is relevant to investigate mechanisms that can trace innovative projects over time to understand their implications for advanced operational performance. Future studies should also evaluate the economic effects of managerial decision making from such innovation activities and how ORB can facilitate and complement existing risk management practices.

Conclusion

In this chapter, I have outlined how operational frontline employees' sensing and leading predictions about operational conditions in the firm can be collected and expressed in simple prediction indices as in the ORB for possible use in a dynamic risk management control system. I argue that the operational frontline is particularly attentive to true uncertainties that can constitute firm risks, as they engage with internal and external stakeholders and are among the first to notice the subtle changes in the way the firm operates. I have provided a detailed account of the design of an approach that aggregates strategic risk information from the operational frontline as a new proactive risk management practice.

Acknowledgements

I am grateful to my colleagues Torben Juul Andersen, Sigbjørn Tveterås, and Carsten Lund Pedersen for their contributions to the development and refinement processes of the operational risk barometer (ORB).

Note

1   Carina Antonia Hallin, Department of International Economics and Management, Copenhagen Business School.

References

Adner, R., & Helfat, C.E. (2003). Corporate effects and dynamic managerial performance. *Strategic Management Journal, 24*, 1011–1025.

Aguilar, F.J. (1967). *Scanning the business environment.* New York: Macmillan.

Andersen, T.J. (2010). Combining central planning and decentralization to enhance effective risk management outcomes. *Risk Management, 12*(2), 101–115.

Andersen, T.J., Garvey, M., & Roggi, O. (2014). *Managing risk and opportunity: The governance of strategic risk-taking.* Oxford: Oxford University Press.

Andersen, T.J., & Schröder, P.W. (2010). *Strategic risk management practice: How to deal effectively with major corporate exposures.* Cambridge: Cambridge University Press.

Ansoff, I.H. (1980). Strategic issue management. *Strategic Management Journal, 1*, 131–148.

Arrow, K.J. (1974). *The limits of organization. The Fels lectures on public policy analysis.* New York: W.W. Norton.

Balogun, J., & Johnson, G. (2004). Organizational restructuring and middle manager sensemaking. *Academy of Management Journal, 47*(4), 523–549.

Barney, J., Ketchen, D., & Wright, M. (2011). The future of resource-based theory: Revitalization or decline? *Journal of Management, 37*(5), 1299–1315.

Behn, R.D. (1985). Cutback budgeting. *Journal of Policy Analysis and Management, 4*(2), 155–177.

Bettis, R.A. (1982). Risk considerations in modeling corporate strategy. *Academy of Management Proceedings* (Abstract Supplement), 22–25.

Bettis, R.A., & Hitt, M.A. (1995). The new competitive landscape [Special issue]. *Strategic Management Journal, 16*(1), 7–19.

Bloom, N., Dorgan, S., Dowdy, J., & Van Reenen, J. (2007, November). Management practice and productivity: Why they matter. *Management Matters,* 1–10. London: Center for Economic Practice, London School of Economics and McKinsey & Co.

Bloom, N., Eifert, B., Mahajan, A., McKenzie, D., & Roberts, J. (2013). Does management matter? Evidence from India. *Quarterly Journal of Economics, 128*(1), 1–51.

Bloom, N., Genakos, C., Sadun, R., & Van Reenen, J. (2012). Management practices across firms and countries. *Academy of Management Perspectives, 26*(1), 12–33.

Bloom N., & Van Reenen, J. (2006). *Measuring and explaining management practices across firms and countries.* Center for Economic Performance discussion paper 716. London: Center for Economic Performance, London School of Economics and Political Science.

Borison, A., & Hamm, G. (2010). Prediction markets: A new tool for strategic decision-making, *California Management Review, 52*(4), 125–141.

Bower, J. (1970). *Managing the resource allocation process: A study of corporate planning and investment.* Boston: Harvard University, Graduate School of Business Administration.

Bromiley, P., & Rau, D. (2014). Towards a practice-based view of strategy. *Strategic Management Journal, 35*, 1249–1256.

Burgelman, R.A. (1983). A process model of internal corporate venturing in the diversified major firm. *Administrative Science Quarterly, 28*(2), 223–244.

Child, J. (1984). New technology and developments in management organization. *OMEGA International Journal of Management Science, 12*(3), 211–223.

Crecine, J.P., & Fischer, G.W. (1969). On resource allocation processing in the US Department of Defense. *Political Science Annual, 4*, 181–236.

Curtin, R.T. (2006). *Surveys of consumers: Index calculation.* Retrieved from http://www.sca.isr.umich.edu/documents.php?c=1

Daft, R.L., & Weick, K.E. (1984). Toward a model of organizations as interpretation systems. *Academy of Management Review, 9*(2), 284–295.

D'Aveni, R.A. (1994). *Hypercompetition: Managing the dynamics of strategic maneuvering.* New York: Free Press.

Deutsch, K.W., & Madow, W.G. (1961). A note of the appearance of wisdom in large bureaucratic organizations. *Behavioral Science, 6*(1), 72–78.

Drucker, P.F. (1988). The coming of the new organization. *Harvard Business Review, 66*(1), 45–53.

Felin, T., & Foss, N.J. (2005). Strategic organization: A field in search of micro-foundations. *Strategic Organization, 3*(4), 441–455.

Felin, T., & Zenger, T.R. (2011). Information aggregation, matching and radical market-hierarchy hybrids: Implications for the theory of the firm. Strategic Organization, 9(2), 163–173.

Fischer, G.W., & Kamlet, M. S. (1984). Explaining presidential priorities: The competing aspiration levels model of macrobudgetary decision making. *American Political Science Review, 78*(2), 356–371.

Gioia, D.A., & Chittipeddi, K. (1991). Sensemaking and sensegiving in strategic change initiation. *Strategic Management Journal, 12,* 433–448.

Graefe, A., Luckner, S., & Weinhardt, C. (2010). Prediction markets for foresights. *Futures, 42,* 394–404.

Hallin, C.A., Andersen, T.J., & Tveterås, S. (2013a). *Who are the better predictors: Frontline employees or executive managers?* SMS 33rd Annual International Conference, Pamela Barr and Frank T. Rothaermel (Eds.). Atlanta: Strategic Management Society.

Hallin, C.A., Andersen, T.J., & Tveterås, S. (2013b). *Fuzzy predictions for strategic decision making: A third-generation prediction market.* CGSR Working Paper Series, No 2. Frederiksberg: Copenhagen Business School.

Hallin, C.A., Tveterås, S., & Andersen, T.J. (2012). *Judgmental forecasting of operational performance: Exploring a new indicator to predict financial performance.* Copenhagen Business School, Department of International Economics and Management, working paper series. Frederiksberg, Copenhagen Business School.

Harvey, A.C. (1989). *Forecasting, structural time series models and the Kalman filter.* Cambridge: Cambridge University Press.

Helfat, C.E., Finkelstein, S., Mitchell, W., Peteraf, M.A., Singh, H., Teece, D.J., & Winter, S.G. 2007. Dynamic capabilities: Understanding strategic change in organizations. Malden, MA: Blackwell.

Helfat, C.E., & Peteraf, M.A. (2014). Managerial cognitive capabilities and the microfoundations of dynamic capabilities. *Strategic Management Journal, 36*(6), 831–850.

Helfat, C.E., & Raubitschek, R.S. (2000). Product sequencing: Co-evolution of knowledge, performance and products. Oxford: Blackwell.

Hodgkinson, G.P., & Healey, M.P. (2011). Psychological foundations of dynamic performance: Reflexion and reflection in strategic management. *Strategic Management Journal, 32,* 1500–1516.

Howe, J. (2006). The rise of crowdsourcing. *Wired.* Retrieved March 18, 2012, from http://www.wired.com/wired/archive/14.06/crowds.html

Howe, J. (2008). *Crowdsourcing: Why the power of the crowd is driving the future of business.* New York: Crown.

Kraaijenbrink, J., Spender, J.C., & Groen, A.J. (2010). The resource-based view: A review and assessment of its critiques. *Journal of Management, 36,* 349–372.

Knight, F. (1921). *Risk, uncertainty, and profit.* New York: Hart, Schaffner & Marx.

Katona, G. (1960). *The powerful consumer* Boston, MA: Houghton Mifflin.

Lam, J. (2003). *Enterprise risk management: From incentives to controls.* Hoboken, NJ: Wiley Finance.

Leavitt, H.H., & Whisler, T.I. (1958). Management in the 1980s. *Harvard Business Review, 36*(6), 41–48.

Malone, T.W. (2010). The new order of business: Decentralization is the new center of command. *Deep Insight,* 1st quarter (4), 38–45.

Malone, T.W., Yates, J., & Benjamin, R.L. (1987). Electronic markets and electronic hierarchies, *Communications of the ACM, 30*(6), 484–497.

Martens, R., Matthyssens, P., & Vandenbempt, K. (2012). Market strategy renewal as a dynamic incremental process. *Journal of Business Research, 65*(6), 720–728.

Molenaar, P.C.M. (1985). A dynamic factor model for the analysis of multivariate time series. *Psychometrika, 50,* 181–202.

Molenaar, P.C.M., de Gooijer, J.G., & Schmitz, B. (1992). Dynamic factor analysis of nonstationary multivariate time series. *Psychometrika, 57,* 333–349.

Monahan, G. (2008). *Enterprise risk management: A methodology for achieving strategic objectives.* Hoboken, NJ: Wiley.

Narayanan, V.K., Zane, L.J., & Kemmerer, B. (2011). Cognitive perspective in strategy: An integrative review. *Journal of Management, 37,* 305–351.

Protogerou, S., & Liukas, A. (2011). Dynamic performance and their indirect impact on firm performance. *Industrial and Corporate Change, 21*(3), 615–647.

Regnér, P. (2003). Strategy creation in the periphery: Inductive versus deductive strategy making. *Journal of Management Studies, 40*(1), 57–82.

Richardson B., & Gerzon, P. (2004). *Emergent risks*. Research Paper. London: Institute of Risk Management (IRM).

Roggi, O. (2014). Value based enterprise risk management practices. In T.J. Andersen, M. Garvey, & O. Roggi (Eds.), *Managing risk and opportunity. The governance of strategic risk-taking* (pp. 68–100). Oxford: Oxford University Press.

Roth, A.V., & Menor, L.J. (2003). Insights into service operations management: A research agenda. *Production and Operations Management, 12*(2), 145–164.

Simons, R. (1991). Strategic orientation and top management attention to control systems. *Strategic Management Journal, 12*(1), 49–62.

Simons, R. (1994). How new top managers use control systems as levers for strategic renewal. *Strategic Management Journal, 15*(3), 169–189.

Slamka, C., Jank, W., & Skiera, B. (2012). Second-generation prediction markets for information aggregation: A comparison of payoff mechanisms. *Journal of Forecasting, 31*(6), 469–489.

Spann, M., & Skiera, B. (2003). Internet-based virtual stock markets for business forecasting. *Management Science, 49*(10), 1310–1326.

Swink, M., & Hegarty, W.H. (1998). Core manufacturing performance and their links to product differentiation. *International Journal of Operations & Production Management, 18*(4), 374–396.

Teece, D.J. (2007). Explicating dynamic performance: The nature and microfoundations of (sustainable) enterprise performance. *Strategic Management Journal, 28*(August), 1319–1350.

Teece, D.J., Pisano, G., & Shuen, A. (1997). Dynamic performance and strategic management. *Strategic Management Journal, 18*, 509–533.

Thompson M., & Wildavsky, A. (1986). A cultural theory of information bias in organizations. *Journal of Management Studies, 23*, 273–286.

Walsh, J.P. (1995). Managerial and organizational cognition: Notes from a trip down memory lane. *Organization Science, 6*(3), 280–321.

Washburn, M., & Bromiley, P. (2011). Comparing aspiration models: The role of selective attention. *Journal of Management, 49*, 896–917.

Weick, K.E. (1995). *Sensemaking in organizations*. Thousand Oaks, CA: Sage.

Weick, K., & Sutcliffe, K. (2007). *Managing the unexpected: Resilient performance in an age of uncertainty*. San Francisco, CA: Jossey-Bass.

Wolfers, J., & Zitzewitz, E. (2004). Prediction markets. *Journal of Economic Perspectives, 18*(2), 107–126.

Wooldridge, B. and Floyd, S.W. (1990). The strategy process: Middle management involvement and organisational performance. *Strategic Management Journal, 11*(3), 231–241.

Wright, G., & Ayton, P. (1987). *Judgmental forecasting*. Chichester: John Wiley & Sons.

Wu, S.J., Melnyk, S.A., & Flynn, B.B. (2010). Operational performance: The secret ingredient. *Decision Sciences, 41*(4), 721–754.

29

Understanding common network patterns to improve management of external and internal stakeholder risks

Eva Schiffer

Risk management often focuses on large catastrophic events which are – at least partly – out of the control of those managing the risk, such as natural disasters or political upheaval. However, a lot of the risks which can seriously damage a company are much less spectacular and are based on the patterns in which people interact (within and beyond the organization) – unmanaged stakeholder relationships can lead to both slow decline and more dramatic clashes which leave the company damaged.

These risks include:

- the engagement and relationships with the clients
- political stakeholders (which is especially complex for multinationals, who have to function in many different national settings)
- competitors
- business partners up and down the supply chain
- internal stakeholders (e.g., the relationships between board and managers, between managers and frontline workers, and laterally between different units of the organization).

In those cases where stakeholder analysis is done, it often focuses on listing stakeholders, and analyzing their characteristics and how they relate to the firm's plans and projects (e.g., how strong their interest and influence is). However, we have observed that many actor-related risks don't manifest because of the individual and isolated actions of actors but because of the way that these actors are connected to each other and the company and the way they use these networks to achieve their goals. Thus, a realistic assessment and proactive management of actor-related risks requires an understanding of the network patterns in which these actors are embedded and the limitations and opportunities that they have because of their specific position in these network patterns (Henisz, 2014).

This chapter introduces a number of network patterns which are derived from extensive work in mapping influence networks in such diverse context as policy development in Africa, business relationships between matrix organizations in the US and illegal logging and wood smuggling in the Far East. This analysis was done using the Net-Map tool for participatory network mapping (Schiffer & Hauck, 2010) which allows participants to map out, in detail, the formal and informal networks (including conflicts), goals and influence levels of all internal and external stakeholders which can influence the outcome of an endeavor. This thinking is based on social network analysis, an interdisciplinary approach to understanding human actions, opportunities and limitations by analyzing the patterns of connections between them (Hanneman & Riddle, 2005). Out of this experience and background I have distilled a number of patterns which I have encountered most commonly across the globe (in Europe, USA, Africa and Asia) and will explore in this chapter the strategic risks and opportunities that each of these patterns carries.

The following examples show that there is no perfect pattern. Rather, each of these very common patterns develops for a reason and their very persistence and common occurrence indicates that these patterns deliver something to someone – or at least that they did, when they evolved (these patterns tend to be very persistent, thus sometimes the benefit is best understood when exploring the history in which the pattern evolved). But, on the other hand, each of these patterns also bears certain risks and the benefits of some patterns are not evenly distributed (e.g., a central actor may benefit while a marginal actor pays the price). Also, some patterns are especially useful for delivering in certain situations or at specific points in the product/project cycle.

Network patterns and their risks and benefits

This pattern describes a situation where one central actor is connected to many peripheral actors who are not connected to each other. We find hub-and-spoke networks, for example, in the way staff relate to a very charismatic and personable leader, companies relate to their clients, new developing projects relate to their stakeholders and traditional media connects with their audience.

This pattern allows the central node to control the messages or products going out and is often useful for distributing standardized goods or messages and mobilizing actors quickly, with a clear sense of direction.

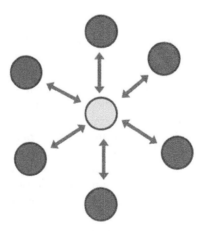

Figure 29.1 It's all about you – hub and spoke network

However, this pattern also has a number of risks, the most dramatic one being its vulnerability to shock. Whether it is a heart attack of the charismatic leader or the end of funding for a project, when the central node is removed from the network, all connections disappear and what looked like a well-organized system of connections turns into disconnected individuals who often don't know who to reach engage to rebuild connections. However, even without the sudden removal of the central node, hub-and-spoke networks can be risky: the structure concentrates control and power in the central node, trusting that they will have the capacity and integrity to do the right thing. Because of a lack of connections between the marginal nodes, the central actor can easily distort information, divert money flows and otherwise play the system for their own benefit. Also, the sheer number of connections this one node has to manage can easily lead to an overload of the one central actor, which slows down the whole system. Finally, what is often overlooked is that a hub-and-spoke network may be effective in moving clear and standardized products and messages through a system, but is very weak at engaging the marginal actors (which may be the frontline workers) in a process of collaborative innovation and problem solving. Thus, organizations which are structured in this pattern tend to be good at giving and following orders but face the risk of being very slow to innovate and adapt to new circumstances.

The cohesive clique is a structure at the opposite end of the spectrum. Everyone is connected to everyone and there is no central node. This kind of structure is often observed

- in teams which are proud of their nonhierarchical collaboration
- in social movements
- in small leadership circles and boards.

This structure allows all participants to be heard and feel embedded in a reliable structure of support. This high level of connectivity can allow companies to benefit from the shared creativity of everyone. Also, cohesive cliques are extremely resilient against shocks. As all members of the clique are connected to each other, the removal of one or more actors will not destroy the network, and often different members of this structure are familiar enough with each other's job that they can replace each other in case of need.

However, just as the hub-and-spoke network, the cohesive clique is a structure which carries substantial risks. The absence of a clear hierarchical structure often makes it difficult to move

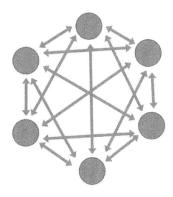

Figure 29.2 Everybody holding hands – cohesive cliques

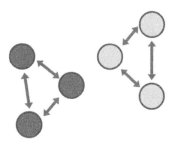

Figure 29.3 Birds of a feather – homogenous coalitions

from discussion to action, because there is a lack of clarity about who can issue a call of action. Also, this kind of structure requires a lot of energy from everyone involved for maintaining all these connections (which is why some people equate networking with not working). This may translate into endless meetings and little time to get other work done. One risk which is especially relevant for cohesive cliques at the leadership level (management or boards) is that cliques tend to be very inclusive for members and rather closed off toward the outside world. Their members tend to be inward-facing and embracing groupthink and may even pressurize or exclude members who dare to express differing views. For those who are excluded from a clique this experience of exclusion may lead to hostility, which erupts when civil society feels excluded from cliquish private sector forums or when frontline workers feel excluded from management cliques. If undetected and managed badly, the results can be public protests or aggressive strikes, where a structure with more openness to outsiders would have enabled collaboration or peaceful negotiations.

Social network analysis describes a phenomenon called homophily (Miller et al., 2001), which means that most people like to hang out with people of their own kind. This can mean that they choose to develop close relationships with others of the same professional, ethnic, cultural, religious, political or economic background. Over time, networks tend to mature towards more and more homogeneity and sometimes disconnect from those parts which are perceived as being too different. While this looks like a simple case of personal preferences, it can have a strongly polarizing effect on organizations and societies, where homogeneous coalitions develop which have little connections to each other. Some examples are

- places where private sector, government and civil society have stopped talking to each other
- companies with strong power distance, where management and frontline workers don't interact beyond the requirements of their job
- organizations with solid silos
- starkly divided political systems.

Some benefits of these homogeneous coalitions are that members feel safe and understood, and this structure can be very useful for developing a new product (without leaking information to the outside world) or surviving as a loyal group in a hostile environment. Homogeneous coalitions are very stable, high trust structures.

However, there are strong risks associated with this structure too. As they lose connection to the rest of the society these homogeneous coalitions are very prone to developing groupthink and radical ideas and to vilifying those who are different. In the example of an organization with solid silos, this structure leads to slowing down of procedures, internal conflict and competition

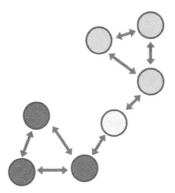

Figure 29.4 A bridge to the outside world – boundary spanner

and a lack of shared direction. If companies are located in a political setting where private sector, government and civil society form homogeneous coalitions which are disconnected from each other, there is a large risk of increasing tensions, misunderstandings and surprise attacks because the company loses its ability to feel the pulse of the society in which it is operating. And finally, an organization where the top and the bottom don't interact can easily fall into an "us-against-them" paradigm, where both sides mistrust each other, loyalty is minimal and a cold war of control and subversion rules the day.

Homophily (the wish to associate with people who are similar, to stay within your "tribe") is a very powerful structuring force of human societies, which cannot be "managed away" by formal decree. This becomes apparent in the many structural reorganizations aimed at breaking up organizational silos. When the dust has settled the new structure often falls into slightly differently shaped silos which staff create as they continue to be close to people who are similar to them.

One kind of actor which can soften and break up the structure of homogeneous coalitions is the boundary spanner. This is an actor who connects two coalitions – either as a free agent who is connected to both worlds, or as a member of one of the coalitions who reaches out to members of the other coalition (Cross & Prusak, 2002). Introducing a boundary spanning position in a silo situation can be like opening the valve and allowing information, ideas, emotions, funds and so forth to flow between the two systems. Typical examples would be

- the individual who works for a company and has family who works in the government, or volunteers in a civil society organization after hours
- the management consultant who brings together the perspectives of top management and front lines.

But also

- the industrial spy who sells corporate secrets to the competition
- the finance officer who slows down or diverts funds as they move from headquarters to the local office to sit in a boundary-spanning position.

The benefits of boundary spanning are that this is where most innovations happen, when ideas and established practices from one domain are moved into a different domain. Often boundary spanners provide the members of otherwise closed-off, homogeneous coalitions

Eva Schiffer

with crucial information about what is going on in the rest of the company or in the stake-holder systems surrounding the company. Boundary spanners can be the glue which holds fragmented organizations or societies together and helps everyone understand the other perspective.

However, one of the risks of this structure is that it gives a tremendous amount of informal power to the boundary spanner. If no one else connects these two coalitions, the boundary spanner may make up information, embezzle funds and use their position for their own benefit, without checks and balances. Also, just as the hub-and-spoke network, a structure which relies on one actor for holding it together is always vulnerable to shocks – if the boundary spanner is removed, the structure turns into one of disconnected coalitions. Further, in some systems there is a strong interest against having something flow between two groups. The most poignant example would be the flow of infections between two communities (Klovdahl et al., 1994) but boundary spanners can also cause harm by sharing confidential information. From the perspective of the boundary spanners themselves, this is a volatile position. While it can come with a lot of power, it also is a position where the person is not embedded in a supportive group; in the worst case, both sides will call the boundary spanner a traitor (imagine, for example, someone who connects management and workers during a strike). To understand this situation it is important to know that while organizations can develop formal boundary spanning positions (e.g., knowledge officer, community relations officer), there is a small percentage of individuals who will always seek out boundary-spanning roles, whether formally mandated or not (Williams, 2002). To reduce the risk associated with homogeneous coalitions *and* to reduce the risk of negative boundary spanning activities, it is crucial to identify who they are and channel their activities in ways which benefit the corporation.

Other common structures

In the scope of this chapter we will not be able to explore each of these structures in detail. In what follows you find a number of other common structures. Each of them, just as the ones discussed earlier, have opportunities and risks and they all have been observed by the author in organizations and societies across the globe. This list is by no means complete but is rather intended to inspire looking at external and internal stakeholder risks in a networked fashion, instead of merely identifying and analyzing individual stakeholders, their characteristics and influence.

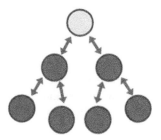

Figure 29.5   The boss is the boss – strict hierarchy

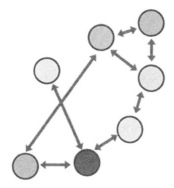

Figure 29.6   Celebrating diversity – heterogenous network

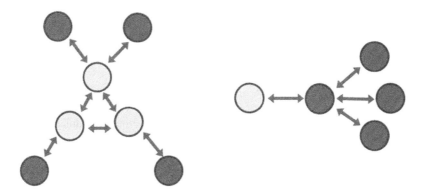

Figure 29.7   The inner circle – core-periphery network and who gets past the dragon? Gate-keeper

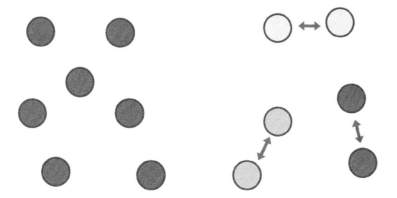

Figure 29.8   Everyone for themselves – disconnected individuals and lonesome twosomes – disconnected pairs

Application

As shown earlier, the ability to identify, name, discuss and judge the network structures of external and internal stakeholders can be a crucial aspect of risk management for companies working in complex and changing environments. By boiling down complex social realities to their most basic, significant microstructures, it becomes easier to understand the stakeholder network risks and opportunities that the organization faces, to engage in a dialogue about the desired future structure and initiate very concrete steps of creating or letting go of connections and growing networks more strategically. These prototypical patterns are used in training managers to improve their network understanding and intuition, in visioning for change processes, to negotiate agreement about how interactions should be structured and to detect, diagnose and strategically manage stakeholder risks. A first step to applying these patterns to a concrete situation can be rather simple: a group of concerned actors from within or beyond the organization reviews all patterns together and answers the questions:

> Which of these patterns reminds us of the situation we are in?
> Why?
> What strengths do we get from this pattern?
> What risks are we exposed to because of this pattern?
> What pattern do we want to strive for?
> What is the first step we can take?

Often this discussion will reveal how different the network looks from different perspectives, and also that there may not be clear agreement about a desired future structure. But by giving the team a language to speak about these issues and a space to deliberate, they will all become more aware of the strategic risks embedded in the stakeholder networks and become more intentional in their risk management strategies.

References

Cross, R., Prusak, L. (2002). The people who make organizations go-or stop. *Harvard Business Review*, Volume 80, Issue 6, pp. 104–112.

Hanneman, R.A., Riddle, M. (2005). *Introduction to social network methods*. Riverside: University of California. http://faculty.ucr.edu/~hanneman/

Henisz, W.J. (2014). *Corporate diplomacy. Building reputations and relationships with external stakeholders*. Sheffield: Greenleaf.

Klovdahl, A.S., Potterat, J.J., Woodhouse, D.E., Muth, J.B., Muth, S.Q., Darrow, W.W. (1994). Social networks and infectious disease: The Colorado Springs study. *Social Science & Medicine*, Volume 38, Issue 1, pp. 79–88.

Miller, M., Smith-Lovin, L., Cook, M. (2001). Birds of a feather: Homophily in social networks. *Annual Review of Sociology*, Vol. 27, pp. 415–444. http://www.jstor.org/stable/2678628

Schiffer, E., Hauck, J. (2010). Net-Map: Collecting social network data and facilitating network learning through participatory influence network mapping. *Field Methods*, Volume 22, Issue 3, pp. 231–249.

Williams, P. (2002). The competent boundary spanner. *Public Administration*, Volume 80, Issue 1. doi: 10.1111/1467-9299.00296

Index

Note: Page numbers in italic indicate figures and tables.

For Product Safety Concerns and Information please contact our EU
representative GPSR@taylorandfrancis.com Taylor & Francis Verlag GmbH,
Kaufingerstraße 24, 80331 München, Germany

Printed and bound by CPI Group (UK) Ltd, Croydon, CR0 4YY
08/05/2025
01864335-0005